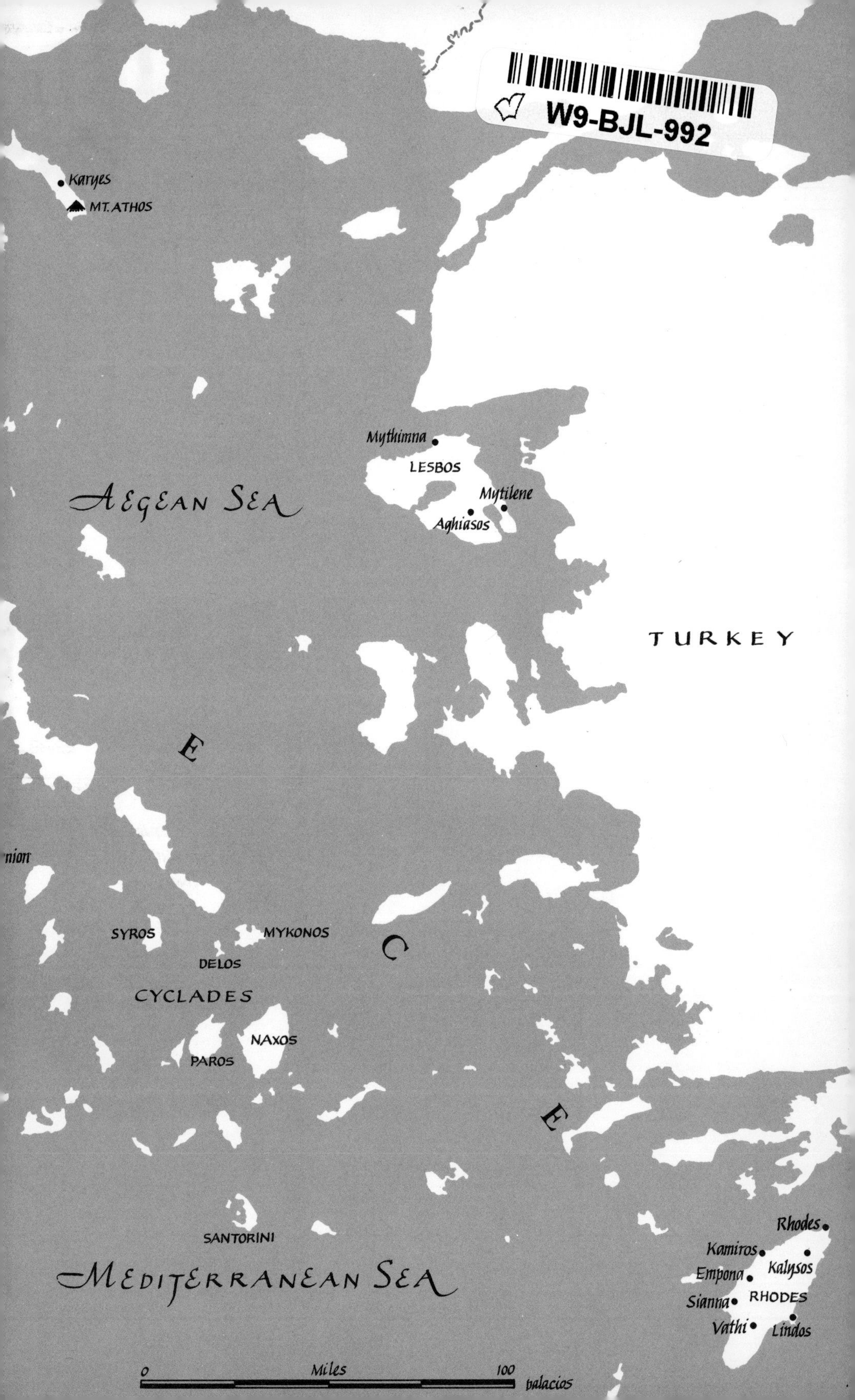

Karyes

MT. ATHOS

AEGEAN SEA

Mythimna

LESBOS

Mytilene

Aghiasos

TURKEY

W9-BJL-992

E

nion

SYROS

MYKONOS

DELOS

CYCLADES

C

NAXOS

PAROS

E

SANTORINI

Rhodes

Kamiros

Empona

Kalysos

Sianna

RHODES

Vathi

Lindos

MEDITERRANEAN SEA

0

Miles

100

balacias

GODS

AND

HEROES

By Herbert Kubly

GODS AND HEROES

AMERICAN IN ITALY

EASTER IN SICILY

VARIETIES OF LOVE

THE WHISTLING ZONE

AT LARGE

ITALY (*Life* World Library)

SWITZERLAND (*Life* World Library)

Plays

MEN TO THE SEA

THE VIRUS (Produced under title INHERIT THE WIND.)

Herbert Kubly

GODS
AND
HEROES

1969

Doubleday & Company, Inc.

GARDEN CITY, NEW YORK

We wish to thank Mr. Ronald Silliman for his permission to reprint his poem "Youra," and Mr. Athanasios Simos for his translations dealing with Kalavryta, in the Peloponnese, and Mt. Athos.

For Alex Marlis, Greek American,
and Ken and Pauline Boss,
who share with me
his surrogate parenthood.

In the Meantime

The Homeric rush of events in Greece since the time of my visit was no great surprise. Anyone in Greece during the confused years before the Junta coup of 1967 could not help but sense the oncoming storm; the shape it would take no one could tell, but its foreshadowing clouds were gathering over the land.

Many of these pages were written before April 1967, and there has been no need to change them. The nature of people and landscape do not alter. The tumultuous panorama of human Greece is eternal and no revolutions or politicians can divert it.

Politically much has happened. Just two years after our meeting in Athens, Andreas Papandreou and I met again on the campus of the University of California in Berkeley. He was, after eight months in prison, in glowing physical and spiritual health, and he seemed a man marvelously restored.

I remembered the Greek Andreas as a tensely harassed and nervously troubled man. Andreas, in America, was serene, self-assured and confident, as if his imprisonment had been a time of self-discovery and focusing of strength. I recalled how in that earlier season, we and many of our friends had been frightened, confused and on the edge of paranoia, a Greek word which describes a chronic Greek condition.

In California, Andreas was among friends. A former economics professor, he was visiting colleagues on the campus he had left four years before to enter Greek politics. His release, before he could be brought to trial on trumped-up charges of treason, had resulted from pressures by foreign intellectuals, especially from the American university community. Free, he became at once one of the most articulate critics of his oppressors, the Junta rulers of Greece.

In the weeks before his American visit, the U. S. State Department had announced a resumption of diplomatic relations and plans to resume U.S. military aid to Greece. State Department spokesmen declared themselves pleased with the dictator's announced plan for the military-supervised referendum of a rigged Constitution—an undemocratic procedure immediately rejected by Greece's respected political leaders. The World Bank, with U.S. blessing, had approved a loan to the dictators at the same time that the European Investment Bank had refused one.

What was happening was altogether too clear. "Truly, the only thing that keeps the Junta in power is the support it is getting from the United States," said Andreas Papandreou. "Without this support the regime would collapse in three months."

The events in these pages come to an end approximately ten months before the coup of April 21, 1967. In any précis of the intervening events, a danger of oversimplification is inevitable. Still, it is now a matter of history that the plans for a coup had been in the works for at least two years, as far back as the July "crisis" of 1965, which resulted from the resignation as prime minister by Greece's most popular political leader of modern times, George Papandreou.

It is a commonly accepted theory that the contingency plan for a military takeover, called "Prometheus," had the approval of Papandreou's onetime friend and now bitter enemy, King Constantine. The plan called for a military coup by the King's loyal military staff, if and when, as was feared, an election scheduled for May 28, 1967, were to result in a victory for the Papandreou Center Union party.

What happened was that the "official" coup was outcouped by the wrong soldiers. A group of faceless young colonels in the Athens barracks, who were opposed to a coup by the King after the elections, decided to strike at once. In the political quiescence of the Orthodox Easter holiday, they seized the reins of government, arrested and jailed thousands of citizens, including a thousand Army officers, dismissed regional governors and mayors, fired university professors, took over control of the Orthodox Church and silenced the press.

The rhetoric of their dictatorial pronouncements was anti-Communism, a cry to which they expected America to respond as a bull to the banderol. Their manufactured villains were the Papandreous, father and son, both of whom were arrested. In a hyperbolic propaganda campaign against the Papandreous, facts were disregarded. In Greece's last free election in 1964, in which George Papandreou had won a record of 54 per cent of the votes, the Communists had received a meager 12 per cent. The concepts for which Andreas was being labeled "pro-Communist" were his Keynesian American New Deal agricultural, industrial and financial reforms to restore the moribund economy of Greece.

Though Greeks insist that certain U. S. Embassy and CIA personnel were aware of the "Prometheus" plan, there is no evidence that there was any official knowledge of it. But there can be no doubt that by its support of the anti-Communism hysteria of the extreme right-wing faction in the Greek military, the United States helped set the stage for the colonels' success.

The reasons given for the State Department's myopic policy of time-marking toleration are familiar ones. America, we were told, could not risk losing an ally in NATO's southern zone during a time of Soviet expansion in the Mediterranean. The Junta, it was rationalized, was a political fact of life with which it was to our benefit to maintain a semblance of friendship. Certain subliminal pressures on policy-making cannot be ignored, such as the lobbying of American business attracted to Greece in the supposition that dictators provide a secure climate for investment and development. And bizarre as it may seem, there was the contract of the Junta with a Manhattan public relations firm for a promotional campaign to improve the image of the dictators in America. The campaign's announced objectives included the discrediting of actress Melina Mercouri and a favorable article in *Fortune* magazine. A spokesman for the public relations firm, corporate clients of which include the Coca-Cola Company, said it hoped to see a bottling plant in Greece, adding, "The Coca-Cola bottle is a symbol of freedom and peace." The contract was later terminated "by mutual consent."

If the little colonels seem at times to be comic opera figures in their banning of classical Greek drama and contemporary popular music, their audacious regime unfolds like a modern Sophoclean tragedy. "In Greece," said Deputy Premier Stylianos Patakos, "we have right people and wrong people. All those who are against the government are Communists." Operating on this premise, the Junta is holding thousands of Greeks in prisons and in concentration camps on the brutally hot, waterless wind-swept Aegean islands of Yiaros and Leros. The prisoners cover the spectrum of Greek society, parliamentary deputies and former ministers, professors and journalists, a bus driver who protested a soldier's free ride and persons who entertained more than five guests in their homes at one time. Many of the prisoners were spirited away during the night in the first weeks of the coup and nothing has been heard of them since.

But their sufferings became known this year when investigators of Amnesty International, a London-based international organization for the relief of political prisoners, returned from Greece with reports of brutality by officers in security police headquarters. The catalog of systematized tortures evokes the forgotten nightmares of Nazi Germany. Following disclosure of the Amnesty evidence, the Council of Europe voted to expel Greece from membership unless it returned to a constitutional democratic government in fifteen months. Sweden withdrew its ambassador from Athens.

No one can predict how long the catastrophic regime will go on. The Greek political scene had been for several years before the coup a mess. Greeks have always been better at political theory than at political practice. Their revolutions have been frequent, their republics short-lived, their monarchy unpopular. The former colonels have estimated that the fulfillment of their mission may take a decade. To disclaim the onus of a military dictatorship they have resigned their Army commissions and taken on the guise of a civilian government. "We shall stay put and succeed," said Patakos.

So their dictatorship rolls on, total, brutal and implacable. In the guise of practical politics, the United States, whose own democracy can be traced through Thomas Jefferson to Aristotle and Polybius of Megalopolis, must share the guilt of democracy's death in the land where it was born. "It is not only the death of democracy in Greece," said Andreas Papandreou. "It is in a larger sense the gathering of clouds in a darkening age."

To those who appear in these pages much has happened. The two most respected political leaders in Greece, George Papandreou and Panagiotis Kanellopoulos, both former prime ministers, have been placed under house arrest for a second time. Greece's most popular composer, Mikis Theodorakis, reported ill, was arrested and then released after signing a statement that he would not further participate in politics; performances of his songs are banned by law. Deputy Paul Vardinogiannis, enigmatic as ever, is reported in bad grace with members of his Center Union party. The dance folklorist, Dora Stratou, whose devotion to Greece is inviolable, was arrested. Eleni Vlachou, who refused to publish her newspapers under censorship, defected to England, and King Constantine is in idle exile in Rome. For one young man the story ends happily. Alex Marlis was graduated last June from Monticello High School in Wisconsin and is planning to become an American citizen.

To each I am indebted. I owe even more to many friends who must remain anonymous because their mention here might be a danger to

them. The single friend who contributed more than any other to this
book did not live to see in actuality the apocalyptic events which he so
clearly sensed were ahead. George Theotokas died suddenly in July 1966,
the month that I returned from Greece.

Herbert Kubly
Wilhelm Tell Farm
Wisconsin

Contents

YOURA

Where the trees never dare to grow. Though I cannot know.
Where the earth begins the slow bruise
to rock. Where the water must be free of blue.
Though I cannot know.

Youra
on the far side of love.
The public side. The side where the heart beats
slow as a march in half-time.
Youra from the distance. Thin line
of an island. Though I cannot know.

What can a man know who lives in a room?
Some men live in the world.
Some men go in boats to Youra.
There, maybe they can feel the sea recede
at night, and know
I cannot know.

I have never seen the fence an island grows.
Where the sun is contained.
Where one talks his poems loudly to the gulls
to keep from going sane.
I have often seen the face that knows Youra.

Whatever sees into the deep that is not forest.
Whatever sees spiders, wild.
Memory of the earlier dead.

Though I cannot know for sure.

What will you do when Youra comes?

Ronald Silliman

> The mountains look on Marathon,
> And Marathon looks on the sea;
> And musing there an hour alone,
> I dreamed that Greece might still be free.

Lord Byron, Don Juan

After shaking hands with a Greek, count
your fingers.

Albanian Proverb

"You have chosen a very decisive year to be in
Greece."

Andreas Papandreou

I

Across the Pindus

The autumn winds whistled; the rain beat down. Huddled under a lifeboat on the deck we watched through a sheet of gray spray the approaching dark hills of Epirus. It took another half hour for our boat to sail between the hills into the small port of Igoumenitsa.

The boat which we'd taken the night before in Brindisi was going on to Patras, and only a handful of passengers disembarked. Drenched officers waved us through customs, interested only in our auto documents. They shook their heads in astonishment at an American girl in blue levis, hair hanging in wet ropes, weighted with rucksacks like a donkey, setting off alone by foot into Greece.

We had chosen to land in this tiny country harbor because we wished to see the country before facing up to Athens. Now we were apprehensive. An Englishman on the boat had said that the only road crossing northern Greece was impassable. We decided to get an official opinion. The tourist office was closed—a voice shouted from an upstairs window that the director was on vacation. A man in a shipping office reassured us softly in English. "The road is driven every day," he said, "but forty miles are under construction and you will need to go very slowly."

My companion, David Greggory, was driving. We splashed through pools of water, climbing immediately into lonely hills. Goats and sheep grazed on green sage and shepherds huddling under sheets of plastic looked like huge iridescent mushrooms. Eroded gullies were bleeding gashes in the red earth. Waxy spears of asphodel brightened the road banks and framed, here and there, a small roadside prayer station the size of a birdhouse.

We came to a halt before a landslide in a pass and had to wait a half hour while workmen with an Allis-Chalmers tractor pushed the boulders and earth from our path. Beyond the canyon the mountains were higher, the roads more hazardous, the rain thicker. We crawled blindly through rolling clouds of fog, colliding now and then with piles of gravel left by the road builders. The unguarded roadside was a bottomless gray pit. Occasional road signs were in letters I could not read. Desolation filled me like a fever. Silently we pushed on.

After two hours we arrived in the walled lakeside town of Jannina, a capital of the Turkish occupation. We passed a mosque and an Oriental bazaar and arrived at the Xenia Hotel in a lush tropical park on the lake. A clerk said the road ahead was worse. In the dining room two German couples and a young Dutch professor with an American wife were pondering our common dilemma. We drank two *ouzos* and ordered lunch, our first Greek meal. The lemon soup, grilled liver and salad were excellent. I tasted my first *retsina* and liked it.

The rains stopped and a sudden burst of sunlight brightened an Alpine landscape. The lake shore was a dripping garden of willows and spruce and a spectrum of flowers. Soft clouds lay on the lake, like a wet day in Switzerland, and high beyond rose the blue crest of the Pindus range. The sunshine and wine levitated our sodden spirits and we decided to push on over the mountains.

The road coiled up the blue and mauve precipices like a great serpent. The road was being built in disconnected fragments and bare rock beds alternated with slippery wash-ins. Buses and trucks were perils—one driver had to halt to let the other pass. We stopped for flocks of sheep. Greggory, driving, at least had his sense of control; from my outside position I could look down unguarded chasms five hundred feet deep. Frequently I had to close my eyes. While fiording a foot-deep slough of muddy water our gear case got wet and our second speed refused to function. Each time we tried it the motor stalled. I had fantasies of being marooned in the terrifying Balkan wilderness.

Suddenly near the silvery summit of a mountain named Mitsikeli, we faced a reassuring vision. An old priest bearing a tall staff, his black robes flying, white beard and hair blowing, strode majestically as a Tolstoian hermit walking on water. He waved us by. We curved around a precipice where we were stopped by a man waving a red flag. He said they were dynamiting ahead, that we must wait for a charge to go off. The man asked for a cigarette, which he smoked while we waited.

Suddenly before us we saw men running. "Papa!" they shouted. "Ho Papa! Ho, ho . . ."

An explosion shook the mountain and rattled through our car. Small stones banged on the roof. When the dust cleared we were surrounded by workmen, collapsing into guffaws of laughter. On the road ahead the old priest was stalking like a Biblical prophet, upwards toward a mauve and blue El Greco heaven. Walking on water would have been child's play to him; he had walked through a mountain.

At four o'clock we came to a sign pointing toward Metsovon. We stopped and consulted one of my reference books. The highest road pass in Greece lay ahead. Metsovon, I read, was "straight from the pages of the Arabian Nights." Its three thousand people spoke Vlach; they were descendants of tribes of nomadic peasants who emigrated in the Middle Ages from Bulgaria and Roumania. Successive sultans during the Turkish occupation had granted them autonomy. Metsovon, said the book, had a government-operated Xenia Hotel.

The steep trail down through a fir forest was hardly more than a donkey path. The village at the bottom was already in shadow. We beat on the locked door of the hotel until we roused the manager, a small soft-voiced man who asked if we were French. His entire hotel was booked that evening for a French touring group; there were no extra rooms. He would, he said, direct us to another hotel. He got into the car and we rattled across town on a rocky road. The last house was a square one-story cement block dwelling, bearing the sign "HOTEL PINDUS." The owner, named Giorgos, was a lean dark man with coiled mustaches. In the doorway, smiling and bowing, was his wife, a small woman wearing dark blue homespun and a paisley bandana around her head. She showed us a small clean room furnished with two cots and a washbasin.

Through chilling dusk we walked to the Metropolis. The low rambling sixteenth-century structure looked less like a church than a hunting lodge in a Carpathian forest. Except for a few flickering votive candles, it was dark inside. We seemed to be alone. Slowly as our eyes adjusted to the dark we grew aware of a hand-carved iconostasi rich in floral detail, a honeycombed wooden ceiling, silver-framed saints with painted faces. In the corner I made out the wood-brown effigy of a man in a praying position. I went to examine it and it moved. My cry brought a black-shrouded hunchback from behind the iconostasi. Suddenly we were surrounded with movement, with human forms lighting candles, bearing epistles, drawing curtains. The evening benediction was in progress. Two old priests were reading in hissing whispers. Soon the entire church flickered with candles. The wooden ceiling turned red and gold; the walls were galleries of saints. The kneeling figure was moaning now and his raised face was like the mask of a saint. We backed into stalls watching the ghostly mysteries swirling around us like a Javanese shadow play.

A few doors away was a museum, a sturdy baronial mansion with stables on the ground floor, built during the Turkish occupation. Upstairs rooms were furnished with hand-hewn furniture, copper and brass and a horde of Oriental rugs and Turkish costumes. The bedrooms had low cushion-covered sleeping platforms and wooden ceilings patterned with relief work.

It was six o'clock. The sky over the valley was a spectrum of mauve, cerise and orchid, the colors of Monet's water lilies, and columns of mist rose like pillars of orange flames to the heavens. The streets were filled with the traffic of women. Women shepherded tinkling sheep and goats from pastures, women led mules bearing logs, women carried pails of milk, gathered bundles of fagots, cooked food in outdoor ovens. Those women not busy with evening chores scurried hither and yon knitting furiously, as if one moment's idleness were a shame.

Their compulsive activity was not shared by men. Stalking singly and in pairs they moved like Byzantine kings through the female bustle, descending toward the square in the bottom of the valley. They were spectacularly costumed in black puff-sleeved wool shirts, black pleated skirts flaring roguishly at the knee, wide black kummerbunds, black— or sometimes white—wool stockings, and on their feet black brogans with pompons large as volleyballs. On their heads they wore black fezzes of fur, or black bandanas tied diagonally in pirate fashion across the eyes. Older men leaned on shoulder-high black crooks which they grasped at the top, and each carried his *komboloi,* a string of worry beads, like an amber rosary. Worry was obviously a man's function. Women had not the time.

The square, an open field, was filled with men talking in low voices, milling back and forth in pairs like prisoners in a yard. The meadow was closed on one side by an arcade of shops and a *taverna,* from which tables and chairs spilled out over the cortile. The shops were lit with dim electric bulbs. In a barber shop haircuts were in progress. A tailor and his apprentice were earnestly stitching. Amplified *bouzouki* blared from a loudspeaker. A man was roasting *souvlaki* on a charcoal grill, filling the air with dark smoke and the delicious smells of thyme and roasting lamb; and his daughter, a thin, agile child of twelve, moved swiftly among the tables, delivering the skewered meat. She was one of two females in the male compound, the other being the mistress of the *taverna,* a rotund wife of Bath in a red plaid skirt, standing in the doorway scratching herself, chomping from a skewer of *souvlaki,* eyes on her three sons, aged perhaps seven to twelve, carrying wine to customers. "Odyssea!" she called and the second boy answered.

"Orestis!" I shouted. To my surprise the oldest boy bounded to our table. Astonished by my success, I called "Electra," but the little meat vendor did not respond.

On the tavern windows were decals for Fix beer, and I ordered some. The boy returned to consult his mother. She came to our table with tiny swift steps. *"Kein Bier,"* she said. I pointed to the window signs. She shook her head vigorously, declaiming in Greek. *"Trinken Retsina,"* she said, pouring wine from a blue enamel coffeepot.

The night had turned cold. I was shivering in two sweaters and a leather jacket. The deep chill was more than night air; it came also from a cool hostility in the fierce faces of men tugging silently on beads, counting them clockwise and then counterclockwise. I wondered what had happened to the Greek hospitality about which I'd heard.

A man got up and began to dance drunkenly, his arms flapping like a scarecrow's. A few of the bead twisters smiled and their gold teeth glittered like stars. In the field men were dividing, like a parting of dark waters. In the open passage two young women appeared. They were wearing stretch pants and sweaters, one blue, the other orange. On high heels they stepped daintily into the lighted area, their breasts and buttocks rolling like sacked melons.

Someone thought to turn off the loudspeaker. *"Gallides,"* I heard a voice say. A glow of eyes watched in silence the progress of the incredible visitors. On younger faces pleasure twitched; older faces were like stone.

The girls entered the arcade and took a table. Madame herded her three boys inside and moved swiftly to the table. I heard the girls order beer. *"Pas de Biere,"* snapped Madame. The girls accepted wine. Almost imperceptibly men began to leave, disappearing into the night. Trying to save the evening, Madame scurried from table to table in tiny gliding steps, as if she were mounted on rollers instead of feet. The manager of the Xenia appeared looking for us. He said the French would be having supper in a few minutes and invited us to eat with them. *"Mangare bene,"* he said. *"Fleisch, patate, salat."* Lowering his voice, he said if we wished he could even serve us beer. In a linguistic mélange he explained that the prejudice against beer was a political one, dating from the "July crisis" when the prime minister, George Papandreou, had resigned. The prime minister had demanded the resignation of the minister of defense, named Petros Garoufalias, a friend of the Queen Mother Frederika and an executive of the Fix breweries. Instead of acceding to Papandreou's demand, the King forced the prime minister's resignation. The people of Metsovon were showing their allegiance by boycotting beer. It was my first Greek political lesson—the lack of friendliness of the men of Metsovon was now clear. By ordering beer we had aligned ourselves with their enemy, the King.

The French girls must have felt it too, for they got up from their table and departed. We stumbled behind them up a dark rocky road that might have been a dry river bed. The hotel manager invited us into his kitchen, filled with a Brueghel crew of aproned cooks, meatcutters and wine bearers, forty chattering French and a dozen local youths there simply to share in the excitement. "What you like we have," a chef bellowed in English. The confusion, the noise, was too much for my nerves. We ordered spaghetti, some veal and a salad and returned to the dining room to wait. Not wishing to make another political statement, we ordered wine.

At eleven we walked across town to the Pindus. A full moon hung over the church; the next day would be fair. On the square, Madame, shrieking with laughter, skated across the field and disappeared; almost immediately she reappeared, streaking back. *Bouzouki* filled the night. Two drunk old men were dancing. Others tugged at beads. The little meat girl and her father were covering their coals with ash. We met some children playing a game. I wondered when they slept.

Three autos were parked by ours and Giorgos, waiting in a euphoric mood, reported his hotel was filled. A German couple, a Greek couple from Athens and two Italians had arrived after dark and gone to bed at once. Many Germans came to Metsovon, he said. German soldiers who had occupied the valley during the war returned with their families for a sentimental reconnaissance. Few Americans came to Metsovon. We were the first to sleep in the Pindus.

An official notice on the door of our room said we were in a "Class E" hotel. Better to start on the bottom, I thought, wondering if there were lower classes, Class Omega, for instance. I read in Greek: "Price of room 52 drs.; price of bed 26 drs.; price of central heating 10 drs." The last line had been crossed out and with reason. The room was bitter cold. Our beds, thin pallets on slats, had single thin cotton coverlets. I wore a sweater and socks to bed. "You'd think with all their sheep and goats they'd at least make some blankets," Greggory was muttering.

We awoke to dazzling sunlight. After breakfast at the Xenia we began the perilous upward trail. We met women leading donkeys loaded with logs. On the highway we passed road crews of women, their eyes peering, Moslem-style, over scarves which protected their nostrils from dust. Women shoveled gravel, hoisted boulders, pounded stones, and a young girl carried a water jar from which the workers took turns drinking. No men were in view.

We crossed the Katára Pass into a sweep of landscape which reminded me of the American West. To our left was a range of massive gray rock peaks, and below us, a broad purple valley which might have been a sage mesa in New Mexico. We descended into Thessaly toward a wide river bed through which coiled a stream of water where sheep and cattle were drinking. In the valley the road suddenly improved. Here and there the river waters were diverted to irrigation, turning the plains into a green garden of corn and grapes. Emerging from the mists ahead was an unearthly forest of pinnacles like lead-colored teeth on the lower jaw of a gigantic prehistoric monster. Molded by a paleolithic sea, the tilting rocks are called "Meteora" because the ancients believed them to be meteors hurled by angry gods. There's another legend that they were placed there by mythical Argonauts to block the passage into Thessaly; still another that they are the remains of castles built by superhuman beings.

In the Byzantine centuries another idea took hold—the formidable rocks were placed there by God as an unworldly refuge for holy men. Hermits moved into caverns on the rocks, turning them into cells. During the troubled thirteenth and fourteenth centuries they organized monasteries on the ledges. Civil wars and brigands sent the monks higher up the precipices and the Turkish occupation drove them to the most inaccessible peaks. Kings and emperors endowed the monasteries with wealth. By the sixteenth century, twenty-four "monasteries in the air" hung over the terrifying precipices. Jealous factions began quarreling over power and property. Corruption corroded moral and religious disciplines. Today only four monasteries are still in use. The others are abandoned ruins, the aeries of vultures.

At the foot of the pinnacles is Kalambaka, where we engaged a room in still another Xenia Hotel. The smiling desk clerk, black-bearded with four gold canines, had the face of a happy beaver. He told us he was a monk known as Brother Bissarion and that he had been for thirteen years in a Mount Athos monastery, to which he still sent most of his earnings. He was also a painter of icons, which were displayed for sale in the lobby. He gave us a large pleasant room with a terrace from which we could look over the red roofs of the town at the startling rocks.

After a bath, lunch and a bottle of cool Demisticha, a clean pale golden wine rather like Neuchâtel, we set out for Hagios Stefanos, one of the Meteora monasteries accessible by auto. Snaking back and forth across the rocks, we could look down on black ravens flying below and deserted monasteries clinging like swallows' nests to adjacent pinnacles. Hagios Stefanos is perched on a splinter which connects to the main massive by a footbridge. Abandoned by monks, it is inhabited by an order of nuns. At the car park we found a covey of angry Germans, women in stretch pants and shorts, and men in sleeveless shirts. An English sign said: "It is forbidden to enter this holy monastery for men dressed with sorts [sic] and for women dressed with sorts with trousers or without jackets."

I was wearing a blue sailcloth yachting jacket over a sports shirt. At the door I was stopped by a tiny nun swathed in black. She said I could not enter without a jacket. I was wearing a jacket, I said, showing my shirt underneath.

"It's not a jacket, it's a pajama," she cried. "No one can enter God's house in a pajama."

"It's a jacket!" I stood in the gate so she could not close it.

"A pajama jacket," she shrilled.

Our cries in German and Greek alerted the disenfranchised Germans, who stampeded across the bridge. Seeing them coming, the nun pulled me inside and bolted the gate. She shrugged, a female Pilate wiping her hands of the affair. I walked through a cortile under a ledge of potted plants, past a kitchen door inside which two nuns were lighting sticks in the open hearth. In the church I caught up with some properly clothed Germans, a noisy ill-mannered crew pushing and rampaging like corralled cattle, buying candles from a mean-looking nun, lighting them before an altar icon. They left. The chapel had fine old wood carvings and many frescoes and icons on which faces were gouged and pocked as if they'd been used for a dart game. The defacing, the gouging of the eyes, was done by Moslems during the Turkish occupation. Not aware of my presence, the nun swept angrily through the chapel, plucking the Germans' candles from the altar like fagots, extinguishing them, returning them to a candle bin from where they would be sold again. I wondered whether it was because the Germans had been Roman Catholics or whether it was policy to resell the cheap brown candles as often as possible.

Obviously, Christian contentment was not the sisters' lot. Swooping about angrily in the high wind, their black robes flapping like wings, they seemed to be infuriated by visitors. Who could blame them? They could not like being perched on their rocklike ravens' nest. Perhaps they *were* ravens, trapped by an evil spell in human form, their wings shorn so they could not fly away. In such an eerie atmosphere one could imagine anything.

The vertiginous view was breath-taking. Below, the great Thessaly plains, the granary of Greece, autumn gold, stretched to the sea, just discernible on the pale blue horizon. To the north the gray Pindus range reached toward the cloud-haloed cone of Olympus.

As I was leaving, Sister Xanthippe of the gate was shrilly refusing entry to two Greek parties. A family was barred because a ten-year-old girl was wearing no stockings. The other party, three men and a woman, was turned away because one woman traveling with three men was immoral. At the sight of me the little creature screamed, "Pajama! Pajama!" A thin young German who had been barred reappeared in a raincoat buttoned to his throat and stood at the gate beating on it. The assorted groups outside began to laugh and their mirth sent Sister Xanthippe into a frenzy. She called for help and in a moment the gate opened and a bearded monk appeared. It was the first evidence that the nuns on the rock were not without male companionship.

The Germans collapsed with laughter. The nun and the monk slammed the gate and we heard the rattle of a bar lowering inside. The young German, clowning now, clung to the door like an impaled bird. Laughter echoed up and down the abyss.

Down one rock and up another and we were at the pinnacled fortress of the Monastery Varlaam. Until the twentieth century the only way to arrive at it was by rope ladder, or, like tethered chickens, in a net attached to a winch hoist. The net, according to old photos, swung over the thousand-foot abyss like a pendulum. Today the human ascent is easier. From the car park it is 195 steps, carved in rock, to the top.

It is a tranquil place. The gate was open and the monks appeared to enjoy their visitors. A young bearded one, his black hair gathered by rubber bands into pony tails, showed us a church frescoed with the life of John the Baptist, and a Last Judgment in which myopic saints on their knees were reading the scales which weighed debits and credits of the judged. Speaking French and German, he led us to two other decorated chapels, a library, guesthouse, hospital, a small garden and the windlass, now operated by a gasoline motor, still used to draw provisions up to the monastery. A clue to the monks' geniality may have been some wine tuns which lay on their sides, as wide as I was tall.

In the morning we set out for Thessaloniki, crossing the Thessaly plains, circling Olympus. Women in fields were picking cotton and harvesting melons and squash. We passed colonies of beehives and met great trucks hauling sugar beets to refineries. Except for some irrigated fields, the earth was a burned desert. Sometimes one side of the highway was green and the other brown. At Larissa we joined the modern toll highway which connects Athens and Thessaloniki. Turning north, we entered the cool green Vale of Tempe, a romantic canyon through which the Peneus River flows toward the sea. Its idyllic beauty inspired myths about Apollo, who came here to bathe after slaughtering Python at Delphi. Coming out of the valley we faced a stunning vista. The blue Aegean was on our right; to our left, the mass of Olympus. On its slopes farmers were burning off dead fields preparing them for the plows. Watching the black smoke spiral heavenward, I felt the presence of ancient gods.

At Katerini, a dusty town on the skirts of Olympus, we lunched at a restaurant called Sotiris. From kitchen pots we selected a variety of exotic dishes: stuffed red peppers, gumbo stew, marinated artichokes, and a bottle of our old friend, Demisticha. A sign above the door said: "Sauber—Clean. Billig—Chear." The Greeks were having the same difficulty as I with "r" and "p." When I discovered that TABEPNA spells tavern I decided I was on my way toward learning Greek.

Back on the toll road we passed a sign which said it was fifty-eight kilometers to Yugoslavia. Tobacco grew man-high and orchards sagged with fruit. At every stop sign bands of children offered us apples and figs. Caravans of gypsies were traveling south for the winter from Roumania and Bulgaria, their wagons loaded with cooking pans, rugs, tethered ducks and turkeys and many dark naked children. Approaching us ahead, trudging in the center of the highway in an upright position, was a huge brown bear. Paying no attention to the swirl of traffic on both sides, the beast lumbered on with solemn dignity behind the little man who accompanied him.

Soon we were in Thessaloniki, following traffic through a hot dusty sprawl of ancient ruins, medieval ghettos and modern high-rises. In the center of the city, a forest of bright unfamiliar flags flew over an international trade fair. We continued a few miles east to the American Farm School, a junior agricultural college for village boys supported and taught by Americans. The young director, Bruce Lansdale, had invited me for a visit. He and his wife were waiting, ready to take me to the final meeting of a National 4-H Club Congress.

On our way back to town I told Lansdale that in my youth I had been a 4-H member in Wisconsin. When we arrived at the concrete-domed sports palace I was seated on a platform among government officials and introduced as "a 4-H member from the United States of America." Applauding below were 150 adolescents, boys in white duck trousers and shirts, girls in green and white uniforms which they themselves had made. They had been chosen most outstanding from a total of 28,000 4-H members in 690 Greek villages. An agriculture minister addressed them, saying, "You will bring to our land a new era of agriculture. You will exchange the primitive methods of yesterday for the mechanized new processes of tomorrow. As you take the place of the peasants of the villages, as you become farmers of Greece, the level of life will rise over all our country. Not only will you and your children live on the land, but you will bring the tired people in our cities back to the villages."

I was asked to present the prizes. A club official read out the names of members and their projects, the same calf and poultry raising and gardening which had been my projects as a boy, and others which were new to me—irrigation, tractor farming, cotton growing, goats and sheep. As the members came forward, I distributed grafting and pruning tools, sprayers and insecticides, fertilizers and cotton planters to the boys; and gas stoves, kitchenware and china sets to the girls.

The grand prize was a three-month-old Jersey calf presented by the Farm School. It went to an eighteen-year-old youth named Giorgos Kerasides, from the village of Thouría, near the Turkish border. Stockily built with straight black hair, high cheeks and copper skin, he looked like an American Indian. Through an interpreter he told me the project for which he'd won the calf was the improvement of the blood lines of cattle in his village. He had raised four calves; there were now three generations of cows for which he was responsible. When the new calf matured he planned to mix its rich milk with the milk of the other cows and raise the butterfat content of his small herd.

He had been to school a total of six years. He lived with his parents, three brothers and a sister on a "farm" of seven and one-half acres of poor mountain land. It supported four cows, two goats and fifteen chickens. The calf, he said, would be a great surprise, not only to his family but to all of Thouría's four hundred citizens. There would be a *yorti,* a celebration. Giorgos burst into laughter thinking about it.

"No one," said Bruce Lansdale, "can imagine the meaning of this calf to this boy, to his family and to his community." I thought I could, for I had been a farm boy myself. I looked at Giorgos, showing his white teeth in a happy grin, and I felt a joy myself, and very much at home.

II

Sons of the Soil

I awoke as I might have in Wisconsin, to the sound of a tractor outside my window. The John Deere, a gift from Lyndon Johnson, who visited the Farm School when he was Vice-President, was pulling a corn picker in a field just below Cincinnati Hall, the lodge for visitors. Beyond the dry golden corn lay the blue Aegean and beyond that the mist-shrouded mass of Olympus.

We were joined at breakfast by Jeannie Woolston from Tuxedo Park, New York, one of the school's volunteer workers. "The Farm School is a way of life," she said. "It grabs you. The teachers are bright young Americans who could have successful careers at home. But they prefer to be here." For girls the dedicated life had problems. Jeannie, who was twenty-one, blonde and vivacious, said, "The students from the Greek villages are not always able to understand girls who are independent, who live alone. So you have to learn the delicate balance of being their friend and keeping their respect, of not being misunderstood."

The Farm School was founded in 1902 by Dr. John Henry House, a Congregational minister who, after three decades of preaching and teaching in desperate mountain villages, concluded that the only way to help the people was to assist them to overcome the terrible misery in which they lived. With a borrowed five hundred dollars he bought fifty-two acres of rocky wasteland, known to Greeks who refused to work it as "the land of snakes."

"Poor land is the curse of Greece," Dr. House wrote. "If I were to succeed on good land I would prove nothing." He began with twelve

12

orphans. A schoolhouse which took ten years to build was ignited by a charcoal heater before it was finished and burned to the ground. During World War II, Dr. House's son, Charles House, who succeeded him as director, was interned in Germany. German troops occupied and destroyed the school. It was rebuilt and reopened during the Greek Civil War. On a winter night in 1949 Communist guerrillas rounded up the senior class of forty-three boys and marched them into the mountains toward Bulgaria. Before sunrise five wily young Greeks had escaped and were back at the school. For several weeks footsore students limped back, starving and in rags. One boy had spent hours submerged in a cold lake. By June every graduate was on hand to receive his diploma.

Their story spread around the world. In 1955 King Paul and Queen Frederika decorated Charles House. Young Bruce Lansdale, a Cornell graduate who had come to the school as a Fulbright teacher in 1948, became the new director. Today the school occupies more than five hundred acres of productive land, much of it irrigated. In its modern classrooms two hundred boys from Greece's poor villages receive a four-year junior college education.

In barns, shops and laboratories the boys learn animal husbandry, livestock improvement, soil chemistry, irrigation, carpentry, machine repairing, food preservation and soil conservation and fertilization. Said Bruce Lansdale, "The last thing we want is to make white-collar workers. We give boys the knowledge, the skills and attitudes which they will need to become leaders in their own village." By selling its agricultural products, including "Golden Guernsey" pasteurized milk flown to Athens for U.S. military and diplomatic personnel, the school has become two-thirds self-supporting, probably a record for privately financed American philanthropies in foreign lands.

Through its extension program the Farm School trains leaders—presidents, secretaries, priests, schoolteachers—to solve village problems without government assistance. It has distributed over seventy thousand American-strain baby chicks, three hundred hogs, Aberdeen Angus beef cattle and calves from its dairy herd, to improve moribund Greek strains. Seeds of high-producing disease-resistant corn, wheat, alfalfa and other crops are distributed through Farm School graduates. The proliferating effects can hardly be calculated. But it is a safe assumption that Greece had become agriculturally self-sufficient for the first time in the last decade to a large degree because of this very unique American aid.

Jeannie took us on a tour. Boys on tractors were plowing and mowing third-crop alfalfa. Others were spraying tomatoes and planting winter vegetables. In workshops they were building wooden beehives, pasteurizing milk, operating a power plant, making cement building blocks and constructing wood-burning hot-water heaters from old gasoline drums for village homes. "We have to start from the beginning, to teach them everything," Jeannie said. "Like showing them how to use a toilet, teaching them not to go to the fields." Several boys were filling a silo with corn. "We want them to learn what many Greeks have lost, a sense of the dignity of manual labor. Our graduates are successful in life because they work harder." In a poultry shed there were thousands of peeping chicks and a twenty-five-thousand-egg incubator in constant use. We saw pens of sheep and hybrid hogs, including a black American sow with eleven newly-born white piglets. "Greece must increase the standards of its products to compete in the Common Market," said Jeannie. "We are trying to help."

I was drawn toward the red brick dairy barn, immaculately clean and smelling sweetly of hay and ensilage. Two rows of cows—Holstein, Jersey, Guernsey and Brown Swiss—were identified by names like Dolly, Harriet, Jean, Kiki, Paola and Thelma. A Guernsey bull was named Caroline Duke, and a fierce Aberdeen Angus bull, Checkerboard Square. I asked a thin youth who was feeding the cows ensilage which breed of cows he preferred. "Holstein," he replied carefully in English without looking up. "They give most milk and they are very peaceful."

I said I had a herd of Holstein. The youth raised his large hazel eyes. "Where?" he asked.

"In Wisconsin," I said.

"Are many cows in Wisconsin," he said. His face had the gaunt leanness of youths painted by El Greco. His black curly hair was cut in a modified Beatle style.

"More cows than there are men to take care of them," I said, thinking of our farm labor shortage. We introduced ourselves. His name was Alexandros Marlis. "Are you a student?" I asked.

"I am graduated, and now I am dairyman," he said. Watching his gentle manner with cows I sensed that he loved them, that he was a born herdsman.

"How old are you?" I asked. From his slight frame and his thinly corded arms I judged him to be about fifteen.

"In two months I will be nineteen," he said. One of the cows was rattling a stanchion. "Excuse me," he said. "If Esther does not have her food with the others she becomes angry."

"Alex is one of our best boys," Jeannie told me. "He is very well-trained and he speaks English better than anyone in his class. But he is one of the luckless ones. Unless a boy has family resources, a piece of land, or a relative or friend who is rich and powerful, there is no opportunity for him. Alex comes from a poor family in a very poor

village. For him there is nothing in Greece. Everyone likes Alex, so he
was kept on until he is called for military service. After that he has
decided to go to Germany."

"Why Germany?"

"To work in a factory. More than a third of the people in Alex's village
are in Germany, including his five brothers and sisters."

The boy was back with the ensilage cart. "Cows get angry and
jealous." He was smiling. "Is little difference from people. What do you
feed your cows in Wisconsin?"

"Exactly what you are feeding them. Ensilage, hay, grain."

"Who takes care of your cows?" he said.

"We have a farmer." Deep behind his large eyes I sensed an idea
slyly being born, the same idea that was lurking within me. "You wouldn't
like Wisconsin," I said. "In winter it is very cold."

He laughed and rolled his eyes. "In my village is also very cold," he
said.

"The snow is deep. No Greek could endure it."

"We have snow in my village," he said. "Sometimes it is deeper than
my boots. And in Germany is even more. My brothers say is very cold. I
will need many sweaters in Germany."

"Do you want to go to Germany?"

It was an unfair question. His impetuous answer, born of peasant
cunning and memories of suffering, must have taken courage to deliver.
"I would rather go to Wisconsin," he said.

In the afternoon I visited the school's English classes. The three
sections met simultaneously in adjoining rooms, the thin walls of which
could not completely separate three groups of voices declaiming loudly
in unison. In the first room, a thirty-year-old Pennsylvania Fulbright
teacher named Martin Runkle was asking, "Did I bring a donkey to class
today?" and a husky seventeen-year-old voice replied, "No you don't." In
the second room Walter Empson, a twenty-three-year-old volunteer from
Princeton, who looked younger than some of his heavily-bearded students,
was struggling with the possessive case. "Whose book is this?" he asked,
and a deep voice replied, "Is me book."

"No, no, no. It's my book. It's mine," said Empson, trying to steer
them through the hazards of the first and second person. "That not your
book, that mine," said a student and another shouted, "They not mine,
they yours." In the third room Philip Foote, a thirty-year-old Texan, was
directing his advanced students in question-and-answer conversations.
"Why did you start the tractor?" one boy asked and another responded, "I
start to cut the hay." A handsome seventeen-year-old named Apostolos
asked, "Why did you touch the body of my girl?" and another replied,

"Because she is very pretty girl." Anxious to change the line of conversation, Foote asked the students to form sentences with the verb "to feel." Undaunted, Apostolos said, "I felt the body of my girl on my dream last night . . ."

In the evening Bruce Lansdale had a welcoming party for first-year students. "New boys from the villages do not mix easily," he said. "They are shy, distrustful and withdrawn. Sometimes we have serious homesick problems and we have no alternative but to send them back."

Seventy boys, aged twelve to fifteen, waited quietly in the recreation room of Lansdale's house. A few seemed exceptionally small and very frightened. "This is Kostas," said Lansdale, introducing one of the smallest. "He brought his harmonica, which he plays before he goes to sleep." The boy, wearing a green crocheted pull-over, brightened for a moment but the loneliness remained in his eyes. Lansdale turned the introductions into a game. Each boy was instructed to confer with the boy on his left and then introduce him to the company.

"This is Gregorious," a boy began. "He lives in Kilkis. His father has twenty-four *stremata* (about six acres), one cow and thirty sheep. He raises corn, wheat and cotton."

The introduced lad blushed and then introduced the new friend on his left. "This is Nikos Dorakis. He is from Lassithi and has nineteen *stremata*, one cow, two mules, ten sheep and twenty chickens." So it continued around the circle. "This is Christos Saliannis. He lives in Pella of Pieria, the birthplace of Alexander the Great. He has three cows, twenty sheep and one sister."

The Farm School's field man is a graduate named Nikos Mikos. The next day I went with him and a middle-aged missionary couple from the United Church Board for World Ministries, to visit school alumni. In Nikos' Volkswagen we drove on dusty dirt roads into arid highlands, through villages of whitewashed houses, communal wells, and cafés where men played *tavli,* a kind of Greek backgammon. Our first stop was at Sedhes, where we visited a short, friendly twenty-eight-year-old bachelor named Dimitrios Aidonides. With an older brother he cultivated ten acres of vineyards, fruits and vegetables. His ownership of an International Harvester tractor and combine astounded me. In Wisconsin where farms averaged twenty times as large as Dimitrios', combines were owned by cooperatives. Greeks love tractors and large machines, and will borrow from banks to own them. The Aidonides brothers harvested eighty acres of neighbors' wheat, from which they kept 10 per cent of the yield as a harvesting fee. The high-yield American wheat was proving a mixed blessing. The hybrid seeds and fertilizers had doubled the crops, causing a surplus and a fall in prices. When they can afford it, Greeks have learned to eat less bread and more protein, which reduces wheat consumption. In his barn Dimitrios showed us a sixty-ton pile of unsold wheat.

In a neat little parlor Dimitrios' sister-in-law served sugared squares of eggplant and the traditional glass of cool water. "Is the water safe?" Mrs. Missionary asked the astonished hostess and her husband asked, "Do you go to Protestant or to Catholic Church?" Dimitrios was full of questions about America. What did we grow in Wisconsin? How much were we paid for our products? How did the American government aid small farmers? "You have so much land in America," he said. "You do not have our problems."

The next graduate we visited was Emmanuel Terzis, a tall muscular poultry farmer thirty-three years old. He was building a new eight-room house on the site of his old home. During its construction he lived with his wife and son in part of a poultry shed. His wife, happy and handsome in late pregnancy, carried a table and chairs into the poultry yard. Surrounded by pecking chickens, we ate candied cherries and drank coffee. At the Farm School Emmanuel had been one of the students kidnaped by Communists. "It was ten thirty on a Friday night," he said. "We had our showers and were in bed when the soldiers marched into the dormitory. 'In the name of the Republic of Greece, we are taking you prisoners,' they said. We walked most of the night. We were near my village and I knew the terrain. Pretending I had to piss, I hid in a swamp. The next day I returned to school."

Before Emmanuel went to the Farm School, the family's ten acres had been planted to wheat. With chickens from the school he turned to poultry. Now he had twenty-five hundred chickens and his own incubator for ten thousand eggs. He was expecting a shipment of White Rock and White Cornish chicks from a New Hampshire hatchery. "They are the best breeds for broilers," he said. "Because of the Farm School, Greeks are learning to eat chicken and chickens are helping solve Greek's food problem." Mrs. Missionary had a question. "Do you farm organically?" she asked. When the question was explained, Emmanuel exploded into laughter.

"Yes, I suppose I do," he said. He asked Mrs. Missionary if she had a farm.

"Oh, no," she said, "but my garden is organic. My tomato yield doubled."

We drove twenty-five miles east to the mountain village of Kato Scholarion. Here we visited Antonios Gavezas, one of the school's most prosperous graduates. He was a tall, lean thirty-two-year-old man with wind-burned skin, a strong, bony face and huge sandaled feet. His farm of seventeen acres, one of the largest in the area, grew wheat, table grapes which he exported to Germany, and twenty-five thousand chickens from which he made enough to pay for the dowry of his sister, Zoe. "The size of the dowry depends on the kind of husband that you want to buy," he said, speaking English in a deep soft voice. Now that his sister was married, he was himself engaged and would soon be married. "When I have picked my grapes," he said, "when I have plowed and sown the wheat, when I have sold my chickens, then is the season for marrying. Maybe it will not be until December 31." He took us to his house in a crowded Turkish quarter where we met his fiancée, a white-skinned dark-eyed beauty named Urania, and his mother, a gaunt, handsome woman, whom he resembled. On a balcony overlooking the roofs of the town, the mother served us still more cherries and coffee. "Nice place you have here," said Mr. Missionary, and his wife, pointing to a Moslem minaret, asked, "What is the denomination of that church?"

"I was a poor boy, very shy, without personality," said Antonios. "But a Farm School graduate who makes a success is admired and becomes an influence in his community. Now I am a candidate for public administrator." The mother said, "We never used to go to Thessaloniki. Last night we went to the circus in our own automobile."

We visited three more alumni, eating sweets and drinking coffee with each, and then at twilight we returned over dusty roads. Nikos spoke of the Greek dowry system, how it was the ruination of Greek agriculture. "The marriage of each daughter requires a division of land, and the impractical small farms grow smaller and smaller." We passed some small boys shepherding sheep. "Children do this work because the men have gone to Germany where they earn more money in factories. The little shepherds do not go to school." Little effort was made to enforce a law requiring all children to have at least nine years of education. "Education diminishes in Greece as the age increases," said Nikos. "More than one hundred twenty thousand boys and girls are graduated annually from elementary schools. Half of these enroll in high schools. Dropouts are high, and only eighteen thousand graduate. Of these only eight thousand enroll in our universities and five thousand graduate. Most of the Farm School students come from villages where there are no high schools."

"Do the children go to church?" asked Mrs. Missionary. Her husband recounted their uplifting tour of "disaster areas"—the earthquake in Skoplje, Yugoslavia, the flood regions of Italy, a refugee camp in Austria. "We found Christians everywhere," said Mrs. Missionary. "Of course there were some Jews in Austria."

When we arrived at the school the sun was setting. The moment it sank behind Olympus the hot afternoon turned into cool evening. On the athletic field the English teacher, Walter Empson, was playing volleyball with the students. Accordion music floated out from a dormitory window. I could hear shouts and splashing of water in the showers. After two days of weeping the little harmonica player had been sent home. The relatives of another homesick boy had been sent for, and were gathered on the dormitory steps. Surrounded by family and by curious students, the child was sobbing pitifully. His father, an excitable dark little man, was raging at the child, making angry speeches to whomever would listen, declaiming the boy a disgrace. He shouted out the sad story of his life. "I am a poor man with only twenty *stremata* of dry land. My whole life I worked to feed my children and my mother-in-law. I made a dowry for two sisters and now I have three daughters who need dowries. This is my reward, a crybaby son who disgraces me before the world!" With a pathetic cry the child ran to his father and embraced his waist. The father kicked the boy away. "You're no child of mine," he shouted.

My heart ached for the boy. His crisis was being handled so badly. If one kind person had spoken to the child, had touched him with a gentle hand, he would have been comforted. In shame the father raged on. In the end he was forced to take the boy home.

Walking to my room I listened to the winds wailing in the dark pines and the splash of water irrigating alfalfa. The lower slopes of the mountains were lost in mists, but the rose-tinted peaks of the Pindus emerged like silvery-veiled breasts of sleeping maidens. One bright star, Venus perhaps, shone over the cone of Olympus.

We dined in town with Jeannie Woolston and went to a *taverna* to hear Vassilis Tsitsanis, a popular composer and singer known as the "father of *bouzouki*." The word, the plural of which is *"bouzoukia,"* is used to indicate a type of music, the instrument which plays it, and, broadly, a form of entertainment. The instrument is of the mandolin type but with a harder tone, which, like country rock 'n' roll in America, is usually amplified to a raucous and deafening clangor. Defenders of *bouzouki* claim it derives from soldier songs in the Revolution of 1821. Its detractors say it is "refugee" music brought into Greece by Asiatic immigrants after the Smyrna disaster of 1922. There is no doubt of a strong Asiatic influence in its monotonously wailing rhythms. Up to ten years ago *bouzouki* was performed only in working-class *tavernas*. Tsitsanis and his followers claim to have made the instrument acceptable in Greek society. In this they were assisted by motion pictures like *Never on Sunday* and *Zorba the Greek* which made *bouzouki* popular abroad. When tourists sought it out in Greece it began to find a grudging social acceptance.

The barn-size hall was called Kalamitsa. When we arrived at midnight it was empty. At one o'clock an orchestra began to play and men filed in, taking places at tables. At one thirty a girl, peering with one eye from under an umbrella of black hair, clapped her hands, stomped on high spikes, and began to sing in a dark voice. *Bouzouki* songs lament life's pathos, especially the cruelty of love and the perfidy of lovers. The girl's keening moved her male audience to a uniquely Greek demonstration. A man threw a plate which shattered with a clatter at her feet. Appearing not to notice, she kept on singing. Wham! Another plate! At once there was a bombardment of crockery which continued through several songs, and the girl shouting into an amplifier raised her voice over the din.

The ritual is known as *spassi,* from the verbal command *"Spas ta!"* or "Break them!" In popular usage the expression means "Be happy!" "It's a catharsis Greek men need," said Jeannie. "They're so emotional they have to do something."

The singer left the floor and there was a moment of calm while waiters with brooms and dustpans swept up the debris, clearing the platform for the next singer. More girls followed. Each was charivaried, each had her popularity gauged by the accumulation of broken plates and cups at her feet. The crockery was tabulated by waiters—profits from the cheap crockery selling at high prices might exceed that from wine and beer. Each time a singer finished there was a sweep-up.

The last girl, named Rosake, was small and provocatively plump with great black eyes, shingled hair and a short tight black skirt slit to the hip. Her keening reminded me of *fado* singers in Lisbon:

> There's no road,
> No path that I can take
> That does not remind me of you . . .

Like flowers around the feet of a Neapolitan diva, the white china spread at her feet.

> No day passes,
> That I do not drink,
> There's not a glass
> That does not recall you . . .

Between singers groups of men danced. Joined together by knotted handkerchiefs, they leaped through the Zorba *syrtaki,* and levitated in the graceful *tsakonikos,* a dance which according to tradition was danced by Theseus in Crete after he had slain the Minotaur.

At two thirty Tsitsanis, a thin, tense man, appeared. Before he could sing a word plates were flying like discuses in an ancient palestra. Like clerks in a chinaware auction, waiters ran from the kitchen with piles of white crockery. Accompanying himself on his *bouzouki,* Tsitsanis began a song. The bombardment of crockery, glasses, beer and wine bottles covered his words so they could not be understood, and it continued for five minutes after he finished. Before the sweepers could clear away the debris a young drunk in a red shirt removed his shoes and began to dance over the surface of broken glass and china, earnestly as a penitent in a religious rite, showing devotion to his idol.

In the morning I set out for still another village. Many Macedonian villages, Bruce Lansdale said, were slowly dying. Their population decline was the result of the migration of young people who escaped the desperation of Greek country life to work in German factories. Most of those remaining at home were elderly grandparents, and children sent back from Germany to attend Greek schools.

Lakkoma, a village on a windy plateau, was an exception. Its youths did not leave, but chose, instead, to remain on the land, to care for it, to labor over it, to make it fruitful. Among its dry and dusty neighbor villages it stood out like an oasis on the desert. Since the war its population had grown from seven hundred to a thousand persons.

I was on my way to see the man responsible for the miracle, a forty-six-year-old graduate of the Farm School named Dimitrios Fliscanopoulos. Because "Dimitrios" is "James" in Greek, he was known by his student name of "Jimmy." I expected to meet a dynamic energetic extrovert. The man who greeted me in the municipal building was short and stocky with blond hair. He had a soft voice and the shy dignity of a scholar. Around him shelves contained the works of Walt Whitman, Edith Hamilton, John Steinbeck, and a row of biographies of Abraham Lincoln.

"I learned about Lincoln at school," said Jimmy. "He became the inspiration of my life. Greece needs a Lincoln. We are in trouble because we have no leaders, no leaders in our villages, no leaders in Athens. Our politicians are not men of vision and spirit, only clerks. It is a terrible thing for a country."

Were there not men like himself, I asked, to bring leadership to the villages?

He shook his head. "We must learn more," he said. "Education is our problem. I do not want to be the only leader in Lakkoma. I do not want to hear them calling all the time, 'Jimmy, Jimmy, Jimmy!' I am so small. I can do so little. But I must continue to think I can. It is the only way."

Jimmy was not a native of Lakkoma. He was a city boy from Thessaloniki, whose ambition was to live on his own land. He began in Lakkoma in 1943 with five acres to which he kept adding, until now

he has twenty-five acres of wheat and grapes. Poultry raising, learned at
the Farm School, is his mainstay. In 1962 his poultry barns were destroyed by fire. With a bank loan he rebuilt and began again. Today he
sells twenty thousand broilers a year. He married a local girl and has five
children. One daughter attended the Farm School's new girl's division.
"Because I am an outsider it has been easier for me to help the people of
Lakkoma," Jimmy said. "I inherited no prejudices, no feuds, no enemies.
I am careful never to take sides. The first problem was to win the
people's trust. A secretary can do a great deal if he solves his own
problems first, if he makes the people respect him."

We were interrupted by a young lady, the local schoolteacher, who
came to use the telephone. "My office is the communications center,"
said Jimmy. "Everything that happens in the village happens right here."
For several minutes we waited, listening to the girl shout into the instrument. "The people do not understand that you can talk softly into a
telephone," said Jimmy. "Because they speak over a distance they believe
they must shout."

"I have some old pictures," he said. "If you see them you will laugh."
He brought out an album of photographs in which I saw a sun-parched,
dusty cluster of houses, like the villages I had been visiting. "The people
wanted to do better but they needed to be shown the way," said Jimmy.
"It took two years of talking to convince them to begin."

A road into the village came first in 1950. A church was next, and
then the municipal building with a warehouse to store surplus crops and
an auditorium for lectures and films. A deep well was sunk two kilometers away and its water piped into the village. A fifty-acre community
forest was planted. A new school was the current project and there were
plans to bring electricity into the village and macadamize the road. The
improvements were made without government aid or loans. To each
project, every family in the village contributed money and labor.

We walked through the town, beginning at the warehouse piled high
with three million kilos of surplus wheat. "We have learned how to grow
more wheat, but we have not learned to sell it," said Jimmy. "Everywhere
warehouses are filled. Farmers don't know how to plan their future.
Grapes give a good yield, but the first crop is four years after planting.
The only fruit trees that grow at our elevation are apricots, and they
take eight years to produce a crop. No one can wait that long."

The main street was filled with trucks and tractors, of which there are
forty in Lakkoma. In a shed outside the town women were sorting and
packing golden *Rosaki* grapes, loading them onto a huge Austrian truck
to be hauled to Vienna. Kicking up a clod of dry earth, Jimmy said, "If
we had irrigation it would be a rich land. But in our high altitudes we

have only one crop a year." A black-shawled old lady scurried out of a house to shake my hand. She was about to fly to America to visit her son, one of Lakkoma's few émigrés. The boy had married an American girl who visited the village with her Greek father. Now he was a prosperous baker in New York.

Jimmy invited me to lunch. We passed through the front rooms of his house to a tiny low-ceilinged kitchen, part of an original Turkish house. Jimmy's wife, a pretty, young-looking woman, served a steaming dill soup and excellent fried chicken. Her mother, a smiling, bright-eyed old lady, watched from her chair in a corner. There was wine and Jimmy toasted America. "To Greece's best friend," he said. "To Americans, who are free, who can do what they wish, who can think what they wish and who can say what they think."

I raised my glass, toasting Greece.

"For Greece there will be no easy solutions," said Jimmy. "We must work hard, very hard, to build our country. We must earn all the good things which America has earned. All the countries of the world want America to give them her riches. But I don't wish to say to my friend, 'Give me, give me, give me!' It is not possible. To my people, I say, 'Americans don't sit in *tavernas* and play cards. They work.' In Greece we must begin with education and that will take much time. Our young people must be persuaded from leaving. Greek youths don't want to leave. They love their home. But they see the hoplessness, the political confusion of Greeks always fighting Greeks. To them I say, we must stay at home and try to make something better. Perhaps if we try hard enough one day we will achieve democracy."

More wine, another toast. "To democracy," said Jimmy. "Democracy is a great word. You cannot speak it easily. It is too great." His eyes shone.

On Sunday morning David Greggory and I went into Thessaloniki to see the Byzantine churches. From the Roman triumphal arch we followed the narrow Street of St. Paul to the rotunda of St. George, built in the fourth century as a mausoleum for Emperor Galerius. When it became a Christian church a century later it was decorated with mosaics, a few shadowy fragments of which still shine against a glittering gold background—a Christ, some saints and apostles and graceful airborne angels.

In other churches, Our Lady Built without Hands, Our Lady of the Coppersmiths, the Church of the Holy Apostles, mosaics have been hacked over by Moslems who, motivated by what strange furies, always gouged the eyes from celestial faces. In the cupola of the Cathedral of St. Sophia there is a restored mosaic of Christ on a rainbow in an olive grove with angels and apostles, and in the basilica of St. Dimitrios an eighth-century mosaic, also restored, shows Thessaloniki's patron, Dimitrios, as protector of children. The saint and the two children have the same delicately rounded chin, the same long straight nose, the same grave, wide eyes. It is the face, the gaze of Byzantium which, walking in the city, we met again and again.

The streets had become rivers of people flowing like a tide toward the center, to greet George Papandreou, the prime minister whose resignation King Constantine had forced in the "July crisis." We parked the car and fought through a feverishly emotional crowd toward Queen Sophia Avenue, over which the political leader would arrive from the airport.

In an explosion of revved motors and sirens he came, riding on the top of the seat in an open car, his hand raised in salute, the wind blowing his gray-white hair, his aquiline profile cameo-sharp against the blue sky. Like an ancient god astride Pegasus, he swept the human mass with him into Aristotelous Square. Standing at a corner of Franklinou Rousvelt Avenue, I heard, between roaring waves of applause, the explosive slogans. "March to freedom!" "Democracy will triumph!" "The people will rule!" I remembered the patriarchs of Metsovon disdaining their beer, and I thought if I were king in Athens I would be very nervous.

III

In the Beginning

It was time, before going on, to return to the beginning.

There was no creation on Olympus. Unlike monotheistic Judaeo-Christians, who believed that in the beginning was God who created the earth and then man, the Greeks believed there was Gaea—Mother Earth—who gave birth to the gods, who in union among themselves or with their own offspring, begat men.

This they did in human fashion with lively disregard for filial lines. Incest, a practical necessity, produced a chaotic clan of squabbling mortals and immortals. Gaea's randiest and most fertile grandson was Zeus, the king of heaven. His untiring and indiscriminate matings filled Olympus with deities and earth with men.

To establish the center of the world, Zeus freed two eagles, one in the place of the sun's rising and the other in the place of the sun's setting. They met at Delphi over the *omphalos,* a stone navel of the earth. Beneath was the sacred cave of Mother Earth's oracle, guarded by the monster Python.

Zeus' most famous son, Apollo, killed Python, an act interpreted as the defeat of barbarism and brute strength in the world and the birth of civilization. Over the sacred cave men built a shrine to Apollo, god of light and reason. Thereafter for one thousand years the liberated oracle ruled the fate of mankind. Delphi, on a ledge between Parnassus and the Corinthian Gulf, was the holiest place in Greece and the religious, political and cultural center of the world.

On the morning David Greggory and I left the Farm School, Avghi, the housekeeper, sloshed us with water from a pitcher, a traditional ritual which, she said, would bring us back. We drove south through the Vale of Tempe where springs named for Daphne, Venus and Apollo kept a river flowing throughout the year.

The day turned to rain. We passed through Larissa and Pharsala, where a decisive battle, in which two hundred of Caesar's legionnaires routed fifteen thousand of Pompey's soldiers, elevated Caesar to the mastery of the world. From the Othrys Pass we looked across the great Thessaly plains spreading toward the horizon like a mauve sea. A Jacob's ladder of diagonal sunlight broke through a chasm in the clouds and shone on a riderless horse galloping across the fields. My heart leaped, my brain reeled. Was it Pegasus I was seeing flying into the heavens? A steed of Pluto's leaping into the underworld? Or a rampaging centaur fleeing a Lapith hunter? The flying shape, mane and tail flowing, appeared to have wings; it soared on, fading into the horizon mists.

We descended to Lamia and entered Parnassus country. A burst of sun turned the gray clouds on the mountain into flames like a fiery portal to the heavens. Circling around it, we came to Livadia, the capital of Boeotia, where we joined the ancient Sacred Way from Thebes to Delphi. After thirteen miles we arrived, in a barren valley, at the Triple Way, a road junction where, according to Sophocles, Oedipus, returning on foot from Delphi, met his father, King Laius, and killed him, an unintentional patricide which set off the chain of calamities which destroyed the House of Thebes. The road spiraled higher through canyons of gray rock. We passed through the town of Arachova, bedecked like a festival with bright tapestries and blankets, and after eight more vertiginous miles, we were in Delphi.

Within moments I was standing on a hotel balcony, suspended between misty cliffs and dark sea. To the west the gorge of the Pleistos opened on the Sacred Plain of Amphissa, a silvery sea of ten thousand olives closed in by a curve of snow-peaked mountains which faced the aquamarine Gulf of Corinth. Beyond the waters silver-bellied clouds floated over the massive snow-covered mountains of the Peloponnese. Though the sun was blinding bright, a crescent moon hung in the sky above. Ravens flew below and an eagle soared overhead. Surrounded on every side by wild primal beauty, I had no doubts that gods once lived here. In such a place, the myths are palpably alive.

For the mysteries by which men guide their lives are truths truer than facts. Paul MacKendrick says there was no sacred crevice in Delphi, no guiding vapors. Looking into the canyon I believed in a cave guarded by Python. Watching tendrils of mist rise from fissures like an exhalation from the earth, the welling of fumes with which the oracle guided civilization seemed altogether plausible. Looking at the turbulent mountains I could almost hear the groaning earthquakes from which plundering Persians, believing them to be rumbling warnings of the gods, fled.

From the next terrace a blast of *bouzouki* clobbered my ear. Peering over the lattice I saw a bikini-clad Ganymede, lying on a mat beside a portable phonograph.

"Am I disturbing you?"

"Not exactly. I've just arrived."

"Excuse me. You're under the spell of Apollo."

"I was brooding."

"He must have been a creep. Never made out. Daphne, Hyacinth, those nymphs. They all got away. I have the impression he couldn't run very fast."

He stood up and extended across the lattice a small pink hand weighted with two large rings. "I'm Welkin, retired poet, professional voluptuary. What do you do?"

"Not retired," I said.

He was probably a youthful thirty-five. He had black curly hair and a hollowed face, and a jeweled crucifix hung on his smooth chest. Irish, I thought.

"Welsh," he said. "I follow Bacchus, explore the life of the senses. Have you had lunch?"

Driving wildly a Jaguar, his delicate hands hugging the steering wheel as if it were a resisting woman, he hurled us like a Zeus thunderbolt down through the olives. "You're good news," he shouted. "I was bored." He tooted at a shepherd and waved an arm. "Good news!" he cried. "Pan and his satyrs came down from Parnassus to romp in the valley. You may find yourself in a bacchanal."

With a screech of brakes we careened against a shack on the beach. "Best restaurant on the gulf," said Welkin. The restaurateur and his family greeted us at the door like Japanese servants, saying, "Good day, Mr. Welkin. Sole very good this morning. Lobster very fresh."

Welkin ordered both and a program of wines. During the superb lunch he kept up a torrent of words, punctuating them with shrills of tortured laughter. The loneliness pouring from him like a fever infected me, filling me with despair.

"My wife is over there somewhere," he said, pointing across the gulf to the mountains of the Peloponnese. "We see each other now and then. I sleep. I take baths. I burn candles. I collect jewels. Sometimes when the spirit moves me I write a poem. Just back from Istanbul. The baths in Turkey were subtle, man, subtle. The lights were candles fastened to the backs of turtles swimming in shallow pools. The loveliest jewels were inlaid in their shells. Good news."

Drunk with wine, he hurtled us through the olive groves back to the belly button of the world. "Welcome to the Pythian games," he shouted, jolting to a halt before the entrance to the ancient city. He introduced me to a guide named Pavlos, who said, "Very happy, Mr. Welkin. He is a follower of Dionysius." The guide and I started up the slope of the Sacred Way. The path in ancient times was lined with statues, porticoes, and twenty-three small temples built by Greek cities as repositories for their gifts to Apollo. The avenue of treasuries, competitively displaying the wealth of rival powers, must have been the most dazzling sight in the ancient world. One monument of which no trace remains was a bronze palm tree with gold dates, surmounted by a golden statue of Athena. Only one treasury, the Athenian, survives in its original state. Its sculptured panels celebrate the exploits of the hero, Theseus.

Fifty yards up the Sacred Way is the great Temple of Apollo. Today only a few of its columns stand in place, but the ground plan is clear. Built on the spot where Apollo battled Python, the temple was the center of the Delphic mysteries. The first was destroyed by fire and rebuilt by the powerful Alcmaeonidae family of Athens. Destroyed again by an earthquake in 373 B.C., it was rebuilt once more by contributions from throughout the Greek world, from Italy, Asia Minor, and continental Greece.

My guide pointed to an opening in the floor, saying, "Here came up the prophetic exhalations. Only the Pythia priestess was allowed to breathe the fumes which gave messages. At first the Pythias were young women but they were not very chaste, so the priests chose women over fifty with whom there was not so much difficulty. Before the Pythia entered the temple, she washed herself in the Castalian spring. She chewed daphne leaves which made her crazy in the head, like hashish. The consultant asked his questions to the priests in the next room and the priest called them out to the Pythia. She breathed deep the gases until she was in a trance. She would babble strange words which only the priests could understand. The priests were very foxy."

They were also wise and experienced politicians, for the answers they translated from the hysterical babblings were based on political expediency and common sense. Kings asked the oracle where to found colonies and when to embark on voyages. Merchants sought advice about commercial enterprises, and young men on marriage plans. In the wars between Greek cities, the oracle was a successful mediator, imposing rules of international law. Rival states were forbidden to destroy enemy aqueducts and wells. They were restrained from killing prisoners. On the oracle's word the Megarans, led by Byzas, emigrated to Asia and founded Byzantium, and in the Persian Wars the oracle predicted the enemy's crushing defeat at Salamis.

The oracle's success brought more trophies to Delphi; more temples were built. The accumulation of wealth aroused the envy of enemies, and Delphi was attacked in a series of debilitating wars. Priests, moved by venality, began to translate the answers which rich consultants desired to hear. Apparently unable to prophesy their own end, they had no good advice for averting the final decline. Sulla plundered the rich temples, Nero carted off five hundred statues to Rome, and the soldiers of Constantine carried off more to Constantinople. The end came finally when Theodosius, the great destroyer of classic Greece, forbade the worship of Apollo.

The next morning it rained, so I went to the museum. Before French archaeologists could begin uncovering Delphi in the 1890s, they had to build a new village to the west. Fortunately for them, fortunately for Greece, the Romans, Byzantines, Franks and Turks who looted the marbles of Delphi and forged the bronzes into armor were unaware of the treasures which lay buried under the earth. "I saw a forest of statues in Delphi," wrote the historian Pausanias. Though less than one per cent of the ancient treasures remain in the museum, it is still one of the best collections in Greece.

Friezes record the feats of Hercules and Theseus. There is the statue of an indomitably proud wrestler named Agias, champion at Olympia and Delphi. Marvelous dancers and horses fill the rooms, and there is a melancholy Antinoüs, the beloved of Hadrian; his soft womanly beauty can be seen in every museum in Greece and Rome. Lording it over the collection like a young god is Delphi's prize, the bronze charioteer. Felled by an earthquake, his existence was not known until 1896. A youth who has just won the Pythian race, he stands in his chariot, gripping the reins, fatigued, modestly surprised at his triumph. The onyx pupils of his enameled eyes, inscrutable, visionary, hypnotic, watch so intently it is difficult to turn one's back on him.

Below the Temple of Apollo in an olive grove on the upper slopes of the Pleistos gorge is a group of ruins called *Marmaria* or "marbles." Here I wandered in the mist-haunted afternoon, beginning at the Castalian spring which gushes out of a narrow chasm between two peaks of the Phaedriades. From the summit of these cliffs, where eagles nest, the Delphians executed their criminals by hurling them into the valley below. Aesop, the fable teller, found guilty of some monetary indiscretion, was one of their victims. A downward path took me by a series of foundations, almost hidden in the thick grass, which my guidebook said were a

gymnasium, the treasury of Marseilles and two temples to Athena. At the
end of the lane, was the loveliest, the most familiar monument in Delphi,
the Tholós Temple. I had imagined this frequently photographed rotunda
to be the seat of the oracle, had indeed once listened to an illustrated
lecture identifying it as such, and I was surprised to find it so remote
from the Apollonic center. Its exact purpose has never been determined.
The three restored columns with a portion of the epistyle frieze is one of
the purest, most exquisite sights in Greece. As soft rain washed the rose-
tinted marble and wisps of clouds rose from the dripping olives up
through the columns like ancient ghosts, I seemed to be enveloped in
primal mysteries.

Just before dusk the sun broke through the clouds. I returned to the
sanctuary and climbed to the ancient theater to watch the drama of day
turning into night. The cliffs of the Phaedriades glowed red and the ravine
of the Pleistos was filled with a deep purple light. From a seat in the top
row I tried to imagine the setting two millenniums ago, the glitter of gold
and enamel, the chanting pilgrims moving slowly along the Sacred Way
to the temple, and then scurrying higher to the theater to watch the
re-enactment of Apollo's slaying of Python, and higher still to the
stadium for the games.

The world was so quiet I could hear water running in the springs and
the tinkle of bells on goats returning home for the night. A caravan of
black-robed women appeared with donkeys laden with baskets of grapes.
The sun slid behind the peaks and the mauve hills turned gray. A dog
barked.

Below me the navel of the earth was dark and silent as a tomb. It had
been silent like this a hundred years when the Emperor Julian the
Apostate, desiring to revive the ancient mysteries, consulted the oracle
and received this conclusive reply:

> Apollo hath no chapel left, no prophesying bay,
> No talking spring. The stream is dry that had so much to say.

We departed in the morning. At the Triple Way we turned left into a
valley of vineyards. A caravan of sheep, winding single file around a
mountain as far as the eye could see, was followed by a cloaked shepherd
carrying, like a baby, a newborn lamb. After three miles we were in
Distomon, a sad dusty town, where in 1944 the Germans, like an army of
vengeful Herods, slaughtered in one hour a male member from each
household. Crossing another pass we faced a broad fertile valley which
extended to the base of Hellikon Mountain. Below us, in a grove of

almonds and cypress, was the cluster of red-cupped domes of the monastery church, Osios Loukas.

Built in the eleventh century by the Emperor Romanus as a tomb for a hermit known as Holy Luke, and finished by the Emperor Basil II, it is the world's most beautifully preserved Byzantine monument. With a majestic regality it soars on a multitude of porphyry columns, its glories the golden mosaics which cover the walls of its domes and apses. The total is too rich for the stunned senses to take in on one visit. To know it all one would need to return again and again and begin each visit as if it were the first. In the center dome Christ the King, gouged by Moslem vandals, is weirdly faceless, but surrounding panels representing the annunciation, nativity and the baptism of Jesus are perfectly preserved. In a baptism, the nude Jesus has the short-legged wide-hipped frame of a Boeotian peasant. There are also paintings in the church—five icons painted by the Cretan Damaskinos, teacher of El Greco. In the narthex the mosaics are closer to eye level. The crucifixion and resurrection have the immediacy of Renaissance painting. In a Doubting Thomas panel, three disciples are white-bearded, one is blond and the others are brown-curled trimly barbered youths. In their huge eyes a silent astonishment shines forth. The incredible moment is filled with fear and wonder and with love.

Returning through Distomon, we saw a restaurant on the square called Ambryssefs. Its owners were two bachelor brothers, Athansios Dardanis, thirty-one, and Angelos, twenty-eight, who were providing dowries for five sisters. Three sisters were married, one was engaged and one was still to go. Not until all sisters were safe in a matrimonial harbor, said the brothers, would they themselves be free to think of marrying. From steaming kettles in the kitchen we selected an eggplant *moussaka,* a *stifado* of beef in onions and red wine, and creamed celery, which we ate with a large salad and native red wine. After the wretched food prepared for tourists in Delphi, it was a feast. "We have no tourists in Distomon," said Athansios. "But sometimes they stop on their way to Osios Loukas. Yes, even Germans. To them we are polite, that is all."

"In one hour two hundred and seventy-six people were killed," said Angelos. "Small boys, old men. Is very bad peoples, the Germans. To kill a soldier is one thing but to kill children and grandfathers is a badness too big to think."

Outside, over a movie theater, a sign said: *"Ce lieu fut abreuvet sanctifié de sang precieux de Distomites massacrés le 10 Juin 1944 par les envahisseurs de Hitler."*

I was copying the words when a dark little man approached and asked

me in French if I were German. Vexed at his question I abruptly
replied, "No, Amerikani."

The man's face brightened. "Ah, good people, Americans," he said,
offering his hand. "You must drink some wine with me." His name was
Nicholas Papatheodorou and he was the local butcher. At a table
screened by freshly slaughtered carcasses of lamb, he poured wine and
laid out food. He summoned his children, two pensive little girls and a
coy boy. "Come! See who is here," he told them. "Look well. They are
Americans." Dancing around the table the little man said, "You will
sleep in my house. You will hear music, you will dance."

We could not, we explained, for we had appointments to keep in
Athens. "You will come back. We will make a fete for you." We left in
the flush of warmth which comes frequently to the traveler in Greece, the
sense of being cherished and loved because some humanity in oneself
has been recognized and met.

We crossed the Boeotian plains, which are the cotton belt of Greece.
Men on tractors were plowing the ancient black earth and black-robed
women carried the stones from the fields. Bushes and trees along the way
were flecked with cotton puffs caught from trucks on their way to gins
and balers. At Livadia we turned onto a new motorway toward Thebes,
the ill-fated kingdom of Laius and Oedipus, Jocasta and Antigone. What
we found was a provincial agricultural town crowded with tractors and
walls of cotton bales. It was time for the *volta,* the evening stroll, and the
streets were filled with soldiers from a neighboring base aimlessly seeking
what there was not, surcease from ennui. "This is Thebes," I said to myself. "Thebes. Thebes."

Ahead lay Mt. Parnes and beyond, Athens. Passing through forests of
pine, I had a vision of a verdant Greece, of a rich green land before its
desolation by builders of ships for the ancient wars, by voracious plundering Turks, and finally by hungry earth-shearing goats. Trees are brother
and sister to man; they give him water, rich soil, fodder, fat cattle, fruit,
shade, all the things for life's fulfillment. Perhaps it was for this, the death
of trees, that the gods, loving trees, also died.

Soon it was dark and we faced for the first time the astonishing
experience of Greek night motoring. I remembered reading in a British
journal that the Greeks were the most chaotic autoists in the world, with
the highest accident rate. For most Greeks, auto ownership became a
possibility only since the war, and especially in recent years. The result is
a middle-aged generation of inexperienced drivers, wildly euphoric over
vehicle ownership. At night they drive with parking lights or with no lights
at all. A Greek's explanation for this incredible behavior is that it saves
battery wear and tear; Greek eyes, he says, are like cats' eyes, able to see

in the dark. Hurtling through the night, we tried to ignore passing
motorists' wild signaling and shouting, trying to tell us our lights were on.
As we approached the city, traffic thickened and the swirl of dark machines was like a film negative of a Keystone comedy run in double
speed. When we arrived at our hotel near Omonia Square our nerves
were in shreds.

Some drinks and a bath soothed us for dinner, which we had on the
roof terrace of a three-story *taverna* in the Plaka called Bacchus. The
music was no roaring *bouzouki* but a gentler combo of guitars and
accordions, and the singer was a sultry-voiced beauty named Lena Daina
who sang the songs of Mikis Theodorakis, a Renaissance-type man, who,
in addition to being one of Greece's two most popular composers, was a
left-wing deputy representing his native Crete in parliament. His film
score for *Zorba the Greek* had made him world-famous.

From our table we looked up on the Acropolis where *Son et Lumière*,
a pretentious light show prepared for tourists, was in progress. The changing flow of light on the ancient columns was striking. The amplified sound
track was another matter. On the hill a recorded voice with a British
accent was declaiming, "Valiant songs of Greece, go forth. . . ."

In a low-keyed passionate style that reminded me of Billie Holiday,
Lena Daina was singing earthly lines that might have been written by
Bessie Smith:

> Make your bed for two,
> For you and for me . . .

"I do not agree with you, Pericles," boomed the voice above. "You
have covered Athens with costly stones, like a harlot you have painted
her . . ."

Lena Daina sang:

> I embrace you, you embrace me,
> I take you and you take me . . .

"Come to me, all ye truth seekers, come to this consecrated rock,"
summoned the voice, and Lena Daina sang:

> "Make your bed for two. . . ."

IV

A Rare Vintage

"Be prepared to go barefoot," Spiros Nicodemou said on the phone when he invited me to the wine-tromping. I caught his veiled suggestion that I bathe my feet.

He fetched me at four thirty in the afternoon and we set out for Piána, a village in Attica near the sea. Spiros was a travel agent, friend of a friend in New York. He was an Egyptian Greek, one of the thousands driven back to Greece by President Nasser's economic discrimination against aliens. Educated in Alexandria, he spoke English perfectly.

We discussed politics. Both King Constantine and his political enemy, the popular former prime minister, George Papandreou, were touring islands and both were being welcomed by enraptured crowds, according to newspapers partisan to each. One journal had published a photo of a peasant woman kissing the King's foot. He was carrying his three-month-old daughter. "The purpose of the trip," said Spiros, "is to show off the baby. For months we read obstetrical details about the baby's birth and the names of professors in attendance. The publicity had an adverse effect—too many women die in childbirth without assistance. For these island trips, the King carefully picks the smaller ones. If *I* went to them *I'd* draw a crowd. Everyone on these islands meets *every* boat. Naturally, when it's a royal yacht they wheel out the grandmothers and babies.

"The King is a dull young man, badly educated and a playboy. One can't feel deeply about him one way or the other. It's his mother the people can't abide. Eventually there will be a plebiscite. The King will lose and the Papandreou party will win."

We were on our way to the vineyards of Michalis Kanakis, a vintner-restaurateur who each year invites Athens' foreign diplomats to his trompings. "Diplomatic wives," said Spiros, "are happy for the opportunity to *help out* and be photographed in the tank." We parked in a lane of pink oleanders crowded with Mercedes-Benzes, favorite car of diplomats, and walked under an arch upon which was printed "Kanakis Garden, Very Nice." Inside, it appeared as if a funeral were in progress. A large crowd was standing at solemn attention while two priests in gold surplices, one old and one young, chanted sonorously behind an improvised altar covered with flowers. "They're thanking God for grapes," whispered Spiros. An incense pot smoldering on the altar sent tendrils of white smoke into the branches of the plane and cypress trees canopying the garden. I looked over the strange company. There were many Teutonic types, tall, blond, and elegantly clothed. One very tall Scandinavian was accompanied by his wife and his mother, a thin old woman in a straw hat, gauntly regal as a Swedish dowager queen. There were a number of black-skinned African diplomats in formal afternoon attire. Their wives in pink and orchid saris bloomed like a flower garden. There were also a few high-chested Greeks, including a uniformed army general. Around the outside of the garden, groups of workers from the Kanakis vineyards clung together, genuflecting piously. There were also many restless children. Four small German boys in *Lederhosen* waited with bare feet.

The young priest, his hair and beard shining black, led the antiphony; the old one, his white beard blowing in the wind like Noah's, read the responses. "They're praying for a good vintage," whispered Spiros. The candles, burning low, sputtered; photographers' bulbs flashed. The old priest dipped a sprig of basil into a bowl of holy water and waved a moist blessing over the company. "*Amin,*" he wailed. Bearing the basil, the priests led the people in a procession out of the garden and into a white-washed barn. Garlands of vine leaves were looped over the rafters. The procession came to a halt before a four-foot-high concrete vat extending the width of the barn, filled with red and white grapes. The priests waved the basil over the grapes, chanted some phrases, and then they disappeared.

A buoyant march tune from a phonograph filled the barn. Michalis Kanakis, a dark, stocky little man, removed his shoes and stockings and the jacket of his blue suit, rolled his pants legs above his knees and leaped into the tub. Inviting his guests to follow, he reached out for the hands of ladies who nervously withdrew them. He beckoned children to join him and with them there was no hesitation. They scrambled into the tub like monkeys. When some smaller ones became mired in grapes and began to shriek, several mothers removed nylons and shoes and climbed in to

rescue them. Finding the sensation pleasant, the mothers encouraged
friends to plunge. Several ladies with good-looking legs hiked their skirts
to their hips. Watching them scramble over the wall, I remembered an
Italian fresco, probably in Ferrara, of a troupe of possessed elders leaping
into a fountain of youth. A Danish lady, holding her skirt recklessly high,
started several male diplomats fumbling with their shoelaces. Outside the
tank, servants were setting up a huge buffet of stuffed vine leaves, eggplant, cheeses, fish, pickles, and bottles of old wine. Kanakis was pulling
at the hand of one of the African ladies in a pink sari. Shrieking girlishly,
she allowed friends to hoist her over the wall. At once she became
ensnarled in the folds of her gown, lost her balance and fell screaming
into the flood. Several black men leaped in to rescue her. They carried her
out and the sari hung from her body in wet dripping strands. Servants
dressed as Greek peasants kept filling wineglasses for everyone inside and
outside the tub. The phonograph played a wild cha-cha. The combination
of wine and music stirred hesitating souls. Men and women leaped into
the purple pool.

Someone was tugging at me; my time had come. I kicked off my shoes
and socks, rolled my pants and plunged. The effect was eerie. By now the
grapes were a soup without bottom and I felt as if I were sinking into a
swamp, sucked into purple quicksand. The feeling was sensuous, like an
erotic swim in a lake with springs, cool here, warm there, depending
where the stomping had been heaviest. The texture was soft and sinking,
solid only when one got through to the wooden floor. Children leaping
gleefully up and down spattered the purple slop on themselves and everyone else. "Dear girl, don't dooooooo dat," said a Germanic male voice, and
a mother yelled, "Phyllis, stop it!" I watched two dark young Greeks,
obviously experienced, and did what they did, dancing the cha-cha,
flailing my arms like windmills to keep my balance. Legs seemed covered
with blood, like the legs of victims in an orgy of torture. The serving
ladies kept handing around glasses of another year's stomping, a beautifully ruby rosé called kokkinelli, very strong. Some of the senior citizens,
bobbing like Humpty Dumpty, had to be set up again, their clothes a
dripping mess. "You'll never get it clean," one lady said to a friend, who
replied, "That's why I wore an old dress." Spiros, who had followed me
in, said that stained clothing was a mark of honor, indicating valor in
battle.

Kanakis' persuasions were directed primarily to women. More and
more women succumbed to his blandishments, and leaping, gave themselves over to the ecstasy of warm pulp rising around their thighs. A
perilously pregnant American wife stumbled about, shrieking with joy.
She called for a cigarette which someone handed her. The mire, turning

darker, was, on top at least, all juice. A lady, hoisting skirts above huge
scarlet-streaked legs, looking like a figure on an old Coney Island postcard, shouted as if a lobster were pinching her toe.

Except for Kanakis, Spiros and the two swarthy bucks, there seemed
to be no Greeks in the tank. Outside four generations of them were
watching with glistening eyes the antics of the foreigners. The music
changed to *bouzoukia*. The two youths placed me and Spiros between
them, grasping our shoulders, and began to dance the *tsifteteli,* an
Oriental belly dance. The music spurred others and we were joined by
Germans and Danes and a black African. The line became unmanageable
and our leaders, turning it into a kind of conga line, began a series of
rabbit-hops called the *yanka.* I was floating in juice; it was hard work just
to keep in motion. Under my legs, the children seemed to be sinking
away, their heads bobbing on the surface like gourds.

Dancing now between two strange ladies, I recalled friezes of Bacchus
and nymphs. Feeling debauched and silenus-like, I clutched at my ears to
see if they were pointed and I wondered if down there deep in the
purple, my feet might be turning cloven.

They were not, I found, when we lined up at a watering tank outdoors
to clean ourselves. Spiros, who was carrying both our shoes, said that in an
earlier year a Norwegian man and a German girl were discovered making
love in the tank. It seemed farfetched but at that moment I was ready to
believe anything. In ancient times, Spiros went on, trompings had sometimes been in the nude. Looking at the irretrievable condition of my
trousers, I agreed that would be practical. A herd of goats on their way
home for the night, waiting at the tank for a drink, were watching in
baffled astonishment. The water in the tank was the color of wine.

V

Many Pressures

Athens was a percussive tragicomic opera with a libretto by Franz Kafka.

It had a handsome chocolate soldier king, a lovely young queen, a dowager queen cast by her subjects as a villainess, a government that rose and fell with alacrity and a vociferously clamoring population.

The setting was *al fresco*. Apollo provides three hundred bright days a year and on most of the others the sun makes a token appearance. Crowded in tiny apartments which provide little more than sleeping space, Athenians do most of their living in the streets and cafés.

Standing one day with the French ambassador on a terrace facing the Parliament Palace, looking down on some political tumult on Amalias Avenue, I said, "Next to Tokyo, where I've never been, Athens must be the noisiest place in the world." The ambassador replied, "On the contrary I have lived in Tokyo and I assure you, Athens *is* the noisiest place in the world."

The problem is a population explosion, probably the greatest in the world. One-fourth of all Greeks live in Athens, which has increased in size by 50 per cent since the last war, to almost two million people. Western nutrition and medicine have spurred the birth rate and slackened the death rate. Lured by a Western illusion of the urban good life, village Greeks from mountains and islands stream to the capital. Throngs of repatriated Greeks pour in from politically hostile Turkey and Egypt. The sleepy provincial town of 200,000 which huddled in the bowl of a valley in 1920 has climbed up the surrounding mountains, Hymettus,

Pendéli and even distant Parnes. When you add the million and a half tourists who arrive each year and an unspecified number of foreigners who were more or less settled there, you have a human swarm as varied and animated as anywhere in the world.

The most recent and one of the more disrupting of Greece's many invaders was progress. The Greeks are an Eastern people who since the war have been plunged pell-mell into the Western world. Their mentality, inherited from three centuries of Turkish occupation, is Oriental. With little comprehension and few controls, Greeks are trying to emulate Western bureaucracy. They were finding it very difficult to cope.

My first confrontation with Greek bureaucracy was at the Alien Registration Bureau. Foreigners who plan to remain in Greece for more than six weeks are required to register with the police. An American lady who lives in Athens warned me, saying, "You relax and you call on your sense of humor. You do what everyone tells you, you flow with the tides and you must be prepared to spend limitless time."

Following her instructions, I had four passport photos made and one Monday afternoon went with David Greggory to the bureau in an office building just beyond Omonia Square, a short walk from our hotel. It was four thirty, the hour when the city rolled up its shutters and reopened its doors after siesta. An elevator man pointed to a sign which said the bureau would be open from six to eight o'clock. We took a walk, had an *ouzo,* and returned at six. The same elevator man told us the office would not be open until Tuesday. This time we pointed to the sign. He shrugged. "They decided not to open today," he said.

The next morning at eleven the same man directed us into a labyrinth of small offices on the fourth floor. We entered one in which a young man was taking a roll of toilet paper out of a filing cabinet. He spoke no English. With the toilet paper unfurling like a banderol behind him, he led us to a girl who told us to go to the second floor. We found a stairwell and descended two flights. A middle-aged woman with a beehive of jet hair was sitting at a table in the hall.

"Que voulez?" she snapped.

"We wish to register." I was not understood. *"Enregister,"* I said. *"Pourquoi?"*

I waved my passport, which the woman grabbed.

"Tourist?" she asked.

"Ecrivaint," I said.

"Tourist!" she repeated.

"Professeur," I said, thinking academe might impress.

"Tourist!" she shouted.

"Oui," I nodded, remembering the advice not to resist the tide.

She thumbed the passport, scrawled some notes on a paper, collected twelve drachs, and let out a yell. A bedraggled-looking little man in baggy pants shuffled into the hall. The woman gave him the passport and memorandum, and with a thrust of a finger, indicated for me to follow him. The old man shambled into a room filled with people. At one end was a counter with shelves of files. Forming a horseshoe around the room were seven interviewing desks, all with queues. My Charon deposited me in one of the lines and disappeared.

There were five persons before me and each interview took fifteen minutes. For more than an hour I stood. I noted that my interviewer spoke English. He was soft-voiced, neatly groomed and seemed a gentle man. Most of the interviewees were Greek-speaking refugees from Turkey who, like all aliens, were required to renew their registrations every two months. They were extremely pushy and rude. Directly ahead of me a blonde Brigitte Bardot shepherded by her father—at least she called him *"Baba"*—was confronted with some insoluble complication and burst into tears. An old woman waddled up and elbowed into place ahead of me. With each exhalation of breath she moaned. The interviewer raised compassionate eyes to me and said softly, "You have been standing a long time." He drew out a chair and invited me to sit. When the old lady's interview drew to a close a pale blond youth with girlish features stepped into my place. I got up and saw from his passport that he was born in 1943, that his name was Corwin Digglesworth.

"Surely, Mr. Digglesworth," I said, "an Englishman understands about queues."

The interviewer raised his eyes and said, "Don't speak to each other, speak to me." He looked at a file which had mysteriously appeared with my name on it. He yelled. In a moment Charon appeared. The clerk spoke to him angrily in Greek and told me to follow Charon, who led me back to the virago in the hall, where I found David Greggory also back. The woman scolded Charon, whose abject role seemed to be the object of everyone's fury.

"What is your father's name?" she asked me.

"Nicholas," I said, giving it the Greek pronunciation.

"What is the name of the father of your mother?"

I told her that also, and she wrote it down. She asked Greggory his father's name.

"David," he said.

"That is your name," she snapped.

"It is also my father's," he said. The idea was an incomprehensible one for Greeks, who are named for grandparents but never for parents.

Charon was tugging at my arm. I followed him. Behind me I heard Greggory insisting, "David! David!"

"Not your name," the woman cried. "Your father's."

With a wink of his eye to indicate he was doing me a favor, Charon left me at another queue, marked "Artists." If not a writer or professor, at least I was an artist. We were making progress.

The line was made up entirely of voluptuous young ladies with blonde (or red or jet black) hair, wearing bright-colored stretch pants and fluttering long beaded lashes. The examiner, a lean, oily-haired man, was enjoying his assignment, languishing over each interviewee, admiring their four identical photographs separately. His jovial blandishments sent the whole row into undulating spasms of giggles. Slowly the situation became clear to me. I had been assigned to a queue of belly dancers from Turkey. The interminable and meaningless repetition began to have a fascination for me, as if I were in a play by Samuel Beckett. Perhaps I, too, was a belly dancer.

When I made it finally to the head of the line, Mr. Pomade looked up, scowled and whooped. Slowly, sadly, Charon appeared, took his verbal beating and nodded for me to follow him to the line in which I had already stood for an hour. The interviewer, whom I desperately hoped was My Friend, looked up, frowned and asked, "Who sent you here?" I fluttered a hand in Mr. Pomade's direction. The two men shouted to one another across the room. Ahead of me an Indonesian girl with an Israeli man who appeared to be her husband, did not know her mother's father's name. The husband tried to help, but he didn't know it either. My Friend told her she would have to come back another day—when she knew her grandfather's name.

He picked up my file and I thought I heard him sigh. Was I a tourist?

"A professor?" Some self-destructive impulse prompted me to say it.

"Of what are you a professor?"

"Of literature."

"You have professors of literature in America?" His face was sad and tired. "What will you do here?"

"Study," I said.

"What? Where?" The voice, I noted, was friendly. I took a deep and desperate breath.

"Archaeology," I said. "Delphi, Olympia, Mycenae . . ."

He smiled and began writing. Both of us, it seemed, were safe in port. He asked for the names of Greek friends, which I gave him. Then he asked their phone numbers.

I did not know them. He smiled sadly and told me to come back the next day with the phone numbers. I should come directly to him, and would not have to wait.

On the way out I met Charon and I felt the sympathy in his gaze. I hoped he was aware of the sympathy in mine.

Promptly at eleven the next morning I was back with the list of phone numbers. Unwilling to let good enough alone I had brought also a letter of introduction from the prime minister's office. Jauntily I moved around the line to My Friend and smiled in greeting. He looked at me darkly.

"What do you want?" he asked, no recognition in his eyes.

"My alien permit. You said . . ."

He nodded and rolled his eyes. He shuffled through a drawer and brought out my file. I presented the ministry letter. He looked at the official seal and the signature. "Is this yours?" I nodded. He leaped up from his desk to show it to some men behind the counter. Several heads bent over it.

"We shall need two copies of this letter for our files," said My Friend. I replied that I didn't have any copies. "Photocopies," he said. "Come back tomorrow with two photocopies."

I returned next day with two copies. After giving My Friend my father's and grandfather's names I was sent to the counter where a man checked through lists of undesirable persons. When he didn't find mine I was sent back to My Friend and he prepared my alien permit card. "Have you ever read Kafka?" I asked.

"I am writing every day all the time," he replied. "How can I read?" We smiled like old friends and he said, "See you in two months."

A Greek friend in New York had given me two letters, one to Odette Adamopoulos, manager of the El Greco Hotel, and another to George Frangopoulos, public relations director of the Greek National Tourist Office. When I arrived, Mrs. Adamopoulos was on a holiday in Italy and Mr. Frangopoulos was in the hospital. After a fortnight Mrs. Adamopoulos, an Egyptian Greek of Italian ancestry, returned. She was an attractive young woman whose charm and helpfulness persuaded me to make the El Greco my home. One morning I received a call from the tourist office inviting me to call on Mr. Frangopoulos.

At eleven o'clock I went to his Stadiou Street office and knocked on the door. There was no answer. Inside I could hear a voice booming out in Jovian rage. The door opened and a girl came out weeping and ran down the hall. I pushed open the door which she'd left ajar and entered. Behind a large desk a burly giant was shouting at a thin young man in front of the desk. I waited unnoticed through the abuse, which I did not understand. The man's great dark head and massive shoulders

reared like a fighting stallion's. The heavy arms flailed and banged on
the desk, over which the man leaned as if he were about to eat his
quivering victim. A telephone bell rang. The man picked up one of three
instruments on the desk, crashed it down, picked up another, shouted
into it and hung up. Catching his breath, he resumed his bellowing. I
decided to leave. My movement toward the door caught the giant's
attention.

"Who are you?" he shouted in French. I gave my name. "Sit down!"
he ordered. The roaring ended finally when the young man fled. The
man with whom I was now alone in the room picked up a pipe from
the desk and sucked on it. "Where are the matches?" he boomed. I
handed him a packet. He lit the pipe and put my matches in his pocket.
"I am sorry," he said, his voice normal. "Your name, please." I repeated
it. He shuffled through some files, found one with my name on it and
leafed through it. "You must forgive," he said. "Are many pressures."
The phones kept ringing. Between calls he directed unfinished sentences
to me.

"I know you will write about me. . . ." A phone rang and he yelled
into it in French. ". . . my terrible temper. It is already written in a
book . . ." A phone, this time in Greek. ". . . by a countryman of
yours. My temper is famous. What islands will you see?" I explained I
had come for help in arranging a trip to the Cyclades. "No, no, no. Is
best islands for you Lesbos, Chios, Skyros . . ." The phone. German.
"You write about islands not well known, people will read more . . ."
A girl entered and with trembling hand deposited some papers on the
desk and ran out. "Is good you bring tourists to new islands. You must
write about the human fauna of Greece. I talk with you like colleague.
I am also poet . . ."

A young Englishman, probably a journalist, entered.

"I am busy," said Frangopoulos.

"But I must see you."

"Come back another day." The Englishman left.

"Soon I will make a reading of my poetry. You must come." He
sucked on his dead pipe. "Where are the matches?"

"In your pocket," I said. He ignited the pipe. "I will introduce you
to many poets and writers. You will see how we enjoy ourselves . . ."
A phone, in Greek. He bellowed into it so loudly, it occurred to me, that
if he'd open a window he'd have no need of the instrument. When he
finished with this he said, "Now you must excuse me, I am meeting with
my minister." I began to repeat the purpose of my visit but there was no
chance. The huge form of him hovering over me was pushing me toward
the door. "You think I am crazy," he said. "Don't you?"

His rages, I learned, had provocation. Greek civil service was a great pork barrel and after a recent government shift most of Frangopoulos' trained employees had been discharged to make way for a corps of untrained, incompetent relatives and friends of new ministers. I saw Frangopoulos once more in January when I was planning a trip through the Peloponnese. "Where will you go?" he asked. I told him—Epidaurus, Olympia, Sparta, Andritsaina.

"Ah, Andritsaina," he boomed. "Very spiritual place. Our office operates a hotel there, the Xenia. I will phone them to receive you as our guests."

I thanked him. Some weeks later, after a harrowing auto climb up through rain-soaked mud trails, I arrived with two friends at dusk at the mountaintop town, eager for a bath, a meal, a comfortable bed. A small boy playing in the courtyard of the shuttered hotel said it was closed for the winter, that it would open in May.

VI

Athens by Night

Quite definitely I was living at the wrong end of town.

Most of commercial Athens is contained in a sloping quadrangle lying about two-thirds of a mile between two squares—Constitution in the west and Omonia in the east. Constitution, which slopes like an elegant terrace from the former Royal Palace, now the Greek Parliament, is the tourist center of Athens. Filled with outdoor cafés, it is bordered on three sides by hotels, shops, airline offices and the American Express. On the right side of the palace are the Royal Gardens and to the left is broad Queen Sophia Avenue, street of embassies.

In contrast to this island of hedonist luxury, Omonia was a hive of cheap workers' restaurants, cafés and hotels swarming with peddlers, news vendors and shoeblacks. Incongruously, Omonia means peace, of which there was none. Beneath the square is a vast subway station fed by escalators which, like the hoppers in a Last Judgment, elevated and lowered souls to and from an underground inferno of pimps, thieves, gamblers and touts. A block away on Athinas Street is the El Greco Hotel. It looks out on smaller Kotzia Square, meeting place of unemployed workers, and is bordered by the City Hall, the National Bank of Greece and rows of cheap shops and kiosks. In the area were several shabby movie houses in which, friends warned, I would catch fleas.

After the first few weeks I stopped apologizing for my address. Greek friends were reconciled to my choice of domicile as the bohemian eccentricity of a writer, or an American, or both. Because Constitution was on a higher elevation than Omonia, I sometimes thought of the two squares in terms of a medieval fresco, as heaven and hell.

One day I met the manager of the Grande Bretagne, Athens' most elegant hotel. When he learned where I was living, he was incredulous. Foreign writers always stayed at the GB, he said. He invited me to move there at a rate no higher than that I was paying at the El Greco. For several weeks I considered it.

But clearly I preferred hell. I did not wish to part from my friends at the El Greco, from Odette Adamopoulos; from Kostas, a bellboy from Epirus who looked after me like a personal valet; from Diane, dark-eyed, smiling telephone operator in whose cubicle I spent many hours gossiping. The teeming excitement of Omonia had become a warm mother. I could not leave my terrace from which I looked across to the Acropolis, rising over the city like a golden crown. Nor could I part with the sunsets over Mt. Parnes, a daily spectacle, evolving from afternoon gold to fiery coral flames which seemed to consume the earth, to purple twilight and mauve dusk and finally, when lights appeared on the distant slopes, a milky way of stars. Especially I did not wish to give up the crowing cocks. On a rooftop below my windows someone kept a flock of chickens. Each morning I was awakened by roosters, just as if I were in my own bed on the Wisconsin farm.

Off Omonia Square I had a favorite restaurant, a workers' establishment named Hara—"Joy," which I knew as "Ted's Place." Greek friends whom I took there did not share my enthusiasm. A first impression was not favorable. One entered by a steaming caldron of the house specialty, *patsas,* the tripe soup which Greek workers eat for breakfast and sometimes for lunch and dinner. Though I became accustomed to the milky sweet odor, I never could bring myself to eat the stuff. Inside the floor sloped, causing the paper-covered wooden tables to tilt. The walls were gray with smoke and flyspecks. Most of the customers were workmen, who in cold weather ate in their overcoats. There were also seamen from Greek and foreign ships, shy country families who found the place a welcoming island in the overwhelming city, and blind persons from an institute in the area. Now and then there was a party of adventuresome tourists from Germany or Sweden. The waiters, with one exception, were shuffling old men who changed their aprons on Saturdays and looked by week's end like a crew of unsanitary butchers.

The exception was Theodoros, known as Ted, a young man tall and broad as a fullback. Because he was studying English, I was sent to him. "Come with me," he said. Lumbering ponderously, as if the large frame of him were almost too heavy to carry, he led me into a dark, windowless kitchen where two gnomelike little men uncovered steaming pots. "You like fish, meat, chicken?" Ted asked. "Is very good *moussaka* today. Nice veal. Chicken?" He shrugged—he was not recommending it. "What kind of fish?" I asked.

"Greek fish," he said. I laughed and so did he. "I promise is good the fish." I ordered *moussaka,* the fish with a beet salad, some beer and a compote of spiced fruit, and it was all excellent. The bill was thirty drachs, just under a dollar.

As often as three or four times a week I lunched there, sometimes alone, sometimes with friends. Always smiling, Ted would advise me on the delicacies of the day. Once I remarked about his happy disposition. "I am gay," he said. I suggested several less hazardous adjectives— happy, merry, jolly—and he wrote them down.

Once a week he attended a night class in English, and he frequently asked me for words, which he laboriously wrote into a notebook. In our fragmentary conversations I learned that he was from a village in Epirus which was accessible only on foot or by donkey. Mysterious about his domestic life—he had eight brothers and sisters and a mother who some-times seemed to be with him in Athens and at other times in Epirus— he was not shy with details of his love life. On his left hand I saw the gold band ring which signifies an engagement. I congratulated him and he shrugged. "Maybe I will marry," he said. "Maybe not. Is a problem. I am thirty. No like but is necessary marry and children before too late. My girl is many hots. I do not always. Little hots, yes, but she is many. Always, night, morning, afternoon, always wanting. I have much tired. Greek girls is too hot. I cannot to cool. . . ." It was a problem with which I commiserated.

Since most of my business and social engagements took me to the vicinity of Constitution Square I sometimes walked the distance between Omonia and Constitution four or five times a day. They are connected by two avenues, Venizelou, which passes the classic temples of the University of Athens, and Stadiou, avenue of theaters, fine shops, and kiosks selling guidebooks, American toiletries, worry beads, foreign lan-guage newspapers and paperback novels. The kiosks always displayed garish English-language male nudie magazines entitled *Muscle Boy, Male* ("Black Boots, Booze and Highway Broads"), *Male Annual* ("Five Cruelest Men in the World"), *Man's Action* ("Will your job wreck your sex life?"), *Man's World, New Man, For Men Only, Muscle Teens,* and so on, an ad infinitum compendium of narcissism and incipient pederasty. I wondered who bought them. Presumably the Greeks.

Midway between the two squares is a third, Klafthmonos, or "Weeping Square," a name dating from the reign of Greece's first king, Otto, before whose residence clerks and government officials gathered to voice protests. The large shaded square, surrounded by newspaper offices and electronics stores, is still used for political meetings. My favorite route from the El Greco took me through a labyrinth of narrow streets and diagonally across Klafthmonos to Stadiou. Another route I favored was down Athinas Street through the swarming produce market to Monastiraki Square, then left up Ermou Street, around the lovely Kapnikarea Church, which stands in the middle of the street, and on to Constitution Square. On this narrow, crowded backway I met few tourists. The only foreigners who prowled there were the international hippies—American, German, French and English youths and girls wearing the same patched levis and pull-overs. Disheveled, unwashed, sandaled or barefoot, they carried their string bags of food, books and cameras aimlessly around the city, gravitating twice a day to the mail line of the American Express, hoping for the remittances which would move them further. Their mecca was Nepal. "Nepal is the last place in the world where you can think," said a youth from Chicago. He had long hair, a full beard and mustache, muttonchop whiskers and rabbinical curls, all bright red. Except for the beards, it was sometimes difficult to tell males from females. Greeks never ceased being flabbergasted at the sight of them. Traffic came to a halt when a band of them passed, pedestrians turned and collided and cars climbed curbs. Walking behind an especially sloven pair on Stadiou one day, I was relieved to hear that their accents were British. "They're not Americans," I felt compelled to say to two Greek girls walking beside me. "For your sake I hope not," said one.

"Athens by Night $7," said broadsides on Stadiou Street. I used to see the night-living faces of timid middle-aged couples, frequently American, pressed against the window glass of special buses and I wondered what esoteric delights they were offered for their money. For the more adventuresome there were other opportunities. On Omonia soft-voiced con men murmured, "Spik English, American, Australian. Take you to Plaka, show everything." The best way was to go by oneself. From the El Greco it was only fifteen minutes to the Plaka, Athens' oldest quarter and night-life center. One night David Greggory and I took a lady anthropologist from California there. Appearing unmistakably American we fought the "battle of the Plaka" through a mob of grasping, wailing hustlers and shills pulling us toward open doors, babbling, "Good food, good dancing, good all things." Most persistent were the flower women. One stuck a sprig of jasmine in my lapel and when I walked away with it she screamed I had robbed her. I plucked the blossom from my jacket and threw it on the pavement. At once another clutched at my coat and I relented. No one would direct us to the restaurant we were seeking, named Erotokritos. We found it finally, a four-story complex with an open roof with a fine view of the city.

A black ram with a green jewel affixed to its forehead, turning it into a terrifying three-eyed monster, stepped on dainty hooves from table to table smoking cigarettes, drinking *ouzo,* eating bread and—cannibalistically—roast lamb. More women arrived with trays of jasmine and gardenias, but most customers were already as covered as well-kept graves. The blossoms filled the room with a heavy funereal scent. Another woman wandered among tables with a clutch of balloons, saying, "Break them all for forty drachmae." Someone did, exploding a short cannonade with a cigarette, and in three minutes the woman was back with a new supply. A man dining alone ordered twenty dinner plates which he threw like discuses at the musicians' feet. A great baroque desert, a kind of cupola built of bananas, watermelon wedges and pineapple slices and canopied with cherries, cream and nuts, arrived at a table and the ram began gulping it. Undoubtedly the beast thought it was human. His identification was complete. I wondered what would happen if he met a sheep.

Later we wandered through the Plaka's narrow up-and-down streets. The medieval hodgepodge of houses turned into taverns and clubs, lighted with strings of colored lights, had a festival atmosphere. At an outdoor discotheque called "The Nine Muses," young Greeks, Swedes, Americans and Germans were frugging. "It was never so wild in Madagascar," said our anthropologist. The music changed to *bouzouki* and a row of youths dipped and dove through the Zorba *syrtaki.* Outside two Greeks, bound together by a knotted handkerchief, danced a solemn *tsamiko.* The great shadows of them loped across the dark walls, and above, the illuminated caryatids, the stone maids on the Acropolis, smiled like a row of Mona Lisas.

My favorite *tavernas* were not in the Plaka at all, but east of Omonia. The first, called Psatha, was in Kypseli; a ten-minute ride from the El Greco. The entrance through the kitchen took guests past the bubbling caldrons and smoking grills which contained the fare of the day. What brought me there was a singer named Keti Apostolatou, a large warmhearted woman from the island of Cephalonia in the Ionian Sea. Her soft Italianate voice, accompanied by a mandolin and a lute, had the sweet enchantment of the sirens against whose lures Ulysses had himself bound to the stake. It kept drawing me to the Psatha.

My other haunt was even closer, a five-minute walk from the hotel. It was a steamy *bouzouki* cellar called Verlouchi after a village in Epirus and was patronized almost exclusively by natives of the northern province. David Greggory and I found it one Sunday night prowling in the dark casbah behind Omonia Square. Hearing music, we looked down a deep stairwell into a brightly lit crowded cellar. We descended into an orgy of Greek dancing. The brightly lit room was jammed to the walls with tables at which guests, mostly men, were drinking beer and wine. On a platform sat eight musicians: three *bouzouki* players, two violinists, two clarinetists and a girl with a tambourine. In front of them was a dancing area perhaps eight feet square. Signs on the walls said, "Dancers are expected to pay musicians" and "Don't break glasses."

According to the dance impresario Dora Stratou, Greek dancing relates closely to the Dionysian rites painted on ancient vases in the Archaeological Museum. Verlouchi's left no doubt that she was right. With the intense solemnity of ballet dancers four men waited for their musical cue. The leader, a tall, fiercely gaunt fellow, was linked to his three friends by a twisted handkerchief. Suddenly he leaped into the air, and landing, began rocking and dipping, his eyes focused in a kind of ecstasy on the ceiling. His friends followed with restrained movements, offering physical support and balance. The leader dropped to the floor and elevating his groin, rotated it in abandoned sexual movements. He leaped up, gyrated slowly under the raised arms of his companions, twisting, bending, lowering on his right foot with his left leg extended, tearing the handkerchief to shreds. His body dripped sweat, his hair was a disheveled thatch, his face, earnest as a priest's, reflected a secret and sublime joy.

The orchestra stopped and I felt, as if it were my own, the dancers' frustration. One dropped a banknote into the musicians' till and the music began again. A woman entered with a basket of narcissi which she promptly sold. The dancers placed the clusters of blossoms behind their ears and from the tables men pelted them with flowers. The floor was covered with crushed blossoms and the hot air turned nauseously sweet as the narcissus dance continued.

When it finished other groups took turns buying dances. A round-faced round-bellied little man with a beautiful smile, rocked and quivered like a spastic Humpty Dumpty. Sometimes a wife would join a line and walk passively through the steps demonstrating that women's bodies aren't designed to cope with the lithe primal movements, why Greek dancing is a male art.

Near the door a plump dark-haired woman in a plaid dress was shepherding a table of eight drunken adolescents, like a den mother with a cub pack. One black-haired lad, probably her son, and a blond friend kept levitating from their chairs in quivering ecstasy, shaking their bodies and arms, and after each spasm they fell into one another's arms, kissing and nuzzling like lovers.

A family entered the room, two small gray parents leading their blind son, a fat boy in his twenties. The great hulk of him swayed to the music, his round face beamed. The family took a table near us and ordered food, which they fed to the youth like bird parents, the mother dropping morsels of meat into his open mouth, the father bread, and as he gulped he rocked to the music, waving his arms and snapping his fingers. I guessed they were poor working people visiting the boy at the institute for the blind which was in the area, that the evening in Verlouchi's was a weekly treat. Fondling and petting the boy, the parents poured wine, holding the cup for him, and when he had drunk the father wiped his lips like a priest at communion.

When they finished the food the father got up and gave some money to the musicians. The mother led her hulking son between tables to the dancing area and the three danced, the little gray father leading, whirling and turning, the mother shuffling behind and the great blind boy, one hand on his hip, smiling sublimely, dipped and swayed over the narcissus carpet. My eyes filled with tears, as if I were watching a mysterious and holy rite.

Then it was over. The father had no more money to count out to the musicians, and the boy, his disappointment clear on his face, was led back to the table. They tried to comfort him but his disappointment would not be cajoled away. I asked our waiter the price of a dance—it was twenty drachs—and I gave him the money. But I was too late. Four of the den pack were on the floor, quivering their shoulders and arms like drunken satyrs, rolling their pelvises like harem catamites. "Get ready for a raid," murmured Greggory. The boys leaped over one another and whirled like dervishes. The curly dark Pan embraced another dark lad and his blond friend, berserk with jealousy, impinged himself against the wall, flailing his arms, rolling his eyes, flailing his arms in an operatic pantomime of stabbing himself. The musicians stopped. The den mother paid her bill and herded the drunken troupe toward the exit. As they climbed the stairs the blond turned back and threw kisses, making a diva's farewell. On the floor a handsome dark youth in a wine-colored turtle-neck sweater was dancing in mesmeric solitude. "Remind me," said Greggory, "to come here New Year's Eve."

In Athens were many resident Americans. With the diplomatic corps, colonized in the suburb of Psychico, which was known to Greeks as the American Gold Coast, I had no contact. On my arrival I presented my letters to the ambassador, including two from former ambassadors, and nothing had come of that. One day I lunched with an American correspondent whom I shall call Bolton, who, I was told, was one of the arbiters of the American colony.

A man in his sixties, he had been in Greece for more than twenty years. He was, I was warned, a proper Bostonian, so I dressed for our meeting in a proper blue suit. He met me in the Grande Bretagne bar, looking like a vigorous Scotsman blustering in from the moors. Red-faced, sandy-haired, he wore a tweed jacket patched in leather and an assortment of silk scarves and handkerchiefs.

"Have you made your travel arrangements?" he asked. I replied that I'd barely arrived.

"The revolution is coming in March," he said. "In six months none of us will be able to live here. For Greeks, politics is a national sport. They don't have baseball leagues or college football. So they play politics and their games will take them over the brink. They all live in a fever of envy. Envy is strong in the Greek character. Every Greek is envious of every other Greek and of every other country. Particularly, they envy America.

"The King is absolutely right in holding off an election as long as possible. There's no doubt an election would give Papandreou a large majority. But he's old, a sick man who is grooming his American son to take over. When the son does, it will be as dictator and Greece will move behind the Iron Curtain. Greeks are totalitarian-oriented— they need a strong leader. The only alternative to Communism is a strong military dictatorship under the King. Greece needs the monarchy for at least another fifty years. If it goes now, it will mean the end."

Not all resident Americans were so political-minded. There were the remittance boys, sustained by monthly checks from families and foundations in their pursuit of Athens' homoerotic smorgasbord. Some had crossed the Adriatic from Italy, in involuntary flight from Italian police. They collected icons, decorated their apartments with antique furniture, and gave their afternoons over to an incestuous cycle of cocktail parties and their evenings to nocturnal prowling. Their haunt was the Kaladiou, an all-male bar just off Constitution Square, meeting place also of a special genre of well-dressed English-speaking young Greeks in their teens and early twenties. An American lady professor called these Greek boys "tricksters" and said, "They stalk you like a detective. Once a woman gives in to one she's not free until she leaves the country." Simultaneously with their pursuit of male and female foreigners, the youths were exploring the Greek marriage auction. "It's entirely a seller's market," said the professor. "Some of the boys are from good families. The handsome personable young bachelor is the only mobile member in Greek society. He compares marriage offers from Greek fathers, hoping for a better settlement, a better social position. The haggling over dowries would curdle your blood."

No doubt. On the jukebox, John Lennon was bawling, "I wanna hold your hand." A row of fortyish Americans were standing at the bar, including several writers whose names were known to me. One who had a thin mane of straight black hair folded over his bald pate like a black fringe, was saying, "I can't bear Italy any more. Italians are too sophisticated, too corrupt. Greeks are the last true Europeans, the only ones not corrupted, not Americanized." A score of Greek youths milled about or leaned on the jukebox. A dark-haired boy wearing a reefer jacket zoomed in on me. "Do you have a friend?" he asked. At the bar a thin pink-cheeked American in his sixties was saying, "It was so bad in Italy I was averaging one orgasm a month. Here I have at least ten a week." The boy, his face close to mine, was whispering, "I know a hotel we can go . . ."

"Cool it!" I said. He moved away and immediately another, a shaggy blond in a German ski sweater, took his place. "I'm hot, I'm burning," he said, slurping his lips. "I got to have sex." He went on with it in scatological language. The aging Pan was saying, "You might call me a lover of innocence." He was an American photographer seeking out "The unconscious phallicism of Greece," the penis-shaped lions of Delos, the columns of Olympus. A poet recited from his works (privately printed in a limited edition of 175 copies):

> I piss a crescent of gold,
> Into the brink, I drink. . . .

A eunuch-like fat man was discussing literature in a squeaky voice. "I empathize for Dick and Perry," he said. "They're American Raskolnikovs and I'm mad for the type." My blond solicitor had moved on and the brunette was back. "He is the shark, a bad Greek boy," said the brunette of the blond. "He has knife and gun."

"No one who is anyone goes to Naxos any more," the poet was saying.

"I am good boy, a student at the Polytechnic Institute," my apostrophizer whispered. He handed me an embossed business card with his name and two phone numbers. "Did you think I wanted money?" The thought hadn't entered my mind. He opened his wallet to show me a swatch of bills. "See, I have money." Then he asked if he might borrow a two-drach piece for the jukebox. I reached into my pocket and gave him one, wondering why, with his ample resources, he should ask for it. He watched the movement of my hand and I understood. The boys of

Kaladiou were expert pickpockets, I had heard. With this ploy he had established where I kept my money. "The hotel is only one block," he was saying.

I had the scene. When I left a young Fulbright scholar, goaded by friends, was singing an old American folk ballad: "I want a boy, just like the boy, that married dear old mum . . ."

On Constitution Square I sensed I was being followed. I turned into Stadiou toward home and the steps persisted, moving faster. After a half block a new face was beside me, asking me the time. It was 2 A.M. "How long you stay in Greece?" The shutter mind was prospecting, reconnoitering. I walked faster and the boy kept up with me. He was slim and young, perhaps seventeen, and clean-cut, almost pretty, with well-groomed black curls and pink skin. He was immaculately tailored in an Ivy League blue jacket, gray trousers and a scarlet waistcoat. "I am student at Polytechnic Institute," he said, softly, politely. "Would you like to come to my house for a coffee?"

"It's much too late," I said. "What would your mother say?"

Walking away, I thought they must teach a very good English course at the Polytechnic Institute. And other courses also, like International Relations.

The outside world kept intruding. No quasi resident in a foreign capital can avoid the short-term visitors who expect you will be delighted to see them, to show them around. One weekend I had three such visitors, an American and two Swiss. The American was a TV producer on a four-day "scouting visit." The Swiss were partners in a small Lucerne hotel which they'd closed in the off-season for a holiday of their own. The three had one thing in common. Each urgently had to find a woman.

The American, whom I shall call Huck Finn for reasons which will become apparent, arrived on Thursday. "Not a whore, you understand, but a *nice* girl," he said. This might be difficult, I said, explaining the Greek moral code, the zealous fathers and brothers. "Money's no consideration, I'm on an expense account," he said. "What I want is to get in on an orgy." What exactly had he in mind. "You know, like in *Dolce Vita*."

To aid him in his scouting the Greek National Tourist Office provided him with a car and driver, and an extraordinarily pretty and able guide named Thallia, which he invited me to share. I rode up front with the driver. In the back Huck Finn was showing Thallia photographs of his wife and two boys in Bucks County. His respectability established, he put the photos away. Thallia said she'd been married one year and had no children. Her husband, a lumber importer, was on a business trip to Helsinki.

"I'll bet he has a nice big blonde up there in Finland," said Huck Finn. Thallia said a wife could never be absolutely sure, but she didn't think so. "It gets very cold up there," said Huck Finn. "I know a way you can get even with your husband."

"Why should I when there is nothing to get even for?" I admired Thallia's cool parrying control of the situation.

"Apparently you don't know about traveling men," said Huck Finn. "I have a wife in every capital of the world and one at home when I'm there."

"Doesn't *she* mind?" asked Thallia.

"American wives understand. I don't expect her to be any more faithful to me than I am to her."

"You must have a very confusing life," said Thallia. We were driving up the Acropolis hill. "Parthenon means 'virgin,'" she said, beginning her discourse.

"Most interesting," said Huck Finn, his downcast eyes on the trim legs beside him. "It's a temple to Athena," she said.

The driver drew up beside a parked Lincoln Continental, sleek, silvery gray, shining like an unidentified flying object, and flying an Arabian flag above a headlight. Surrounding it was an admiring circle of sponge, postcard and pistachio sellers, murmuring to one another, "Eight thousand dollars, eight thousand dollars." Our driver said the machine was one of a fleet of Ferraris, Maserattis, Mercedes-Benzes and Buick Rivieras imported by Greece's most famous tourist, ex-king of Saudi Arabia, ibn-Saud, for his numerous sons. Reports of the lusty Saudi boys' tavern brawls and traffic accidents appeared regularly in Athens' newspapers. No one seemed quite sure exactly how many sons there were. Our driver, who told us he had once chauffeured the exiled king, said there were forty-five. I asked what happened to Saudi's daughters. The driver didn't know. The royal retinue in the beach-side resort of Kavouri, he said, included a harem of dark beauties from home, and I remembered a recent news story about the arrival from Arabia of a herd of female camels to provide the exiled family with camel's milk. Away from papa's chauvinist eye, his sons were known to prefer buxom blondes, preferably German, known in Athens as "saudikrauts."

We climbed the ancient steps. Continuing her discourse, Thallia spoke of optical illusions in the Parthenon. "If you will look carefully you will see that the columns slant slightly inward," she said. "If they were extended far enough they would meet like a cone. Without this, the temple would appear wider at the top and seem to be spreading apart."

"How about that?" said Huck Finn. "Do Skidmore, Owings and Merrill know?"

"The columns are elliptical," said Thallia. "If they were not thicker in the center you would think they are narrower."

"Sure as hell beats the hell out of the Parthenon in Nashville, Tennessee," said Huck Finn.

Thallia continued, saying, "The columns are graduated in size, becoming narrower as one goes in from the corners. This makes a greater width between the center columns and gives a sense of space." Huck Finn was looking at a voluptuously buxom blonde walking with a dark thin Arab. "The slightly curved floor combats the illusion and makes it seem flat. It also drains away the water and prevents erosion of the stones."

"Do you suppose your office could find me a saudikraut?" asked Huck Finn.

It rained on Saturday afternoon when the Swiss arrived in my hotel from Istanbul. A letter from a Zurich friend introduced them as Karl Geisli and Eric Hirsch, names which mean "goat" and "elk." The Goat was young, perhaps twenty-five, husky and blond. The Elk was twenty years older, short, fat and smiling. With them was Elk's wife, a ponderous tweedy woman who announced she was going to bed to rest up for the next day's sight-seeing. What did one do evenings, Elk asked. Could I take them to a native *lokale?* Lowering his voice, the Goat said they hadn't had a woman in two weeks, not since Tel Aviv, where they'd both had the same nice clean girl. She was nineteen and hadn't cost much.

A bellhop gave me the name of a workers' *taverna,* the Ellenike on Mezonos Street. I phoned a Greek friend, a young importer called Johnny, who did business with American firms and had a brother studying law at the University of Minnesota. At nine o'clock, Huck Finn, Elk and Goat and Johnny and I set out for the jungle beyond Omonia Square. When I gave the taxi driver the address he said there must be some mistake. Johnny also was apprehensive. Mezonos Street was no place for tourists, he said. The lower-class neighborhood was not even for respectable Greeks.

The *taverna* was old, low-ceilinged and almost empty. On a narrow platform an orchestra of horns, pipes, mandolins and drums was roaring away. The music was not *bouzouki,* said Johnny, but a type of mountain music popular in the 1930s. Sitting with the musicians were three girls, scantily clad in long black fringes. "Are they whores?" asked Huck Finn.

I asked for a corner table as far as possible from the decibel onslaught.

It was next to the door of the toilet as my nose quickly told me. Pastel frescoes of hedonist abandon in pastoral settings covered the walls. They appeared to have been painted by a lesbian—the shepherds and satyrs were all simpering Mary Pickfords with mustaches. "In all my life I have never been in such a place," said Johnny. "An American must show me."

We ordered *souvlaki* and two bottles of wine. Our conversation, I could see, was going to be rudimentary. Huck Finn spoke only English and the Swiss only Schweizerdeutsch and German. Johnny spoke a fragmentary German and English. Huck Finn decided to scout impressions. Taking out a pencil and pad he directed rhetorical questions at Johnny.

"Why don't Greeks hate Germans? Isn't it because they believe in today and not yesterday or tomorrow?"

Understanding not a word, Johnny nodded, and the fact finder wrote it down.

"That makes Greece an existentialist country!"

The confused oracle nodded and Huck Finn scribbled away.

"Isn't it true that Greeks are more human than Italians because the Greeks have suffered more?" Yes, yes. It was recorded.

"The United States helps Turkey more than Greece because the Turks are more aggressive, better politicians." Dictating to himself now Huck Finn was covering pages.

The place was filling up with workmen wearing dark shirts and no ties. One of the fringed girls stepped down from the platform and, raising her arms, began to quiver and rotate her belly. A flutist followed her about the floor like a snake charmer. "That girl with black curtains are good dancer," said Johnny. The Goat's eyes shone like blue scarabs. I could hear him breathe.

Two elderly men got on the floor with the girl and began the handkerchief dance. Silly drunk, grinning foolishly, they staggered after the girl. Her fringes trembling, the fake jewels in the high bouffant of her black hair flickering, she whirled artfully around them.

Our food came and with it a cloud of hovering flies. It was not very good. Elk said he didn't think it was clean, and Goat, all appetites hammering, ate both his and Elk's. Another girl, her hair falling in long twining ropes, descended from the platform and slowly began to roll her belly.

"Is she one?" asked Huck Finn.

Johnny said that in his opinion the dancing girls were not prostitutes but probably relatives of the musicians.

Where, asked Goat, chomping on beef, could he get a woman? Johnny said we were only a short distance from Aristotelous, a street of houses.

"Let's go," said Huck Finn, wiping his mouth.

It had stopped raining. Like the leader of a hound pack, Johnny steered us through a maze of silent dark streets to Aristotelous. It was dark and hushed but, unlike the other streets, it was not empty. Silent shadows of men lurked everywhere, moving in singles and pairs, and gathering in soft-voiced colloquies on corners.

"Where are the girls?" asked Goat.

"Inside the doors," said Johnny. "Is very strict the police for them coming out."

"Where are the houses?" asked Huck Finn, looking down the row of six- and eight-story apartment buildings.

"Is very difficult to find the houses because the houses is all the time in the middle of other houses," said Johnny. He explained that both streetwalking and bordellos were illegal and girls lived in pairs, like roommates, in small flats. "Where you see red button, there is house," he said. Tiny red lights glimmered the length of the street, like a long string of Christmas bulbs.

"What do we do?" asked Huck Finn.

"You squeeze a light," said Johnny.

"How much will it cost?" asked the Elk.

"One hundred, maybe two hundred drachmae," said Johnny.

"A little expensive," said the Goat. I reminded him of the fees charged by the girls of Zurich. We started down the street, between the rows of dark forms many of whom were in military uniforms. Some of the apartment houses had Christmas trees in the foyers, and baby carriages. Quite obviously it was Saturday night. Before the basement doors as many as six or eight men waited. Our Don Juans were growing apprehensive.

"What are they like inside?" asked Huck Finn.

"They are girls," said Johnny.

"Are they clean?" asked the Goat.

"Is expected girls see doctor," said Johnny.

"But if they're illegal how can you be sure?" asked Huck Finn. The thought had occurred to me.

"Well, you have to do something," said the Goat, pressing a red bell. "You can't tie a knot in your parts." There was no answer and he moved down the street and pressed another. A cardboard sign said "Kliston," "Closed." At a third an ancient grandmother popped her gray head out for a second and said her daughters weren't home. We found a basement door slightly ajar. A man beckoned us in. We entered a long barren corridor lit by a low red light. Along the walls sat two rows of sullen men. Others stood in the corners. It struck me as being very like the waiting room of a National Health dentist's office in a London slum. The difference was that only men had toothaches. "It will be two hours," said the man who'd invited us. "I can't wait that long," said the Goat.

We left. In a burst of desperation Huck Finn rang a bell and another grandmother's head appeared.

"*Germani?*" she asked.

"*Amerikani,*" Johnny replied, and like the gates of Troy, the door opened on still another dismal corridor, smaller than the first and occupied by two middle-aged men smoking cigarettes. The floor was littered with butts. We took chairs facing a glistening lithograph of Christ rising from the tomb. In a moment two soldiers in uniforms several sizes too large slunk out and Grandmother signaled the two men into an inner chamber. They stomped on their cigarettes and disappeared. In ten minutes one of the men shuffled out as if he were carrying a hod of stone on his back. Grandmother beckoned and Huck Finn, deliberating, followed her. Two minutes later the other man passed by and the Goat charged in.

The Elk went to the outer door and looked into the heavens. "It's going to be a nice day tomorrow," he said. "One will be able to make little color pictures." I could not take my eyes from the Christ, floating upward in a swirl of white muslin, bearing a white flag. His eyes were lowered to a dark circle of bearded men cowering around the stones.

When the visitors had left I dined one night with Thallia and her husband, Cleon Stathis, in the Plaka. Thallia apologized for not entertaining me in their home. "We're ashamed to have strangers see how we live," she said. "We have three rooms. I suppose we are more fortunate than most." I spoke of the warm hospitality with which I had been received in Macedonian villages. "Don't speak to me of Greek hospitality," said Thallia fiercely. Her husband, trying to subdue her, was unable to stop her from talking. "It's all nonsense, it doesn't exist," she said. "No Greek ever does anything without thinking what he may gain. We're a predatory people utterly incapable of trust and friendship. Whenever a Greek extends hospitality, it means an involvement." As a child during the Civil War, Thallia had been sent to live with relatives in a Peloponnese village and the experience had turned her against all villagers. "They're the meanest, the most petty, the nastiest people in Greece," she said. "Certainly they're nice to tourists. You can bet they're plotting ahead, thinking how they will use you."

"We are different from Europeans," said Cleon. He was a balding man in his middle thirties, a cultivated Alexandrian who looked at Greece through the eyes of an outsider and with the insight of a Greek. "We are very close to the East and our confusion is Oriental. It is true, a Greek is shrewd," he said. "He is always looking for an advantage. He wants immediate gain without responsibility. During America's prohibition it was the Greeks who made the stuff but the Italians sold it, they shot the guns. We haven't changed. We want the rewards but someone else must assume the responsibility. You Americans work and sleep and if there is any time left over you amuse yourselves. We amuse ourselves and sleep and if there's any time left over we work. A Greek trusts no one and an American trusts everyone. It's a cause of many difficulties between us. We seldom say of anyone, 'He is an honest man,' because we don't believe anyone really is honest."

Cleon was chewing Tums to relieve the gnaw of an ulcer. On the paper tablecloth he slowly drew the outlines of a fish and shaded the head. "We have a saying in Greece that a rotten fish always smells first in the head," he said. "Our so-called upper class, those who rule us, are illiterate, stupid, uneducated and arrogant. They care only for themselves, nothing for the people. Unless one has contact with this power group, there is nothing for him in Greece. So our youth leave in every direction—to Australia, Canada, Germany, South America. Anywhere, to escape the terrible trap of being a Greek." Cleon left no doubts as to his politics. "There are perhaps one hundred rich families who own property, who support the King," he said. "All our admirals and generals come from this group. They pretend to democracy. But in Greece where democracy was invented, there is none. The King is their tool. He forced the resignation of Papandreou who has the support of seventy-five per cent of all Greeks. Papandreou is the only one in politics who cares, who offers any hope."

The somber and depressing report was quietly and gently offered. Cleon's bitterness was in his words, not his tone. Perhaps the ulcer from which he suffered was paining him. Certainly, the ulcer was a result of the pressures in his life. He and Thallia were of the class—white-collar professionals—who most felt the squeeze. The lower classes, more deeply rooted in, and sustained by, tradition, probably survived more easily.

"The going salary for a white-collar worker is twenty-five hundred drachmae a month," Cleon continued. It was about eighty-three dollars. "Five thousand drachmae is affluent. A family seldom pays rent. The home with its linens, blankets and kitchenware is usually provided by a wife's dowry. The husband provides the furniture and maintains the home. In this way we manage. But dowries are a crippling burden for men who must marry off their sisters before they can themselves marry. Sometimes a man unfortunate enough to have a large family of sisters cannot marry until he is fifty or more years old.

"Slavery," said Cleon, "is outlawed in the Western world. But when such a wide difference of economy exists as between men like Onassis and Niarchos, and the workers of Greece, when government workers earn less than seventy-five dollars a month, when police must abet crime and prostitution to supplement their incomes, then slavery exists and the West has a problem that touches everyone."

"We have been thinking of emigrating to America," said Thallia. "Cleon's firm has an office in New York. How much salary would we need to live in New York?"

A considerable one, I said. They too, I sadly thought. Our table on an upper floor looked over a brightly flickering city. On Lycabettus the lights glimmered like jewels. A full moon was shining over the Parthenon, which crouched above us like a great golden cat. How could anyone bear to leave such beauty?

"To see the beauty requires a contented life," said Cleon. "Many have lived in Athens their entire lives and have never climbed the Acropolis. To them it is a pile of stones of interest to tourists."

VII

The Circular Isles

1
"BEATNIKS DON'T SWEEP"

We were on our way to the origins. A ship named *Leto* for the mother of Apollo was taking David Greggory and me to the Cyclades, or "Circulars," a ring of islands around Delos, birthplace of Apollo and a religious and political center of the Aegean civilization.

One-half hour out of Piraeus we passed a sister ship, the *Aphrodite*. It was a Sunday in early October. The human profusion on the *Leto* was unnerving. A medley of German waltzes and polkas roared out of the ship's amplifiers. The light was too blinding to read, even with dark glasses. A lovely French girl with the pointed lobes of a nymph, removed her sweater, closed her faun eyes and lay on her bikini bra, exposing her back to the sun. I removed my shirt and quickly put it back on. The *meltémi*—wind of the islands—was strong and cold. Abandoned deck chairs flapped about like blue kites and the paper wrappings from passengers' picnics took off like birds. The sea was high. Spray broke over the rails, and myriads of silvery pellets struck our faces like shot. A fat woman, clambering over bodies, reaching starboard in the nick of time, vomited into the gale, unaware in her misery that she'd chosen the wrong side. The French girl rose and crossed the deck. I followed and discovered the larboard sea was bluer.

In midafternoon Mykonos appeared on the horizon. Its stone landscape and square little houses, some with flattish domes, shone gold and white in the cerulean sea like Sunday-school pictures of the Holy Land. Furls of windmills revolved. Waiting on deck in the harbor to be ferried ashore, we saw at the water's edge a hotel named "Delos." When the little caïque disembarked us we walked around the arc of the harbor to its doors. A man inside invited us to sit down while he went to see about rooms. The salon, which seemed to be the hotel's only public room, was decorated in peasant style with wide windows open to the sea. Its white walls were covered with green ivy and philodendron, and in its high arches was an aviary of small chirping birds. Several children were playing. A wide-eyed nymphette, three years old, brought us an ashtray. On the hotel desk I saw a bust of President Kennedy, a photograph of Mrs. Kennedy taken on Mykonos, and a dog-eared copy of the telephone directory of Joliet, Illinois, a town I associated with a prison to which, in my Wisconsin boyhood, Chicago gangsters were frequently committed.

The man returned. "Who do you know in Joliet?" I asked, pointing to the phone book.

"Many," he said. "Used to live there."

He was a dark little man, wiry and tense, about forty years old. He introduced himself—his name was Nicholas Fiorentinos and he was owner of the Delos. He called his wife, a placid, smiling woman who was born in Joliet. The Delos, she said, was headquarters for Mykonos' "Joliet Club," a society of former Illinois residents, most of them American citizens. The bond between the two very disparate towns, Mykonos and Joliet, began in the early 1900s when a Mykoniat mechanic named George Polycandriolis emigrated to America and settled in the Illinois town. His success spurred a succession of young male relatives and friends to follow. All returned to Mykonos to find wives whom they moved to Joliet. They worked as truck farmers, on railroads and factories, and when they saved enough money they bought their own small farms. The Mykoniat colony in Joliet grew and prospered. Children born in America became lawyers, teachers and doctors. At least one Joliet Mykoniat, a hoteliere, became a rich man. Some who did not become rich finally returned to Mykonos, where they were able to live like rich men on American Social Security checks. They met in the Delos to recall their life in America and sometimes to make transatlantic telephone calls to their children in Joliet.

Their club has its counterpart, a Mykonos Club in Joliet, the affluent members of which recently endowed Mykonos with two deep wells and two reservoirs, the best water system in the Cyclades.

Anna Fiorentinos, who was born in Joliet, reversed the migratory pattern by marrying Nicholas and returning with him to Mykonos to manage his family hotel. Her father, a 1911 immigrant to the United States, owns a farm outside of Joliet. A brother teaches mathematics in the Joliet High School and a sister teaches history in Plainfield, Illinois. "Sometimes I miss my family," she said, "but I'm never homesick for Joliet. Mykonos is a happy island."

After taking possession of our rooms, we stepped out into the town, into the carnival of Sunday afternoon. Mykonos is the favorite island of Greeks as well as of foreigners—its five thousand citizens entertain eighty thousand visitors a year. Though the high season was one month past, we would never have guessed it. The esplanade, a crescent extending twenty yards back from the sea, was filled with a colorful human mosaic. Pink-skinned Germans and Scandinavians wore the brightly-colored knitted gear which Mykonos women knit for tourists. Hippies from America and North Europe and local fishermen were similarly barefoot and similarly dressed in blue denims and sweaters. English-language signs on shops said, "Trousers tailored in one day," "Art of the Silver" and "Music Dancing." In the background were the women of the island in brown and white homespuns, tending their stalls of sandals, embroidery, sweaters and toy windmills. In the center of the square, a large pelican named Petros, internationally famous ever since he was photographed with Jacqueline Kennedy, was showing bored contempt by ruffling his feathers.

We found a table and ordered *ouzos* which came with a plate of *mezédes*—olives and bits of smoked octopus. The sun was setting. The whole town had been whitewashed a fortnight before for the King's visit and now in the twilight the white buildings were curiously luminous, as if they were giving off light absorbed during the white-hot day. Green shutters appeared phosphorescent. The sky was flecked wth fleecy cirrus fans, cerise on top, silver on the bottom. The sea splashed over the quay, driving tourists from the forward tables. A happy old drunk, weaving between tables, was singing in a cracked voice and everyone applauded him. A young boy, probably a grandson, came to get him. The old man kissed several tourist girls and permitted himself to be led away, turning back to bow and wave his hat.

In the jovial atmosphere there was no indication of irritation. No doubt this was due to the amiability of the natives. Mykoniats like the foreigners who have brought them prosperity. Preserving their own individualities, in the interests of commerce sometimes even accenting them, they are amusedly tolerant of foreigners' eccentricities. In such a mood of toleration, both natives and visitors fall easily into a relaxed spirit of live-and-let-live permissiveness. Language is an aid. There is no place in Greece where the natives are linguistically so prepared to meet strangers. English is a second language with many Mykoniats, some of whom also speak French and German.

Behind the harbor façade is a bewildering network of alleys and this we set out to explore. So narrow were the alleys that when we met a donkey, we had to lean against a wall. The paths, leading often as not to dead ends, were laid out as traps for pirates, enemy pirates, that is, since on other islands and on passing ships, Mykonos' pirates were known as the most terrible. We passed several churches, doll churches they seemed to be, with flickering candles visible through small metal grills. Mykonos has more than 350 churches, few of which are used for worship. Many were built as votives of gratitude by seamen survivors of shipwrecks.

A path up and then down a hill toward the water brought us to Mykonos' most famous church, the extraordinary Paraportiani. This strangely organic mass seems at first sight to be self-proliferated like a capricious white mushroom. To Mykoniats, the complex of Byzantine curves and angles topped by a dome and arch is a haphazard, untidy accident, and the tourists' fascination for it strikes them as odd. Le Corbusier discovered it after the First World War—every cubistic form which he introduced to modern architecture is there in the primitive masterpiece. Standing in the diminishing twilight, watching textures and shapes change, like a white cumulus cloud about to take off over the sea, I pondered how a primitive peasant, the unknown builder of the Paraportiani, had influenced Western thought and art.

The night had turned cold. We returned to the Delos for some warm clothes and found there a delegation of the Joliet Club, summoned by Anna Fiorentinos to meet us, two homesick old men eager to speak to Americans.

"I voted for F.D.R. and I voted for John Kennedy," said one lively little man named George Vilablangas. A sixty-seven-year-old bachelor who worked as a truck gardener in Joliet for forty-six years before he returned in 1963, he is known in Mykonos, because of his ardent American patriotism, as "George Washington II."

"I did not know it," he said, "but I lived in America too long to come back. When I returned my parents, brothers, sister and friends were all dead. In Joliet, I have many friends."

Didn't Mykoniats in their landlocked town in the center of America miss the sea? I asked.

"In Mykonos we were too poor to enjoy the sea and in Joliet we never think of it," George replied. "It is not the Greek way to enjoy the sea. The sea is work. It is danger."

In Mykonos, where they are in demand as tourist guides, life was not entirely boring for George and the other former Americans. "But there is the homesickness," said George, who recently renewed his passport to return to Joliet. "I will have to find a job. Social Security is not enough for living in America. But I want to go home."

The other man, whose name was Dimitri Asimonitis, had no plans to return. "But I cannot forget the beautiful U.S.A., honest to God, I can't," he said. A fat, round man of sixty-six with a white crew cut, he was sent to America when he was thirteen to live with an aunt. At the age of twenty-six he returned to Mykonos to visit his mother, married there and had five children.

He was the owner of a grocery store, which he invited us to visit. We came to it at the end of a maze of alleys, a crowded dark little room smelling marvelously of spices, vinegar, soap, cheese and dried fish. A dark, thin man, one of Dimitri's sons, was behind the counter. On the counter was another battered copy of the Joliet telephone directory and newspaper photographs of the Kennedys were pasted to the walls.

"Mrs. Kennedy speak to me when she is here," he said. "I tell her America is best country in world. When anyone says bad things about America, I bust his goddamned nose." Laughing and crying simultaneously, he said, "Always my heart will be American. Always I feel sorry to come back."

I was relieved that his son seemed not to understand English.

"If I had not come back, I would be a goddamned happy American."

The man's self-pitying nostalgia was becoming unbearable. Trying to break away, I backed through the door into the alley outside. He followed, clinging to my arm, urging me to eat some chocolates which he offered from a box. "Always I shall love the stars and stripes," he sobbed, his tears dripping on the chocolates. At that moment, we were bathed in a warm shower from above. Looking up, I saw a small boy peeing through the iron grillwork of a balcony.

It was the moment to escape. We ate dinner in a seaside restaurant and returned to the Delos. The sky was a dome of stars. Naked street bulbs, swaying like pendulums in the wind, cast shadows which leaped back and forth over the quay. My mattress was hard and lumpy but the rhythmic swoosh of the sea against the wall of my room was like a soothing mother and I slept.

In the morning, the sea awakened me. A "bell wind"—so called because it rings church bells—was driving the surf against the ramparts, against the hotel, washing the jetty with it and spattering my window. I heard shouting. Getting up, I saw crowds of men, women and children running on the beach with baskets and buckets, gathering small smeltlike fish which the surf was washing up. Flipping on the sands, the fish, called *kefanos,* glittered like dancing coins, and the people of the town were harvesting the miraculous draught like manna.

At breakfast we met a young Australian couple, an architect named David Mercer and his wife, Beryl. They were tall, handsome people; he was blond and she had brown hair and eyes. Like us, they had planned to take the boat to Delos, only two miles away. Anna Fiorentinos urged us not to go. The sea, she said, was too perilous. Passengers in the small caïque would be soaked with spray and many would be seasick. So we decided instead to go to a beach. One named Santa Stefano was an hour's walk on a cliff road. The wind battered at us all the way. Inside the Santa Stefano bay, the water was calm, the sand warm. A half-dozen Swiss were there and a blond Danish family, lean, sinewy parents with five naked golden children, all so beautiful one could not help looking at them. We swam in the turquoise lagoon and at noon lunched on shish kebab, salad, and wine on the terrace of a little restaurant. The wind, growing stronger, tattered the canvas awning over our heads. Out on the sea we saw a large ship bobbing like an apple in a tub. We dressed and started back, clinging to one another to keep from blowing away, thinking of Icarus taking off from just such a ledge. Another myth had come to believable life.

Back in town, we set out to find Mykonos' smallest church, called the Church of the Cat. Its legend is that it was built by a sailor who made a vow during a shipwreck off Gibraltar. Unfortunately, he spent so much money on his way home—who knows, perhaps in cat houses—that all he could afford when he arrived was a church large enough for cats. At once we were lost in the network of passages. Each time we asked directions we were sent deeper into the labyrinth. One man directed us to "go to the church where I have sung for thirty-nine years and turn right at the apple tree." We saw a group of women, black-robed knitting Madame Defarges, cackling among themselves, and they beckoned us forward. The next man we asked said we had passed the church, that it was behind us. I was beginning to doubt the existence of the Church of the Cat. We saw many cats, all of a singular breed with mustaches which appeared to be painted on their faces. David Mercer suggested we follow them, since they were probably parishioners. But all seemed to be going in different directions. Finally, a man offered to lead us. He walked fifty yards back in the direction of the knitting women, and pointed upwards to the corner of a house roof, where there was a minuscule projection in the shape of a church. It had a red roof and was the size of a small dovecote. A few yards away, the knitting women were laughing.

"Is this the Church of the Cat?" Greggory managed in Greek.

"Ne, ne, ne," the old ladies nodded in unison, and then collapsed into shrieks of mirth. The eldest in the pack began to skirl, "Meeeeee-owwwwww, meeeeee-owwwwww . . ." Her black-robed friends responded with a cackle of mirth. I remembered that Hallowe'en was three weeks away.

"There's no cross on it," said Greggory to the women.

"You don't put crosses on animal churches," one of the ladies shrilled. "Only on people churches." We started down the street, hearing behind us the old women screeching "Meeeee-owwwww, meeeeee-owwwww . . ."

I saw a sign which said *Vienoula,* and I remembered that I had a letter for Vienoula Kousathanas, owner of a weaving shop. At once I knew I was in the right place. Shelves and tables were stacked with bolts of homespuns and tweeds, and with sweaters and scarves. A large white-haired woman was pouring tea. I told her the name of the friend who sent me and she said, "How is Helen? Why doesn't she write? I am angry with her. For two months I have received no letter. I am very angry. Doesn't she know how much I love her?" The deep resonance of her voice, its overpowering warmth, made each commonplace word ring as if it had been written by Aeschylus.

A sandaled blond German youth was sitting in the shop laughing at everything Vienoula said. "He is like a son," she said. "He has been here since spring and soon he must return to go to school. We are sad." She had been reading a book about Greece by an American who misquoted her as saying she disliked tourists. "How could I have said such a foolish thing?" she said. "I love tourists. I live from them. In my shop I see all the tourists. When winter comes I am sorry, it is so lonely. Thank God a few still come."

Stories about Vienoula in American and European magazines have made her famous. As a young woman, she lived in England. She returned to Mykonos, married and had five children. When her husband was ill ten years ago, an American artist who was visiting Mykonos suggested that she organize the women of the island into a weaving cooperative. Vienoula designs the fabrics and garments which the women make in their homes, when "they are not busy with seeding or harvesting." Friends spread the word; the shop was a success. "Too successful," said Vienoula. "I have also sold my three daughters in the shop. They married tourists, one a Norwegian, one an Athenian, and the third an American professor on Long Island." Two sons were with her. Panagiotis, twenty-five, was in charge of the dyeing. Nicholas, nineteen, was bookkeeper.

Panagiotis was there now, tending shop. A tightly-knit young man with black curly hair and dark, knowing eyes, he was waiting on a red-haired American girl, who was bossily ordering yards of fabrics "for my boutique." When she had gone, Panagiotis said, "She is crazy. She has no boutique. But she has enough money to pretend she has and it gives her importance. She buys and buys and buys. She is very arrogant. Someone should take a *vourdoula* to her." He was speaking of a long, leathery whip used by donkey drivers. "It would be fitting," he said, his eyes alight with innuendo. "Perhaps you do not know that a *vourdoula* is a dried bull's penis."

To start us on the right path back, Panagiotis walked with us a short distance. Weaving through the labyrinths we met dogs, strange furry creatures like brown caterpillars. Others were lean and luminously white. "The dogs of Mykonos are shadow dogs who have forgotten how to bark," said Panagiotis. "They are always silent." It was true; the creatures were unlike any other dogs on earth. They were moon dogs like the unnatural beasts under the tables in quattrocento paintings of the Last Supper, or sniffing at the damned in frescoes of the Last Judgment. We arrived at a well and Panagiotis said, "There is a legend that any male tourist who drinks from it will marry a Mykonos girl." I pointed to a chain and lock sealing the well. "The mayor is worried because of the dowries. He does not want all the property in Mykonos to be owned by foreigners. So he locked the well."

He left. Our route took us by a windmill. From a window near the hub of the revolving wheel the miller beckoned us inside. The door was open; we climbed a steep flight to a platform under the cupola. The ceiling was so low we had to crouch to enter. The place had a fine nutty smell and everything was dusted with white flour, including the mustachioed old miller. Flour poured from spouts like liquid. The miller was on his knees, stirring it with his hands, explaining the process of milling to two blue-eyed blondes in tight blue slacks. "We are from Holland," said one of them. "We know about mills." The great gears creaked like wagons crossing a wooden bridge.

In the morning the sea still raged. In spite of it, the Mercers, Greggory and I decided we would take the boat for Delos. If we were going to be so foolish, said Mrs. Fiorentinos, it would be necessary to dress in swimsuits under raincoats.

No one else on the dock was dressed in our peculiar way. Fortunately, we were carrying orthodox clothing into which we wriggled on deck. On the open sea, whitecaps rolled over us, pitching us about like the small craft in Japanese prints. A party of young Swiss made a game of the turbulence, merrily tumbling over one another. The Greeks tugged anxiously at their worry beads, and a German woman closed her eyes and gripped her seat, her face pale and sweating. The two-mile voyage took an hour.

Delos lay before us like a fan, rising gently at first and then steeply, toward a rocky peak. We entered by a rampart of weathered rock into a long, narrow, serenely calm harbor. In the foreground was the ghost of a Roman city, its columns, broken near the earth, like rows of white footstools. Above, ascending to sacred Mt. Cynthus, were the remains of an earlier Greek city. Marble fragments scattered over the island shone white in the sun. Delos, I remembered, was known as the island of light.

Legend credits its origin to a miracle of lusty Zeus who needed a place for the accouchement of his mistress, Leto, which would be hidden from the prying eyes of his wife, Hera. As a center of the cult of Apollo, most characteristic of Greek gods, it became a sanctuary equal to Delphi and Olympia. Sacred festivals were celebrated with processions, games and religious rites which brought thousands of pilgrims, many of whom settled on the island. There were also practical reasons for Delos' hegemony. Its harbor was a safe stopping place for ships on the way to Asia. When the Romans made Delos a free port it became a great commercial center, dealing in grain and slaves. A rich international society built temples, colonnades, agorae, theaters, and stadia.

The end came quickly in 88 B.C. when the city was sacked by an Asiatic invader, King Mithridates VI, who destroyed its buildings, slaughtered its twenty thousand citizens and left Delos a dead city. Pirates carried off treasures and scavengers from neighboring islands mined the marble for building stones. In 1873, the French School of Athens began excavations which are still going on.

Because the winds blow more fiercely in the afternoon, our skipper warned that the boat would leave at noon. We took off by ourselves, hoping to cover the three-mile island in two hours. At the temple of Apollo giant lizards crawled over fragments of columns lying like sliced sausages on the earth. The marble pediments were carved with cattle skulls like the paintings of Georgia O'Keeffe. In the shrine to Dionysius large stone phalli pointed to the sun like loaded cannons. Beyond the agora, we saw Delos' most beautiful monuments, the sacred lions, silhouetted against the cloudless blue. At least sixteen once guarded a sanctuary and a sacred lake. Today there are five, lean and graceful as white panthers. In the residential quarters, the small houses and narrow lanes were like the houses and streets of modern Mykonos. The importance of water was everywhere apparent. The sacred lake was a communal reservoir and deep rain wells lay under the floors of temples, public buildings, and houses of the affluent. In one of the wells we found a fig tree heavy with juicy, purple fruit which we ate. The wind was whistling among the sacred stones and birds sang. Sheep bells tinkled among the ruins—for centuries Delos has been a pasture for Mykonos livestock.

The archaic city on the slopes of Mt. Cynthus is better preserved. Trotting breathlessly from monument to monument, we saw the wind-swept little Doric temple to Isis, the House of the Dolphins and the House of the Masks, both with mosaicked floors, the House of the Trident with two lions on its columns, the house of a patrician Athenian couple named Dioscourides and Cleopatra, with their headless statues, a theater of five thousand seats facing, of course, the sea, and a great rectangular reservoir covered with eight Roman arches. All of it had a marvelous richness of intimate detail. Marble tables and chairs, mortar stones, bathtubs, household utensils, gave a vivid picture of a vigorous civilization. We made the 368-foot ascent to the summit where we looked out on the circle of Cyclades—Mykonos, Syros, Naxos, Paros, Tinos—rising from the indigo sea like the silvery backs of gigantic dolphins. The wind was driving the sea against the stones of the nearest island, Rhenea. Below our skipper was blowing a horn and we saw our fellow passengers scurrying out of the passages and lanes like coveys of quail. Running pell-mell down the rocky slopes, we had our last view of the lions, the profiles of their jaws thrown open to the skies, seeming to break the eternal silence with roars. On the boat the German lady, anticipating the voyage back, sat pale and stiff; a friend was wiping her brow. Delos was a speck in the sea.

The next day we took one of Mykonos' antiquated buses to the island's second village, Ano Merá. We jogged up through a stony landscape cut into tiny patches by a disorderly network of stone fences. On the bus was a large women in a florid print dress and straw hat, who spoke to us, saying, "Would you mind dreadfully if I tagged along?" Without waiting for an answer, she introduced herself. "I'm Lily Marsden. It can be very sticky for a lady alone. The Greeks, you know."

She followed us off the bus and into a monastery where we were greeted by a good-looking, smiling monk. When he discovered we did not speak Greek, he called another, a frail, hunched little fellow who spoke French. He had long, disheveled braids which he shook loose, letting the hair fall to his hips, and began to rebraid. "I do think," said Lily Marsden, "that long hair in men is very untidy." I said I supposed it need be no more untidy than long hair in women. "Women wash it more," she said starchily.

The monk, his fingers kneading hair, showed us a miraculous icon he said was painted by St. Luke. What, I asked, made it miraculous?

"It cures people," he said.

"Silly superstition," said Lily Marsden. The church had lavish chandeliers and paintings in an eighteenth-century Italian style. "Thank heavens it's clean," said Lily Marsden. "One thing, you can always tell an English church by the way it's kept."

"That's how I tell an English woman," said Greggory. "By the way she's kept."

The monk led us up an outside staircase to the roof, from which we looked over craggy brown hills, abandoned windmills, and the stone fences like a nervous system gone berserk, to the sea. In the unpaved village square beneath us, the eucalyptus trees were bowed southward, bent in right angles by the unceasing winds. The empty, barren place filled us with desolation. We wanted to leave at once. The bus had gone, said the monk, and there would not be another for two hours.

In a café we asked the waitress to telephone for a taxi. She was young and beautiful with her black hair gathered in a white shawl and a smile showing perfect teeth. She asked to borrow Greggory's Greek-English dictionary, and as we drank our coffee, she stood in the doorway forming English words with her lips. After ten minutes she came to our table and addressing Beryl Mercer, asked, "What has the name of your aroma?"

Beryl replied that her perfume was Le Dix, by Balenciaga.

"I like very," said the girl, her dark eyes shining.

Returning in the taxi I could not forget her, dreaming of Paris perfume in such an utterly desolate place. What, I wondered, would happen if she ever escaped Ano Merá? I thought that when I arrived in Athens I might send her some Le Dix. But I did not know her name.

Back in Mykonos Lily Marsden's idiotic chatter was beginning to unnerve us. When she sat with us at a café table, Greggory took a plastic sack of multicolored pills from his pocket, saying, "Miss Marsden, I wonder if you could help me. My doctor gave me all the pills I would need for the trip, but they've gotten all mixed up in my bag, cold tablets, diarrhea pills, aphrodisiacs, birth control pills . . ."

He spread the spectrum of pellets on the table. "It would be dreadful taking one and not knowing which it was until too late. Can you tell them apart, Miss Marsden?"

Miss Marsden tugged nervously at her hat. "Mercy, it's lunchtime," she said. "I have an appointment. Well, thank you. Hasn't it been jolly?" She tripped across the esplanade.

In the afternoon I sought out Panagiotis Kousathanas, the one person whom I guessed might know the name of the perfume-dreaming girl of Ano Merá. He was tending his mother's shop. "Know her well," he said, rolling his eyes. "Like to know her better. But she has four brothers and I think it safer to let them buy her perfume." I wrote down the name, Kokona Boutioury. A small unsigned parcel from Athens I felt would be safe enough.

Vienoula was in her garden, said Panagiotis. He offered to take me to her. "My mother is cleaning her houses," he said. "She rents rooms to tourists." We entered a courtyard of flowering trees and a grape arbor. At a well in a corner Vienoula was washing linens with a servant. She wiped soap from her hands and drew back her hair. She plucked some grapes from the vine and we sat on a stone bench eating them.

"Beatniks don't sweep," she said in deep visceral tones which might have been Iphigenia's discussing the housekeeping in Aulis. "There were two beatniks sleeping in the open air, in the cold, and I said to them, 'Why don't you sleep in my room which is empty? You need not pay. I only ask that you keep it clean.' They did not sweep, they did not clean. It is like a dirty stable. The girl is from Holland and the boy from England. I thank God they are not Americans. I should not like to change my opinion of Americans."

That evening the Fiorentinos invited us to a party. A long table was spread under the aviary of twittering birds. Seated around it, along with our hosts and ourselves, was the entire Mykonos police force—the chief and his assistant and the assistant's wife. The chief, a bachelor in his early thirties, had a cockatoo's crest of black crew-cut hair, bright dark eyes and a trimmed mustache. His colleague, a few years older, was athletically built with brown hair, also cut in a brush. His wife, seated beside me at the table, was a birdlike brunette with flashing eyes and a face small and perfect as Nefertiti's. The chief struggled uneasily with English; the assistant and his wife were silent. The banquet began with a variety of *mezédes* and a white wine from Rhodes. "Bottoms up," toasted David Mercer, and we emptied our glasses. The phrase caught the ear of the police chief who was anxious to broaden his English. The glasses were refilled.

"Up the bottom," the chief bawled out.

Our guffaws pleased him. More wine was poured. "Up the bottom," the chief bellowed again, joining in the laughter. For one demented hour, through courses of fish and lamb, and a variety of four wines, the inanity continued. Fiorentinos filled glasses, and the chief, delighting in his social success, bellowed, "Up the bottom!"

Deciding the madness had gone far enough I tried to explain to him that he was saying it wrong. "Is not the same, bottoms is up, up the bottom?" he asked. The next time he roared, "Bottoms is up!" Associating freely, he asked, "What means to keep up your sunnyside?"

To distract him from his semantic chaos, I asked what happened to law and order in Mykonos when the entire police force was at revelries.

"Is always law and order in Mykonos." Speaking Greek with Fiorentinos translating, the chief said, "There are no poor people here so there is no crime. Our people are proud of their honesty. If you lose something, it always comes back."

"Then why a police force at all?" I persisted.

"There are many duties," the chief replied. "A Swiss lady cannot find her room. A goat climbs a fence into a neighbor's garden. A Frenchman drinks too much wine. Many duties."

Fiorentinos interrupted with a complaint about the nocturnal habits of his young lady guests. Since he never went to bed before all guests were in their rooms, he sometimes got no sleep at all. "The hour depends on their success," he said. "This morning three B.B.C. girls came in at seven, eight, and ten A.M. 'Why didn't you tell me?' I asked. 'I could have locked the door and gone to bed.' 'How did we know?' they said."

The door of the hotel opened and in a gust of wind and sea there entered two tiny, wizened old ladies, both carrying large suitcases. *"Haben sie Zimmer?"* one asked in a timid voice. It was after one o'clock and they had just arrived on the last boat. Fiorentinos called a maid who took the little ladies upstairs. Within five minutes they reappeared, dwarfs wearing raincoats and shawls over their heads, their spectacles glistening, and went briskly out into the night.

"See how it is," said Fiorentinos. "No sleep again tonight."

Suddenly the assistant policeman's wife broke her silence. "Poot out the light," she commanded huskily.

Fiorentinos dimmed the lights. "Tenk voo veree much," she said and without any announcement she began to sing in a deep contralto about an island maid abandoned by a sailor. Leaning on my shoulder she sang sad song after sad song, like a musical Hecuba. Drunk, I tried to focus on the bowl of hibiscus on the table. She was young and very lovely.

The next day David and Beryl Mercer and I went by taxi to a distant beach called Platy Yialos, a lush cove with brightly painted schooners marooned on the sand, and Germans and Swiss in the water. It was a sadly bittersweet day for I was leaving by the afternoon boat and the Mercers were starting the next day on their journey home to Brisbane. As sometimes, not often, happens to travelers, we had in our week together become abiding friends. We spoke of my coming to Australia, of their visiting me in Wisconsin, trying to dispel the heartbreak of parting, of the eight thousand miles that would eventually separate us. Below on the beach we saw the ubiquitous trio, the police chief and his assistant and the assistant's wife. She was swimming alone and the two men,

vigorously chesty, were romping on the sand with a little girl of four or five
years, the daughter of the assistant. The Mercers and I speculated over
the perplexing bonds of this handsome *ménage à trois*. I leaped up to pick
a red hibiscus for Beryl's hair. The three down by the sea saw me and
waved and we realized they were quite probably also speculating about
us.

"Up the bottom," called the chief, rocking with laughter.

"Up the bottom," I shouted back.

2

THE SYMBOLIC THINGS

Approached by night, Hermoupolis, with its thousands of lights
flickering on two levels, appears to be a great city. As the port of Syros
and capital of the Cyclades, it very nearly became one. Hermoupolis was
the first port of Greece until Piraeus surpassed it in the late nineteenth
century. Its government buildings are the most imposing outside Athens.
There are elegant villas in the countryside and automobiles on its roads.

Yet tourists shun Syros. A reason may be the attitude of its people
toward foreigners. "Of course, we love tourists," said the lady who
registered us at the Hotel Ermis. "But we are not dependent upon them.
We have clubs, cinemas and concerts and a very nice society in winter."
With a touch of envy she added somewhat primly, "In Mykonos I hear
there are many *Dolce Vita* types."

It was the time of the *volta* and the esplanade was crowded with
evening strollers, many of them soldiers and sailors from training bases on
the island. The busiest ports of call were the *loukoumia* parlors, a row of
white shops like Fanny Farmer stores, selling the saccharine confection
known in English as "Turkish delight." Each shop was stacked with
mountains of the stuff in a great variety of *"parfums"*—including rose,
jasmine and violet. I asked a saleswoman who consumed it. "The people,"
she said, causing me to wonder about the incidence of diabetes on Syros.

She directed us to Syros' best restaurant, called Kosmikon Kentron
Asteria, "Social Center of the Stars." It was a large room facing the port
with a pyramid of wine bottles covering a wall like an iconostasi. The
place was nearly empty. An idiot in a corner laughed, and at a table
four men wearing hats tugged at their worry beads. We had been
promised native music and a *bouzouki* band was waiting. Our entrance
was the musicians' cue to begin. The owner, a large heavy man who
looked like Robert Morley, paced by our table sighing audibly. A cluster

of his relatives, dressed in black, stood in the kitchen door listening to
the music. An almost unbearable despair settled on both of us. We seemed
to be in a room without exits, from which we could not leave. I asked for a
boat schedule and found there was no boat leaving the island for two days.

The waiter was pushing "bifsteak," which turned out to be salty ham-
burger served with a tasteless pasta. The wine was an old friend,
Demisticha, and we drank two bottles. Finally some guests arrived, a party
of seven men, and their entrance was like a liberation, freeing us to leave.

Hermoupolis has a famous church dedicated to St. Nicholas. When
we went there the next morning the front door was locked. A side door
opened and a fat, bald little man waved an arm, calling, "Come, I show."
His face and hair, and a jacket which he dragged behind him, were dusty
white so I assumed he must be a plasterer or concrete worker. The
décor of the church was Russian rather than Greek, with many paintings
in an Eastern style. Our guide pointed to a Byzantine madonna with the
child on the left side, and an Italian madonna with the child on the right
side, which he explained was the rule of the two confessions. As the
tempo of his explications increased he began to stammer, repeating some
words four or five times. "From Roosia Roosia Roosia Roosia," he
gasped, pointing to a jeweled icon. Foam gathered at the corners of his
mouth. Spraying us with saliva, he sputtered, "Everywhere you see see see
see is beautiful." He crossed the church. "Come come come come," he
commended, pointing to some cherubs floating over a Christ. "Angels with
six winks winks winks winks. Count please." Wherever he moved, the
jacket stirred up a cloud of dust. I had decided that he was mad. Pointing
to the painting of an eye under the ceiling he cried, "Look! Everywhere
is watching eye of Gott Gott Gott Gott. . . ."

Moving toward the antrum doors, I remembered they were locked. I
drifted toward the side door but each time I came close, the guide took a
position between me and the door and steered me in another direction.
"Look, is Saint Dimitrios Dimitrios Dimitrios all gold from Roosia Roosia
Roosia. Is very very very . . ." Unable at once to think of the word, he
grabbed my arm and shouted at the top of his lungs, "Ex-press-EEVE!"

Feigning interest in a gold lamp I was able to move closer to the door
which Greggory was approaching from the opposite side. Making a wide
circle around us, our guide arrived at the door before either of us. "See
paintings holy holy holy," he shouted, his voice echoing through the high
nave. The three of us watched one another like a trio of Japanese
samurai.

"Look at eggs eggs eggs," said the fellow, pointing to an egg-shaped
lamp base. "Represent our re-re-religion. Eggs make small birds birds
birds. Birds make eggs eggs eggs. We must believe in God like eggs eggs

eggs and birds birds birds." Running low, guarding all doors, including the locked one, he shouted, "Oh oh oh oh, look at the good marble of Tinos and Paros."

"Get me out of here before I crack up," Greggory murmured.

I was making stealthy gains on the door. The man, his eyes darting like a cat's, swung back and took a position directly before it. Rolling his eyes toward the ceiling, dropping to his knees, he burst into a spell of mono-syllables crying, "Oh oh oh! Is Jesus Christ Christ Christ!" Shaking in a kind of fit, he pointed a hand to the dome cupola inside which was painted a Christ in Ascension magnificently lit by the morning sun. The Raphaelesque figure rising from gray mists, surrounded by a chimera of silvery cherubs, was the most beautiful thing in the church. "Jesus there there there," the man was crying. His knees rattled on the floor and his eyes were weeping. "Is never in same place place place. Sometimes is here here here. Sometimes is there there there. Sometimes is no place. Sometimes is large. Sometimes is small small small. . . ." The guide's face was purple. Leaping to his feet, he began jumping up and down. "Today is here. Jesus Christ is here here here here . . ."

The door of the church creaked open and an old woman padded in. Not comprehending her role of rescuer, she watched with amazement as we leaped toward her. Caught off guard, the guide shouted, "You want to go from this door door door?"

"Any door," said Greggory.

"Not yet yet yet. Come to see the angels flying. . . ."

He was too late. We were in possession of the door.

"Angels from Roosia Roosia Roosia." The voice was pleading now. We threw some drachmae at the man and ran into the sunlight. Bowing in the door, he was saying, "I salute salute salute . . ." We ran down the alley and he called, "Sometimes I see in dream dream dream the symbolic things . . ." Some workmen were tearing up the pavements with pneumatic drills and we could no longer hear him but we saw his lips continuing to move.

3

THE CARDIAC WALTZ

Our boat was late. For two hours we drank *ouzo* on the quay, watching the revels in the *loukoumia* parlors. Finally the boat, named *Pandelis,* arrived and with it a cargo of new army and merchant navy recruits from Athens. A young seaman carried two cages, each with a canary, down the gangplank. For his sake I hoped they would sing on Syros.

The heavy steel vessel plowed the waters slowly and smoothly. Our second class was packed with Greek islanders who unpacked lunches of cheese, salami and olives. A couple beside me energetically disjointed a chicken which disappeared in minutes. I slept.

When I awakened it was night. I went out on deck, crowded like a cattle boat with sleeping Greeks. On the horizon I could see islands. I heard singing and I followed the voice to the prow. A girl was filling the night with tender music. Spread over a coil of rope at her feet were two sailors and three girls who beckoned me to join them. I took a place beside one of the girls who translated into English the words of a song, whispering in my ear, "My room is a yacht when you are there . . ." Clinging to a cable for support, her head thrown back, her breast high, her hair flowing, the singer seemed to be serenading the moon, and her sweet song floated over the sea like a siren's luring mariners. When the lyric was familiar, the sailors and girls joined gently with their own voices, taking care not to cover the girl's soft contralto. A small hand folded in my own and soft breathing warmed my face. "My room has a blanket," I heard. "Will you come?" I seemed to be in a dream, no longer sure whether the words murmured in my ear came from the song or from my interpreter. The lights of Paros lay ahead. I was disembarking in fifteen minutes.

From a guidebook we picked the only Class A hotel in Paros, named Meltemi, which is equivalent to calling a hotel "The Hurricane" or "The Hilton Tornado." It stood outside the town, behind a windmill which had long ceased to function. Except for a candle flickering at the desk, the hotel was dark. A young clerk said it was closing for the season in a week. The kitchen was shut, the power plant already turned off. A solitary chambermaid led us by candlelight to our rooms. We were the only guests.

Nearby was a third-class hotel bright with lights, from which we could hear music and voices. Hoping there would also be food, we walked the short distance there. Outside we found a band of children, little girls wearing halos of flowers and boys with bow ties, throwing stones at one another. The provocateur in this pitched battle was a frilly-pantsed girl perhaps three years old who picked up handfuls of gravel and threw them at the boys. After each foray she ran screaming behind an adult for protection. A very nasty type, I decided, wondering why someone didn't swat her lacy bottom. Several of the bow-tied boys were reeling drunkenly and shrieking like banshees. One got a pebble in his eye and began to bawl. We asked a man watching it all if there was any food for us.

"Many foods," he replied in English. "Welcome to the feast." He was a strongly built young man with long mustaches. He ushered us inside and seated us at a table covered with fish, roast lamb, potatoes and beakers of wine. We were at a wedding. At a center table, surrounded by women, a large buxom bride wearing a red dress and white flowers in her black hair was smiling serenely. "Where is the groom?" I asked. Our host pointed to a small thin fellow on the dance floor. He was, said our informant, a lighthouse keeper on the tip of a satellite island called Antiparos. Watching his happy, buoyant levitations with a girl, blonde and small as himself, while his bride gossiped contentedly with her relatives, I tried to imagine the domestic years ahead.

A phonograph played Western tangos and waltzes. The men leaped about like colts and women followed them with tight-lipped tolerance, as if dancing were a necessary foolishness to appease the male. Our host introduced himself, saying, "I have a mule," by which he meant he guided tourists. He presented us to two ladies, pleasant plumpish matrons who spoke no English, so there was nothing to do but dance. The record, a long-playing medley of German waltzes, seemed to go on forever. Couples kept dropping from the floor. Determined not to lose face we swooped and whirled to the end. "The cardiac waltz," gasped Greggory when it finally finished.

The next record was Greek and the relieved ladies relaxed to voyeurism. Men linked arms and began leaping through the *syrtaki*. Showing off for us, our muleteer seemed borne by invisible wings. The dance was interrupted by an ear-shattering scream from outdoors. The voice was the little provocateur's. Bending over to pick up a handful of stones, she had been kicked in the rump by a drunken little boy. She was, it turned out, the daughter of our muleteer.

The next day, Sunday, we swam on a rocky beach below the hotel and explored the town. Whitewashed Paros is a quieter Mykonos without the tourist stampede. Barbers were busy with Sunday shaves and in a tiny piazza a town crier was announcing deaths, births and marriages. The men who heard him were wearing white kummerbunds. At a seaside café fishermen were eating roasted octopus. The creatures hung grotesquely over the grills and each order was filled by drawing a dangling tentacle into the flames until it was cooked. We drank an *ouzo* and asked for a menu. The English list of "boilet eggs, meat bulls, fat guts and fruit compost" did not entice us. In the town we found a more orthodox bill of fare at a restaurant called Starfish, where we ate grilled veal in a garden.

In ancient times the island mined a beautiful white marble used in the temples of Delos. On Paros the stone can be seen in the Ekatontapyliani— Our Lady of the Hundred Gates—the most famous church in the Aegean.

Actually it is not one church but a multi-orificed complex of three churches built over a temple during the reign of Justinian. Here again we were victims of a maniacally egocentric guide who slapped each column, shouting, "Marble before Christ." Raising a stone in the floor, he pointed into a black pit, crying, "Temple of Demeter before Christ." He continued his fugue in a marble baptistery where there was a cross-shaped tank for immersion. Architecturally confusing, the church has been made more so by its alterations. Seventeenth-century baroque piers and arches were overlayed on an early Romanesque gallery extending around three sides. Taking it all in with a sweep of an arm, the guide shouted, "Before Christ!"—apparently the only English phrase he knew. In exasperation we left. The fellow followed us into a courtyard where there was a gnarled old cypress. Beating his fist on the trunk so hard birds flew out of it, he cried, "Before Christ, before Christ!"

The next day we hired a chauffeur named Stavros, a smiling bustling man who also knew one English phrase with which he managed a kind of communication. It was "Bye-bye." Greeks are geniuses at keeping old boats afloat and old cars on the road and Stavros' twenty-year-old Chevrolet was, obviously, an object of love. He drove us through a green valley toward a cluster of cloud-covered volcanic peaks. Our first stop was in the interior village of Lefkas, an empty silent place where Stavros took us to a "factory," a dark room in which four girls perhaps fifteen years old, with long black braids, were looming rugs. Working silently, swiftly, each girl knotted wool on her own ten-foot warp of 740 taut threads. Their fingers moved like the fingers of harp players but the only sounds they produced were the sharp little snips of knife blades. I counted one girl's movements—each minute she tied and cut twenty-four knots of colored wool, creating a richly Oriental floral design. There was no light in the room. Each three-meter-square rug took a month to finish and sold for 5500 drachmae, less than $185.

A priest bustled into the place to ask if he might borrow our driver to take him to a house in the country where a man had just died. We walked down an empty street toward a café. A man came out of a door, calling, "Welcome America!" His name was John Milonas, and he was a retired engineer from Flatbush who had returned with his wife to spend two years in the house from which they had emigrated thirty-five years ago. With two pensions—Social Security and U. S. Army—he was a plutocrat in Lefkas. "We live very good," he said. "Eat meat or fish every day. But my wife is homesick for Flatbush." There were, he said, two hundred American pensioners on Paros. He walked with us through the town, pointing out the empty houses. "When I was a boy there were two thousand people. Now there are one thousand. The rest are in Germany." I watched him tugging worry beads and asked him if he had needed them in America. "Of course not," he said. "In America there were things to do. Here one must make the time pass."

Stavros returned. "Bye-bye," he waved in greeting. He drove us over a rocky trail toward the sea to the fishing town of Marissa. Fishermen were repairing bright red, orange and yellow nets which were festooned over the quay like gay lace. At a fountain Stavros put water into the Chevrolet and checked the motor, and then we headed back toward Paros, stopping on the way at the ancient quarries. Locking the car, Stavros led us on foot up a stony path to a dark opening in a cliff. An ancient inscription and some human figures carved into the red stone looked as if they were cast in iron. Stavros dropped a rock into the open shaft and we heard it ricochet downward to infinity. "Bye-bye," he said smiling and then he picked some herbs, oregano and thyme, for us to smell.

There was still a monastery to see, called Longovarda, where the monks were famous icon painters. Hidden in a canyon, it was white-washed and bright with potted begonias and geraniums. In a richly frescoed chapel, Stavros crawled on his knees kissing icons. We entered a courtyard and climbed some stairs to a balcony. Cats slunk in and out of doors. Finally we met two dusty-robed monks, one old and one young. Immediately Stavros was arguing with them to show us the painting studios. Tourists, said the old monk angrily, stole icons. We left and the young monk followed, mumbling apologies, saying he did not think we were thieves. He showed us a donkey with which, he said, he transported the monastery's supplies from Paros. The donkey's name was Icarus.

We had plans to take the *Elli*, a boat scheduled for 5 P.M., to Naxos. In the booking office there was a large stall of American paperbacks, including *Fanny Hill, Dr. Spock Talks with Mothers, A Man Called Peter,* and *My Years with General Motors* by Alfred Sloan, Jr. Waiting in line I took up a book by Kazantzakis and the young man in charge of the establishment said scornfully, "An anti-Greek writer. Americans like him." He was a thin sour-faced fellow who made no effort to conceal his hostility. "The *Elli* has been canceled," he said, smiling, showing his pleasure. "There will be a replacement at nine o'clock."

The replacement was named *Despina*. We went down to the dock at eight and ordered some food in a seaside restaurant. At nine, a boat arrived and we scurried up the gangplank. The ticket taker said the boat was not the *Despina* and was not going to Naxos. We returned to our table in the café and ordered coffee. The night turned cold and windy. A full moon lighted the sea. The restaurant filled with characters, each

of whom had a different opinion as to when the *Despina* would call.
Perhaps ten thirty. Or midnight. We asked a tourist policeman who wore
an armband saying "English." He shrugged. "No spik," he said. Someone
was playing a transistor radio, a Voice of America broadcast of Teresa
Brewer bawling,

> I got a boy friend,
> Oh la la la la. . . .

A chubby little man in a soiled white jacket, carrying a wicker basket,
sat down beside us and placed his hamper on the table. It contained
cookies and *loukoumia*. He smiled amiably and we bought him a drink.
He said he was a vendor and was waiting for the *Despina*. When would it
come? He shrugged. Who could tell? I was imagining Theseus trying to
get away from Ariadne, telling her, "Dear, I have a little business in
Athens and am taking the *Elli*. Take the *Despina* and follow me."
Finally it was midnight and the Voice of America sobbed,

> Don't you feel like crying,
> Don't you feel like crying . . .

In black despair I replied, "Yes." The wind whistled. Suddenly at
half-past midnight a murmur went through the crowd and our *loukoumia*
salesman grabbed his basket and ran toward the quay. We followed,
stepping after him onto a tiny caïque. It chugged into the harbor. Out on
the sea a light was approaching. It was the *Despina*.

4

ARIADNE'S ISLE

Naxos is not a tourist island so most of the passengers were Greek.
The deck was covered with them sleeping in blankets like a cargo of
mummies. Here and there tethered chickens kicked helplessly.

From the ship's cables loaves of bread suspended with string swung
like pendulums in the moonlight. There were also some of the youthful
wanderers known as "Island Troubadours"—German, Scandinavian and
English youths and maidens, who drift from island to island, sometimes
with motorcycles which are loaded on boats with winches, eating out
of rucksacks which they use as pillows, writing in journals, reading
from paperbacks of Freud and Jung, Gide and Mary Renault.

In the second-class lounge the little *loukoumia* seller was organizing
a raffle selling chances on a toy windmill for two drachs. The lottery

provided a moment of excitement and was won by a white-haired old man. Later I saw the salesman on the deck sleeping, his hamper between his legs.

When we arrived at 3 A.M. the port of Naxia was dark. On the jetty we were assailed by a covey of men offering us rooms. We asked directions for the Ermis Hotel and a man offered to guide us there. We followed him across the quay. When he turned into a dark side street I became apprehensive. Silently he beckoned us on. Another turn and he stopped before a small house and unlocked the door. Turning on a light, he bowed grandly, saying, "Welcome to my home." Bowing still, he did not see us turn and run. Behind us we could hear him crying, "Welcome, welcome." On the desolate sea front we saw one small figure, the *loukoumia* seller, carrying his basket. His face lit up at the sight of us. Of course he knew the Ermis. He offered to take us there. Trudging beside him, noting that he was wearing sandals, it occurred to me that his name must be Hermes, that he was the ubiquitous messenger of Zeus.

The hotel, a restored Venetian palace on the edge of town, was locked and dark. I rang a bell, holding my thumb on it, and Hermes pounded on a side door. After a long wait a light went on and a tall young man appeared wearing a bathrobe. Naxia was built by Venetians, and the young man in the door, black-haired with a thin, pale face, might have been a doge's son. He took us into a parlor in which were hanging several paintings of the Venetian school and a portrait of an aristocratic-looking gentlemen, clearly an ancestor. Someone was beating on the door. It was Hermes who had been left outside. Smiling sweetly, pathetically he asked, as a reward for delivering us, a bed for the night. The young man disappeared. Smiling reassuringly, making a sign with his hands that everything would be O.K., Hermes said, *"Buona. Dormez gut."* Chattering in a German-Italian polyglot, he told us his grandfather had been from Naxos. He was thirty years old and lived in Piraeus with his wife and seven-year-old son named Nicholas, whom he visited "always on Sunday." During the week he rode the boats with his basket. It seemed a sad sort of life and I wondered how he could support a family on his poor earnings. Feeling sorry for him, I remembered what Thallia Stathis said in Athens: "Once you feel sorry for a Greek you're lost." The young man returned and said there was a room for Hermes. It was almost four o'clock.

In the morning a cold wind blew off the sea. The town, an arc around a hill, was dazzlingly bright. The tart air seemed charged with ozone, making me want to run and leap like a boy. Directly across the bay, connected to Naxos by a breakwater was an islet with a solitary marble portal where a temple once stood. I had seen the tiny island reproduced

on an opera stage in Salzburg and recognized it as the reef on which
Dionysius found Ariadne abandoned by Theseus.

I ran across the breakwater and, soaked with spray, climbed to the
white gate. My heart throbbed inexplicably, as if I were arriving at a
holy place where I'd been in another time, perhaps in another life. By
the incredible portal to nowhere—perhaps to everywhere—I spent the
morning. Fragments of the fallen temple lay about me, the wind whistled,
the dark sea rose around me in white geysers. What instinct had brought
me to this bleak empty hill in the sea, what strange sorrow and joy were
battling in my heart? Beyond the water the whitewashed town shimmered
and behind it the brown hills rose toward mountain peaks. On the quay
I saw a man trudging alone, carrying a basket. Recognizing Hermes, I
knew what it was about this place which held me, I knew why Strauss's
opera inevitably shook me to tears. It was an essence of solitude, the
inescapable condition of life, which was here so pure and eternal.

I sent a postcard of Ariadne's isle to Lotte Lehmann in Santa Barbara,
and met Greggory for lunch in a restaurant on the waterfront. As we
were eating, Hermes padded to our table, his face a fan of smiles, his
open shirt showing a V of black wool like a Chios sheep. We invited
him to join us and he ordered a carbohydrate lunch of spaghetti, rice
and potatoes. He asked if we'd slept well, if we'd found our beds soft,
how much we'd paid. He showed us a photo of his son. "So *grande*," he
said, measuring from the floor. The pathetic little wanderer aroused my
compassion. I wondered how he managed with his small basket, if he
always found a bed, whether he rode free on the boats. I wondered if his
Saturday homecomings in Piraeus were joyful events, or whether his
disgruntled wife was relieved to see him trudging away on Mondays.
Naxos, he told us, was the best of the Cyclades. It had the bluest sea,
the most beautiful beaches, plenty of good fresh water from its high
mountains, and its own electricity "all night long." Its people were so
honest doors were never locked at night.

In the afternoon Greggory and I hired a car to take us over the island.
We found Naxos greener and less rocky than the islands we had visited.
On a road lined with maguey agave, as in Mexico, we passed through
terraced mountains of olives and grapes. Our driver, a silent man, drove
to the end of a road and led us, Indian file, up a forest path into a canyon
thick with olives, fruit trees and dark cedars. We crossed a glen and,
climbing an embankment, came upon a path of marble slabs in a cove of
oleanders. There our guide stopped and pointed into a hollow in the
earth. Lying in the olives and cedars like a youth asleep in the forest
was a *kouros*, a gigantic stone figure of young Apollo. Its legs were
broken but the right one lay in place. The changing colors of the stone's

gray-lichened surface made it appear to be throbbing with life. An old marble quarry was nearby—quite certainly the youth had been carved here in the valley where he now slept. The figure—perhaps twenty feet long—was early Doric, almost Egyptian with its long hair and arms at sides with palms turned inward. Centuries of corrosion had made it nearly faceless, but the strong pectorals, the navel and the sex were clearly outlined. We stood silently over it, held by its haunting loneliness. It is believed that an earthquake felled the youth, but who, I wondered, had raised him in this secret Eden?

Two inquisitive black goats were peering at us from a ledge. The wind sighed in the cedars. Birds twittered in the branches and flecks of white clouds sailed across the sky. Cypress trees brought a cemetery mood to the place, an air of forever and never, and when we walked away finally it was like a leave-taking from the grave of a friend.

5

THE DEVIL'S ISLAND

I stood at the rail, still under the island's spell. The boat was taking us to Paros to catch an overnight boat to Santorini. On the deck, Hermes was trying to sell his *loukoumia* but there were no buyers. Moved by pity, I filled a duffle bag with the stuff. Realizing he would probably not see us again, he asked for more money, not for himself, he said, but for his son. He wailed a repertoire of woes—there were no tourists, business was bad, he had many expenses and there was nothing for his son when he went home on Saturdays.

We gave him some coins but they were not enough and he turned on us, making a speech which awakened the sleeping passengers, shouting out to them of our ingratitude, our betrayal. Angry, filled with despair, I walked to the prow. The brown peaks of Paros appeared, and the lighthouse tended by the new bridegroom.

Disembarking, we went at once to the shipping office to inquire about our Santorini boat. The unhappy young man who disliked Kazantzakis examined our tickets.

"So you go," he said. "On the *Karaiskakis* to Piraeus?"

"No, on the *Kanaris*," I said.

"Ah, but you go to Naxos."

"No. We went to Naxos last night."

"But the *Kanaris* goes first to Naxos. Why did you come back here?"

"Because you didn't tell us," I burst out in anger.

He shrugged and smiled. "So now you must go again to Naxos," he said, laughing happily. "Maybe never to come back to Paros again."

The *Kanaris* was two hours late. On deck we tried to find out what time we would arrive in Santorini. From the crew we got a variety of answers—at five, at seven, maybe ten. We rang for a steward. One appeared, saying, "I am second class. You are first class."

"Just tell us when we arrive. *A che ora? Um wieviel uhr?*"

"Is better first-class steward," he said and disappeared. We gave up and went to bed.

At seven we were awakened by a clamor. We went out on deck where it seemed as if we'd sailed into a harbor on the moon. The boat, moored to a buoy, lay parallel to a sheer black cliff four hundred feet high. Gaunt dark rocks jutted around us and on the starboard side a rust-colored crater of a volcano rose from the sea.

Quite understandably, the Greeks call Santorini "Devil's Island." The fantastic archipelago around us appeared in prehistoric times when a volcano emerged from the sea, forming a single circular island. Successive eruptions changed its shape. New craters rose, the center of the island sank, the sea poured in, leaving fragments of a broken crater. Cataclysmic eruptions continued through the sixteenth, eighteenth, nineteenth and twentieth centuries. Islets appeared and disappeared. In 1956 a devastating earthquake destroyed most of the inhabited island. Persisting in their purgatorial existence, the stubborn islanders rebuilt after each destruction. The volcanic earth was rich, producing fine wines and the best tomatoes in Greece. Few tourists choose to spend a night on Santorini, but cruise boats include it in their ports of call, disembarking hundreds of one-day visitors. A path zigzags across the face of the cliff to the island capital, Phirá, a row of buildings on a ledge to which visitors ascend on the backs of mules and donkeys.

The babble on deck was the voices of the muleteers, an aggressive devil's tribe that boards each boat to snare tourists. Their saddled donkeys and mules waited on the jetty. A scrawny boy with an old man's wizened face grabbed my bag and pulled at it. I won the tug of war. Like a beagle stalking game, he followed me on to the ferrying caïque and when I put down the bag he grabbed and refused to surrender it. Aware of all the menacing eyes watching me, I capitulated. The urchin was the youngest of the company and obviously the most enterprising. With narrow eyes too far apart, his large mouth open in a grin, showing the absence of an important tooth, he looked incredibly like a jack-o'-lantern. He had strong wide hips like one of his donkeys. His pants and shirt were filthy and patched, his sandaled feet were caked with dirt. I asked him his name and he replied, "Apollo."

He led us to the donkey herd where he sorted out three, loaded our bags on one, and the two of us, sidesaddle, on the others. We led the climbing caravan. For Apollo, spurring the donkeys with curses and a whip, it was a triumphal procession. For us it was a back-cracking jog up 587 steps with numerous stepless inclines between.

Though the blinding white town was new, signs of destruction were everywhere. From the top the view was even more unnerving than from below. Now we could look into the dark cone of an active crater. Apollo delivered us to the door of the Atlantis Hotel which turned out to be headquarters for a film company making a motion picture on the island. The lobby was hung with cages of twittering canaries. Through a glass door in the lobby I saw a beautiful black-haired woman being made up by several young men. I recognized her as a famous Greek actress, Leda Kyrou. In the dining room the English-speaking manager introduced us to a middle-aged French actor named Jacques Rigour, who invited us to his table. He told us the company had been on Santorini for two weeks and that most of the actors and crew were already stir crazy. Several had fled the island and replacements were being recruited in Athens. "No one speaks," he said, enjoying an opportunity to gossip. "The problem, naturally, is sex. Elias Amadopoulos, the leading man, is hot for Leda but she won't have anything to do with him so he runs amuck each evening. We all do. The only ones who don't run amuck are the mules. Mules are sexless." The film, called *Purgatory,* was a fantasy based on an old belief that the mules of Santorini are the reincarnated souls of local dead. The climax called for the eruption of the volcano, which was going to be simulated by throwing several tons of old rubber tires into the crater to make it smoke. "We have thirty boys playing muleteers," said Rigour. "If you like boys you may find Santorini amusing."

We asked for a driver to guide us over the island and one was sent for. He arrived in a half hour, a large-framed lean man named Antonios Mavromatis, who drove a twenty-year-old Chevrolet station wagon powered by a German diesel engine. We were given the choice of calling him by either of two nicknames. One was "Adenauer," by which he became known after he chauffeured the German prime minister over the island. His other name was "Adonis," and he was known by it because he was handsome. He had a ruddy round face tapering to a pointed chin, large black eyes under heavy brows and a small mustache over heavy sensual lips. He was an earnest and dignified man who walked like an American cowboy, throwing his knees outward.

In the Chevrolet-diesel, which chugged like a tractor and threw off black fumes, we followed a cliff road toward Ía, a ghost town destroyed by the 1956 earthquake. Below us on the left was the sea. To the right were fertile black lava fields which, were desalinization ever to become practical, might be transformed by irrigation into a year-round Eden. As with most islands, water on Santorini was collected from sparse rains and there was never enough. New houses on the island were of a single design, a white half-cylinder lying on its side with windows only in the ends. The style, authorized by the Greek government, was resistant to earthquakes.

Ia once had 5000 people. Because most of its able-bodied population was working in the tomato fields on July 5, 1956, only 48 persons were killed, but two thousand homes were destroyed. Today, 600 persons live in a new town rebuilt over the rubble. As usual, when new civilizations are built over old ones, there were several layers of buildings —sometimes the floor of one was the roof of another. Solitary arches and isolated stone stairways led to nowhere. In the desolation men with bare feet in the dust and women in black robes and kerchiefs lashed by the winds stood like monuments from the past. There were also small children, born into the ruins, and I wondered about their view of life and the world in this terrible place where no new reconstruction can ever be more than a façade over the irrevocable destruction. Across some dark straits below lay a satellite island of Therasia, a whorl of gray lava.

We returned to Phirá and continued southerly to a place called Episcopa where we stopped at a church overlooking the sea. A barking dog aroused a hunched old woman, a walking bundle of rags with only one eye who tottered on a stick which she tapped like an antenna on the stones. Her high squeaking voice was exactly like Papagena's in *The Magic Flute.* She opened the church and, following us inside, watched closely as if she feared we might be thieves, knocking her staff on the fluted columns, screeching, *"Marmo! Marmo!"* Adonis explained that the church had been a pagan temple; he pointed out delicate inlays and carvings and fragments of frescoes.

Outside the church we looked down on a series of concave black stone circles in the earth, like Druid holy places. I asked Adonis what they were. When I did not understand him, he pantomimed with his hands a process I could not comprehend. Shrieking with joy, the old lady hobbled off and returned in minutes with a handful of wheat which she held out in one hand, pointing with the other to the round floors below, and suddenly it became clear. The shells in the earth were threshing floors.

I gave the old woman some coins and she fell to my knees, kissing my hands. I could not get it out of my mind that she was a beautiful maiden bewitched by a spell. How else could she have been so ugly?

We drove through the new town of Kamara with rows of cylindrical white houses like halves of tin cans on their sides, and began the climb up Mt. Elias toward ancient Thera. It stands on a mountain twelve hundred feet above the sea and a new road goes two-thirds of the way.

By an old stone hut in a canyon, Adonis stopped. A woman waved and a little man wearing a leather jacket and a guide's cap bounded out, followed by a small long-haired black dog. Both got into the car. The man's name was Giorgos and he was the official guide of Thera. "Wind no gut," he said, pointing to the mountaintop.

At the road's end I discovered what he meant. So did Adonis who chose to wait in the car. A bitter gale blew from the west with cyclonic intensity. As Greggory and I followed Giorgos and the little dog up a steep loose path of pumice and gravel, I had the very real fear I would be blown, like Icarus, into the sea a thousand feet below. I saw the dog, his black hair blowing eastward, and I thought if the dog didn't sail away, neither would I. Finally we reached a natural terrace a half-mile long and less than five hundred feet wide, the site of the ancient city. Its Dorian beginnings date to the ninth century B.C. Later it was the capital of the Egyptian Kings Ptolemy I and II during their Aegean rule, and still later, a Roman and Byzantine capital. Abandoned, finally it was forgotten until the beginning of this century when German archaeologists, exploring through a meter of lava, discovered it.

At the entrance of the city Giorgos pointed to the profile in stone of a Ptolemaic admiral named Artedidorous. *"Er hat traum,"* said Giorgos, turning a linguistic exuberance into a language uniquely his own. *"Er shlaft and hab dormitio zu bau ein temple."* Cut into the stone was an eagle for Zeus, a lion for Apollo and a dolphin for Poseidon. Fragments of white marble from the Naxos quarry were scattered about and broken columns of native granite lay like fallen trees among the dandelions and autumn crocuses. I tried to conceive the compulsions that could bring such stones to this disquieting place, the armies of slaves that raised temples, built theaters and gymnasiums in such an inaccessible aerie. The inaccessibility quite probably was the reason. From such a lofty lookout, kings and emperors could survey their Aegean empires with little vulnerability to attack.

Life on the mountaintop does not seem to have been boring. Evidences of hedonist self-indulgence were everywhere and Giorgos, conditioned to tourist prurience, did not fail to point out a single one. A gigantic phallus carved into rock was touchingly inscribed by the artist in Latin, "To my friends." Leaping into a stone bath and demonstrating it with a frenzy of animation, Giorgos said, "A guten appareten for washing. Komen water zu fire. Canal zum abgehen. Bon hot bad. Is people sehr sauber." We saw a theater for a thousand persons, stone sacrificial tables, temples to Apollo Boreas—"the wind"—and his huntress sister,

Artemis. The climax of our tour was the famous gymnopaedias where Giorgos wiggled his hips to show how "les boys dence nekid." He showed inscriptions which he said were carved by dancing boys in Phoenician— the letters were Greek but in reverse, going from right to left. "Molte naughty," said Giorgos. "Boys sind alles pederasts." They were also bitches if Giorgos' translations of the graffiti can be trusted. "Antonios is a bad dancer," he read to us from the stones. "Alex is a poor lover." Women, said Giorgos, did not find life on the windy mountain very congenial.

A young couple—a Mexican boy and a Dutch girl—appeared and Giorgos, introducing himself, recommenced the tour with them. Descending alone, we missed the reassuring aplomb of the little dog. Adonis seemed relieved to see us. He coasted us down the mountain and drove to the village of Pyrgos where he showed us an old church from which, he said, some valuable icons had been stolen. "Very bad tourists," he said, shaking his head and crossing himself. He kneeled before an icon. Then he drove us to his own town of Emporium by the sea. On the way we stopped to pick up a hunter with a gun. He was Adonis' cousin, an English-speaking ship captain from Piraeus who was spending his vacation hunting and fishing on Santorini. He told us he and Adonis had hunted rabbits all night and that two days ago on the neighboring island of Kristiana, Adonis had shot a mountain goat.

Adonis took us to his house, one of the white cylinders. His wife, a smiling, black-haired girl younger than himself, served us candied grapes and *ouzo,* and we thanked her. "Don't mention it," she said, her eyes dancing, proud of the English which the cousin was teaching her. The arched house was divided into three whitewashed rooms, a living room between a bedroom at one end, and a kitchen at the other. In the back yard Adonis showed us a wire cage in which rabbits, chickens and partridges were living peaceably together. The young partridges were with their "father," he said.

"Mother," I corrected him. Patiently he corrected me, explaining that the partridges were reared not by their mothers but by their fathers. He showed us the long-antlered head of the mountain goat which he planned to have mounted. It was shot, he said proudly, with an American Winchester rifle. Adonis apologized for the dryness of his garden—the rainy season would begin soon and last year's supply of water was nearly finished. In these weeks, he said, water was dearer on Santorini than wine. Life on the island, he continued, was difficult, the population was diminishing. Many of its youths became, like George, sailors. Sons of affluent families went to Athens to study and make careers. When we left, Adonis' wife, apologizing that there were no roses, pinned anemones to our lapels. "Next year when you come I will spik better," she said.

For the drive back to Phirá, Adonis put on his hunting cap and a belt of English shells and packed a two-barrel shotgun. At a knoll which looked out over a dark circle of small islands, he stopped. "The best place for quail," said George. Adonis gave me the gun, and, beating the brush, roused a covey to flight. I shot one and he took the gun and brought down two. With the three plump birds warm on my feet we drove back to town. White mists were rising around the island like volcanic steam. They were, said Adonis, clouds of wind-borne lime from island quarries.

In the hotel, the *Purgatory* company was beginning its evening of running amuck. Jacques Rigour, red-eyed as if he'd been weeping, was drunk at the bar. "It's the bloody cats," he sniffed. "I'm allergic and we have two in the film." The day had gone badly, he said. "Leda threatened to jump over the cliff. If she had it would have been a better ending than the six we already have."

Two Greeks, both casting assistants, arrived in the bar, a simpering beady-eyed little man known as Nellie, and Jack, a fat dark-skinned man wearing dark glasses. "Actually they're company pimps," said Rigour. "Nellie was hired as a grip." The word was not in my vocabulary. "It's Hollywoodese for boy-of-all-trades," explained Rigour. "Nellie speaks the queen's English. She's supposed to take care of the men when things get tough, keep them from cracking up. We've still got a month on the island." He spoke of the two Greeks in feminine pronouns. "Jack recruits boys from the local gymnasium. She's casting the muleteers and there's no dearth of applicants. The whole high school is seeking a film career. She brought us an eighteen-year-old this afternoon. Beautiful, yes, but stupid."

Scowling darkly at the other end of the bar was the leading man, Elias Amadopoulos. He was wearing tight beige trousers, white socks and Hush Puppy shoes, and looked haggard and miserable. "He's bought himself all kinds of fishing gear and he's going to be a great sportsman in the morning," said Rigour. "I hope a shark gets him. He's priming up and you'll see some action tonight at Gregorios'. It's the only place in town to eat."

The restaurant, down some steps from the main street, was small and dirty and had a cement floor. It appeared makeshift, as if it were built of cardboard. Wine bottles stood on shelves fashioned from wooden packing cases. We sat with Rigour near an open window. "I'm cold," he said. "Close it." Gregorios, a desperate hand-wringing little man, stuffed an old rug in the glassless pane and brought us a bottle of dark wine which

Rigour found sour and poured on the floor. "Bring another," he yelled, and Gregorios ran for a new carafe. Apologizing for the place, he described how it had been before the earthquake. "Very grand, very elegant." He brought a guest book with comments from visitors in a variety of languages, including an English one, "The wine was divine," signed by Sean and Mimi Howard of Bluebell, Pennsylvania.

Elias Amadopoulos arrived with two tall girls, so much alike they might have been sisters. They had high foreheads and golden hair and both wore green Eisenhower jackets and tight levis. "He wants them both," said Rigour, "and can't have either. They're Swedish lesbians and mean as hell." At a table two ruddy German men, also blond, were wearing crocheted white and blue sweaters and gold crucifixes at their throats. A dozen or so curious young men were standing about, some fingering worry beads. "All waiting to be discovered, all wanting to be muleteers," said Rigour. The two Greeks called Nellie and Jack arrived and chairs were brought for them to our table. I had an uneasy feeling of being in a company of malefactors. Two mangy cats rubbed against us. "Get those bloody beasts out of here!" Rigour screamed, and Gregorios quickly complied. "My corset's too tight," said Rigour, squirming in his chair.

The food was dreadful. Our waiter, Gregorios, Jr., a boy in a filthy apron, picked his nose when he wasn't changing records on a phonograph. The dance floor was about five feet square, hardly room for one man. Elias Amadopoulos got up, stalked around it once like a king and began to dance. He was holding a glass of wine from which he drank while he danced. One of the Germans threw a plate which crashed at his feet. Others began throwing plates which clattered on the concrete floor, covering it with broken crockery. When the plates were finished they threw glasses and bottles. Amadopoulos danced on, flapping his arms like wings as if he would like to fly away, growing more and more sullen. "He's about to run amuck," said Rigour.

He did. The two Swedish girls got up to leave and Amadopoulos in rage began slapping his hands together and leaping like a wild thing. He picked up Nellie who bawled and kicked like a calf, kissed him on the lips and dropped him. Then Amadopoulos gathered new plates from tables and began throwing them at himself, still dancing, shattering them around his moving feet, plates filled with food, half-empty wine bottles, turning the floor purple. Gregorios, wringing his hands, sobbed like a child. When there were no more plates to throw, Amadopoulos snapped his fingers and began to pound his fists on the ceiling, making it buckle. Pushing a hand through the thin composition, he crumpled to the floor, his knuckles spurting blood. He was taken away by members of the company.

The rumpus brought Santorini's police department, two gold-toothed dark-haired men about thirty, in gray uniforms. They were greeted with cries of welcome. Assuring themselves that the disturbance had passed, they took chairs at our table and drank some wine. Nellie was telling stories I did not understand which sent the officers into fits of giggles. At that moment a black cat stepped inside the door, looked around, arched its back, snarled and leaped back out. The officers got up and left.

Outside a cold moon was shining over the white town. The wind whistled and luminous white clouds moved swiftly across the blue night sky. Near our hotel a new cathedral was under construction on the site of another destroyed by the earthquake. A row of skeletal arches formed a lacy silhouette in the moonlight. The church would never be so beautiful again. Near the hotel a little man was darting about in the night like a wraith. Stopping by a small marble obelisk in the street, he made strange movements with an oil lamp. He placed the lamp before the stone and knelt by it in a praying attitude. I watched him, wondering what strange rite I was witnessing. Seeing me, he murmured, *"Église . . . église. . . ."* He continued to pray audibly.

In the hotel I asked the manager what it was I had seen. He said that before the earthquake a church had stood on the spot marked by the obelisk. The shaft of marble had been part of the altar, the only fragment that remained. A few pious people continued to keep the bit of pavement sanctified by praying there. In the lobby Leda Kyrou was entertaining some guests with parodies of Katina Paxinou, Irene Pappas and other actresses in roles from the classic plays. Her voice was blood-curdling.

At 8 A.M. we were awakened by the mule boy, Apollo, telling us a boat was arriving. We jogged down the steps on his mules. At the dock Elias Amadopoulos was fishing with a spear gun and fly rod.

Our boat, named *Limnos,* might more appropriately have been called *Limbos.* Ponderous and dirty, it had been scrapped by the British and rebuilt in Nova Scotia for the Greeks after the war. Coal smoke churning from its chimneys covered the deck with soot. The crew, ragged, filthy, with brutish faces, looked like pirates. A messmate spent most of the voyage fishing from the keel. Our cabin near the furnace was an inferno. When we opened the porthole, the sea poured in. On the deck third-class passengers lay moaning and vomiting among boxes of live chickens. Greeks are hopelessly bad sailors—expecting to be sick they begin at once, even before a boat leaves the harbor. I heard a voice, and turning, saw a member of the film company, a gray-haired Greek actor, yelling into the wind. There was no one to listen to him. When he saw me he flushed. "I speak to friend I think is here," he said. He was going to Athens for a rest—it was probably too late. He continued to pace and shout, and later I saw him, pale and sick, on the deck. We stopped at Naxos, where I had a glimpse of Hermes on the quay with his basket, and in the evening at Syros, where the *loukoumia* parlors were burning brightly. From the ship's amplifiers blared a Voice of America broadcast of Perry Como singing "On Blueberry Hill." The trip to Piraeus took sixteen hours.

VIII

The Colossus

The phone rang and a great voice rolled out of it, filling my room, saying, "This is George Katsimbalis."

I was a moment understanding. The Colossus of Maroussi had seemed like an old man in 1940 when Henry Miller wrote his book, an old man complaining of his ailments, "talking about himself as of someone who was done for." Now, a quarter of a century later, I was hearing his voice, almost superhumanly recognizable, saying, "I heard you were coming but I was leaving for France to visit Larry Durrell. Just got back." He invited me for lunch and asked me to meet him at noon at the Apotsos, on Stadiou Street.

I arrived early. I was seated at Katsimbalis' table and ordered an *ouzo*. The crowded room was small and paneled in dark wood like a Victorian English pub. The stand-up bar had a brass rail. Walls were covered with tin posters advertising bloater paste, snuff and biscuits. It was a male crowd—English journalists, American expatriate poets and Greek businessmen were drinking *ouzo* and beer and munching from plates of chips, salami and bits of octopus.

Suddenly he arrived, larger-than-life, a bald-headed, great-bellied Buddha entering ponderously on a cane. Buddha? The impression changed when he spoke. It was Falstaff rampaging his way into the Boar's Head, bellowing, "Sorry I'm late. Came in a Charlie Chaplin cab Hollywood would pay a fortune for. Every time I closed a door another flew open. Finally had to bind it with wire." He looked at my glass and roared, "What kind of *ouzo* are you drinking?" I didn't know.

"Take it away," he bawled at the waiter. "The only *ouzo* to drink is Lesbion *ouzo!*" Slowly he lowered himself into a chair and his stomach jostled the table. A bottle was brought, from the island of Lesbos, and he poured from it into two glasses. "Celebrating my fiftieth year in the place," he said. "Came here as a schoolboy from the gymnasium."

I was about to put water into my glass. "Don't do that," he roared. "You *never* put water in Lesbion *ouzo.*" He put an ice cube into each glass and we bolted it straight. "The only way," he purred, pouring more. He ordered salami from the Ionian Islands. "The only salami a man can eat," he said. "None of this Italian and Bulgarian donkey meat." I said that in Macedonian villages *ouzo* was called *raki* and I'd never learned the difference. "There isn't any difference," Katsimbalis said. "It's all *raki.* That bloody name *ouzo* came from the Italian *al auza* which means 'for use.' They stamped it on cases of the export stuff. The name caught on—first-rate *raki* became *ouzo.*"

Miller says that listening to Katsimbalis was "like watching a man write a book expressly for you," and Katsimbalis' friend, the writer George Theotokas, called him "Greece's greatest oral writer." His monologue was a great free-association proliferation woven into a kind of art by his own Gargantuan presence in every sentence. He spoke of himself without vanity and with the ribald humor of a true tragedian. He was his own Rabelais, his own Cervantes. In his cycle of tales he was Gargantua, Don Quixote, Baron Munchausen. His language, British in phrasing and accent, included terms like "jolly well" and "bloody."

"I was brought up by an English nurse named—I feel I must mention it at the risk of embarrassing you—Miss Allcock. She sang me to sleep with 'Little Brown Jug.' The bloody song has been a great influence in my life. I was fifty years old when I went to England for the first time. Walked into a pub and felt right at home. Lovely time.

"Emptied a few jugs in your country too. Invited by your State Department on a cultural tour. That blighter, Miller, you know. Never told me a word about his book. Wasn't until after the war someone told me I was famous in the United States. In Washington they assigned a Pekinese, a certain elderly lady, to take charge of me. Kept me moving. Wheeled bottom. Forty states in three months. The Pekinese asked me where I wanted to go. To the wilds of Florida, I told her. Oh, I know, she said, you want to see girls. You're bloody right, I told her. How could I say it was because Miss Allcock used to read me a book called *In the Wilds of Florida.* Miss Allcock also read *On the Banks of the Amazon,* but the State Department wasn't about to send me there so I refrained from mentioning it. You want to see those bathing beauties, said the Pekinese, giggling wildly. So she sent me to colleges and ladies' clubs where I met a lot of Pekinese like herself.

"Visited Miller on Big Sur. I made you famous, George, he said. Famous, hell! Made me a lot of trouble. Said I was a drunk and a woman-chaser. He said nothing about my being a scholar. I'm tracing Poe and Whitman in Greece, first notice of them, critiques, rise in popularity, influence on Greek thought. When Miller knew me I was working in the library until midnight. Then I'd meet the boys, the young writers and take them to a brothel. I lined them up. In they went, one after the other. Some got so they liked it, turned into pretty good writers. I was only forty in 1939. Sixty-seven now and not the man I was, I must admit. Couldn't do it now.

"Henry's book got me in trouble with my wife. He hardly mentioned her, you wouldn't even know I was married. She didn't care for that. I want you to meet her. If you write about me, write about her, set things right. My wife's a Cretan. Smart woman. She's never asked any questions, never where have you been? She got her revenge with Hitler. During the German occupation curfew I had to stay home nights. Hardly blame her for being partial to Germans. Very peculiar race, Cretans."

A wizened little man with a briefcase moved softly among the tables selling razor blades. With a great hullabaloo Katsimbalis greeted him. "My dear friend," he said. "I admire him. He survived the famine, not only he, but all his family. He kept them alive and for this I honor him. Three hundred thousand Greeks starved to death in one year. On Christmas I had thousands of pounds and couldn't find anything to eat but some stalks of celery. Not a drop of oil, not a crust of bread." He spoke in Greek and the little man grinned. "Those razor blades are a front," he said to me. "What he's really got in that briefcase are pistachio nuts. Since the government put a tax on pistachios, the poor bastards have to hide their nuts in briefcases and pretend they're selling marijuana or hashish. Have to follow them up a dark alley to get pistachio nuts."

Another man passed selling bouquets of hyacinths, filling the place with sweet scent, and a third carried a string of a dozen dead birds, decorated with ferns. "Very peculiar fowl," said Katsimbalis. "They're not quail, they're not turtledoves, they're not ducks. Never saw anything quite like them." He spoke to the fellow. "He says they're a special partridge, more delectable than the ordinary variety."

He asked from where I had come to Greece, and I said Rome. "I envy you," he said. "Wish I could go to Rome. Can't possibly. My mother, my beautiful sweet mother would never stand for it. Says she'll have a heart attack if I leave and I'll never see her again. My mother

is eighty-eight. A real beauty. She'll bury me for sure. When she does
it will be in Paris, in Pierre Lachaise. Most elegant cemetery in the
world. My father and sister are there in the family tomb. We were
people of property. The Germans confiscated everything in Maroussi. All
my books. Got the land back. It's sold now and I'm building a little
house on Constitution Square. Come along, I'll show you."

Slowly he led me lumbering around the corner and pointed with his
cane to the "little house." It was a new high-rise office building in a
row of airline and travel offices. "More trouble than it's worth. Carpenters
and masons are getting your American ideas. Always striking. They're
telling *me* how to do it." We moved on up Jan Smuts Street to Zonar's
where he ordered a Lucullan lunch of hors d'oeuvres, soup, sole, salad
and wines, beginning with a white Pallini from Attica.

"I drink three liters of wine a day, can't survive on less," he said.
"With all the casks I've drunk in my life, I've a liver like a newborn
babe. Had a bit of a shock last month. A nosebleed, first in my life.
Doctor said I had diabetes. Put me on an old man's diet. To hell with it!
I'm from indestructible Dorian stock. Look at my Dorian head. Can't
you see it? Very dull people, these Dorians. Fortunately Crete's in my
blood, wears down the Dorian dullness. Long line of shepherds, both
sides. Came from a village in the Peloponnese called Katsimbali. Never
been there. Very depressing place I'm sure. Near Tripolis, in the center
of mythical Arcadia. The mountains are like Doré's for Dante's Hell.
Forests of fir trees.

"You're going to find Greece a very confounding place. Geographically
we never existed. All the races of the world have passed through us.
Yet we are the country with the greatest unity of language and religion
in the world. Everyone understands one another."

What about political unity, I asked.

"Never had it. Never will. Everything in Greece is individual. No
two trees are alike, no two goats, no two *retsinas,* no two Greeks.
Not like your Switzerland where every goat, every fir tree, every Swiss
is exactly like every other. Not like your America where everyone tries
to be like everyone else. At least we know who we are. You don't
because you are nobody. One of your ambassadors was telling how he
couldn't find out anything about Greece, no one would tell him a thing.
Would I, Katsimbalis, help? I said it's his job, it's not my responsibility.
I refused to see him again. You're such simple types, you Americans.
How could you ever understand anything as complex as a Greek?

"He called me one day, the ambassador. Said he had an American
poet who had all those Pulitzer and Guggenheim things, who wanted
to meet me. Let him come, I said. So he did with tears in his eyes. I

thought it was overexcitement at meeting me but it turns out to be a physical defect. He's a weeper. I'm . . . , he said. Yes, I know, I said, that Guggenstein one. I teach history, he said. What happened in Greece in 1921? I asked. I don't know, he said, I only go to the Congress of Vienna. And you think we're a race of Slavs, I said, so you think we speak Russian. You can't talk to me like this, he said, tomorrow I'm lunching with the King. Good, I said, you'll find him your intellectual equal. Tell him about the Congress of Vienna. I want to see more of you, he said. The feeling is not mutual, I said. I'm living at the American School, he said. Naturally, I said. So he started weeping all over me, like a bloody monsoon. Said he wanted to love me, to hug and kiss me. Kiss the King, I said, he welcomes American kisses. I tell you, the fellow was like Chaplin, up, down, splashing tears. He's been writing me pathetic letters ever since. Doesn't seem to know he's sick.

"Beware, young man, beware," Katsimbalis said, addressing me. "You don't know how terrible we can be."

The Pallini was finished and he called a waiter to bring a bottle of *Boutari*, a rich burgundy type. "The only drinkable red wine in Greece," he said. "I'm a pagan, a son of Dionysius. No priest ever called me a lamb who's gone astray. I've never been a lamb and I've never gone astray."

Whenever a woman entered the restaurant he appraised her. "Is she back?" he said of one. "Dreadful German, always hanging around. Germans are not bad tourists. Rather generous like you Americans. Much better than the French and English." A woman hailed him and he bowed. "Her breasts are like empty tobacco pouches," he mumbled. He began an account of bordello adventures which would have brought blushes to the cheeks of Rabelais. The language was visceral, the participants famous people still alive. A waiter brought dessert, a huge cream-filled pastry covered with honey. I remembered the diabetes. Coffee and brandy followed. "I hope you haven't been drinking that kerosene Metaxa puts out. The only brandy worth drinking in Greece is Botry's Three Star." He asked what islands I had visited and I named them. "Ah, Santorini, very enigmatic place. You can look at it in one of two ways: a dark picture of hopelessness or a promise of rebirth. Why don't you go to Andros? Best of the lot." He began to recite from Byron, *The Isles of Greece* and some stanzas from *Childe Harold*. "Read Byron if you really want to experience islands. An awful lot of bad books have been written about Greece and I'm sure you're going to add to them."

A Greek writer of whom Katsimbalis spoke with respect was the novelist and dramatist, George Theotokas. "My dear friend, the only

honest man in Greek letters. But he's gone insane." His evidence for
Theotokas' loss of reason was political. Katsimbalis, a tory rightist, supported the monarchy. "Theotokas professes to admire Papandreou. They
call Papandreou left. Left my arse. He has the support of the bankers
and rich men. Like Theotokas, a very rich man. Compared to them I'm
a sniveling pauper." I remembered "the little house" on Constitution
Square.

It is a characteristic of rich Greeks to insist on their poverty. Their
self-respect and survival in the human community seems to depend on
it. Since Greek fortunes are frequently stashed away in American, English and Swiss banks, rumors of fortunes are not easily verifiable. When
I met George Theotokas he told me how rich Katsimbalis was. In the
curious little comedy in which I found myself between Katsimbalis and
Theotokas, I was inclined to believe Theotokas, not because I mistrusted
Katsimbalis, but because everything he said, his very language was a
grandiloquence of hyperbolism. In contrast, Theotokas was calm, percep-
tive and straightforward as no other Greek I met. He was one of a
half-dozen persons who in my year in the land I learned to love and to
cherish.

I met him at a party of writers and artists. Most of the guests were
upwards of fifty years in age. In Greece a writer of forty-five is considered young and insufficiently proven to be included in the cultural
establishment. Of the poets, novelists, painters and others introduced
simply as "intellectuals," the one who impressed me most was Theotokas.
He was a bookish man in his sixties, remote and reserved, yet we
established a contact at once. His bald handsome head had the linear
strength of a Roman senator's. He had cool blue eyes which turned
warm and friendly when he spoke. He had also been to America as a
State Department guest and had written an enthusiastic book about his
visit.

He invited me to lunch in his apartment across Queen Sophia Avenue
from the American Embassy. His rooms were lined with books. On the
walls hung oil portraits of his wife, a woman of legendary beauty who
had died. A collection of jade, onyx and coral worry beads were strewn
on his table. Beneath the outward calm, the cool logic, one felt the inner
tensions of a deeply feeling man. He was a lawyer, recently retired as
director of the Greek National Theater, and he was devoting his time
to writing, including political articles for a liberal newspaper. He was
the foremost political theorist and apologist for the Center Union, the
party of the former prime minister, George Papandreou.

Theotokas did not, as the mass of Papandreou supporters, see the
leader as a faultless savior. "Papandreou is a politician," he said. "He

has a politician's faults and makes a politician's mistakes. But in the dangerous period in which our country now finds herself, the Center Union is the only hope, the only party that represents the people of Greece, that cares for the future. The majority has a right to rule. You cannot say, because you disagree with it, that a majority cannot be trusted to rule, that it is incapable."

Across the street the American flag was waving over the Embassy. "As in so many places," Theotokas continued, "America insists on riding the wrong horse in Greece. In the same way that our government does not represent our people, I believe that your representatives here do not represent the point of view of your people. There are widely circulated rumors in Greece that the U.S.A. is running our country and there is certainly evidence that pressures are exerted. The small hard core of rightist power which is running our country is exploiting America's fear of Communism to continue their control. Their fear that Papandreou will lead the country toward Communism is foolish hysteria. As our first postwar prime minister, Papandreou fought Communists in our civil war. An old man who has fought the enemy during his lifetime does not in his last years join it. Nor could his son, Andreas, an adviser of President Kennedy. The Papandreou concept for democracy in Greece is close to America's own. To our rightist government this is a threat. United around the King, they will not voluntarily give up their power. They know Papandreou's popularity so they delay an election as long as possible. As a last resort they would establish a military rule. This is a very real danger. Toward this end there are frequent dismissals of non-loyal military officers, a tightening of the ruling circle. The King is in command of the army, which he believes he controls, but an army is made up of young men from the villages and the islands and no one can tell what they may do.

"It is an irony that our country, which gave the world democracy, is ruled by the only king of Hohenzollern blood still sitting on a throne in Europe. If our King had remained out of politics, if he were a figurative head as the English, Scandinavian and Dutch monarchies, no one would object to him. But in taking up the leadership of the right the King has fallen victim to the undemocratic forces in Greece. By doing so he may have certified his doom. It is a dilemma for which I still wish a peaceful democratic solution, but I fear bad times. It is ironic that America, which fought a king for its freedom two hundred years ago, should in the twentieth century support over a subjugated people an absolute monarchy which would have been considered medieval two centuries ago."

As I became more and more absorbed by the intricate mesh of Greek

politics I went like a pupil to a master, to Theotokas' study for help
in understanding. It was not as a result of our conversations that my
political attitudes grew close to his own. Rather the conversations were
a result of a natural sympathy of mind. He read my books and I read
those of his which were translated into English and Italian, including
his fine novel *Argos*. In a climate as fiercely emotional as Greece's,
Theotokas was a rationalist, a calm Aristotelian intellect. He was a student
of Thomas Jefferson and the two Greeks after which Jefferson patterned
his American Constitution, Aristotle and Polybius of Megalopolis.

Athens had its grand guru of the arts, the retired poet Nikos Gatsos.
His fame as a lyricist had been firmly established in the 1930s. Some of
his poems, including *Amorgos,* named for an island, are translated into
English. Since the war he had written little—a few essays, some successful
lyrics for his composer friend Manos Hatzidakis. Now, in his sixties, he
was known as a kind of Mikado of creativity. He was a suavely handsome man with pale skin, black hair and brows and heavy-lidded dark
eyes. Wearing a dark blue suit and tie, he held daily soft-voiced court
at a corner table in Floca's Café to an international company of writers
and artists. To these conversations the press had given the name "Flo-
casophy." There were usually Americans—Gore Vidal over from Rome,
Eugene Istomin in Athens for a concert engagement, and Elia Kazan
on his way to Africa. I met Yaël Dayan, in from Israel, as well as
English novelists, French composers and many Greeks, including Hatzidakis, and frequently journalists and photographers interviewing the famous visitors. The talk in Greek and English, which Gatsos spoke well,
was a mixture of international gossip and an earnest discussion of
contemporary theater and literature.

In this group I was never quite at ease for a very personal reason. I
was puzzled by the scorn, frequently expressed in the circle, for the
work of the contemporary Greek writer I admired most, Nikos Kazantzakis. The contempt for the great Cretan, so prevalent among Greek
literati, was, I believe, based on envy; it was the peckings of sparrows
against the wings of an eagle. In a small country like Greece a literary
life is difficult. Except for a handful of classic scholars, no one outside
Greece reads Greek books. Royalties are minuscule—a book seldom
sells more than two or three thousand copies. Literature is not a vocation
but an avocation. Except for a fortunate few who had family resources
like George Theotokas, Katsimbalis and Gatsos himself, writers are first
professors, lawyers or businessmen.

The one exception to this was Kazantzakis, whose books won both
fame and fortune in Europe and in America. For this the establishment

could not forgive him. Among the youth, the generation of students, Kazantzakis was greatly admired. From them I heard that Kazantzakis, frequently a candidate for the Nobel prize for literature, never received it because of Greek political opposition on the grounds that he was sympathetic to Communism.

IX

"Never Wither"

Our passage on a ship called the *Minos* was calm. Looking through my porthole on a Sunday morning, I might have been watching the creation. From the mists shrouding the sea, a mauve spine of mountains was taking shape. The sky turned silver, and then rose. Suddenly the sun rolled over the horizon, turning the peaks to flaming volcanoes. I remembered the allegorical truth that somewhere in these mountains Zeus was born.

Where else? It was Crete upon which I looked, one of the great wombs of civilization. When the West was still in primordial shadow, a brilliant culture grew and flourished on this island bridge between Europe, Asia and Africa, brightening the Mediterranean like a comet for almost twenty-five centuries. Crete's story is a fusion of myth and history, the sorting out of which goes on and on. Its mythological King Minos, son of Zeus, who gave his name as honorary title to succeeding rulers, became a historical personage when archaeological excavations in this century confirmed Homer's claim that Minos was Europe's first lawmaker, and Thucydides' evidence that he founded the world's first navy.

No other place had I approached with such anticipation and apprehension, with such a sense of awe. El Greco, the painter who moved me above all others, was a Cretan; so was the great Nikos Kazantzakis, who wrote, "I thank God for allowing me to be born a Cretan." Crete, said another of her poets, "is one great heart. You must bend down and listen to its beating."

For an hour the *Minos* followed the coast of the 150-mile-long island.

With her three mountain summits, Kazantzakis describes Crete as a triple-master schooner sailing in the foam. Eagles live in her lofty plateaus, and eagle-like men. On Athens' streets I had seen Cretans, prouder, fiercer, taller, straighter than all other Greeks, walking with long strides, moving like kings through lanes which other men intuitively cleared for them.

The morning sun glowed on the red earth, colored, said Kazantzakis, by centuries of Cretan blood. Crete's desperate fight for freedom has continued unrelenting from neolithic times into our own century. A son of the last king of Crete, Idomeneus, fought in the Trojan wars with eighty Cretan ships. For more than a thousand years Crete was prey to invaders—Romans, Byzantines, Spanish Saracens and crusading Venetians. The Venetian occupation, beginning in 1211 and continuing almost five centuries, was the most enlightened. Trade with Europe brought prosperity. The Italian Renaissance spread art and literature across the island; schools were founded and monasteries became centers of learning. The Cretan painter Domenicos Theotocopoulos went by way of Venice to Spain where he was known as "El Greco."

In 1669 the Cretans fell under their cruelest oppressors, the Turks. For more than two centuries they endured executions, atrocities and rebellion. On November 9, 1866, three thousand Turks attacked the monastery of Arkadiou. When they demolished the gate with cannon fire and poured into the courtyard, the Abbot Gabriel ordered a powder magazine blown up. The explosion killed nine hundred Cretan defenders and three thousand Turkish soldiers. The event is celebrated each year as Crete's national holiday. Cretan autonomy was finally won with English aid in 1898, and Prince George, son of the King of the Hellenes, was appointed governor of the island. In 1912, when a Cretan, Eleutherios Venizelos, was prime minister of Greece, liberated Crete was finally welcomed into the Greek state. In the Second World War, Crete suffered still another cruel occupation, by the Germans.

Our ship was entering the walled harbor of Iraklion, known to Cretans by its Venetian name of Megalo Kastro, or "Large Castle." A stone lion representing San Marco scowled from the ramparts out over the sea. We went down the hatch to claim our car. The hold was filled with autos, trucks, tractors hooked to plows, and fifty donkeys standing in a welter of manure, many with plastic flowers braided into their manes. In five minutes we were driving across the quay and through the walls into a bustling Oriental casbah of narrow winding streets. We were seeking a hotel and selected the Candia Palace because of a woman who was in charge. Her name was Giorgia Balzaki. Small with black hair and large black eyes, wearing a black dress, she looked like a haunted and beautiful child drawn by Käthe Kollwitz. Her frail appearance was a deception. She was tough, humorous, incorrigibly tempered, quixotic, and wondrously efficient and kind. She telephoned a young newspaper editor, and before we could unpack our bags, the editor, Kostas Grammatikakis, arrived at the hotel with his fiancée to invite us to lunch. Kostas was the son of the owner of Crete's leading newspaper, *Ta Messogia*. He was a small, brown-haired young man of twenty-five. The girl, Marita Gabrilaki, a stunning black-haired beauty, had studied as an exchange student in California and was employed as a secretary in the United States Air Force Base near Iraklion.

They drove us along the northern sea to a small restaurant on a beach called Tobruk, where the owner served us charcoal-grilled red mullet and a thyme-flavored *souvlaki* prepared by his wife. The wine was a rosé called Minos. The man asked the inevitable question, *"Sind sie Deutsch?"* I asked Kostas why a Greek never asked, "Are you American?" Or English. Or simply, "Where are you from?"

"The first foreign country in Greece is Germany," he replied. "More tourists come from Germany than from any other country. Germans make themselves known, they go to the islands, to the villages. Many country people have never met a stranger who is not German. Because of the occupation, many Greeks know a few words of German which they like to show off."

How was it possible that Greeks did not hate Germans? I asked, thinking of occupation atrocities, how in the Viannos district southwest of Iraklion the Nazis had in one day executed a hundred men and set fire to fifteen villages.

"We have learned that survival cannot afford hatred," said Kostas. "We have been so much in war, so constantly occupied that it would be necessary to hate everyone. Perhaps our big quality is a short memory. We can forget anything, everything, and begin again.

"With the Germans you might say that we have a love-hate relationship. Our experience is closer to the Germans than to any other people. Our royal family is of German blood. German archaeologists excavated Greek ruins and opened up tourism in Greece. Almost every Greek has a member of his family or a friend working in Germany. More than three hundred thousand German workers are sending money to their families at home.

"If there is anyone we dislike," Kostas continued, "it is the Americans. We don't know Americans, we are insulted by their indifference. We think they are materialistic, without heart. Americans pass by us very quickly, meeting only other Americans. Germans, French and Swedes go to villages, they are interested in meeting us. A Cretan is by nature an enemy. History has made us suspicious, hostile, lonely. But we also have warm hearts. We want desperately to be friends."

In America, Marita had been homesick for Crete. "California was exactly as we believe America to be," she said. "Rich, rushed and self-indulgent. It was an experience I wanted, but only for a short time. Americans seemed to me a very provincial people who care about nothing but themselves." As she spoke I was looking at a colored rotogravure picture of John F. Kennedy hanging among the icons on the restaurant wall.

"We don't think of Kennedy as belonging to America," said Kostas. "He belonged to us, to the world. Greece is a land of heroes and Kennedy is the only Greek hero of our time."

Marita said, "When Kennedy died we all cried together as if a member of our family had been murdered. At the American base there was no great excitement and few spoke of what had happened. At home everyone wept for weeks, no one could speak of anything else. I asked a lady in the market why she loved Kennedy so much. 'He is like my husband, my son,' she said. 'He is my own.'"

I wondered how he, looking down from the wall, so comprehending and articulate, would have explained to these well-educated cultivated young people a problem that seemed clearly one of understanding and communication. Who was at fault? The Greeks, so emotional and demonstrative? Or Americans, tempered by their northern puritanism to believe the show of grief a weakness.

In the afternoon we went to the Archaeological Museum. The repository of Minoan treasures unearthed by archaeologists is one of the most astonishing collections in the world. Because of the minuteness of things, recreating with infinitesimal detail the ancient culture, it is also one of the most exhausting to see. Unlike modern Cretans, the Minoans were small people. Their burial tombs are child-size. The mother and daughter snake goddesses, fertility deities with milk-swollen breasts, are hardly ten inches tall, and the wonderful bull's-head libation vase of black soapstone with rock crystal eyes and gilded horns, is even smaller. Stunningly beautiful jewelry, vases, idols and bronze utensils filling more than 130 cases, are all in proportion. Minuscule seals and amulets are difficult to see without magnification.

After two hours my eyes burned and I went upstairs to rest them on the extraordinary Knossos paintings. I found an elegant cosmos of dolphins, flying fish, blue monkeys gathering crocuses, holy bulls, pheasants, red and white lilies, slim-waisted princes with peacock feathers in their hair, and almond-eyed broad-shouldered priestesses entwined with sacred snakes. Gender was discernible only by skin coloring, chocolate dark for males, radiant pink for females. Kazantzakis called this world the revelation of an Atlantis "issued from the depths of the Cretan soil."

The stately dignity and grace of the people are Egyptian, but the Minoan figures are freer, more animated and joy-filled, more beautiful. They are closer in stature to living men. And women! A group of palace ladies, fashionable bare-bosomed matrons wearing elaborately jeweled coiffures and brocaded jackets, are gesticulating with daintily tapering fingers. *"Les Parisiennes,"* these chic red-lipped wide-eyed beauties were called by Sir Arthur Evans, the excavator of Knossos, and the name clings to them.

An acridly musky odor lay on the air of the city. It came, said Giorgia Balzaki, from the smoke of distilleries which used olive pits as fuel. The evening streets were filled with the Sunday *volta.* Outside the hotel, on King Constantine Street, a black-clothed crowd moved like two turgid dark rivers beside one another the three short squares from Nikiphorou Phoka Square to Eleutherias Park. Women in black dresses, stepping on spiked heels daintily as mannequins, clung possessively to dark-suited men who twirled worry beads. Couples stopped now and then at café tables for an ice or a caloric pastry, or halted to gossip with friends. Striding like knights through this dark mass of middle-class conformity were country men in dark boots and black fringes over their eyes, moving independently of their wives in brown homespuns, who followed Indian-fashion a few steps behind. The difference between city men, capitulating to Western matriarchy, and village men maintaining their Eastern sexual status, was unmistakable and it was easy to see which men—and women—were more content.

Across the street from the hotel was a small piazza we named "Jukebox Square," because of the machines in a row of small cafés, outblaring one another with recorded *bouzouki,* Beatle sobs and Elvis Presley wails. The square was a bus station and gathering place for servicemen who danced on the cobblestones while they waited to return to their camps. The din never stopped. Rock 'n' roll was my lullaby, and a sobbing ballad called *Kennedy* filtered into my dreams. The words translated:

> Birds don't sing,
> And fields don't bloom,
> All the people of the world,
> Mourn for Kennedy.

> Kennedy, Kennedy,
> Your name will never be forgotten,
> Your immortal deeds will never die. . . .

In the morning we drove three miles through groves and vineyards to Knossos. With us was a guide, a silver-haired gentleman named Theodoros Karoussos. The Knossos valley, he said, was the most fertile in Greece. Until 1900 the palace was covered with olives and grapes. A farmer named Minos Kalokairinos had plowed up some vases in 1878, and the great German excavator Heinrich Schliemann guessed that a Minoan city lay under the rolling hills. But the Turkish rulers of Crete would not permit Schliemann to dig, and in 1899, nine years after his death and the first year of Cretan independence, excavations were begun by a rich English amateur, Sir Arthur Evans, who financed the project with a quarter-million pounds of his own money. As Schliemann had done in Troy and Mycenae, Sir Arthur brought Homeric legend to historical life in Knossos. Unlike Schliemann, a purist who took no liberties with his discoveries, Evans also restored. His reconstructed palace still provides scholars with an archaeological controversy.

We approached on foot over the Minoan road, a gully in the red earth. The vintage was completed but the scent of grapes and of figs hung in the air. To our right the peak of Mt. Ida was hidden in clouds. Theodoros halted to begin his indoctrinating lecture. His tone was reverential, like a cathedral custodian's. He told us that Minoan history was divided into three periods: Early Minoan, from 3400 to 2100 B.C., during which the civilization grew out of neolithic Crete; Middle Minoan, from 2100 to 1550 B.C., when it flourished; and Late Minoan, from 1550 to 1100 B.C., when it declined. The late period is also known as the Mycenaean because it was then, during Crete's decline, that its civilization was transferred to Mycenae in the Peloponnese. The first palace was begun about 2000 B.C. but it was twice destroyed and rebuilt before its final destruction about 1400 B.C. Reasons for the Minoan decline are still conjectured. Achaean and Dorian invasions, and earthquakes caused by eruptions of the volcano on Santorini, all seem to have played a part. In the last centuries, surviving Minoans lived in poverty among the ruins, unable to impede their end.

We entered by the south stairway through a procession corridor, where, in a fresco copied from the original in the museum, eight hundred persons converged on a goddess in white ceremonial robes. It led into a central courtyard where the bright Cretan sun shimmered in a tide of color. Frescoed walls were painted in bright mineral hues, columns were red and black, rows of clay jars were bright ocher. In the stones on which we walked, the mica shone like jewels. A flowering vine, called "Arabic jasmine" by our guide, poured over the stones, blanketing them with green leaves and blue blossoms.

Except for the rectangular court, the ten-acre palace had no fixed plan, and was not built in symmetrically balanced portions. Rather, it proliferated through its centuries in all directions on many levels. Scholars have counted eight hundred rooms spread over five floors, illuminated by light wells and connected by corridors and stairways. The Minoans built for themselves instead of for history, and with time the palace of soft gypsum and wooden columns simply crumbled away. The reinforced concrete which Evans used in the restoration serves a practical function of strengthening and supporting the ruins.

We descended into the lower chambers, passing walls painted with fish, flowers and birds, and princes and princesses wearing necklaces of lilies. We walked through corridors of vases, some man-high, which were found filled with wheat, lentils and peas carbonized by fire, and the sediments of oil and wine. In Minos' throne room the king's alabaster throne was standing against a wall painted with griffins and lilies. The queen's chambers were a sea of swimming dolphins.

Theodoros kept diverting our attention from paintings to examine plumbing details. Cretan guides have an obsession for hydraulics and drainage—no doubt it has something to do with the abysmal plumbing in their own homes. Theodoros showed us septic tanks, filter chambers, baths and toilets, similar, he said, to those in use today. He took us into a network of gloomy cellars in which, he said, were found the great double-headed axes known as "labrys," which we had seen in the museum. The word has entered into the languages of the world as "labyrinth." Theodoros told us the story of Prince Theseus, the Athenian prisoner who, he said, slew the half-man half-bull Minotaur in these very chambers and then was guided from the labyrinth by a silken thread laid by Minos' daughter, Ariadne. The story continued with the young lovers' escape to Naxos where Ariadne was abandoned by Theseus, who later married her sister, Phaedra. In the dank halls the Minotaur, symbol of man's uncontrollable forces, the ithyphallic young Theseus and the love-struck princess became credible as life.

Like resurrected Lazaruses we rose from the tomb's darkness into light. Leaving by way of the north portico we sat in the amphitheater, absorbing the warm sun, breathing the sweet warm air. Crickets chirped beneath the stones and birds twittered in the pines. Minoans gathered in the theater for bullfights, said Theodoros. These bloodless spectacles, more dances than fights, can be seen in one of Knossos' most beautiful frescoes. I imagined young Theseus grasping the bull's horns, the angered beast rearing its head, the youth flying into the air, somersaulting twice over the beast's back, and landing on his feet, more gracefully than any modern toreador, embraced by a girl waiting for him with open arms.

Cretans are singers. They improvise songs called *mantinades,* pouring into them their ambivalent gaiety and melancholy, their loves and their hates. One evening I visited a collector of Cretan songs, a soft-voiced college professor named Nicholas Petroulakis. For an hour we played tape recordings of heroic and sad mountain songs called *ritzikia.* "They express warriors' emotions," said Professor Petroulakis. "Like Christ in His parables they speak in metaphors so the enemy cannot understand what is being sung." Against a background of lyres, violins and bagpipes, vigorous male voices sang of the beauty and betrayal of women, of courage in battle, of death. A warrior made his farewell:

> Mother, if our friends should come,
> Do not tell them I am dead, making their hearts heavy,
> Lay the table for them to eat and the bed for them to rest,
> Give them a place to stack their arms,
> And in the morning when they say good-bye,
> Tell them I am dead. . . .

Hearing this I remembered a story told by Kazantzakis, how, arriving in a village at night, he was welcomed by a priest who prepared food for him, and a bed, and apologized that his wife, suffering from an indisposition, could not welcome him. Leaving in the morning, Kazantzakis learned from a stranger that the priest's only son had died the day before and was being mourned in an inner room. In Crete the stranger is a god to whom all doors are opened.

Crete's longest song, probably the longest in the world, is a popular sixteenth-century ballad from the Venetian occupation which tells the story of a singing Romeo-warrior named Erotokritos. The varied lyrics of his travail would fill a five-hundred-page book, and his story has been made into an opera by Manos Hadzidakis. The professor précised the story:

"Erotokritos is in love with Aretousa, daughter of the King of Athens. He asks for her hand. The King says 'No,' and orders Erotokritos exiled from his kingdom and his daughter to prison. Three, four years later, Athens is attacked by an enemy. For months the war goes on. Finally it is agreed that the war will be concluded by the single combat of two men, one from each army. When Erotokritos heard of this, he painted his skin black with ink, returned to Athens and asked to be the fighter. After many days of fighting Erotokritos won and Athens was victorious. 'Now you are the real king of my kingdom,' said the King to Erotokritos. 'What would you like as a reward?' Erotokritos said, 'I don't wish for anything except one. I want your daughter for my wife.' So the King sent word to Aretousa in prison that someone wished to marry her.

'No, I cannot,' she said. 'I love only Erotokritos.' 'I will see about this,' said Erotokritos. He washed himself and became again white. Then he went to the prison. Of course, Aretousa changed her mind. Marriage was the reward for all their suffering and they became happy ever after."

One morning Greggory and I set out for Hagios Nikolaos, seaport capital of Crete's eastern province of Lasithion. A tumult of black clouds churned over Mt. Dicte, the birthplace of Zeus. The coast road took us through jungles of banana groves and plains of windmills used for pumping irrigation water, looking like a crop of gigantic daisies. We saw a small boy, a Toby without an angel, carrying a fish in his bare hands, and we drove by a gypsy camp where dark women were delousing children. We met few cars and many donkeys bearing swaddled women.

Our first stop was at the Minoan palace of Mallia, built at the same time as Knossos, a flat area of ruins in which the architectural plan remains clear. A *kernos,* a circular stone offering table, was carved with thirty-four small receptacles in which the first fruits of the harvests, in the form of seeds, were offered to the gods.

Turning inland, we entered through a pass into a valley surrounded by mountains. Ahead in a burst of light lay the town of Neopolis. We stopped on the square where two young men greeted us and asked to examine our car. We inquired for a restaurant. "You should not eat here," said one of the youths. "Better to go to Hagios Nikolaos." After ten more perilous miles we were once more on the sea in a small harbor surrounded by hills. We had reservations at the Minos Beach Hotel, and here we lunched on a terrace from which we could look eastward over misty Mirabella Bay at a range of mountains. In an olive grove behind the hotel donkeys brayed and turkeys gabbled. Under the trees an idiot boy was talking into the mouthpiece of a red plastic telephone. "Don't bother me," he said, dialing. He listened and hung up. "I'm trying to call myself up," he said. "But my line is busy."

In the afternoon we drove through six miles of olives to the village of Kritsa, setting for the film *He Who Must Die,* made from Kazantzakis' novel *Christ Recrucified.* Our walk through the familiar settings had the sad sweetness of a pilgrimage. Wimpled old people keened and moaned in the sun, only the upper portions of their faces visible. Men wearing Turkish bloomers slept in front of cafés. Hundreds of white doves fluttered about the olives and murmured in the branches. The tranquil atmosphere was curiously depressing because of an absence of young people—gone, no doubt, to Germany, to Australia, to Athens.

We stopped at the country church of Panaghia Kera, where, someone had said, the fourteenth-century frescoes were the most famous in Crete. The fragments of paintings on the buckling walls were faded, mildewed, and darkened by centuries of candle smoke. Still, the visible portions were marvelously animated. Sinners in purgatory included water thieves, sheep stealers and harlots. In an abject scene of the Virgin's annunciation, Joseph has turned away in doubt, obviously disbelieving the busybody angel explaining the situation. "A likely story," Joseph seems to be saying. "Who is the man?"

In the morning we drove thirteen miles to Gournia, still another Minoan town. It lay on a lonely hill facing the sea, with only a tinkle of sheep bells and the distant banging of hunters' guns to break the stillness. A tiny orchid-colored flower grew over the ruins, covering them like a pink carpet.

A guard appeared. "I am Marco," he said, extending his hand, laughing, showing his joy over our arrival and his pleasure in the anticipated conversation. A heavy man with a round face, trimmed mustaches and gray wavy hair, he spoke uninterruptedly a strange and original English in a soft voice filled with a suspenseful dramatic excitement which seemed to turn everything into a revelation of secret mysteries. His heroes were two deceased Americans, a certain Miss Boyd, the archaeologist who excavated Gournia, and a Mr. Seger, whose money paid for the excavations.

"Only Americans can have to give money archaeology," he said. He showed us a small gourd-shaped vase found in the ruins. "Is how comes name," he said, laughing. "Little people from little village find little *vasen* like this so is named all place here, Gournia. Before Miss Boyd, was not ruin but one big *feld*." We were walking through a maze of narrow lanes. "Is all two stories high," he said. "Why? There is little steps up going down and down going up. Up has maybe big rooms, down, small. Here in Gournia is only people in houses. Not like in villages today where live in one room people and in other room sheeps. In Gournia they put animals in little houses below."

We stood on a summit looking out over the blue gulf and some islands named Psira and Mochlos. Marco took a long breath, waited suspensefully and then began an astonishing performance, saying, "Crete was once big land like Africa with elephants and birds and trees, and then . . ." Hesitating, building empathy, he continued with the slow eloquence of a preacher. "Then three thousand before Christ is one big earthquake and island Creta make dive into sea." Standing on a rock with his hands in the air, Marco pantomimed a jackknife dive. "Earthquake make collapse! Trees go fire! Tidal wave all over!" He made a washing sign, waving his hands. "Then comes big shake." A tremble passed through his body. "When big waves wash on rocks a little carpenter say, 'I don't think I stay here. I go up there on mountain. I will take my tools and put under one big stone and when sea go back I return and take.'" On his knees, Marco made with his hands the motions of raising and lowering a stone. He got up and in mournful cadences went on, "But water cover all the land. Carpenter finished like everyone." Marco stood on his tiptoes, gasping for breath, reaching his arms upward like a drowning man. "Gone forever. . . ." Watching and hearing him, I was filled with a strange recognition, a memory of Atlantis which had been haunting me ever since I had looked upon the beautiful walls of Knossos.

"But is not all gone," said Marco. "Is left a little Creta. Pass five thousand years and come Miss Boyd and find the carpenter's tools." Smiling radiantly, his arms extended like a blessing, he seemed to be describing a miracle. "Miss Boyd and a little student found fishhooks and a harpoon." Marco threw the harpoon like a javelin. "She found *vasen* and bronze from Egypt. Many year Miss Boyd work to bring *gournia* up. Came Mr. Seger, gave Miss Boyd money. 'I will stay in Gournia forever,' said Mr. Seger." A dark cloud crossed Marco's face, foreshadowing tragedy. "Mr. Seger make journey to Egypt. Come back he die from malaria of pyramids. Money stop. Miss Boyd stop. Mr. Seger leave paper which say, 'I give my house with all things to my very nice Greek friend, Nicholas! Come father and sister of Mr. Seger, look at paper, say 'O.K., all is for Nicholas.'"

"Miss Boyd came back from America in 1924 two weeks. Look at Gournia. After never came back. Miss Boyd died." Marco's eyes filled with tears. "Die also Nicholas. Villa is broken up. Come little soldiers from Germany." Marco was using the word "little" to indicate youth. "Then is here little French and little American boys. Like Gournia. Very nice clime, many sun. Stay bring money to make like it was before. War stop. Money stop. No longer care people. Is left to die villa."

With Marco in the car we drove two kilometers to the villa, a large quadrangle built in hacienda style around a cortile of roses and geraniums. "Mr. Seger very big man, very big money," said Marco. "Had every night many people sleep." We walked through rows of rooms in which the woodwork was crumbling away. A room which had been a library now had a dirt floor. "Germans make ammunition depot," said Marco. On the sea below us stood a small church outside which two old ladies were engaged in a colloquy. "Mr. Seger give money to make church. Today go three families." Marco's voice choked, his eyes grew misty. "Is die, all die. Everything finish. I have thirty-eight years." He plucked at his own gray hair, and said, "In two-three years my head will be white like marble."

Back in Iraklion I went to the Historical Museum, to the Kazantzakis room, a restoration of the writer's study in Antibes as it was before he died in 1957. It was an inside room, windowless, dark and silent. Wall shelves were filled with Kazantzakis' library, the works of Freud, Dostoevski, Shakespeare and Nietzsche. On a dark wooden desk lay pens and inkwells, and manuscripts, written in ink in a small firm hand. There were funeral photographs. The coffin carried by men in Cretan costumes with scarves covering their heads, was followed by similarly costumed men carrying copies of Kazantzakis' books. There were earlier photographs of a school performance with the youthful Kazantzakis playing a hero in classic costume. Who was he? Agamemnon? The god Zeus? I could not tell.

In the afternoon Kostas Grammatikakis and I climbed to his tomb on the Martinengo Wall, that part of the Venetian ramparts which stood over the oldest quarter of the town. Below the city spread out along the sea. Turning southward we looked on Mt. Ida, covered with snow, and Gioekthas, the mountain with the human face, a profile of sleeping Zeus.

On the grave was a raised slab of dark mountain stone, and at the head, an uncarved boulder. Over it stood a plain unpainted cross of peeled log with a laurel crown hanging from it like a crown of thorns. No name, no dates were there, only some words carved on marble from the author's own pen: "I do not fear anything so I am free."

On the tomb lay a small tightly-woven wreath of wild blue flowers. Kostas said, "Young men come up from the town each day to pick up the papers, the cigarette butts, and see that there are flowers."

While we were standing there a band of school children, herded by teachers, the boys first and then the girls, trounced noisily up the steps. As they came closer their voices hushed. They pressed in a thick circle around the grave and listened silently while a teacher told them the story of one of the greatest of all Cretans.

Kostas did not know the names of the little flowers braided into a wreath. Various Cretans I asked replied "wild flowers," or "weeds," or "field flowers." A girl at my hotel whose English was ephemeral said they were "wild animals." Weeks later in Athens I saw some of the same blossoms in a flower market near Constitution Square. I asked the woman selling them and she said they were amaranths, a name which means "never wither."

X

The Legacy of Lilijoy

"I defy you to make the story credible," said David Greggory. It had begun in San Francisco, at a dinner party at which I met a young banker named Channing Steele III. He asked if I would seek out the grave of an aunt who had died unexpectedly of a heart attack the year before in Crete. When word had reached California of her death, the body had already been buried. He gave me a memorandum which said "Choraplata, Crete. Lillian Joyce Steele. Demos Stratakakis."

Demos Stratakakis, said Steele, was a family friend. In Iraklion I showed the memorandum to a Cretan friend. "I remember," he said. "It was a very strange story. Will you go to Choraplata?"

On a map he pointed out the village on the southern coast. "The fishermen and farmers are Dorians who have hardly changed their way of living in three thousand years," said my friend. "They are always killing each other in feuds so the women never stop wearing black. It's a very wild place."

I wrote a letter to Demos Stratakakis. Four days later I received his reply, hand-blocked in English, giving road directions, telling me he would wait in his house outside the village. One morning I drove through Rethymnon and, turning left on a narrow dirt road into the White Mountains, climbed upwards through olive groves where women were gathering the first windfalls. I passed shepherds' hamlets where, I remembered my friend saying, "when there is a wedding they steal sheep to give to the bride." I plowed through red dust which hung so thickly in the air I seemed to be driving through fog, and I could hardly breathe.

The dust colored the day, turning the leaves of vineyards the color of roses.

Emerging from a pass in the mountains, I faced, far below, the silver mirror of the African sea. I descended by a coast road to the village of Choraplata on a ledge a half mile above the water. It was a small place of three hundred people with a main street and a single square. Standing outside a café were a half-dozen men, blond, tall and fiercely mustachioed, wearing baggy black breeches and boots, braided vests. With fringed black kerchiefs twisted at rakish angles around their heads, covering one eye, they looked like a crew of pirates. Following the directions in the letter, I continued through the town and descended toward the sea, and arrived behind a vault in the mountain, at an old whitewashed house enlarged with a modern wing, set behind a stone wall. Over the wall I could see a garden of roses and asters. The house was larger than any in the village.

I pulled a bell rope and in a moment the gate was opened by a young man, tall and blond, with wide shoulders and sun-browned skin.

"I am Demos," he said, softly speaking English. "Chan wrote you were coming. How is he?" He was dressed in northern clothes, corduroy trousers, English tweed jacket and a soft blue flannel shirt. On first impression he might have been a Scandinavian tourist. But the inscrutably solemn gaze of his hazel eyes were a Cretan gaze, and I remembered the blond men on the square and someone telling me that the people in this part of Crete had preserved the racial purity of their fair Doric ancestors.

He led me into the house, through a long hall with doors opening on both sides, and out again into a cortile garden with a fig and a medlar tree and some potted begonias. There was a table with chairs. "Would you like a drink?" he asked. He disappeared and I took a chair. Some birds chirped in the trees and a sleek orange cat crossed the patio and entered the house. My host returned carrying a tray with a bottle of Johnnie Walker, glasses, ice and a plate of shrimp, cheese, olives and tomato wedges. "You will say when," he said, pouring Scotch. "Chin, chin!" he said, raising his glass.

"It is very pleasant here," I said.

"I like very much San Francisco," he said. I was surprised to learn he had been there. "Two years ago at Christmas we were there," he said. "Pebble Beach. Hillsborough. How is Lucius Beebe?"

"He is dead," I said.

A dark cloud passed over the young man's face and lingered there. "I did not know," he said. "I would like one day to go back," he said. A pregnant young woman appeared in the door of the house. She came to me and offered her hand.

"My wife," said Demos Stratakakis.

"How do you do," I said.

"She does not speak English," he said. I greeted her in Greek. She had a lovely high-cheeked round face and brown hair and she wore a gray wool dress and sandals. Taking a chair, she sat silently. "You see," said Demos, his eyes settling on her stomach. "It is no longer simple to go to San Francisco." The girl said something in Greek and Demos translated. "My wife says she is sorry she cannot speak English with you." I nodded to her and apologized for not speaking Greek. She rose ponderously from her chair, walked to a rosebush, picked a pink bloom and brought it to me. "It is a custom to greet visitors with a flower," said Demos. I thanked her and she returned to her chair, smiling shyly. Demos poured more Scotch. "When will come Chan?" he asked.

"I do not know," I said. "He asked me to . . ."

"I know," said Demos swiftly, not letting me finish what I had started to say, that I was to make some photographs of Miss Steele's grave. "We will have lunch first," he said. He nodded to his wife, who got up. "My wife would like to know if you will eat here in the garden."

"Of course. It's beautiful."

The girl nodded and smiled and started slowly back into the house.

"She is lovely," I said. Demos' eyes, hard as steel, focused on the bare branches of a pear tree, stunted in the shape of a cross against the wall. He sat, spare, stiff-spined, silent, his face a bronze mask. Only his bony fingers, twitching on the glass, seemed to be alive. I had the uneasy feeling that my visit was spurring some inner crisis. I tried to imagine his age but it was difficult. About thirty, I guessed.

"A man must have sons," he said. "I am twenty-seven years old." He emptied his glass and took up the bottle.

"No more," I said, covering my glass with my hand.

"You will excuse me," he said, splashing whisky into his own glass, saying, "When a man marries he must establish early his rule." He made a cutting gesture across his throat with his thumb. "If you do not cut the head of the cat, your own head will be cut," he said. "I have cut the head. I am boss."

I had no reply to that. "Can you ride a mule?" he asked. I replied that I could. "After lunch we will go to the mountain," he said, emptying his glass, standing up. "Now I will show you the land." He stepped into the hall and took a rifle from the wall. "For hunting," he said. "Sometimes there are birds." Carrying it, he led me back through the house and out the gate.

I followed him over a rocky path from which we looked down toward the sea over slopes terraced with vineyards, and groves of olives and lemons. "All Lilijoy's," he said. "The best land in the Nomos. 'I must have this land,' she said. 'This is the place to end one's life, this is the place to die.' The fields belonged to many people and when they heard an American millionairess wanted to buy it, they made the price high. I bargained for her. It took five years."

Out on the sea the hump of an island rose through the blue mists. "Bread Island," said Demos. "It is shaped like a half bread loaf. Once when a big fish swam in from the sea to eat the people of the village, Zeus dropped a loaf of bread into the sea for the fish to eat instead. The fish could only swallow half the loaf and spit up the part which you see." The island appeared deserted. "Only foxes live there," he said.

Leading me on, through an arbor of olives, Demos spoke in sudden bursts of words, between which he brooded silently. "When Lilijoy came to Choraplata she asked for someone to take her to Bread Island. I was twenty-two and I had a boat. It was the first time we met." He shook a branch with the nozzle of his gun and one or two olives dropped. "Two more weeks," he said.

"We went to the island many times," he continued. " 'I will be buried on this island,' said Lilijoy. 'Why do you always speak of dying?' I asked. 'Because I am old,' she said. 'You are young, you have life to think about. When one is old, one lives with death. We will buy the island. Then one day you will bury me on it and it will be yours.' The island was not worth much but at once the price was increased ten times. She never bought it. Still, we went there, and she called it her island." I tried to imagine what had stirred a California spinster to buy property and settle here in this inaccessible place. I knew very little about Miss Steele except that she had been a sportswoman, a tennis champion, that she had lived with her mother and when the mother finally died in her eighties, she had traveled to the Mediterranean, to Spain, Italy and finally Greece. "Write of her," said Demos, his voice passionate. "Write that she was a great lady. Great! Great! Say that Demos Stratakakis said so."

We turned back. Behind him on the narrow path I saw how like a soldier he walked, precisely in measured steps. In the garden an elderly woman served us a fine lunch of fish and lamb grilled with lemon and parsley, and a cucumber salad. We drank a rosé wine. The people of Choraplata, Demos said, were both fishermen and farmers, according to the season. As a young man, when Miss Steele had met him, Demos had been a fisherman. Then when she had bought the land he cared for her vineyards and orchards.

"And now the land is yours?" I asked.

"It is not yet decided," he replied gravely. "I take care of it."
We finished lunch. "I will take you to your room and you will rest," he
said. He took me into a whitewashed room with a large hand-hewn
bed, a clothespress and a washstand. One wall was taken up by a fireplace.
Icons hung on the walls and a bowl of flowers stood on a table. "In an
hour we will start for the mountain," he said. It was always the mountain
to which he said we were going, never to the cemetery. I removed my
shoes and lay on the bed, trying to assemble what I had heard and seen,
trying to understand why my host seemed so remote, so separated from
everyone, including his wife. What dark emotion was hidden beneath
that monolithic dignity? Was it grief? Even, as it seemed apparent, he had
been the lover of Miss Steele, it seemed doubtful that he should mourn so
profoundly one who had been dead a year, a year in which he had taken
a young and beautiful wife. Was it fear? I could not imagine one such as
he fearing anyone. Anger? I recalled everything I had heard of Cretan
passion, the loyalties and hatreds, the intensity of friendship as binding as
marriage, the inherited feuds.

For a half hour I dozed and when I went outside my host was waiting
at the gate with two mules. We mounted and started in the direction of the
village and then, at a fork, took an upward path, climbing through poor
dry earth. The hoofs of the mules slid on loose shale or were buried in
dust. I tried to imagine a funeral procession up the steep path, the bearing
to the heights of a coffin in the hot Cretan summer. Miss Steele, I
remembered, had died in August.

We passed through a tiny village. Women's eyes watched from beneath
black wimples and men nodded silently, aware I had something to do with
the grave above. Cats slept on low-sloped roofs, a hen with splints on a leg
hobbled across the path. Sewage drained from vents in walls and its odor
mingled with the scent of the jasmine growing over the stones. Ahead a
single perfectly-coned cypress was silhouetted against the blue sky, and
around it came a small girl leading a donkey loaded with kale. A cock
crowed, and below Bread Island seemed to float on the sea. Ahead
Demos rode in dark silence. Of what passed through his mind I had no
clue. Slowly, more slowly, we climbed.

And then there it was, the cemetery, so small, so pitifully poor, a
slope of shale seventy feet square on which nothing grew except some
cypress. We dismounted. Bleak white crosses of wood carved with names
marked a few graves. The unmarked others were simply ovals of whitewashed stones laid in the red earth. On each was a tin cup of ashes of
cedar burned on the feast of All Souls. The graves, said Demos, were
turned every three years and the processes begun again, the dust of each

generation mingled with the dust of ancestors like flour in a bin. At the foot of the plot, a stone wall kept it all from washing down the mountain. Demos put down his gun and with quickened steps moved to the wall, to a large marble vault standing three feet above the ground, the only one like it in the cemetery. With a soft cry he crumpled to his knees before it. He genuflected. Moaning softly, he embraced the tomb with his long arms and kissed the dark marble over and over. Hardly daring to breathe, I turned away, looking down over the silvery olive slopes to Bread Island. I could hear children shouting at their games and in the cypresses birds chirping. The wind sighed. Now and then I heard his lowing behind me, nothing else, only the soft keening, on and on, and I had a spine-chilling sensation that it was Antigone I was hearing mourning at the tomb of Polynices.

The mourning ceased and I turned back. The tomb slabs, like everything else, were covered with dust and Demos was wiping the black marble with a handkerchief, washing it with his tears. I read:

LILLIAN JOYCE STEELE
February 2—1897
August 30—1964

Below the simple legend an eye-shaped incision carved two inches into the marble was filled with an assortment of multicolored pebbles. Demos picked up some of the stones, and closing them in his trembling hand, said, "A week before she died we took a boat to Bread Island. We followed the cliffs and the rocks and we stopped at the beaches. It was our last happy day together. Lilijoy collected these stones and when she died I found them in a dish in her room. They are hers forever." I looked at the handful of dusty gravel and imagined them as they were, washed by the sea, bright and colorful. He returned the stones into the niche and I made some photographs of the tomb. Against the cemetery wall I saw the crumbling remnants of discarded coffins and here and there in the shale, gleaming in the sun, the white fragments of bones. "She will not be disturbed," said Demos, his voice calm now. "I have paid the priests enough, they have promised me the tomb will be permanent, that she will rest here forever. And when I die I shall be here with her." The tomb was his own design, he had paid for it. "It was not here she wanted to be buried but on Bread Island. When she died this could not be arranged, the land could not be purchased. The police delayed the funeral to investigate her death and then, because the weather was hot, they ordered it at once. I remembered this cemetery which looked over the island that Lilijoy loved and I asked the people of the village for permission to bring her here. They were proud to have such a distinguished lady buried with their own dead. Because she was not of the Orthodox faith the priests objected, and I paid them too. My friends and I carried the coffin up the mountain on our shoulders. The priest from the village and a United States Navy chaplain read the service." I could see it, the caravan of wailing black-robed village women, the murmuring men, walking in the sweltering sun, following the suspended coffin like a procession for an ancient hero. "At the funeral feast the cheese was bad and one hundred people became ill," Demos said.

Crossing himself, he kissed the marble twice and then rose. "Shall we go?" He took up his gun and led me like a warrior out of the cemetery to the waiting mules. In the village children waved, chanting, *"Yasou, yasou,"* and in the crumbling passages toothless old women smiled, taking pleasure in the drama of death, in their own anticipation of it. We passed a flock of sheep with clanging bells descending from summer highlands to winter meadows. Their shadows were long and when we arrived at Choraplata the sun had dropped behind the western mountains.

A fire was burning in the hearth in my room. There was a knock on the door and Demos entered carrying the tray of ice and glasses with a bottle of *ouzo* as well as the Scotch. I chose the *ouzo* and he poured some over ice for both of us. He had changed into a dark jacket with a white shirt and blue tie, black whipcord trousers and shining black boots. We sat drinking by firelight.

He broke the silence, saying, "You know Lilijoy killed herself." I had thought of this. "A suicide cannot be buried on consecrated ground so I had to bribe the doctor 15,000 drachmae to falsify the death certificate, to write that it was a heart attack, and I had to pay the priest and the police." He emptied the glass and taking up the bottle poured more over the same ice. "She died the day before her marriage to Stratos Penalis," he said, his voice dark. He waited a moment. "Are you not surprised?" he asked.

"I am trying not to be surprised by anything you tell me," I said.

A shadow of a smile passed across his lips. The anguish returned. "She was going to marry the brother of my mother, Stratos Penalis." Our eyes met. I waited. "It was my fault," he said, his voice low. "We had many quarrels. When we made our journeys, when we were in London, in Rome, in Paris and Lisbon and especially in America, we often quarreled. But they were not angry fights and they always came to an end. Then in the last six months our quarrels became angry, they burned like fire. It began when I told her I wished to marry. She did not want me to marry as long as she was alive. When she died, she said, there would be time enough. How could I wait for that when I could not think of her death, when I did not believe it would ever happen? It was necessary for me to marry, to have sons. My younger brother already had two sons and I had none. This Lilijoy could not understand, that I could not wait, that the law of life is to marry and have sons. I had been affianced to Leda since she was sixteen, five years before I met Lilijoy. The father of Leda was speaking to my father, her brothers were showing their anger. Wedding plans were made. Lilijoy cried. She didn't stop crying. 'You have given me the happiest years I have known, the only happy years of my life,' she said. I tried to say to her there would be no difference, that I could marry and still live here, that I would bring my wife to live here too. She said I was mad, I was a beast. I could not make her understand that what I was doing was necessary, that there was no other way, that if I did not marry Leda I would have to leave Choraplata forever. I told Lilijoy I did not love Leda, I loved only her.

"Then one day she told me she was going to marry my uncle, Stratos Penalis. I laughed, I thought she was joking. I did not think she even knew my uncle. Because he was my uncle I had always thought of him as an old man, even when I was a boy. He was retired from the army, a widower with three sons close to my own age. I could not believe she was serious. I made a joke of it, I offered her my congratulations. 'I don't love you any more,' she said. 'I hate you.'

"Then I knew she was serious and I began to understand how this had come about. My mother, worrying about my marriage, had introduced her brother to Lilijoy. My uncle, who knew no English, went to Chania to take lessons and his sons paid for them. I do not know if it was my mother or the sons of my uncle who thought of it, that my uncle should ask Lilijoy to marry him, but everyone was in favor of it."

Demos poured more *ouzo,* which his trembling hand caused to drip on the table. Listening to him I had abandoned my Anglo-Saxon credulity. His story had its own passionate logic and it suddenly seemed quite plausible that Miss Steele should accept Stratos Penalis' offer of marriage. The stake for which she gambled was a passionate protest from Demos, a commitment of love, perhaps even a plea for her to marry him. Not understanding the Cretan code she had lost.

"She asked me what she should do," Demos continued. "I told her I had no opinion, that she must make up her own mind. I went to Athens where I was drunk every night, thinking only of her. My mother wrote that the marriage of Lilijoy and Stratos Penalis was arranged, that Lilijoy had signed the marriage agreement, giving my uncle the right to the house and the fields. All I could think was how happy Lilijoy and I had been, how she had given me the only happiness of my life.

"Two days before the wedding I returned. I found Lilijoy crying. She had been crying for many days. I asked her how she could do it, how she could sign the agreement giving the house and the land to my uncle. She threw a cup of coffee at me. 'Now I know why you have been my friend,' she said. I told her it was my fault, my mistake. I told her to stop the wedding, that I would go away with her, to Japan, to Peru, any place where we might be alone together. I said she must sell the house and the land. We would never come back. She would not listen. 'I no longer trust you,' she said. 'Please go away.'

"I went home and I spent the night in my parents' house. My mother was happy. She was making plans for my marriage with Leda.

"In the morning I came here. The gate was locked and on it was a card which said 'Very tired. Resting.' The card was still there when I returned in the afternoon. I sat by the gate an hour and then I came in. I ran up the stairs to her room. The door was locked. I called. And I broke open the door."

In the dark I could hear Demos' soft moans. "She was as if asleep," he said, his voice muffled by his hands covering his face. "We were one body, one soul. She said once she would kill me and she did, she killed my soul. I wish also she had killed my body." In the shadows I could hardly see his form. But I could not shut out his softly moaning voice. Then it stopped and I was aware that he had stood up. "We will go to the café," he said. "Come."

At the door he slid a leather-covered revolver into an inner pocket of his jacket. It was night and the stars seemed unnaturally close. Demos seemed to have thrown off his tragic mood. Leading me up the path, he spoke of the redwood trees in California and the seals at Carmel. On the square there was light only in the café. Walking toward it we met some dark figures who passed softly without speaking as if we were both strangers. The incident was unsettling. I remembered what I'd heard of the enigmatic Cretan character, of a suspicion and hostility toward strangers.

In the café men were sitting at tables arranged around a glowing charcoal brazier. Two or three nodded but the rest took no notice of our entrance. In a corner outside the circle a man was playing a lyre, holding the instrument like an upside-down violin, the sound box resting on his knee, the keyboard under his chin. The bow which he drew over it had rattles like castanets.

Taking chairs at an empty table, we joined the circle. The lyre player put down his instrument and shuffled to our table. Demos ordered food and wine. The man disappeared into a back room and then returned with a bottle of wine and two glasses. He went back to his instrument and resumed his playing. Two young men, looking very dour, stood up and without ceremony walked out of the café. The disquiet I had felt on the square returned. No one was speaking and all eyes but the musician's were upon us. I remembered hearing that in Choraplata a man might be shot for picking up another's drink, for accidentally clinking his own glass against his neighbor's.

Demos poured some wine. "The men who left," he said softly, "were the sons of my uncle." The eyes watching us in the room were like cat's eyes.

"Where is your uncle?" I asked.

"He is dead."

I felt a weight on my chest like lead and my blood turned to ice.

"Lilijoy left many letters," said Demos. "A letter to me. A letter to my uncle. Letters to relatives and lawyers in California. All the letters said the house and the land were to be given to me, that my uncle was to have an income of two hundred dollars each month for the rest of his life. At first my uncle was happy. Two hundred dollars each month in Choraplata would turn him into a rich man. But all the relatives were talking, especially the women. The sisters in my mother's family could not stop talking. They told my uncle if the marriage had taken place everything, the house and the land, would be his. With their talking there was always an excitement."

"And your mother?"

"She said she was on my side. But when they talked together, the women, she would change her mind in a woman's way. The village was in confusion."

While he spoke men were getting up and silently leaving, singly and in pairs. Soon there was no one in the room but Demos and me and the lyre player sawing on his strings, ringing his rattles like sleigh bells. A woman brought our food, good roast lamb, and then he said, "The sons of my uncle took the marriage agreement to a lawyer in Athens who told them the dispute over the land would have to be settled in an American court. It is now more than a year and still nothing is decided. I have been working the land, taking care of it. When there were grapes to be harvested, and olives, I could find no one in the village who would help me so I paid some Spaniards who had come to Crete to work. One day when I was picking olives with the Spaniards my uncle and his sons appeared and ordered me to leave. The olives belonged to them, they said. I replied that I would wait for the decision of the American court, that I would not leave until then."

There was a question I felt compelled to ask. "How did your uncle die?"

Demos' hard eyes penetrated mine like steel and he said, "With a bullet in his head. He was found one morning in his orchard."

I tried to eat but my gullet would not function, my jaws would not move. I swallowed some wine.

"You don't eat," said Demos, smiling faintly. "When you refuse food in Crete you offend the house and make an enemy of your host." I ate, choking it down, thinking of the walk back across the square, down the dark lane.

"The sons of my uncle are either going to kill me or I will kill them," Demos said calmly. The smile was still on his lips and I did not know if he was serious. "Sometime. Not now. And their sons will kill my sons unless my sons kill theirs first. They have between them five sons and I have none. I need time to make sons, enough sons to equal theirs."

He interrupted the musician to pay the check and we began our walk through the darkness. I imagined forms lurking by every wall, behind every tree. I clung close to Demos and then decided to linger behind. I began to talk to make clear which of our two forms was my own, and my own voice frightened me. Finally we arrived at the gate. When we had let ourselves into the house, I felt able to breathe again. Demos took my hand, clasping it so tightly in his I thought my bones would break. "If only I could have her back for one hour," he said. "I would give my life for that. My life is over. When she died, so did I die . . ."

I strained for a cool voice. "You're speaking nonsense," I said. "You're a married man, you have a baby coming. Perhaps you will be rich. Your life is just beginning."

"My life!" The voice was a cry. "You think I am happy, that everything is peaceful because I have a wife. My wife is a peasant, an ordinary person. *She* was not ordinary. She was everything extraordinary. She was my life. And now she is nothing and I am a dead man."

We parted for bed. The fear which was there in the house like a shadow gave me no rest, allowed me no sleep. I tried to comprehend the legacy of violence and death which a California spinster had left to a village of cousins, committing them to murder, perhaps for generations. Could she have planned it as a revenge for her own frustrations, for the lie of her life? Like a child appealing to a saint, I called out to Sophocles, but no voice came to me and I did not know. I thought of the life of the girl who had welcomed me with a rose, and I prayed that the child she would bear would be a girl and that it would bring some joy to her and to the house. I waited for the light.

XI

Donkey Serenade

At a fork in the road we asked a hunter the way to Anoghia. He pointed toward a thick cover of clouds hanging over the crags of Mt. Ida, and directed us on a recently blasted rock roadbed, through a gray-walled canyon.

Midway in the canyon, like a sentinel in the road, stood an eagle. Unruffled, the bird let us pass, spreading his wings which brushed against our car.

Not a phoenix but an eagle, superbly Cretan, invincible as the landscape and the people who live in it. In 1944, a German army marched into Anoghia and, in reprisal to resistance, killed every male at home that day and burned the town to the ground. From its ashes Anoghia was rebuilt. Today it is known for its revival of the old crafts, for its weaving and woodwork, and for its vigorous hospitality to strangers, especially at weddings.

The cold wind-driven rain was unfortunate weather for a wedding. Our invitation had come from Iraklion's director of tourism who told us that wedding celebrations in Anoghia were the most exuberant in Crete. Marriages were on Sundays, and usually in the fall of the year. Since August there had been more than thirty. I had heard that for a guest to leave a celebration before the bride and groom was considered an insult and that a fortnight ago four Danish archaeology students, wearying of the interminable drinking and dancing, had left, one by one, on the pretense of having to urinate. Corralled by a brother of the groom, the guests were returned at gun's point for another four hours of eating and drinking. The official who arranged our invitation had assured me that the wedding to which we were going would end before evening.

The pass opened into a sloping valley of olives and vines. We climbed through a village and into another cloud-filled pass. We drove through Synikismos Anogiou—"the Settlement of Anoghia"—built by a handful of survivors of the German slaughter. Most of the survivors had chosen to rebuild their new homes on the ruins of the old, two kilometers further on. The fog was so heavy we could barely make out the dark swaddled forms walking under umbrellas up the muddy road.

We had been directed to a local café where we were to meet a certain Vassilios Spachis. We found him, a dark heavy young man with a mustache, sitting at a corner table with four other foreign guests, a television cameraman from Hollywood named Roberts and his wife, large blond people, and a very small old couple, both of whom spoke English in precise north European accents. The Robertses had driven out in a rented car with an English-speaking guide called George who was also at the table. The small couple had traveled to Anoghia by bus. Not understanding their names, I guessed they were Swiss or Scandinavian, since it seemed highly unlikely that anyone would invite a German couple to a wedding in Anoghia.

I was wrong. Roberts addressed the little man as "Doctor" and I asked if he was a medical man. "I am *doktor* of engineering in Frankfurt," he replied. With their identical light blue eyes and crinkled pink faces, their short gray hair—hers cropped as closely as his—they looked like a pair of small gray mice.

The dank steamy room was filled with men in tentlike black and brown shepherd's capes, drinking *raki* or coffee, silently watching our table. Mrs. Roberts and the German lady were the only two women in the room. The Robertses were talking uninterruptedly, sometimes both together, and the little Germans nodded their heads to everything that was said like agreeable children, smiling endlessly as if they were frightened not to smile. Mr. Spachis, who it turned out was the director of a weaving cooperative which had a membership of eight hundred home weavers, told us that Anoghia had a population of four thousand people, mostly farmers, herdsmen and shepherds. The wedding, he said, would begin with a procession of friends and relatives carrying the dowry of the bride, a farmer's daughter, to the home of the groom, a cattle farmer who lived in the Settlement of Anoghia. Because of the rain this was being delayed.

Spachis herded his guests out of the café, across the muddy street to the municipal building. Outside was a white marble tablet in the form of an open book engraved with a text which we did not, because of the rain, stop to read. We entered a room called "The Sporting Club," a center not only for sports, but also for folklore and tourism. Several officials were waiting to greet us. The large room had walls of books, a shelf of stuffed game and birds, comfortable furniture and a glowing electric heater. A large framed photograph of President Kennedy hung over the desk.

"Wonder why they don't put up Lyndon and Ladybug," said Mr. Roberts. No one replied. The interpreter, understanding, remained discreetly silent. "At least Shaggy Jack had hair," Mr. Roberts said, going on with a series of Lyndon Johnson jokes, all in execrable taste. Mrs. Roberts, a helpmeet worthy of her husband, joined with some tasteless gossip about Mrs. Kennedy and Mrs. Johnson. "Can't someone shut those Chowderheads up," murmured Greggory. Apparently no one could. Eager for approval, happy to be included in the confidences, the Mice nodded like puppets, laughing at everything the Chowderheads said.

Some women arrived with trays of food, pieces of barbecued lamb and slices of bread, sent from the house of the bride, and a man poured glasses of wine. Mrs. Chowderhead refused the food, saying, "You can't be too careful in strange places." The delicately seasoned meat was excellent and the Mice chomped on it hungrily, smiling with full mouths at anyone who bothered to look at them. The men in the room seemed to assume the Germans to be Americans. Spachis and George, who knew they weren't, said nothing. Spachis was showing us some embroidery. "I bought some lovely lace in Bavaria," said Mrs. Chowderhead, and Mrs. Mouse could hardly contain her excitement over Bavarian lace.

The mayor, a trim young man in a black suit and dark-rimmed glasses, arrived. Speaking through George, he said, "The people of Anoghia welcome you from the heart and are sad that it rains."

"We've been very lucky with the weather," said Mrs. Chowderhead. "This is our first rain since Austria."

"In Anoghia we love very much President Kennedy," said the mayor.

"Tell him Nixon would have been a better President," said Chowderhead.

"I don't think the people would understand that," said George wisely.

Mr. Chowderhead was showing the mayor his plastic folio of credit cards. "Weren't worth a damn in Bucharest," he said. "They put me in the bastille for photographing their railroad station." Outside the rain was subsiding. I went out and translated as best I could the Greek words on the marble tablet. On one side I read:

"Because the village of Anoghia was a center of English espionage

on Crete and because the men of Anoghia directed sabotage and executed
a German sergeant and because the guerrillas of the resistance made
Anoghia their station and because through this village passed the kid-
nappers of Gen. Von Kleip, we order the complete annihilation of the
village and the execution of every man of Anoghia who is found in the
village and within a radius of one kilometer. 13-8-44. H. Miller, general
commander of Crete."

Beside it on the second tablet of the open book I read:

"According to the order of the King on May 3, 1946, there is presented
to this village the Military Cross, for its suffering during the occupation
by the Germans, and for the admirable conduct, patience and the in-
comparable heroism of its people. Minister K. Manetas."

Standing there in the soft rain, writing it down, I could not stop
weeping. I remember what they had told me in Iraklion, that two hundred men had been slaughtered, as well as the old and infirm women
who could not walk. Cattle, sheep, donkeys and horses were destroyed.

Through the window I could see Mrs. Mouse smiling at the Chowderheads, a whimpering Wilhelmina wringing her hands in a kind of perpetual anxiety, and beside her Dr. Mouse was nodding his assent to everything being said. If they read the tablet, I thought, they would have
reason for their anxieties. I was wondering who had sent them here, by
what crude mischief they had been dispatched to Anoghia. They were
innocent, of course, of the events carved in the marble, they were innocent as Germans are always innocent, always being Mice, always
unknowing.

I went inside where Mr. Chowderhead was showing the Mice his
German tape recorder and telling them his rented car was a Mercedes-
Benz. Finding voice at last, Dr. Mouse said, "I am glad to hear not
everything in the world is made in America." I held my peace. Between
the Chowderheads and the Mice a friendship was springing and the
Chowderheads were inviting the Mice to ride back to Iraklion with them
in the evening. It was now after twelve. Out on the street there was an
excitement. Men came out of the café. A bearded old priest emerged
from the fog and, following him on the muddy street, young men in
whipcord trousers and boots carried chairs, tables and a bed. Behind
them a caravan of women and children under umbrellas carried linens,
blankets, dishes, copper and kitchenware. Girls in traditional costumes
carried embroidery, mattresses and bedding. The procession concluded
with three musicians. A blind violinist was being guided up the slippery
road by a flutist and mandolin player.

We crossed back to the café to await the return of the party. At the
corner table we were served small glasses of *raki* and a bowl of hard

little nuts, called *rovithia*. The men who filled the room watched silently, listening to us speak English. The Mice, nodding toothily, gnawed a small nut each. Their compulsive smiling was becoming a torment. The human steam which filled the room clouded the windows so we could not see out. Now and then my eyes would catch a strange pair of eyes, a glass would be raised and I would be greeted by a friendly smile.

One man stood out from the group. He was lean and straight, with a bony dark face, deep black eyes and black hair and a small black mustache. In black whipcord trousers, jacket and highly polished boots, he looked like a hero out of Kazantzakis. He exhaled and a cloud of cigarette smoke drifted toward the ceiling. Chewing on a hard nut, Mrs. Chowderhead was saying, "I guess the nuts are why they all got gold teeth." Mrs. Mouse laughed. I asked George if he knew the dark man across the room.

"Everybody knows him," said George. "He is a hero of Crete, a soldier of the resistance. His name is Sokrates."

Catching my eyes the man nodded his dark head and with a passionate show of teeth waved his cigarette. I beckoned him to join us. Slowly, regally, he crossed the room. George pulled up a chair and invited him to sit with us. Sokrates acknowledged the introductions with a sepulchral voice, each word a dark liturgy. He called for a waiter to bring more *raki,* and he passed cigarettes and lit one for himself. The index finger of his left hand was stained mahogany from nicotine. He had lean grooved jowls, strong neck cords and thick black brows. From George I learned that he owned a butcher and grocery shop in the town.

"What time is the wedding?" Mrs. Chowderhead asked. Speaking through George, Sokrates said, "Any moment now when the party returns with the groom to the house of the bride." The dowry, he said, included sheep and goats as well as money. The groom paid all the wedding expenses.

"It's just the other way at home," said Mrs. Chowderhead. "The bride's family has to pay." The Chowderheads irritated me; I was in an ugly mood. Now I found the calm strong presence beside me settling. I could even see some humor in the outrageous comedy which fate had cast in the cheerless room. George was explaining that it was the custom for foreign guests to present a gift of fifty drachmae to the bride and groom.

The sum was less than $1.60. "Is it fifty for married couples or are we both supposed to give fifty?" asked Mrs. Chowderhead. George replied fifty would be enough for a couple. Mrs. Mouse smiled happily through her thick lenses. "When do we give it?" she asked, and Sokrates said he would let us know when the time arrived.

"Are marriages *arranged?*" asked Mrs. Chowderhead. "Or do the bride and groom choose each other. I mean, is it *love?*"

"Both," Sokrates said.

"How old are the bride and groom?"

"He is thirty-three," said Sokrates. "She is thirty."

"Well, were they ever married before?" asked Mrs. Chowderhead. I hoped George would not translate the question, but he did. A silence settled around the table which Sokrates broke, saying sternly, "In Anoghia there has never been a divorce. Not one."

"Well, she *could* be a widow," Mrs. Chowderhead persisted.

"In the history of Anoghia, only one widow has remarried," said Sokrates. He ordered more *raki,* and Mrs. Mouse, pursing her lips as if she were going to whistle, said she would have some.

We heard music. The musicians, the blind violinist in the center, the groom, priest and friends were going to fetch the bride and take her to the church. In a few minutes Sokrates said it was time for us to go. We walked in the rain down the muddy road, arriving at the church the same moment as the wedding procession. Small children carried the bride's long train.

The small church filled quickly. "Can we go in?" asked Mrs. Chowderhead.

"Is better to wait," said George uneasily. I noticed he was nervous and beside me Sokrates was frowning. Drawing me aside George explained that the word had spread some Germans were present and this was causing uneasiness. We stood in the rain. Children in rubber boots sloshed around us. The musicians began to play. A group of very tall young men in flashing janizary costumes—voluminous blue bloomers, purple sashes, black boots and black scarves worn pirate-fashion over one eye—began to dance. They were joined by a group of young women in richly embroidered costumes of white skirts with red aprons worn on the side, jeweled bodices and bright turbans.

"Why can't we go into the church?" Mrs. Mouse was wailing. One of the janizaries took a ferociously curved knife from out of his bloomers and, moving through the crowd, began carving from a loaf of bread, handing out chunks of it. Another followed with a pitcher of wine which he raised to the lips of the watchers, like a priest offering communion. The bread and wine, said Sokrates, was a symbolic blessing on the bride and groom. The dancers whirled silently in the mud, the girls' black hair clinging to their olive faces. In the thickness of the fog they were like shadows dancing in a cloud. The crowd watched from under a circle of umbrellas like a ring of black mushrooms and someone held an umbrella over the blind violinist. Some children began to jog in their own dancing circle.

Sokrates disappeared. He returned in a moment with the word that we were welcome after all and he led us into the church. A crowd of women were pressing around the bridal pair, forming a kind of human pool. Most of them were talking. In the back of the church some children were playing a jumping game. Over it all I heard now and then the droning voice of the priest, and Mrs. Chowderhead saying, "This is the wildest wedding I ever saw." Her husband said, "In America we teach kids some respect for religion."

The church, lit by a multitude of candles, was hot. Nudging my arm, Sokrates showed me icons and frescoes. With a minimum of common language, with signs and a few Greek and German words, we were establishing a communication. He explained that two of the three naves of the church were destroyed by Germans who had used the third as a stable for horses. He pointed to bullet holes in the frescoes. Now and then I got a glimpse through the crowd of the bride and groom seated before the priest, both with haloes of artificial flowers on their heads; the haloes were joined together by a white cord. The haloes, explained Sokrates, were symbols of the eternity of marriage—the next time the bride and groom would wear them would be in their coffins.

The priest's voice stopped, and the people in the church formed a line to offer their congratulations to the newlyweds. The couple sat with bent heads so that each person who passed could kiss the haloes. We joined the line. Behind me Mrs. Chowderhead and Mrs. Mouse were clutching fifty-drachmae notes. Mrs. Mouse was trembling with excitement and I wondered how the Germans would be introduced.

Sokrates was up to it. Stepping ahead he presented all of us as "friends from America." For a moment I feared Mrs. Mouse would say, "We are from Chermany," but she was too quivery to speak at all. I kissed the haloes, offered my congratulations and followed Sokrates from the church. "The groom looked old enough to know better," said Mr. Chowderhead and Dr. Mouse laughed out loud.

Outside they were still dancing. The newlyweds emerged from the church and joined the dancers, and the child who bore the train danced behind the bride. It began to rain harder and the dancers gave up. Led by the priest and musicians, the wedding party started on foot the two kilometers to the Settlement of Anoghia.

The long caravan of umbrellas moving through mists was like a Japanese painting. When we arrived in the village the newlyweds disappeared into the groom's house and most of the guests, including ourselves, were directed to a café, a damp dark place where tables and chairs were set

for a party. Watching over me like a guardian, Sokrates arranged a table
to include the Chowderheads and Mice, and the interpreter, George. Mr.
Chowderhead astonished the guests by playing on his machine the music
he had recorded in the rain. Mrs. Mouse was trying to give away two
return bus tickets to Iraklion which, since they were riding back with
the Chowderheads, she and her husband would not be using. "I thought
. . . since we've been offered a ride . . ." Her lips trembled. With a
fluttering hand she extended the tickets. "Perhaps . . . someone . . ."
Listening to George's translations of her words, the wedding guests were
silent. "We don't want . . . any money . . . for them . . . ," Mrs.
Mouse went on. "We don't wish . . . to sell them . . ." No one replied.
"We would . . . give them . . . to a friend . . ." Sensing the coldness
in the place, George struggled on with it. Becoming almost frantic, Mrs.
Mouse went on. "We thought . . . someone might as well . . . since we
won't . . . I'm sure they'll be good for many days. . . ." Still there was
no answer and her voice, trailing off, continued, "We thought . . . someone might . . ."

The silence was finally broken by Sokrates saying slowly, "The tickets
would not be of any use to anyone here." George interpreted his words
which Mrs. Mouse did not appear to understand. Almost in tears, the tickets fluttering in her hand, she whimpered, "Won't someone . . . take
them . . . ?"

"Why is everyone so rude?" asked Mrs. Chowderhead. "You'd think
they'd at least be gracious."

Food came, platters of roast lamb and roast pig, salad, potatoes and
slices of watermelon. Sokrates selected the most succulent pieces for my
plate and kept my glasses filled with *raki* and wine. I remembered someone telling me Cretan friendships were like marriages, that the unfaithfulness of a friend was like the unfaithfulness of a wife, and that one
could not, without jeopardy to his life, be friends simultaneously with
two enemies. I looked about the room and wondered who in the company were Sokrates' friends and who were his enemies. Better, I decided, not to smile at anyone. George was speaking of Anoghia's history
of resistance to invaders. "It is the custom for everyone to carry a knife,"
he said. "And every man to keep a loaded gun under his bed."

On my note pad Sokrates had printed his full name: "Sokrates
Kefalogiannis." The Kefalogiannis was one of two large and powerful
families. The other was named Sbokos. For centuries the two clans
had been feuding and battling in Guelph-Ghibelline fashion. Politically
the Kefalogiannis were rightists who supported the King—a cousin bearing the name was a parliamentary deputy in Athens. The Sbokos were
Papandreou leftists.

The Mice were gnawing happily on bones. Mr. Chowderhead, who was getting drunk, continued to talk of the wedding, saying, "All I can say is the bride and groom didn't seem very happy about it."

"They were very earnest," said Sokrates. "They knew they would be united forever."

"All the same she looked as if she knew her happy days were over, ha ha ha ha . . . ," bellowed Mr. Chowderhead. The Mice stopped gnawing and laughed. "We've been married twenty-eight years and we have two daughters married," said Mrs. Chowderhead.

"And I paid for the weddings and not the grooms, ha ha ha ha," said her husband.

I looked at Sokrates' flushed face. I wondered how much he understood, what was going on behind those inscrutable eyes. A soldier came to tell us that he had two cousins working in a factory in Baltimore. Mr. Chowderhead said, "Well, I'm glad to hear someone's working in America. I thought everyone was on relief, ha ha ha ha . . ." The Mice were finding him hilarious; their shrill laughter rang through the hall. They appeared to be drunk. Watching them eating, drinking and laughing all at the same time, I was thinking of a Katherine Mansfield story called *Germans at Meat*. A circle of children had formed around us, watching us eat. Several were barefoot. The incredible conversation continued. Sensitive to its nuances, interpreting how and when he chose, George managed to keep an edgy amiability. Forking over some potatoes on her plate, Mrs. Chowderhead said, "Are these fried in animal fat? In America we fry everything in vegetable fat."

"I'm surprised they don't all have diarrhea, ha ha ha ha," said Mr. Chowderhead. He poured some *raki* and raised his glass. "Here's to you, Socky, old pal."

"Thirty weddings in two months," said Mrs. Chowderhead. "It seems like a lot."

"We marry in the autumn when the harvest is finished," said Sokrates.

"Crops first," said Mr. Chowderhead. "Marrying is just a hobby, ha ha ha." The convulsed Mice were laughing so hard they spat food across the table.

"They don't seem to mind flies at all," said Mrs. Chowderhead. At this time the café owner, a smiling man in his fifties, introduced himself to us and presented his wife, an elflike little woman with brightly flashing eyes, pink cheeks and two long black braids which hung below her waist. We invited her to join us and she took a chair beside Sokrates. She was dressed in black.

"Tell her," said Mr. Chowderhead, "that I can see why the women of Crete don't need cosmetics."

The compliment was relayed with merriment. The woman sat smiling, relishing her *raki*. She seemed young, almost girlish, and very shy. She took a shank of lamb from a platter and from the folds of her skirt drew out a fiercely curved knife, carved a mouthful of meat from the bone and began to chew. Addressing her through George, Mrs. Chowderhead said, "Why do you ladies wear black all the time?"

Embarrassed, George attempted to answer himself, saying, "Some ladies do not wear black all the time. Black is mostly for ladies overage."

"What do you mean, overage?" asked Mrs. Chowderhead.

"Advanced age?" said George.

"Well, how advanced is she?"

"She is just past forty," said George. "But you see she lost a son seven years ago so she will be wearing black all her life."

"You'd think they wouldn't after a reasonable time," said Mrs. Chowderhead. "Tell her I want the names of all our hosts so I can send them thank-you notes. Of course they won't be able to read them."

I asked George about Sokrates' war activities. I learned that Sokrates was an eighteen-year-old resistance leader when the Germans came to Crete. To escape capture he was hiding in a mountain cave at the time of the massacre. Two days later, on August 15, Sokrates and some companions found sixty women of Anoghia being held captive in a mountain gorge by four German and five Italian soldiers. They killed the soldiers and returned to Anoghia with the women.

While George told the story, Sokrates was pouring more *raki*. We had drunk too much. The fog was thickening and I remembered the long road back. The innkeeper and his wife invited us to their house for a final drink. We tried to beg off but this proved impossible. We walked a short distance up the road, passing some donkeys along the way. Sokrates stopped and pointed toward the foggy heights of Mt. Ida, to a place where, he explained, he had lived in a cave during the war. The innkeeper's house was, like the other houses in the town, a single room painted white and very clean. It contained a bed, a charcoal brazier, a battery radio, a table and several chairs.

"They don't overfurnish these joints," said Mrs. Chowderhead.

The innkeeper's wife served glasses of *raki* and plates of raisins. Dancing with the bottle, her braids flying, she filled our glasses a second and third time. "No," I cried. "No, no!" She laughed merrily and I realized she was like everyone else in the room, roaring drunk. The time for caution was long passed, I decided, and I drank every drop. Outside I heard a cock crow as if he were trying to tell me something. The Mice were still eating. Their eyes had a glazed catatonic glisten. I realized that they would be leaving Anoghia as unaware as they had arrived. Dancing around me, the innkeeper's wife stuffed my pockets with raisins and nuts.

On Sokrates' arm I staggered to the car. Could I come back tomorrow, he asked. No, I said, the next day I had plans to go to the monastery of Arkadiou. We embraced, pledging eternal brotherhood. I got into the car and Sokrates, standing at stiff attention, saluted like a general. In that moment two small boys appeared out of the fog and beat their fists angrily on our car, shouting *"Germani! Germani!"* Sokrates leaped forward and tore the boys from the car. Somewhere in the fog a donkey brayed.

"The donkey serenade," roared Mr. Chowderhead. "Ha ha ha ha . . ."

"Ha ha ha ha!" shrieked the Mice, still innocent, still pure.

XII

All Maybes

It was like going to Independence Hall on the Fourth of July. The date was November 7, the Cretan national holiday, and I was on my way to the monastery of Arkadiou, where on this day in 1866 the Abbot Gabriel blew up a powder magazine, killing its Cretan defenders and three thousand Turks.

It was a day in which Crete celebrated its soldier heroes. A contemporary hero, Sokrates Kefalogiannis, had been the subject of discussion the night before in Iraklion. Kostas Grammatikakis, who knew Sokrates, said, "The leaders of the resistance continue to be our popular heroes. When a man has shown his bravery he is respected and loved by everyone. But precisely because of this, the life of a hero becomes a lonely dedication. Sokrates is one of these. He loves Crete and feels his identity with the land, with the mountains and with his dead companions. He loves the people and the people love him. He is not married—perhaps he wanted a certain woman and did not get her, so his life is a dedication to his love. He cannot mix with the crowd, he cannot loiter in cafés, he cannot play cards. He would never dance in a public affair like a wedding. To do so would be to compromise his leadership. To him dancing is very special. The others of us feel the fact of the dance. He feels the dance. Like Zorba, he will dance only when he feels like it. He will dance alone, in his house, on a mountaintop, or by the sea."

Sokrates dancing alone on a mountaintop! It would be something to see.

It was almost noon. The road from Rethymnon was filled with autos, army trucks loaded with soldiers, buses, bicycles and scooters, and was lined with people waiting for runners in a Cretan marathon to pass on their way from Arkadiou to Rethymnon. The road curved between a cliff and a canyon and then opened on a bowl-shaped plateau encircled by mountain peaks. The autumn landscape bloomed with the bright colors of women's coats and sweaters, and with picnic blankets. Music and singing echoed in the hills. Ahead in a grove of trees stood the monastery. Our car had hardly come to a halt when there was a tapping on the window. It was the face of Sokrates laughing in the glass. Like brothers reunited after the Trojan Wars, we embraced. With our minimal language he explained to me that he had come from Anoghia with friends. He had seen the Chowderheads in the monastery taking photographs (with a lovely Turkish couple no doubt) and he was worried I might not come.

Together we walked to the monastery. It took a long time, for every few steps Sokrates was greeted and embraced by friends. The church had a delicately carved Venetian façade and eight Corinthian columns. The center of three doors was walled up, a reminder of its switch from the Catholic to Orthodox faith. Inside, wild-looking men wearing purple bloomers, fringed head scarves and jeweled curved scimitars knelt before a painting, kissing it. The canvas portrayed the Abbot Gabriel, holding a crucifix in his right hand and a torch in his left.

From the church we went to the powder magazine and here in the roofless stone cellar Sokrates pantomimed history.

"Big powder," he said, outlining with his hands the ammunition pile. "Greeks forty days . . . finish food." He sucked in his lean corded stomach, showing hunger. His flat linear body and face were distorted in agony, like a modern sculptured crucifix. "Drei tausend Turks," he said. "Papa Gabriel fire." Sokrates struck a match and leaped back with his arms enveloping a great explosion. "Brooooommmmm! Boom boom! Alles tot!" He cradled an imaginary infant in his arms—a single baby had survived the blast.

Sokrates' graphic performance was interrupted by a Greek Army officer who, offering linguistic assistance, said, "All men in monastery were blowed because put fire to kill the Turkey. . . ." We went to the museum where Sokrates demonstrated the use of swords, knives and guns, and then we went to a memorial tower where thirteen warriors' skulls were on display in a glass cabinet. Sokrates opened a trap door in the floor and lit a match so I could peer down into the bone-strewn crypt. We walked over the countryside and he showed me where the Turks had encamped. From his pocket he brought out a packet of roast

lamb and some apples which we ate seated on a grassy hillside surrounded by other picnickers.

It was time for the cross-country marathon to begin and Greggory and
I wanted to get on the road ahead of the runners. Sokrates was returning
with friends to Anoghia. He clicked his heels and saluted. "Adios," he
said, and disappeared into the crowd.

The road was lined with spectators. In the first village we were delayed
a quarter hour by a traffic tie-up. When the same happened in the second
village we left our car to investigate. A man was making a speech in
the middle of the highway. Words like "demokratia" and "eleutheria
(freedom)," were greeted with waves of applause. We got a glimpse of the
orator, a ponderously heavy man who rocked on his toes as he talked.
Little children ran forward to present him with flowers and mothers extended their babies for his approval. His automobile, a black Ford, had
an official silver license frame. Quite obviously he was Mr. Big.

By the time we reached the third village the caravan of hooting autos
was a half-mile long. By not letting cars pass, the police were deliberately
making it appear as if the caravan of automobiles were a parade in Mr.
Big's honor. Indeed, maybe they were right, for no one was protesting.
Greggory revved the motor and we zoomed ahead. Caught by surprise
and seeing we were foreigners, the police let us pass. As we got closer
to Rethymnon, the waiting crowds grew larger. Whether it was for the
marathon runners or for Mr. Big that they waited, we could not tell.

Rethymnon looked like a city fortified for a bombardment and was
filled with an unpleasantly musky odor. The walls of brown bags which
lined the streets were not filled with sand but with carob beans, known in
English as St. John's bread. It was the season of their harvest and
Rethymnon was the carob center of Crete. The long brown pods had a
variety of commercial uses—an extract from them was used for a soft
drink, a chemical derivative went into the manufacture of photographic
film, and they were fed whole to sheep and cattle. Trucks loaded with
bags blocked roads, and streets piled with the stuff were reduced to one-
way lanes.

Our hotel, the Xenia, had heat, apparently the only hotel in Crete
that did, and after a passable lunch in the dining room we took a nap,
letting the dry warm air draw the damp and chill from our bones.
When we left the hotel we saw the black car of Mr. Big parked outside
filled with wilting bouquets, like a funeral coach. We crossed town to the
sports stadium where we had reserved seats. Outside, crowds watched
from the roofs of buildings and from distant hillsides. A cold wind blew
out the olympic flame burning on a pedestal in the field and an attendant

relit it. On the field athletes were pole-vaulting and throwing the javelin and discus. A military band was playing.

A gust of excitement swept over the stadium like a wind. The crowd cheered the first runner from Arkadiou, a twenty-year-old Athenian named Demetrios Vouros. Brown-skinned, heavy-thighed, he pranced around the track, waving his arms. The twenty-four kilometers had taken him seventy-three minutes.

In ten minutes number two, also Athenian, panting heavily and covered with sweat, galloped into the arena. Five minutes later when the third, a younger smaller youth, arrived, four young men hoisted him on their shoulders and carried him around the track. He was the crowd's favorite, a boy from Rethymnon, and the first Cretan to finish. The roaring welcome continued for eight minutes. Runners were arriving now at regular intervals but the crowd, losing interest in the race, turned its attention to the athletic games. Then suddenly the crowd rose to its feet and began to shout. I wondered what type of hero could whip up such a storm. A black automobile drove into the field and he who got out was neither an athlete nor a runner. It was the orator, Mr. Big who, rocking on his toes, waving a pudgy hand, reminded me of the late film comedian Oliver Hardy, whose films were still popular in Greece.

I asked a man beside me for the name of the crowd dazzler. It was Paul Vardinogiannis. He was a parliament deputy, a local son representing Rethymnon Province in Athens. In the recently-ousted Papandreou government he had been a minister. A protégé of the Venizelos family, he was the most powerful politician in Crete.

A military band played the national anthem. Platoons of soldiers, sailors, marines and uniformed women trooped by, followed by a review of American-built tanks and Mercedes-Benz trucks. Motorcycle troops rode on their machines standing on one leg, on one arm, standing on their heads on the handlebars and finally in human pyramids of thirteen men on each machine. Rockets zoomed and exploded in the heavens, a troop of military acrobats leaped over platforms, as gracefully adroit as the Minoan bull dancers in the Knossos paintings. Now and then a laggard marathon runner puffed into the arena but no one paid any attention.

It was six thirty and bitterly cold. A full moon rose over the stadium like an operetta prop, silhouetting the crowds on the rooftops. Still the turbulence continued. Bands of costumed folk dancers covered the field. Mr. Big loped into the field and took his place at the head of a chain of dancers. As the crowd hurrahed, the elliptical hulk of him, levitating buoyantly as if he were inflated with helium, led a chain of women across the field. The roar of the crowd, which could have been heard in heaven, continued until an explosion of fireworks brought the day to an end.

We went in search of food. Restaurants were jammed. The one we finally entered had a day's accumulation of litter and refuse on the floor. A grinning mustachioed waiter wearing a filthy apron asked if we were "Cherman." I replied we were Turks and he went roaring into the kitchen. The wine he brought was excellent and the lamb well-roasted.

Back in the hotel the military band was playing dance music on a terrace under our window. Out in the harbor a fleet of anchored battle-ships were strung with colored lights from prows to sterns. The melody was "Two Sleepy People" and among the dancers I saw Mr. Big floating on his toes, a beautifully costumed young woman in his arms. I was wondering about a sense of familiarity which had been haunting me through the afternoon. One so individual in appearance was not easily forgotten, and I tried to remember where I might have seen the man before.

A chambermaid came to turn down our beds and I asked her if Mr. Vardinogiannis had ever been to America. "Yes," she said. "He was President Kennedy's friend . . ."

Then it came to me. In November 1963 I had seen this unforgettable man on the television screen, walking with Queen Frederika in the funeral procession of John F. Kennedy. I watched him now, lilting with a girl in his arms, to "The Anniversary Waltz."

The drive west to Chania took us through a pastoral landscape as busy as an Umbrian painting. The sea was on our right, mauve and green mountains were on our left. Shepherd boys watched their sheep under the olives, two oxen pulled a wooden plow, a donkey carried firewood, an old woman returned from a well with water jars and another gathered herbs in a field. The scene had the innocent purity of Renaissance landscape turned Biblical by the pictures of Perugino and the Lippis. We drove through Episcopi—the birthplace of Paul Vardinogiannis—and Hora Sfakia, Neo Horio and Armeni, green villages shaded by sycamores like the maples of New England.

Chania, capital of Crete, is a handsome Venetian town with a horse-shoe-shaped "Little Harbor," lined with eighteenth-century houses, sailor taverns and an excellent restaurant. We lunched in the sunlight at a table on the quay with Esther Hitchens, one of a group of American writers who lived around the harbor. I asked a waiter the size of a flounder I was considering for my lunch. Measuring with his hands, he stammered, "Is . . . ah . . ." Blushing, he turned to Esther Hitchens, saying, "Excuse me please . . . is ten inches long." No Cretan man, said Esther, ever gave the measurement of anything without first apologizing to ladies present.

"Apparently he thinks every women is thinking constantly of the phallus," she said, "when it is obvious that he is thinking about it."

The flounder arrived not only with its head but all its viscera intact. A wildly mottled clan of fat harbor cats crowded around our table scrambling for the roasted guts. Eating the excellent fish and drinking a fine white wine called Clos Castelli, I felt like a cat king surrounded by courtiers.

Our purpose in Chania was to visit a bishop named Ereaneos, known for his efforts to improve Cretan life. I had heard him spoken of as "a saint" and "the red bishop"; his headquarters at Kastelli Kissamou was called by his critics, "Little Moscow." The next day we circled the blue gulf of Kissamou and were greeted in Kastelli by a young priest whose name was Ereaneos, the same as the bishop's. He had taken it while a student at Rethymnon where the elder Ereaneos was his theology professor. "I wanted to follow him always," said the young man. "So I decided to take his name." Ereaneos, Jr., was small, dark and handsome as an Arab. His beard was trimmed, his curly jet hair was neatly shingled and his teeth were white and perfect. He was one of those rare *religieux* whom the spirit of Christ has touched, who fulfill with their lives the ideal of goodness which is the essence of Christianity. Though past thirty, he had a youthful enthusiasm and buoyance, and a smiling inner radiance which reminded me of Fra Angelico's saints. He had studied in England, read English books, had English friends. Completely self-effacing, he gave all credit to the bishop. "He embraces all of life," said the young man in a softly gentle voice. "He takes care of his people, he changes their lives." When Ereaneos, Sr., came to Kastelli as bishop of western Crete, he found no electricians, no mechanics to provide services for his people. He wrote to the Council of Churches in New York which put him in touch with Pennsylvania Mennonites who sent two teachers, an electrician from Indiana and a mechanic from Germany. With them the bishop organized a class of eighteen boys, and Ereaneos, Jr., translated the lectures from English into Greek. Mennonites provided machines and tools. As the school grew, members of the first class became its teachers and in 1964 the bishop turned his thriving vocational school over to the Greek Education Administration. Now more than two hundred boys, aged thirteen to eighteen, were being taught electronics, printing, automotive mechanics and machine shop by nineteen teachers.

The bishop's next concern was for girls. He enrolled forty-five in home economics classes, training them for rural housewifery. Next he took on the education of the younger boys and girls of the villages. Because there were no high schools in the villages an education beyond elementary school was impossible for many. To meet this problem the bishop built hostels for boys and for girls near existing high schools. His latest project was an agricultural school and model dairy farm to train boys in modern farming methods, at the same time providing dairy foods and meat for the student hostels. In a few days the bishop was expecting twelve Holstein dairy cows by airplane from Pennsylvania, plus a bull and some pigs. Ereaneos, Jr., said, "We wish to bring a new kind of life to our country families. We want boys to get over the idea that it is a curse to work in the fields, we want to dissuade them from going to Germany. With new machinery and new ways we hope to interest them in the land, to persuade them to stay at home."

He showed us a foundry, electric, blacksmith and carpentry shops, a weaving center where girls operated looms and knitting machines, a print shop where students were hand-setting one of the bishop's lectures, entitled "The Political Responsibilities of a Christian."

I asked Ereaneos, Jr., the source of the money which paid for the laboratories and workshops. "The money comes from all over the world," he said, smiling. "Perhaps God sends it." The mysterious force was the bishop. An indefatigable and persuasive letter writer, and a dynamic energist who personally followed everything to its completion, he seemed well equipped for social evolution.

We met him at lunch. He entered the room swiftly, a man in a hurry. He was small with a white beard, graying mustaches, lively eyes and an electrifying personality. He was wearing a black biretta at a rakish angle and gold chains over his vestments. I was startled to see how much the two Ereaneoses resembled one another, how like father and son. They were the same size and had the same wide brow and dark flashing eyes. Their personalities, however, differed. The elder Ereaneos had a solid command of practical matters; in contrast the younger was a dreamer and scholar. Complementing one another, they were able to work harmoniously together.

Ereaneos, Sr., who spoke no English, channeled his conversation through Ereaneos, Jr. "Jesus Christ is not only the bridegroom of our souls and our metaphysical redeemer," he said. "He is also the redeemer of the world. As Christians we are committed to fight for an ideal kingdom on earth. While a church has not the right to interfere in politics in a factional spirit, it has the duty to enlighten its people. It must stand peaceably between the passions and recriminations of powers and governments and bring to them the light of Christianity's great and eternal principles."

The bishop apologized for a "modest" lunch which turned into a banquet of fish, stuffed vine leaves, peppers and tomatoes, cheeses, fruit, yoghurt and a variety of wines and liqueurs. He spoke of his friendship with Nikos Kazantzakis and it was easy to see how the writer, who often criticized the clergy, would have admired this Dostoievskian holy man. The bishop said, "A priest must build his life on a love that is true and real—otherwise the church becomes an obstacle to a genuine human experience." Speaking of his critics in the church, he said, "Anyone who has not married, built a home, or buried someone he loves, knows nothing about life." It did not seem to occur to him that such a statement from a bachelor priest might puzzle a listener. He was worried about the cows flying from Pennsylvania, and he wondered if they would become ill in flight. I suggested that the air-bound animals would probably be given tranquilizers. "Flying cows," he said, shaking his head. "The apocalypse is with us, the millennium will arrive in Crete with those cows." I mentioned the rumors in Iraklion that he might be elevated to an archbishopric. "Ah yes," he said merrily. "Haven't you discovered that every Greek wants to be a captain?"

In the afternoon we went with Ereaneos, Jr., to the bishop's farm where five American Mennonite college students were building a barn and pig stall for the imminent livestock. Their leader, red-cheeked twenty-four-year-old Roger Beck of Ohio, said, "You come here with an undefined reason, not knowing quite why. When you find out how much you're needed, then you know why you're here." His assistant, lanky twenty-three-year-old Harold Groff from Colorado, said, "It's good to get away from America, to meet less fortunate people and to look back at America through their eyes." The volunteers were paid fifteen dollars a month and observed a strict Mennonite regime of no smoking, no drinking and no consorting with native women. Of their influence on Cretans, Ereaneos, Jr., said, "The people are astonished. We have an impression of Americans as being rich, pleasure-loving and self-indulgent. These young men are hard-working, friendly and kind. It is hard for us to believe that Americans can be like this, that they should sacrifice themselves to help us."

Our next stop was the bishop's hostel for boys, on a hillside overlooking the sea. Nearby was the fortified monastery of Goniái, the monks of which fought Turks during the three-hundred-year occupation and in this century battled Germans. The abbot's sister served us *raki* and sweets and showed us Turkish cannon balls embedded in the old walls. Schoolboys were watching an American bulldozer breaking ground for a new International Education Center. Ereaneos, Jr., joined them. "Look," he cried with childlike excitement. "It goes along like a great pig tearing up the earth." In a study hall the schoolboys greeted us with speeches and spirited songs, including a patriotic ballad called "Omalos" about a victorious battle with Turks. Beside me a clean-faced young priest sat with crossed legs, his hands telescoped into his sleeves, his eyes lowered like a shy nun's, and I remembered Henry Miller writing that a Greek priest was a fusion of male and female, a kind of spiritual hermaphrodite. Small boys crowded around the priest and around Ereaneos, struggling to sit on their laps and to kiss them. The blushing priests and happy children were like a painting of paradisaic innocence.

Our hotel, the Xenia, was brand-new, unheated and incompetently staffed by inexperienced natives. It was nonetheless a lively place, for its bar was popular with American sailors stationed at nearby Suda Bay, and the hotel's guests included sixteen adventuresome young Englishmen who were in Crete with helicopters for the purpose of spraying olive trees. It was the sprayers' third season in Crete; they had been there for four months and were homesick for England. They sprayed sugar beets against fungus and wheat against smut but most of their operation was against the *dacos,* a fly which lays its eggs on unripened olives. The trees were sprayed with a combination of DDT and sugar to bait the flies. The sprayers had problems. A shepherd thought a low-flying craft was an attack on his sheep and shot 180 buckshot holes into its fuselage. Up-sweeping air currents in the mountains were a hazard and one helicopter had crashed. When the sprayers missed a village because of defective maps, the inhabitants began a feud with a neighboring village which they believed had instructed the pilots to bypass them. The most critical of the young Englishmen's problems seemed to be a lack of girls. "Cretan girls are pretty and very well developed," said Geoffrey Bond, a twenty-one-year-old sprayer. "But we're not allowed within shouting distance." One young pilot who did get within communication distance on a beach was stalked by the girl's knife-carrying brother and had to be rescued by his colleagues.

The homesick sprayers kept the Xenia lobby roaring with Beatle records which they played on a portable phonograph. The records had an appreciative listener named Edwina Gilbey, eighteen-year-old bride of a gray-haired fiftyish archaeology professor on sabbatical from an Ohio University. She was a poutingly pretty child with long blonde hair who had been the professor's student. She called him "Daddy" and he called her "Baby." When I met them John Lennon's voice was crying:

> I mean I got a lot to give,
> And I'll give it all you you . . .

"Isn't it . . . I mean . . . gee whiz . . . he *relates,*" Edwina gasped. She spoke in disconnected phrases to which she brought a curious rhythm by emphasizing certain words. She tasted a whisky sour. "It isn't *soury*," she said. "I mean . . . what is a whisky sour . . . like when it isn't *soury?*" The golden whorls of her hair lay in loose waves on her leather jacket. Her mascara-laden lashes drooped heavily over her gray eyes. She began to giggle. "Like when I *drink* . . . well, you know . . . *everything* is . . . I mean *real wild* . . . like out there at the digs . . . I mean, well . . . a *luster bath* . . . without any *water* . . . how can you take a bath *without* water?" The professor patiently explained that a Minoan lustra bath was an exposure to the earth's radiant forces. "Well, for *gosh* sakes," said Edwina. "I mean . . . without water it's . . . you know . . . real *crazy.*"

Late that night when I went to bed Edwina was sitting on the stairs winding her long hair around her wrist, listening to a Beatle sobbing:

> Tell me why you cri-aaa-ed,
> And why you li-aaa-ed to me . . .

"Daddy went to bed," said Edwina. "He thinks I'm *crazy* . . . but I just can't *stand* . . . I mean like not hearing . . . my favorite yum *yummiest* record in the *whole world* . . . makes me . . . well . . . you know . . . sort of all *burpy* inside . . ."

We met the Gilbeys for breakfast. Edwina was wearing her hair in a sort of Madame Butterfly bouffant into which the professor had placed a chrysanthemum. Edwina took it out, saying, "This is . . . you know . . . kind of *deadlike* . . . I want a real fluffy *fluff* one." She ordered "something real yum *yummy*" and the waiter brought her fried batter-cakes soaked in honey. After breakfast we set out, Greggory, the Gilbeys and myself, for Crete's most inaccessible scenic attraction, the Gorge of Samaria. The journey took us through rich valleys of ripening oranges and up a winding red dirt road into the mountains. "I guess there's *oil* on this island," said Edwina. "I mean . . . *oil* is in deserty places . . . and this sure as hell is *deserty*. . . ." We passed through Lakki, a windy, dusty village perched on a ridge. Winding through a pass, we saw the shimmer of the southern sea. "I mean . . . well, for God's sake . . . *look,*" Edwina cried. Ahead were three helicopters and two tank trucks belonging to the English sprayers. Geoffrey Bond told us because of the high wind they were giving up for the day. Driving on through the billowing dust, we had to stop for a single file of goats, and then entering into an alpine wilderness, we passed shepherds' huts hardly distinguishable in the stony landscape. The wind was wintry cold and the sky a tumult of black clouds. We entered the Omalos plain about which the bishop's schoolboys had sung, where a band of Cretans had trapped a Turkish platoon. We stopped at a shepherds' hostel, a cement block structure standing in bleak solitude. Inside five shepherds and a policeman were huddled around a stove. The shepherds sat in unclipped sheepskins with crooks between their legs. A woman in dark homespuns served us *raki* and mountain tea. A fat brown puppy climbed into Edwina's lap and went to sleep. "I mean . . . well . . . isn't it just the *cutest,*" crooned Edwina, cuddling the puppy. "Sort of . . . you know . . . it could be a *real* baby. . . ." The tea, called *malotira,* was made of marjoram and thickened with honey. Sipping it, Edwina said, "Isn't it just . . . I mean . . . *mediciney* . . . like it's *got* to be good for you." The woman brought a plate of roasted pumpkin seeds which we painstakingly peeled. Edwina began to giggle. "Wouldn't it . . . I mean . . . well, you know . . . like *what* if they . . . well, sort of *grew* inside you . . . like being *pregnant* . . . with a *pumpkin,* my gosh!"

We drove on across the plateau toward gray Dolomites-like mountains until the road ended suddenly at the northern entrance to the gorge. We got out and looked down into the ravine. "Chrrrrist!" gasped Edwina. "I mean . . . going like up a *gangplank* even . . . makes me feel . . . you know . . . *pukey* . . . I don't *feel* well . . ." She bolted back into the car, slammed the door and refused to come back out. "I'm not . . . I mean like going," she said. "I'm *staying.*" The three of us started down the canyon, clinging to roots and branches to keep from catapulting over the stones. We had walked about a half hour when a great boom of thunder cannonaded up and down the gorge. As we approached the bottom the path became easier. There was another crash of thunder and rain began to fall lightly. We trudged on. The rain thickened. The top of the canyon was no longer visible. All we could see were flat gray walls on both sides.

We gave up and started the slippery climb back. Forty-five minutes later we emerged on the Omalos ledge, soaked to the skin. "You know . . . well, I mean . . . I *told* you," said Edwina. The car heater was on and she had changed the style of her hair, which was parted in an inverted V, a gothic steeple framing her beaded eyes and turning her face into a pouting triangle. We piled into the car. Edwina drew herself into a corner. "You're making me . . . I mean . . . all so doggy *wet.*" Rain was falling in hard gray sheets. We drove slowly to Lakki where we stopped at a café filled with men waiting out the rain. We bought some *raki* and spread our salami, eggs, cheese and fruit on a table. "You know," said Edwina happily, "well, I mean . . . this is . . . but really . . . the yum yummiest *inside* picnic I ever was *at.*" From a bush outside the café the professor plucked a long white blossom known as "angel's-trumpet" and brought it to her. "Really . . . I mean . . . gosh . . . it's just *too*

too . . . you can't . . . I mean put it in a place like your *hair* . . . where
in *hell* would you put it?" We waited for the rain to stop and returned
slowly over muddy roads to Chania.

In the morning Greggory and I departed for Phaestos. A four-lane
highway south from Rethymnon began smoothly, rising up through a rocky
tundra to a high pastoral plateau. We passed over a purple-heathered
mountain and descended into the tree-shaded town of Spíli, filled with
sounds of falling water. After Spíli the good road came to an end. For an
hour we crawled over stones, stopping for bulldozers to clear the way of
rubble or to fill a gully so we might pass. It was night when we arrived
at Timbákion, a flat ugly town near the sea. The road north to Iraklion
was the best in Crete. We followed it for several miles, looking for
Phaestos, which the map showed to be on our right, where we planned
to spend the night in a tourist pavilion. We drove on, looking for a sign,
passing at one point a flock of sheep whose green eyes shone like a
thousand-eyed demon of mythology, arriving finally at the agricultural
town of Mires where a policeman told us we had passed Phaestos.
Backtracking eight kilometers, we turned from the highway into a dark
country lane and drove to its end. We walked in the darkness around a
hill and there, in a glow of light, was the pavilion.

It was small and filled with people. The lady manager gave us the
alternative of sharing a dormitory of ten beds with a mixed party of men
and women, or sleeping on cots which she offered to set up in the dining
room.

We chose the dining room. My bed, a thin pallet, sagged like an old
hammock. In spite of it I sank into a deep sleep from which I was
awakened at eight o'clock by sunlight flooding the room. The ancient
palace was outside the window. The sun beaming through rifts in the
clouds covered the plain of Mesara with golden light. As we were break-
fasting on the porch on bread and honey and coffee, a bus arrived and
unloaded passengers, including a gray sparrow of a man, hardly more
than five feet tall, weighing perhaps a hundred pounds, carrying a rolled
umbrella. Looking around, he spotted us on the porch and hopped up the
steps, saying, "Ich bin Alexandros."

I had guessed it. He was Alexandros Venetikos, the multilingual guide
who escorted Henry Miller over the ruins in 1939 and became a character
in Miller's book. "Sprechen Deutsch?" he asked. No, I said, English.
"Vous are American? Me very good friend mit Henry Miller big writer.
Come letter every month, call me Brother Alexandros. Put in book
Alexandros. Make famous." He was sixty-two years old and he had
been a guide at Phaestos for thirty-three years. "I make for you explains

in leedle English, un poco Italiane, une peu Français, ein bitzen Deutsch."
They were, I said, languages I understood. "Very buon," he said. Taking
a Napoleonic stance beside our table, he waved his umbrella toward the
green plain. "Is Mesara, meaning middle von berg. Mt. Ida on north and
Mt. Asterousia on south." We followed him into the palace. "Alles is
maybes," he began. "Phaestos haben maybe three period. Early before
two thousand Christ is builded King Minos, first city of Creta, schreiben
by Homer. Mittel period to Christ. Hellenistic to three hundred after
Christ. Is four palace, one under other." Phaestos, I had read in my guide,
was discovered in 1900 by the Italian School in Athens and, except during
wars, excavations have continued ever since. The palace, smaller than
Knossos, was more strongly built. Pointing with his umbrella, Alexandros
led us through passages hardly wide enough to pass. "Warum small?" he
asked in school masterish tones. "Very small people. Roads ein meter.
Bench very small, tombs very little. Why? Is all klein peoples like
Alexandros. Maybe sleep sideways." He curled inside a tomb to demonstrate the position of a corpse. Then he pointed to a water reservoir,
saying, "Water is all from rain put together." Using his umbrella as a
vaulting pole, he leaped over stones and darted in and out of corridors
like a child in a game, never stopping his breathless monologue. "Please
look small room. Find here big bronze messer, is maybe to sacrifice.
Maybe. All is maybes. Here find vasen mit black wheat. Another vasen
mit swaztika. Not like Hitler but a sonnenzeichnis. Maybe vasen for
olive oil. Maybe wine. Maybes. In this room is sleeping king's servants."
Alexandros lay down, pantomiming sleep. "Very small like Alexandros."
Leaping up he led us into a tiny cell. "Is olive-oil room. Look please the
drain. Why? Maybe a vasen broken, oil spill, is for drain away. Very
practical people." He tapped his umbrella on a mortar stone. "Here
broken olives for pressing oil, same as in big fabrika today." The
umbrella pointed to a fragment of wall. "Prego schauen. Between stones
and mud is straw. Pourquois? Because is good insulation. Is in winter sehr
kalt in Phaestos. Is summer very hot. So insulation like today in Norweg
and Deutschland. All columns upside down cypress, small under big top.
Warum? So rain run down. Maybe. Only maybes." He led us through a
doorway so small he had to bend his head. "Look, please, Queen's
alabaster toilet. Queen sitzen Turkish style, she not sitzen on toilet, she
sitzen herself on feet. Here lustra bath. Not wash with much water. Come
here all king's family and make wash with little spritz holy water." He
made a spraying movement with his hands. "Maybes. All maybes. When
is kalt all king's family sitzen here in verandah in sun. Maybe is window
alabaster, maybe is goatskin. All maybes." The umbrella pointed to a

fragment of color on the wall. "Look, is once frescoe ganz wall. Now finished. Many years wind and rain. Catastrophes."

I asked what catastrophes had befallen Phaestos. Alexandros shrugged, opening his hands in a gesture of helplessness. "Maybe earthquake, maybe fire, maybe war, maybe Dorians. Maybes, all maybes." We were nearing the end of our tour. "Alexandros is sorry is not very clear the head today," he said. "Full of troubles. Very bad mein leben. My madame is in hospital Iraklion with no knee, only gypsum. In my house is nine people leben in one room." We gave him a hundred drachmae and he bowed us off like a Japanese concierge. "Please come back another day when Alexandros has better head for guide. Please say good greetings from Little Alexandros to his brother big Mr. Miller . . ." As we drove away we heard his voice calling, "Please remember, archaeology is all maybes, only maybes . . ."

From Phaestos it was a five-minute drive to still another Minoan palace called Haghia Triada. The name, meaning "Holy Trinity," comes from a small church standing above the palace site. Here the guard, a sleepy youthful man named Antonios Markakis, seemed to resent having his midday slumbers disturbed. "Phaestos is an army of tourists," he said. "Haghia Triada is solitude." He was a painter who used the small tourist pavilion as a studio and preferred visitors to stay away. His paintings were charming Rousseau-like primitives of the ruins and the local fauna and flora. He was saving them, he said, for a show in Athens. I persuaded him to part with a picture of a pair of partridges against the fuchsia background of a Cretan sunset. We went to see the ruins and he went back to sleep.

With no distracting babble we were able to wander up and down corridors and stairways, through arcades and courtyards, and afterward we sat in the sun on a terrace facing a romantic landscape. In its time the palace faced the sea. Since then the waters have receded two miles, leaving a lush steamingly fertile valley of orange groves, olives and cypresses, with the white solid forms of chapels scattered among the trees. Birds sang in the vines, and the wind sighed in the pines. Beyond in the horizon of the sea lay the African desert. We left on soft feet so as not to awaken the sleeping guard.

Across the Mesara valley on the slope of a snow-covered mountain a bright new village shone in the sunlight. The white and blue houses clustered around a church were no ordinary village. Most of its residents are girls from four to eighteen years of age, orphans brought there by a bishop named Timotheus. Like Bishop Ereaneos of Kastelli, Timotheus is a native of Rethymnon. Both priests studied humanities at the University of Paris and both returned to apply the humanism of Christ to life in their native island. In his western diocese Ereaneos began with a boy's school. In the south Timotheus turned his attention to homeless girls. At the entrance to Timotheus' village I saw a husky priest, his dusty sleeves rolled back, carrying stones for a new wall which he was building with some workmen. I asked for the bishop and the priest, wiping sweat from his dust-streaked face with the back of his muscular arm, directed me to the bishop's office under a long arcade beyond a garden.

The office was empty. It was a large blue and white room sparsely furnished with a desk, two chairs, some holy pictures, and pots of philodendron plants and red amaryllis. The office opened on a garden bright with autumn asters, chrysanthemums and fuchsia. Birds sang from a row of cages hanging in the sun. A pretty girl about fifteen years old entered with coffee and candied fruit for me and then, bowing silently, departed. While I was drinking the coffee a gray-haired grandmotherly woman entered and introduced herself in English. She was Christine Artamakis, a Greek-American from Chicago. She and her husband had come after his retirement to Crete where she served the bishop as translator, English teacher and as a surrogate mother to the girls. She spoke of the bishop with the soft-voiced veneration of a disciple. "When he came here there was only the church and a stable," she said. "All that you see he built with his own hands. Whenever he collects enough money he begins a new building. He started in 1956 with twenty girls. Today there are sixty-five. He has built a school, a convent for the nun teachers, and a home for old people. He works all day and he studies at night. He sleeps very little and doesn't eat much food. We think he must be sustained by the grace of God."

At that moment the priest I had met in the fields entered, scrubbed, combed and wearing a clean robe. "You are welcome," he said, taking my hand. I was not surprised that he was the bishop—the thought had occurred to me while listening to Mrs. Artamakis. A cheerful heavy man, he hardly seemed an ascetic subsisting on spiritual manna. A drooping left eye gave him a curiously diabolical appearance. It was the result, he said, of a wound while fighting Germans in the occupation. "I love you Americans," he said, speaking Greek, which Mrs. Artamakis translated. "America is a proof that Christianity has not died from the earth. For two decades since the war you have held the future of the world in your hands. It is evidence of your Christian love."

He humbled me, this holy man, for I was thinking of other motives sometimes assigned to America. The bishop's favorite subject was ecumenicism, about which he wrote articles in a magazine, *Rebirth,* printed by his students. "The function of the clergy must change if Christianity is to survive," he said. "We learn from the mistakes of Christian history. We must return to the spirit of the early Christians, to the simple service of love which was Christ's mission on earth. The Church has failed in history because of its earthly ambitions, because Christians lacked a mutual purpose to fight atheistic materialism. Now at last the Church is being brought together. Communication and transportation—the mighty jet planes, radio and television, the telstars—all help to bring our ecumenical goal. For the new fraternity of the people on the earth, for a resurgence of human love, we must put aside our dogma differences and meet in the humanistic spirit of our common faith. One shepherd—one flock. That is the Christian goal, and America is leading the way, America is bringing it about."

I was too moved to reply. I wanted desperately to believe what the bishop was saying, to share his vision of the world. But I was not he. He was a holy man from another age, able to bring to the human chaos about him a passion to move worlds.

Mrs. Artamakis took me on a tour of the village, to dormitories with rows of beds, each with a doll perched on its pillow, gifts from the United States Air Force at Iraklion, to sewing rooms filled with whirring machines at which girls were making their own clothes, a weaving room where they operated looms and knitting machines, a new classroom which the girls were whitewashing with lime they stirred in a kettle outside the door, a home economics kitchen where they were cooking the noon meal, a press room where they printed their magazine. We walked through vegetable and flower gardens, groves of ripening oranges, lemons and tangerines and vineyards. "He planted them all," said Mrs. Artamakis. "Every tree and vine." In the home for the aged, old men and women were gathering for lunch. "Old people are more difficult than children," said Mrs. Artamakis. "If one gets a bigger fish than the others, they think you love him more." Finally we visited the museum, a touching collection of pictures and artifacts gathered by the girls, and dominated by a large framed photograph of John F. Kennedy. "He is the hero of the school," said Mrs. Artamakis. "On the anniversary of his death we hold a memorial service."

The bishop was back with the workmen, shoveling cement into a mixer. He invited me to lunch and apologized for its modesty. We ate red mullet, veal chops, potatoes, salad, fruit and plenty of wine. The bishop was in a jolly mood. He had just learned of the engagement of one of his "daughters."

"No doubt you have seen that our girls are very pretty," he said. "We don't hide them. When a boy likes a girl he speaks to me. He is allowed to see her. When there is an engagement we arrange for a dowry. Sixteen girls have been married in our church. Not only do I perform the ceremony, I am also the father of the bride. Fifteen children in Crete call me 'Grandfather.'"

He spoke of the war. "In the village of Skourvoula the men were hiding so the Germans shot thirty women. In Kándanos the Germans molested old ladies in their beds and then poured oil over the town and set fire to it." These were stories I'd heard before. "The Germans are the army of Lucifer in the world," the bishop said. "The Americans are the soldiers of Christ." His view of the world was an Armageddon of good and evil armies fighting a holy battle.

At the gate he embraced and blessed me. When I drove away I saw him roll up his sleeves and pick up a sack of cement.

I joined Greggory at Phaestos and we started north toward Iraklion. After ten miles we came upon a green valley of olive groves on the banks of a small stream. The sun falling between the leaves dappled the green earth where sheep grazed, and here and there, like forgotten tombstones in the grass, stood fragments of marble columns and pedestals. They were the remains of Gortyna, the Doric city which conquered Phaestos and which became the Roman capital of Crete.

It would have been easy to miss. The only monument visible from the highway is a roofless basilica called Haghis Titos, a red-brick arch and dome silhouetted against blue sky, like a set for a romantic ballet.

We descended through rushes toward the stream, called Lethaios, into a Roman odeon where we faced one of the important monuments of Crete, a stone wall carved with the law code of Gortyna. The curved limestone, forty feet wide and man-high, was engraved in the fifth century B.C. with seventeen thousand inch-high characters snaking in a zigzag from left to right and right to left. Scholars have deciphered and translated the Doric Cretan dialect and an English professor, R. F. Willetts, has written a book about it. The laws deal with four categories of persons: free men grouped in hetairiae, free men independent of communal marriages, peasants who were bound to the land, and slaves. The adoption of children (described as an imitation of childbirth) and inheritance are set forth in detail. The paternity of illegitimate children is established. Rape, seduction and adultery were not criminal offenses but matters for monetary compensation. Youths were required by law to marry and a divorced wife was awarded her children.

Few places in Greece moved me so deeply as this foundation of Western law in a quiet cove in the rushes. In the rustic arcadia around us, sheep bells tinkled, water rippled over stones, birds chirped in the cypresses. Two lambs, one white and one black, gamboled like puppies, and butterflies floated like flower petals in the autumn light. We heard a softly wailing pipe, and it seemed for a moment as if Daphnis and Chloë must be there languishing under the trees. Beyond the Lethaios was an old mill and in the doorway, blowing into a flute, was a mustachioed old man wearing Turkish-style bloomers and a fringed scarf on his head. He bounded down the path to greet us, handing us cards which said he was miller, bagpiper, guide and archaeologist. He invited us into the mill, a small dark room like a womb in the earth, smelling sweetly of grinding wheat. The miller's wife, a sprightly little woman younger than he, was spinning thread from wool on a stick. Falling waters chortled over the mill wheel and the grinding stone rumbled. The miller blew on his bagpipe, a white pigskin with its four legs protruding ludicrously. It did not matter that the performance was a show hurriedly improvised for us. We might have been in the cave of a primal Adam and Eve, participating in the creation of bread and cloth and music, of all the needs of man.

Unlike other archaeological places, Gortyna is no mausoleum, no sacred place of death, but a green living valley offering replenishing olives, figs and wheat to the sowers and harvesters who inhabit it. Only 5 per cent of the old city has been excavated. We found columns in a potato field and hidden by vines, a headless armless draped figure of a woman on which the severed neck formed a small bowl in which birds bathed. We followed an avenue of Corinthian pediments resting on the ground, as if the columns were still there in the earth with only the tops visible, and we came upon an agora and the red-brick shell of a Roman temple. In a sunken temple we found a fallen statue of Pan on which the erect phallus pointed heavenward. We heard merry laughter above and we looked up into the faces of three young women who were picking olives. I wondered what those girls, beating so fiercely the branches with their poles, made of the tumescent stone asleep in the grass and if they ever returned at night with real Pans, hot-blooded, with quickening flesh. Imagining the scene by moonlight, the white columns among the olives, I almost swooned.

From Gortyna the road began at once its mountain ascent. Near the summit, in the Askyphou Pass, we were hailed by a dark man standing beside his car. We hesitated. It was a lonely windswept place and no other autos were in sight. Stories of banditry were on our minds. But the man seemed in distress. He was well-dressed in a business suit and his car was a Mercedes.

In Greek and fragmentary German he explained he was on his way to Timbákion from Iraklion where he had forgotten to pay a debt. Would we, he asked, deliver some money to his creditor. He counted out 8187 drachmae and put them into an envelope upon which he wrote a name, Helias Mariakis, and the address of a foundry on Avgoustos

Street. He thanked us, shook our hands and got into his car. Waving, he drove away.

It all happened so quickly that it was only when we were ourselves driving northward, that I remembered the man had not told us his name or had asked for ours, that he had not even looked at our license plates. As we descended through miles of vineyards toward the city, I became suspicious of the envelope in my pocket, suspecting some trick. In the city we drove at once to Avgoustos Street, to the address on the envelope. A large dark man was alone in the shop. We asked if he was Helias Mariakis. He was not. The bearer of the name was his friend and would be back in an hour. We explained our errand and he said he would give the money to his friend. We left the envelope. I found myself haunted by new anxieties. Would Helias Mariakis get the money? Should we have asked for a signed receipt?

So great was my concern that I called on Kostas Grammatikakis and told him the story. I had no need to worry, he said. The favor asked was not unusual, the money would go to the rightful owner. "In Crete we trust," he said. The innocence this time was my own.

XIII

An Agricultural Feast

"Because Thanksgiving is an agricultural feast, it's the only American holiday we celebrate at the American Farm School," wrote Bruce Lansdale. "Why don't you come?"

I had a second reason for wanting to return to Thessaloniki. I had promised the young dairyman, Alex Marlis, to help him go to Wisconsin. In this I had received no encouragement at the American Embassy. "How long have you been in Greece?" a Greek lady secretary in the emigration office asked me.

She laughed when I told her. "Only one month!" she said. "I don't know why, but every American wants to take a Greek home as a souvenir." I tried to explain that "a souvenir" was not quite what I had in mind. "Greeks who go to Germany usually come back," she said. "Those who go to the U.S. are lost to Greece. That's why our government makes it as difficult for young men to leave as the U.S. makes it difficult for them to enter. The whole thing is quite impossible." The opposition of two governments seemed formidable odds. In my mind I was trying to picture the young farmer who loved land and cattle in a German factory. There was nothing to lose and a great deal to gain, and I decided to gamble.

The day before Thanksgiving I drove north through a tumultuous Wagnerian landscape. The low heavens were dark and wet and snow covered the mountains. Banks of blinding white clouds, rising out of the valleys as if from a subterranean furnace, clung to the mountain

157

walls. Sprouting wheat fields were emerald green. In Thessaly women
picked cotton beside a meadow in which wool-bearing sheep grazed.
Gypsy colonies, smoke curling from wigwams, looked like Indian villages.

It was night when I drove through Thessaloniki, and raining. At the
Farm School I found students in a restless holiday mood. The older
boys were rehearsing a Thanksgiving program. In the dormitory Alex
Marlis was monitoring the younger ones who, unable to sleep, were
talking and laughing in their beds. "I try to help them not to make noise,"
he said. "But it is impossible."

At eleven the next morning I joined the American consul general
and other visitors in the school auditorium for the Thanksgiving service.
Small smiling boys ushered us to our seats. The room was decorated with
cutouts of Pilgrims and turkeys, and, wreathed in flowers, photographs
of the King and Queen and President Johnson. A Greek flag hung to
the right, an American flag to the left. Spilling out from a huge cornu-
copia at the foot of the stage was a mound of pumpkins, corn, squash,
melons, potatoes and onions. On the curtain was a painting of a man
sowing and another harvesting, and the words:

> We thank thee then, O Father
> For all things Bright and Good,
> The seed time and the harvest,
> Our life, our health, our food.

The program opened with a blessing by the school's Orthodox priest,
and the hymn, "For the beauty of the earth, For the glory of the
skies. . . ." Bruce Lansdale read the 121st Psalm, beginning, "I will lift
up mine eyes unto the hills . . ." and the consul read the President's
Thanksgiving proclamation. Then it was time for the student pageant.
Like the chorus in a play by Aeschylus, a group of boys, each speaking
a single line, narrated the Thanksgiving story.

> Nearly three hundred and fifty years ago a group
> of one hundred pipple left England in a small
> sheep called the Mey*flower* . . .
> They had traveled a long way . . .
> Some had died . . .
> It was December and very cold . . .
> They had no homes . . .
> And very little food . . .
> But they were thankful . . .
> They gathered together to ask God's blessing . . .

The chorus sang, "We gather together to ask the Lord's blessing. . . ."
Listening to the familiar words so vigorously sung by accented young
voices, my own voice failed and my eyes filled with tears. The story
continued:

> The first winter was turr-ible . . .
> One-half the pipple died . . .
> Some of starvation . . .
> Many from cold . . .
> They hardly had strength to bury the dead . . .
> But they had faith . . .
> And their faith was rewarded . . .

The curtain opened on a scene of cold desolation with four boys in
Pilgrim costumes—black knee-length suits, white socks and collars and
high-crowned black hats, carrying broad-muzzled blunderbusses.
"How can we be thankful on empty stomachs?"
"We must return to England."
A dark-skinned boy in a loincloth and a grand headdress of feathers
approached. The Pilgrims raised their guns.
"What do you want, Red Man?"
"I bring food."
The Indian waved a hand and four bare-skinned youths appeared
bearing fruits, vegetables and a turkey.
"I bring fruit from Injun children."
"I bring corn from Injun squaws."
"I bring turkey from Injun braves."
"We understand suffering too . . ."
The chorus took up the story:

> Spring came . . .
> Pilgrims began to clear the land . . .
> The Indians helped them . . .
> They taught the Pilgrims to plant corn . . .
> And to hunt turkey . . .
> They harvested their crops . . .
> They built houses . . .
> They were safe, they were thankful . . .
> And they had a beeg feast. . . .

The curtain opened on Pilgrims gathered around a table so heavily
heaped with pumpkins, corn, cabbages, apples, oranges and leeks, it
threatened to collapse.
"This winter we will live and eat well."

"We have much to be thankful for."

On stage appeared a most astonishing band of Indians. Young braves in loincloths and feathers had streaked their skins wildly with paint. "Squaws" in blond wigs and Turkish scarves had gigantic bobbing breasts, bawdily parodying Anita Ekberg, Brigitte Bardot and the other mammary queens. The uproar in the hall did not subside for several minutes. In the front row the Orthodox priest shook with laughter.

"We come as friends," said the Indians in unison, and the Pilgrims replied:

> You have saved our lives . . .
> We have set aside today to be a day of Thanksgiving . . .
> With turkey . . .
> And crenberry sauce . . .
> And pumpin pie . . .
> And prayers . . .

An Indian stepped forward and, addressing the audience, said, "Will you please join us in singing 'My Country 'Tis of Thee'?"

I walked in the gardens. It was perfect Thanksgiving weather. The sun was bright. A bitter wind rattled the chrysanthemums on their stalks and bent the zinnias and asters. The terrible sense of loneliness that descends on a traveler in a foreign land at holiday time had been dispelled and in its place I felt another emotion, an overwhelming sense of human warmth. Never in any of the great theaters of the world, nor in any temple of worship, had I been more moved. Never in a lifetime of holidays had the message of Thanksgiving been made so clear to me as it was by these earnest farm boys in a foreign land.

I joined the guests for martini cocktails, and then crossed the campus to the dormitories where three hundred places were set for dinner. The large hall was noisy and festive. Windows were decked with ivy, cedar and ears of corn. I was seated at a table with the consul and Bruce Lansdale, and two sweet white-haired Quaker ladies from England who were shocked that the Pilgrims in the Thanksgiving play had been allowed to carry guns. "It's the American influence," said one wistfully. "You are all so military-minded." Senior students in Sunday suits were waiters, serving traditional turkey, cranberries, salads, pies. One of the Quaker ladies asked me, "Do you keep a *real* Christmas in America?" We try, I said. A chorus of boys began to sing lustily, "When the Saints Go Marching In." "Isn't that a hymn?" asked the Quaker lady beside me and her friend said, "But they don't sing it like a hymn." The time for hymns was over and the boys, smooth-shaven, black-eyed and handsome as cinema stars, sang on, belting "My Bonnie Lies over the Ocean," "Oh, Susannah" and "I've Been Working on the Railroad." In the end the cheering youths carried the school chef, a fat laughing man, through the hall on their shoulders, and the students burst into such a crescendo of hand clapping, yelling and foot stomping that the teachers had to blow police whistles to bring them back to order. "Is it an American tradition?" asked a Quaker lady.

The next day I went with Bruce Lansdale to a community development conference in the mountain village of Sochos, fifty miles north of Thessaloniki. The meeting was one of several sponsored by the Agriculture Ministry in key communities for village leaders of surrounding areas. We passed new oil refineries and an aluminum plant. "Industry has come to a few urban centers," said Bruce. "But Greece will remain agricultural. No Greek is happy working in a factory. He fiercely loves his liberty and no matter how poor he is, he'd rather be his own landlord on a bit of land. That is why these conferences are so important."

Bruce, who has lived most of his life in Greece, said, "To understand the Greek villager, one must be aware of three qualities which are the backbone to his character. He has a deep practical wisdom which does not come from education but from the experience of his hard life. He is passionately devoted to his surroundings, his sheep, his land, and his mountains. Finally, he feels that he and his nation have a divine mission in the world, that he is a bearer of past glories which will one day return. Such instincts do not especially make a man receptive to new ideas."

Sochos was cold and crowded. Ice patches lay in the rutted streets; the dirt square was filled with saddled horses and buses and trucks. The meeting was in an unheated cinema, a dank cold room with concrete floor and walls. About three hundred men and ten women teachers and social workers huddled in overcoats. The men appeared to be of all ages and from all levels of farm economy, from humble peasants in work clothes to prosperous landowners in dark suits, neckties and silk scarves. The conference was opened with a blessing by two priests who waved water-soaked sprigs of basil over the shivering crowd. With respectful attention the delegates listened to a minister ask them to cooperate more closely with government agriculturists, to an economist describe farm and consumer cooperatives in the United States, England and Russia, to an engineer outlining plans for irrigation, a school superintendent discussing lunch programs, and a forester who told them to plant trees "to restore dead rivers and prevent the rains from washing our land away." Now and then waves of coughing and shuffling feet indicated a restlessness in the audience. Still the speeches went on. A priest warned that hardheaded suspicion, egotism and self-interest paralyzed progress and that "only by replacing these dark shades of the human soul with Christian love can we achieve new roads and bridges, schools and a clean water supply."

At noon the men ate packed lunches or crowded into Sochos' three cafés. We found places in one at a table of priests and ate a hearty meal of bean soup, boiled beef and spaghetti. For the afternoon session a small wood stove had been moved into the theater. Seated next to it, warmed by a crackling fire, we listened to a schoolmaster speak of his school's role in community development, describing how his students planted a forest, brought chicks from the Farm School to improve poultry strains, inaugurated a school lunch program, landscaped the cemetery and organized theatricals to raise money to buy library books. "Our young men do not sit in the cafés," he said. "They are too busy with 4-H clubs, the library, with lectures and football games." A man from the public health service spoke on home hygiene, telling the farmers not to slaughter animals outdoors, "where dogs eat the offal and spread disease." He urged them not to share family habitations with livestock and to spread manure over fields instead of heaping it outside houses where it provided breeding places for flies. The fly as a disease carrier seemed a new and strange idea to the delegates. The speaker instructed them to keep flies from cheese-making areas and to keep milk animals clean.

Finished with flies, the health official, a dapper suave type with long sideburns and heavy brows, spoke earnestly on another subject—the building of toilets. "You should realize the need to do this without being forced by law," he told the villagers. "I believe you can do it, that you can build toilets, and I implore you to take this seriously." Some priests in the first row leaned attentively on their umbrellas, paying attention to the speaker as he outlined the steps. "First you select a place which is below and away from your water supply. Next you dig a pit, which you cover with cement or wood, putting a hole into it. Then you build a dry house over it and make a cover for the hole to keep the flies out."

The time had come for an open discussion. It developed quickly into a free-for-all with men leaping up, and calling attention to themselves by waving their arms. An elderly man complained that the commercial fertilizer distributed by the government was not sufficiently concentrated, that a more potent product would save him trips to his fields, eight kilometers from his house. A sleek-haired young man said that government agriculturists overlooked his village and another complained the government offered his village no help in road building and well digging.

A prosperous-looking man wearing leather gloves said, "If we do not build toilets tourists will not come to our villages." A burly young village president said, "In our village we have two cooperatives, two churches, a school and ten cafés. Our problem is we can't cooperate, we can't work together. Tell me, if you can, how do you make Greeks cooperate?"

He was wildly applauded. In the first row the priests covered their faces with their hands to hide their laughter. The answer came from Bruce Lansdale who in perfect Greek spoke of human brotherhood as a basis for the cooperation with which all human problems could be solved, from the building of village toilets and bridges to the administration of the United Nations. The priests applauded him.

We drove back through cold dusk over a brutal terrain of rocks and steep slopes, meeting herds of cows returning for the night, and donkeys carrying on their backs the plows they'd been pulling all day. "The peasants of Greece are like the land," said Bruce. "Hard, intractable, resistant. How can one not admire a stamina which has survived for centuries under the most adverse circumstances? How can we expect to change in a moment, the habits and patterns of history? The villagers are a product of history. Their worship of their own past is one force which above all others they hold in common. For them the present is only beginning to stir."

XIV

"Somewhere Where
the White Chickens Are"

On Saturday I went by bus with Alex Marlis to his village of Kastaneri. It was a rainy gray day. As we rode over flat agricultural plains toward the mountains facing Yugoslavia, Alex spoke of his family, his two sisters and three brothers, all working in factories in Cologne, his parents living with two small granddaughters in Kastaneri, supported by money sent from Germany. The little girls were the daughters of Alex's sister, Katerina, and his brother, Dimitros. The children's mothers worked in factories alongside their husbands. All the brothers and sisters were married except a brother next to Alex, an American Farm School graduate whose name was Christos. The brothers and sisters were trying to persuade the parents to move to Germany. "Maybe they will go," said Alex. "Christos says he will marry a German, that he will never return to Greece."

We crossed the Axios River, which flows from Yugoslavia, and climbed a dirt road toward the border mountains, at one point fiording a stream. The bus went as far as Goumenissa, an agricultural town. It was market day. Dirt streets, muddied by rain, were lined with stalls of slaughtered meat, and bins of apples, grapes, chestnuts and vegetables. The old houses were in Tudor style with red tile roofs and low brown eaves, and red brick and white stucco walls reinforced with brown logs. Porches were painted blue. The curiously Elizabethan atmosphere gave me the feeling of having been dropped into Shakespeare's town and century, no pretty complex of cottage gardens and cowslipped meadows, but a hub-bub of braying donkeys, scratching hens, crowing roosters, manure piles, gutters flowing sewage, dogs sniffing slops emptied from upper chambers, saddled horses, sharp-eyed peasants bartering with tradesmen, children running in games and pink-cheeked old women clacking in doorways. The country fair bustle could have been painted by Brueghel. It was the season of the leek harvest and great bundles of the vegetable, thick as corn-stalks and high as sugar cane, bound at top and bottom like Roman fasces, lay everywhere. Two of the sheaves burdened a donkey.

In a steaming restaurant we had a strapping lunch of roast lamb and boiled leeks and strong red wine, and then we met Alex's father, a slight little man with worry beads whom Alex resembled. He had come to market by horse and asked if I preferred to go the twelve kilometers to Kastaneri on horseback or part way by auto taxi and then on foot. Since it was raining, I chose the taxi. Arrangements were made. A flashily dressed man with a mouthful of gold teeth introduced himself and inquired if I were German. Germans were the only foreigners who came to Goumenissa, Alex explained. The dapper man was the com-munal secretary of Kastaneri. He asked if his wife might ride in our taxi. She had come to town with him on a horse, but would prefer, since it was raining, to return with us.

The driver said we must leave at once or the trip would be impos-sible. His taxi was a Mercedes-Benz. He guided it up a roadbed upon which men seemed to have been working recently, and skirted an un-guarded ledge which dropped off into a canyon. "Meester," said the driver, pointing into the abyss, "like Texas."

We passed a donkey loaded with leeks and caught up with a young man in a dark overcoat and offered him a ride. He was going to Kastaneri for the wedding of a cousin next day. We halted before a mud pool, and the driver and Alex got out and built two narrow bridges of rock for the wheels to pass on. The secretary's wife, a hearty woman in her thirties, expressed skepticism about my visit. "Is he going to *sleep* in the village?" she asked. Shaking her head incredulously, she began to laugh. Ahead was a mist-covered mountain and on a narrow plateau, the red-roofed houses of Kastaneri.

"In summer it is beautiful," Alex said. The brown wintry village shaped like a horseshoe on a curve of the mountain stood in a forest of chestnut trees from which it took its name. We arrived at a stream which the driver could not fiord. We paid him, leaped from rock to rock across the stream and climbed toward the village. We heard the cries of children, sounds of chopping wood and—at 4 P.M.—a rooster crowing. The first houses we passed were boarded up. The owners were in Germany, Alex said. From other houses, blue smoke poured from holes in the walls. The houses, like those in Goumenissa, were in haphazard Tudor style. Scrawny multicolored chickens scratched in the dirt.

The Marlis house was, like many others, over a stable. We climbed to a balcony and there Alex's mother met us, embracing and kissing Alex on both cheeks and greeting me the same way. She was a large woman, taller than her husband. She wore black homespun, a head scarf, and heavy outdoor shoes. I liked her at once—she had an innate refinement which she had passed on to her son. Two blond children, Maria, aged nine, and Erne, two, peered out of the door. There were three rooms. The largest, a sort of summer kitchen and storeroom, had an earth floor and contained a loom, bins of potatoes and chestnuts and a rack hung with drying raisins. The other two were tiny dark bedrooms. One also served as a kitchen and dining room and it was into this I was taken. A two-burner wood stove no larger than my attaché case, stood six inches off the floor. The mother lowered herself to the floor before it, strong and gracefully as a dancer. Sitting on her feet, she fed little sticks into the fire to warm the room. On one side was a double bed and on the other, two children's beds. Cold wintry air came through broken panes in the single window. Alex served some *raki,* made by his father, potent stuff which helped warm me. He was quietly pensive as if he were seeing through me for the first time how sad things really were.

We took a walk, plodding through twilight lanes of dark, padlocked houses and as we walked, Alex, speaking in a kind of litany, said, "This is the house of Christos Kachagia. He and his wife and children are in Frankfurt. The doors are nailed on the house of Stavros Passalis. He is in Cologne. The Bojardeni house is the nicest in town. My sister, Annette, is married to their son, George. Five of seven Bojardenis are in Germany, and Dimitrios, the youngest, is preparing to go." A grizzled old man and a chubby pink child about three were watering a donkey at a fountain. The man's name was Demos Samaras; the child, his grandson, was also named Demos. "I have two sons and a daughter and all are in Germany," he said.

It was dark now and we went to a café. Old men were playing cards at several tables around a hot stove. Two pressure oil lamps hanging from the ceiling filled the room with white light. It was a country store with shelves filled with canned goods, salt, sugar, soap, lamps, *raki,* beer, wine, oil, crockery and hardware and kitchen utensils. Sheep bells and bundles of brown and white candles hung from the beams. The owner, Giorgos Pappas, was a handsome man with curly gray hair and mustaches, a young face and gold-toothed smile. "In America does every man find work?" he asked. I replied that most men had jobs. "In

Greece, no one," he said, looking around the room at the gathering of old men. "My two daughters are in Stuttgart. Now my boys want to go and they are only sixteen." Other men arrived. Each greeted the company with a murmured *"Kalispera,"* took a chair and silently began tugging at worry beads. An old man bowed before me, and said in English, "How are you, sir?" He was Dimitrios Pappas, uncle of Giorgos, and he had worked on the railroad in Columbus, Ohio, from 1910 to 1919. "I went American President Wilson," he said. "America, God's country." He was eighty-four years old, had thick hair, bright eyes and a lean bright face. His hands tugged at beads. The oil lamps hissed.

Giorgos' sons, strapping black-haired twins, arrived with two horses and a pack mule loaded with produce which they carried into the store, boxes of canned goods, bottled soft drinks and sacks of flour. Giorgos set up a round of *raki.* The small glasses were emptied neat in one gulp and refilled. The stuff landed hard and burned inside. Alex's father arrived and took a chair beside me, twirling his beads. Sitting in silence between father and son, I thought how much alike the two faces were, the boy's young and handsome, the father's lined by worry and work, a foreshadowing of what the boy's would become if he lived his life in this place. Like an illness I felt the claustrophobia of the place, its threat to Alex, his young despair.

The lights flickered and the twins, named Dimitrios and Christos, pumped the lamps which hissed and brightened. They sat down backwards beside one another, resting their healthy scowling faces on the backs of their chairs, waiting like everyone in the room. Several adolescents arrived, murmured greetings to the twins and, finding chairs, joined the silence. Formally dressed in suits, white shirts and ties, they sat whirling beads. Sometimes through the window I could see the slinking dark forms of passing women but none approached to the door, none thought to intrude on the male sanctuary. The silence grew oppressive, as if it had been going on for eternity, and I had the eerie feeling I was in a congregation of men awaiting death, or of men already dead, expecting a summons to judgment. "Sometimes they sit until morning," said Alex.

About thirty men were in the room now. Whenever the light faded one of the twins would pump the lamp. Beside me I heard the click of Mr. Marlis' beads. He cleared his throat to speak, and his voice was like a file, ordering more *raki* and plates of *mezédes*—olives, cheese, pickled fish, tomatoes and cooked beans. The village secretary, whose wife had ridden with us in the afternoon, arrived and greeted me with a handshake. His name was Christos Dartsis and he was forty years old. His arrival was a welcome intrusion. He was a smiling, slightly comic dandy in a natty tweed suit tailored too tightly to his pudgy frame. Toasting the "historic occasion" of my visit, he made a welcome speech, saying, "We are grateful to you for coming to our village. We wish for visitors but none come. You are the first American." He showed me a letter from a relative in Columbus, Ohio. In 1910 a hundred men had emigrated from Kastaneri to America, most of them to Ohio. The old uncle was the only one who had returned. The secretary had one brother in Germany and another preparing to go. He said, "A few years ago there were nine hundred and fifty people in Kastaneri and now there are six hundred. The rest are in Germany. In two years you will find no one here—we will all be in Germany. Kastaneri will be a ghost town." There were still some youths in the village because "they cannot go to Germany until they have done their military and they cannot do that until they are twenty. So they sit here waiting for birthdays." I remembered Bruce Lansdale saying Kastaneri "has no economic validity, no reason to continue its existence and it should be permitted to die." The town's only industry was agriculture. Alex's father owned six arid acres in small patches, a three-hour donkey ride up the mountain. His livestock consisted of five sheep, two horses and twenty chickens. The secretary also owned six acres and, he said, "one donkey, one goat and some hens." It had been a dry year with poor yields of wheat and potatoes. There had never been an auto in Kastaneri, only a few motor scooters. "We have a river," said the secretary. "But no bridge."

Uncle Dimitrios, who had been in America when Wilson was President, called for more *raki,* saying, "America, she dry." Feeling a little drunk, I said, "She very wet." This exchange, translated by Alex, broke the ice. The silent men moved their chairs in a circle around me and began to ask questions. Who murdered President Kennedy? Was it Communists or Cubans? How far was Cuba from America? How far from Dallas was Texas? Was President Johnson loved in America?

For an hour they continued the questions and answers channeled through Alex. Being American, I was expected to be omniscient, to know everything.

"Why does America not build us schools to educate our children?" a young man asked. I told them of American colleges in Athens and Thessaloniki, of the American Farm School. A man asked, "In America are there Negroes in high places in the government?" I racked my brain for the names of Negro congressmen and judges. "Why does America like Turkey better than Greece?" I did not think it did. "Why does America help Turkey more?" NATO—not America—had defense bases in Turkey which it was necessary to maintain. There were questions I could not answer, like, "If all the young people leave Greece, what will happen to us old ones? Are we to starve?" The men drew closer around me until I could feel their strong breaths on my face and heard the soft whirs and clicks of their beads, and they asked the inevitable question, "Why does America make war in Vietnam?"

To this I tried to answer by quoting John F. Kennedy and by speaking of the long conflict between powers committed to opposing political philosophies, of which Vietnam was simply one more battlefield. The men listened silently, as if they were aware there was little conviction in my words.

The twins were forgetting to pump the lamps. In the dim light the eyes of the men shone white like animals' in a forest. Many smoked pipes and the hot room reeked with the gamy odors of sweat, unwashed bodies and strong tobacco. There was grim, noble beauty in the faces grizzled by work, weather and time, tools that sculpt flesh. A child burst into the room, a blond curly-haired boy with an angelic face and slightly askew eyes, like a cross-eyed Della Robbia. He was the brother of the bride, sent to invite me to the wedding the next day. It was ten o'clock, time, Alex said, to go home to supper. Snow was falling. Alex and the secretary led me over the dark and muddy path with a flashlight. Alex asked if I needed to go to the toilet and directed me into a smelly alley between two buildings. Facing a wall, I remembered the urgent speeches on toilet building at the community development conference. Music and songs from the bride's house filled the night and far away I saw the lights of Yugoslavia.

We washed on the porch in an enameled basin, and poured the slops over the rail. Inside the mother was on her haunches blowing on the fire, cooking something in a pot on the little stove. The two children were asleep, a table set between their two beds almost filled the little room, which was warm as a womb. A kerosene lamp burned, rugs were on the floor, two dark cats curled in the corner. The father, sitting silently in the shadows, seemed shrunken, used up.

The table was set with linen napkins and, because there was no room for chairs, we sat, father, son and I, on the edges of the beds in which the children slept. The mother served steaming bowls of fish stew with more *raki* to drink, and afterward some apples and walnuts and finally coffee which she cooked in a small dipper over the fire, and chestnuts which she roasted on the stove lid. While we were eating the baby awoke and making not a sound, sat up to watch, peering at us like a baroque cherub.

It was time for bed and Alex took me into the second small room, which was unheated and marrow-chilling. I put on a sweater, blew out the kerosene lamp, crawled under a load of blankets and fell asleep.

When I awakened at eight everyone was up. The room in which I lay
was painted blue. A string of dried pomegranates was festooned across
one wall and on another was a family photograph, the parents with their
six children, Alex an infant, and an old grandmother, mother of the
father, whose home the old house had been.

Alex brought a tray with my breakfast—scrambled eggs, bread and
coffee. When I finished I went to the other room where the mother was,
as usual sitting on the floor before the little stove, blowing on the fire. I
could not remember the location of the "toilet" of the night before and
asked Alex. He took me out on the steps and, pointing to an area beyond
some houses where hens were scratching, he said, "Somewhere where
the white chickens are." I set off, trailed by several curious children.
The morning was bitter cold and below the valley was filled with white
clouds. When I returned the mother was chopping wood with a fierce-
looking double-bladed ax and Alex was cutting the head from a chicken,
which he carried up the stairs, leaving a trail of blood. The father had
left at six o'clock with friends to hunt boar.

Alex and I walked to the church, a single-level squared structure, like
an adobe ranch house. The yard was a mass of brambles. An old
woman arrived carrying a shovel of smoking ashes which she strewed
over her husband's grave, to commemorate the fortieth day of his death,
Alex said. Her mission accomplished, she left quickly. We climbed up
among the chestnuts to a second, smaller church called Elias Prophet.
Outside two woodsmen were cooking food over a campfire. Nearby
were fifteen donkeys loaded with firewood which the men were bringing
down to sell in the village. Inside the church was bright with icons
painted in a naïve style. St. John the Baptist, one head firmly on his
shoulders, held another on a platter in his hands. St. George rode a
horse with both of its eyes on the same side of its head, like a
flounder, or a horse by Picasso.

It was starting to rain, so we returned to the village, to Giorgos Pappas' café for coffee. One of the twins brought a four-month-old London
Times, asking, "Can you read this?" He seemed awed that I could.
A dozen men who had been there the night before were playing cards.
I met the new schoolteacher, a large, deep-voiced young man with a
dour melancholy expression. He told us he had arrived three days before
on foot from Goumenissa to replace a woman teacher who, finding
Kastaneri unendurable, had abandoned her pupils in mid-term. His pay
was two thousand drachmae a month—about sixty-six dollars—and he
had not been able to find a comfortable room. Sniffling with a cold, he
seemed wretched. I asked why he had come, and he said there had been
no choice in the matter, that teachers in Greece were hired by the

government and assigned to posts. He asked how many pupils a teacher in America taught. I guessed about twenty. He had fifty-two pupils, most of whose parents were in Germany.

Conversation in the café was about the wedding. The groom had just arrived with his relatives and friends on a hayrack drawn by a tractor. The prenuptial feast was midday in the bride's home but the actual marriage was to be in the church of Stathe, the groom's village fifteen kilometers away. The entire wedding, the groom with his party and the bride with her family and friends, were going to ride to Stathe on the hayrack and on the back of a Mercedes-Benz truck which somehow had been brought as far as the river below. It sounded like a complicated marriage, especially in the rain.

On the street outside the secretary's office a long line of women and old men waited for the postman. The office was also a post office to which the mailman came three times a week—on Sundays, Tuesdays and Thursdays—by horseback from Goumenissa. Since it was the first Sunday of the month, money orders were expected from relatives in Germany. Much of Kastaneri's mail came from Germany and more than half of the village income came from German remittances.

The office was a small room painted green, furnished with a desk, several cases of books and the only telephone in town. A wood stove filled it with heat. The secretary was talking with a blue-eyed blond young man named Christos Itas, who was going to Thessaloniki for a physical examination which would make it possible for him to immigrate to Australia. He was, Alex said, very poor and the community had helped him, raising money for his clothes and passage. Since we planned to return to Thessaloniki in the evening I asked the secretary to arrange for a taxi to fetch us and I offered the young immigrant a ride. The secretary cranked the phone. In a moment he was shouting into the mouthpiece, trying to persuade the taxi driver to come for us. The fellow refused, insisting it was impossible in the rain. The secretary's voice and manner were solemnly official, befitting his role as nerve center for six hundred people. Alex said that he was paid fifteen hundred drachmae a month —about fifty dollars—and when there was no money in the treasury he willingly forfeited the salary.

A line of women had letters to Germany for the secretary to address in Roman script, which they were themselves unable to write.

The mailman arrived with two saddlebags of letters which he un- packed on the table. Women and men filed by him, collecting their letters. When the mail was distributed the persons who had received money orders lined up a second time with the pink slips and the postman opened a leather envelope of money, from which he counted currency

and coins into opened palms. It was like a factory payday. One of the
young women who cashed a money order was the secretary's sister-in-
law. With her were two small blond children wearing identical Bavarian
sweaters in snowflake designs, sent by the father. A pregnant young
woman told the mailman that her baby would be two months old when
her husband came home for a visit at Easter. An old woman, small,
walking with a cane, broke into tears and her voice choked as she
received the money from her sons. Alex's mother was in the line,
collecting fifteen hundred drachmae from her son Dimitros and her
daughter Katerina.

Through rain and mud we sloshed toward the bridal house. In the
courtyard two musicians were blowing shepherd pipes and a third was
beating on a drum. We climbed into an upper hall and were shown into a
dark room filled with long tables around which men, in dark suits and
wearing caps, were drinking *raki*. A man, one of the bride's relatives,
served us roast lamb with potatoes and a variety of sweets and cheeses.
The men were quiet, but from another room, I heard a clamor of voices
and music. I asked Alex where the women were and he said, "In the
women room where the noise is."

A white apparition appeared, like Ophelia, in the doorway. It was the
bride, young and beautiful, in a billowing white dress spangled with
silver threads. She had red hair in which silver sequins glittered like stars.
She entered in a kind of trance and stood in the center of the room, eyes
shut, hands folded before her. An attendant carrying a basket of small
packages followed her. Approaching like a somnambulist, the bride bowed
stiffly before me and taking my right hand in hers, kissed it, and did
the same to my left. She moved on to Alex and the attendant handed me
one of the packages. Watching the bride move down the line of guests,
kissing hands, I saw that each man slipped the bride some folded
currency, that the curious ceremony was actually an exchange of gifts
between the bride and her guests. I quickly drew some money from my
pocket and Alex signaled the attendant who nudged the bride and the
bride returned and, repeating her ritual, bowed and kissed my hands,
accepting the money. She moved on, doing the same to every man in the
room. We opened our parcels and each contained a pair of socks and a
hand-hemmed white linen handkerchief. "In the old days," said Alex,
"the bride would have knitted the socks herself. Now they buy them."
We met the groom's father, a tall white-haired man, who said sixty
persons had traveled from Stathe on the hayrack, that the trip back,
beginning at two o'clock, was expected to take one and a half hours and
that the ceremony in the church was scheduled for four o'clock. I asked

how many from Kastaneri would accompany the wedding party and he said, "As many as there is space for."

We walked through the rain to Alex's house for dinner. I was cold and wet and anxious about our return. Other visitors had arrived, an old man from the groom's village who was a cousin of Alex's mother, and two of his granddaughters. The secretary arrived to tell us that because of the rains the wedding party would leave earlier than scheduled and he had arranged for Alex and me to ride with the guests on the hayrack. While we were eating the chicken cooked in a thick soup, we heard pipes and beating drums pass the house. We finished the meal, Alex's mother kissed us good-bye, and we ran after the wedding. Beyond the river, the party, loaded on the truck and wagon, was ready to depart. The caravan waited while we slid down the mountain, leaped across the stream and climbed on the wagon. The two drivers decided not to take the road upon which we had arrived, but an "old road," which was believed to be less muddy.

The truck, a huge eight-wheeled affair, led the way. The bride and three friends rode in the cab with the driver, one of the girls sitting on his left between him and the door. In the back under a canvas canopy were the groom and some sixty relatives, mostly female. The canopy was so low only the smallest girls could stand upright and since there was no room to sit, most of the passengers stood in the dark with stooped shoulders and bent heads. In addition to the human cargo, the truck carried the bride's dowry, trunks of linens, blankets, dishes and furniture.

Still the truck passengers were the lucky ones. The tractor-drawn hayrack had no covering and we rode in the soaking rain. All the passengers were men, most of them young and several were roaring drunk. The "old road" turned out to be no road at all, but a rocky trail that had once been a road. Because it sloped perilously, the tractor driver commanded us to stand on the upper side to keep from sliding. Men with umbrellas stood under them in pairs, face to face, grasping each other for support. As the wagon rolled and lunged, the embracing couples, careening across the slippery boards, seemed to be engaged in a bizarre dance. One of the musicians began to blow his flute and several men started to sing. Their ribaldy lewd lyrics about cuckolding wives and unfaithful husbands were hardly wedding music. Some younger ones began a bawdy belly dance which was hilariously applauded. Alex's old cousin, grinning toothlessly, wearing an old army overcoat which went almost to his feet, whirled wildly with a boy in his teens. The wagon rolled and pitched and the rain beat down.

One man became sick and jumped off to vomit. He followed on foot with two friends who walked with him. Up to this point the

experience had been a kind of lark but now the fun was turning to
terror. The hairpin curves were ledges of soft mud. Looking over the
side into a bottomless abyss filled with fog, I felt sick with vertigo. Fog
rising from the depths like steam covered everything. Behind us Kastaneri
was hidden by it. With no earth visible anywhere, we seemed to be riding
in limbo.

At a widening in the trail, the truck driver drew aside and stopped.
His cargo of bride, groom and dowry was less expendable than our
wagonload of drunken men, and he beckoned us ahead. The trail, gullied
by erosion, disappeared completely. Our wagon, riding on a bias, began
to list and the driver ordered us off to pull at it on the upper side to
keep it from falling into the abyss. The strategy worked. Suddenly, the
truck behind us began to slide. A girl in the cab screamed. Her cry
was heard under the canvas where passengers opened a flap and became
aware for the first time of their danger. A chorus of screams, muffled by
canvas, rang through the canyon. The men on the wagon ran back to
support the truck from which screaming women were leaping. Mired in
mud, the women continued their cries. The bride, an attendant holding
the billows of her silvery veil, stood calmly, magnificently poised, in the
rain. She seemed not to hear the clamor raised by the women, who were
concerned now for the dowry still on the truck. Supported by fifty men
above and below, the truck slowly crossed the gully.

Ahead the trail dropped into a valley. The two drivers agreed to
undertake the descent without passengers. Only the bride and her retinue
were allowed to ride. The wedding party continued on foot, a human
caravan trudging under umbrellas through mud. The sobbing procession
was more funereal than bridal. A bridesmaid with sequins in her hair,
walking barefoot in ankle-deep mud, carried her high-heeled shoes.

My own shoes were greased with mud and I seemed to be on skates.
A man in a black overcoat took my hand, as if I were a child. Like a
sure-footed goat he led me down the mountain, calling me "Komrade,"
murmuring a litany of assurance, saying, "Ah, what courage, Komrade . . . you are doing so well . . . it is no longer far . . . easy,
Komrade, lean on me. . . ." He asked how old I was and when I told
him, he said softly, "Ah, but I thought you were much younger. You are
walking, Komrade, like a youth. . . ."

In the valley there was a river to wade across and beyond it the
tractor and truck waited to take up their passengers. I was invited to
ride in the canopied truck where I met the groom, a very tall thin youth
doubled up under the canvas as if in a cramp. The dowry trunks heaved
about like crates on a tossing ship and in the corner I saw the angel-faced
cross-eyed boy who had invited me to the wedding. The terrors now past

were forgotten and a merry spirit prevailed. Someone started to sing. The groom insisted I continue to Stathe for the ceremony and the feast.

For a moment I considered it. But I was soaked, muddy and sneezing. Alex had his cows to milk in the morning. We said good-bye and stood waving on a corner in Goumenissa, watching the truck pull away. I saw the bride smiling and I said a prayer for her happy life. She had certainly earned it.

We walked to the house of a friend of Alex's where we cleaned our shoes, dried our clothes and warmed ourselves with *raki*. On the long ride to Thessaloniki the bus was delayed in four villages with wedding parties filling the streets. "Greeks," said Alex, "marry on Sundays, usually in the autumn season between harvest and Christmas." A passenger on the bus was Christos Itas, the young man who hoped to go to Australia. He had walked from Kastaneri to Goumenissa in the rain in two hours. It was a feat of good health and I had no doubt he would pass his physical examination in the morning.

XV

The Welcome Wagon

Dr. Norton Wilson is a distinguished diagnostician in a Midwest American clinic. I met him in the El Greco bar on his first evening in Athens, and I recognized the type—warmhearted and outgoing, a man who loves and trusts people and is trusted by them. He seemed to embody all the commendable American qualities—youthful vigor, idealism, generosity— with none of the irritating characteristics which sometimes make Americans abroad seem absurd. He was a tall rugged man who in the 1930s played football for Purdue. Had he been an actor, his handsomely lean face and gray curly hair would probably have had him cast as a doctor on a TV medical series.

It was his first trip outside the United States since World War II when, as a medical officer in the Pacific, he had been awarded the Distinguished Service Medal. He had flown to Rome the week before to deliver a paper at a medical conference on the diagnosis of malignant tumors through blood analysis. Persuaded by his colleagues and his family to take his first vacation in eight years, he purchased a twenty-day excursion ticket which brought him to Athens. After checking in the hotel he had wandered into one of the workers' cafés on Omonia Square where he talked to anyone who spoke English. "A great people," he said, enthusiastically. "So friendly, so kind. I had three drinks and couldn't pay for one. And they're so poor." The doctor's disarming company was a welcome respite from coping with Greeks and made me a little homesick. I accepted his invitation for lunch the next day.

In the morning I worked until eleven and then decided to pick up my mail. Walking toward Constitution Square, I increased my pace to avoid the shills. They were there, on Stadiou Street and outside the American Express, stalking tourists, offering come-on cards to nightclubs in the area. I had a collection of thirty such cards, inviting me to the Copacabana ("fabuloys girls"), the Miami ("international strip-tease"), the Canada ("beautiful starlets will entertain you"), the Black Cat ("most beautiful girls in Athens"), the Themis ("We honor Amerikan Express Credit Cards").

A young man blocked my path, bringing me to a dead stop. "How do you do," he began. "Where are you from? Do you like Greece? How long do you stay?" The line, spoken softly in English, was familiar.

"I have been here three years, I live in Psychico and I work at the American Embassy," I said. Sometimes it worked but not always since no one fitting such a description would be picking up mail at the American Express. My interlocutor, small and dressed in a brown tweed jacket, wasn't buying it. "Are you looking for something?"

"Yes," I said. "The bluebird of happiness."

Dark eyes smiled roguishly. "What you like best?" It was a question which I sometimes answered with imaginative specifications from Krafft-Ebing which, to my surprise, were usually taken seriously. "You like to come to my bar and have a drink with me?" he asked.

"Never before noon," I said, passing around him.

"Coffee?" Following me, he extended a small yellow card, inviting me to the Broadway Club. "Twenty girls open from 11 A.M.," I read, "All kinds of traveler checks we accept."

At one o'clock I was back in the El Greco waiting for Dr. Wilson. He arrived in the bar at one thirty, looking pale and shaken. He ordered a double Scotch and told me the story of this morning.

"I was coming out of the American Express," he began. "A nice-looking well-dressed young man stopped and asked if he could help me. I thought it was very kind of this young man to bother. You know, sort of like a Welcome Wagon back home. I said, 'Yes, I am looking for TWA.' He said he'd take me there. He asked where I was from and how long I was staying. I asked him how he knew English so well and he said he worked in England and had many American friends. He told me he owned a bar and he invited me to have a drink. I said 'No,' that I had to go to TWA to confirm my reservations.

"When I came out of TWA there he was waiting. He asked if I'd come to his bar now to celebrate our friendship with a drink. It seemed very decent of him. There was no one else in the bar. We sat at a table and my friend asked what I'd like. I ordered a vermouth. A pretty blonde girl came up and asked if she could sit with us. Did we mind if she had a drink? She ordered a bottle of champagne. I thought it was a funny time to drink champagne but it was none of my business. Then another girl, who said she was a sister, came and also ordered a bottle of champagne. I couldn't help thinking for such small girls they were drinking an awful lot very fast. They said they were from some village in Thessaly and that they lived alone in an apartment with a view of the Acropolis which they'd be glad to show me. I said I had a date for lunch and they asked if I'd like to come for a drink about seven o'clock. I noticed that the friendly owner had disappeared and I began to think maybe it wasn't quite a Welcome Wagon after all. The waiter brought a third bottle of champagne. He was a tough-looking young guy who didn't speak.

"I decided I'd better get the hell out and got up. The waiter said 'Just a minute' and brought me a check. I said I'd been invited, that I was a guest. 'For vermouth,' he said. 'The bill is for the champagne.' The girls got up and left. The bill was for twenty-two hundred drachmae. I said I didn't think I would pay it. 'You pay or I call police,' said the waiter. I was pretty nervous. I wanted to get the hell out. I looked in my wallet and saw I didn't have enough money. The waiter was looking in my billfold. 'You got travelers' check?' he asked. I gave him a fifty-dollar check and the rest in drachmae. When I got outside I looked at my watch. I'd been in there less than twenty minutes."

I looked at the doctor and wondered why one so tall and powerfully built hadn't kicked over the table and walked out of the bar. "I don't know," he said, "I guess I was scared." His story angered me and I said he must go to the police.

"No, I want to forget it," he said. "I had to learn my lesson. Maybe it was worth seventy-five dollars."

I told the doctor it was his duty to go to the police, his duty to other tourists, and I said I would accompany him, taking with me my letter of reference from the prime minister's office. He finally agreed to go.

After the siesta, at four o'clock, Dr. Wilson, David Greggory and I set out for the office of the Tourist Police. We crossed Constitution Square and entered Philellinon Street. The bar which Dr. Wilson pointed out was, as I had suspected, the Broadway Club. While we stood there looking at photographs of seminude girls, appearing no doubt like three foreigners on the prowl, a dark seedy-looking man approached and asked if we'd like to meet the girls.

"Perhaps," said Greggory. "Twenty lovely girls," he read aloud from the sign.

"What is the price of champagne?" I asked the fellow.

"Six hundred and seventy-two drachmae a bottle," the man said. "Six hundred plus twelve per cent."

"Is it French champagne?"

"They call it French," the fellow replied. "But it's Greek imitation. Real champagne costs one thousand one hundred and twenty drachmae."

I wondered why the fellow was being so candid. We wore dark suits and Greggory was carrying a leather folio. Perhaps he suspected we were some kind of officials. "It sounds not logic," the man said, suddenly very nervous. "But we have so many poor families of so many children so it is not so much. . . ."

I said I did not want to hear about the poor Greeks and their starving children. The man suddenly switched roles and assumed an attitude of moral indignation. "Whoever enters into such a place is illogic," he said angrily. "For a man to enter a place so dubious is illogic logic. All these places where women is working is feelthy." Dr. Wilson was nodding in agreement. "My dear friends," the fellow continued, "they has their tricks everywhere. They has to. It's fraudulent, it's tricky. They always win because they pays to police and police supports them."

It was what I hoped to find out. We walked one block up Nikis Street to the headquarters of the Tourist Police.

The lieutenant at the desk was a balding shifty-eyed man in a heavily epauletted uniform. Understanding no English, he phoned someone who did. Greggory got on the phone and told our story. "Yes, yes," a bored voice replied, "you went to a nightclub." In a moment a plainclothesman with a mane of black hair arrived and said he spoke English "a leetle." Both men showed their boredom and annoyance. It was time, I decided, to produce my ministry letter. The lieutenant read it to himself, forming the words with his lips. Excited, he dialed a number and read the letter to someone on the telephone. While this was going on I looked at a picture hanging directly over the officer's desk of an anguished Christ in a red cloak wearing a crown of thorns. To the left was a framed photograph of the young King in royal regalia. Finished with the telephone conversation, the lieutenant asked us to return in an hour at five thirty when he said an English-speaking officer would be there.

We went to Constitution Square for coffee and on our way were accosted by four young men inviting us to various nightclubs, including the Broadway. When we returned to the police station at five thirty we found it filled. A dark plainclothesman, apparently the one who had been telephoned, was in charge. He was polite and cautious. Accompanying him was a younger taller officer, an interpreter, who spoke English well. The officers passed my ministry letter among themselves, as if it were holy writ. The interpreter asked Dr. Wilson to tell what happened.

He began with the meeting of the young man outside the American Express.

"Yes, yes," said the interpreter. "There are many like him in Athens." As the doctor told his story, the interpreter translated it into Greek. I had the feeling he was sympathetic toward us. The men in the room listened with a kind of stoic neutrality. Now and then the officer in charge smiled superciliously as if to say, "Yes, yes, we know all this."

"It was the Rosemarie Bar?" he said.

"No, the Broadway," I said, repeating the name which by now had been spoken at least a dozen times.

"Did you look at the menu?" the officer asked Dr. Wilson.

"No one offered me one."

"Why did you not ask for one?"

"Why should the doctor have asked for a menu when he was invited for a free drink?" I asked. Turning to Dr. Wilson with the patient air of a kindergarten teacher scolding a backward child, the officer said, in Greek and the interpreter in English, "All those fellows who walk on Constitution Square are tramps and you must not trust them." It was apparent that the officer was not believing Dr. Wilson. "What did you speak with the man?" he asked. For the third time Dr. Wilson began his story. "What did the boy look like, what was he wearing, what kind of necktie?" the officer asked. Unable to remember the necktie, Dr. Wilson repeated his description of a brown tweed jacket and dark brown trousers. The officer interrupted to ask a second time why the doctor had not asked for a menu or inquired for the price of champagne. The repeated pursuit of this point annoyed me and I asked, "Is it customary in Greece, a country famous for its hospitality, for an invited guest to ask the cost of refreshments offered by his host?" My point seemed to get through to at least two of the gentlemen who began a heated discussion between them. I made some shorthand notes which spurred everyone in the room to excited conversation centering around the word "stenographia." As I continued writing the officers, watching from the corners of their eyes, became increasingly restive. I was aware of a new man in the room, a small dapper fellow with a cinematic quality which reminded me of David Niven. I had not seen him enter. He was apparently an important personage for he assumed a position in the center of the group. He was smoking a cigarette from a long holder and, between thumb and index finger, he held a small glass of clear liquid, probably *ouzo*. He had sleek black hair, mustaches pointed with wax and wore a navy-blue suit rather too sharply cut. He sipped from his glass while the interpreter briefed him in Greek. Turning to Dr. Wilson, speaking

British-accented English, he insinuatingly asked, "My dear fellow, why did you stay when you discovered you were in an ill-famed place?"

"He didn't stay," I said. "He was there only twenty minutes." Ignoring me, the man continued to hammer at the doctor, saying, "I am not a policeman but I have traveled in other countries and what I do not understand, my good friend, is why you went into this bad place at all." Though his English words were not understood by most of the officers, his supercilious tone was and the men in the room smiled at one another. "Surely you are aware," the man continued, "that such dubious people as you found there exist not only in Greece but in every land. Is it your first stay in Greece?" he asked, exhaling a jet of blue smoke, sipping daintily from his glass.

"I arrived yesterday," said the doctor.

"Do you like our country?" asked the man, waving the cigarette holder with thin bony fingers.

"Yes, very much."

"I think you are going to have a very worst impression from what happened to you today," said the man, laughing suavely. "Where will you go in Greece?"

"I hope to make an excursion to the Peloponnese."

"The Peloponnese! I'm *from* the Peloponnese! From Sparta. Will you go to Sparta?"

The doctor did not know.

"I'm from Kalambaka," said the interpreter, who seemed to have been replaced by David Niven. The commanding officer said, "I Crete. You go to Crete?" The doctor said he wouldn't have the time. "But you will see Olympia," said David Niven. "Ah, Olympia," he sighed, trying to kiss his fingertips, nearly dropping his glass. "I pray for your sake the weather will be kind. In December it rains a great deal." The lieutenant at the desk offered us cigarettes which we accepted and coffee which we refused. Speaking through David Niven, he asked, "If you were in our position what would you do?"

It seemed a strange question. Greggory answered it, saying, "It might be desirable to prevent a repetition of the incident. Constitution Square is full of tourists—"

"But those fellows who work outside are illegal," interrupted David Niven, his cigarette cutting the air like a scimitar. "We always catch them and send them to the courts. If we catch this one we shall prosecute him at once."

It was increasingly apparent that nothing would be accomplished so we got up to leave. "Ah, but wait," said David Niven. "We have telephoned the manager of the Broadway Club and he is sending someone over." We returned to our chairs. David Niven sipped from his refilled glass. I asked him if he was a policeman. He shrugged away the question and laughing merrily said, "I am a professor. I teach English at Athens University. You see I am the police English teacher and I was just giving a lesson when you arrived with your little problem. I was invited to assist in the communications." I asked him where he had learned to speak English so well. "In Australia, my dear fellow," he said. "I sailed there in my youth." Turning to Dr. Wilson, he asked, "Where is your home?" The doctor replied with the name of his city. "Ah, very big, very beautiful," said David Niven. "Surely you have some bad people there, people who play tricks." The doctor admitted there were some. "Surely you have known before you came here of the pitfalls of Greece, that Athens is a *very* bad place . . ."

A burly thick-shouldered young man entered. "That's him," Dr. Wilson cried. It was the waiter from the Broadway Club. Speaking fair English, he turned to Dr. Wilson and asked, "You came to our place and did not know what it was?" He laughed incredulously and the men in the room laughed with him. Their common attitude seemed to be that the doctor was either naïve and stupid, or that he was dishonestly pretending to be. Greggory made the point, for the fourth time, that Dr. Wilson had been invited for a free drink. His voice mocking, David Niven said, "And you accepted this invitation without asking what kind of a place it was? Now that is very incredible." The conversation was moving too swiftly and too confusedly for Dr. Wilson to follow. "He was told it was a bar," I said. "That seemed clear enough."

Addressing the doctor, David Niven asked, "As soon as you realized you were in . . . ah . . . well . . . a suspicious place, why did you not leave?"

This was too much for me. "He did leave, for Christ's sake," I bellowed. My outburst started the men talking to one another like a meeting of the Japanese Diet. "But you must understand in such places they are crafty, they are cunning," David Niven continued. The investigation was turning into a shambles; procedural control was no longer possible. Once more, for the benefit of the waiter, Dr. Wilson was asked to tell his story. Listening as if he were hearing it for the first time, David Niven kept interrupting. "Oh, he disappeared in the bar, then he was not the owner?" he said, his lips curling. "He *deceived* you, in other words." The doctor agreed he had been deceived and the waiter said to him, "This is something all over the world, my friend." I asked the waiter if he knew the young man who had posed as manager and brought the doctor into the club. Picking lint from his lapels, he replied he'd never seen this man. The officers repeated this to one another. "You see," said David Niven, shrugging. "It would be very difficult to find him."

"I don't think so," I said. "I think you are all lying. I'm sure that anyone who has delivered a twenty-two-hundred-drachmae victim to the Broadway Club will return for his commission."

"May I ask you a question?" the waiter said to Dr. Wilson. "You came into this bad place and you didn't know what it was?" He threw his head back and laughed. Red-faced and ashamed, the doctor looked like a repentant child. The commanding lieutenant, trying to restore some order to the chaos, spoke in Greek to David Niven who addressed the doctor, saying, "The lieutenant expresses his big sorrow for what has happened and is sorry there is no way we can help you." The point seemed to be that no money would be returned to the doctor, which was not entirely what we had in mind. "You must remember," said David Niven, wagging a schoolmasterish finger in the doctor's face, "when you are in Greece you must be a little more . . . cautious. You must learn not to trust us."

This aroused Greggory who said, "You are chiding this man because he is a good person and I don't like it."

"I don't know what you mean, sir," said David Niven.

"He is a good honorable man." Greggory was shouting now to make himself heard. "It just happens that there are many people like the doctor in America. He is of such basic goodness that he approaches all men as if they were also good. He is, as a matter of fact, so honest that he even believes you are honest!"

The room was silent. We got up to go. The policemen crowded around us, smiling, shaking our hands, expressing to Dr. Wilson their wishes for a happy visit in Greece. The waiter clasped the doctor's hand and invited him to return to the Broadway Club with him for a drink.

"Noooooo," shouted Greggory and I in unison. We ushered the doctor out into garish neon-lit night streets and fought our way through ranks of young men who followed us to the square, murmuring, "You like pleasure . . . nice young girls . . . very good time . . ."

The next day Greggory called Athens University and learned that no Greeks taught English there, that the professors were either Americans or Englishmen. I phoned the officer in charge of tourist relations at the U. S. Embassy and he said tiredly, "It happens all the time. You should be here in June and July. My phone is ringing at five A.M. Last week a visit to a club cost a Catholic priest one hundred and thirty-five dollars." My friend, Spyros Nicodemou, said, "The policemen are partners in the clubs and the bad condition goes on and on. It will only get worse."

Some days later I read a letter in the Athens *News* from which I quote in part:

"I am an American businessman and I love Greece. . . . Yesterday a friend and I walked half a block from Constitution Square. A nice man invited us to his bar. We went in politeness, explaining we never drank until sundown but we would see his bar.

"There we were begged and cajoled to have something until we ordered two cups of tea. Then two of the three girls in the place came over, sat down, cuddled up to us, begging us to buy them drinks. . . .

"Our total expenditure for two cups of tea in fifteen minutes was 1450 drachmae. . . . Later we were accosted five more times by men in the street inviting us to visit their bars. . . ."

XVI

Winter

In January Athens turned into a cheerless and unhappy place. It began on the first day of the year with King Constantine's New Year's Day message to his subjects.

The King said, "During the year which is ending I saw to my regret healthy and creative political discussion being turned into immoderate passion and distortion of the truth. Distortion of the truth was also systematically indulged in by the organized internal enemies of the nation."

The object of the King's attack was the political left. He said, "Communism is a miasma, born outside of Greece, inspired and motivated from the outside." But since the Communists represented no more than 5 per cent of the voting Greeks the King appeared to be attacking Greece's largest political party, the Center Union, led by his most-hated enemy, George Papandreou. The controversy over the proclamation filled newspaper columns through the month.

It rained in January and one day it snowed. The city was stagnated by a chain-reaction series of strikes. Taxis, trolleys and buses halted. Grocers, restaurants and amusement places closed. Bakers struck and the government ordered policemen to bake bread. Teachers closed schools and postal employees stopped the mail. Christmas greetings were delayed until February.

Most appalling was a strike by garbage collectors. The narrow streets turned into mounds of rubbish; pavements were covered with reeking offal and rain made the walks slippery with it. Rats came out of hiding

185

to reconnoiter the refuse and health officials issued epidemic warnings. Doom prophets of the political right called the strikes a "warming-up by Communist unions for revolution."

A direct result of the King's proclamation was the banning from radio broadcasts of the music of my favorite popular composer, Mikis Theodorakis, known through the world for his film score for *Zorba the Greek*. A political man, Theodorakis was also a parliament deputy from Crete. Greece's two other famous composers, Manos Hadzidakis and Stavros Xarhakos, neither of them political activists, withdrew permission for performances of their own works until the government rescinded the "obscene, stupid and illiberal measure" against Theodorakis. Orchestras and singers were silenced and radio stations broadcast a monotony of *bouzouki* and country bagpipes and lutes.

The ban had the reverse effect of making a martyr of Theodorakis. A record distributor said that sales of recordings doubled even though police attempted to extort from record sellers the names of purchasers. Labor unions sponsored a series of concerts of Theodorakis' music in Athens' Center Theater, and tickets were immediately sold out. I finally got one through a friend in the Foreign Ministry. The theater was filled with a young crowd of white-collar workers and office girls. It seemed unlikely that they were Communists.

They were there to show their appreciation for music written for them. More than any other of Greece's composers, Theodorakis addresses his lyrics to the lower and middle classes. He appeared, a mighty man lumbering like a young Thomas Wolfe, and they welcomed him like an Olympian hero. The smile on his boyish face was like a clown's smile, curiously poignant. Turning his back, he raised his long arms and with a majestic sweep signaled the musicians to play. His left arm soared with the melody, cutting figures in the air, and his right chopped out the rhythm. So did one of his long legs, slightly extended, jog the beat, causing him to bob as if he were on a horse. A singer, a dark sparrow-like Edith Piaf named Maria Pharantouri, sang *The Ballad of Mauthausen*, a setting of four poems by a Greek prisoner in a concentration camp. She had great dark eyes and sleek black hair and she wore a plain slip of a brown dress, brown lisle stockings and simple black slippers. On her pale child's face there was no make-up. Her voice burst forth in a cry of despair, forlorn and dark, singing:

> Girls of Mauthausen,
> Girls of Belsen,
> Have you seen my love . . .

The tumult of applause seemed to frighten her. Theodorakis grinned, happy now, a man among friends. The concert's climax was a group of nine songs entitled *The Greek Race,* sung by a gray-haired dapper little man named Gregorios Bithikotsis who was a plumber before Theodorakis discovered him and made him one of the most popular singers in Greece. Beside the giant composer his body seemed no larger than a child's. But his voice was mighty, an effortlessly rolling baritone singing:

> For those in the prisons, and those under the earth,
> Silence! The bells will toll at any moment . . .

The lines were lost in a salvo of whistling and cheering. Theodorakis began again and the crowd, standing, sang:

> This earth belongs to them, and to us,
> No one can take it away. . . .

Kostas and Marita Grammatikakis arrived in Athens from Crete on their honeymoon and one day I lunched with them. The only salvation for Greece, they insisted, was a strong leader, a "dictator." I shuddered, remembering better than these attractive and intelligent young people what the word "dictator" meant in our century. They said there was no leader in Greece strong enough for the role and they saw no hope.

During this time I was having a suit made by a tailor on Stadiou Street. He spoke no English and one day when we were having communication problems during a fitting another customer, a dark-haired young man, interrupted in perfect English, saying, "Could I be of some help?" His name was Mike Serapoulos, he was twenty-eight and he had just returned from five years in an Illinois university where he had studied engineering. He was also a poet, an admirer of my friend, Nikos Gatsos. After the fitting we had a drink and he told me his family home was in the Peloponnese where he had been picking olives on his father's land. He had turned down job offers and a career in America to return to Greece. "Though I have become American, I am still a Greek," he said. "I have roots in this country which gave its roots to the Western world." By returning to Greece he had made himself liable for military service and he was enlisting in the Greek Air Force at the end of March.

The euphoria he felt on returning was running out. Looking at Greece through American eyes he could feel only despair. "Perhaps I had to come back because it is my last chance to find out what has gone wrong with my country, to understand what has happened in the Greece I see around me now. It is like running a film of history in slow motion.

In the country, in the Peloponnese, I still find Greece, the elements of greatness which I love, the closeness to nature, the identification with humanity. But the city is a twentieth-century phenomena and the Greek is lost in it. He is too easily demoralized, too easily corrupted."

He spoke bitterly of the King's New Year's Proclamation, "so idiotic it's not to be believed," of the strikes and of undemocratic economic policies. "The Midas-rich shipping tycoons fly Panama and African flags and bribe officials to escape taxation," he said. "They own châteaux in Switzerland and apartment houses in New York, while the masses of the Greek poor must leave their homeland to seek a living in other lands.

"Still there must be something real here, something of value," he said. "I cannot die before I know."

Walking home from our meeting, I was robbed. As often happened when I walked along, a stranger spoke to me, a small man in work clothes. Where was I from? New York? Ah, a wonderful city! He was a merchant seaman who had been in New York and had friends there. Walking with me he followed the usual conversational gambits, telling me of his travels, showing me postcards from American friends. He discussed the hard life in Greece, the shocking state of Athens with its mountains of odorous garbage. In Kotzia Square, outside the post office, he said suddenly, "You have dropped your newspaper." He handed me the *Time* magazine which a moment before had been in my jacket pocket. Before I knew what was happening he had slashed my trousers pocket with a knife and disappeared with my money clip and about seven hundred drachmae. It was not much and I had not been hurt. But I was angry with myself and with Athens. I had been a fool! I had let down the bars as was my habit, forgetting that one had to be on guard every minute. The experience haunted me for days and sent me into a depression.

On a Sunday morning I went to the agora, which was excavated and restored by the American School. On the way I passed through the flea market of Monastiraki, reconnoitering the Oriental-like bazaar spread out on the little streets. The disarray of products included furniture, old eyeglasses, all manners of used clothing which customers tried on in the streets, watches, awful jewelry, stoves, bathtubs, used auto parts, old *Playboy* magazines, icons, cameras, rugs, phonograph records and all types of machinery. One stall specialized in monogrammed athletic jerseys and jackets, among them garments labeled Green Bay Packers, Wheatley College, Kappa Sigma Fraternity, Cleveland-Pittsburgh Freight Lines and Fussball Club München. I stopped at a shop of icons where, mixed among the saints, were some obscene bronze satyrs with huge upright phalli. A woman tried to sell me a taxidermist's triumph of a mongoose fighting a cobra. "How much?" she shrilled. My language was not up to explaining that even if she paid me I would not carry away the horror.

The agora was green and springlike with small pink and white flowers. I climbed a hill to the Theseum, Athens' most perfectly preserved temple, and looked out over the multitude of Sunday strollers, imagining the bustling agora when Socrates and Plato discoursed there, and perhaps St. Paul. It began to rain.

In the hotel lobby I met Mrs. Schlossmacher of Cincinnati, a winter resident in Athens. "I'm an out-and-out damned capitalist," she said. "And I don't care who knows it. Capitalism gives jobs and nothing else does. All those other things are for bureaucracy." She looked the role. A great buxom glowing woman with a high beehive of white hair, she was dressed in pink and red. Crossing her fat legs, linking pink satin-slippered feet, she said, "I've lived in Greece for two years and all my friends want me to come home. But I'm having too much fun, the Greeks are too entertaining and I wouldn't miss a minute of it. You've no idea what a Greek will say to you. The other day in a beauty shop a perfectly nice woman asked me how many lovers I had. Imagine! Not did I have lovers, but how many? Can you imagine—me a respectable widow for ten years. No one would ever ask you that at home." She was shaking with laughter. "I have so much fun over here I just nearly die laughing."

My depression persisted. I was concerned about the book I was to write. How could one describe a country for which one's emotions were so deeply a mixture of love and hate? Any account of such a love-hate relationship indubitably would be tempestuous.

The time had come for a trip.

XVII

Spring

The guidebook said one might go to the Peloponnese in any month except February when the weather could be bad. On February 2, David Greggory and I set out, taking with us Mike Serapoulos, the Peloponnese who after five years in America wanted to rediscover his native heath before enlisting in the Greek Air Force.

We left Athens under a cloud of smoke. Five years ago, said Mike, no smog had blurred the famous Athenian light. In his absence the twentieth century had cast its cloud over the city. In the country it was a sunny spring morning with green meadows and almonds in pink blossom. The light off the silvery Saronic Gulf was blinding. We passed Kakia Scala, the narrow ledge between cliff and sea where Theseus killed Sciron, a pirate giant who harassed travelers. Crossing the Corinth Gorge, Greece's Panama Canal, we faced the shallow turquoise Corinth Gulf. Ahead lay the solitary mountain of Acrocorinth.

On that impregnable summit in a temple of Aphrodite a thousand priestesses were dedicated to sacred prostitution. Called *hetairae,* the famous whores were well educated and their houses were centers of learning in which the symposium was developed. The city at the foot of the mountain was the richest and liveliest in the Greek world. No wonder St. Paul wrote letters and dropped in to preach! On the *vima,* or platform, where he spoke we looked across the city, carpeted with small yellow and white daisies. The showpiece of Corinth, seven Doric columns of the temple to Apollo, stood in pristine solitude against blue skies and the deeper blue sea beyond. The pillars shone like a row of golden idols and between them we could see the snow-capped mountains across the gulf. We crossed to the temple and found the fluted columns were carved from a soft sandstone which eroding winds were eating away. Swallows nested in the crevices.

Most of the treasures of Corinth have been moved to Athens but enough remain for a small museum. In the grave of a youth, presented as discovered, an adolescent's bones lie with five vases for libations, five drinking bowls and six metal "strigils"—body scrapers used by athletes for scraping oils from their bodies. I wondered how the boy had died and if he'd been old enough to climb to the temple on the mountain.

An owl screeched in the ruins and a rooster crowed. My watch said exactly twelve o'clock. Greek roosters always crowed at noon, Mike said. I wondered why. On our way to the car Mike carved our names on a maguey plant. "A nice young one," he said. "It will last a long time." He was wearing American cowboy boots and a Mexican belt.

We stopped at a country *taverna* in a place called Dervenakia, where we ate *souvlaki* in an open yard and drank a good red wine called "Blood of Hercules." At another table three hunters were eating. Clusters of gray and blue woodcocks were flung over a chair, and their dogs visited our table, begging gristle and fat. A tiny steam train chugged by, clouding us in dark smoke.

Through a green valley of olives and new wheat we drove toward Mycenae. The fertile plain was the strength of the Atreus kings, making them for a time the equal of Egypt's Pharaohs, with whom they shared a veneration for death. In the modern town we passed the "Orestia Bar," "Restaurant Iphigenia" and "Hotel Atreus," and Mike moaned, "My God, what is happening to my country." The hilltop palace stood forth like Babel's tower in a strong landscape of mountains, facing the plain across which we had come. The famous headless lions at the gate have a sleek grace; otherwise the stone-age compound is a labyrinthian pile of gray stone which reminded me of nuraghi, the tribal dwellings of ancient Sardinia. With what engineering ingenuity, I wondered, did they elevate the huge stones, sometimes six feet thick? Asphodel and other flowers grew on the sunlit floors, but in the canyons of stone it was easy to imagine dour roofed-over rooms as settings for the bloody saga of Atreus.

I climbed to the top of the pile and found a stunted almond tree, rooted in the rock. Its arthritic branches, twisted by the prevailing northwest winds toward the southeast, were covered with thousands of pink buds. I lay under the tree, looking up through the pink branches at a three-quarters moon visible in the blue afternoon sky, listening to sheep bells echoing on the mountain walls. The wind blew cold. The tree growing on the bleak summit was a triumph of resurrection and life, a pink living fragrance growing out of death.

We visited the two beehive tombs incorrectly called Agamemnon's and Clytemnestra's. Entering the vaginally orificed entrances was like an entrance into an earth womb, and I felt the same terror and fascination when as a child I saw for the first time an entrance into a railroad tunnel. When we came out the sun was sinking below the high horizon and on a facing mountain the red flames of a shepherd's fire leaped up the gray rocks. We drove by twilight to Nauplia, the first capital of modern Greece when the Bavarian King Otto settled there for a short time in 1833. We took rooms in the Xenia Hotel on a promontory surrounded by the sea.

In the morning we drove to Epidaurus, the sanctuary where six centuries before Christ, Asclepius, son of Apollo and a mortal woman, Coronis, performed his miracles of healing and raising of the dead. We walked through a thick pine forest to the theater. Its gray-lichened stones were covered with green moss. I climbed to the top and listened to the conversation between Mike and an animated guide who performed his bag of tricks to demonstrate the acoustics—clapping hands, dropping coins, whispering, striking a match, and all of it came clearly to me on the top tier of the marvelous arena. Mike précised Aristophanes' *Lysistrata,* saying, "The women of Sparta declared a strike on fucking. So the men sent a messenger to the Athens parliament, asking for advice in the solving of their problem. At the gate of Athens the messenger was told to check his weapons. What weapons, he asked. Your spear, said the guard. That's not a spear, said the messenger, that's my cock." The guide's laughter filled the theater. When it subsided the place was so quiet I heard a bumblebee circling my head.

A cock crowed. It was noon, as Mike pointed out. We walked to the sanctuary zone, a vast acreage of foundations and scattered stones carpeted with a myriad spectrum of anemones. Never had I seen such a rich variety of floral colors—reds, pinks, mauves, lavenders, blues, yellows. There were also hyacinths and crocuses, but it was the anemones to which the place belonged. Asclepius' hospital was a field of stones fallen among the blossoms. In the temple to Zeus, fragments of fluted white columns and pedestals lay in a great jumble in the rainbow of color, a vision of paradise painted by Fra Angelico. To the west of the temple was the mysterious Tholos, a temple of cult practices containing six concentric walls, the outer three of which have no doors. The question of how its worshipers entered remains unsolved. One of the many theories is that the subterranean labyrinth housed sacred snakes.

We returned to Nauplia, passing men with mules plowing fields of stone, cutting red fissures in the thin soil. Youths were killing birds with slingshots, a common method of hunting in the Peloponnese. What kind

of birds? "Any birds," said Mike. "They put them in an omelet. Haven't
you ever eaten a sparrow omelet?" We climbed to Nauplia's eighteenth-
century Venetian citadel, an astonishing Sir Walter Scott compound of
ramps, stairways, gun turrets and enclosures large enough to contain an
entire population during an attack. There were dungeons for prisoners
and a chapel in which candles were burning. Descending to the town,
we sought out Greece's first parliament building, now a music school,
before which an old witch in a shawl was sweeping the stones with a
short broom. Helping her was a cat. Nearby, on a small square we found
San Spyridon Church in front of which Greece's first president, named
Ioannes Kapodistrias, was murdered in 1831. Inside was a primitive
painting of the stabbing by white-skirted assassins. Across the street from
the murder spot, in a dark little shop hung a colored picture of John F.
Kennedy.

In the evening we found a restaurant on the waterfront. Its walls
were lined with wine barrels and it was owned by three brothers named
Nikos, Giorgos and Kostas. Only two were on hand. The youngest,
Kostas, was in Switzerland for the winter. "A girl wrote him a letter,"
said Nikos. "So he went to be her fiancé." Fiancing seemed to be
Kostas' dilatory occupation—last year, said Nikos, he had been a fiancé
in Holland. Fiancing, I was thinking, was an "n" short of financing. I
was sitting under a framed picture of King Otto, a light-complexioned
man in lacy skirts, the expensive pleats of which covered wide northern
hips. Most of the kings of Greece have been of Germanic blood. "Germans
are methodical, disciplined and organized," said Mike. "Being none of
these things, Greeks admire the qualities in others." We ordered fish
which was excellent and as he ate, Mike spoke of his hungry childhood
during the German occupation. "A kilo of meat, probably dog, cost five
million drachmae, and at one time an egg cost two hundred million
drachmae. I was very hungry many times." Mike sucked out the white
pearly eyes of his fish, a delicacy, he assured me. When I disdained
the eyes of my fish he ate those too. The experience of hunger makes a
Greek respect food; he scavenges everything, letting no morsel go to waste.

In the morning we left Nauplia, stopping at Tiryns, another stone-age
palace with walls even more Cyclopean than Mycenae's. Tiryns' origin
goes beyond history; according to legend it was the setting for the
twelve labors of Hercules. Great vaulted passageways of unmortared
rock, unfelled by five thousand years of earthquakes, were polished to
an oak sheen by the oils of centuries of sheep stabled inside. The rock
on which the palace stands rises over a plain of orange groves and directly
below was a barbed-wired prison farm. Armed guards stalked over the
rooftops like Herr Obermeisters, pointing their rifles at denim-clad workers

crouching on the earth, planting vegetables. A young man stood at the fence watching us. He waved and I waved back.

It was the season of orange harvest. Sheep nibbled at oranges thrown over fences into roadside ditches and our car pulped the fruit and skidded on them. We drove on toward Argos, where there were ruins of Roman baths and the largest of Greece's theaters. Its curved slope almost faded into the hillside from which it was carved. Between Argos and Tripolis we crossed a chain of mountains dividing Argolis and Arcadia, descending at one point into "Pear Valley," a fertile plain surrounded by mountain peaks. A small black train chugged through it like a fuming dragon. Men stalked over the fields sowing wheat, hand-flinging the seeds like Biblical sowers. We crossed another mountain and arrived in Tripolis, capital of Arcadia. The modern commercial town was without charm. We lunched there, in a steaming basement restaurant, and continued on to Sparta. After six miles we arrived at Tegea, the religious center of the ancient Arcadian Confederacy. A village was huddled around the sunken ruins of a Doric temple to Athena, one of the most beautiful in the Peloponnese. Great black segments of fluted columns lay about. Mike said the marble was originally white, that the black color was a patina of lichens and "marble rot." The temple was felled by earthquakes and sank into the earth, hidden there until it was discovered in 1880.

We were in an area known as "Morea," famous in the past for its thriving silk industry. The Greek word means "mulberry," and we passed miles of trees, their pruned branches cut back to the trunk making a strange sight, like rows of brown columns with slightly askew Corinthian pediments. The branches are cut, said Mike, to provide fodder for sheep. We crossed a mountain range and descended into Lacedaemon, "the hollow land."

Ahead, snow-covered like Swiss Alps, were the peaks of the Parnon and Taygetus, from which Spartans dropped their weakling boy babies and unwanted girls. Ancient Sparta was a city without walls, taking pride in its human army of "moving walls." Boys were taken from their parents at an early age and submitted to a military regime unparalleled in human history for austerity and aggressive ruthlessness. Silence was a discipline, verbosity a disgrace in the greatest military state of Greece. Sparta's rivalry with Athens resulted in the Peloponnesian War (431– 404 B.C.), which Sparta won. But her brutality aroused the hatred of all Greece and the Spartans were finally defeated by the Achaean League, and the city was destroyed by the Visigoth King Alaric in 396 A.D.

Understandably, ancient Sparta was greatly admired by Greece's nineteenth-century Germanic kings who ordered the modern town built.

Greece's most modern city resulted. Neatly squared with wide boulevards, it has large uncrowded markets and comfortable bourgeois houses. The streets were shaded with orange trees heavy with golden fruit—not edible, as I discovered, but bitter oranges, planted deliberately to prevent pillage. Edible oranges filled the town. Street gutters were clogged with rotting fruit, the Eurotas River washed them away, and a donkey was eating them.

In a new hotel, the Dioscuri, the young manager promised us heat and hot water. But he did not say when and in our three days in Sparta we were never to experience either. Across the street was a statue of Lycurgus, the organizer and lawmaker of Sparta, erected by an American society. We walked through the twilight town, inhaling the delicious smells of oranges, baking bread, pine and cooking pots, and we dined in a restaurant called Semiramis, where I ate *stifado,* a marvelous stew of beef and onions marinated in wine and spices. The waiter said it was even better with rabbit.

In the morning the sun breaking through the clouds fell across the city in striated Jacob's ladders. I ordered orange juice and was served the chemical stuff called *portocalada.* Though oranges lay like fodder in the streets, the idea of squeezing one remained alien to a Greek. After breakfast we drove three miles through groves of olives and flowering almonds to Mistra, described by Kazantzakis as "the Greek Pompeii." Mistra's castle-fortress was built in the thirteenth century by the Frankish lord, William de Villehardouin, on the summit of a hill at the foot of the Taygetus. The Frankish conquerors, themselves conquered by the beauty of the dark-haired local women, forgot their homeland and founded a city. In the next two centuries a town of forty thousand grew up around the castle. The silk industry prospered, an academy of philosophic thought was founded, and a school of painting developed distinguished for its graceful elegance. Mistra survived until 1740 when it was burned by Albanian troops. Restored in our century. Mistra is the world's most beautiful monument of the Byzantine Renaissance.

It began to rain and under umbrellas we trudged up lanes of cypress, climbing through crumbling houses to Mistra's red-domed churches. In the Metropoli and Aphendiko only fragments of frescoes have survived the Moslem vandalism and the ravages of time and weather. In the Theodori, a ceiling Christ is caught in wide-eyed consternation; an upstairs gallery was for women and unbaptized men. In the Perivleptos, "Church of the Mother who sees all," the door was so low we needed to bow our heads to enter. The frescoes were the best preserved in Mistra. Beautiful panels portrayed the Nativity and Ascension, and the life and death of the Virgin. In a painting of Jesus' baptism, exorcised little demons swam away like a school of nasty little fish.

We climbed above the churches to the "Grand Palace," a roofless fortress of arches and walls, as haunting as Tintern Abbey. It covered a small plateau halfway between valley and mountain. Wandering through its vast silent halls I tried to imagine the courtly bustle. Through its empty windows I looked across the blue-misted valley, the fields of olives and oranges divided by rows of dark cypress, the tendrils of smoke rising from cottages. Birds chirped in the grass, and on the red church domes below white doves fluttered.

Through narrow lanes we continued to the convent of Pantanassa, "the Queen of the World," where seven nuns, the only inhabitants of Mistra, still kept house. Outside the cell doors were pots of flowers, fuchsias, lilies, cyclamens, geraniums and roses, each reflecting the personality of the one who cared for it. The nuns came out of their doors offering embroideries, the sale of which enabled them to buy food. Well-preserved chapel frescoes showed Christ raising Lazarus and entering Jerusalem on his donkey, and the Virgin receiving the annunciating angel. In the cortile an almond tree was in flower and under it a spring flowed. By it was a cup for drinking and a bar of soap for washing. Crowded on a ledge above the tree was a small cemetery.

The sun was shining. Returning to our car we passed an open restaurant in which a radio boomed *bouzouki* over the valley and hillside. A solitary waiter began to dance in the sunlight. Whistling, snapping fingers, his arms outstretched like a swooping angel's, he abandoned himself to the pleasure of the music, the warm sunlight, his joy in being alive. Sheep passed with tinkling bells and a walking tree turned out to be a donkey laden with branches and foliage, harvested for fodder.

In the afternoon we sought out ancient Sparta. It is not surprising that the warring Spartans did not distinguish themselves in the arts. The historian Thucydides observed, "If one day there remained nothing but its sanctuaries and the foundations of its public buildings, future posterity would never believe that this city was as powerful as is supposed." In the museum were a number of statues relating to the Dioscuri, the twin sons of Zeus and Leda (turned into a swan). Sparta's most famous sculpture is a helmeted warrior. The play of light on the beige marble gave the covered face a whimsical prudish quality. Only the hollowed eyes, the nose and a slightly prissy mouth are exposed. But the features, like those of Delphi's charioteer, are unforgettably human. The shoulders are slightly curved by strain and the neck vertebrae stand out.

Old Sparta is difficult to find. In an olive grove where women were beating the branches, recent excavations had uncovered a basilica of

Roman brick and some fragments of columns. For an hour we wandered among the trees seeking a theater. Night fell and we never found it. Owls hooted.

We dined that night with the manager of our hotel, whose name was Nassos, in a crowded *taverna* in the nearby village of San Giovanni. The place was decorated with Christmas bells and tinsel which Nassos said would remain through carnival and Easter. In a bower of crepe paper on the wall was a mask of Mrs. John F. Kennedy. Though a native Peloponnese, Nassos, a bachelor, had lived in Athens and after two months in Sparta did not think he would be able to endure his post much longer. "There are villages around Sparta without a single young person in them," he said. "Spartans are emigrators. Every family has one or two old men who have been in America and have come home to live on their pensions." After several drinks, Nassos' conversation turned to political matters. "Greece's problem is the King," he said. "The people will never forget what he did to Papandreou. He is king not for the down-people but for the up-people. He does not seem to understand that Greece is ninety per cent down-people." He introduced us to a young soldier who said, "In the army all recruits must swear an oath of allegiance to the King. I am no fool, I took the oath, but the first chance I get I will fight the King."

The next morning, a Sunday, we set out for Monemvasia, sixty miles from Sparta in the southeast corner of the Peloponnese. A bad mountain road took us through a springtime landscape of blooming almonds, thousand-year-old olives gnarled like free-form sculptures, fig orchards with wheat growing under the trees, and old houses covered with roses. After two hours we faced the sea and Monemvasia, a Gibraltar-like rock standing nine hundred feet in the silver sea and connected to the mainland by a bridge. Called Malvoisie by the Franks and Malmsey by the British, it was famous for its wine. According to a legend, when the Duke of Clarence was condemned to death by Richard III, he asked to be drowned in a cask of Malmsey. The vineyards were destroyed by Turks and today Monemvasia, with its impregnable Venetian and Byzantine fortresses, is a sun-warmed ruin. In recent years artists bought property there, stirring in natives a hope for a real-estate boom similar to Mykonos' and Hydra's, but the remote loneliness of the claustrophobic rock defeated them and many of the restored houses are boarded up. The houses cascaded with bougainvillaea and birds sang in cages outside the open doors. But no people appeared on the narrow streets and when we found a restaurant it had no food.

We returned to the mainland village and found a table at an outdoor café facing the sea. Drying octopuses hung on lines over our heads like grotesque laundries. A woman cooked fish for us on a grill and Mike consumed the head of his, sucking out the eyes, inflating them like bubble gum until they popped in his mouth. The performance was too much for me and I took a walk. A Sunday afternoon ennui had settled over the streets. A woman came out of a house and offered me a small loaf covered with powdered sugar which she said was "forgiveness bread," distributed in church that morning in memory of someone who had recently died. When I returned Mike was talking to a fat lady who was trying to sell him some property. Lots were selling for 200,000, drachmae she said; she just happened to have two which she could let us have for 20,000 drachmae. We passed up her opportunity for quick riches and turned back to Sparta.

The valleys were pink with almonds. I could not tell whether more trees had burst into bloom during the day or whether it was simply their softer illumination by the oblique afternoon light. We stopped to talk with a shepherd and his two sons watching sheep under some blossoming trees. The boys' sandaled feet were brown with dirt and calluses. "Don't be fooled by how they look, because they're here with sheep," said the father. "When I was a boy there were no teachers, no schools. Now my boys go to school and they're smarter than I am. The clear air washes out their brains. They know many things." We passed some youths lying in the sun doing nothing, and Mike said, "Philosophy would never have been born in Greece without such afternoons." Hunters passed with guns. "All Greek men have a shotgun," said Mike. "In my village there is not a house that does not have at least one gun."

The westward road to Kalamata through the Langadia Gorge was closed for the winter so the next morning we turned northward to Tripolis. Stopping to buy food for a picnic, we met an ex-Chicagoan with a curious problem. He had returned to marry in Tripolis and his two sons, born when he was still an American citizen, were Americans. Because he had stayed in Greece too long his own citizenship had lapsed, but his children, who had never been to America, remained Americans. "I want to take them to America," he said. "I want them to have the advantages to which Americans are entitled."

After twenty-three miles we arrived in Megalopolis—"large city"—once the capital of ancient Arcadia and now a moribund village of three thousand people. A mile from town are the ruins and here on the green arena of the most beautiful theater in Greece, we ate cheese and salami and drank a bottle of the Blood of Hercules. Curiously, no great fuss is made about Megalopolis and few tourists visit it. Its emptiness enhances its mountain-enclosed majesty. I climbed up through the grass-covered theater to a grove of pines and looked across the tree-bordered Elisson

The American Farm School, Alex Marlis second from right. For poor boys there were no opportunities.

Delphi, the navel of the earth. Clouds rose through columns like ancient ghosts.

Sokrates on butchering day. A hero dances alone on the mountain top.

The tablet of Anoghia. The general ordered a complete annihilation.

A man of Crete. "History has made us suspicious, hostile, lonely."

Bishop Timotheus. "America is proof that Christianity has not died from the earth."

Mistra, Greek Pompeii. White doves fluttered over red domes.

The theater of Megalopolis.
A shepherd grazed his sheep
among the ruins.

The temple of Vassae. A thank offering to Apollo in a lunar landscape.

Citrus grove in the Peloponnesus. The lemons were as large as footballs.

Carnival in Patras. Pagan and
Christian gods were at war.

Vardinogiannis in Crete.
Handshaking villages, weeping villages and kissing
villages.

In Selia. Manolis carried the flowers.

Easter. "Christ is Risen."

River to the ruins of a temple and the ancient city. Like Washington, D.C., Megalopolis was a planned capital, built in four years from 371 to 368 B.C. To populate it the inhabitants of some forty Arcadian villages and cities were moved there. It was not a happy enterprise, for internal dissensions between the assembled clans began almost at once. The city, enclosed by a wall, was built on both sides of the river which was spanned by a bridge. The federal assembly met in a building next to the theater, called the *thersilion*. The statesman Lycortas was born in Megalopolis, and his son, Polybius, whose works were studied by Thomas Jefferson before he drafted the American Constitution. The flourishing city was frequently besieged and destroyed. With characteristic alacrity, like a colony of ransacking and ransacked insects, the citizens kept rebuilding. Eventually they gave up. In Pausanias' time, Megalopolis was a heap of ruins known ironically as the "Large Solitude."

We crossed the river and wandered through the ruins. White fluted columns from a temple to Zeus lay like white fallen logs in the green wheat. A shepherd brought some sheep to graze among the ruins. I raised a question which frequently tantalized me—about what did shepherds think during the long days with their sheep? Mike said that shepherds were sensitive men in constant silent communication with nature, that they were aware of each bird and small animal, each growing thing. For them simply being out of doors was a fulfilling communion.

We drove on, coming after a few miles to the village of Katsimbali, the family heath of my friend, George "The Colossus" Katsimbalis, who himself had never been there. We stopped to make some photographs for him. It was a mean place of crumbling stone houses, of mud streets inhabited by barking dogs, wailing sheep and scrawny chickens. A woman scolded from a second-floor window at her son for letting some sheep get into a wheat field and the son raged at the sheep. Most of the men were in Germany, working in factories, and we saw only women, vestal viragos shouting to one another from windows and balconies. We found a café called "The Good Heart" but the door was locked and a woman called from an upstairs window that she had not the time to open it.

We had been told that the road to Andritsaina was bad and such an admission by Greeks was warning enough. We followed the Albios River through a classically beautiful Arcadia of green fields, terraced hillsides of flowering almonds and cypress forests. At Karytaina, a hilltop village with a Frankish castle, the steep upward road turned into a channel of mud. With Mike acting as copilot, instructing Greggory when to rev the motor, what ruts to straddle, we chugged on, fiording pools, bumping over rocks. At the top of a mountain we came upon a three-forked split in the trail with no sign to tell us which to take. A taxi miraculously appeared. The driver suggested one of us ride with him to lighten the load in our own car. When we declined he speeded up and lost us, but we were on the right path, which continued to grow worse. At four o'clock we arrived in Andritsaina. We found the Xenia Hotel to which the director of the Greek National Tourist Office in Athens had invited us as his guests. With a sinking feeling I saw that the place appeared to be shuttered. Some children were playing ball in the parking area. Overcome with laughter, they told us the hotel was closed for the winter.

We asked for another hotel and a boy directed us to the Vassae, at the opposite end of town. It was a cold weather-beaten place. In a down-stairs room old men in overcoats were playing cards and *tavli*. The manager welcomed us with an unctuous smile. We were in a hurry to get to the temple before sunset, so we declined his invitation to see the rooms. In the desolate square I saw for the first time a Greek woman tugging at worry beads, and I didn't wonder.

We went on, up through a lunar landscape of stones, past canyon walls whorled like old wood, with crisscross striations indicating geologic up-heavals. Clouds lay below us. Suddenly we were at the end of the road. We walked up a curved path and faced the loneliest temple in Greece, Vassae's shrine to Apollo. Constructed from the gray stone lying all around, it seemed to be part of the landscape, born, as indeed it was, of the mountain. It stood like a tree in harmony with the fierce earth in which it was rooted. It was built about 420 B.C. by Ictinus, architect of the Parthenon, and paid for by the Phygalians as a thank-offering to Apollo for delivering them from a plague during the Peloponnesian War. Except for its collapsed roof and several fallen columns it stands in eternal and forsaken isolation.

Below the temple was a stone hut. A caretaker appeared, wearing a heavy dark coat, and invited us into his little office to sign his registry. There had been only two visitors since January 1, a lady archaeologist and a professor, both English. The last American, a teacher from Boston, had arrived on Christmas Eve and stayed four days, passing Christmas with the caretaker and his family in the village.

Damp clouds rolling up the valley enveloped the temple in a cold gray mist. We walked perhaps two hundred feet and turned to look back. Like a ghost, the temple had disappeared and I felt a deep, inexplicable sorrow.

We returned to the Hotel Vassae for some *ouzo* in the public room. The old men were playing a card game called *xeri*. Others read news-papers or stood tugging at beads, watching us. We looked at our rooms. The beds were beat-up pallets on boards. The "running water" was a bucket of cold water with a slop pail on the floor and the "sanitation" was a hole in the floor up through which the cold wind whistled. There were no window blinds and on the walls someone had written, "You are very beautifull," and beneath, in another handwriting, "Vous ets boceau bon." The writers, I hoped, had warmer weather.

We walked the empty streets looking for a place to eat and found what appeared to be a combined butcher shop and restaurant. To enter we crouched under carcasses of beef dripping blood. The small room, blackened from smoke, was lit by a feeble unshaded bulb. The water supply was contained in an old Caltex oil can fitted with a small faucet. The manager, a grizzled unkempt little man wearing a blood-caked apron, was cooking something on a gas burner. At another table five youths without plates were eating grilled mutton from a common platter. A small boy, the owner's son, sat quietly on a wine barrel, watching. The room was filled with steam from a kettle of tripe which gave off a nauseous odor. Mike ordered the tripe and Greggory and I ate an oily soup and then the beef which had been boiled in it. We drank liberally of some resinated red wine which was not bad.

The youths at the next table told Mike they were high school class-mates, seventeen years of age, celebrating the unexpected holiday of a teachers' strike. Suddenly one of them began to sing, filling the little room with plaintive vigorous melody. His friends joined in, repeating in unison each line which the leader, who was blond and handsome, sang alone. Mike joined in the responses. The songs were "demotic," music of the people, he said. I asked him to write the words in English.

> I should not be happy,
> I should not be drinking wine,
> I should be in a cave,
> Living alone . . .

We bought the youths a liter of wine and they continued their dithyrambic improvisations, the leader giving a line in his loud baritone, the chorus taking it up in low key, developing it in a new direction with new themes which the leader in turn picked up and carried on. Between phrases they keened, like baying dogs, in monosyllabic wails which chilled the blood. They drank wine and puffed fiercely on cigarettes. The leader's eyes were shut, his face was red, and he seemed to be in a trance.

> I can't go on,
> People around me are not loving,
> I cannot live without love,
> I'll take a long path,
> A long path to a foreign land,
> To keep my heart from burning . . .

The leader's voice sagged and a new leader took over, the chorus following him. Their melic strophes seemed to have a Turkish influence, like
an imam wailing prayers from a tower.

> My golden heart is eaten by sorrow,
> The girl that I love is with someone else,
> I'll drown my pain in wine,
> Come into my arms,
> Sweeten my burning heart . . .

Drunk now, the singers interlocked arms, swaying as they sang.

LEADER: Underneath an oak tree, three old people were resting . . .
CHORUS: Three old people were resting and a captain of
    the sea passed by . . .
LEADER: A captain of the sea, the sea so wide, so far . . .
CHORUS: Why do you take our youths, the old people
    asked the captain . . .
LEADER: What do you offer them at home, asked the
    captain, what life, what love . . .
CHORUS: We will sail on the sea, the wide sea, but
    we will never forget our village . . .

Then, suddenly as they had begun, the singers stopped and reeled out
into the night. They were poor farmers' sons, said the butcher, and would
soon be leaving their homes. "Few youths remain on the land," he said.
"These boys will go to Athens, to Germany or to Australia. All of them
will leave." The butcher's name was Vasilis Fianoulis and he had been
in his youth an unsuccessful suitor for the hand of one of Mike's aunts
who taught school in Andritsaina. He remembered Mike's grandfather,
who as the Peloponnese representative for a German patent medicine
firm, had been well known in the area and a popular best man at
weddings and godfather at christenings.

It was too early to retire to our cheerless rooms so we joined the
old men in the public room where Mike taught me to play *tavli,* a game
somewhat like backgammon. A patient teacher, he let me win two games.
In a conversation with the manager Mike discovered that his grandfather
had stayed in the hotel. The man offered us a drink and in return we
listened to his desolate report of life in Andritsaina. The people were
sheepherders who, because their wool was prized by the Turks, had
prospered during the occupation. Extending their domains a hundred
kilometers to the sea, they became the landed gentry of the Peloponnese.
In the nineteenth century Andritsaina had five thousand people and one
of the most famous libraries of Greece. "The families still hold the land,"

he said. "But they have moved to Patras and Athens. The government has no interest in the farming population, there's no dignity left on the land. Andritsaina is a dying village of one thousand people and no young men remain here." The Greek shepherd, he said, was disappearing. With growing industrialization and a gravitation toward urban centers, a shepherd was the lowest of citizens, hardly more than a slave in ancient times. Because Communist leaders acclaimed the dignity of agricultural workers and shepherds, those few shepherds remaining on the land were turning to the political left, to Communism.

We went upstairs. The rooms were icy cold, the sheets clammy damp. "Imagine what it would be like in winter," said Mike. I suggested we examine the graffiti on the wall for Grandfather's initials. Shifting the seasons, Mike said, "Are we lucky it's not summer. In winter fleas are in hibernation." He started moving his bed, making a great racket. Pointing to a hole in the wall, he said, "I had a mouse in my face once when I was a little boy." The landlord chose the moment to appear with registration sheets, demanding among other things our fathers' birth dates and mothers' maiden names. I asked Mike to inquire if the man had an electric heater, for which I would happily pay a supplementary fee. The idea struck the fellow as funny. I put on two sweaters, a cap, gloves and a muffler, bolted a glass of brandy with two Nembutals and I slept.

In the morning, braving the toilet, I found for my use on a nail in the wall, the registration sheets. At last I knew for what purpose Greece required a never-ending supply of mothers' maiden names. We had a decent breakfast of eggs, bread and coffee and asked for our bills. The government rate-card posted in the rooms gave the price as twenty-four drachmae and the bill said thirty-three. It was not a great difference but I was feeling querulous and demanded an explanation. The official price list, said the manager, was two years old. He was lying, of course. I got no support from Mike who could not forget that the manager had been Grandfather's friend. He said, "When a Greek lies it is because he is polite. He is really thinking of you, he doesn't want to hurt your feelings. You must try to see through your wall of Calvinism and remember that " I pondered.

It had rained in the night and pools of water in the road reached the car doors. We stopped to rouse a donkey curled like a dog in the mud. But it was all downhill and we made it by noon to Megalopolis where Greggory planned a visit with the family of a friend, a girl in Los Angeles. The father's name was Antonios Kallianotes, and we had no trouble finding the house. He was a friendly white-haired old man with horn-rimmed glasses who had lived for thirty years in Boston where he owned a grocery. In 1958 he returned with his wife to their old home where they lived comfortably on his American veteran's pension and Social Security. Four of his five children remained in the United States and one, a daughter, lived with her husband and son in the house next door.

Within a half hour after our arrival Antonios' wife, a motherly smiling woman, had spread a table of food and wine for us. Framed Currier and Ives prints hung from walls in which there were wide cracks, the results of an earthquake the previous April in which fifteen houses in Megalopolis were destroyed. After the meal we were taken to the daughter's house for dessert and a liqueur made from distilled orange blossoms. A Christmas tree in the corner was lit up for us.

In the afternoon we turned south across the Messenian plains toward Kalamata. The prosperous commercial town on the sea was, according to my guidebook, a swinging resort in summer. In winter it was an empty place with nothing to do. We stopped at a seaside bar for drinks and were its only customers. An excellent hotel, the Rex, with heat and baths, was a sybaritic joy after our Spartan night in Andritsaina. We passed the evening listening to Mike discourse on women, a natural subject for three bored bachelors. When he returned from America he had found that some girls he had known in high school were prostitutes. "They were simple village girls who are victims of The Dream," he said. "They were corrupted by cheap magazines in which they read about Hollywood, and an easy rich life with beautiful clothes, cars, cocktails and bikinis on the beach. Prostitution became a problem in Greece in 1955 and 1956 with the arrival of America's Sixth Fleet. A simple Iowa sailor represented to a girl all the things which she associated with American life. Managers of clubs and bars promised the girls money and the opportunity to meet Americans. In those days Athens was like the American old West— all you needed for a bar was four walls, liquor and girls. The girls were living out The Dream, and the managers made the money.

"In Athens, there are daughters from best families who are call girls. A girl will say to her mother, 'I'm going to the library to make some notes for mathematics.' Or, 'I'm going to my girl friend's house.' Instead she goes for an hour's rendezvous with a man and earns five hundred drachmae. It is an entirely separate world from the one in which she lives, the world of her family and a respectable boy friend. In a month she will earn more money than her father.

"In such a situation there is no trust between the sexes. My friends have all had shocking experiences and say they will not marry in Greece. The girls are no longer trained in cooking, home economy and house-wifery as in the old days. They want the freedom they think American girls have. But they misunderstand this freedom—to them it is only self-indulgence. They will marry only men who can afford servants. They are not, like American girls, intellectuals. They have no interest in learning. They have given up all the old values without finding new ones.

"So it is not surprising that we have a high divorce rate. Until recently marriages were always arranged. Natural selection did not exist. The parties were brought together by their families and if they liked one another they were lucky. Sometimes a girl is allowed to say 'I don't like that one' and her family will look for another. The rich families are only concerned with not letting the wealth out of the family. No one of lesser fortune is eligible. In shipping families cousins marry cousins inside the small shipowning circle. Divorces are usually in the forty-year age group. The men have discovered with money they can do anything and their wives find out they also can have fun."

In the morning we drove through hill country to Pylos. Small farms were bordered with cypresses, and the roads had a festive air with people traveling either on foot or by donkey. An old man with three goats waved; a woman was shepherding twelve sheep and leading a hog on a leash.

Because of its strategic location on a natural harbor, Pylos was an important city in the ancient world. Until its destruction about 1200 B.C. it was, under the rule of King Nestor and his descendants, one of the rich cities of the Mycenaean world. The harbor is blocked by a rocky island where, in an engagement of the Peloponnesian War, an Athenian expeditionary corps forced the surrender of Sparta. In the same waters in 1827 the allied fleets of England, France and Russia routed a Turkish-Egyptian fleet and established the independence of Greece. Today Pylos is a pretty hillside village of twenty-five hundred persons with a small park in which captured Turkish cannons are mounted on concrete pedestals. We stopped for coffee and then drove ten miles north to Nestor's Palace. The two-story structure was built of wood, and only the foundations remain. Excavated since the last war by the University of Cincinnati, it is one of the best-preserved monuments in Greece. To protect walls mortared with mud a steel canopy covers the area. In the center is a great throne room with a circular hearth and around it are waiting rooms, lavatories, pantries and storage cellars. Living quarters were on a second floor.

We continued north along the Ionian Sea. Fields of blue iris with yellow gorse, mustard and sorrel were almost too beautiful to bear. The burst of spring flowers covered the land, turning it into an everlasting garden—iris, anemones and primulas bloomed everywhere and almonds covered the hills with pink light. In villages the road narrowed into stony paths. We saw a shoemaker, a Greek Hans Sachs, pounding a sole outside his shop, surrounded by children. In Kiparissia we lunched on fish and "boiled weeds," a wild green served cold with vinegar. Near us two large tables were filled by a party of country folk ranging in age from several small babies to old men. One of their number, a house painter who had visited Canada as a seaman, introduced himself in English. The old man was his father, the others were brothers, uncles, sisters and a variety of in-laws and friends. They were Spartans who had arrived in Kiparissia two days before by bus to testify at the trial of the painter's brother in a local courthouse. The brother had shot a woman, said our friend, not only the woman who was dead, but twelve other persons who had survived. He said it was accidental, the brother had been hunting rabbits. How the woman happened to be where a rabbit should have been was what the jolly family was there to explain. Because of high public feeling about the case in Sparta the trial had been moved across the mountains to Kiparissia. In the meantime the family was enjoying its holiday with gusto, eating great platters of fish and calling for more wine. Our informant, better dressed than the others, had a carefully-nurtured inch-long nail on his small finger. The nail, said Mike, was a status symbol indicating he was foreman of his paint crew, and it was useful "for cleaning out the ears."

We passed villages with tents which Mike said were issued by the government to families whose homes were destroyed by the earthquake a year before. In the branches of oak trees I noticed wooden floors with thatched canopies which Mike said were "summer beds" for sleeping in hot weather. Old women spinning wool in doorways appeared to be fluttering sticks of cotton candy. Near the village of Kakóvatos we stopped and walked through dunes of pine to the sea. The air was filled with a variety of smells, sulfur from a thermal resort, resin flowing into little pails attached to pine trees which would be used for resinating wine, and thyme and marjoram which, Mike said, "is gathered by girls to pack their dowry linens so their beds on their marriage nights will smell of the fields."

At Pyrgos we turned inland toward Olympia, where we arrived at dusk, just as the gates to the sanctuary were being closed. We stood by the fence looking at the sacred grove in a hollow of wooded hills. The sky turned purple, the light grew soft and the temple columns shone like white ghosts. Gradually the noises of the day died away. The river murmured and crickets chirped. Sheep bells tinkled and stars appeared.

Above us, on a hill, was a hotel, where a beguiling chorus of doll-like girls, smiling like geishas, opened doors for us and carried our bags. One of them, small and firm-breasted, showed me to my room. She spoke not a word but the articulation in her eyes sent my head spinning. The hotel was old-fashioned, with elegant Victorian lounges and high-ceilinged rooms. It seemed that wherever I walked in the long corridors I met the same girl, smiling sweetly. In the bar I found Mike engaged in a colloquy with another, and he reported that the girls were hand-picked from neighboring villages, that the one who had taken me to my room was sixteen years old and her name was Anita.

We walked into the town. There was an air of desperation in the empty streets. Shopkeepers, restaurateurs and souvenir sellers seemed to be crouching in doorways waiting to spring out and draw us in. Olympia's season would begin in a month, said Mike, and the streets would be so crowded one could hardly pass through them. We found a restaurant that had a handful of customers. The manager recommended chicken, which turned out to be almost inedible. Back in the hotel I met Anita carrying the bags of a newly arrived guest. For a moment she raised her lashes. Some of the other girls had changed into carnival costumes and were dancing in a salon, presumably to give the impression there were people in the hotel. I went to my room to read my guidebooks, and Kazantzakis, who called Olympia "a sacred landscape" and said, "No other place in Greece incites a feeling of peace and concord so gently, so compellingly."

Peace was the role of Olympia. Driven by ambition, hatred, and jealousy, the passionately brawling Greek tribes and colonies tyrannized, enslaved and exterminated one another with unflagging persistence. The miracle of Olympia was a sacred truce which automatically stopped wars. Suddenly every fourth year the Greek world forgot its quarrels and aggressions and gathered to worship the gods and spend their competitive energies in athletic games. Friends and foes came from the powerful cities of the mainland, from the Aegean Islands, the Greek colonies of Asia Minor and from Italy, Sicily, Egypt and the Black Sea. If a war happened to be in progress, athletes from both sides put aside their arms and traveled to Olympia to compete in a friendly way. In Olympia the Greeks came to their maturity and gave the world Panhellenism which was to glow like the Olympian torch through Western civilization. So important was the assembly that Greek time was reckoned by "Olympiads," the four-year spans which passed between games.

Games were the heart and core of the assembly and civilization was matured by them. No other people have understood the function of sports so completely. Gymnastics were a requirement in a Greek's growth as a social being. A strong healthy body was necessary for a healthy vital mind. Harmony between the two was the goal.

The gods competed at Olympia before man. Zeus wrestled his father, Kronos, for the kingdom of the world, and his son, Apollo, defeated Hermes in a race. The sanctuary began as a purely religious center, a home of the gods with Zeus as presiding deity. In the fifth century B.C. a great temple was built. So lavish were the gifts of worshipers that the shrine became Greece's richest museum and eventually an archive of Greek history and a diplomatic center to help bring peace to warring cities. Orators, writers and artists turned Olympia into a center of humanism. Herodotus and Thucydides read their works, Pindar recited odes to a background of twanging lyres and Plato conducted symposiums. The official epoch of the Olympiads began in 776 B.C. As the popularity of the primitive religion declined, the games grew in importance and continued for more than one thousand years. Olympia's decline began with Roman pillaging in the second century B.C. Sulla carried temple treasures to Rome and games were run according to the caprices of the conquerors. The Emperor Nero competed in the chariot race—despite his falling off his chariot twice and not finishing the race, he was awarded first prize. The last festival was held in 393 A.D., the year the Emperor Theodosius ordered the outlawing of pagan rites. Thirty-three years later Theodosius II destroyed the pagan temples. Whatever the Christian marauders left was felled by earthquakes in the sixth century. Earth was hurled upon Olympia from Mt. Kronion and the flooded rivers covered it with sand. Olympia was forgotten until 1875 when the Greek parliament authorized Germany to excavate, and the treaty between the two countries has continued to the present time. It is ironic that Germans, driven by god cults of their own, should have raised their extraterritorial flag over Olympia, but hardly surprising. The Germans, who developed physical strength and endurance to make war, could hardly comprehend the Greek's balance of body and spirit, nor his concept of athletic games as the beginning of peace. The scholars and diggers did their work well, excavating and restoring with integrity and taste. They planted oaks, poplars and cypresses, turning the sanctuary into the shady grove it once was.

I got up from my bed and went to the balcony. The wooded hills made a dark circle, like a protecting wall, around the sacred acres. Stars flashed on the rippling waters of the river; the stones among the trees glistened like a cemetery at night. Owls hooted and bats swooped around me. I seemed to be hearing what Kazantzakis called "the voices beneath the soil." The Greek land was "a deep tomb with layer upon layer of corpses whose varied voices rise and call you." I wondered if what I was looking upon was really a graveyard and if it was dead, the Olympian dream. Or would it rise again, taking men upward toward a plateau of wisdom and a noble vision for human peace?

I felt oppressed, like a mourner. A key rattled in the lock, the door opened and there was the child, Anita, lashes lowered, pink rising in her cheeks, filling the room with quickening life.

"Excusez-moi," she said, speaking words she'd been taught, wishing me to understand that she did not know I was in the room. She waved a hand toward the hall—she had thought I was with my friends. She had come, she explained, to turn down the bed. With her head turned slightly to watch me, she drew down the coverlet, fluffing the indentation of my head from the pillow.

In the morning I rose early and went down into the mist-shrouded valley, crossed the bridge over the river and waited for the gates to open. I looked across the acres of gray-lichened columns, squat heavy Doric, gracefully slender Ionic and elegantly fluted Corinthian with acanthus capitals, standing among the oaks and pines in a meadow of blue iris. A madness of bird song filled the damp morning. What kind of birds, I asked the guard who arrived with a key. He shrugged and replied, *"Tsiropoulia,"* meaning "skinny-birds." "Half a bite," he said. "We don't listen to birds, we eat them. There are only two kinds, those big enough to eat and those too small to eat."

Below the gate and outside the sacred Altis, or temple zone, were the gymnasium and palestra, open quadrangles where athletes trained for a month before the games. Only free Greeks were allowed to compete, neither slaves nor criminals nor foreigners. Women were excluded under penalty of death. One noble lady named Kallipateira disguised herself as a trainer and remained undiscovered until her athlete son won a race and she betrayed herself with weeping. Because she was the sister and mother of Olympic victors, the judges spared her life but decreed that henceforth trainers as well as athletes must remain naked. I tried to imagine the scene—hundreds of oiled-bronzed youths scurrying through the energetic preparations, running, leaping, wrestling, watching one another with sly, jealous eyes, feigning indifference, their tempers tensing as the day approached.

The games began on the dawn of the first full moon after the summer solstice and continued for five days. As the sun rose trumpets pealed in the valley and priests performed sacrifices. The first contest was a foot race of speed and endurance. The second was a military race in which the athletes ran twice around the stadium in full armor with shield in hand. After that came boxing, wrestling, jumping, and discus and javelin hurling. The contests concluded with chariot races in the hippodrome at the end of which riders were required to jump off and continue alongside their horses, not letting go of the reins. On the last emotionally charged day the victors were crowned with laurel and given prizes of money and valued objects, and then they rode on chariots hitched to four white stallions past forty thousand cheering spectators to the temple of Zeus. Their nude statues were placed in the Altis, which turned in time into a forest of gleaming manly forms. Returning to their native cities they were welcomed with triumphal receptions. Sometimes city walls were torn down for their homecomings. They were granted special privileges which continued through their lives.

South of the palestra are the ruins of the Theokoleon which was the home of the priests, a small temple called the Heroon, believed to be the tomb of a dead hero, and the Leonidaion, a hostelry for distinguished guests. A wall separated these buildings from the Altis, a zone too sacred for human habitation.

The squared sanctuary area is dominated by the huge temple to Zeus. The broken columns lie where they fell, like great sausage slices, still keeping their column form. I lay against one of the fragments, measuring its width, which was seven feet. The native sedimentary rock from which they were carved was formed from millions—trillions—of sea shells, tiny as peas. Inside the temple reaching to the roof, had stood one of the seven wonders of the ancient world—Phidias' statue of Zeus, carved of gold and ivory and inlaid with precious stones. It was removed to Constantinople by Theodosius II and there was destroyed by fire.

Crowding the sacred zone were smaller temples dedicated to Rhea, mother of Zeus, and to Hera, his wife, to the heroes Pelops and Hippodamia, and to Philip of Macedon, the father of Alexander the Great. At the foot of Mt. Kronion, just inside the north wall, stood a row of treasuries built by Greek states. The temples, the building of which continued for ten centuries, reflected every variety of Greek and Roman style. I wandered as in a dream through stoas and agoras, taking care not to step on the iris which covered the earth like a carpet. The blue blossoms were everywhere, covering the home of the gods even where there seemed no earth, out of cracks in the stones, from old clay vessels lying among the marbles. The sunlight on the green grass and blue flowers was iridescent. People were pouring into the area and human voices silenced the birds. Women picked iris like children in a meadow and then, bored with the bouquets, they threw them away. The dead flowers lying everywhere angered me. It made no difference to me that the supply had no end, each ravished blossom was a pain. A woman arrived with a band of children and spread a picnic on the grass. I tried to tell myself that my purist irritations over the human defilement was absurd and I thought how it must have been with thousands of athletes and poets and priests, with the crowds bustling to temples and theaters and to the stadium.

I climbed the hill to the museum, which was just below our hotel. On a table inside the door was a scale model of Olympia. Looking down on it was like soaring over the valley in a helicopter. The temple dominated the scene like the Parthenon dominates the Acropolis. Outside the south wall was the palace of the Olympian senate and several Roman buildings; outside the east wall was the hippodrome and the 650-foot stadium.

I entered the museum in a kind of panic, afraid of what I knew was inside, afraid of my responsibility to myself. I remembered Kazantzakis' admonition that "a traveller must see everything as it is the first and the last time . . . hail and farewell." In no other museum was each stone so perfectly a masterpiece, in no rooms did the voices of the past speak so directly. My fear was that I might not be able to see, to perceive it all. Standing before me in the hall was Apollo, surveying with calm serenity a drama of tumultuous violence around him, raising his right arm, casting over the uproar, like a blessing, his mystic peace. I relaxed.

The scene from the temple's west pediment presents the battle of the Lapiths and Centaurs at the wedding of the Lapith King Pirithous. The cause of the turmoil is women. Inflamed with wine, the half men, half horses have suddenly burst into a rampage of rape. A Centaur grabs the bride in passionate embrace and the bridegroom splits his skull with an ax. Other Centaurs are trying to carry off women; one is abducting a boy. The howling combatants bite, stab, and wrestle. In the panting frenzy men and beasts are roaring with pain. Rising above it all, the god gazes over the turbulence with unruffled majesty. By his glance barbarism is soothed into civilization, the divine light of reason triumphs over man's primal animal nature.

I turned to the east pediment, a stately formal frieze representing the chariot race between King Oenomaus of Pisa and the Achaean Prince Pelops. Oenomaus, according to the myth, forced the suitors of his daughter, Hippodamia, to enter a chariot race with himself, the loser of which was to be killed. Thirteen suitors had already lost their lives when Pelops presented himself. He bribed Oenomaus' servant to unfasten a wheel of the king's chariot, won the race, killed the king and claimed both kingdom and daughter. The fragmented panel is a calm one with Zeus in charge. The horses are at ease. But the scene troubled me. I could not accept Pelops' victory, so flayed by trickery. The Greeks' admiration of the trickster nettled me. Zeus turned himself into a swan to make love to Leda and to a white bull to seduce Europa. Hermes stole fifty cows from his brother, Apollo, and drove them backwards to Pylos, leaving hoofprints pointing in the opposite direction. Ulysses, the greatest trickster of all, devised the stratagem of the Trojan horse and had his enemy, Palamedes, stoned to death as a traitor on the false evidence of a letter planted under his bed. The mythology of gods and heroes is a never-ending saga of deception. The trickster, so greatly admired, is still very alive in the Greek character. It accounts for the Greeks' inherent mistrust of one another. A Greek trusts no one. Business and social relations are maintained in an atmosphere of suspicion, surveillance and accusation. A Greek will forever try to trap you in a lie—to do so gives him a sense of power. Mistrust is so deeply rooted in the national character that not only does a Greek trust neither Greek nor foreigner, but the Greek nation has never matured to the point of trusting another country.

Other great statues were in the room, the Winged Victory Nike and sculptured panels showing the twelve labors of Hercules. The most spirited was a terra cotta of Zeus abducting Ganymede. The god, smiling ribaldly, stalks triumphantly off with the youth, and the nude boy, wearing only a sunbonnet and clutching a chicken, is curiously bemused.

Olympia's most famous single work, sometimes called the most perfect statue in the world, is Praxiteles' Hermes. It stands in a room of its own on a platform of sand in which someone had written with a finger, "Zorro." The body is strikingly virile, yet there is a womanly softness about it. In a bust photograph offered for sale, the god, cradling the infant Dionysus, might pass for a madonna and child by Michelangelo. Blood seems to flow under the silken white skin. The mouth, with a strong lower lip, is petulant, the eyes gaze remotely past the infant, a brother for whom Zeus the father has ordered Hermes to be baby-sitter. The child demandingly extends an arm but Hermes is not interested. He seems to find caring for the child a bore and will be glad to deliver it to the nymphs and be rid of it.

The statue creates a powerful and mysterious spell. A man in a dark cape entered the room and fell to his knees, kissing the sand at Hermes' feet, exactly as he might have bowed before a church icon to kiss the feet of a saint. I heard a sigh, and turning, saw a blonde woman, probably Scandinavian. Catching my glance, aware that I could see the tears in her eyes, she said, "His *thing* is broken off." So it was. The testicles were there, however, like a pair of ripe plums, and I remembered a professor lecturing in California, describing them as the most perfect in the world. I had wondered how the professor knew. Now, seeing them, I had to admit he had a point. In the outer room I watched the woman passing one emasculated statue after another, her grief accelerating. "All their *things* are broken off," she wailed, checking off Apollo, some Lapithae and Centaurs, and a youth lying on his stomach. "Even the horses' *things* are broken off. Who did it?"

"Christians," I replied, and she asked, "What did the Christians do with all the *things?*"

I could only theorize. To the right of the east pediment the woman found a youth with his parts intact and, comforted, she smiled through her tears.

Late in the afternoon I returned with Mike to the sanctuary. We sat on the steps of the temple watching the shadows lengthen across the stones. A schoolteacher was herding a class of pupils through the zone. Mike listened to her spiel and said, "She misses completely the spirit of Olympia, she turns it into a symbol of supernationalism. She does not understand that the temples, that all the ruins in Greece, stand for one thing, human freedom. In our elaborate mythology the gods are human gods with a passion for individual liberty. Each stone speaks of it.

"Our last war ended in 1951. Before that it was occupations—Turks, Venetians, English, Germans. The past fifteen years have been the first in which we were free to act as a nation. Now is the time, the opportunity to teach the lesson of Greece to our young. Education should be our salvation. But education is wrong, it fails. What the woman is speaking about is glory without meaning, pride without soul. She creates a fascist dream and for her sin Greece will suffer."

He wandered away, leaving me alone on the steps. A young man joined me. "My name is Angel," he said, smiling insinuatingly. "And that's what I am." He was a guide, he said, and asked if I'd like to go for a walk. Not right now, I said. Would I meet him for a drink in the evening? I said I would see what my friends had planned. "I think it would be better if you met me without your friends," he said, leaving no room for misinterpretation.

He left. Guards were scurrying about, rounding up visitors, preparing to close the gates. Workmen going home from their diggings carried their shovels on their shoulders. A lean dog loped over the ruins and a caravan of sheep passed outside the wall. The wilted flowers on the paths made me wince.

We dined in the hotel, waited on by the plump little geishas who giggled at Mike's drolleries. The dessert was an elaborate pastry of cream and sugary nuts. I asked for a plain dish of ice cream and one of the girls said, "Not in winter. You would catch cold." They invited us to join them for a carnival frolic in a nearby village. I begged off and returned to my room, not wanting to miss the turning down of the counterpane.

In the morning we set out for Patras. On our way we stopped at an orange grove owned by a friend of Mike's. The rows of oranges reaching across the plains to snow-covered mountains were like California. The owner, named Konstantinos "Kostas" Kaoukis, had been a schoolmate and was a friend of King Constantine. He was a tall, darkly handsome young man of twenty-five with gentle manners and voice. He owned five thousand orange trees. It was near the end of the harvest and 600,000 kilos of fruit had already been shipped to Holland and Germany. Drop-offs were not gathered and the irrigation ditches were clogged with rotting fruit. On the ground the oranges turned into balls of green mold which sent out clouds of green dust when I stepped on them. A dozen men were picking and piling oranges on a wooden platform where four shawled women packed and sorted, throwing the discards on a rotting pile. The cavalier waste of fruit pained me. I was remembering my first orange, a Christmas gift from my father. In our Wisconsin winters an orange was an event. "Will you permit me to present you with some oranges?" Kostas asked gently. He ordered two workmen to fill our station wagon. The oranges from new trees imported from California and Israel, grew large as cannon balls in the Greek earth. Some lemons were shaped like footballs and were just as large.

We stopped in a village called Andravida and in a steaming workers' restaurant, lunched on nutmeg-flavored meat balls called *sutzukakia*. After the dismal food of Olympia, they were a feast. The attitude of restaurateurs in tourist meccas is that visitors who stay a day or two have to eat and are probably not coming back, so no effort is made to please them. The worst food in Greece is served in Olympia and Delphi.

Our incredibly good fortune with weather seemed to be coming to an end. Dark clouds hung ominously over Patras and the snowy mountains beyond. We had come for Greece's greatest bacchanalia, the Patras carnival. "Live again the years to remember," said an English-language brochure. "The younger ones of both sexes are flooding the streets in masquerades all the evenings. In many cases behind these masks wrinkled faces and gray hair find also the temper to jump around." Newspapers spoke of egg and chocolate wars between the American and Russian ambassadors. Hotels had been reserved for months. Ours was classified as "de luxe." Its bathless small rooms and hard lumpy mattresses were hardly that, but it faced the square and beyond, a great pier in the sea. A tiny railroad locomotive kept passing on the main street and now and then an airplane appeared on the horizon. The chugging trains, planes, autos, donkeys and harbor ships recalled the transportation calendars which were a delight of my youth when I dreamed of leaving the Wisconsin farm. The choked streets roared with the din of amplified phonographs blaring Greek, German, Italian and American popular music. Patras is a modern middle-class city with excellent shops little different from prosperous commercial towns in Germany, Switzerland or the U.S.A. Arcades over sidewalks protected the crowds from rain which had begun to fall. Squares and fountains were decorated with glistening gargoyles made of waterproofed plastic.

A *taverna* we visited in the evening was called "The Jungle"—its walls were decorated with paintings of tropical forests inhabited by lions, tigers, monkeys and coiling snakes. On a platform fronting a *bouzouki* band, a girl was wagging her hips like a wound-up doll, and a second girl sang. An "egg war" continued through the evening. This consisted of pelting everyone with soft wax eggs which broke on contact, showering the victim with multicolored bits of confetti. Children wandered among the tables with bowls of the eggs, selling them. As foreigners we were popular targets and the cannonade had to be endured with humor. The eggs were solid enough to sting—one properly aimed could have blackened an eye. Open mouths were invitations for bombardments which resulted in an epidemic of coughing and spitting. Confetti lay deep on the floor and guests were covered with it. Bits of colored paper clung to hair and clothes.

The real entertainment was on the dance floor. The dancers were youths in their teens and early twenties, some in military uniforms. Groups took turns on the floor moving earnestly, intently performing a rite. One tall thin lad lay on the floor, arching his body, thrusting his groin upward in lewd pivots and a friend lay on him, joining in the writhing. Finally the noise and the eggs became too much to bear and we left. Outside the door several young men were urinating in the rain, further dampening the damp night. In the hotel my lumpy bed was a rack; the street roar filled my dreams.

It was still raining in the morning. A clerk told us that the bishop of Patras, "an enemy of the carnival," was praying for rain, that pagan and Christian gods were battling for control of the skies. We went to the United States Information Office where I presented a letter to the director, an explosive volatile little man named Dimitris Plessas. Photographs of Abraham Lincoln, John F. Kennedy and Lyndon Johnson decorated his walls. For an hour we listened to Mr. Plessas' pro-American, anti-Greek discourse. "We're a lazy people," he said. "You Americans work hard for your luxuries. We prefer not to work, our aim is to enjoy life. But we want it both ways, we want your luxuries without working for them, we want you to give them to us. All Greeks are individuals with strong wills. In parliament we have three hundred stubborn mules." I was thinking of newspaper stories of parliamentary sessions in which deputies picked up their chairs and threw them at one another and had to be subdued by police. "The Greek will must be kept under some sort of control," Plessas went on. "What Greece needs is a dictatorship with a strong whip." Did he know what he was saying, I asked in astonishment; had he forgotten recent history? "I can phone forty or fifty of my friends in Patras right now," he said. "And each one would say the same thing. A dictator is necessary to save Greece." The people of Patras, he continued, were the aristocrats of Greece. "Athens is our Sodom and Gomorrah," he went on angrily. "Eighty per cent of the Athenian women are prostitutes. Thank God in Patras we are still morally sound." I remembered Athenians describing Patras as the most licentious city in Greece. "Poor Greece," Plessas wailed, breaking into a fit of sobbing. "Oh, poor Greece." Over his shoulder I saw a huge rain-soaked rat walk across a stone ledge outside the window.

He guided us on a tour of the city, beginning with the monument to Archbishop Germanos on the spot where the priest-hero rallied followers to rise against the Turks in 1821. We continued to a Venetian castle to which the Archbishop marched his troops to attack a Turkish garrison and begin the Greek revolution. Nearby was an old Roman theater handsomely restored in white marble. We went on to the Church of St. Andrew on the site where Patras' patron was crucified. The saint's mortal remains were spread from Constantinople to Scotland. In the ninth century part of the head was returned to Patras. A finger came back in the last century and the skull, accompanied by a Roman cardinal, made its triumphant return home only the previous September. The richly decorated church with a Byzantine grandeur of icons, chandeliers and relics, including a bleeding madonna, put me into a Tolstoi mood and I had a sudden desire to reread *Anna Karenina.* Nearby is a new mosquelike cathedral which was begun about 1900 and would not be finished for another ten years. It would be the largest church in the Balkans.

We dropped Plessas at his office and drove outside the city to the Achaia Claus winery, founded in 1883 by a German named Gustav Claus. An old sparrow-like guide named George Mallios told us the story of the origin of the winery's most famous product, called Mavrodaphne. "Gustav Claus was walking one hot day in the country and was very thirsty. A beautiful dark-haired girl offered him water and other little things. Her name was Daphne and young Gustav fell in love. A marriage was arranged and they were happy and joyful. Then she died and he made the wine in her memory." We drank some of the heavy sweet stuff. On the wall of the dark-timbered tasting room was a photograph of King Constantine, upon which someone had made a political comment by drawing a great "X" across it in red ink. The guide took us through a series of baronial towers and underground caverns, including a Westminster Abbey of wines where great sealed casks were marked with plaques, celebrating visits from Bismarck in 1873, King George I in

1882, King Paul in 1949. Recent tuns were dedicated to Constantine and his queen, Anna Maria.

The next day the sun shone; it appeared that the praying bishop would lose his contest with Zeus. We were invited to lunch at the home of Eva Papangeloutsos, owner of a newspaper, *The Peloponnese,* and a novelist. A female servant led us into a salon which was decorated like an Oriental seraglio and filled with several dozen bouquets of pink and red flowers, the scent of which made me dizzy. Much of the woodwork was gold and the furniture was upholstered in pink and red. Fine paintings hung on the walls. In a moment our hostess appeared. She was a pretty plump blonde woman wearing a blue dress, bespangled with jewels. She greeted us and began at once to tell us her view of Greece. "Unfortunately our new generation of young people are materialists and concerned only with making money," she said. My eyes wandered over the gold mirrors and cabinets filled with rare bric-a-brac, the crystal chandeliers. She said, "The older generation which is concerned with tradition and culture is disappearing. Here in Patras we try to keep the traditions of an aristocratic life. But unfortunately our youth imitate the bad wild life of the United States. Or worse, they are Communists who would destroy everything."

The "traditions," I was happy to discover, included a superbly stocked bar. As we sipped Scotch a young woman, delicately built and lovely, wearing a sable hat, entered like a poltergeist. "If you want to know about Greece don't listen to Mother," she said. "She looks at everything through gold spectacles." The daughter, Lillian, had arrived for a visit from Torino where she was married to an Italian doctor. Both mother and daughter were Italophiles; Torino, their favorite city, said the mother, "is so aristocratic." Lillian said, "Greeks are a nation of Zorbas—first-, second- and third-class Zorbas. All they are concerned about is today. They philosophize too much and they don't think of the future."

Mr. Papangeloutsos arrived and another daughter, Nan, with her husband, Spyros Doukas. The young people complained about the rigors of carnival. Yawning, his voice hoarse, Spyros said they had danced through three consecutive nights. "And still another week," he groaned. "How will we stand it?" Lunch served by three servants in a pink dining room was a seven-course banquet. The talk was of the carnival, of balls at which only men masked and others at which only the women masked. Lillian confided a "beeg sicrit." The male dressmakers of the town would attend a ball in the opera house that evening masked as women in order to confuse the men. The stories of flirtations and infidelities, of neglectful husbands falling in love with their masked wives, were out of Boccaccio.

Lillian suggested a ride. In her Mercedes she drove us fifteen miles along a reedy coast to a seaside summer house. When we arrived she discovered she'd forgotten the key to the iron gates. A caretaker's wife, apparently experienced in such crises, brought a chair by which Lillian climbed to the top of the fence, then hung there, impaled on an iron spear, until the chair was lowered on the inside for her descent. Each of us made the same perilous entry. Inside a large garden had grown jungle-wild. In the center stood a Halloween castle which might have been designed by Charles Addams. "Last year at Marienbad," I heard Greggory murmur. Through a moatlike mire of swampy earth we trudged toward the towered stronghold. Its doors sagged; the gothic windows were broken. "Communists destroyed it," said Lillian. "They took everything just like in Zorba." We continued through thickets of palm trees, untrimmed box hedges, blossoming almonds and a rampage of blooming roses to a pair of identical "pavilions," stables with quarters upstairs. "You see how it is," said Lillian. "How Communists destroy the old traditions." It was starting to rain. Fortunately the caretaker's wife had found a crevice in the fence through which she was able to pry us out.

In town the crowds were fighting a "chocolate war," pelting one another with sweets. We watched from a balcony of the hotel, collecting a harvest of candy. At five o'clock we were invited to Mrs. Papangeloutsos' opera box for a "matinee" masked ball. Masked women and unmasked men were twisting in the horseshoe-shaped theater and five levels of tiers and boxes were jammed with onlookers. Groups of women similarly disguised in long black gowns and black dominoes wandered quietly through the crowd, like members of an eerie burial society. Masked women pursued laughing men up and down stairs and in and out of boxes. A girl in a grotesque rubber mask singled me out, speaking English in a gentle voice. She was small, soft and young but the ugly face terrified me. She asked me to dance and the sensation of dancing with a mask was not pleasant. From boxes people were throwing wax eggs at the dancers, covering them with confetti. A blonde singer in a bikini was fronting the orchestra and her navel was a bull's-eye for a volley of eggs. When the dance was over I excused myself. I met Lillian on the stairs and she invited me to explore the upper levels. They were occupied mostly by working-class men watching the upper-class revels below. "Of course they're all Communists," whispered Lillian. The orchestra was playing a song by Theodorakis, and she said, "It's a song about poor people." We returned to the family box where her mother, wrapped in mink, was feeling the breasts and rumps of two masked female figures, making sure, she said, they were not *makaronis* —a popular term for female impersonators. Passing muster, the girls zoomed in on me, sitting on my lap and kissing me.

At nine o'clock it ended, and an hour and a half later we picked up Lillian, costumed in trim black tights and a cat's mask, to go to still another ball at a seaside resort. The floor was crowded with American Indians and cowboys, Roman gladiators, a Noah's ark of animals, Negroes and Bedouins, all twisting and shaking. Small boys wearing Roman legion helmets passed among the tables selling eggs with which the revelers pelted one another. The floor was deep with confetti. We were joined by Spyros and Nan Doukas. He was a safari explorer in a pith helmet and she, like her sister, was a cat, a tiger-striped blonde one. They led a "yanka," a kind of rabbit-hopping conga line. Lillian and I fell in, and she said, "Isn't this just like *Dolce Vita?*" How could I explain that it was more like Halloween at the country club? The difference was that this frantic pursuit was in its second week and had still a week to go. The little egg-sellers, walking about with their eyes shut, probably wouldn't make it. "We try," Lillian said, "to keep up the old traditions."

XVIII

Earthquake

The Greeks' favorite spectator sport is politics. Even more than usual, it was a political time and wherever I met with people, at dinners, parties, cafés, the conversation was about the latest political scandal. One ineffectual coalition government was replaced by another. Ministers resigned and politicians changed their party affiliations to fill the vacant posts. Parliament recessed sessions simply to cool deputies' tempers.

Newspapers were filled with politics. The right press accused the center left of Communism; the left press charged the promonarchist right of suspending the democratic processes. Freedom of speech ceased to exist— hardly a day passed without a news story of a farmer or worker arrested for "insulting the King" or for "offending the honor of the Queen Mother." The "insults" and "offenses" were usually careless remarks, made frequently under drink, and overheard by an informer. An island mayor had been sentenced to six months in prison for shouting, "Long live the Nation!" instead of "Long live the King!" and an Athens worker was jailed for cheering former Prime Minister George Papandreou.

To a foreigner the unremitting turbulence was often incomprehensible. In order to understand some of the things that were happening, I read books, especially one given me by George Katsimbalis, entitled *A Short History of Modern Greece,* by a British professor, Edward S. Forster.

The birth of modern Greece took place on March 25, 1821, the day that Archbishop Germanos of Patras unfurled a flag in the Peloponnese monastery of Haghia Lavra, an act which signaled the outbreak against the Turks who had occupied Greece for almost four centuries.

Volunteers came from throughout Europe to fight for Greece; the most famous was Lord Byron who died at Missolonghi in 1824. The war ended in 1827 with the battle of Navarino (Pylos), in which Great Britain, France and Russia finally defeated the Turko-Egyptian fleet.

The tempestuous Greeks proved incapable of governing themselves and after the assassination of their president, Kapodistrias, in Nauplia, the three protecting powers concluded that Greece should be governed by a monarch with a non-Greek king. The throne was offered to the second son of Ludwig I of Bavaria, Prince Otto. He was eighteen years old when he arrived in Nauplia in 1833, with a retinue of Bavarian bureaucrats and troops. For ten years every office was filled by a German. A revolution in 1843 forced Otto to dismiss his Bavarian entourage and replace it with a constitutional government. A second revolution in 1862 ended with Otto's abdication.

The Glücksburg dynasty, which has ruled Greece intermittently to the present time, was established in 1863 when the British government chose as the new Greek king, Prince William George of Denmark. He was seventeen years old when he ascended the throne as King George I. During his stormy reign, which lasted fifty years, the Cretans revolted against the Turks who still occupied their island, and finally won autonomy in 1899. Greece declared war on Turkey and was disastrously defeated. In 1909 a constitutional government was elected under the premiership of a Cretan, Eleutherios Venizelos, the greatest statesman of modern Greece and one of the most influential political wizards of modern Europe. King George was murdered in Thessaloniki in 1913.

He was succeeded by his son, Constantine I, a headstrong prince who had been educated in Germany and was married to the Kaiser's sister, Sophie. Unwilling to cooperate with the pro-Allies Venizelos, he was deposed during the First World War for his pro-German sympathies. Greece fought with the Allies and after the war Venizelos battled at conference tables for Greek territories held by Turkey in Asia Minor.

Constantine was succeeded by his son, King Alexander, who died in 1920 of blood poisoning resulting from the bite of a pet monkey. In an election three weeks after his death the main issue was the recall of King Constantine, or "Constantine vs. Venizelos." When his Liberal party lost its majority, Venizelos resigned the premiership and left Greece, and Constantine was restored to power.

With Venizelos no longer negotiating for Greek interests, Allied support of Greece waned. England feared that any support of Greece against the Moslem Turks might arouse her Moslem subjects in India and other areas. Neither France nor Italy was prepared to oppose the growing power of nationalist Turkey. Abandoned by the Allies, Greece declared war in Asia Minor. A disastrous campaign ended in the massacre of the Greek population of Smyrna and the expulsion of 1,500,000 Greeks from Asia Minor. King Constantine was deposed a second time and died in Sicily. He was succeeded in 1922 by his son, George II, who abdicated and went to Bucharest in 1923. Three months later, in March, 1924, a republic was established by plebiscite.

In 1935, King George was restored to the throne by plebiscite. The following year Army General Joannes Metaxas suspended the constitution and set up a dictatorship which continued until Metaxas' death in 1941. When the Italians and Germans invaded Greece in World War II, King George went into exile in Egypt.

In 1944 an exile government was formed in Cairo under the prime ministry of George Papandreou, leader of the Social Democrat party, whom Winston Churchill considered the only Greek statesman qualified for the job. With the help of British troops Papandreou began the fight against Communists in the Greek Civil War.

After the war the Greeks voted in a plebiscite to return King George from his London exile. He died in 1947 and was succeeded by his brother, King Paul, a moderate man who in the difficult years of Civil War and reconstruction, restored the dignity of kingship. With his German-born Queen, Frederika, a granddaughter of Kaiser Wilhelm, he traveled by jeep and donkeyback over the impoverished war-ravaged countryside, rallying the loyalties of his subjects. During his reign the U.S. provided Greece with $300,000,000 of Truman Doctrine aid, and sent General James Van Fleet to supervise the reorganization of Greece's military defense. King Paul's death by cancer in 1964 came at an unfortunately critical time in political Greece. The conservative government of Constantine Karamanlis, which had brought a stability to Greece for eight years, fell when its political foes charged that the elections which had kept it in power were shams. In an election less than a month before the King's death, George Papandreou, seventy-six years old, was elected to the premiership with a 53 per cent vote, the second highest majority in Greece's history.

Into this situation Paul's young son, twenty-three-year-old Constantine, succeeded to the throne. A handsome youth with a reputation as a playboy yachtsman—he had been the only Greek in modern times to win an Olympic race—the young King, strongly influenced by his hard-minded mother, Frederika, revealed an arrogance not inherited from his father. Greece's royal emblem depicts two sheepskin-clad, bearded men with clubs defending the crown. Above the figures appear the words, "My strength lies in the love of the people." From the beginning it was apparent that Constantine had decided his power lay not in the love of

The pascal lamb. Cradled in arms like children.

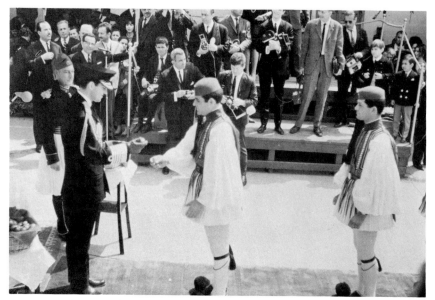

Cracking red eggs with the King. A nervous youth was the hero.

Evzones. Dancing for the King.

Two grandmothers of Rhodes. The leather leggings protected against snakes.

A royal journey. "My strength lies in my people's love."

Pirates of Katerini. The people wanted elections.

Young dancers of Veria. "Compared to country girls, all city girls are withered leaves."

Jon Emerson on the boat to Athos. "God provided beards for men to wear."

A monk of Athos. Once there were 10,000 strong young men.

The monastery of Dionysiou. Souls striving for salvation in inacessible cells.

The apocalypse of Vatopedi. The infernos were livelier than the paradises.

Father Nifon. "All things crumble to dust."

The fire dancers of Langada. "Konstantine tells you to do it."

Alex in Wisconsin. Monticello's educative life was enriched.

people but in the loyalty of the Greek Army. Unlike the monarchs of England, Denmark, Sweden and Holland, he was unwilling to reign as a figurehead. Like his grandfather, Constantine I, whom he was reported to admire, he involved himself in politics. In his leadership of the political right he had the support of England which was interested in maintaining Cyprus as a military base and preventing the unification of that island with Greece, and of the United States which wished to continue a friendly climate for NATO defense installations in Greece.

A power battle between the impetuously willful young King and the proud uncompromising old premier, who was determined to reduce the influence of the crown, was struck almost at once. The conflict between them centered on control of the army and it came to a climax when the Greek Army commander on Cyprus, General George Grivas, claimed to have uncovered a plot among junior army officers to overthrow the monarchy. The code name of the fabricated hoax was *Aspida* (Shield) and Grivas claimed that its leader was the premier's son, Andreas Papandreou,* a naturalized American who had been a professor in American universities for twenty years and who, before returning to Greece at the request of Premier Karamanlis, had been chairman of the economics department at the University of California in Berkeley. In the election in which the father became premier, the son won a deputy's seat in parliament, and he was appointed by his father to a ministerial post.

An impasse between the King and the premier occurred finally when a pro-King minister of defense, Petros Garoufalias, accused the premier of seeking to influence the investigation in order to cover up for his son, and described Papandreou as "a danger to the nation." The premier called on the King to demand the resignation of the defense minister. The King refused. Papandreou accused the King of unconstitutional meddling in politics and offered his verbal resignation, which the King accepted. The King called on the parliament speaker, George Athanassiades-Novas, to form a new government. Failing to win a vote of confidence it quickly fell. In the meantime Papandreou's fight with the King had turned him into a national hero. His charismatic effect on crowds was well known. His followers rioted in the streets of Athens and other cities. It was July 1965—the most tense time in Greece since the Civil War. Two months later, on my first night in the land, the people of Metsovon refused to serve me beer because beer in Greece

---

* In 1967 the Junta government dropped the charges and released Andreas Papandreou from prison, thus conceding what Papandreou supporters had insisted from the beginning, that the charges were contrived and without validity.

had become a political pawn. Defense Minister Garoufalias, who had
brought about the downfall of Papandreou, was in private life a brewery
executive and a friend of the Queen Mother Frederika.

On February 16, 1966, the second anniversary of George Papandreou's
election, the deposed prime minister addressed his followers in "the place
of tears," Athen's Klafthmonos Square. For weeks the city had been
tense with anticipation. Pro-Papandreou newspapers predicted the rally
would be a renaissance of freedom, and the opposition press warned
that the event might be the beginning of a revolution and should not be
permitted. I was warned by friends that as an American I should not get
into the crowd; in case of riots my life might be in danger.

The day before the rally I went with Mike Serapoulos to the newspaper *Athinaiki,* the fourth-floor editorial offices of which looked down
on the square, and I asked if we might watch the meeting from its
windows. The editor was a Papandreou supporter who had recently
served a prison sentence for publishing some stories "insulting to the
Queen Mother." He had, he said, refused hundreds of requests for
a place at his windows. I showed him my American press credentials
and he relented.

The rally was scheduled for eight o'clock. At six thirty downtown
Athens was a human sea. Outside my hotel, Kotzia Square was filled
with policemen and soldiers waiting calls to action with portable radios,
their poised antennas gleaming like fly rods. We had been warned we
might not be able to leave the news offices for hours, so we bought
sandwiches and chocolate bars. We pushed through a tidal wave of men,
all of whom had small blue cards pinned to their lapels, saying simply
"114," the number of the last article of the Constitution, which says,
"The safeguard of the Constitution depends on the patriotism of the
Greeks." Elections and the constitutionality of the King's acts were the
issues of the rally. Papandreou was expected to demand an election
which the King would oppose because the certain Papandreou victory
might be interpreted as a plebiscite against him and a possible end to the
monarchy.

The besieged guards at the newspaper offices shouted, "Go away!
This is not a circus!" We showed our credentials and were taken to the
elevator. The editorial offices were filled. As an American I was warmly
greeted and quickly we found ourselves at an open window. It was a
mild spring evening. The dark mass of human heads below filled the
square and every street leading into it; in the dusk it looked like a great
insect colony. There were a few women in the crowd and some children
riding on their fathers' shoulders. From windows above us men were

emptying boxes of the little papers saying "114" and they fluttered over the square like blue confetti. The square was illuminated by neon signs advertising Metaxa brandy, and another newspaper, the right-wing *Messimvrini*. A speaker's platform was set up on a stone balcony over a florist shop and above it a neon sign said, "Hail Feb. 16! Hail democracy!" A party leader was making a warming-up speech, shouting "Hail Freedom!" and the crowd echoed the words like a roll of thunder. Rockets streaked across the heavens and red and green flares lit up the night. Hundreds of balloons were released and wafted gently westward. "George Papandreou will once more be leader of Greece," the speaker shouted and the crowd began a chant, repeating over and over, "Pa-pan-dre-ou! Pa-pan-dre-ou!" A man beside me said the police had ordered him to close his appliance shop at six o'clock and ordered his customers to go home. Another said he had been stopped by a policeman and told to turn back. A searchlight was passing over the square like a beam seeking a drowning man at sea. It lit up a kiosk, the roof of which was covered with men. Like clusters of Zacharias, men hung from the branches of trees and covered the roof of a public toilet.

At a signal the crowd lit thousands of candles which flickered across the square like a milky way. Candles—lit at midnight on Easter Eve in all the churches of the land—symbolize resurrection and their light now was intended as "a resurrection of democracy," the return to power of Papandreou. The fireworks were also a part of Easter celebrations celebrating resurrection. I was reminded of the Fourth of July nights of my childhood.

Police began moving through the crowd, putting out the lights, but as quickly as they extinguished them in one section, hundreds more of the "freedom lights" burned in another. The men on the kiosk unfurled a flag and the silhouette of them in the night was like the statue of the flag-raising at Iwo Jima. Some photographers crowded into the windows to make pictures and a short stout woman holding a little girl with ribbons in her hair, wailed that she was the sister of an employee of the newspaper and her child could not see.

A reporter was making a human count. He said that Constitution and Omonia squares and the streets connecting them were all filled. At the rate of eight persons to a square meter he estimated the crowd at 700,000, the largest, he said, ever to gather in Greece. A new speaker on the balcony, a suburban mayor, was calling for "democracy through elections." He compared Papandreou to Bishop Germanos, leader of the 1821 revolution, and called him "the true ruler of the Greek people," an obvious insult to the King. The crowd began a new chant, *"Ena-ena-tessera!"* the number "114," repeated over and over, accompanied with a rhythmic clap of hands. A flock of white doves were released over the square. Confused, frightened by the lights and the noise, the birds fluttered up through a shaft of light, circled over the square and disappeared. On rooftops, terraces and in windows, dark forms were clustered like bats. It was eight o'clock; the tension was almost unendurable. New rockets were fired, a new surge of candles flickered and the crowd waved handkerchiefs which were like a white surf rippling across the square. The speaker, shouting hoarsely, could no longer be understood because of chanting by students in the corner of the square next to the University. The students unfurled a Greek flag and the crowd roared. Whenever the human thunder subsided in one area it rose again in another. Standing in the safety of the window frame, I remembered old films of Hitler rallies in Nuremberg and Mussolini in Rome's Piazza Venezia, and I trembled for fear of the faceless force below.

Then, in a burst of white light, the old man appeared. In the brightness only the dark shape of him could be seen, and his white hair glowing like a phosphorescent halo. The crowd roared. The old man waved his hands benignly, a faltering Moses trying to quell the human tide. A cannonade of rockets boomed in the heavens.

"This is not a rally, this is an earthquake . . ." The sound of his voice over the amplifiers stilled the multitude, but only for a moment. Every phrase he spoke was tumultuously applauded. "The question before Greeks today is who governs Greece. . . ." The chant resumed. Like a kindly bishop chiding a disorderly congregation he waved his right hand for order. "The King may reign but the people will rule. . . ." His old man's monotone might have been the voice of Polonius. Because of the shouting I could not understand him at all and was dependent upon Mike for fragmentary translations. "With strength, with courage, we will overthrow the oppressors," he said.

Behind me the child was crying and the little woman wailed, "My cousin works here." She asked me to raise the child to my shoulders, which I did. "Can you see him?" the mother asked the child. "Can you see Papandreou?" The child happily waved a lollipop which became glued in my hair. The mother, who could not see at all, beat her hands in applause.

In the square a man fainted and a caravan to rescue him pushed through the amorphous crowd monster like a parasitic eel burrowing into a whale. The stricken man was raised overhead and carried out like a fallen hero.

The old man told a joke about himself and the laughter went on for a minute. The mother handed the child on my shoulders a penny whistle which shrilled in my ears. In the square, tree branches bent to the earth with their burdens of men, like rows of dark ravens. After an hour a rise of emotion in the crowd indicated that the old man was nearing the end. "He's simply repeating himself," said Mike, "he's keeping the fires burning." The applause would not let him finish; the clapping was like the beating of rain and the moving hands gave off a white light. The old man raised an arm but it did no good. Finally he simply stopped and, shoulders sagging, turned his back and walked off. The shouting, the singing, the chanting seemed to move the earth. More doves were released. Frightened, they shot almost vertically into the night and disappeared. Copies of newspaper extras were brought from the presses and the front page was covered by a photograph of Papandreou.

This was the time which I had been told would be dangerous, when there would be rioting and violence in the streets. The crowd dispersed quietly, like the waters of a subsiding whirlpool. Human streams flowed peacefully away in every direction. Within a half-hour the square was cleared except for some students chanting "Pa-pan-dre-ou. . . ." Then they too slipped away. The Place of Tears was deserted. A car drove across the pavements stirring a wake of rustling paper like a ship through foam. We walked back through quiet streets. On Kotzia Square the policemen's antennas were poised for the signals which never came.

The next morning even the anti-Papandreou press reported that there had not been a single unruly incident. The *Messimvrini* said that the quiet dispersal was "fearsome and sinister," proving beyond question that the rally had been "organized and controlled," presumably by Communists. An editorial described the crowd as "apathetic," and said the rally was Papandreou's "swan song." Newspapers, depending on their politics, estimated the crowd as ranging from one hundred thousand to a million persons. A compromise guess—one probably close to the truth —was a half million people, almost one-seventh of all the voters of the land.

XIX

The Shepherd Queen

The waiter who brought my breakfast was a sullen young man who seldom spoke. On this morning he put the tray on the table with an abrupt thud. At the door he turned back and in a dark voice said, "You go see Frederika today?"

"Yes," I said, and he replied with something so shocking I thought I had misunderstood. He repeated the epithet a second time. I looked at him, stunned. "Frederika is enemy of Greeks," he said. "If you visit her you are enemy of Greeks." He raged on. "She will tell you lies, only lies. She is not a good woman. She has lots of money and the people of Greece have no money. She thinks all Greeks are Communists. When people say, 'We are hungry, we want food, we want to work,' she says they are Communists. If you Americans like her so much you can have her. Greece will be glad to give her to you. Her, the King and his wife. Take them to your country. You can have them all." He turned to leave. "Well, God bless you. I hope you have a good time and please tell her how we Greeks feel about her." He slammed the door.

It was February 21. The week before, a call had come from the American Embassy. "The Queen Mother," said the voice, "will see you at eleven o'clock on Monday." Why this particular day had been picked was a mystery. It was "Clean Monday," the first fast day of Lent, a day of symbolic spiritual and bodily purification when housewives cleaned their pots and pans with hot water mixed with ashes. It was also a festival devoted to picnicking, dancing on the green, kite-flying and a variety of

228

Dionysian merriments to welcome spring. Because of my invitation, friends jokingly called it "Queen Monday."

For weeks I had been pondering the enigma of the controversial woman I was about to meet. My interest began in a movie theater during a screening of a documentary on the life of her husband, the late King Paul. I saw films of the quietly dignified King and his vivacious young Queen riding donkeys and jeeps into destitute villages during the Civil War, playing children's games in camps of war orphans, participating in a grape harvest, dancing Greek dances in native costumes, climbing mountains to seek out earthquake victims. "A shepherd king and queen," said the commentator, "dedicating themselves to the poor." In every situation the Queen had been vibrantly responsive, reaching out to people with love and sympathy. Wherever she went the adoring crowds had cheered and wept and pressed forward to kiss her hand. In the theater there had been no applause. While the crowds on the screen applauded, the movie audience—they might have been the same faces—booed and whistled derisively.

What Greeks were saying about Queen Frederika was appalling. In their attacks they synthesized her into a combination of Clytemnestra, Lady Macbeth and Lucretia Borgia. I was told she ran the country through the King, her son, that the ill-advised New Year's Proclamation had been her idea. I heard rumors that it was she who had two prime ministers fired, Karamanlis and, in the previous "July crisis," her hated enemy, Papandreou. There were stories that she collected taxes for a "Queen's Fund" and stashed away in Swiss and American banks private fortunes bled from poor Greeks. She was, they said, fanatic on the subject of Communism and labeled her political opponents Communists. After five months in the country, I knew, of course, how Greeks were given to hysterical hyperbolism, especially in political matters, and I did not believe much that I heard. But I could not find more than two or three persons who spoke kindly of the once-beloved Queen, and I wondered what had happened in the less than two decades since the documentary films had been made.

A history professor said, "The story of Frederika is a study in the rise and fall of a public figure, a phenomena not uncommon with us— our dramas and myths are full of it. After the war Communists were our big concern and Frederika with great courage went around to the battle sites and suffering villages, bringing food and medicine and winning respect and love. But this epoch passed and times changed. Something else began to become apparent—the Queen's manipulations in government. Perhaps it had been going on all the time and we were not aware. The death of King Paul, which put her into the foreground, had considerable to do with it. But it began long before. As she matured she assumed a stronger role and became more active in things from which, in our country, women are excluded. Basically our problem is a weak king with an Oedipus complex for a mother who has a strong power drive. You've seen it all, alas, in the old plays."

A retired general said, "Frederika is responsible for the corruption of Greek political life. As granddaughter of the Kaiser, she clings to an old German concept of absolute power. She forced the election of 1961 which re-elected Karamanlis. Then when he tried to reduce the power of the palace she had him fired. When Papandreou tried the same thing he also had to be sacrificed. In these matters Frederika is a mother, fighting for her family. Though we believe Americans support the Queen in her palace manipulations, the Americans cannot be held responsible. I blame the Greeks. We are vulnerable, we are at your mercy. We survive, we live by American assistance. So we must offer ourselves to please you. We are completely corrupt, no longer believing in anyone or anything, and the palace is the cancer of our corruption."

A journalist said, "No one who does not remember can imagine Frederika's popularity at its height, and the extent of her influence. A great part of her problem now is the advisers she chooses, her intimates, those with whom she surrounds herself. She is a snob. The most trivial hackneyed pretender is more important to her than any distinguished untitled person. She has formed a sort of mutual-benefit society of courtiers who rely on her influence for self-preservation and she depends on them for hers. They are all yes-men who tell her the truth about nothing so she is constantly misinformed. Frederika has a mania for money and in a French sense she trafficks in influence, using her position to help foreign businesses get a foothold in Greece, and for this she is paid in cash and corporate stock and in a variety of ways."

A society woman whose family was royalist in its politics, said, "It's her German personality. There is no question of loyalty. She is strong and German in a country where women traditionally play a background role. Perhaps it's simply an incompatibility of national temperaments. She completely disregards the social mores of our country. Our women wear black mourning for at least two years after a death in the family. This custom she flaunted; everyone talked of the long earrings she wore at her husband's funeral. Two months later she appeared at her son's wedding in her usual chic. Our people say she does not mourn because she is German and not Greek."

A woman editor said, "This is a mother-loving country and we can't forgive Frederika for her treatment of her own mother whom she's never allowed in Greece and did not permit at her son's wedding. Her mother

may be an unpleasant woman but even so, Frederika should never
have made the mistake of showing her hatred in Greece. Her attitude is:
I am Frederika! I am the Queen, I can do as I wish and people must
admire me. She's alienated our people with her constant demands for
money. They have too many cars, too many boats and I don't know how
many palaces they never use. Queen Juliana of Holland, the richest
woman in the world, rides among her people on a bicycle and Frederika,
queen of the poorest country in Europe, insists on all the royal pretensions
and trappings. Her friends are not the good people of Greece, but the
richest, the shipping billionaires. We are after all a puritan country and our
Queen should never be the guest of notorious tax evaders and adulterers.
We can't stop talking about her in Athens, the conversation never lags.
She could be our Jackie Kennedy, one of the great women of the world.
But somehow things always go wrong. She has great courage. In danger
she is a lioness. She does much good. But somehow she destroys it all. She
has been a good mother, a tireless worker for Greece. But because of her
personality it all comes out wrong. Like that perpetual silly fuss about her
earrings."

A social worker in the Ministry of Welfare said: "No person has ever
been so victimized by such a campaign of organized lies as Queen
Frederika. Her passion has been her great and genuine love for her
people. In Piraeus she came with us into the slums disguised as a Red
Cross worker in dark glasses, a simple coat and a shawl over her hair.
Unrecognized, she went alone into the worst possible places, into hovels
steeped with human filth where the odors were so strong the social workers
were turned away at the door. She sat by the bed of an old woman from
Turkey who could hardly speak Greek and she took the old woman's
hand and spoke gently to her. She arranged for the woman to be taken
to a hospital. She insisted on going into dangerous areas at night with only
a woman companion, visiting the quarters of prostitutes and junkies.
Afterward she telephoned the Minister of Welfare and threatened not
to leave the area until he agreed to do something. A slum clearance
program was begun. Frederika is injuriously honest. She says exactly
what she is thinking. It is amazing how bad a politician she can be."

Paul Vardinogiannis, a parliament deputy and former minister, who
accompanied the Queen to the funeral of John F. Kennedy, said: "Frederika is a tragically misunderstood woman. She hasn't changed as much as
the times have changed. We Greeks are very emotional, we are not a
logical people."

An embassy secretary instructed me to arrive at the Queen Mother's
villa in Psychico a few minutes before eleven. I asked about what I might

be expected to speak and the secretary said, "She is very interested in space." It was not a field about which I felt informed. "You will probably not have to say much," I was told. "She will do the talking." From a friend in the Foreign Ministry I received some instructions in etiquette. On meeting the Queen Mother I was told to make a token bow, take her hand and almost but not quite kiss it. I would address her as "Your Majesty." For a sleepless hour the night before I repeated to myself "Your Majesty," to make certain I would not address her incorrectly as "Your Highness."

At ten thirty I phoned the concierge to call a taxi. He sent a boy into the streets which, it being a holiday, were empty. The urgency of the event spurred the manager—for a quarter hour he, the concierge, two boys and I raced around Omonia Square trying to find a cab. There were none. A policeman was recruited. At five minutes to eleven an ancient Buick rattled into the square and was sequestered from another passenger by one of the policemen. The incredulous driver began driving in the wrong direction toward the *Mitera,* a word meaning "mother," the name of an orphanage sponsored by Frederika. "No, no, no," I shouted, "the house where the Queen lives." He looked at me as if I were a lunatic, but he turned around.

At eleven twenty we rattled up to the sentry box outside the Royal Villa. Two petticoated evzones saluted me. Trembling and sweating, I rushed through a row of functionaries and was presented to the chargé d'affaires, a small man as nervous as I, who hurried me inside. Her Majesty would be down presently, he said. The large-beamed room had a baronial air and was comfortably furnished with a piano, soft chairs, and a divan with many puffed cushions. Not especially lavish, it had a pleasant lived-in homeyness. An album of Bach fugues lay on a table; a silver-framed photograph of the late King was on the piano. Glass doors opened on a bright garden where I saw a table with hi-fi equipment. Beyond the garden was another villa, the residence of ladies-in-waiting and members of the Queen's court.

I heard soft steps. A youthful woman, astonishingly beautiful, descended the stairs. She was wearing a short gray suit woven with silver metallic threads which matched her bouffant silvery hair and a great deal of flashing jewelry, including the famous dangling earrings. I had seen women like that—poised, radiant, with a self-assurance that just touched on arrogance—in the Vierjahrzeit Hotel in Munich, and at the opera at Bayreuth. No photograph did her justice—the camera was no match for her glowing pink color, her youthful radiance. She was, I remembered, forty-eight years old.

"Good morning," she said in softly accented English. I went through my rehearsed routine of almost-but-not-quite kissing her cool extended hand and she invited me to sit in one of the cushioned chairs. She took another facing me and crossed her trim legs. She was wearing soft bedroom slippers with blue pompons.

I said I bore greetings from an old friend, the widow of a former ambassador to Greece. Frederika laughed. "Oh, yes, she was always very busy, always organizing marches. And all the women of Greece were so fascinated they followed her. But they never really knew for what they were marching. They simply thought it was what women did in America."

Where, she asked, had I been, what had I seen in Greece? I told her my impressions of Epirus, Crete and the Peloponnese. "My husband and I were in all those places, we traveled everywhere on donkeys and jeeps," she said. "How happy the people were to see us, how they loved us, how they adored their King." Her eyes were like amethysts. "We slept in cold rooms without comforts, without water. In one village we were the guests of a priest who had removed an unsightly stove from his own bedroom in our honor. The room was terribly cold and I asked the priest to return the stove. Four priests carried it back and I tended the fire myself." She stopped. "Now my son goes in a Mercedes and in his airplane. Things are very different."

I asked what language was spoken in the family circle. "English, of course," she replied. "It is the only language my son and his wife share." Then, remembering one of the frequent criticisms of the royal family, that it did not speak Greek, she added, "My son speaks Greek very well. He is the first king of Greece to master the language of his people." I commented on the presence of music in the room. "My husband was very musical, the piano is his," she said. "My daughter, Princess Irene, has been studying the piano for only two years and recently she played a concert of duets with Gina Bachauer."

She asked who I'd been seeing, who my Greek friends were. I pondered the question, wondering whom I should name.

"George Theotokas," I began.

"An intellectual!" she said with scorn. "I don't like intellectuals. They're all weak and they have no courage. When my husband and I were fighting the Communists to save Greece they sat in the cafés. They're still there and they're all against me."

I said I considered myself an intellectual, and added, "As a matter of fact my impression is that you are rather intellectual yourself." She blushed—queens, I thought, were after all, women—and she asked who else I'd met, what members of the press. I named George Papageorgiou, the editor from whose windows I had watched the Papandreou rally.

The Queen's face hardened. "I sent him to jail," she said fiercely. I had heard the editor incited Frederika's wrath by sending a reporter to Germany to interview her estranged mother. It was a rough moment. Thinking hard, I said, "I'm seeing Eleni Vlachou tomorrow." The credential was a good one—Mrs. Vlachou, owner of two newspapers and a popular magazine called *Eikones,* was considered, next to Frederika, the most powerful woman in Greece. "My dearest friend!" said Frederika. I had heard stories of their on-and-off friendship, of periods when they did not speak. She asked if I had been at the Papandreou rally and what I had learned from it. I said I had been handicapped by not understanding the language, but that I had the impression of an old man rambling in the manner of Polonius. With surprising vehemence that seemed to be a defense of Papandreou, she said, "His mind is very clear. You must realize he is eighty-four years old. He does not admit to it, of course." I remembered that before Frederika and Papandreou became bitter enemies they had been good friends. Gratuitously she added, "Papandreou could never win an election without the help of the Communists. That is his danger to Greece."

She uncrossed her legs, showing trim knees, and she raised a jeweled hand to her face. She talked freely, covering a variety of subjects. "I have always been interested in social works," she said. "It's so necessary when a people are so poor." She spoke of the Queen's Fund, from which, I had heard rumors, she held back monies for her own use. "Only one per cent of the fund goes into its administration," she said. "There is no organization in the world that operates on such a small percentage." As she continued I realized she was in a subtle way defending herself, offering explanations for all the charges against her.

"My son was very carefully trained for his responsibilities," she said, recalling another criticism, that young Constantine had been inadequately educated for kingship. "From the time he was twelve he was always with his father, always being taught. My husband took him into his confidence and asked his advice. He has understood the problems of a king since he was a boy. In ruling families this was unique. The boy grew up in his father's way of thinking, his father's judgments. And when my husband died and my son became king there was not the slightest doubt that he was ready."

She began to speak of Makronisos, a penal island upon which political prisoners had been held after the Civil War in brutal circumstances. The stories about it were among the bitterest I'd heard in Greece. "How sad it was, how terrible that it was necessary," she said. "When my husband and I visited the island three hundred thousand Communists broke rank and cheered. You can't imagine what it was like when he spoke to them, when he said, 'I need all of you to help me.' They wept." The Queen's blue eyes glistened as she seemed to relive the moment. "When they were released and returned to Athens and there was a rally in Olympic Stadium, everyone of them volunteered to defend our country and fight the Communists in the bandit war. It was the most moving experience in our lives." Whenever she spoke the word "Communist," her voice sharpened. Communists, it was apparent, were her bête noire, the object of a particular hatred. "It was incredible," she said. "The Communist bandits were kidnaping children from the villages, they snatched away fifty thousand of them into Albania, Bulgaria and Yugoslavia to educate and train them as Communists. They were kidnaped, simply stolen." I had heard many versions of the "stolen" children and the number always varied. "How I suffered because of that terrible island, worrying about those stolen children. For years I tried to get them back. I suffered so much that I had a serious nervous breakdown in Switzerland. My illness was not generally known. But now I don't mind speaking of it."

What, I asked, had happened to the children. "They're coming back," she replied vehemently. "Those youngsters are returning according to the plan, full-fledged brainwashed adult Communists, a great fifth column attack, a phalanx in the scheme to make Greece Communist. The families from which they were stolen have long since forgotten them. They've had other children and are not pleased at the invasion of these troublemakers."

At this moment a pretty child of about two years toddled in from the garden. She was very blonde and blue-eyed and was wearing blue jeans. The Queen swept the little girl up in her arms, speaking to her in English. "My granddaughter, Elena," she said. "Her parents are on a tour and I am the baby-sitter. I have three, all girls." Implying a royal family's desire for boys, she said, "There's still time for grandsons. My children are all so young." She cuddled the child for a moment and then freed it and it returned to the garden. Turning to me, the Queen asked, "Are you a Christian?"

The question startled me. I replied in the affirmative.

"What faith?" she asked. As I had been told she might, she was interviewing me. I said I was of the Episcopal faith but that I had been brought up in the Swiss Reformed Church.

"Zwinglian!" she said. "That's worse than mine. I was a Lutheran. Did you suffer through those long sermons, those cold services as I did? Didn't you hate it?" She laughed; we seemed in that moment to be friends. "These churches of our childhoods lacked feeling," she said. "Christianity should be warm and loving. Now I am Orthodox. Did you know that the Orthodox Church is very friendly with the Episcopalian?" I did, and I spoke of the close cooperation of the two Churches in New York. She began an attack on the Greek clergy which was at that time engaged in a power struggle with the government. "They are not good men of the spirit," she said, fiercely. "They are corrupt, they are not even Christians. A time will come when priests will not be distinguished from other men in their dress and appearance, when Church leaders will not be set apart from common men, when the Church will return to the simple spirit of Christ and his followers."

Then, her voice subdued, yet gently urgent, she said, "I want to give to you my favorite passage from the Bible. It was also my husband's favorite. It's from Jesus' prayer before the high priest when he is taken to be crucified." She hesitated, putting the words together in her mind and then she quoted, "I am in the Father as thou, Father, are in me, that they may be one in us, that they may be one even as we are one. . . ."*

She paused. In the deeply moving moment it seemed she was identifying with the words she had spoken, that in some way she intended Jesus' prayer to be her own for the people who seemed in these times to be betraying her, even as one disciple betrayed Jesus and another denied him.

"I will tell you the real problem of Greece," the Queen Mother said. "There is only one problem. All the others you will hear about—Cyprus, the Church, tax evasion, poverty—are only fronts to distract the people from the great problem, which is Communism. The problem is in the north, in Thrace and Macedonia, where the Communists plan to take over, through which they would move into Greece. It is the ageless problem of the Balkans, the conflict of Slav and Greek. The aim of all Slav Communists is to take over Greece, and if we don't understand this, if the world doesn't understand it, then Greece is lost.

"Monarchy is the only defense we have in Greece against Communism. If the monarchy ever left Greece it would become Communist at once. It would not be Russian Communism. Russia is a country where one can reason, it has become a great European state. The Greek Communism would become like China's, a ruthless Communist dictatorship.

"I know! I know! To save Greece from Communism has been the great cause of my life. As it was my husband's, as it is my son's, as it is the cause of all people who love Greece. And how the Greeks loved

---

* The passage, which I found in the Oxford Bible, King James version, is from Jesus' prayer for his disciples before he was betrayed by Judas and taken to the high priest. It appears in St. John 17, verses 21 and 22, and reads, "That they all may be one; as thou, Father, art in me, and I in thee, that they also may be one in us: that the world may believe that thou has sent me. And the glory which thou gavest me I have given them; that they may be one; even as we are one . . ."

my husband for it, how in the country and on the islands they love my son and his wife. They are so young, and Greeks love the young."

She was speaking now of the King, asking me what I had thought of the controversial New Year's Proclamation. I said I thought it was a mistake. She became angry; obviously I had touched a sensitive nerve. It was the only time in our conversation that she seemed for a moment to lose her poise. "Are you for Communism?" she asked fiercely.

"Certainly not," I said.

"Then why did you not like the proclamation?"

I thought, and I said it seemed to me that the New Year's message had made unnecessary problems for the King by alienating many of his people, that it had given strength and impetus to his opponents.

"My son is a man, not a puppet," she said, her voice imperious. "He is a courageous King. He does not say what people wish to hear, he speaks what he himself believes, even if he knows it will not make him popular, if he knows it will cause him problems." I replied that I did not think this judicious, that it seemed impulsive rather than courageous. Still angry, perhaps betraying her involvement in the affair, she said, "But the government approved the speech. If the government did not believe in it, why did they not stop the King from making it?" Then she spoke of the idea, popular in certain Greek circles, that the country needed a dictatorship. "Those who want a dictator could never agree on the man," she said. "They would not be satisfied with anyone but themselves."

She recalled the funeral services for President Kennedy. "I was the only one who could go," she said. "My husband had a government crisis, my son was in school. What a terrible day! We were all exhausted and we had nothing to eat from breakfast until seven o'clock. Up to the church everything went very well, but after that it was all confusion. At the cemetery no one knew what to do. There were all those bodyguards such as your American gangsters have. There were five around me. De Gaulle had twenty."

She asked, "Do you believe Oswald killed Kennedy?" I replied that I did. "I'm not surprised you believe it," she said. "It's part of your American naïveté. You absolutely refuse to believe it was not the deed of a single man. You do not understand conspiracy. Why do you insist on suppressing the truth, why can you not see it?" The "conspiracy" was Communism. She sighed. "It was his time," she said. "If you are religious you must believe that. The great achievement of his life, the deed which will make him immortal, was Cuba. Kennedy was sent into this world for that one moment and having accomplished it, the time had come for him to go."

She told of other trips to the U.S., "to study nuclear physics, my hobby," she said. "I am deeply impressed by the dedication and earnestness of American scientists. Your professors are the best of America, the real America which the world admires. My last trip was in January, 1964, to receive an honorary degree from Columbia University. I was called back by the illness of my husband. It was our first awareness of his failing health."

I spoke of the compulsion of young Greeks to leave their country. "The young are one of our big problems and my son is devoting himself to it," she said, skirting my point. "We have this terrible problem of Teddy Boys—it's just coming to Greece from England and America. They see it in your films. Why are your American films so bad? America is not like that. Your films are bringing a bad influence to the whole world. These Teddy Boys need a purpose, they need to be put into danger. They must have something to fight for, even if they kill themselves. There is always the need for volunteers which the young can fill. There is always a fire to put out, a flood to be controlled. We must organize our young people into volunteer organizations to help."

I sensed in her the beginning of restlessness and I said I must leave. We stood, and she asked, "What will you write about me in your book?"

"For one thing, I'll say you are more beautiful than I expected."

"I've had all kinds of flatteries in my life," she said. "Flatteries as well as insults. Neither means anything." Then, her voice almost wistful, she said, "I suppose you think like everyone else, that I'm a bad woman. I don't mind. When you fight for what you believe you can't expect everyone to be your friend. I am used to it."

It saddened me, her final urge to defend herself, the need to be humble. It was also terribly human, indicating many things: loneliness, arrogance, insecurity. I found it difficult to break away, to leave her alone. I was reacting in a very male way, with a male impulse to comfort this beautiful, this appealing and bitter woman. I was feeling deeply her tragedy.

I said good-bye, and was at the door when she turned and spoke once more. "Where are you planning to go in Greece?" she asked. Several places, I replied, and mentioned Corfu where the royal family has its holiday villa, called "Mon Repos." "Wait until May," she said gently. "Corfu is loveliest in May."

XX

Joy in the Air

The chargé d'affaires was waiting with a car and driver to take me into town. Athens was welcoming spring. Kites floated over the hills like great birds. I was on my way to the house, under the Acropolis hill, of the painter Spyros Vassiliou, where more than two hundred artists, writers, government officials, diplomats and unclassifiable celebrities were celebrating Clean Monday.

A *bouzouki* band was playing, files of men were dancing and tables were spread with wines and a "feast of fasting"—seafoods, cheeses, the new vegetables and fruits of spring—everything in fact but meat. George Katsimbalis was telling stories of his visit to Hollywood. "It was the week after Sydney Greenstreet died," he said with booming voice. "I was having dinner with a producer and when we entered the restaurant a lady screamed and fainted dead away. All the women in the bloody place began to shriek. They thought I'd been resurrected, that I was Sydney Greenstreet."

A young woman was carrying a white lamb which was sucking milk from a nipple attached to a wine bottle. "Why doesn't she do it properly?" roared Katsimbalis. "Why doesn't she open her dress?" An American poet arrived with a bevy of handsome young Greeks. "Ganymedes!" Katsimbalis snorted. An American from the Embassy was swishing about the room with a red-checked tablecloth tied about his waist. "Look at that silly ass behaving in such a foolish way," bellowed Katsimbalis. "The future of Greece depends on such drunken idiots. You bloody Americans want to be loved and you do everything to make us loathe you. We're

239

a perverse people. We like the British because they're shits and we understand them. But with you Americans it's hopeless."

He introduced me to his wife, a gentle little woman entirely unlike what I would have imagined as Mrs. Colossus, and he introduced me to a famous beauty, Leto Katacousinos. I had come to Greece with a letter of introduction to Mrs. Katacousinos and her doctor husband, but they had been in Paris so we had not met.

She invited me for supper. Leto was a novelist and her husband, Angelos, was a Byzantine prince, descendant of an emperor, and one of the most distinguished neurologists in Greece. Their penthouse across Amalias Avenue from the Old Palace was filled with books, paintings and flowers. They were lovely people, warmhearted and enthusiastic. Leto invited me to go with them, the next Sunday, to a kite-flying party. "Kites welcome spring," said Leto. "It is our way of throwing our joy in the air." On Saturday evening she sent her maid to buy kites. The maid returned to report there were no more kites to be bought in Athens. "I found an old kite-maker," Leto reported in the morning. "He worked all night."

The day, bright and warm with a brisk wind, was made for flying kites. In the fresh green country we passed gypsy camps roasting lambs on spits, and bands of women with burlap bags gathering "boiling weeds." In an hour we arrived on a ledge over the sea at the holiday villa of an Athenian doctor and his American wife. A young shepherd was turning a spit on which a lamb had been roasting since dawn. The guests included a navy admiral, a U.S. minister, dapper in ascot and tweeds, and Paul Vardinogiannis, the parliament deputy whom I'd seen dance in a stadium in Crete. After Scotch highballs and some *mezédes* which included the liver and kidneys of the roasting lamb, we climbed to the top of the hill and released our kites. They shot into the heavens, their tails snapping in the wind. Admiral, psychiatrist, parliamentarian and minister ran and leaped like demented children, and the kites, pulling toward Sounion's temple, tugged on the cords until our hands bled. After an hour we were called to lunch. The lamb was excellent, the salad the finest I'd eaten in Greece, the wine from our host's own vineyards. Paul Vardinogiannis ate the lamb's head, breaking it with his hands, sucking the skull dry and when he was finished his plate was a mound of glistening bones. Below some young people were swimming and surfing on the glittering sea. The shepherd who had roasted the lamb and the admiral's chauffeur were untangling the snarled kite lines, preparing them for the afternoon.

I longed to wander among temples and one day I drove to Eleusis, center of the cult of the fertility goddesses Demeter and Persephone.

According to legend Demeter was sheltered by King Celeus of Eleusis while she mourned her daughter, Persephone, who had been abducted into the underworld by Pluto. To show her gratitude for the King's hospitality, Demeter presented his son, Triptolemus, with the first grain of corn and she taught him how to till the soil. The shrine commemorating the gift was a center of worship for more than a thousand years. Eleusis stood at the end of a twenty-two-mile "sacred way" which began in the Ceramicos Cemetery in Athens and over which, each September, a procession of pilgrims marched to participate in the "mysteries" or sacred rites.

That compulsive leveler of Greece, Theodosius, finally destroyed it. The modern town is a grimy industrial port. The ruins of the agricultural shrine are surrounded by stacks belching smoke and choking cement dust which covers the area like a blanket. At the gate a little guide introduced himself. "I am Jim," he said and bustled me into the sacred area. The hillside was covered with fragments of marble which, once white, were tinted with time to lovely shades of beige and pink.

"When Persephone was stolen by Pluto, Demeter was very very angry," said Jim. "Then Demeter teaching son of king for growing corn and the king was very pleasant for that. Every September come here three thousand peoples from Athens with small pigs for sacrificing."

We were entering the Propylaea, the sacred entrance built on the same design as the Propylaea of Athens' Acropolis. Beside it was the 2500-year-old Callichorus Well, the fresh water of which, so close to the sea, was considered a gift from the gods and a holy place.

"Girls danced around and made many ceremonies for praising Demeter," said Jim. "All the peoples bring wheats and other foods for Demeter and the priests who live around, they eats." He pointed out sheaves of wheat carved in the pink marble and a rose which he said symbolized the straying Persephone. "When she was down was winter and when she was up was spring," he said. "Demeter is the mother of earth and Persephone the life on earth. Has to come Persephone up to bring the spring." We moved on to the Ploutoneion, the temple over Pluto's cave. "In Sicily is another cave they tell tourists is Pluto's cave," said Jim. I told him I had been there. "Romans come to Greece to conquer but Greek spirit conquer Roman spirit," he said. "They steal everything to make for themselves." We entered the Telesterion, sanctuary of the mysteries. "Here the people not come out for two days and two nights and what they do nobody knows." Jim was unable to offer much specific detail concerning the mysteries. "Maybe they pray, thank Demeter for good harvest," he theorized. "Maybe is all freemasons having ceremonies. Maybe sex, having big orgies. I read many books from writers who believe each of these things. Freemasons write is for Masons and people who like orgies they write is for sex business. I am thinking is maybe the sex. Is more pleasant than praying for two days and two nights. Whatever is, people who are initiated go away very pleasant and those who are not initiated go away unpleasant." Jim seemed to be paraphrasing Homer who wrote, "Happy among the inhabitants of the earth is he who has gazed upon these things. But he who is not initiated does not have a like fate to the initiates when he has died and is below in darkness." In his book *Les Mystères d'Eleusis,* P. Foucart describes the ceremonies as a sacred drama in which the legend of Demeter and Persephone was re-enacted to show the human soul's journey into the underworld. After the drama the initiates' own journey was joyfully concluded with a torchlight procession through an initiation hall simulating the underworld, into the Elysian fields to the temples of Demeter and Persephone. "We take today same things from the old religions," said Jim. "Is the same, the Easter resurrection."

One evening Mike Serapoulos and I attended a session of parliament. When we arrived at the convening hour, seven thirty, only a few deputies were in the hall. The subject scheduled for discussion was a fairly innocuous one, the relief of victims in a recent earthquake. A bell clanged harshly and nine more men ambled into the chamber. By eight o'clock about fifty men and one woman were scattered among the three hundred deputies' seats. The reason for the small attendance was a boycott of parliament by the Papandreous and their supporting deputies, who did not recognize the government of "Palace puppets," as they called them. Only one in a row of thronelike ministers' chairs in the front was occupied. Four policemen huddled in the right front corner of the chamber. They were there, I knew from newspapers, to restore order in the case of any disrupting arguments.

A deputy arose to speak. He droned on until the ear-shattering bell clanged a ten-minute limit. The deputy continued to talk. The bell clanged, the president of the parliament shouted for him to stop. The speaker shouted to the president and neither could be understood. Finally the speaker slumped down and the pandemonium subsided.

A second deputy leaped up and began to speak in a loud voice. The president shouted that he was out of order and commanded him to stop. Ignoring the order the deputy went on about "condensing villages" —a proposal to build new and larger villages to consolidate many small ones. The man was describing the advantages of the plan, such as better schools, a stronger rural economy. The time to consolidate was now, he said, when the small villages had been destroyed by the earthquake. The bell clanged like a fire truck. The president shouted. The speaker on the floor continued to gesticulate but his voice could no longer be heard and he finally gave up.

A new speaker got up to protest the plan for condensing villages which he said was simply a stall while earthquake victims were suffering. Simulating the victims' distress, he flapped his arms, clutched his chest as if he were in agony and raised his hands in prayerful supplication. His voice rose and fell, moving from anger to sobbing to pleading. It was his idea to give earthquake victims building supplies so they could restore their own homes.

The supporter of village consolidation leaped up to say that the supplies could not be delivered because there were no roads over which to haul them. The speaker accused him of obstructionism, of permitting people to die, of "murdering them with words." From their places five seats apart, the two parliamentarians began to shout at one another. The epithets "Idiot! Donkey! Calf!" rang through the chamber. The president also shouted and no one could be understood. The bell clanged like a three-alarm fire. The frenzied orator climbed on his desk, one arm folded across his body, the other waving a fist. His antagonist threw a sheaf of white papers into the air and they fluttered onto the empty seats like feathers. Several deputies got up and left the room. The orator stopped his flailing, leaped from the desk and moved toward the other who was emptying his briefcase, throwing more papers. Two policemen moved down the aisles.

The bell was shattering my ears and we left. It had been a routine session, said Mike. I reminded myself I was in the land of Demosthenes and I tried to imagine what it would be like during a crucial session, during a fall of the government, for instance.

From the parliament we drove outside the city to a workers' suburb where, we'd been told by the dance expert Dora Stratou, we would see the best dancing in Greece. Though Lent had begun, a carnival spirit prevailed and the café, called Stelios, was festooned like New Year's Eve. When we arrived at ten thirty the large barnlike place was almost empty. The manager, a thin dark Cretan with long curled mustaches which reached out from his face like a black yoke, was sitting on a platform behind the cash register. We had come to dine and a waiter offered us two specialties, a lamb's head roasted complete with eyes, or grilled sheep guts. I demurred on both and ordered chicken which, as usual in Greece, was underdeveloped, undercooked and barely edible. Within twenty minutes the place was filled, mostly with family groups, including children, and in another quarter hour guards at the door were turning people away. Music blared forth from a jukebox. A toothless little man, barely weighing a hundred pounds, began the dance with a small girl, obviously his daughter. She was fragile as a bird with great brown eyes and a lovely smile, and she wore a loose blue sweater which draped from her pointed breasts, a pleated miniskirt barely ten inches long and a wide floppy straw hat. Probably fourteen, she looked ten. Encouraged by her father, she bent backwards, touching her head to the floor, shaking her pelvis, rotating her tiny upright breasts. The crowd applauded and the father grinned in paternal pride. A small boy, the girl's brother, perhaps eight years old, entered the floor and duplicated her movements, the bending, the gyrations. Finally the mother, a pretty small blonde woman, joined her family and began to shake. Watching the paroxysms of the family orgy, I thought of the stories of incest, of fathers raping daughters which appear now and then in Greek newspapers.

The record changed to a roistering song called "Hi George Papandreou!" It was greeted by a charivari of applause. The little girl, her eyes wide, her face serious as an Eleusinian princess, led the dance. Dropping backwards, her skirt slipping up her thin black-stockinged legs, she held an inverted saucer position and began to quiver arms, legs, pelvis, breasts, shoulders. In a moment she was hidden by a circle of drunken men, who shouted, leaped and hoisted their groins. Paper streamers flew through the room and fell across the prostrate child.

Suddenly shouting filled the hall. A man was on the floor and another was astride him, pummeling him with his fists. Women screamed and men leaping into the fray upset tables, crashing dishes and silver to the cement floor. From his pulpit the manager pulled the cord on the jukebox and shouted for everyone to sit down. The fight, explained Mike, had begun because a man had made an indecent gesture toward another man's wife, the kind of incident, he said, which sometimes provoked murder.

The manager started a languid Viennese waltz which failed to subdue the turbulence and the fight went on. We started for the door and the manager followed and shook our hands. "It's not a normal night," he said. "Perhaps you will come back on another, a more peaceful time. . . ."

XXI

Escape from Prison

Twenty-five girls were learning English. "Eleni, have you a sister?" the teacher asked.

"Yes, I have a sister."

"Who is your sister?"

"My sister ees Katerina."

"Anna, have you a fiancé?"

"Yes, I have."

"Who is your fiancé?"

In a burst of giggles, Anna replied, "My fiancé ees Thanos Kristas."

"Thallia, have you a fiancé?"

"Yes, I have a fiancé."

"Who is your fiancé?"

"My fiancé ees Telefero . . . Telefero. . . ." Blushing, Thallia could not remember her fiancé's full name. It was not surprising. The plump pretty nineteen-year-old girl from a village in the Peloponnese was on her way to Sydney, Australia, to meet a fiancé she did not know. He was a twenty-six-year-old carpenter whose parents lived in a village near her own and the match had been arranged by their families. Thallia had seen only her future husband's photograph. Her emigration and her lessons in a school in the Athens suburb of Kyfissia were arranged by the Australian government, which imports up to fifteen thousand young Greeks a year.

Was she happy to go? Was she looking forward to meeting a fiancé she had never seen? Thallia shrugged. "If I see him and don't like him

I will throw off the ring," she said, removing the ring from her finger to show how she would do this. "I will take a job as hairdresser." Smiling, she said, "But yes, I am happy to go for the better life." If she approved of her fiancé, would she marry at once? "As he wishes," she said. "I don't know."

Thallia's story was not unusual. Through the Intergovernmental Committee for European Migration, the Australian immigration office in Athens operated nine schools throughout Greece to prepare young men and women for life in Australia and New Zealand. In the Kyfissia school fifty girls from eighteen to twenty-two years of age, from villages all over Greece, were studying a concentrated two-month program of English and home economics, after which they would be sent to Australia in chartered planes. "There are many Greek workers in Australia without women," said one of their teachers, an American-educated young woman named Rose Linaki. "So naturally the girls will get quite a reception. Greek workers prefer to marry their own nationals."

"Since most of the girls are actually going out to be Greek wives, we teach them homemaking rather than professional home economics," said Miss Linaki. "They learn sewing and cooking, the use of automatic laundry and ironing machines, the scrubbing and waxing of floors. In every way possible we try to simulate Australian conditions.

"Their first lessons are in hygiene. Many of the girls insist on sleeping in their underwear because in their villages only prostitutes remove their underwear at night. Some of the girls refuse to shave their armpits for the same reason. Naturally we insist on it. One girl wrote home and two brothers arrived to defend her honor. It took quite a bit of persuasion. We order daily showers and we teach them the use of deodorants. We have nightly inspection to see that all are bathed, have used their deodorant and are sleeping in pajamas."

The girls' day began with a seven thirty breakfast and continued through thirteen hours of lessons and work. "We give them a very difficult schedule to prepare them for the active life ahead," said Miss Linaki. "Village girls have certain problems. In their homes they are accustomed to an indolent life with no responsibilities and no awareness of time. They are used to doing very little. Some of them like our regime from the beginning and most adjust quickly when they begin to feel the incentive of opportunity which does not exist in Greece."

The girls are not permitted to speak Greek in the school. In a trial-and-error method devised by the Australian Office of Education, English is turned into a noisy game in which each pupil is an active player. In one class a girl was given a nurse's cap. Others were patients, with a variety of ailments. Leading an antiphonal dialogue, the teacher asked, "Where are we?"

"We are in a hospital. Everyone ees sick."

"Is Wanda sick?"

"Wanda ees not seek. She ees the nurse."

"Paraskevi, what is the matter with you?"

Paraskevi (who has cotton in her ear): "I have ear ache."

"Paraskevi has ear ache."

"Alexandra, what's the matter with you?"

Alexandra (holding stomach): "I have stomach ache."

"Give Alexandra her pill."

"Alexandra ees taking her peel. . . ."

With bottles and spoons, bandages and thermometers, and with spasms of laughter, the lesson continued. When it was over it was lunchtime. "What are we having for lunch today?" asked Rose Linaki, and fifty girls replied together, "We are having macaroni pie, lettuce and carrot salad and cakes." Across the table from me the prettiest girl in the school was smiling like a Japanese doll. She had black hair, large blue eyes and deeply dimpled pink skin. In my honor she had put some lipstick to her lips. Her name was Panagiota, she was eighteen and her home was in a village near Olympia. An older sister, an alumnus of the school, was married to a carpenter in Australia and worked as a dressmaker. Panagiota could hardly wait to join them. "I will find a nice fiancé," she said, smiling beautifully, leaving no doubts that she would. Beside me was a prim womanly girl with brown eyes and soft brown hair. Her name was Chryssanthi, she was twenty-one and she was from the island of Euboea. She was going to Melbourne where she would be married at once to a twenty-five-year-old stone mason named Ioannis who was from a neighboring village and had gone to Australia nine months before. While the arrangement was not a romantic love match, she did at least know him and was happy with the prospect.

More than two thousand girls had passed through the school on their way to Australia in the three and one-half years of its operation. "Few of those who write letters are homesick," said Rose Linaki. "Sometimes a homesick one will make a trip back to Greece. When she has been here a short time she begins to long for her good life in Australia and she is happy to go back forever."

Several evenings later I attended English classes in downtown Athens for Australian-bound young men. The men studied only English, did not live at the school, and many had daytime jobs to support themselves. After six months they would go to Australia by boat, continuing their studies during the three-week voyage. Signs of "Don't shout" on the walls and blackboards proved useless; nothing could subdue the students' enthusiasm for their new language. Four lusty groups shouting all at once produced a deafening vocal din. One teacher opened a kit of tools and distributed them.

"What is Kostas doing?"

"Kostas ees mending the chair."

"What is Stavros doing?"

"Stavros ees painting the door."

Another teacher held up a magazine picture of a football game.

"What are they doing?"

"They are footballing."

"No, no, no. They are *playing* football."

A second picture showed a girl with a bowl of soup.

"What is she doing?"

"She ees eating soup."

In the next picture a woman was feeding a baby with a bottle.

"What is she doing?"

"She ees eating the baby. . . ."

The students were impatient to get to Australia. A lean fair-haired boy from Tinos said, "On my island we are very poor. In Australia I will work on a many-cow farm and make a big life." A darkly jowled boy from Epirus said, "In Greece there is no work, no opportunity to make a life. For young men it is a prison. So you see it is like we are escaping."

Boys, said an Australian administrator of the school, have no problem of homesickness. "We have only to provide them with girls," he said. "Some of the more venturesome ones will marry Australians. There are Greek communities in our cities, with churches and clubs, which keep the Greek language alive. Most of them keep their Greek citizenship and we do not press them to become Australians. Being proud Greeks they become better Australians than they are aware."

XXII

Prayers in Thebes

I needed a bilingual cicerone, a companion interpreter to accompany me on some journeys and help me with translations. I called on a friend at the British Institute, which conducted classes in English for Greeks, and he introduced me to Thanos Simos.

Thanos was twenty-three years old, and had just finished three years in the Hellenic Royal Navy. His English, studied at night while in the service, was limited but he spoke it freely with uninhibited imagination and invention, creating a language uniquely his own, always making himself understood.

He was more than six feet tall—unusual for a Greek—and had black curly hair and flashing black eyes which were the barometer of his mercurial temperament, registering a variety of moods—merriment, melancholy, humor and anger—in bewildering succession. Exasperating and ingratiating, he added a dimension to my experience and valuable assistance in my work.

He was unique in another way. Of modest middle-class family, he identified with the privileged and the wealthy. His political attitudes had a childish piety which seemed misplaced in the twentieth century. The King, Queen and Queen Mother were godlike figures whom he adored with a passion which the young usually reserve for sports heroes, popular musicians and film stars; George Papandreou and his Center Union party were "microbes which the King has to fumigate from the government."

I learned to understand the reason for this one day when he invited me to his home for lunch. Before Thanos' birth the family had been prosperous; the father owned a factory in Athens. Four months after Thanos was born in 1943, the father died of tuberculosis. The mother lost the family property and was left a poor widow with three small children. For reasons never quite clear she blamed all her misfortunes, the death of her husband, the loss of her property, on "the Communists," an attitude which she passed on to her children. In time the mother remarried an executive of a small shipping firm which operated a fleet of four merchant vessels between Greece and the Scandinavian countries. "My stepfather did a thing unheard in Greece," said Thanos. "He married a widow with three small children and no dowry. For this we are grateful and we love him."

The lunch—a Lucullan feast of Greek delicacies—went on for three hours. Not surprisingly my hosts were all large people. The stepfather was a heavy man accustomed to good living. Thanos' brother was as tall as he; his sister almost. The hub of the monumental family was the mother, named Vasiliki and called "Kiki," a Rubens-contoured earth-mother who, despite her size, had preserved a womanly figure. "She has never worn a corset," boasted Thanos. The mother had a brother in Seattle she had never met—he had emigrated as a young man before she was born—and her image of the United States seemed to be drawn from American films, of which she was a dedicated follower. She asked if I had cowboys on my farm and whether there were any *gigantia* (redwood) trees. I was shown family photographs, including some of the first husband, the father Thanos had never known, and whom he startlingly resembled, photos of the mother in her youth, extremely slender with an exaggerated cupid's-bow mouth, looking like a cinema vamp, of Thanos as a curly-haired infant ("I was mother's darling baby") and another of him as a thin youth carrying the class flag at his graduation, a valedictory honor given to the best student. After three hours at table, during which I ate soup, shrimp salad, spinach pie, *dolmades* (stuffed vine leaves), chicken, and roast lamb, and drank a river of wines, I was in very real agony. With a sweet wistfulness, the mother asked, "How do American women stay so thin? Is it the American climate? Is it because they make so many sports?"

The next Sunday Thanos and I went to Aegina, closest of the Greek islands. Though it was a season for rain, the sun had shone uninterruptedly for weeks. Farmers feared a drought and in Thebes they were praying for rain in church. Our boat was called the *Neraida,* which, said Thanos, meant "a sad fairy which we meet very often in children's tales." He was in a querulous mood following an argument with his family that morning in which he had been urged to marry. Two wealthy shipowners had suggested to his stepfather the possibilities of his marrying their daughters. Thanos had refused both. "They are foolish girls but have much dowry and my father cannot understand why I will not," he said. "I do not wish to be thankful my whole life to a wife. I will not be the captive of a foolish girl and her rich father. I want to build my life for myself and until I do it is impossible for me to marry." The plot to marry Thanos was being complicated by an aunt in Canada who had in mind for him a Montreal restaurant owner's daughter. "I do not prefer to accept her proposition," he said. "I prefer to marry in the American way with someone I love."

The deck of the *Neraida* was crowded with young picnickers, attractive couples, casual and free as American collegiates. The boys were dressed in American blue jeans and plaid flannel shirts; the girls were in sweaters and skirts. Though it was just after eight o'clock, they were already singing and dancing to the music of transistor tape recorders. Finger-snapping youths leaped through a *hasapico* in which they seemed suspended in air, levitating as gracefully as the gulls following the ship. A girl thought she saw a shark and her companion said to me, "You Americans have brought the sharks to us. We didn't have any and now we have many. They follow from Spain your navy ships which throw out the garbage."

We were in open sea and the lurching boat heaved the dancers across the deck. A cluster of dark clouds crouched like cats over the mountains of Aegina. In ancient times the island had been a maritime power with an affluence which, said Pericles, "blinded Piraeus." Its fleet covered the seas to Italy, Egypt and the Black Sea. Now the island lay sleepily under fog. A tiny red-cupolaed church stood on the end of the quay.

As we disembarked the sun disappeared, turning the day ominously gray. We took a bus five miles inland to the Doric temple of Aphaia. Standing in solitude in a pine-enclosed aerie, surrounded by the misty pine green island and its dark seas, the restored temple was as hauntingly beautiful as Vassae in the Peloponnese. Pink-stalked asphodel grew among the limestone columns which, in the curious gray light, shone like bleached bone.

A cold wind keened in the pines, causing branches to snap and groan. The sea was smoke-colored, the horizon dangerously white. I felt an uneasy sense of peril until I remembered that the temple had been there, majestically inviolable, for more than two thousand years. Waiting for the bus, Thanos began to sing and we danced in the road to keep warm. An old priest came shuffling up the road and Thanos made some quick movements with his hand across his groin. "Is three things in Greece to meet are bad luck," he said. "Black cats, snakes and priests. When you meet a priest is necessary to make the cross over the balls to throw off the evil spell." The bus came and took us quickly to the resort village of Haghia Marina. German signs read *"Fleischwaren"* and *"Zimmer zu melden— fliessende Wasser."* The restaurants had German names. The one we chose was filled with youths from the boat playing their transistor radios so we moved on to another perched on a ledge above the sea, called "Blauer Delphin." It was filled by a family group, four generations of children, grandchildren and great-grandchildren of a wizened little patriarch with one jack-o'-lantern tooth. They were eating stiffly crisp fried fish and drinking beakers of white wine. The old man went into the garden and with a knife cut an armful of lettuce leaves and green onions which he distributed among his descendants like a priest giving out palms on Palm Sunday. A young man turned on a transistor radio to *bouzouki* music. Chairs were cleared and the old man unfurled a hand-kerchief and began to dance. His relatives clapped their hands and shouted *"Ola! ola!"* over and over. Tired of dancing alone, the old man grabbed two granddaughters, one pretty and plump, the other tall and flat-chested, and with one in each arm, leaped about the room like a nimble satyr.

We ate our "steaks"—thin veal chops over-fried in oil—and went out into the afternoon. Rows of half-finished houses and new hotels lined the streets, every meter of space filled with new structures to prepare for the springtime invasion of German tourists. Foaming breakers exploded against the cliffs and mists covered the afternoon as in a Japanese land-scape. Two donkeys, one carrying a man and the other a woman and child, appeared out of the fog and it was like a painting of the Flight into Egypt.

We returned by bus to the port, passing the temple, now a ghost in the mists. Fields of asphodel, bent by wind, seemed to cover the island with pink gauze. When we arrived in the harbor, rain was falling and waves rolled over the jetty. The quay was filled with tourists waiting for boats. We bought first-class reserved seats on a boat leaving in an hour and ran through the rain to the little church at the end of the promontory. It was dedicated to St. Nicholas, patron of sailors and Christian heir to Poseidon, King of the Sea. Thanos kissed an icon and prayed for a safe voyage back. Our boat appeared out of the fog. We ran back to the port and when we arrived the gates were closed. I waved the tickets. "Impossible," said the guard. "The boat is overloaded." He pointed to another, a smaller craft named *Hydra* toward which the crowds were running through the rain. This gate also was closing. Thanos, who was ahead of me, made it inside but I was left behind. He told the guard I was a "minister" from the U. S. Embassy and the gate was opened for me to squeeze through.

Outside the crowd was splashing pell-mell in yet another direction, like a crowd in a René Clair film run too swiftly.

The *Hydra* was as crowded as an undersized ark. The tiny first-class salon was jammed and a large woman, waving her ticket, was screaming "Throw them into the sea." We pressed into third class and found places at a table with a family group, a mother with two sons, the wife of one of the sons and their child. As the little craft chugged out to sea, lightning forked across the black skies and thunder boomed. Waves splashed over the window at which we were sitting. The tiny vessel rolled with the waves, tossing people from their chairs. Children cried, men shouted, women screamed. The mother beside me laid her head in her arms and began to pray. His face pale, Thanos looked out on the lethal green sea and said, "It is very fierce."

A lottery seller swinging a string of pink mullets entered the cabin and shouting, offered chances on the fish. The boat heaved, he fell over me and I could feel the cold wet fish slapping on my back. At another table a woman became ill and began to vomit. A cabin boy arrived with a paper container. Within moments dozens were sick and boys raced back and forth, emptying the containers into the sea. The mother beside me fell ill and her son, pale and sweating, murmuring softly, comforted her and then himself began vomiting on the formica table. Fanning them with a newspaper, the second son told a story of another voyage, from Andros, when the motors stopped and the anchor chain broke. He was interrupted by a moan from his wife who called for a container. The frantic husband gave me the newspaper to fan his ill family, slid his sleeping son to his brother's lap and took his wife in his arms. Turning white he also became ill.

A sobbing young woman, tall and dark as Electra, her black hair uncoiled, her head back, her eyes closed, was embracing a column as if it were Orestes. Men and women without chairs embraced, clinging to one another, chanting prayers. An elderly woman fainted and was supported in her chair by a stranger. A man came in from the deck and began to shout insanely. Thanos explained, "When he came back from his seasickness he sees his mother and thinks she is dead. He is shouting, 'Mama, get up from those arms! Get up!'" The woman feebly opened her eyes and the son, taking her in his arms, bellowed louder than ever. Thanos' head dropped to the table; the drops on his brow shone like pearls.

A man wiping steam from a window with his hands began to shout and point into the night. A flash of lightning showed a bright rainbow arched over the sea. Like Noah's cargo, the passengers took heart. The lottery seller shouted "One sixty-one," the winning number. Checking their tickets the people forgot the storm. The hysteria and illnesses

miraculously subsided. A woman, shrieking with joy, took possession of
the string of fish and her friends congratulated her. Everyone looked out
on the bright rainbow arched over the sea and, in a lightning flash, the
silhouette of Piraeus, a white crescent on the horizon. I felt strangely
serene, as if I had sailed with Odysseus. "I think in Thebes they have
prayed too much," said Thanos weakly.

XXIII

Kalavryta

1
"VIDOWS AND WICTIMS"

I read in the newspapers of a controversy in the Peloponnese. "A serious dispute"—said the story—"threatens to break out between the inhabitants of Kalamata and Kalavryta following a government decision that official celebrations to mark the anniversary of the 1821 Greek revolution against the Turks will be held in Kalavryta this year. Official celebrations were up to now held in Kalamata. . . ."

In the dispute between the two towns over which should be the first shrine of Greek independence, history is on the side of Kalavryta. There, in the monastary Haghia Lavra, the revolutionary priest, Archbishop Germanos of Patras, raised Greece's first flag of rebellion against the Turks on March 25, 1821, the day celebrated as the anniversary of Greek independence.

The case of Kalavryta was inviolably confirmed on December 13, 1943, by Germans. On that day, as a reprisal to history, the Nazi 68th Infantry Division in one hour razed Kalavryta with fire and massacred its entire male population over fourteen years of age. Because of this horrifying single episode in an unbelievably brutal occupation, the name of Kalavryta fills Greek hearts with shock and loathing and forever will.

In Germans it stirs a nervous guilt. In Athens I heard stories of German efforts to aid the stricken town. To discover the extent of German retribution I went one day to the German Embassy and spoke with the commercial attaché, Dr. Karl Pfauter.

He was a large man with blue eyes and a large head, nearly bald. "Ah, Kalavryta," he began and stopped to pick nervously on a hangnail. "I have not been. I could not go. I am too ashamed for all the terrible things." Speaking in a nasal lisp, moistening his lips with his tongue, he continued with unrelated things, about a Belgian nun who had done relief work, and, he said, "had many troubles with the Grik authorities," and a curious tale about the Nazi—not German but *Nazi,* implying the exclusion of himself—killing of fifty thousand Jews in Salonica. "I was then in Athens," he said, "I was in the *Geheim Dienst* (Secret Service) and I warned the Griks that Jews would be transported, and believe me, they would not believe me. There were Grik Jews who delivered the names of all the Jews in Salonica. So they were destroyed. Horrible people these Grik Jews. They were spies for the Nazis. Jah, jah."

I kept trying to return the conversation to Kalavryta but he seemed not to hear me, speaking instead what was on his mind, saying, "Those fifty thousand Jews in Salonica was Spanish subjects." They were, I remembered, descendants of Jews who had fled Inquisition Spain and had been Greeks for almost five hundred years. "I went to the Spanish Embassy," he continued. "The chargé d'affaires was a priest. I see him in my eyes still. . . ." Dr. Pfauter shuddered with the horror of his memories. "You must go to the Cherman Embassy and claim them as Spaniards I say to him. He was shaking with fear and he did not do anything. He had the possibility of saving the Jews and he did nothing. So the Jews of Salonica disappeared."

As he spoke, Dr. Pfauter moved about the room, loping rather than walking, like a large animal in a small cage. "Griss was a very complicated picture," he said. "You can't imagine how careful one has found it necessary to be. The Griks were very difficult. They had a bad fault. Jah, jah."

I asked Dr. Pfauter what the Greeks' bad fault had been. He hesitated, rubbing his hand over his bald dome. "Gossiping," he said. "They talk all the time, always gossiping about people. Griks don't discuss subjects or problems like Chermans. They discuss only personalities. So if something is said to a Grik, the next day is known by all Griss." He sighed. "Is still a great problem."

I interrupted and asked again if he would tell me of the German aid to Kalavryta. He stood still for a moment, thinking intently, breathing deeply.

"Jah, jah," he began. "A great Cherman lady made this business for Kalavryta, is name Frau Ehrengard Schramm of Göttingen. Her husband, Percy Schramm, is famous professor of history, a friend of mine, a scholar always writing books. He kept a diary during the war when he was a commander in the Wehrmacht." Dr. Pfauter's voice deepened. "He has written a very fine book, *Niederlage 1945,* about the last days of Hitler."

"What did his wife do?"

"Jah, jah. She is the Baroness von Thadden from Pomerania. Her sister, Elisabeth von Thadden, is arrested and executed for the July 1944 assassination attempt of Hitler. I don't remember whether she has been hanged or shot. Jah, jah, jah." Dr. Pfauter stopped to page through a great file. "She is also a writer about the *Griechenland im zweiten Welt Krieg.* You read Cherman? Is very interesting. An exactly written history about the unlucky fate of poor Griss to be pushed into the war through the stupidity of Mussolini."

Now Dr. Pfauter found that for which he was searching, a photograph which he handed to me. It showed a commanding woman with a high-browed face, wide-spaced eyes and a stern expression.

"She appears very strong," I said.

"Jahwohl, jah, jah. She come from the east where the Cherman woman is like man, big and strong with very great power. She is friend of Griss and come many times before the war. So she is single Cherman person who could appear as first Cherman in these poor Grik villages. Jah, jah. She felt entitled to make herself the first Cherman friend to these poor Grik vidows. Is not only Kalavryta she visit, is other villages. . . ." Dr. Pfauter took a paper from his file and handed it to me. It was a list of eight Greek villages, four of them in Crete. It was a fraction of the total villages destroyed by Germans.

"Tell me about Kalavryta."

"Jah, jah. Kalavryta is village of ruins and vidows and wictims and orphans, many orphans. Frau Schramm learned Grik so she could speak with those poor wictims, so she could explain how the Chermans also is wictims of the terrible Nazi regime. She is very commanding with much authority. Like a queen. Jah, jah. When she comes into a village she assembles it around her and she says now we will discuss. She discusses. She being always anti-Nazi, she found the entrance to the souls of these poor vidows and wictims and found their confidences."

"In Kalavryta?" I persisted.

"Jah, jah. In Kalavryta she assembled the vidows and wictims around her and asked how is your economic situation, how can you earn your living? She explained bluntly and frankly her own experience and suffering and how she became to speak to them. For it has been very difficult for Chermans to get contact with Griks. In every village she visited she asked the required and the need, what could be done.

"Jah, jah. Frau Schramm was all alone, she had no big organization.

She organized some friends, and she has genius for raising money from private citizens and organizations and even from Cherman government. From Kalavryta she takes almost a hundred of the orphan wictims, and from other villages also many, and she take them to Chermany for schools where they have good Cherman technical and vocational training. Any Grik boy who writes she says come to me. Her house in Göttingen is like from rubber, always full with Grik boys. Her husband, the Herr professor, is so patient, always having in his house Griks. A young man who had been wounded by Nazis she take to Chermany for operation. Jah, jah. Always she ask what can be done for your village and of course there were many foolish and idiotic Grik requestions which were not feasible. Like tractors and machines. They ask for tractors very expensive which is much too big for their bad little fields and when she send the tractors . . . well, do you know the Griks a little bit? They sold the tractors. Jah, jah." Herr Pfauter was beginning to sputter with the strain of our interview. "Frau Schramm, she have had Griks trained in kettle herding. You know how Grik cows are meager and degenerate, and she sent them good strong Cherman cows. In hills of Macedonia she found all this *Unkraut,* how you say, veeds, like a fern, covering the land and could not cows eat. She get experts, good Cherman experts, to make research for eradication of this horrible fern which is eating up all the fields. In many village she give *Röhren* for running water. She make houses, churches and irrigation systems. To help the vidows and wictims she sent a young Cherman agriculture expert. He had all kinds of terrible problems. He had to live in a Grik village with all the gossipings and awful jealousies. He needed the intervention of a minister to make his work.

"Jah, jah." Dr. Pfauter took back the photograph and looked at it admiringly. "Frau Schramm is like an angel. A good Cherman angel, very dedicated. Every year she come twice to Griss to visit the poor vidows and wictims of the Nazis and now she is being older and ailing, poor one, and she cannot come any more. I am arranging to get for her some Grik decoration. Jah, jah . . ."

2

THE BEAUTIFUL SPRINGS

The next morning, a Saturday, I set out with a car and driver for Kalavyrta. With me were two companions, Thanos Simos, my interpreter, and a young secretary from the Foreign Press Office, a serious young man who had been born in Kalavryta and whose name was John

Athanasopoulos. He had left Kalavryta the day before the 1943 massacre, as a two-year-old baby in his mother's arms, and he had no memories of it. The trip with me was his first return and he was making it with mixed emotions.

He told his story. "My father died of malnutrition after being wounded in the guerrilla war. My mother had two children, my brother who was fourteen, and myself. Both of us were ill with malaria and starvation. So on December 12 my mother took us on the train to Athens where she had relatives. If we had stayed one more day it would have been too late. My brother would have been killed."

We were following the shores of the Corinth Gulf. The sea was high, the sky gray, the mountains snow-covered. We passed through Diakopton, from which a small cog railway went to Kalavryta. The eighteen-mile ascent took two hours. By car we would circle the mountains, passing through Patras, and approach Kalavryta from the south. I asked John to tell me of the massacre.

"It is a confused picture," he said. "I will try. There had been fighting between Germans and Kalavryta guerrillas, and the Germans began burning villages around Kalavryta. The bishop went to the German commander and asked him not to destroy the villages. 'Go home or we'll shave you,' the Germans said, making the worst possible insult to a priest. The Germans arrived in Kalavryta on December 11 and a schoolteacher who spoke German made a speech, telling the invaders that Kalavryta was a peaceful town, that the people lived quietly and the Germans had nothing to fear from them. The Germans were very grave. They demanded the names of the guerrilla fighters and the mayor provided them. The commander issued an order that no one was to leave Kalavryta. Two peasants left for their homes outside the village and were shot.

"On December 13, in the morning, the church bells rang and everyone gathered in the square. The Germans ordered the people to go into the schoolhouse. There the men were separated from the women and children and ordered to march to a field on a hill behind the cemetery, a half mile from the village. The field belonged to a man named Kapi. All boys fourteen years of age and older were taken with the men.

"In Kapi's field the men were forced in a circle against the wall of the mountain. Germans with guns surrounded them so they could not escape. The men were ordered to 'heil' Hitler. They shouted *Zito i eleutheria* (Long live liberty) and *Zito i Hellas* (Long live Greece). A priest, Papa Panagiotis Demopoulos, shouted 'Kill me and free my people,' and the Germans marched him away and shot him. He is remembered forever as 'The Good Priest.' The men could see other Germans setting fire to the

village and to the schoolhouse in which their women and their children
were locked.

"A man shouted, 'We'll die as brothers. There is no greater death than
to die for Greece.' The German commander ordered his men to start firing.
The machine-gunning took fifteen minutes. Afterwards it took the Germans
another hour to make the *coup de grâce* with their pistols into the skull of
each fallen Greek. Thirteen men recovered from their wounds and one
has written a book.

"Down in the village a German soldier panicked and opened the doors
of the burning school, letting out the women and children. The Germans
shot him. The whole massacre was later reviewed in the Nuremberg
trials where it was stated seven hundred men were killed. In Kalavryta
they have the names of over twelve hundred."

We stopped in Patras for coffee and then we began a climb through
barren rock-strewn mountains, passing flocks of sheep and a few crumbling
villages. We drove through a canyon of glistening mountains and entered
into a broad fertile valley, blue with spring flowers. Men and women on
donkeys and mules were going home from market.

Kalavryta, said John, meant "beautiful springs." The town lay along
a valley stream in a circle of mountain peaks. Here and there among the
modern streets a charred shell remained. We went to the town hall
where a dozen dignitaries, stern dour men, were sitting around a council
table like a quiet and solemn jury. With one exception they sat stiff and
straight. One across the table from me slouched comfortably in his chair,
puffing on a pipe. The unheated room was cold. The men's black suits,
white shirts and dark ties made me self-consciously aware of our casual
sports gear, our sweaters and caps. In the uneasy silence I felt the dark
gaze of a dozen pairs of eyes pressing on me. Most penetrating were the
eyes of the man across the table. He seemed different from the others,
a lean wiry little man, alertly handsome with shining black hair, heavy
brows and a mustache. His black suit was excellently tailored, his knit tie
appeared to be imported. His appearance seemed very English. He
filled the black pipe in his hands with good Dutch tobacco and he
sucked the flame of a match into it.

Coffee was served and an awkward conversation began which Thanos
translated. I was introduced to the town secretary, an explosive little man
named Panos Polkas, who seemed angry even in welcoming us, and a
schoolteacher named Dimitrios Kaldiris, a thin tense man who seemed
filled with pain and resentment. We continued with courteous amenities,
making little conversational progress, and Thanos struggled with the
translations. The subject I had come to discuss was approached cautiously, obliquely, with odd facts given loudly by the secretary and quietly

by the schoolmaster. To break the ice I commented on the comfortable-appearing modern town.

"Only seven houses were left," the secretary said angrily. "Some women and children went to live with relatives in Patras and Athens, but most chose to stay in the burned town. Twenty guerrillas came down from the mountains to help the women. Thirty Kalavryta men who were living in Athens and Patras could not stay away. They were brought back by a responsibility." And perhaps guilt, I was thinking. Guilt for having been away, for not having died in the massacre with their brothers.

"As time went on other men moved to Kalavryta," the schoolmaster said. "They came from other villages and they married the girls and started families. After the liberation the town slowly began to live again. Kalavryta was rebuilt with American aid and gifts from American Greeks. A rich man in San Francisco named Angelos Pampoulis, who was born in Kalavryta, sent money to build houses. Also in San Francisco, an old widow named Katina Gellepis, who worked in a laundry, sent forty thousand dollars to build the hospital."

"Names changed in Kalavryta," said the secretary. "Old families disappeared. Only eight of the widows remarried. The rest preferred to live with their grief, to keep alive the memory. The widows were forced to sell their lands and their properties to the new families. The new took from the old." With Thanos translating every word the conversation continued slowly in a formal manner. Outside some men were raising arches of laurel over the street in preparation for the national holiday. The secretary said there would be a parade and a church service with a representative of the King present. Through the conversation I had been uncomfortably aware of the penetrating, mildly amused eyes of the silent pipe-smoker watching me. On the wall over his head I noticed for the first time a framed photograph of King Paul and Queen Frederika made on Kapi's field. The Queen's face, distorted in agony and stained with tears, moved me deeply. The pipe-smoker's eyes across the table followed my gaze. Removing his pipe, he exhaled a ring of smoke, smiled cynically, and in perfect Oxford-accented English said, "Do you think the sorrow is real?"

My astonishment caused the man to laugh. "May I introduce myself?" he said. "I am Thanos Tsaparis. I publish a newspaper, The Voice of Kalavryta."

Recovering, I said, "Obviously you also like to play games."

"Not at all," he said. "I hope you shall let me help you."

"Thank you. You must have lived in England."

"I have never been out of Greece."

"I find that hard to believe," I said. "Where did you learn English?"

"From listening to B.B.C. broadcasts on the short-wave radio. I suppose I have rather what you would call an accent."

"Rather," I said. We laughed. Thanos Simos and John began to giggle. A few of the men around the table smiled faintly at the joke that had been played on us. In spite of my irritation I found myself liking the native Thanos, and we were friends almost at once. I asked where he had been on the day of the massacre.

"In school in Athens," he said. "I was seventeen. On the night of December 13 I had a dream that I was standing in Kapi's meadow and in my dream I could see Kalavryta burning. I saw the red flames and black smoke. Ten days later I learned what had happened, that my brother had been shot. I have never been able to forget that it is because I was in Athens that I am alive today."

The Tsaparis family, said the schoolmaster, had been the most distinguished and richest in the town. The father, who had died before the massacre, owned an electrical plant, a bank and a department store. "But the Germans destroyed all the property and inflation finished the bank," said Thanos Tsaparis. "I am a poor man. I could have stayed and worked in Athens but I felt I had to come back to rebuild the electrical station, that it was my duty. I did that and then I could have left. But I didn't. In order to fight my personal war with another gun, I started my little newspaper. We are about thirty men now who fight to keep the old Kalavryta alive."

The price of his fight was high. His wife who was from Thessaloniki and who was unhappy in Kalavryta, with its melancholia and its nursing of grief, pleaded to leave. Three children were growing up and needed to be moved from the dour atmosphere to be educated. His mother, a survivor of the massacre, now in her eighties, lived in seclusion. "She has become quite strange," said the son. "She locks herself up in her little house and sees no one but me once a day." He himself had an ulcer and six months before had almost died from hemorrhaging. "Always I have felt I must do what I can for Kalavryta. Sometimes it seems I have botched it all, that I have done nothing for anyone, nothing for myself and nothing for my family. But it is impossible to leave."

I spoke of the German woman, Frau Schramm. Thanos Tsaparis' eyes narrowed, the lines of his mouth tightened.

"Schramm is a very clever woman," he said, harshly accenting "clever." "After the war Germany had to renew her commercial relationships with the countries with which it did business before the war. To open such relationship they had first to change the feelings of the people. So Germany used every possible contact, every individual that knew Greece. I think that in back of Schramm were the big German factories, corporations like

Bayer, Siemens and Osram." The explanation was coldly cynical and behind it I felt the hatred boiling in Thanos Tsaparis' blood. He referred to the German woman only as "Schramm."

"Schramm took more than thirty Kalavryta youths to Germany," he went on. "Ten married and stayed there—in Kalavryta we consider them traitors. One died, presumably of a heart attack while swimming, but in Germany anything is possible. Some twenty returned to Greece and none are in Kalavryta because the technical training they received in Germany is of no use here. Most of them are in Athens, working for German firms. Three girls also went to Germany. One came back immediately. She has a curious story. She was born on the day of the massacre. The German soldiers entered the house and found the mother in labor. They did not set fire to the house but the father was taken with the others and shot. When the girl was in Germany much was made of her in the German press. She felt guilty for being there and in two weeks she returned. She is now working for me."

I asked about the Germans who had visited Kalavryta.

"They come as tourists," said Thanos Tsaparis. "Only Germans would have the gall. No one speaks to them. We do not show our anger, but we cannot pretend to welcome them. A German minister came and made a speech, saying 'Germany is different from Hitler's Germany. We want to forget, we want to help.' The German ambassador brought some chemical laboratory equipment for the high school. He went to Kapi's field with a wreath, but not one man of Kalavryta would accompany him and he had to go alone."

3
THE SCHOOLMASTER'S STORY

More deeply than it did any man in the room, hatred and rage possessed the thin pale schoolmaster. His dark eyes flashed in his white face and he could not speak the word *German* without flushing and trembling. Now and then during his long story other men, overcome by emotion, got up and left the room.

"The memory of that day," he began, "will burn in my brain even after I am dead. It was cold and gray. The Germans ordered everyone to stay in their houses. In our house we were nine, my father and mother and seven children. I was ten, the second oldest. The day before the Germans had gone from house to house and into all the shops, stealing everything, food, clothing, tools. Our little train was going up and down all day and all night, taking our things away.

"When the church bells rang, the people ran out of their houses in panic. German soldiers with pistols ordered each of us to take a blanket and food enough for one day and told us to go to the schoolhouse. There they sent the women and children into the north rooms of the school and the men and older boys into the south rooms. My brother, Panagiotis, who was fifteen, wanted to go with my father, but he was carrying a smaller brother so he was pushed in with us. The doors were locked. Through the windows we could see the soldiers.

"A woman screamed, 'Fire! Fire!' We crowded to the windows and we saw the whole town burning. Buildings were collapsing. Children cried and women fell to the floor to pray. Smoke coming up from below filled the room—the Germans had set their fires in the cellar. 'They are burning us like dogs,' a woman cried and she began to scream. Breathing the suffocating smoke caused everyone to cough. We began to break windows and we tried to break the doors. A teacher who spoke French begged a German guard outside to free us. 'I will be killed for this but I cannot let it happen,' he said. 'I am a father. I will open the door.' He opened the door and another German shot him. We ran screaming from the school and a poor old woman, Krina Tsavala, was killed by the hundreds of feet trampling over her. Germans with machine guns would not permit us into the burning town so everyone ran away from the town, down to the river. A woman whose house was in the upper town, near the cemetery, escaped and began running toward her house. She met German soldiers marching down the hill, carrying their guns and their bloody axes. They were singing. Down by the river we could hear their voices, yodeling 'hol-de-i-o-la-la-la . . .'"

The schoolmaster stopped. His lips moved but no words came from them. His face was white, his shoulders shook, tears were flowing from his eyes. After a time his shoulders stiffened and he went on.

"In Kapi's field the woman saw a strange heap which she thought were the blankets which the soldiers had stolen from our houses. She asked the soldiers, 'Where are the men?' and they laughed and said, 'They've gone to Athens, to Patras.' The woman started up the hill and she noticed she was walking in blood. She was walking in blood to her ankle. She ran into the butchery, seeking her husband and her sons. She found her husband and two sons dead and a third son still alive. She put him across her shoulder and she brought him to the river. In spite of her load she flew like a bird, crying, 'There, there up on the hill our husbands and sons are slaughtered like sheep.'

"We ran up the hill. What we faced I cannot describe. All the earth was covered with blood, with heads split open, with spattered brains and parts of bodies. No one can tell it, no one can imagine what we saw.

Four priests had been murdered with axes. Women crazy with grief ran over the field, searching for their men, trying to find their own dear dead, to caress and kiss them for the last time. Their lamentations filled the world. Women and children carried the bodies down to the cemetery. Night fell. When we could see no more we returned to the burning town. The houses flamed like great candles. Seven houses were not burned and in these the women put their children.

"My mother took us into St. George's Church. She tried to comfort us. But we could not sleep. All night children screamed in their mothers' arms. They were frightened by the icons so my mother covered them with blankets and the children could not see them. All our lives we had been taught to love the icons, but now we were frightened even of God. The cathedral was burning and sometimes in the night it crashed with a great noise, like a tree in the black night. My mother left us there, returning to the hill where she found my father. She covered his body and she sat with it.

"In the morning a German plane passed low, close to the ground, making photographs and we ran to hide until it was gone. The women told the children to remain below and they went to Kapi's field to bury the men. The Germans had taken all our spades, our trowels, and there was nothing with which to dig. The corpses were dragged down to the cemetery in blankets and on wooden ladders, and the women buried them with their hands. Women with four or five dead and with no one to help them, covered the dead on the execution place. Shepherds came down from the hills, bringing bread and milk.

"That night the valley was filled with hungry wild dogs. The smell of blood had brought them from all around. They licked up the blood covering the ground and the brains, and they dug up the corpses and ate from them. The next day the women tried to bury them deeper. On the third day the Red Cross arrived with food and clothing and medicine. The women built stone huts from the ruins. Winter came and snow covered the valley."

The schoolmaster stopped, as if he were out of words and out of strength. "That is all," he said. I had been thinking, as I listened, of the ancient dramas, of *The Trojan Women,* and of *Antigone.*

"It is not all," said the secretary, carrying it on with angry words. "The ground froze and the burying and reburying went on for two months. Having to dig graves with their hands, the women dug them shallow and the hungry dogs dug them up at night and ate from them. Our soldiers guarded the cemetery at night, shooting the dogs. Some women had as many as six corpses to bury. When they were finished they washed the blood from the blankets and covered their children with them for they had no others."

Other men began to speak and one of them said, "Several times in the months that followed supplies arrived from the Red Cross and from Americans, and always the Germans would raid the village and steal the food and the clothing. It went on all winter and each time the women would flee with their children into the mountains."

"My mother found a goat," said the schoolmaster, "and she fed us by suckling on it. But we were seven and there was never enough and we were always hungry."

The room was silent. I raised my eyes to the window and saw that the afternoon sun was casting long shadows. The clock on the church tower said 2:33. I checked my watch which said 4:25. The schoolmaster saw me and said, "The church is new but the clock is the same. It will remain forever at the moment time stopped in Kalavryta."

4

THE FIELD OF KAPI

It lies one kilometer east of the village, a kind of alcove in the side of Mt. Helmos. From its leveled surface soar five abstract concrete forms, panels and arcs, covered with lists of names and placed in a circle, symbolizing, said Thanos Tsaparis, "the resurrection of the rising soul." The monument was built with contributions from the school children of Greece. Inside the circle was a single modern sculpture of a weeping woman and on a knoll above stood a large white cross.

It was a serene place and in the late afternoon utterly peaceful. Birds were singing and bells tinkled on sheep grazing above, beyond the cross. To the right on a mountaintop were the ruins of a Venetian castle. A short distance below was a crowded cemetery, and beyond to the west, on the side of Mt. Erimanthos, stood a monument of the 1821 revolution. Below and between the two monuments, at the bottom of a bowl of snow-covered peaks, lay the town.

From one of the concrete panels Thanos Simos read and translated, "On the thirteenth day of December, 1943, in this place, all the male population of Kalavryta was executed by machine guns of Germans revenging national resistance. This is in everlasting memory of the Greek battle for victory."

The encircling pylons carried the names of stricken families. Fifty-two boys from the ages of twelve through seventeen were listed individually with their ages. So were four priests, the old woman, Krina Tsavala, who was crushed to death, and thirteen men who were shot but did not die. In the mountain wall was a dark door leading into the earth, a newly built crypt prepared for the bones of all massacre victims which would, according to Greek custom, eventually be taken up from their graves. The crypt had filled with the water of melting snows and some workmen were draining it. Around the memorial was a thickness of pine and cypress. "I have planted them," said Thanos Tsaparis. "I am arranging to bring to this place a vase of earth from all the other terrible places of massacre— from Lidice in Czechoslovakia, from Setif in Algiers, and Montecatini in Italy." As he spoke, I felt in him the obsession of the heroic ancients and I understood it, this need of all Kalavrytans to nurture their grief and their hate, to tend them like flames and never give them up, and I felt they were right in their dedication to never let the world forget this unfathomable carnage by the swine of the earth.

Scattered among the trees were small white crosses and other grave plots outlined with whitewashed stones. "These graves were made here by women who had no assistance and who could not carry their dead to the cemetery," said Thanos Tsaparis. One grave plot lovingly kept within an iron fence had a cross on which I read, "Here lies a father and his two sons. Everything I have loved in this world here on this slope I have buried alone." Other small crosses had no names. "They are the unknowns," said Thanos Tsaparis, "the strangers in the town no one knew were here."

The sun slid behind a peak and the shadowed ledge turned cold. Above the white cross still gleamed in sunlight. The sheep, bells tinkling, passed by the plot, homeward bound. We were an assorted group, standing hushed inside the circle, three of us from Athens, the men from the municipal office and some strangers. One of the strangers was a ruddy-faced gray-haired man in a heavy overcoat. He had a high-browed aristocratic head, bald in front, and he stood alone, silent and intensely nervous. Thanos Tsaparis brought him into the group and introduced him. His name was Panagiotis Nikolaidis, and he was one of the thirteen who had not died. His body, said Tsaparis, had a total of seventeen bullet wounds, three from the massacre and fourteen from the 1948 Civil War. His flushed complexion and strong worker's hands gave the impression of robustness. He was nervous because he had been brought there to tell his story.

He began by pointing to a spot on the earth, saying, "I was there, and I have never been able to believe that I am still alive. Near me were the director of the gymnasium, the professor of French, Konstantine Athanassiadis, the lawyer, Panagiotis Georgantas, our priest, Panagiotis Demopoulos and others whose names I cannot remember. . . ."

He spoke with a terrible emotion, the torrent of his words flowing rapidly, halting only when he had to gasp for breath. "We were standing or sitting on the earth, here in this circle where the Germans brought us, where they surrounded us with their guns. Standing below was the German Commander Tenner, eating almonds from a bag. There was a machine gun beside him. We were all wondering what would happen, we were asking one another, what will they do with us, what will happen to our wives and children. They told us we were waiting to go to another place. They told us, swearing on their soldier's honor, that we were in no danger, that our families would not be harmed. We were talking amongst ourselves how we might escape and we thought of a plan. We tried to move toward the edge of the circle, thinking we would suddenly run, and then we saw that we were surrounded by machine guns hidden under branches. We knew the Germans were lying and we did not know what was happening to our wives and children. We were too afraid to try to escape, afraid for the reprisals against our families. A man shouted, 'Look, they are burning our houses,' and then we saw the village all in flames. A rocket was sent up from the village, exploding a green light in the skies. It was a signal. The Commander Tenner dropped his bag of almonds and moved to his machine gun, and then we knew, we understood what was happening. A second rocket burst, painting the sky blood-red. Tenner raised his hand like a salute and he dropped it and all the machine guns exploded at once, vomiting fire. Men crawled close together on the earth and some tried to escape and were shot down."

Speaking more and more swiftly, his face flushed, Nikolaidis began to run about the circle, pointing out places, and his voice broke with emotion.

"The lawyer, Panagiotis Georgantas, shouted, 'Brothers, death for liberty is not death," and he fell to the bloody ground. Near me Konstantine Athanassiadis was lying dead with astonished open eyes. The Good Priest shouted, 'German pigs, where is your honor?' To the men he said, 'Be brave—to die together for Greece is to live,' and then he fell and a soldier butchered him with an axe. The boy, Konstantine Alexopoulos, thirteen years old, cried, 'I am a very little boy. I do not want to die, why do you kill me? What is my crime?' and then his voice faded away, saying, 'Quiet, quiet, quiet . . .' I tried to run and I felt a pain in my neck and I fell. I rolled into a ditch and covered myself with bushes. I thought: this is the way death is. Death was around me, I could hear its voices, the dying words of my friends. I lay on my back thinking philosophically of the entrance from life into death. I thought: this is murder, not execution. The Germans planned everything. They picked

Kapi's field because it is surrounded by mountains, because no one could escape. They asked us to bring the blankets for our coffins.

"Above the barking of the guns I heard loud singing. The Germans were driving the sounds of their murder from their ears with their own strong voices. In fifteen minutes everyone had fallen, the guns stopped. From everywhere I heard cries, the moans of men not dead. And then there were more explosions. The Germans were inside the circle, putting pistols to the heads of the men who still lived, splitting skulls with axes, finishing their macabre deed. I did not move and they passed me by. Then I heard music. The Germans were marching away, singing, yodeling, 'Hol-de-ri-hol-de-ri . . .' until they were so far away I could hear them no more. I could not move. Everything was quiet. All my life I shall hear in my mind that yodel, 'Hol-de-ri . . .' "

All eyes in the circle were lowered to the ground. Nikolaidis could not stop, but went breathlessly on, repeating things he'd already said, saying, "The Germans marched us up here in double file with guards beside us. The Commander was eating almonds, making a path with the shells."

My eyes met the eyes of Thanos Tsaparis, which were filled with tears. Thanos Simos had disappeared. Looking up I saw the large frame of him standing by the white cross above and his hands were covering his face. Nikolaidis went on, "Late in the afternoon when it was growing dark, women and children came to search for their husbands, their fathers and sons. My wife, my mother and my mother-in-law carried me down in my blanket and I lay that night in the cemetery beside my dead comrades. I spoke to the mother of the boy, Konstantine Alexopoulos, and I said, 'Brave woman, you must be proud. Greece has lost one of her noblest children. . . .' "

Someone said, "Let's go down to the cemetery," and silently, in single file, we left the field of Kapi.

5

THE CEMETERY

A caravan of bent old women, robed in black, some walking with sticks, were passing through the gate and moving softly among the graves and crosses. "Every Saturday they come to visit their dead," said Thanos Tsaparis.

The cemetery, with cypresses and blue hyacinths, was the most carefully kept I had seen in Greece. The more elaborate graves were covered with white marble. The modest were simple rectangles of whitewashed stones. In the descending dusk the stones among the green shone ghostly white.

The black-hooded women, moving softly up and down the rows like dark spirits, carried candles and small vials of oil with which they lit grave lamps, which, burning, one by one, flickered like stars. When they had lit the lamps and weeded the graves, the women sat quietly on the tombs, using them as benches, talking softly with one another. Some knelt by their graves and moaned softly, watching us through tear-filled eyes. "It is blood they are weeping," said Thanos Tsaparis, "the blood of their hearts which drops day after day forever, as they try to understand what has happened to them." We walked up and down rows of graves, all with one date, "13–12–43," over and over and over again. Fathers were buried with sons under stones which were covered with names. I read:

> Apostolis Theophanopoulos — 57 years old
> Theophanis — 33 years old
> Mitsos — 32 years old
> Panos — 22 years old
> Theodoros — 13 years old

And another:

> Kyriakos Ballalas — 56 years old
> George — 24 years old
> Nick — 22 years old
> Andreas — 14 years old

Under these I read:

> With dry lips, with eyes filled with tears,
> In my arms I long to embrace you,
> My tears and pain water this ground,
> My voice will always call you, Kyriakos, our father,
> George, Nick, Andreas, my brothers.

Thanos Tsaparis said, "See that little girl? She is lighting candles at the grave of her grandfather and uncle whom she has never known. All our children are taught never to forget their terrible heritage. That old woman is Maria Liberi who lost her husband and three sons, and that is Ourania Oikonomou, who was a young woman in 1943, who lost her son, her brother and a nephew."

He introduced me to Ourania, a heavy handsome woman, fifty-five years old. Standing over a grave, holding a lamp in one hand and moving the other back and forth across her breast, speaking in soft melodious rhythms, she said, "We carried the men down until night fell and then we sat all night in the cemetery and in the morning we went again. We had nothing to dig with and we took the cold earth up with our hands, placing it gently like a blanket over a child. For four days and four nights we carried them down and then we had to do it all over again because of the dogs. How did we do it, how had we the strength? Where did we find the courage?"

Across the cemetery wall was a school and on its athletic field some boys were playing football. Thanos Tsaparis called out a name and a boy dropped from the game and came into the cemetery. The boy, his son, a smiling brown-haired youngster, gravely shook my hand. "When he is older the smile will disappear from his face," the father said. The boy, not understanding English, continued to smile. "He knows, they all know," said the father. "Our children grow up in the shadows of this terrible cemetery. Every Saturday they must come here with the women to light the candles." Thanos Tsaparis went on, smoking his pipe and weeping, and the boy, seeing his father's tears, looked down to the grave at his feet. "For the sake of our future generations we must move the cemetery further from the village," the father said. "We can't have it so close, the children still to come cannot be expected to live forever in its terrible shadows. But as long as the old women live, it is not possible."

Nearby an old woman with white hair and soft brown eyes called out, crying, "Look! Look here, my son!" Addressing me, she keened softly, saying, "Is not this grave beautiful? I water it with my tears and for this reason there are always flowers."

Another, bent and small, kneeling by a grave, began to shout. "Do you see me? I'm all alone in the world." Her voice rang like a bell in the hushed place. Her eyes were like a madwoman's. "I carried my dead sons, one by one, on my shoulder and I buried them with my hands, my nails, my feet, with all that I had at the moment I buried them." As she continued her crying I felt someone touch me and I looked into the tear-stained face of Thanos Simos and I heard him whisper, "Antigone buried her brother with her hands."

As quickly as he had appeared, Thanos Simos fled. Following him, my eyes came to rest on still another stone, and I read:

> What I loved in this world,
> And what I nursed,
> I brought down from the mountain,
> And buried alone.

Other women were crying out to me, calling for my attention, and I knew I could remain no longer in that place. I saw the lean form of Thanos Simos hurl through the gates as if on wings, and I followed it.

6

THE MONASTERIES

In their week-long debauch of murder the German soldiers also massacred the monks in two monasteries near Kalavryta. The first was Megaspélaion, richest and most famous of all Greek monasteries, and the second was Haghia Lavra, where in 1821 the flag of revolt was raised.

With Thanos Tsaparis, in his pickup truck, I drove on Sunday morning to Haghia Lavra. The road ascended for four and a half miles in a southwesterly direction toward snow-covered peaks. "The Germans," said Thanos, "arrived at Haghia Lavra on December 14, the day after the Kalavryta massacre. They slaughtered the monks and burned the monastery. After the war it was rebuilt as a national monument."

The new monastery covered a ledge between two mountains. Outside stood a huge plane tree more than thirty feet in circumference. "Under this tree Bishop Germanos hoisted the banner," said Thanos. "Actually, March 25, when we celebrate the raising of the flag, is a symbolic date. The revolt began as early as March 10 and became official on March 17 at a meeting of revolution leaders in Haghia Lavra."

In the monastery museum framed under glass, we saw the improvised flag, a section of red and gold brocade from Smyrna, portraying, curiously, the death of the Virgin. Bishop Germanos chose this Christian banderol as a fitting emblem of revolt against the Moslem Turks. It contained more than fifty hand-embroidered faces. In the forehead of an angel was a charred bullet hole. Also in the museum were lacquered candelabra and a gospel bound in gold and jeweled with diamonds, gifts of Catherine the Great of Russia. Haghia Lavra, founded in 961, was a sister monastery to an original Haghia Lavra in Russia and to the first monastery of Mt. Athos, also called Haghia Lavra. At one time the monastery had nine hundred monks. Today there are twenty.

A monk welcomed us into a sunlit salon and served us small saucers of a rose-colored jam. "You have in America?" asked the monk, and, believing it was strawberry jam, I said, "Yes." Its curious sweetness was strangely transcending and had a lingering perfume.

"No," I said. "In America we do not have this."

The monk laughed with delight. The sweet, he said, was *rodozáchari,* preserved rose petals. He served us small glasses of pink brandy, sweet and pleasant, and I wondered if it too were made of roses. Monks distilling and preserving rose petals were surely a creation of Fra Angelico.

We entered the cozily-heated apartment of the prior and were greeted by the prior's *mikró,* or "small one," a blond and slightly built servant named Andreas, nineteen years old. In a voice startlingly deep, he told us he had been in the monastery six years and had only recently decided not to be a monk. "Life is more fun in the towns," he said.

The prior bustled into the room. He was a vivaciously merry and handsome man eighty-two years old. He showed us a framed citation, signed by Joseph McNarmey of the U. S. Army Commandery General, "for help given to the soldiers and sailors of the United States which enabled them to escape from or evade capture by the enemy." As the prior talked, Andreas served us still more preserved roses and brandy, and coffee. There were many empty rooms, said the prior, and he invited me to return and stay for as long as I wished—there would be rose petals every day. He took us into the chapel which was fired by the Turks in 1770 and by the Germans in 1943. The walls were covered with faded frescoes, the figures of which peered like ghosts from out of the charred mortar.

Driving down the mountain, Thanos discussed Greek politics. "The Greeks don't need the King," he said, "but the King needs the Greeks. Our royal family lives like German kaisers a hundred years ago. If the King did not have a special plane which Greece cannot afford, if he could learn to be like democratic Scandinavian kings who go about the streets alone, he might regain his popularity. But our royalty will not do this. Frederika is a very clever woman but she is not clever enough to understand the Greek people. She sees them through the eyes of a German aristocrat."

In town we stopped in his newspaper office for coffee, pastry and still more brandy. Across the street was the schoolhouse. "In 1946 the school was rebuilt," said Thanos. "We made the mistake of building it like the old and the children were so nervous they could not study. The children of that generation were not strong. Even today as adults they suffer from neurosis, neurasthenia, anemia and all the weaknesses of malnutrition. Men of my generation cannot seem to do anything with their lives. They have no will to learn, no ambitions, no desires. They are failures as men because they will always be destroyed by their memories. Just to hear the word 'German' makes us ill with anger and with hatred so that we cannot think clearly. None of us will ever be able to live in a normal way. Our melancholy will go on forever. We go through the motions, we even laugh, trying to behave as if we knew joy. But it does not work. We do not feel it." He sucked on his pipe, relit it, and said,

"We are doomed. But we hope for the next generation. One thing we must try and that is to change the climate for our children so they can live like normal men and women."

We set out in a northerly direction for Megaspelaion, driving six and one-half miles over a perilous zigzagging road. We forded water-filled ditches and splashed with revved motor through pools of mud. Several times we had to stop to remove fallen rocks from our path. Rising to a higher level, we were marooned in snow and I had to push. On the way I told Thanos of my visit with Herr Pfauter in the German Embassy and of his plan to obtain for Frau Schramm a Greek decoration. Thanos groaned, and then he doubled up over the steering wheel, bellowing with laughter. "Sometimes if you don't laugh," he said, "you go crazy."

We were approaching a mountain of vertical rock with rows of windows. They were the windows of the monastery which was actually a great cave gouged into the mountain. Here on December 9, 1943, the monks were executed in a novel manner. Roaring with laughter, the Germans had simply pitched them into the abyss.

Megaspelaion ("The Great Grotto") owes its name to the hollow in the rock into which the eight-story monastery is built. By an industrious cultivation of lands and a genius for soliciting legacies and donations, the monks amassed lands and real estate in Constantinople, Smyrna and Salonica. "They have many fields, forests of lumber and office buildings in Athens," said Thanos. "There is a saying that if all the Peloponnese were destroyed, Megaspélaion could rebuild it, but if Megaspélaion were destroyed, the Peloponnese could not afford to restore it." It was destroyed several times by fire, in 1400, in 1640 and in 1945, and each time it was rebuilt. The new monastery is of modern design with bay-window balconies in all the rooms facing a spectacular mountain view.

We parked on a ledge and trudged through wet snow toward the gate. Like children we scooped up snow and began a snowball fight. Looking up we saw monks watching us on their balconies. They signaled us to a door where we were greeted by a plump young blond monk with a chain of keys. He would guide us through the monastery, he said, and he began by telling the story of its founding which Thanos translated into English.

"One night in the fourth century," he began, "two monks in Palestine named Symeon and Theodor had a dream in which the Virgin told them, 'Go to Kalavryta and find an icon painted by St. Luke in a cave by a spring.' The two monks traveled to Kalavryta but they could not find the icon. So the Virgin came to them again in a dream and told them to look for a little shepherdess named Euphrosyne. They came to this mountain and they met the girl who knew where the icon was because her billygoat one day disappeared into a cave and came out with his beard wet. So the two monks went where she sent them and they saw the spring and beside it the icon. When they tried to remove the icon there appeared a great dragon in a flame and tried to eat them. The Virgin put out the flame and killed the dragon, and the two monks built the monastery. It was the year 361."

I could not tell from the soft-voiced solemnity with which he retold the story whether Thanos was being pious or gently ironic. But there was no doubt about the piety of the monk. Smiling rapturously, his hands folded as if he were in prayer, he led us into a dank chilly cave to show us the running spring and from there to the monastery library to view some grisly relics, the skulls of the two founders encased in silvered caps and their hands wearing silvered gloves. The climax of our tour was the icon itself. With a great clanking of keys, he unlocked heavy bronze doors and took us into still another cave, a cruciformed chapel hollowed out of rock. It was lit by sputtering candles. The walls were frescoed, the floor was covered with a deep red rug into which Byzantium's two-headed eagle was woven. Rattling keys, the monk opened the crypt containing the icon. Holding up a candle, directing its light on the image, the monk murmured, "Painted by St. Luke forty years after Christ."

The black relief of pitch and wax was barely visible under its covering of jewels. On the head was a gold crown bursting with diamonds. There were many bracelets, pearl necklaces and at least fifty watches, "gifts to the Virgin," the monk said. In a cabinet beside the icon were another two hundred watches.

"Why watches?" I asked. The little monk did not answer. Apparently piqued by what he seemed to consider an impious attitude, he slammed shut the door of the crypt and bustled us out of the cave. He left us in an unheated reception room where a round-faced laughing monk with huge rolling buttocks served us still more brandy. Thanos asked for a crust of bread to ease his gnawing ulcer and I also was given a piece. It was dark, nutty and very good. Outside the wind wailed in the pines and I heard a cock crow. It was twelve o'clock. As we drove away, the monks stood on their balconies waving. "I would like to have been a monk," said Thanos. "But I did not have the faith. I believe in a Supreme Being but after that I do not know."

When we returned to Kalavryta it was time for lunch. The restaurant Thanos chose was the back room of a store. From our table at the window we looked out on a roof where more than twenty cats were sleeping in the sun. The owner, whose name was Katerina Athanasiou, was a small plump blonde woman with dancing blue eyes, pink skin and a merry face, the first laughing face I'd seen in Kalavryta. "But I am not from Kalavryta," she said, her laughter filling the room like song, "I'm

from Rogus." It was a village of the valley in which, five days before they
came to Kalavryta, German soldiers had killed the entire male population.
"Life is such a sorrow that if you did not laugh you could not endure it,"
she said. She introduced me to her children, a boy and girl, both blonds.
The boy, George, seventeen years old, was wearing an American sports
shirt and blue jeans. "He wants to be an American," said the mother.
"He is sad because his godfather in Chicago was going to send for him
and last month a Negro killed the godfather in a *taverna*. So he can't go
to America."

She ran to get the letter which had brought the news a week before
and Thanos read it. The godfather, she said, had grown up in Kalavryta.
An old woman wearing a soiled oilcloth apron appeared from the kitchen
to say that she had brought up the godfather. "It must be awful in
America where people are always being killed by Negroes," she said. She
began to weep. Katerina sent her back into the kitchen and with her
high girlish voice went on with the story. We ate lamb with noodles and
drank strong red wine. Thanos said, "Katerina is the only happy woman
in Kalavryta. She is like a medicine for all of us. She has a very old
husband and that's why she is so happy." How, I asked, did an old
husband make a young happy wife? Thanos smiled and did not answer.
The old woman in the kitchen was the sister of the aged husband and
when we left she came to say good-bye, weeping still, sobbing, "I raised
he whom the Negro killed like my own son. . . ."

7

RIGULA SINI

Thanos Simos had disappeared. Since his flight from the cemetery the
day before, he had hardly spoken. Remote, silent, he darted through the
streets of the town like a possessed Myshkin. I had started our driver on
the long auto road around Patras to Diakopton where we were to meet
him three hours later at the railway station. The arrangement gave us
extra time in Kalavryta, and now, in the hour that remained, Thanos
Tsaparis took me to the home of a friend, a woman named Rigula
Sini. In 1943 she had been a young woman. The Germans had killed her
fiancé, her brother and several nephews and cousins.

She was strongly built and gray-haired and she was wearing a green
sweater. Except for Katerina Athanasiou, she was the only woman I
saw in Kalavryta who did not wear black. Her tiny two-room house
was spotlessly neat. Rugs covered the stone floors. There were beds in
both rooms and a stove and a radio in the first. "These are the houses

built for us by the state," she said. "They are so small that when someone dies you can't get the coffin around the corners, you must take it out through the window."

Sitting by the stove, speaking in a calm voice, she told her story. "The bells rang," she began, speaking the words with which everyone begins his story in Kalavryta. "Women and children were locked in the school, the men were marched away. We saw the flares in the sky, first the green, then the red. A great smoke came from the cellar and we couldn't breathe. Children cried, women screamed . . ."

She began to speak rapidly and her face flushed. I noticed what small feet she had for a heavy woman. Above her on the wall I looked on a framed lithography of the Last Supper. In Thanos' eyes I saw tears and I braced myself for what was coming.

"A German soldier opened the door and we rushed out. Krina Tsavala was stomped to death. I also stepped on her, I couldn't help it." Rigula Sini paused and with a shaking hand wiped the tears from her eyes. "There was fire everywhere. The women started to run toward the river, crying, 'Where are the men?', calling out the names of husbands and of sons. With two friends I climbed past the cemetery to Kapi's field. The first things we saw were our priests lying on the ground, their heads cracked open . . ." Rigula Sini's hands moved aimlessly, as if they were trying to tell the story without the help of her voice. "Then we saw them all. We stepped through blood, each seeking our own. We found the wounded men who were still alive, with bullets in their throats instead of their heads." She paused, breathed heavily, and she went on. "It was dark and we decided to go back to the women to bring them the news. They would not believe us, not until we showed them the scarves, the handkerchiefs and the caps we had taken from the bodies. The women began to scream. All that night in the burning town you could hear women wandering through the streets, calling out names, crying 'Kostas, Nikos, Giorgos, Manolis,' all the names of our village. An old man, Panagiotis Sarantavgas, who had returned from his fields and found his three sons gone, began to sing the *Mirologia,* the lament for the dead, and he sang all night.

"In the morning the women went together to the cemetery. The bodies were in great heaps, bodies covering bodies, all with a bullet here . . ." Rigula Sini pointed with her finger to her temple. "Their blood and brains were soaked in the earth, their bodies were dismembered. There are no words, no words to tell what the Germans had done." She stopped and I thought she would not go on. But she did, saying, "Each woman helped every other to carry bodies to the cemetery. Not until the third day did I find my brother. There were no bullets in his body. His face

278 GODS AND HEROES

was in the earth, his blood had flowed from his mouth. He had died from asphyxiation under other bodies." She stopped and wept, and then, drying her tears, she said, "Each day we had to put more earth over the bodies because they were dug up by dogs. Nikos, my fiancé, was one of the last to be found. With his mother and his sisters I carried him down the hill. I must have carried fifty bodies on my back. There was no water to wash and I could not get the blood from my skin. For a month I looked like a butcher, and then I went down to Aegion to stay with some relatives, and I washed. . . ."

It was a half hour before my train. Rigula Sini rose and went into the other room, returning in a moment with coffee, little bowls of candied orange peel and some brandy. I drank and I ate, resting my eyes on the Last Supper on the wall. And then we left.

The tiny cog railway was waiting in the station. So were Thanos Simos and John Athanasopoulos. I asked Thanos Simos where he had been and he said he had knocked on the doors of the town, seeking out old ladies and talking with them. I understood his commitment, his need to seek out as much of Kalavryta's pain as he could and make it his own.

As the train jogged down canyons and crevices Thanos told the story of his afternoon.

"In a small room, poor and clean, an old woman lay on her bed. Her name was Maria Tsokana and she was ill, not from bodily sickness, she told me, but from a sickness of the soul. 'My child, I'm tired,' she said. 'I have suffered enough, I cannot endure more. Why does God not take me? Why does my heart not stop its beating?'

"Two women came into the room and quietly sat beside her. One was named Diamando Koyvelioti, the other, Vasiliki Ballala. 'My child, where do you come from?' said the first. 'What do you want us to tell you? With these crooked arms I buried my dead and ever since they have hung from my body, unable to do anything else.'

"'My son, my son,' said the other, and she took my hands and she kissed them. 'My sons had the same age as you. With my own hands I carried their broken bodies to the cemetery. Their blood covered my fingers and my feet and colored the soil of their graves.'

"Suddenly the old woman on the bed sat up. 'Speak, my child,' she said in a strong voice. 'Tell the world about our pain. Let everyone know the Germans' terrible deed. Tell about our bleeding hearts, how we who still live have died.' She began to cry out in heart-rending sobs and her two friends also cried. All three bowed their heads in their hands in joining together their lamentations.

"In another small house Antiopi Handronikola, sixty-five years old, pointed to some pictures on the wall. 'Look! Look, my son,' she cried. 'Look at their faces, my husband George, my Anthony nineteen years old, my Stavros sixteen years old, and Christos, my Christos, such a small angel, only fifteen years old. Oh God, oh my God, why Christos?' She wept and I stayed with her, holding her hand until she stopped. She said, 'Since then there has not been one empty night that they have not come back to me, that I have not seen their empty dead eyes looking at me.' She put her arms around me. 'My son,' she said, 'permit me to kiss you. It will be a kiss for them, for my sons.' Her kiss of pain and tears was a living burning brand of pain which will burn on my cheek, in my soul, for as long as I live."

In the train in front and across from us, I saw three red-faced blond young men in knitted sweaters, knee pants and hiking boots. I moved up in the car and, as I expected, I heard them speaking German. Amiably, with eager friendliness, they pointed out Megaspelaion, where they had hiked. *"Phantastisch!"* said one of them. They had, like us, been in Kalavryta for two days. "The scenery is wonderful," said another, "but the people seemed melancholy. They are not friendly." Sensing an innocence, I asked one of the youths if I might see his guidebook and he gave it to me. A single paragraph on Kalavryta told of the monasteries and the spectacular railway ride and of the waters in a famous spring which, it said, were a cure for madness. "Was there more?" asked the young man to whom the book belonged. "Did you see something we didn't see?" Shaking my head I returned the book.

XXIV

Without Feet

On March 25 I was awakened by the booming of rockets over the city. In the streets below I heard shouting and music.

At nine forty-five I crossed town to the cathedral. Police had raised a fence around the square, outside of which crowds were waiting the arrival of distinguished persons for a national holiday requiem. I showed my pass from the Foreign Ministry and was saluted into the plaza. Armed forces units and several military bands stood at attention. I joined the press corps on the cathedral steps. A French correspondent said the service inside had been going on for a half hour but that most of the important guests had not yet arrived. The trick, he said, was to arrive as late as possible but not later than the King. Like a procession in a Steinberg cartoon, a caravan of chauffeured flag-flying Lincolns, Mercedes, Jaguars and an occasional Buick or Chevrolet, rolled slowly up to the cathedral steps. A brass fanfare met each one, a snapping of guns and a flurry of salutes.

Watching the ponderous disembarkations of generals and admirals weighted with medals and ribbons, top-hatted fat diplomats in morning coats and women in picture hats and fluttering dresses, I remembered an old film of a mythical Balkan duchy, the Marx Brothers' *Duck Soup*. Backs arched, stomachs protruding in front and rumps in back, the invited guests climbed portentously up the cathedral steps. From inside I heard, like soft thunder, the basso rumblings of priests. At the fence the people were shouting and children waved paper flags.

The comedy turned slapstick. A rattling taxi, a fifteen-year-old Chevrolet, appeared quivering and sputtering in the limousine procession with a gold-fringed flag unfurled above it. From such an absurd-appearing vehicle I half expected Groucho to leap without his pants. Instead a dark little man flashing with medals, his swallow coat almost brushing the pavements, stepped down. It was the Ethiopian ambassador.

At ten thirty a squadron of white motorcycles roared into the square, followed in a moment by a cavalry unit on white horses. A band played the lilting measures of the national anthem. A Rolls-Royce zoomed in and stopped. The King, wearing a field marshal's uniform, leaped briskly from the royal vehicle and saluted. With him were the Queen, radiant in pink dress and hat, the Queen Mother and the Princess Irene.

From outside the fence I seemed to hear chanting. I wondered if I might be mistaken. But the staccato syllables were altogether clear. "Pa-pan-dre-ou!" the people were repeating in measured syllables. The chant might have been the crowd's answer to the arrest, some weeks before, of a young man who had shouted "Pa-pan-dre-ou!" when the King was passing. Even if it were a crime to cry out the name of the leader of the majority political party in the land, which it was not, police could hardly arrest a crowd on the national holiday. The King climbed the cathedral steps, followed by his ladies. In ominous counterpoint to the singing inside the chant went on and the police did not seem to hear.

I walked up Mitropoleos Street, crossing police lines to Amalias Avenue where I was invited to a parade-viewing party at the apartment of Angelos and Leto Katacousinos. It was also Angelos' name day and the Katacousinos' national holiday party was one of the most famous in Athenian society. Their terrace was perfect for parade watching. Fifty guests were drinking *ouzo* and Scotch highballs. Across Amalias Avenue on the steps of the palace, was the parade reviewing stand. Beyond on Mt. Lycabettus rockets boomed, sending clouds of smoke rolling over the city.

The American minister consular asked me how it had been at the cathedral and I told him of the chanting. "All spontaneous, of course," he said sharply, implying in his tone that the shouting had been an organized Communist campaign. In the street below, sixteen invalided soldiers, several without legs, waited in wheelchairs for the parade to begin. White uniformed nurses stood ready to push their chairs, which gleamed silver in the sun. Amalias Park was covered with a hazy smog; the palms and pines were enveloped in misty Turner-like light. Parliament Deputy Paul Vardinogiannis arrived and told me that on Constitution Square the police had stopped the crowds from yelling *"Demokratia!"* "In the country where it was invented, democracy has become a dirty word," he said.

The King rode a black horse into the palace plaza, and sat at attention, flanked by six guards on white horses. A band played and the veterans in their silver chairs began to roll. On the terrace, Vardinogiannis and I were joined by an admiral's wife. "Look!" she cried, pointing below. "Do you see without feet?"

The grand marshal leading the parade was a veteran in khaki, strutting stiffly on two peg legs. "Just to show what is the war," said Mrs. Admiral. "Please notice this man without the feet." The man goose-stepped like a rigid puppet. "Look, how is elegant," cried Mrs. Admiral in my ear. "No feet, no legs! Is all wood!"

The parade moved forward. After the veterans came troops of boy scouts and then in a cloud of blue smoke, a cordon of roaring motorcycles. "Look!" shrilled Mrs. Admiral. "Look, how is beautiful." What we were viewing was a patriotic show of military muscle. For an hour it passed—tanks, trucks loaded with rockets, mounted machine guns and cannons. A secretary from the Danish Embassy identified the war machines: blue-nosed rockets, Hurley trucks, antiaircraft rockets, guided missiles. As they passed below, jet planes zoomed overhead in V formations, streaking the skies with blue smoke. "It's not real," murmured Paul Vardinogiannis. "It's all fantasy."

"See all the people in the streets," Mrs. Admiral shrilled. "Every year is same thing, the people never have enough of admiring."

A hundred tanks increasing in size, rumbled by. "It's all American equipment, everything is American," said the American minister.

"Everything?" I asked, feeling a damp chill.

"Ninety per cent," he said. "Maybe some of the trucks are German." A small Greek boy raised himself on his tiptoes at the railing. "Is it all the King's?" he asked his father. The father replied that it was and the child asked, "But should it all be?"

The weapons caravan moved slowly on. A United States Information Service officer identified "Sams" (surface to air), "Honest Johns" (surface to surface) and other names strange to me. After the weapons came manpower. Sailors were hitched to huge cannons which they pulled, in teams of sixteen, like horses. White-uniformed snow paratroops carried bazookas and machine guns; signal corpsmen flashed flags. Companies of military cadets, marines, soldiers, and Women's Army Corps, called "Stratiotines," marched briskly by, and the Dane, observing the tightly fitted uniforms on amply curved figures, said, "The uniform is not very fair to the shape of Greek ladies."

The parade concluded finally with a procession of limousines, the same ones I had watched arrive at the cathedral. At the very end, like a clown trailing a circus parade, rattled the banner-flying Ethiopian taxi.

The marshal, jogging on peg legs, brought it all to an end at the reviewing stand. The wheeled veterans rolled swiftly, the wind blowing the white headdresses of their nurses like white flags. "Look!" squealed Mrs. Admiral. "A noble son of Greece walking on street with wood."

The parade dignitaries had been invited to the party. The Danish ambassador, in red and gold uniform, arrived first; then the Belgian in blue and gold. Both wore boat-shaped hats with sweeping plumes. "All the countries have diplomatic uniforms except the United States, Switzerland and Canada," said the wife of the American minister wistfully. The admiral arrived, a chesty little man looking like a pigeon in pheasant's plumage. More trooped in and with all the saluting, embracing and kissing, it might have been the presentation scene from *Der Rosenkavalier*. After lunch I went for a walk in the park. Tanks and guns were returned to barracks. Troops of soldiers and sailors wandered disconsolately, stalking diversion. Children were feeding ducks and babies waved paper flags with pictures of the King and the Queen.

I could not wipe the picture of the wooden-legged parade marshal out of my mind. From the press office I learned his name was Ghikas Tripos, that he was forty-nine years old. Several days later I went to the Athens suburb of Perisos to seek him out. His wife, a handsome friendly woman, greeted me in English. Her husband, she said, was in the hospital. As a result of the parade, in which he'd walked five kilometers in two hours, the bone ends of his amputated legs had become infected.

The wife introduced me to her children, a twenty-one-year-old daughter and thirteen-year-old son, and she served me brandy, chocolate pastries and coffee. She told me her husband had lost both feet in a rocket explosion in the Albanian war. His legs had frozen in the snow, and after many operations in which more and more of his legs had been removed, he had learned to walk on the pegs. To support her family Mrs. Tripos told me she worked in the Ministry of Coordination. Her husband had raised the children and he cared for the house. In his spare time he painted icons and small landscapes which she showed me. They were simply and tastefully done. Proudly she brought out photographs of her husband, tall, thin, dark, leading parades, not only on March 25, but also each Ochi Day, October 28, when Greeks celebrate their victory over the Albanians. "He is a fine man," she said gently, lovingly. "A good husband."

XXV

Herding Sheep

"A Greek politician," said Parliament Deputy Paul Vardinogiannis, "is a shepherd herding sheep. He has to watch over his constituents, take care of them and convince every last voter that his is the one single vote that will win his election."

The successful officeholder is first of all a professional *koumbaros,* a best man at endless weddings and godfather to hundreds of namesake children. Vardinogiannis had been best man at more than five hundred Cretan weddings and had christened eighteen hundred babies. On occasions when he could not return to his native Crete for a ceremony, a brother in Rethymnon acted as his proxy. Every ceremony included a gift. "It is very expensive being a politician," said Paul. "It is the responsibility of my secretary to see that a congratulatory message is sent on every name day. To the parents of course. Children don't vote." The bond is an intimate one—the *koumbaros* is considered a member of the family who comes to visit, who breaks bread. "Every peasant considers you his personal mediator in Athens," Paul said. "In no country in the world is a politician expected to make so many grass-roots trips."

Early in April, Paul invited me to accompany him on a weekend visit to constituents in the Rethymnon province of Crete. In the morning of the Saturday before Palm Sunday a car arrived at my hotel and drove me to Paul's apartment in the Kolonaki section of Athens. Three young Cretans were waiting to make the trip. A butler served us a breakfast of coffee and rolls. While we were eating, Paul appeared in open shirt and slippers. A crisis had arisen in the government, he said. The four of us would go at once to catch our scheduled plane and he would follow on another in two hours and meet us in Rethymnon.

My companions were Paul's private secretary, Evangelos Papadakis, who was twenty-seven years old; a student of politics and economics named George Perakis, who was twenty-three, and a thirty-three-year-old magazine editor named Manolis Douglerakis. Paul's name for me was "Kublaki," which, he said, made me his Cretan brother. The suffix "akis" indicated a Cretan, just as the ending "poulos" indicated a Peloponnese. Both in their separate dialects meant the same thing: "the son of."

Since Manolis was the only one of my three companions who spoke English, he established himself at once as my interpreter for the trip. On the way to the airport we speculated about the crisis which was delaying Paul. The student suggested Cyprus; the secretary thought it might be the new scandal about a Greek ship caught pirating oil through a United Nations blockade to Rhodesia. In the airport we saw the newspaper headline "CONCERN FOR THE GRAVE HEALTH OF GEORGE PAPANDREOU," and decided this was the reason for Paul's delay. For weeks Athens had been covered by rumors about a serious illness of the former prime minister. In rumor-rife Athens I had even heard that Papandreou's son and heir, Andreas, was ill with cancer. Since their Center Union party was the popular people's party such rumors spread rapidly and caused great apprehension and confusion. It also aroused hopeful excitement in the opposition. In the case of the old man, his advanced age and a recent illness with pneumonia were valid causes for concern. Any decline in his health almost certainly would result in a party crisis.

In the political power structure Paul was a formidable force. Born into a large and poor Cretan family, he was adopted as a political protégé by Sophocles Venizelos, son of Greece's great premier Eleutherios Venizelos. Until his death from a heart attack in 1964, Sophocles Venizelos had been the political leader of Crete. After his death Cretans turned to Paul as their *meson,* or intermediary, in Athens. In the Center Union's landslide election of 1964 Paul had headed a slate of three Cretans elected to parliament. In the Papandreou government he was appointed "minister to the prime minister," an office which is a kind of exalted executive secretariat. After the 1965 "July crisis" downfall of Papandreou, the other two Cretan deputies had defected from the Center Union party to join the "salami government" of Stefanos Stefanopoulos, so named because it was made up of defectors slicing themselves from their parties in return for ministerial appointments. One of the two, Kostas Stefanakis, was minister of justice, and the other, John Tsouderos, was minister of coordination. Their defections were looked upon as betrayals by Cretan followers of Papandreou, and on a visit to the town of Anoghia,

Stefanakis had had to be rescued by police when former constituents attacked him as a traitor and threatened him with his life. For Paul, the defections of his colleagues had resulted in a rise of popularity and solidified his position as the most important political leader of Crete. His strength lay in his appeal to the uneducated majority and a perpetuation of the favoritism characteristic to Greek politics. Mistrusted by members of his own party, he was considered by political opponents as an unavoidable evil.

A driver with a car was waiting in the Iraklion airport to take us to Rethymnon. The burgeoning green spring, the red earth and snow-covered mountains were shrouded by chartreuse mists. Fruit trees bloomed and Judas trees glowed pink. Blocking our way were flocks of sheep and goats en route from winter lowlands to the summer highlands. Our driver, a grizzly dark little man, was vehemently vocal. Shouting in dialect, he seemed to be engaged in an argument with the secretary and political student. Manolis assured me that everyone in the car was in agreement. "In Crete, which is the castle of democracy, you will not find anyone not of the Center Union party," he said. I wondered what would happen if there were a disagreement. The driver's articulation included his hands. Driving wildly over perilous cliff roads, he frequently abandoned the steering wheel to flail through some conversational climax. Suddenly he forsook his Cretan torrent and shouted in English, "I fuck the King's house!" It turned out that he spoke excellent English, that his father had lived in England and he had fought with English soldiers in the war.

I was relieved to hear a suggestion that we stop for lunch. In a valley by a stream we found a café called Drossia, which means refreshment. Sitting at a table in the sun we ate freshly roasted pig, bread and salad and drank a heady red wine. Another freshly killed pig hung in the doorway dripping blood. From a radio boomed a *bouzouki* ballad called "Our Pavlo." A male voice was singing:

> Vardinogiannis is a son of Crete,
> Pavlo is our brother,
> He will not betray us . . .

Black-turbaned shepherds surrounded our table, offering us wine, toasting "Pavlo." One said, "They come to ask me, why not support Tsouderos? I tell them Pavlo's my brother, my best man, and I will never betray him." A farmer threw some frozen grape blossoms, soft fuzzy things like dead worms, on the table. A frost, unprecedented for April, had been catastrophic for wine growers and he seemed to expect "Pavlo" to do something about even his blossoms. The café owner asked Papadakis to tell Paul he needed thirty thousand drachmae from the Greek National Tourist Office to expand his establishment. A shepherd asked us to "have Pavlo send me a letter beginning, 'My Good Friend' and I will show it to everyone."

We drove on through a valley of olives, through fields of asphodel ripened to cottony puffs, and we stopped in a village where a half-dozen men, all taxi drivers, surrounded our car and angrily discussed a recent police order issuing seven more taxi permits. There was not enough work as it was, said the drivers, and Paul must do something about it.

At two o'clock we arrived at Paul's office in Rethymnon. The streets were littered with blue and green leaflets, dropped from an airplane that morning, announcing that Paul Vardinogiannis was coming to Crete accompanied by an American writer. A large crowd was waiting. The office, a high-ceilinged room, was filled with bouquets of wisteria and calla lilies. Its walls were covered with photographs of various Venizeloses, including one of the great Eleutherios dead in his coffin, and of Papandreou and Vardinogiannis. Word spread quickly that Paul had been delayed because of a sudden illness of the old man, and the crowd was hushed. A fat, near-sighted man, the office manager, brought a book for me to look at. It was called *The Bible of Venizelos—The Story of Modern Greece*.

I went for a walk. The musky odor of carobs, as pungent as in November, filled the air. Men wearing white hoods were carrying the bags of beans in and out of warehouses. I amused myself at photographers' windows, looking at hundreds of wedding pictures of sternly mustachioed young men and solemn plump brides, their wedding bouquets wrapped in plastic, and I speculated on the size of each dowry, which one was the dominating partner and how many children they would have.

I arrived at our hotel, the Xenia, and found that Paul had arrived. The desk clerk, a young woman who was married to a bank clerk, was complaining to him about her low wages—she said the two thousand drachmae she earned was hardly "milk money" for her three children. Paul promised he would look into it. We had a drink and I began with him a slow journey back to his office. The words "Paul is here" had spread through the town like a wind. The streets were rivers of people waiting to greet him. Men abandoned their creaking carts of beans; shopkeepers ran from their doors. Others, more shy, waited in their doors for him to notice. He always did. In a zigzag course we moved from one side of the street to the other, missing no one. We were pulled into a tavern and served black bread soaked in salt water, symbolic, Paul explained, "of what Jesus Christ served to his pupils." A mechanic held

back his grease-covered hands, but Paul took them, saying, "Your hands
are a lot cleaner than my politician's hands." Through the emotional
effusion he moved on with masterly self-control, slapping backs, embracing men, kissing godchildren. In his curious levitating lope he seemed to
be floating, a human shuttle weaving a formidable warp of good will.
He knew exactly with what degree of intimacy to greet each individual.
Hearty thwacks, kisses, pinchings, hugs were meted out and happily
received. Over and over he was asked two questions: "How is Papandreou?" ("As healthy as you and I"); "When will there be elections?"
("When Greece returns to democracy"). On the waterfront a fat pink-
cheeked jolly woman, her hair in gold ringlets, ran out on high heels to
embrace him. Her arm interlocked in Paul's, they walked together a short
distance, and Paul apologized for not having time to visit her. "She is a
public woman," he murmured to me in English, "and has much influence."

The long journey ended finally in the office where he was welcomed
like a messiah. He made a speech, reassuring the crowd of Papandreou's
good health, and then, for a half hour, he embraced, kissed, and shook
hands, and gave his *koumbaros'* blessing to dozens of children. Soft-
voiced petitioners whispered in his ear, saying, "My daughter is finishing
school. Can you find her work?" "My son goes into the national service.
He wishes to be in the air forces." "I am ill and must go to Athens.
Will you give me a letter for the hospital?"

An old man who said he was the town historian arrived to take me on
a tour. He led me through narrow streets with their wartime German
names still painted on corners, showing me statues, doorways, minarets
and domes that were a précis of history: Minoan, classical, Byzantine,
Venetian, Turkish. He told me the 1941 war in Rethymnon had lasted
five days, during which New Zealanders had killed 1641 Germans. When
we returned to the office at dusk Paul was still hearing petitioners. A
young man who had applied for admission to Athens' Polytechnic Institute
wanted Paul to see about his acceptance and Paul said he would.

A driver was waiting to take us to a village but it was difficult to get
away. Paul got into the car and the crowds pressed around, clutching at
him. We started moving slowly and men ran alongside, talking. Finally,
when we left them behind Paul lay back in the seat exhausted. "Oh
Kublaki," he sighed. "In our complicated bureaucracy they need help in
everything. Licenses for trucks, taxis and bars. Children into schools,
sick into hospitals. Nothing can be accomplished without influence and I
am expected to work all miracles."

I asked why it must be so. He said, "Because in our history of revolutions, of uprisings and crisis, we've never had a moment to develop a

political life. In democratic countries elected legislators pay close attention to the temper of the constituents and their governing acts correspond with the hopes and wishes of the people. But in Greece our rightist government makes this impossible. Our first really free elections were in 1964 and you know the results."

The village, ten kilometers in the mountains, was called Armeni. There was no electricity and it was completely dark. A four-year-old child named Dimitrios ran up and down the shadowy single street crying "Pavlo is here!" Shadowy clusters of shepherds and farmers, wearing white sheepskin cloaks, converged on a café which filled in minutes. The owner and his wife greeted us. A pressure oil lamp hissed under the ceiling. Paul was seated at a table between the village president and the priest, an unkempt old man, with snarled beard and hair, wearing a brown overcoat. Trays of *raki* were passed and the priest drank eagerly. Paul took a glass, touched his lips with it and returned it to the tray. He drank little and seldom on political trips. Someone asked about Papandreou's health and Paul said, "He draws strength from you, the people. That is why he is alive. The important thing is the torch, the flame which he gives us and which we must keep alive." Godchildren were presented and a man described a dilemma—his son, a policeman, had been sent from Athens to a village in Macedonia because he was a supporter of Papandreou. It happened all the time, said Paul, and he promised to see what could be done. He stood up and began a speech, coolly with un-emotional eloquence, looking with his black hair and small mustache, very like Zero Mostel. While he spoke more *raki* was passed and the priest reached eagerly for a glass. Beside me Manolis translated Paul's speech, whispering, "I regret coming to you not as a representative of the government but as a voice of the minority. It is our tragedy in Greece that George Papandreou has been banished from the government. He is the only leader in Greece with your interests at heart, who can solve your problems. Today the government has no plan, it can do nothing for you."

Paul was loudly applauded. A shepherd in a black turban made a loud speech about Papandreou under whose administration, he said, school lunches were inaugurated in Greece. "My two boys were thin and sickly," he said. "We thought they would die. Then came the Papandreou lunches and now they are large and strong." He was applauded and a man shouted, "We want an election." The crowd took up the cry, chanting, "We want an election." Paul raised his hand and the clamor subsided. "So do I," he said.

There were long handshakes, interminable farewells in the night. The moon was full but it had a ring around it and the air was chilly. As we pulled away a soldier ran alongside the car, clinging to Paul's hand, saying, "Though I wear the King's uniform, don't think I'm not on your side." Riding back through the night, Paul said, "I try not to mention personalities, I speak only of issues, always of 'the government.' But it is difficult. What the people want is an opportunity to sell their products at a better price, a doctor to free them from their fear of sickness, and an education for their children. They have a passion for education." Paul recalled his meetings with President Kennedy. "I saw Kennedy four times," he said. "On each occasion it was to have been a short interview which stretched out as long as two hours. He was especially interested in the United States' international image and the relations of his country with Greece. Once he spent a half hour explaining to me the difference between the Republican and Democratic parties. Then he laughed and said he wished he understood the difference himself."

An itinerary of ten villages was scheduled for Sunday. When I got up Paul was already in the streets, greeting people leaving a church after Palm Sunday services. A procession of children was kissing his hand. One of them gave him a palm frond which he carried into the car. Our auto caravan traveled the same road as the night before, passing through Armeni. The road continued upward through a rocky landscape patched with bits of cultivation. Finally there were only shepherds on the ledges, their white sheep indistinguishable from the stones among which they foraged.

"Villages vary greatly in personality," Paul said. "Not only do they have different dialects, but also different ways of greeting. There are handshaking villages, embracing villages, kissing villages and weeping villages, and you dare not forget which is which." Casually he continued, "In one of the villages, I can't say exactly which, you are going to meet a famous bandit. He escaped last year from Iraklion prison and has been hiding out in a number of villages where no one, not even the police, who are his friends, will report him. His crime was one of family honor— he attempted to murder a man who had betrayed a niece—and in the villages he has become a hero. His popularity is great enough to have political meaning. It seems Tsouderos offered him amnesty but he refused, saying, 'I don't want freedom at the price of your friendship.' Whether he actually said this or not I don't know. But the report that he said it has increased his following. Recently he communicated with me, asking for help to get him into the Greek Army on Cyprus, which would mean an automatic pardon. He's really quite a fellow. Incidentally, he speaks English and you'll enjoy him."

We entered a small village, called Mixorouma, the ancestral home of Manolis Douglerakis. It smelled of sheep and goats. Though no visit had been scheduled, Paul told the driver to stop. Word spread quickly and in five minutes a crowd was gathered. Down from the hills and lanes people came running. An old man shouted, "Hurrah, our minister is here!" Bent old men in dusty turbans lined up to shake Paul's hand. A priest arrived wearing a pink plaid shawl, and a woman, her eyes filled with tears, gave Paul a great bouquet of iris, calla lilies and pink stock. Against a background of cackling hens and braying donkeys Paul made a speech, saying, "You must make your decisions on principles and not on personalities. Don't fight for me, fight for your interests. If you know a better man than Vardinogiannis, vote for him." The applause which greeted this indicated he was in no danger. I remembered that an Athens journalist had described Paul as "a diabolically clever man."

In the car Paul threw the flowers on a ledge behind the seat and asked for a cigarette. "You're seeing what is wrong, you're seeing our immaturity," he said. "People are children seeking a parent-leader. I don't want to be a cult. I want them to think. Until Greeks learn to think for themselves, to follow ideas instead of running like sheep after a leader, Greece will never exist as a democratic country. Greece defined and built the first democracy. But five centuries of Venetians and Turks have destroyed everything."

We crossed a mountain pass and descended along a southerly flowing stream. At an isolated villa, surrounded on all sides by a sweeping view, we stopped. It belonged, said Paul, to a worldly priest whom he wanted me to meet. The priest, who was just returning from Palm Sunday services, greeted us with hearty exuberance. He was a ruddy energetic man in his fifties with great waves of groomed hair and beard, a flashing gold-toothed smile and sensual eyes and mouth. A young woman served us candied fruit and coffee. Interrupting his conversation with the priest, Paul turned and speaking in English said, "She is one of his nieces. He has quite a few." A small child toddled into the room. Paul exclaimed on the child's beauty and the priest beamed. Paul said, "The child belongs to the niece. The Holy Ghost was the father."

Our next stop was in Spíli, a pretty tree-shaded agricultural town nestled like a Swiss village on a ledge between snow-covered mountains and a green valley. It sang with the cadenzas of many small waterfalls. We were greeted by the town president, a prosperous young landowner, tall and darkly handsome, immaculately tailored and groomed. He took us into a café, a large glass-walled room with pink ceiling. The crowd inside was equally divided between old men in turbans and young men in Sunday suits. The physical and facial types were astonishingly varied. There were lean dark Berbers, round-faced Oriental faces, and a group of gold and silvered-haired men, descendants of ancient Doric invaders whose lean bony faces were like aristocratic Scandinavians'. Almost every man had a mustache. One man began to speak, asking, "Who will be leader if Papandreou dies?"

"You," Paul replied. "You must be your own leaders." The answer did not seem to satisfy. Paul went on, saying, "Papandreou cannot be your government, Vardinogiannis cannot be your government. Only if you accept your responsibilities in a democracy can Greece become a democracy."

When it was finished we were taken to a restaurant and served an excellent meal of roasted meats, potatoes, salads and wine, which we ate in ten minutes. In other villages people were waiting and we were already more than an hour behind schedule. Our caravan was joined by a car filled with cameramen and reporters with tape recorders, including a sultry beauty named Maria who was wearing a tweed skirt and sweater. We drove back toward Mixorouma, where a roadblock stopped us. In the house of the village president, one of Paul's *koumbaros,* a dinner had been prepared. Paul groaned. "To refuse would be an insult, a political catastrophe," he said. Holding his round stomach, he said, "You see why politicians are fat. I was once a very thin young man." Like marauding locusts we bolted another Sunday feast of chicken, cheese, good brown bread and red wine.

It was six miles to Agousseliniana, "a kissing village," Paul said. In its dusty little square an assembly of tall straight old men in turbans and capes, with flowing white hair and beards like gods', were waiting. Paul leaped from the car. They crowded around him and he kissed them all. Dark huddles of women on terraces and rooftops watched. Their curiosity was centered on the reporter Maria mingling freely with the men. In a surge of high spirits we were ushered toward a café where we were served *raki* and bowls of sunflower seeds. "The men here are very poor," said Manolis. "No drachmae." Hanging on the walls, like icons, were photographs of Venizelos, Papandreou and Vardinogiannis. "Our dear friend, you are superb," said one of the brawny gods to Paul. "We are all crying for your situation." Godsons, wide-eyed crew-cut little boys, lined up for the *koumbaros'* blessing. A toothless grinning priest with two goatish beards flying off in different directions, wearing a rakish tam-o-shanter and a U. S. Navy pea jacket, spoke to me in English, saying, "The jacket is gift from American professor." A wizened red-faced little man with watery eyes and pale purple-veined hands was introduced as the town poet. With quavering voice he read an ode to Paul.

> As long as your eyes weep for us,
> So long we can hope,
> As long as you walk among us,
> So long we will not lose courage.

The next was a weeping village, said Paul. He told us to go ahead, that he would follow in another car. Manolis whispered that he was in search of a water closet, not a common convenience. The village was named "Ai Yiannis O Kamenos" (St. John the Burned), because it was once destroyed by Turks. Our car was the first in the caravan to arrive and the crowd, which had been waiting for two hours and believed Paul was in the car, sang as we drove up and threw flowers in our path. A second car arrived in a welter of flowers and song but Paul was not in it. In five minutes a third car arrived, still without Paul. The situation turned tragically comic. Villagers were breathless from singing, the street was paved with flowers. Children ran into the fields to gather more. The village poetess, a fourteen-year-old high school girl named Stella Kitraki, was waiting, a poem in her hands. I counted 127 people, and a man explained that twenty shepherds were in the hills with their sheep. For the first time women were mingling with men, tall lovely girls, blonde and dark, were like stately vestals bearing roses. Older women were decorating our cars with pine boughs, turning them into a camouflage for Birnam Wood. A fourth car, bearing a banner of the Papandreou youth organization, rolled up but Paul was not in it. Twenty restless minutes passed and then, like the climax in a French film, a tiny Opel filled with the great form of Paul came through the hills, and flowers fluttered in the air. Taking a position in the middle of the road, the young poetess began to read:

> We come to welcome you, worthy son of Crete,
> In you we hear the voice of our land,
> We feel the spirit which surrounds you,
> Which tells us you are not like the others . . .

Around me I saw tears coursing down fierce shepherd faces. Paul also was weeping. The girl's voice, like an impassioned Electra's, surged on through several stanzas:

> Wake up, people of Venizelos, sons of Democracy,
> It is cowardly to be betrayed by leaders,
> Hear your heart's thundering voice,
> Hear it shouting, "Defend your native land . . ."

There was no time for the refreshments which ladies of the village had prepared. As we drove away they ran alongside the car with trays, throwing us walnuts, olives and chocolates which we munched on the way. Other women had filled the car with flowers, surrounding us with melancholy sickening sweetness. Driving deeper into the mountains, into a canyon of twisted olive trees and asphodel, we met six women on a country road and Paul told the driver to stop. When the women saw who it was they became hysterical. All of them tried to embrace Paul simultaneously. "I pray for the King to be under the earth and not on it," cried one.

Emerging from the pass, we faced the waters of the Libyan sea. On a plateau above us glistened a white village, named Selia. Its free-form houses with outside spiral staircases were like African houses beyond the sea. Our approach had been noted. When we arrived a town crier, an old man with one eye and a great bellowing voice, was loping through the town, crying, "Come! Come everyone! Vardinogiannis is here! The leader of Crete is among us! Come, come, come!"

From every street people poured into the square. Women brought bouquets which Paul handed to Manolis and the political student, who holding them looked like abject bridesmaids. A local farmer, small, deceptively mild-mannered, began reading a welcome speech from a swatch of papers in his hand. His voice droned on and on in iambic monotones. Paul's hands were folded, his eyes were lowered to the ground. Shifting his weight, he murmured in English, "The fellow's a menace. He seems to have convinced everyone he's smarter than they are." Still it went on with tenacious persistence. Manolis looked down into the lilies in his arms as if he were going to be sick into them. Paul lit a cigarette. "Now the bloody fool's reading my biography," he whispered. "He doesn't have to convince me I'm Paul Vardinogiannis." I looked at the people, handsome dark Bedouins, blue-eyed blonds like Vikings, brown-haired mahogany-eyed girls with bright head scarves blowing in the wind. Women with children in their arms pointed toward Paul, directing their gaze on him.

When it ended finally after twenty-five minutes we were escorted to the house of the community president, another *koumbaros* brother. An outdoor stairs took us into a whitewashed upper chamber where a long table, covered with a lace tablecloth, was set for eighteen places. It was our third dinner of the day. I told Manolis I didn't think I could manage. "Breathe the fresh air, drink some fresh water," he said. "Good air and water make you hungry. I know a monastery where the water is so fresh it makes the monks eat five or six times a day. With plenty of fresh water Greeks can always eat, drink, dance and make love."

I drank the glass of water he handed me and attacked the red mullet in the plate before me. The fish roasted with thyme was delicious; so were the salad, the olives and cheeses and the dark red wine. An agricultural village, Selia had the added blessing of the sea and was more prosperous than inland villages. I asked the size of the village and

Paul said, "They say about three hundred. But two things you will never find out in Crete. One is the population of a village which they always make larger. The other is the distance from one village to another which they always make less. They'll say to you, 'It's one cigarette' or 'two cigarettes away,' as if every man walked at the same pace or smoked with the same speed." Outside I could hear the people chanting, "Pa-pan-dre-ou . . . Var-din-o-gian-nis . . ."

In the next four hours we stopped at five villages and in each there was a floral welcome, followed by speeches and refreshments. In Mirthos Paul spoke from one flat housetop to people gathered on other flat roofs and the scene was like an illustration from the Bible. In Lefkogia, Paul was photographed with fifty godchildren all wearing identical blue-and-white pull-overs. They were, he said, "propaganda sweaters" sent by the defected minister, Tsouderos. "The people knew that he did not pay for the sweaters so they accepted them," he said. "Americans paid for the sweaters." I asked how, and he looked at me mysteriously, saying, "America pays for many strange things."

In a tiny dark room in a hamlet named Yianu an old musician played a lyre and Paul and the political student, bound to one another by a handkerchief, leaped, dipped and whirled through a *hasapiko,* buoyantly as swooping birds.

It was now eight o'clock and utterly dark. We were three hours behind schedule with two more villages to visit. We were seeking one called Koxare. We had been directed on a trail through an olive grove and seemed to be lost. And then suddenly, from out of the darkness we heard a chorus of children's voices, softly as katydids, chanting "Var-din-o-gian-nis. . . ." Without seeing it in the dark we had arrived in Koxare. People were standing all around chanting softly in the sibilant night, converging on our car, reaching inside to shake our hands. It seemed to be a children's village. Children were everywhere, making a game of the event, murmuring happily over and over, "Var-din-o-gian-nis." A café, lit by a single oil lamp, quickly filled. *"Zito,"* the children cried, "Long live Vardinogiannis!" "You do not stand alone," a village official said. "We stand with you. Give us the name of the traitors. We will revenge you." The threat was rhetorical; the names of forty-five defectors from the Center Union party were a matter of public record. "The names! The names!" voices chorused. Paul made his plea, telling the people to forget personalities and consider the issues. But they would not be appeased and as we drove away, we heard the chorused cries behind us in the night, "Death to the traitors!"

A full moon was rising. We were on our way to the last village, a very small one high in the mountains, called Atsipades. Our course was a

donkey path. As we crawled slowly in low gear, olive branches, silvered
by moonlight, brushed against our car. Our lights were seen from above
and bells began to ring. There was a volley of artillery fire and then
as we came closer, we heard the familiar chant, "Pa-pan-dre-ou! Var-
din-o-gian-nis!" echoing through the hills like some celestial fugue. At
the road's end a great arch of olive and laurel branches had been built.
It was lit by oil lamps and underneath the road was scattered with
flowers. It was after nine o'clock and the people had been waiting on
the ledge for more than three hours. Children leaped like fauns in the
night; their faces when the lights caught them were filled with frenzied
excitement. "O Pavlos irthe," they cried. "Our Paul is here." Then, as
if they had been rehearsed, they began to shout, "Elections! Elections,
elections!" making a game of it. The village was a kissing one and the
salutes took several minutes after which Paul, standing under the arc,
made his speech and each time he spoke the words "Demokratia" and
"Eleutheria" (liberty), the crowd shouted *"Zito! Zito!"*

The village was not there but higher up on the mountain. A man
carrying a single oil lamp, followed by two *koumbaros* supporting Paul,
led the dark human caravan up a rocky stream bed. Clouds covered
the moon and it was dark. Each silent man clung to one ahead, straddling
the stream's water. Sheep, aroused in the night by the strange procession,
bleated plaintively. I had the sense of being in an opera, of being part
of a band of thieves furtively making my way to a gypsy camp in
Il Trovatore.

We arrived finally at some dark forms of houses and we climbed an
outside stairway to an upper room where rows of women waited to
greet us, whispering softly, *"Kalispera, kalispera. . . ."* We entered a
small room lit by a single ceiling lamp, filled by a set table. The roof
was thatched with bamboo and beautiful lace covered the shuttered
windows. It was the home of a *koumbaros,* a farmer named Stelios
Manalakis. A parade of godchildren, including the son of our host,
squeezed into the room to greet Paul. The table was set for sixteen, but
twenty squeezed around it. Across the table from me, Paul was kissing
a large burly fellow who kissed him back. Turning to me, Paul pointed
to the man and murmured something in English. I leaned over the
table. "The bandit!" I heard Paul whispering. "The famous bandit!"
The robust fellow shook my hand and in a thin womanly voice said,
"How are you? How is New York? Is good the America!" Paul sat
down between the bandit and a black-turbaned white-haired priest.
Women began to carry in great platters of roasted meats, whole chickens,
rabbits and lambs. There were no knives on the table. The men tore at
the roasted carcasses with their hands. Bones cracked, tendons snapped.

Ripping, crunching, they battled over joints and chomped on legs of lamb as if they were drumsticks. A five-liter carafe of wine stood at each end of the table. Beakers were filled and drunk like water. No one spoke. The only sounds in the room were the sounds of slurping and gnawing. The men stopped now and then to wipe faces and hands with lace napkins, and went on with it as if they feared if they did not hurry they might not get enough. More than ever, I had the feeling I was at a feast in a gypsy cave. Feeling a slight visceral unrest I ate fastidiously a bit of lamb and a chicken leg, washing it down with the good wine. On one side of me a uniformed police captain was stuffing himself with the fury of a machine; on the other side, Manolis, complaining he was full and could not eat any more, disjointed the leg of a rabbit and chewed noisily. A pile of bones mounted by each plate. As honored guest Paul was served the head of a lamb. It crunched like a shellfish in his hand and he loudly sucked in the contents. He dropped a small dark sphere on my plate. I saw what it was and in a surge of nausea, pushed it aside. A guest took up the dark blue eye and swallowed it whole. The frenzied race of ingestion went on.

When the meats were gone and only bones remained, the women brought platters of fish, which were reduced in minutes to lacy skeletons. For dessert there was a platter of sheep livers and hearts. "I can't eat any more," groaned Manolis, grabbing a sheep liver. Some guests were roaring drunk.

Paul and the bandit stood up. Supported with their arms on each other's shoulders, they sang, "This is a time when captains are sailors and sailors are captains . . ."

"It is a song of *demokratia,*" whispered Manolis.

Other voices joined with antiphonal improvisations. Paul or the bandit would sing a line which the men in the room repeated, adding lines of their own praising Papandreou, attacking the King and the government, and each new theme was cheered with a volley of shouting. The bandit kissed Paul and in his high voice sang, "We wish you to live as long as the mountains. Under your protection we walk free, we live, we work . . . ," and Paul, kissing the bandit, boomed out, "What can one man do when he has so many traitors around him?"

A chorus sang, "Small birds hate the eagle because they can't fly as high. An eagle never dies, he is always killed. Before he is killed he pays his debts, he kills his killers. . . ."

At this point the chief of police beside me could stand it no longer. Throwing off his jacket he crossed to the other side of the room in the only possible way, by crawling under the table which rose and fell, creaking and clattering like a table in a seance. On the other side he

placed one arm on the bandit and with the other he embraced Paul
and he sang, "When you speak passions come out of your voice and
all your words are true. . . ." His powerful bass was the strongest voice
in the room.

"Don't you think this is dangerous?" Paul sang to the policeman and
the policeman sang, "What's the matter, are you afraid?" The men in
the room roared with laughter. The three swayed in one another's arms.
"Look!" Paul called out to me, throwing back his head in a burst of
joy, looking twenty years old. "One arm around the policeman, and the
other around a bandit. You are seeing the brotherhood of Crete!" With
vocal grandeur the policeman sang, "Our soil will be fruitful—in the
same way human rights will grow over the land . . . ," and Paul responded, "Where the wheat grows the mule will work, where the people
go the leaders must follow. . . ." The room shook with the applause,
and the bandit piped, "Your words have a very good odor. . . ."

It continued a half hour, during which the wine flowed. The priest
kept emptying his glass and his red face glowed with beatific sublimity.
The names of Papandreou and Vardinogiannis rang over and over. Outside the door godchildren watched with wide eyes, their faces like ser-
aphims. On the ceiling the lamp swayed and hissed. The time was late
and a new theme—one of farewell—entered into the singing like the
Benedictus of a mass. Paul's joy-filled abandon had turned to melancholy.
With tears flowing from his eyes he sang, "Thank you, my good friends.
Thank you very much. I wish you all happiness. . . ." The convict, his
eyes glistening, sang, "I am happy, happy with what I see." The policeman took up the theme, singing, "I have had good food and I have
seen beautiful friends. . . ." "We must go," sang Paul. "We must leave
for other places where the fight is hard. Farewell. . . ." A chorus of
men answered, "Farewell, God keep Crete, farewell. . . ."

Like drunken disciples leaving the Last Supper we stumbled after Paul,
supported by the secretary and the political student, down the outside
steps. A single file of villagers accompanied us down the rocky path.
Tree frogs sang, a startled lamb bleated and small boys leaped around
us. Under the arc of laurel the men halted to relieve themselves, making
a ritual of it, and in the moonlight their silvery scimitars of piss shown
like a spraying fountain. In silence Paul embraced the policeman, the
bandit and all the others. As we rolled away, the priest, a cigarette
glowing inside his beard like a trapped firefly, ran alongside the car,
calling out, "When will they have an election?" Behind us gunshots
rang out. The flower-filled car smelled like a new grave.

Below in Koxare the people were waiting to wave good-bye. It was
dark but we saw the shapes of them huddled in the night and we heard

their voices. Paul was sunk back into his seat in deep melancholy. "The people are afraid," he said, his voice breaking with emotion, "Kublaki, the people are afraid."

The next day in Athens I read in a newspaper of the crisis which had delayed Paul on Saturday. Political enemies were accusing Vardinogiannis of "adventurous profiteering," of holding an owner's interest in the Greek tanker *Joan V*, which was pirating oil through the United Nations blockade to Rhodesia. The captain of the tanker was one of Vardinogiannis' brothers; another brother was an officer in the shipping company. In a letter to the press, Vardinogiannis wrote, "I have no participation or share in any shipping business and if anyone can prove otherwise, I will turn the ships over to him as a present. With honor, Paul Vardinogiannis."

XXVI

"Christ Is Risen"

"Of course I fast," groaned George Katsimbalis after three days of starvation. "I'm anti-Christian, but I'm a good Greek. It's in me and I can't help it. I weep not for that pale simpering Nazarene who spoiled everything, who loused us up. I weep for the death of Adonis."

Something happens. At Easter a basically anticlerical people ordinarily indifferent to religion suddenly surge into churches, plunging pell-mell into an exhaustive excess of ritual and ceremony. "I never go to church," said Thanos Simos. "Except on Easter I go seven times." The compulsive Holy Week orgy of fasting and feasting, of pageantry and ceremony, is in no strict sense a Christian indulgence. It is a festival in which Christian myth and rite are incorporated into the ancient ceremonies to celebrate a God who dies in the bloom of his youth, rises from death and is acclaimed as a source of renewed life.

Not only Jesus, not only Adonis, but Lazarus. The day before Palm Sunday on the "Saturday of Lazarus," children lay on the ground pretending to be dead and then leaped up in laughing resurrection. Mothers baked special sweet buns kneaded into the shapes of winding sheets. During Holy Week a morning and evening service was held every day in every church of the land. On Palm Sunday priests handed each parishioner a palm-woven cross and a branch of myrtle called *vaya* which were hung with the family icons, to be used during the year as talismans against the evil eye. Newly married brides are touched with the evergreen leaves to invoke fertility.

300

The fasting and mourning began on Monday. At evening services, called *nymphioi* ("bridegrooms"), an icon of Christ was carried through the sanctuaries while priests intoned, "Behold, the bridegroom cometh in the middle of the night."

Tuesday was the day for whores to go to church. Gospels and hymns were dedicated to Mary Magdalene and the service included the reading of a poem by Kassiani, a legendary Byzantine abbess who wrote pious verse to expiate the worldly life of her youth. According to a secretary in the Foreign Press Office it was traditional for prostitutes to rest from their labors and devote the day to piety; the girls' favorite church, he said, was St. Nicholas, in the roaring red-light district of Piraeus.

With Thanos Simos I set out in the evening for the port town. My guide was out of sorts. Fasting since Sunday, eating only some occasional boiled vegetables without seasoning, he was, he said, "beginning to feel very bad in the stomach." When we arrived in the vast dimly-lit church it appeared to be filled with respectable working-class family groups. Men and women were separated, the men filling the right side and the women the left. Small children were lighting candles and arranging flowers.

"It's a bad sign," said Thanos. "Even the whores are losing faith." Looking over the black-robed women we saw scattered among them a number of flashy young ladies wearing make-up, fur jackets and spiked heels. One carried a baby which kept flailing its arms, fighting for freedom and another held a carafe of wine in a string sack as she knelt to kiss an icon. A priest was singing the hymn of Kassiani, which began:

> Lord, I who have sinned greatly,
> When I understood your divinity,
> I became a perfume bearer,
> Now I bring you perfumes . . .

The voice, beginning gently, soothingly, rose to a torment of agony and continued:

> Alas, I cry because I have within me darkness,
> I have within me a sinful desire, a dark urge to sin,
> I beg you to accept my warm tears,
> You who have the power to change the sea to clouds . . .

Across the aisle tears were flowing from the eyes of the women, those in black robes as well as those in bright dresses. I caught the gaze of a buxom blonde in a white chinchilla jacket who eyed me with interest through opaqued eyes. The priest's voice, now comforting, lyrically sweet, sang:

> Show mercy to the beatings of my sinful heart,
> You who have caused the sky to tremble,
> I kiss your feet and wash them with my tears,
> You who understand my soul,
> Never forsake me, your faithful servant . . .

We left when the hymn was finished and walked up notorious Notara Street, where it was apparent at once why so few girls were in church. The American Sixth Fleet was in port and sailors in summer whites filled the area. Doorways were lit with red bulbs; some opened into hallways lined with red wallpaper, and the entire street glowed like a fiery avenue to an inferno toward which sailors, supporting one another physically and morally, lurched drunkenly. Girls beckoned us from windows and called down from balconies. One queenly Lorelei, walking with cool steps, led six sailors laughing and tumbling sillily over one another, up a flight of stairs. Music blared from cheap cabarets, gaudy movies and seedy hotels. The walls of bars named "West Coast," "Chicago" and "Rio" were plastered with pictures of nude girls in acrobatic poses and at the end of the street a doorway advertised "motorcycles for hire." Mounted youths burst forth in fusillades of explosions like demented centaurs.

Wednesday was a day of anointment. Crowds lined up outside churches, waiting to be touched by the priest with oil on the forehead, chin, cheeks, and hands. Women received wads of oil-soaked cotton to send to husbands at sea and to sons living in foreign lands. Thanos reported that he was "beginning to feel a little crazy in the head." I suggested he might be feeling the beginning of the ecstasy of the saints, a prefix to visions. He accompanied me to a Plaka restaurant where he munched on a dry piece of bread and became immediately drunk on two glasses of wine. He began to sing, in English, "I am Jesus' little lamb, therefore, glad and gay I am. . . ."

The daytime hours of Thursday were devoted to the preparation of the Easter feast. Women baked pastries and dyed baskets of red eggs. Miraculous powers were ascribed to the first egg dropped into the dye —it was called "the egg of the Virgin Mary" and was preserved to protect children against the evil eye. Miraculous virtues were also credited to eggs laid during the day, especially those laid by a black hen, or a pullet producing for the first time. Late in the afternoon Thanos appeared in my hotel with a basket of red eggs, and a *tsoureki,* a braided Easter loaf with a red egg baked in the center.

In the evening the city was silent; like a foreshadowing of tragedy, the tension was mounting. The Easter cycle with its symbolic re-enactment of death and resurrection grew more intimate, the grief more personal. Women thronged black-draped churches, where they mourned as they would for a deceased member of their own family. "It is women's duty to cry all night," said Thanos. "And if they can weep no longer they rub their eyes with an onion to make more tears." The women were singing funeral hymns and spontaneous songs describing the grief of the mother of Jesus. Addressing one another antiphonally, they sang:

"Do you see that naked man hanging on the cross, a bloodstained shirt upon his shoulders, a crown of thorns upon his brow?"

"He is your son and my teacher."

"Why do you not speak, my son?"

"What am I to say, Mother? Wait for me until Saturday when bells will ring and priests will sing. Then you too, Mother, will rejoice."

Holy Friday, a day for total fast, was devoted to the funeral of Christ. The day was sunny and fair. Flags flew at half-mast, offices were closed and government officials participated in the ceremonies, as if the deceased were a national hero. In the churches the day began with the removal of the body of the dead Christ from the cross. At ten o'clock Thanos and I went to the First Cemetery of Athens, which was filled with crowds bearing flowers and candles. Inside the gate was the cemetery chapel and there the symbolic body of Christ, a panel of gold embroidered cloth, was laid on the *epitáphios,* a canopied bier of flowers. The jammed church was stifling with candle heat. Women were weeping, men stood mutely solemn. A policeman moved through the crowd, clearing a path for an old, swollen-eyed priest who wore a long cape supported at its corners by white-robed boys. Into the cape, deep as a tarpaulin, the people threw their bouquets of roses, stocks, violets and lemon blossoms, building a great mound of flowers to decorate the pall. The procession moved around the church, circling the pall three times, and women, bearing holy water in small pitchers and perfume bottles, covered everyone with spray.

Outside, the cemetery had a bustling festive air. At the gate a wailing gypsy woman, nursing a baby from a full brown breast, offered candles for sale. She was ignored and Thanos said, "Greeks believe it was gypsies who made the nails that were put into the body of Christ." All over the cemetery women were scrubbing and polishing family tombs and decorating them with flowers. The tombs were the most pretentious in Greece. Some with white marble colonnades were like small villas. I watched an old man and woman sweeping the steps of a tomb as if it were the porch of their house. We passed a large marble temple on which was

carved, "The home of Ioannis and Koula Koufogiorga." Many were
decorated with statues of the dead. Doors of the tombs were opened
to expose the boxes of bones inside. At several tombs priests were holding services for the relatives of the dead. When a priest finished at one
tomb, he bustled to another tomb and another family to begin the ritual
again. The sunlit cemetery was filled with singing birds and the heavy
scent of flowers and smoldering incense.

All day people crowded into churches, paying homage as they would
for a king lying in state. In the afternoon we drove halfway up Mt.
Hymettus, to the twelfth-century monastery of Kaisariani. Its red-tiled
roofs, tufted with green grass, were dappled by sunlight which shone
through cypresses and pink-flowering Judas trees. Men, women and
children stood in a long line waiting their turn to move through the
chapel and kiss the *epitáphios*. The four posts of the bier were braided
with pink and white stock; the canopy was covered with a variety of
field flowers. A covey of seated nuns formed a circle around the bier
and chatted with visitors, turning the event into a social occasion. Free
on this day to receive hundreds of guests they seemed almost jolly.
The high-domed chapel was richly frescoed and pleasantly cool. Little
girls brought fresh flowers.

The long day climaxed after dark with the funeral processions. In
Athens the most spectacular cortege began at the Church of St. George,
on the top of Lycabettus, and moved slowly down into the city. A larger
official procession began at the cathedral, making its solemn journey
around Constitution Square. From the roof of the Grande Bretagne Hotel
we had a superb view of both. The city was dark; the only lights were
thousands of flickering candles carried by the marchers. Rockets soared
over the town, exploding showers of blue, silver and ruby stars. The
Lycabettus procession of candles zigzagged across the mountain and
descended slowly toward the city. The cathedral cortege, led by the
Athens Police Band playing a slow funeral march, moved up Ermou
Street. The two processions seemed like two slow-moving rivers of burning lava converging on the center of the town.

Only men were permitted to march in the official cortege. It was led
by officials bearing banners and Christ's empty cross. The procession of
parliament deputies, ministers, soldiers, sailors and boy scouts was paced
to drum rolls so solemn and slow it was an agony of suspense to
watch and to listen. Other military bands picked up the mournful refrain, making an eerie effect over the town. A great flower-laden
epitáphios, carried by priests in golden robes, halted briefly before the
Old Palace and then continued at snail's pace around the square. The
incense which covered the city rose in nauseating swells to our rooftop

aerie. Bells began to ring. Rockets spewed stars in the heavens and Lycabettus glowed like a giant Christmas tree festooned with lights. On the front steps of the hotel a small frail-looking man of thirty-five, wearing a threadbare suit, waved a Bible and, in the manner of an evangelist, shouted with a terrifying intensity to the rich and elegant hotel guests, "God will judge you! He will punish you!" Policemen came to take him away.

The gloom lifted on Saturday. In the morning Thanos arrived to take me to the market "to see the men carry the lambs on their backs." In the churches noisy ceremonies of exorcism were taking place, demons which might hinder the resurrection were being cast out. At a given moment in the service the priest emerged from beyond the iconostasi bearing a basket of laurel leaves which he threw at the congregation and the women caught the flying leaves to take home as talismans against the evil eye, to drive away mice, and to put among the winter woolens to protect them against moths. After the service attention turned to the preparation of the paschal feast. Women hurried home to bake. In the country men would kill the pascal lamb but in cities where men had no lambs of their own, they selected them already slaughtered in the market place.

The market was a pandemonium. Men trapped in the inert mob fought over carcasses, the naked blue eyeballs of which seemed to look with chagrin and astonishment on the turbulent madness and on each other's mortification. The men cradled the bloody lambs in their arms like children, and I had the sickening sense of being at a Herodian massacre. A caravan of soldiers, carrying two lambs each, were loading a great army lorry for their barracks feast.

At eleven o'clock that evening bells rang out, calling the people to church for the last time. We drove outside the city to Thanos' family church, St. Nicholas in Filothei, in a small pine forest on a hilltop overlooking Athens. Police ushers squeezed us into a low-arched grotto-like chapel, hot with human heat and dark except for altar candles. Each person was holding an unlighted candle. I wondered how the candle-bearing swarm would avoid setting fire to each other and the claustrophobia which had oppressed me now and then during the week returned stronger than ever. A priest was chanting. As midnight approached the crowd grew increasingly restless. Voices began to keen along with the priest's, gently and sweetly.

Then, at a signal from the priest, the altar candles were extinguished and the church sank into total darkness, the darkness of the grave. The crowd hushed waiting. Exactly at midnight the priest appeared with a newly lighted white candle, and his words, deep and sonorous as if God were speaking them, filled the church.

"*Christos Anesti!* Christ is risen!"

Those who stood near the priest pushed toward him to light their candles from his and then they turned to light the candles of those behind and the flame passing from one to another, moved back through the church, and each time it was passed the bearer embraced and kissed his neighbor, murmuring happily, "*Christos Anesti*" and the receiver replied, "*Alithos Anesti,* He is risen indeed!" The wonderment and joyful bewilderment with which the words were spoken made them seem as if I were hearing them for the first time, as if I were there outside Jerusalem in the company of Jesus' friends. The moment was almost unendurable. I felt faint, and tears filled my eyes.

The doors of the church opened and the people, following the priest, surged out of doors, crying over and over the words, "Christ is risen!" The forest slope was a moving sea of light, as if a cloud of fireflies had suddenly descended on it. In all the churches of the city bells were ringing. Men and children lit rockets; the heavens boomed and the skies were showers of stars. People were chattering joyfully, as if each person were happy to have the agonies finished, relieved that the suspense was over and done with, as if he had actually feared the miracle might not take place, that Christ might not rise.

People began to leave, breaking up into small processions, toward their homes. Each cupped a hand over his candle, protecting it against the winds, for to succeed in bearing home the new light was a good omen for the coming year. The caravans of candles dispersing from all churches and in every direction glimmered like stars and were the only lights on earth. At home, said Thanos, a sign of the cross would be traced over the doorway with the candle, which would then be used to ignite the lights before the family icons.

The speed with which the crowd broke up must have been spurred also by hunger. In homes feasts were waiting and after a week of fasting everyone was rushing to them. We went to a restaurant where we began in the traditional way with a red egg after which Thanos ate *mayiritsa,* an Easter soup made of lamb's intestines, eggs, rice and dill. We had roast lamb, salad, sardines, cheese pie and lots of red wine. Thanos ate for an hour. When we returned to Athens after two o'clock, the streets were filled with people bearing candles, greeting friends, gossiping, and the restlessness continued through the night.

Sunday was a day for secular pleasure. I was invited to the Royal Palace Guard's Easter party for King Constantine. Outside the barracks gates, across Herodou Attikou Street from the Royal Palace, a crowd was gathered to catch a glimpse of the King. I showed my invitation and a soldier opened the gate. A band was playing. The courtyard inside was decorated with huge cutouts of chicks and colored eggs, and with garlands of flowers and greenery. In this kindergarten setting the two hundred tall guardsmen were preening like peacocks. Protectors of the royal family and royal property, the guards are selected for stature (over six feet tall), bodily strength, good looks and intellectual alacrity. Proudest and most elite branch of the Greek military, they are divided into three squads, two of them evzones, famous for their costumes of short white-pleated skirts, embroidered tunics and jackets and long-tasseled red fezzes. A third squad of fiercely handsome Cretans, called *vrakofori*, wore bright blue bloomers and shirts and white boots and carried curved Turkish scimitars. Older officers, their *tuttis* flaring out over fat paunches, looked as if they were pregnant.

A long red carpet led to a flower-decorated table in the center of the court and on the table was a huge bowl of red eggs. Under an arcade rows of tables were set for the feast. The traditional Easter fare was lamb roasted on a spit, and in the barracks' back yard, evzones were turning twenty lambs in charcoal pits where they had been cooking since dawn.

In the street shouting signaled the King's arrival. The bandsmen tuned briefly and began the sprightly "King's March." The guardsmen fell into stiff-spined lines, their eyes as glassy and unflickering as dolls. The King zoomed in, driving his own Rolls-Royce, bringing it to a crunching halt. An officer opened the limousine door and the King, tall and boyishly good-looking in an admiral's uniform, stepped out. He shook hands with the officers and then, smiling amiably, bowing to his right and to his left, he walked up the long carpet and took his place by the bowl of red eggs.

The guards, each bearing a red egg, fell into line for the ceremonial egg-cracking. Moving forward, one by one, each man snapped his heels in attention, saluted, shook the King's hand, murmuring, *"Eftihismeno Pascha,* Your Majesty, Happy Easter," and then offered his egg to the King for combat. When neither of the two eggs broke the King cracked his against the soldier's a second time. The crowd watched each meeting of eggs with breathless suspense. When an egg cracked, the guardsman clicked his heels and stepped away, taking his egg with him as a souvenir, and other guardsmen snapped into place. When it was the King's egg that broke, he dropped it on the table and took another from the bowl. Relaxed, laughing, the King was obviously enjoying himself; his feeling of soldierly comradeship was unmistakable. One strong egg gave him a run of more than a dozen victories. A trembling youth with a nervously bobbing Adam's apple finally broke it and was the hero of the day.

When the last egg was cracked the band struck up a mountain tune and the Cretans, their sabers flying, danced the *sousta,* a simulation of a military attack, and then the evzones, their skirts flaring, whirled through a circular *syrtos,* alternating coquettish lilts with vigorous dervish leaps. When they finished the King saluted, leaped into his car, revved the motor and roared away. He was going on to crack another six hundred eggs at army, navy and air force barracks.

Tables were spread with the roasted lambs, with bowls of red eggs, with salads, honey pastries and beakers of wine, and when the feasting was over, the proud guardsmen danced until the afternoon shadows fell across the courtyard.

There were paschal feasts everywhere. One block from the Royal Guards in the courtyard of the Athens Fire Department the elevated ladders from two fire trucks formed an inverted V one hundred feet in the air, and from it hung a large board cutout of Jesus, nude except for a red sash at the loins, held up by two ropes tied to the upraised hands. On the cobblestones under the ascending Christ firemen were dancing the slow *tsakonikos,* a dance which, according to tradition, was first danced by Theseus and his companions in Delos as a thanks offering to Apollo after the slaying of the Minotaur. The afternoon had turned gray and cold. A fireman pouring a glass of wine for me, said, "Christ is risen," and I replied, "He is indeed!" Above us a wind rocked the resurrecting Christ with the flowing sash which creaked on its lofty moorings.

In the week that followed newspapers tolled the holiday casualties. In Athens twenty-two persons were seriously injured by fireworks; in Thessaloniki seventeen. In the town of Serres, Father George, priest of the Church of the Evanghelistria, had his beard burned off from a fire-cracker thrown during the resurrection service. The service had to be interrupted so he could be rushed to the hospital.

XXVII

Island of Poetry

On Easter Monday I took a plane to join Angelos Katacousinos on his native island of Lesbos. During the hour-long flight I read newspapers filled with rumors of still another political crisis.

The new unrest concerned Cyprus and, like every Greek political scandal, it was incomprehensibly complex. For several months Cyprus' president, Archbishop Makarios, had been feuding with General George Grivas, Greek chief of the Cypriot Armed Forces, over the command of the Cyprus National Guard. Suspecting that General Grivas was co-operating with the Greek government and the Palace in a plot to over-throw the Cyprus government and assume military dictatorship, Makarios had asked the Greek premier, Stefanos Stefanopoulos, to withdraw General Grivas. The situation was curiously similar to George Papan-dreou's July 1965 dispute with King Constantine over control of the army which ended with the resignation of Papandreou from the prime ministry. Several ministers in Stefanopoulos' makeshift government, including Foreign Minister Elias Tsirimokos, were known to be sympathetic to Archbishop Makarios. One of Greece's many political turncoats, Tsirimokos had defected from the Center Union party when he accepted the ministry. In a public statement on Easter eve, Premier Stefanopoulos had invited the resignations of any ministers disagreeing with his Cyprus policy.

Though parliament, which was adjourned for Easter, would not convene for another week, Athens was buzzing with rumors of secret caucuses and plots. Since the makeshift government had the support of less than half of three hundred parliament deputies, there was a possibility that the Cyprus dispute might collapse the government. I thought of the gay, smiling young King blithely cracking eggs on Sunday and I wondered if he had had a premonition of what lay ahead.

The plane descended slowly into green hills. Unlike mainland Greeks and the dwellers of Greece's many barren islands, the people of Lesbos have preserved their forests and because of them they are prosperous. One of the largest of Greece's islands, Lesbos is also one of the richest and most beautiful. The light over Lesbos is always silvery and on its eastern slopes, facing Turkey, olives, chestnuts, sycamores and cypresses grow down to the edge of the sea.

Lesbos' fame goes back to the sixth century B.C. when it was the home of the lyric poetess Sappho. It was the fashion in those times for women of patrician families to devote their leisure to the composition and recitation of poems. Inventing her own Sapphic meters, Sappho wrote so passionately of the loves and hatreds which simmered in the sultry feminine atmosphere that the name for the citizens of Lesbos came to designate throughout the world the pursuers of homosexual female love. Understandably, the natives prefer to be known as Lesbions.

Lesbos' second most famous citizen lived more recently, in the twentieth century. He was the folk artist, Theophilos Hadzimichael, a Greek "Grandpa Moses," who after his death in 1934 was recognized as one of the great painters of Greece. He was born in the capital of Mytilene in 1868 or 1873, depending on which of two conflicting birth certificates is the correct one. A strangely possessed little man, he painted during a lonely and impoverished bachelor life more than three hundred pictures of Greek mythology and history on cotton cloth, boards, pieces of tin, whatever materials fell into his hands, and on the walls of cafés, taverns and friends' houses. In 1965 a permanent gallery of one hundred collected works was opened on Lesbos and it was this that Angelos had invited me to the island to see.

We went at once to the gallery, a peasant-style house of four white-washed rooms in an olive grove near Varia, the village where the artist had lived and worked. The road led through tall grass, under wisteria arbors and groves of flowering Judas trees. Across eleven kilometers of blue sea were the rolling gray mountains of Anatolia.

Inside was a child's fantastic comic-book world. Naïvely drawn and boldly colored, the paintings surged with life and energy. Living only in his art, Theophilos with his burning brush induced a frenzy of color. No wonder his neighbors believed him mad. A small neurasthenic man who was slow of speech and painted with his left hand, he portrayed virile warriors, fierce pirates, and lordly kings. In love with costume, he not only painted them, he also wore them, using himself as model for evzones wearing foustanellas, Macedonian soldiers and Alexander the Great. Frequently hungry, he painted bakeries with rows of loaves and butcher shops with slaughtered lambs. Dogs were his companions and he painted them constantly, a curious Lesbos species of mongrel white terrier with brown spots and an intelligent, almost human face. No subject escaped him. Brigands and warriors, revolutionary heroes, mythological gods and Biblical prophets, Samson slaying a lion, Adam and Eve in a peaceable garden, Moses in the bulrushes, the famous lovers Erotokritos and Aretusa, Turkish pashas, priests, fishermen and shepherds, Sappho reading her poems, orgiastic wine festivals and clashing battles, all brought to life in a fantastic human panorama. Detail was his passion. In an olive-picking scene, thousands of olives are clearly outlined in the trees and on the ground; a view of Constantinople shows every minaret and dome. In a picture entitled *Patrisson Family from Chicago,* probably painted from a photograph sent to Lesbos relatives, a prosperous immigrant family is portrayed on Easter Day. Four children are cracking eggs. The father, wearing a hat, is seated at a table loaded with traditional Easter viands; the mother, wearing a red hat and red net stockings, is nursing a baby. A jungle hunting scene, a miniature painting in itself, hangs from a wall, and a variety of pets—cats, rabbits and a parrot—fill the room.

Critics like to compare Theophilos to El Greco. Considering the differences between the two artists, the comparison is valueless. A contemporary Greek painter, Yannis Tsarouchis, spoke more meaningfully when he said, "Theophilos had the courage to open the pomegranate of Greek genius to disclose the eternal seed."

Art and poetry are life to the people of Lesbos. Dedication to creativity is especially strong in the inland town of Aghiasso. In the afternoon we drove there, climbing through olive groves in which thickets of red poppies bloomed like spatterings of blood in the green landscape. Blue iris, white daisies, pink and purple anemones turned the island into a vast garden.

It was cool in the mountains. In Aghiasso men were dancing on the cobblestones, celebrating Easter, and women sat in the doorways watching them. Lesbions are the most reserved, the gentlest of Greeks. Impetuous excitability is foreign to them. The cultivated, soft-voiced people are proud of their island and happy to be living on it. I met an English-speaking student home from Athens for the holiday. He said, "Life is too quickly in Athens. I prefer enjoying. Lesbos has all the things I want. I can live near the mountains and the sea at the same time. In Athens people need much time to go home from work and back in the afternoon. In Lesbos you go by foot, three minutes from house. I prefer my life not so quickly and in Lesbos I have all year a joy."

We visited the pottery kiln of a family named Kourtzis, friends of Angelos. Mrs. Kourtzis served us holiday sweets and showed us an article published by her in a Rotary Club magazine about Theophilos, who had once worked in Aghiasso as a potter. When we left she loaded us with gifts of pottery and hand-loomed rugs. Mr. Kourtzis and his son, an engineering student home from Athens, took us to the library and introduced us to actors of the local theater who performed ancient plays, Shakespeare and modern plays written by a local priest, Father Christos. "I am writing a new play," the old priest said. "I am not hurrying. It will be my last and I want it to be my best."

In the evening Angelos and I were invited to dinner by the bishop of Mytilene. His palace on a hill over the town was illuminated like a theater set. Inside there were red rugs and drapes, crystal chandeliers, baronial oaken chairs carved with the two-headed eagle of Byzantium, and a collection of Byzantine and Renaissance paintings. That the bishop was devoted to good living was apparent. He was a heavy good-looking man with a gracious and worldly manner and a gently Rabelaisian smile. Under his neatly groomed gray-streaked black beard he wore a ruby and emerald lavaliere. He was, said Angelos, a politician in the Church and the first contender for the archbishopric of Athens, highest Greek office in the Orthodox Church. He served Scotch highballs. Speaking German with a few English phrases, he took me on a tour of the palace, which included a small red and gold chapel richly frescoed with the lives of Lesbos' saints. In the drawing room he introduced me to the other guests, beginning with a black-haired handsome man in his fifties. "This is the minister of farewell," he said.

"I'm sorry," I said, wondering if I had misunderstood.

"The minister of farewell, Mr. Michael Galinos." I recognized the name which I had seen frequently in newspapers. Galinos, a friend of Foreign Minister Tsirimokos and a defector from the Center Union party, was minister of welfare in the Stefanopoulos government. The bishop introduced his other guests, Galinos' male secretary, the Communist mayor of Mytilene, an ex-minister of welfare during the right-wing administration of Karamanlis, who, said the bishop, was making a study of Christianity in the theater, the bishop of Mithimna, a town on the other end of the island, Lesbos' governor who was a member of Papandreou's Center Union party, and the governor's wife, who was the only woman present. It seemed an astonishing assembly to be breaking bread and I wondered on what common conversational grounds they might meet.

The banquet began with a cheese soufflé and continued, forever it seemed, with fish, chicken, lamb with vegetables, salads, pastries and red eggs, all served by two young men in business suits who kept renewing flagons of wine. Using Angelos, a doctor, as a kind of catalyst, the subject which the guests, all of them middle-aged, found in common was the state of their own healths. The ex-minister had an ulcer, the governor had gout and his wife had migraines. The mayor's liver was in distress and the minister of farewell had a slipped disc. The bishop wondered how much prussic acid was normal to the bloodstream—he feared he had too much.

"You should follow Hippocrates," said the minister of farewell to the mayor.

"I don't know what he said," said the mayor. Turning to Angelos, he asked, "What did Hippocrates say?"

"I'm not a student of Hippocrates," said Angelos. "I don't really know."

"He said we must keep the spirit of youth alive inside," said the minister of farewell. "That if you wish to remain a young man you must love a young woman."

"Hippocrates said *that?*" The ex-minister was incredulous.

"It's a fine rule," said the minister of farewell.

"In Switzerland there are doctors who follow Hippocrates," said the ex-minister. "They have medicines which turn a man of seventy to twenty-five years of age."

"Really," said the bishop. "Must one go to Switzerland? Couldn't the medicine be sent here?"

Angelos said he'd never heard of the elixir. "You have to go to Switzerland," said the farewell minister's secretary. "The treatment includes an operation in which they insert glands from goats."

"Where do they insert the gland?" asked the bishop of Mithimna. No one knew. The mayor said he supposed medical science would soon discover many rejuvenation medicines and he hoped that each of the guests would live long enough to benefit from them. Everyone was speaking at once. A young priest entered the dining room to call the minister of farewell to the telephone. In five minutes he returned, pale and shaken. The call had been from a member of his Athens staff, with the news that Foreign Minister Tsirimokos had resigned from the government.

The party, which minutes before had been merry, now hushed and quickly broke up. The next day newspapers announced a second resignation, that of Minister Galinos.

In the morning Angelos and I set out for Mithimna on the northern end of the island. We followed cliff roads jutting over the sea and stopped halfway in Kalloni for coffee, which we drank under an arbor of dripping wisteria. On a garage next door a sign said, "Wisconsin Heavy Duty Engines." We continued to the fishing village of Petro where we climbed to the Church of the Virgin, perilously perched on a rock, to see a miraculous icon of the Virgin and Child which, according to legend, floated in from the sea three times, at which point it became apparent to the exasperated fishermen who kept returning it to the sea, that the Virgin wanted a church built on top of the inaccessible rock.

It was a short distance to Mithimna, a town of two thousand persons which rose almost vertically from the sea. The spectacular town is a summer center for artists from Germany, Holland and Scandinavia. Its large and fanciful wooden houses are famous for their richly frescoed interiors. We lunched in a restaurant over the sea and while we were eating, a local doctor, a friend of Angelos', arrived with his son, who was home for the holiday from an English-language prep school in Athens. The boy, whose name was Stavros Tsakyrakis, offered to guide me through the town. A sturdily built fifteen-year-old, he had an awesome intelligence and an ebullient personality. "I like everything," he said, smiling happily. "But mostly letters and books. I am going to be a writer." Tromping up and down the lanes of the town, he talked about literature, asking me who I thought was the greatest modern Greek writer. I replied, Kazantzakis, and he was pleased. What, he asked, did I think of Somerset Maugham. "Sometimes very good," I said, "and sometimes bad."

"Yes," said the boy. "He is sometimes bad because he wrote too much, he tried too hard to amuse." We saw the public baths, built of white marble in mosque style. "It is used by men in the morning and ladies in the afternoons," he said. "But not many ladies come. They are ashamed." He took me into an abandoned house, built in 1833. The ceilings and walls were painted with marine scenes.

"Do you ever go down to the sea and sit there alone, looking at her?" asked Stavros. "I do. When I feel a fear, an agony I have never felt before, when I must think about life and its problems, I go down to the sea. My mind is calm, my heart is quiet and I want to shout, 'Thank you, God, for the sea!' I think it must be because I am born on an island. I know I could never live without the sea. I've written a poem about it. It's very romantic. But I'm really not romantic."

Then why, I asked, had he made his poem romantic?

"Well, it's much a lie," he said. "I think at least half of all things writers write are lies."

He took me into a barbershop to meet the barber who had worked for two years in New York. "He made much money," said Stavros. "But he had a very bad life. He worked all the time and only drank coffee and ate sandwiches. Of course, he didn't like it."

We were seeking a house in which Stavros promised even more beautiful frescoes. "What kind of God do you believe in?" he asked suddenly. Startled, I replied that I believed in a Christian God. "I suppose I do too," he said. "But I don't think priests are much help. They get in the way. I find I believe better without them."

He knocked on a door. It was opened by a young girl with bright red hair who led us silently into an upstairs dining room. The walls were paneled with seascapes done in a graceful French style. While we were looking at them, the girl's mother, a heavy ponderous woman who had been aroused from sleep, entered. I said I was surprised to find such elegant pictures in such a remote place. Stavros interpreted my words. The woman rolled her eyes and burst into angry complaints.

"She says she doesn't like the pictures," Stavros said. "She doesn't understand them and they only bring her troubles. You see the house has been registered as a national monument and the Archaeological Service will not let her change it, to make it comfortable. It is cold in winter and the rain comes in. And she does not like people beating all the time on her door, wanting to visit. She says if you like the pictures so much, you can buy the house. She wants to sell it and buy one without pictures that is comfortable."

As we trotted down the hill Stavros said, "She is obviously a very common woman who thinks only of money." Below the sea, blinding bright in the afternoon sun, washed against the rocks. "Listen," said Stavros. "Do you hear the waves? They are whispering. Can you imagine a world without the sea? She is my best friend. No words I can say would be enough to tell how I love her." When we said good-bye he gave me his poem, inscribed in ink in English on lined paper.

> The rough waves
> Crash on the shore,
> As my agonies
> Beat on my heart.
>
> I bring my pain to the sea,
> My heart quiets,
> My mind calms,
> I am happy.
>
> I will judge,
> Sometimes I'll solve,
> I may fail,
> But I will live.

XXVIII

To See the King

I was returning to Athens to see the King. Early in April I had received a call from an Embassy secretary relaying a Palace invitation for a royal audience on Friday, April 15, at 10:45.

On Wednesday, when I returned from Lesbos, I received another call, from Mrs. Margaret Papandreou, inviting me to meet with her husband, Andreas, also on Friday. I told her I could not come because I had an appointment with the King, and she invited me to call a day sooner, on Thursday, April 14.

Known simply by his first name of "Andreas," the son and heir of George Papandreou was the most controversial man in Greece and the most difficult to see. His numerous enemies said he was a Communist and accused him—falsely—of a sinister association with the secret leftist organization given the name "Aspida." The purposes of the contrived society was said to be the undermining of the crown by purging the army of its rightist control and putting it under the command of the extreme left. Twenty-five army officers had been arrested and charged with "Aspida" membership. Andreas could not be arrested because of his political immunity as a parliament deputy. That the King considered him an enemy was well known. Much of the political resentment against Andreas seemed to be based on his American background and against his beautiful American wife. Curiously, a cabal against him existed in the embarrassed American Embassy.

On Thursday I took a taxi to Psychico and arrived a few minutes early at Papandreou's home. I was greeted by an elfin blond boy,

Andreas, Jr., aged seven, who showed me his Easter gifts from his grandfather, some chocolate eggs and toy chicks. Chattering engagingly, he
described the roasting of the Easter lamb on a spit in the yard. He was
missing a front tooth which he said he had put under his pillow where
it had miraculously turned into a coin.

The father arrived. He was a sturdily-built tense man with thinning
black hair. I had heard that he was ill, wishful rumors began, no doubt,
by political enemies. Except for an apparent nervousness he appeared in
excellent health. "You have chosen a very decisive year to be in Greece,"
he said. He had received a letter about me from George Theotokas, and
said, "You are lucky to have as your friend the finest mind in
Greece." Pacing the room, unable to settle, he said he was surprised that
the Embassy had permitted me to visit him. I said that the Embassy had
nothing to do with my visit, that I had no diplomatic contacts.

"I must tell you before we begin that this house is probably bugged,"
he said. I asked how this was possible since the house, set off from the
street, stood in a large garden. "Surely you've heard of little receivers
without wires which they throw about, that pick up conversations." I
said I considered this unlikely. "Perhaps you are right," he said, "but
my phones are tapped." This was certainly possible. I sensed his anxiety
and strain.

I remembered Freud writing that paranoiac fears are frequently justi-
fied and I felt a deep sympathy for the torment of this learned man. The
thought struck me that he was unsuited to the cloak-and-dagger atmosphere of Greek politics, that he should never have left the academic life.
His manner with me was pedagogical. I seemed to be listening to a lecture
rather than participating in a conversation.

He said, "The Greek monarchy has always had the protection of a
larger power. For a long time it was the British monarchy, but now it
is the protection of the United States which is preserving the Greek
monarchy. The influence is not through the Embassy, but the CIA. The
two seldom work together, nor do they get on very well. The CIA is the
club."

I spoke of the seemingly capricious reversal in the Greek attitude
toward Queen Frederika, and he said, "It isn't that Frederika has
changed. It's her position from Queen to Queen Mother that has made
the difference. Greece has changed, the people are becoming more enlightened, more aware, and they see Frederika in a different light. As the
major adviser of the King, Frederika is a destructive influence, the
source of most of our political problems."

At this point Mrs. Papandreou entered the room and in her presence
Andreas seemed to relax. She was tall, poised and handsome. Andreas

went on, saying, "The King is intelligent, but badly educated. Being the last king of the Orthodox faith, he believes himself in the direct line of the first Constantine whose name he bears. He thinks of himself as holding a divine mission, certainly a dangerous attitude in one so young and unwise. He believes the army belongs to him personally. His attitude toward Greece, toward the military, toward labor and education, is paternalistic. He is the guardian and all should be grateful and loyal. His view of the political left is irrational—he doesn't see it as a valid political movement, but simply as criminal gangsterism, the aim of which is to take over what rightly belongs to him. The people don't count. He has contempt for politicians and a cavalier attitude that they should perform to his bidding. He is an athlete, with an athlete's competitive, stubborn and persistent spirit, an athlete's determination to win.

"In modern Greece we have had democracy only once, under my father's ministry. And because it interfered with the King's autocratic image of himself, he needed to unseat the real leader of the people. There has not been even a pretense of democracy since. That victory made the King cocky and arrogant. He decided he would be the political leader. Failing to understand his role as a figurehead, a symbol, as do the monarchies of England and Scandinavia, he assumed monarchical privileges which are archaic. He does not understand that by doing this he is actually hastening his own end."

I asked Andreas about the health of his father who had been ill. "He is quiet and aloof," said Andreas. "While the doctors say he is recovered, his spirit does not improve. He is feeling his age, and he is depressed. No doubt he knows they are waiting for him to die, that the government plans to delay elections until he is gone in the hopes that his death will weaken the Center Union, that there will be no new leader to replace him."

Did he see himself as his father's successor? Skirting the question, he said, "I could pick up two-thirds of his support today. About the rest I don't know." I spoke of Paul Vardinogiannis' conviction that Greece would not know political rest until Greeks learned to comprehend issues instead of personalities. "Of course, Paul is right in theory," said Andreas. "But Greeks will always follow personalities."

At this moment two parliament deputies arrived. As I was leaving, Mrs. Papandreou, who was from Iowa, asked about my Wisconsin farm, and she said, "I wish we had a farm in Wisconsin."

A cab returned me to my hotel. The fare was fifty-two drachmae. I gave the driver a fifty-drachmae note, plus a twenty. He returned the twenty, saying fifty was enough. He was smiling. It was the first time I had had a taxi tip returned and I understood what the driver was trying to tell me, that he approved of my visit. In the hotel, the concierge, the telephone operator and the busboys welcomed me like a returning hero, eager to know what Andreas had said.

The next morning as I was dressing for my visit with the King, I received a call from an Embassy secretary saying that my appointment had regretfully been cancelled due to an unexpected rearrangement of royal conferences. I would, said the secretary, receive a call within a day or two notifying me of a rescheduled appointment.

Considering the climactic political events of the week, I was not surprised. The possibility that it might be cancelled had occurred to me and I was surprised only that the cancellation should have been made at such a late hour.

In the never-ending game of political musical chairs, the "minister of farewell," Michael Galinos, had resigned from the government and two days later announced that he would rejoin it. He was known as "the defector of defectors," the undisputed champion. When the government appeared to be losing its cliff-hanging majority, it was suddenly saved by the defection from Papandreou's party of an obscure deputy named John Yamas. The next day two Center Union deputies alleged that they had rejected bribes of five million drachmae each to switch their allegiance to the Stefanopoulos government. It was said that the money was offered by rich Americans. The rumor, never proven true, was nonetheless believed. Blaming the defections on American pressures, Marika Venizelos, daughter-in-law of Greece's great political leader, said, "Don't you Americans know you cannot buy honest men? Don't you understand that you buy only traitors who will betray you as easily as they betray Greece? Americans are fine people, they are the strength and the hope of the world, but they simply cannot understand how their diplomats betray them."

When I heard rumors that Paul Vardinogiannis was considering defecting to the tottering government, I telephoned him. He invited me to lunch. I arrived in his apartment while he was in conference with two politicians. A butler brought me a highball and I waited, trying to concentrate on the fine paintings on the walls. In a quarter hour Paul appeared. "I am joining the government on Tuesday and becoming the new foreign minister," he said. I did not speak. "Do you believe me?" he asked.

"No," I said.

"Why not?"

"If you say so, I suppose I must. But I find it difficult."

He laughed. Embracing me he said, "Kublaki, I'm glad you still have faith."

I sank into a sofa. "I'd like another drink," I said.

"Greeks will believe anything," he said. "I'm glad to see you've not turned Greek. The offer was made to me but I turned it down."

I mentioned the rumors of American bribes and he said he did not believe them true. "Americans are always exerting their little pressures," he said. "But they never directly attempt to control us. The only real guilt of your diplomats is that they do not see deeply into our problems. They see us only as a photograph, and they expect things to be easily and quickly solved. Of course, without a deep knowledge of the Greek personality, of Greek history and economy, nothing can be understood. If things are in a bad way it's our own fault. We have no government, only a mass of corruption."

He confessed to being in doubts about his own career. He had spent the morning with Tsirimokos who, he said, had resigned the government to save face when he heard the King was planning to dispose of him. Paul said, "The pattern of ousting a minister who fights the Palace is a tradition in Greece. A great prime minister, named Trikoupis, was forced to resign in the 1880s under George I in circumstances almost identical to Papandreou's last year. The only way a politician can survive is to flatter the King, to be a courtier. Unfortunately for me I'm no yes-man."

Weeks passed during which I received no word on the rescheduling of my appointment with the King. Finally I called the Embassy secretary. "The Palace has not been able to make another appointment," he said. The message had come, he said, "in terse language," and he added, "This has never happened before."

I discussed the situation with a journalist friend and to him the circumstances seemed perfectly clear. Quite obviously, he said, my visit with Andreas Papandreou, the one man whom the King hated more than any other, was known by the Palace. Either my telephone conversation with Mrs. Papandreou, during which I'd spoken of my appointment with the King, had been monitored, or I had been seen entering the Papandreou house. "There is no doubt," said my friend, "that the King makes and breaks his own appointments. He may act, of course, on outside advice, but the decision is made by him. In your case you've been caught up in the biggest power struggle in Greece. Its two key figures, its two polarities, are Andreas and Frederika. In a sense neither is wholly Greek, one has adopted the country and the other repatriated to it, and both hold to the Greek conspiratorial view of events."

I was unable to put the matter of the broken appointment to rest. Two weeks before I planned to leave Greece for good, I telephoned the

Palace and asked for the King's public relations secretary, a Cypriot named Stelios Hourmouzios. He invited me to see him the next day.

He was a dark heavily-browed man with the energetic exuberance characteristic to press agents. Before he had joined the Palace corps he had been employed by the shipping billionaire Stavros Niarchos. He greeted me with gusto, saying, "I hear you were on Mt. Athos. How did you enjoy it?" I wondered how he knew. "I am also an author," he said. "I am writing with Queen Frederika the official biography of King Paul. She told me of your visit, how much she enjoyed talking with you."

He was sorry, he said, that it had been necessary to cancel my appointment with the King. "Unfortunately cancellations are sometimes necessary. The King is a very busy man and emergencies always come up." He paged through a calendar book, pointing out red-inked cancellations. "Sometimes there are as many as eight a month," he said. "In your case an appointment had to be moved up so the King could receive the new ambassador from Uruguay. Then he had to rush to lunch with the directors of the Bank of Greece. Something had to give. Unfortunately it was you."

I asked why a rescheduling of my appointment had been refused.

"But it hasn't," he said. "Obviously, there's been a misunderstanding."

Had the Embassy secretary lied, I asked.

"I don't wish to contradict your Embassy. But surely you know diplomats are the same the world over, they use their couched language."

I reminded him that my appointment had been broken more than a month ago and I asked if foreign visitors ordinarily remained in Greece so long waiting for an appointment to be rescheduled.

"You must remember the King is a very busy man," said Hourmouzios, speaking rapidly, giving me no chance to break in. "He has to change his clothes so often, sometimes five times a day, and some days he hasn't as much as a half hour for himself and his family. Please don't think there is anything personal about your case, anything sinister."

The thought had occurred to me, I said, that the cancellation might relate to my visit with Andreas Papandreou.

"An absurd idea," he said. "Who could have suggested such a thing? Naturally, since you are a writer, you should see representatives of all parties. We would *expect* you to do that."

A secretary entered and announced in conspicuous English that someone was waiting. Recognizing my signal to leave, I got up. Hourmouzios shook my hand, saying smoothly, "I'm so sorry you're leaving Greece, that we'll not have the opportunity to schedule another appointment. You could have seen for yourself what a mature young man the King is, how intelligent, how earnest, what a fine leader he is developing into."

As I left he said, "You will remember, of course, if you publish anything, to send it to us first for approval."

When I reported the interview to my journalist friend, he said, "If you were staying longer in Greece, the Palace would now be embarrassed into remaking the appointment. But by delaying they have the idea, since you are leaving Greece, that everything will straighten itself out, that time will take care of things. But they are not, of course, being as bright as they think."

In the government foreign press office there was at this time a crisis only peripherally political. Two young Americans had arrived in Greece from Iran with their pet parrot which customs officials refused to permit in the country. The distraught young men called daily to plead for the release of their pet which, they said, spoke only Persian and was miserable in its quarantine incarceration.

The director, a kind and gentle man who devoted much of his busy time solving the personal dilemmas of visiting foreigners, said, "I must try to get the poor boys their parrot. It would be a small thing, and if we make them happy we win their good will. That is a purpose of this office."

For a week there were urgent calls between the offices of the foreign minister and the minister of health. The minister of health would not relent. The bird, he said, could under no circumstances be legally admitted, and he ordered it destroyed. After an emotional scene by the Americans in the press office, another call was made. The bird was given a two-day stay of execution. Appeals were made to a parliament deputy and other influential officials. The minister of health would not be moved, and after a farewell with its masters in the customs office, the bird was sent back to Iran alone.

XXIX

Conversations

Greeks dearly love to talk and the subject they talked about more than any other was politics. In evaluating what one heard, it was always necessary to take into account the Greek instincts for dramatic exaggeration. Violently partisan in all things, a Greek seldom makes a point the same way twice. He believes nothing is as it appears to be. Holding to a "plot theory," a conspiratorial view of life, nothing is believed to happen according to natural laws. Everything is assumed to be contrived and manipulated.

I was invited to a Sunday family dinner. My host, whom I shall call Stratis, was a deputy in parliament. His wife Diane was from a rich and distinguished family. The guests included her father, a banker, a lawyer uncle and his wife, named John and Minerva, and a bachelor cousin, a businessman named Nicos. All spoke English fluently.

Before we had finished our Scotch highballs and *mezédes* an argument developed over the royal family. The intensity of feeling and the political alignments astonished me. Stratis, who as a member of the Center Union might be classified as politically left center, was defending the monarchy. The lawyer and his wife, supporters of the right wing ERE party, and Nicos, a right extremist who favored dictatorship, were attacking the monarchy.

"The King is a stupid uneducated boy," said Aunt Minerva. "He does not understand anything."

"The King is not stupid," said Stratis. "The people are not willing to give him a chance."

"Why do we need him?" asked Uncle John.

"The monarchy is absolutely necessary to keep this country from chaos for at least another ten years," said Stratis. "Where there is no real government, no solidity at the top, the crown gives us at least an atmosphere of order and authority. We have nothing else."

"Greece's periods of greatness were all under dictators," said Nicos. "The age of Pericles, Alexander the Great . . ."

"My dearly beloved cousin," said Stratis, showing his contempt. "I love you and I respect you. But I do not respect your ideas."

A waiter served the fish course.

"Why don't the King and his mother go away?" asked Aunt Minerva, her voice shrill. "I don't want them in Greece, I don't want them taking my money."

"What money?" asked the father.

"I don't want to pay four thousand dollars for a car which costs two thousand dollars in Italy." Aunt Minerva's reference was to the high excise tax on automobiles that are not manufactured in Greece.

"My dearly beloved auntie, listen to me . . ."

"I know many things I can't tell . . ."

"What do you know?"

"The money that is taken out of the country and sent to Swiss banks."

"The Queen collects money for people who need to be cared for," said Stratis.

"What people?"

"The peasants!"

Through the meat course, the salad and the dessert, the shouting continued, growing shriller, more vehement.

"Frederika has shown that she is a very courageous woman," said Stratis.

"Courage!" cried Minerva. "Courage is all the Greeks have. Aren't we all courageous? We who stayed in Greece during the war, who could not find enough to eat. Didn't we have courage? Don't speak to me of Frederika's courage! She came back after the war and went to Jannina and put on a peasant costume. Is that courage?"

"I realize there are very few people in Greece who like the Queen Mother," said Stratis. "There are also few in Greece who like the truth."

Uncle John said, "Greece was thrown into its present confusion by the King, when he forced the resignation of Papandreou."

"The King was badly advised," said Diane's father. "If he had been wise he would have let Papandreou finish his four years."

"Let's face the truth," said Stratis. "Papandreou should never have insisted on taking over the defense ministry and controlling the armed forces. He should not have pushed Andreas into the foreground."

"The King takes all the wrong advice from all the wrong people," said Aunt Minerva. "If he weren't so stupid we would not have had the crisis."

"The July crisis was created by my party, by the Center Union," said Stratis. "If its members had remained loyal instead of defecting to the crown, there would have been no crisis."

"Of course," said Nicos, sarcastically. "Everyone knows the intelligence of our parliament is below the normal Greek intelligence, and we know what *that* is."

"My dear cousin," said Stratis testily. "If you know perhaps you will enlighten us."

"There are three and one-half million illiterates in Greece, about half of the adult population," said Nicos. "I daresay in parliament the illiteracy is even higher."

"Villagers may not read or write," said Diane. "But they are civilized, they have inherited the old wisdoms."

"And the old egos," said her father. "Our trouble as Greeks is that we're all drunk with egoism."

"You're forgetting our silly illusions about our own cleverness," said Stratis. "If we, the crafty sons of Odysseus, have one besetting sin it is that we think we are too clever by twice."

"If we're so clever, why can't we have a democracy like other countries?" said Aunt Minerva.

"Plato proved a democracy is unworkable for Greeks," said Nicos. "His republic was ruled by an oligarchy of aristocrats."

"Of which you doubtlessly fancy yourself one, my dear cousin," said Stratis.

"Democracy is a delusion invented by an inferior majority," said Nicos.

Everyone was shouting now, no one was listening.

"We have a parliament of donkeys . . ."

"The palace is our infection . . ."

"Why can't we have an election?"

Stratis rose from his place and supporting himself on the table's edge with his knuckles, outshouting them all, said, "My dear sweet family, I love you all but you are nonetheless fools." And then he walked from the room.

There was the sound of scraping chairs as the guests pushed away from the table. Aunt Minerva's eyes filled with tears. In seconds the dining room was empty and the guests were driving away, Uncle John and Aunt Minerva in a yellow Mercedes, Cousin Nicos in a blue Jaguar.

Stratis reappeared. He was laughing. He poured two Scotches, and he said, "Another Sunday dinner. It happens in thousands of houses every week. They leave angry, frustrated, exhausted, like soldiers from the field of battle. We may not speak for a few days but next Sunday we'll go through the whole thing again. Thank God we're so heated about politics. It's our national sport, a safety valve. If we talked about the cinema or football in this way we would be doomed. It is the still waters that are dangerous. As long as we keep the sea ruffled we can hope." He drank from his glass and said, "As you have seen today we have no real right in Greece, no real left. Just a lot of Greeks fighting in the middle."

The next week I was at a gala in a garden. The United States minister consular had invited more than one hundred diplomats, parliamentarians, ex-ministers, Greek and American millionaires and international society persons to drink martinis and Scotch under the trees.

I met Gregory, a newspaper editor, who pointed out Tom Pappas, American director in Greece of the Standard Oil Company of New Jersey. He was talking to a Greek shipping tycoon. "Behold the conspirators," he said. "The fate of Greece is being plotted under these trees this afternoon. One might even guess, a revolution."

"It's hardly the setting to plot a revolution," I said.

"That's where you're wrong," said Gregory urbanely. "It is opposition to evolution which brings revolution. As you can see, Greece is really an American colony. And Americans who practice democracy at home do not believe in it for their colonies. Your efforts are directed at keeping democracy out of Greece, at preserving an order which disallows the social reforms which might prevent a revolution."

"Why don't you throw off the conspirators, why don't you act for yourselves?" I asked. "All this talk of conspiracy, of everyone plotting against you, is a national paranoia."

"Ah, yes, paranoia is a Greek word, describing a Greek condition. But what of you Americans, your paranoia? What is more paranoiac than your fear of Communism, your seeing it everywhere? Is not that paranoia on a national scale?"

An old woman dressed like the madwoman of Chaillot in a black net cap with silver sequins tied with a bow under her chin, a native embroidered cloak and enough costume jewelry to drape an icon, broke into our conversation, saying, "They're terrible, the Communists. They're doing awful things."

"What are they doing?" I asked.

"No one knows exactly, that's why it's so sinister," she said. A handsome American woman with chestnut hair wandered into the circle, saying, "Personally, I love George Papandreou, he's my secret passion, the most fascinating man I've ever met." She struck me as a minor character out of *Dodsworth*.

"Fortunately the King can deal with him," said Mrs. Chaillot. "What a fine young man he is. So courageous, so wise. He's saving the country, he's preserving democracy."

"It's hardly a democracy when the majority of people have no voice in the government," said Gregory.

"The majority are misled by Communists," said Mrs. Chaillot. "That's why it's so sinister."

The buzzing under the trees went on. I saw Panagiotis Kanellopoulos, leader of the ERE party and a former prime minister,* one of the most highly esteemed politicians in the land. "You are hearing many dialogues," he said. "You must be very confused."

"The symposium is not exactly a Socratic one," I said. Kanellopoulos smiled. He was a thin, debonairly handsome man wearing a blue pinstripe suit. A former professor of political science, he was known for his coolly Aristotelian logic. George Katsimbalis called him "the only gentleman in Greek politics," and George Theotokas said of him, "He is the Hamlet of Greece—an aristocratic intellectual torn between his humane logic and his loyalty to the right-wing party of which he is leader. He is a first-rate, honest politician and a torn, unhappy human being." In his youth Kanellopoulos had been a revolutionary, a political prisoner on an island of exile. In those days he and his most powerful rival, George Papandreou, had been close friends. When Papandreou was prime minister in the first postwar government, Kanellopoulos had been his deputy minister; a year later he had himself been prime minister. In September 1965, after the "July crisis," King Constantine had asked the two old friends to join forces in a new government but an agreement between them could not be reached.

"It is not Papandreou's fault that he is a danger to our land," said Kanellopoulos. "His charismatic influence, which one hears so much about, certainly exists. It has also brought him Communist support. At least half of the crowds that he draws are Communist."

"I was not aware," I said, "that there are so many Communists in Greece."

Speaking intensely, his dark eyes flashing, Kanellopoulos said, "Our youth clubs, among which Papandreou is very popular, are Communist.

---

* Kanellopoulos was to be prime minister once more, in April 1967, at the time of the military junta take-over. Because of his courageous criticism of the new regime he was placed under arrest.

It is impossible for youth to follow a middle party like the Center Union. Youths are extremists. They follow Papandreou because they are Communists. Communism becomes a threat because of those who accept its help."

I said that if Communism existed to the degree which he insisted—which I did not believe—it was because of the failure of Greece's successive governments to meet the social needs of an underprivileged population, and I pointed out that in the United States Communism was not a serious political problem because of the American government's adaptation to the needs of social change. Kanellopoulos disagreed, saying, "Communism in Greece is not a result of economy. In Cyprus where the economy is five times better than in Greece, thirty-five per cent of the people are Communists. Our Communism is part of a great international campaign and the enemy must be fought, just like any other invaders into our borders.

"Papandreou," he went on, "has always been a very vain man who cannot bear to hear anything but good about himself. This personality defect has increased with age and keeps him from being the leader he would like to be. He has always to be on stage center, it is his driving force. Perhaps, now in his last years, this is enough, perhaps it is no longer important to him that he win an election, perhaps he does not really wish for one. As long as he can be a martyr, a hero, he is fulfilled. And this is far easier out of office, than in."

There was, I suspected, truth to what Kanellopoulos was saying. If he was Hamlet, there was indeed, a touch of Polonius about Papandreou. I tried to imagine a dialogue between the two old friends, a dialogue that would never take place.

At the garden party I met an economist from the United States Embassy, and on the condition that he would remain anonymous, he invited me to see him. I went next day.

I said to him that everywhere I had been, in Crete, in Macedonia, in Epirus and the Peloponnese, the people were clamoring for an election and everywhere the people were blaming American influence because no election was being held. I asked if there were truth to the rumors.

"The Embassy policy is one of passivity," he said, "of sitting it out. The weak, corrupt and decrepit government now in power is buying time which is absolutely necessary to save the crown. A semblance of government is, of course, better than no government. What the United States wants in Greece is a government that will be friendly to us, which will look warmly on NATO and which will have stability and effective leadership. If there had been an election this year, it would have been an overwhelming victory for Papandreou. This would have been a disaster. The army would support the King and civil war would result. Stefanopoulos is a puppet, but as long as the Papandreou party attacks him, the heat is off the King. Of course, there must be elections eventually but the longer they can be delayed, the less acute will be the situation.

"Papandreou's personal charm wins you. He has charisma, that mystical hold over people which is the strength of great leaders, leaders like Venizelos, Roosevelt, Churchill and Kennedy. He articulates all the vague yearnings, the aspirations of the Greek people. More than anyone else he is aware of the needs of the common man. He has consciously tried to lead his backward people into the twentieth century. A good example is his program for free education. He tried to raise Greek education up to European standards, to make it compulsory through the ninth grade, to raise teachers' and professors' salaries. Unfortunately, he is no longer the man to follow through, he is no longer capable of action. I admire him and like him more than anyone in Greek politics. But unfortunately, he has come twenty years too late.

"The plan is to ride out the crisis until George Papandreou dies, or at least until he and his son can be discredited, until the attitudes about them can be changed. The Aspida affair, with its purpose of suggesting Andreas as guilty of treason, is part of the effort to diminish the popular support of the Center Union. In the past winter the old man has deteriorated visibly, his health has failed."

I said, "If Papandreou were to die before an election, isn't it possible that the people will blame those who opposed him for his death and the national grief will help elect the son? Why not let him be elected? Wouldn't it be better for the country than to continue martyring him, making him a hero?"

"Perhaps," was the reply. "But the hope is that with Papandreou's death, the factions within the Center Union will come to odds and the party will fall apart. The death watch seems to be a fact. I look to the future with gloom and see nothing decisive ahead for a long time."

Of all the leaders whom I had hoped to meet in Greece, the only one I had not seen was George Papandreou. A visit with him was arranged by his daughter-in-law, Margaret Papandreou. On the morning of the day I was to see him she telephoned. "I'm sorry," she said. "He doesn't feel well and he's simply not up to it. He was good for a day and he did too many things and tired himself out. He's so old and his strength is so slow in returning. I'm terribly disappointed. It would have been a good experience for both of you."

XXX

The Valkyries
and the Minotaur

The scene was the beach of Rhodes' Hotel des Roses, where I'd just finished my swim. Beside me two beauties in bikinis appeared to be asleep.

A lean youth in dark glasses about twenty years old broke away from his companion down by the water, loped up the sands and circled the maids lying spread-eagle, their long blonde hair fanning out in Medusa ripples. He hovered over them, lighting a cigarette. They pretended not to notice. Discouraged, the youth flipped his cigarette at their feet and rejoined his friend.

In a moment the other accepted the challenge and started up the slope. Short and muscular, he stopped a moment to arrange his swimming trunks, taking care to give himself a Brueghel codpiece profile. Taking an offensive stance beside the unresponsive naiads, he began to whistle softly, all the time moving in a circle around the delicious bodies, flexing his knees in vaguely sexual movements. For a half hour he danced patiently around them like a rutting pigeon, or a partridge.

Finally one of the girls opened an eye.

"Hallo," said the youth, flashing white teeth. "You are Swedish?"

The answer was yes.

"How do you like Rodhos? Is beautiful, no?" The second girl opened her eyes. "You have friends on Rodhos?" Down by the water the other boy watched.

"Oh, yes," said the first girl. "We have friends."

"Grik friends?" The young man went into a series of poses, flexing his biceps, turning his body to show the knobby contour of his groin. "You think I am handsome?"

The girls burst into laughter. Making sure their bras were secure, they sat up. Confident now of victory, the boy said, "I am also very nice for dancing." He demonstrated a few steps. His companion came bounding. "Is my friend Stavros. You like to make dancing tonight, you like we show you Rodhos?"

Variations of this little comedy were repeated on Rhodes beaches many times each day. The youths were members of an association called "The Hundred Parrots" because its members followed more or less the same conversational gambit. Their organizational purpose was "to render service to our single beautiful visitors."

The god of Rhodes is Helios, the Sun. The first inhabitants, sons of Helios and the nymph Rhoda, were known as Heliades. In Hellenistic times the Rhodians called their island "Heliousa," and each year they flung four horses and a chariot into the sea for Helios' use. Their celebrated Colossus was a statue to the Sun God. The young Julius Caesar, Augustus, Tiberius and Cicero all made carefree student visits to the sun island.

The young were still coming, 130,000 a year, to the island of the sun. A majority of the pilgrims were young women from offices and shops in the cold cities of the north. "They come," said my Greek guide, Xenagos, a veteran parrot, "for the sun and they come for the sons of the sun."

The modern Heliades are ready. The obsession to please lady tourists surges like lava through the blood of the entire male population, regardless of age, whether married or not. "The men of Rhodes go about like dogs and the wives wear horns a meter long," said a mother of three, extending her hands above her head as far as they could reach. Xenagos boasted, "In the customhouse, Socrates, an old watchman, is getting girl friends all the time who send him presents from Stockholm."

The parrots, who held frequent council, made certain that every beach was patrolled. Their favorite stretch was the half mile from the municipal bathhouse, past the des Roses, to the aquarium promontory. Over this they loped with persistence, showing off their bodies by leaping about with a beach ball, taking running dives into the breakers, and sliding over the waves on surfboards. They sought girls in bikinis because "they are easier." Nights they roared about on motorcycles and scooters, making ports of call in all the places tourists frequent, and when they were successful they zoomed away, skirts and blonde hair flowing from the seats behind them, like lusty centaurs carrying their prey on their backs.

They believed their services to female tourists "help tourism." Xenagos explained, "Every happy young lady who flies to the north fulfilled tells her friends at home what a good time she had. Next the friends come and then more friends. It seems that the men up there in Sweden are very cold. That's why their women come to us to be warmed."

The evidence would bear him out. Though visitors came from Germany, Switzerland, England and the United States, most were Scandinavian. In the high season Rhodes was virtually a Swedish colony. Menus and shop signs were printed in Swedish—and sometimes Danish. Because Rhodes was one of the most distant of Greece's islands, most visitors came by air. In 1958 when Rhodes had a half-dozen hotels, a Stockholm travel agent flew five hundred Swedes to the sun island. Last year some eighty charter flights arrived each week from Sweden and Denmark. Rhodes had sixty hotels and more were being built at the rate of ten a year. The most popular resort in Greece, Rhodes' tourism was its only industry.

Not all the traffic between Stockholm and Rhodes was one-way. The polarity of north and south resulted in one of the most successful exchange programs in the world. About a thousand male Rhodians were in Sweden, many as guests of ladies. Said Xenagos, "Sweden collects all the good boys from Rhodes. One of our most famous lovers has left his wife and children to go with a rich old Swedish lady. Now his children will die from hungerness."

A capsule of Rhodian history may not be necessary for the northern ladies' enjoyment of an extravagantly beautiful island, but I found it a help. In the prehistoric period the island was settled by Minoan Cretans, and before the Trojan War by colonists from Attica and the Peloponnese. About 1100 B.C. the militant Dorians built three cities named Ialysus, Camirus and Lindus, all of which became centers of maritime trade. In 408 B.C. the three cities united to build a new capital, Rhodes, on the northern point of the island. The geographer Strabo called it the most beautiful city in the Graeco-Roman world. The 105-foot-high Colossus took twelve years to build and stood only fifty-six years before an earthquake tumbled it into the harbor in 227 B.C. In 89 B.C. Rhodes surrendered to Rome. Five centuries later it fell to the Byzantines. In 1309 the island was sold to the militant order of the Knights of St. John. For two centuries the knights resisted Turkish attacks, capitulating finally in 1523 to Suleiman the Magnificent. For almost four centuries Rhodes was a Turkish province. In 1912 the Italians captured it and in 1948, after more than two thousand years, Rhodes was finally reunited with Greece.

Most of the modern town was built by the Italians. Believing in his final monomania that he was descended from the knights, Mussolini restored the old town and built the new as a seignorial retreat for his retirement. The result is not Greek at all, but Italian, with a gracious use of space and light around the waterfront. Government buildings and a theater are in Mussolini's drab neoclassic style, but they are of a neutral color and one is hardly aware of them. The fact that I found the port area beautiful distressed Xenagos. "To restore something not as original is to destroy it," he said. "The Italian barbarians destroyed everything."

A chauvinist Rhodian, Xenagos never, during the week that he accompanied me about the island, stopped talking. The nickname meant "guide," or literally, "he who shows around a foreigner." He was tall for a Greek, with a long square jaw and dark mournful eyes. He was a smeller. His tilted nose, sniffing like a setter's, established the presence of roses, bougainvillaea, hibiscus, jasmine and all the floral myriad of Rhodes. His favorite flower was *angelika,* the mock orange blossom which drenched the town in swooning scent. "If you put out your tongue," he said, "you can taste the smells." As a tour guide on Greek ships, Xenagos had been to America, where he had learned English.

My tour began with the knights' old town, a large medieval quarter inside a fortification of towers and ramparts. The heavy Gothic buildings overlayed with influences from the knights' native lands—Norman, Venetian, Byzantine and Tudor—fuse into a strongly masculine fortification style suitable for knights. Light playing on the squares and streets turns them gold in the sun and gray-mauve in the shadows. The cobbled street of the knights, lined by the inns of the "tongues" or ethnic knight groups, rises at the top to the Grand Master's Palace. Everything I found impressive in the palace—high-arched halls, alabaster windows, a sculptured frieze of the Annunciation—sent Xenagos into a rage. "See what the Italians have accomplished with their vulgarity," he mumbled. The only details to which he gave approval were some mosaic floors which the restorers had moved from the island of Kos. "*They* danced on them," he said.

The knights' compound also contains the old Turkish town and here Xenagos led me through a labyrinth of narrow streets, past domes and minarets, markets, fountains and a sauna bath. From under arches and flying buttresses young girls in loose shifts without undergarments smiled and beckoned. Xenagos' ribaldries sent them into skirls of laughter. "Ever since our ten years of war with Troy over a woman, Greeks are afraid of women," he said. "We know is better to fight a hundred devils than one woman. What we learned is that women must be like slaves, kept always below." I asked if he had a family and he said, "I have only one mother and that is quite enough."

We toured Rhodes' three ancient cities. Of Ialysus, on a high hill fourteen kilometers from Rhodes, little remains. There are some excavations of a temple of Athena and a fourteenth-century Franciscan monastery in which a group of adjoining chapels of various shapes were like a cluster of golden flowers. To the east we looked across eight miles of sea to the mountains of Anatolia. "Was once same, Turkey and Rhodes," said Xenagos. "Came earthquake and broke off." The hill was covered with cedar and cypress. "The cypress which are pointed are males," said Xenagos. "Those that are round with skirts are ladies. They come to contact and have babies. The cedars can't have babies. A change of climate has turned them all widows. When die is finished with cedars in Rhodes."

From Ialysus to Camirus, the distance was "thirty kilometers beeflight." On a winding coast road it was somewhat further. The day was bright and warm. Xenagos, who was driving our rented car, sniffed the air and said, "Be glad you are here. Is now in London eleven degrees, in Stockholm twelve, in Zurich thirteen, and in New York forty-nine." His passion for such detail had developed during his service on cruise ships. We passed fields of vegetables lying wilted on the earth. "Was big windstorm last week," he said. "I don't know the reason but Apollo is angry with us. We shall not eat fruit this year, we shall not eat tomatoes and cucumbers. The people cannot pay the Agriculture Bank, the Bank will take the land and the people will go to Australia."

We were passing through a village called Paradhissi. "Is a place to fall in love. The women are the most beautiful in Rhodes." He drove slowly, "to estimate the girls." None appeared. "They have a bad custom," said Xenagos. "They always stay in their houses." He sniffed. "If you pay attention you can perhaps smell them." He began a curious tale of a friend who struck an old woman of the town with his car. "She was a Turkish woman sitting down in the street, eighty-three years old. No bones broken, no bleeding. Next day she died of frightening. She was frightening to die so she was fighting the death so hard she died from tiredness. Is now a trial. Very bad for my friend. They say he wants to kill Turks."

Camirus, excavated by Italian archaeologists in this century, lies on a green slope facing the sea. There are ruins of a Doric temple, an agora, a colonnade, some Hellenistic houses and a series of sacrificial altars. Xenagos was fascinated by the wells and the plumbing. "It was once healthy to drink the natural waters. Today is all suffering from the kidneys and I don't know what because the water is no more natural." The desolate ruins had a haunting melancholy quality. Birds sang. The ripe heads of wild oats showed hoary white between the rocks and on a path by the sea a woman was leading a walking haystack with a donkey inside. "Was very flourishing, very beautiful city," said Xenagos. "But cities happen like people. If successful and famous will die quick. Someone will kill him, like Cassius killed Camirus. He murdered the people, he stole the statues." I was unable to verify in my books that Cassius had destroyed Camirus but it was possible. The record shows him to have plundered ancient Rhodes. "Romans were the worst for Greece," said Xenagos. "We lost two thousand years. That's why we are very back."

From Camirus we crossed the island ("thirty-eight kilometers beeflight") to Lindus, third and most famous of the ancient cities. Women working in the fields wore goatskin leggings as protection against poisonous snakes. Rhodians cherish deer because of their reputation as snake-killers —a bronze statue of an antlered buck stands in the harbor. The men were gathered in village cafés. "Men kings, women slaves," said Xenagos. "The right way, like the Bible says. In cities it is different. Men must work to keep their lazy women in the houses. Very bad for civilization."

We entered a rock canyon and there, suddenly, before us lay Lindus and the sea. The cramped plaza was jammed with excursion buses— beyond it no car could enter. The modern town in a bowl-shaped valley is a complex of tourist shops. Walking over the pebble-mosaicked lanes, we passed women in doorways softly pleading for us to buy pottery, embroidered blouses, lace and knitted woolens. "Like beggars," said Xenagos, hurrying past. "It is a disgrace." We hired donkeys and joined a caravan of tourists snaking upward toward the ancient city.

Silhouetted on the crest of a bluff against the blue sea, the acropolis is a stunning sight. The stairway and colonnade, familiar from hundreds of photographs, lead to a plateau which is taken up by a temple of Athena with its propylaea, and a theater carved in rock. On the edge, like a précis of history, was a Byzantine church, a castle of the knights and some Turkish fortifications. The effect, unfortunately, was diminished by throngs of tourists filling the area like a market place, following like sheep after female guides outshouting one another in Swedish, Danish, German and French, and by hundreds of photographers focusing on the familiar ruins. "A circus!" grumbled Xenagos.

We descended on foot over spotless pebbled streets which rolled like waves on the sea. From a courtyard mosaicked in stars and flowers a toothless old woman in black shouted, *"Ich bin Mama Lindos. Ich habe das aelteste Haus in Lindos."* At the bottom we visited a Byzantine church in which the human frenzy was duplicated in lively primitive frescoes covering every inch of wall, like a holy comic paper.

Returning up the west coast to Rhodes we passed Mt. Tsambika, on the summit of which is a monastery about which Xenagos told me a legend. "All the ladies who cannot have babies go barefoot up the mountain and spend the night praying. Many babies made this way. Is why so many boys on Rhodes is named Tsambikos and so many girls Tsambika. Naturally everyone is wondering. There must be a very strong young monk up there." At the foot of the mountain there was a beach on which "the Swedes go nudist."

We made our last stop at a deserted mineral spa called Kallithea. This time I agreed with Xenagos—the colonnades spread over a lunar landscape of black lava were a colossal monument to bad taste. Fountains were dry; pools rank. Arcades contained rows of toilet stalls marked first and second class. The waters were highly laxative; in its heyday the spa had been an excretory carnival. "An Italian idea," said Xenagos, sniffing the *angelika* blossoms. "Is now popular only with bees. From here comes the best honey in the world."

The next day was Xenagos' thirtieth birthday. Nicholas Sarri, one of Rhodes' thirty-five travel agents, invited us to cruise on his forty-five-foot schooner, the *Trident*. Sarri was owner of Rhodes' best restaurant, a pavilion floated on pontoons in the harbor, called The Kon-Tiki. We sailed at eight o'clock with thirty-two passengers, mostly Swedes. Xenagos mournfully reflected on birthdays. "I am not happy, I am not dancing," he wailed. "Is like an old man I am feeling, thinking only is another less year in my life." He had been up most of the night in a nightclub called "Rhodes by Night." "Very crazy," he said. "Drunk Swedes were flapping around like fish." He and a married friend had taken two Swedish girls to greet the sunrise on the aquarium beach. "Is best place. Always on one side not windy. When wind changes you change to other side."

On deck an Aphrodite in a green bathing suit, legs curled under her as if she'd just risen from the sea, was combing her long blonde strands. "In Sweden it is always so cold," she said. "Right now there are three meters of snow." She was Karin Persson, twenty-three years old, from Malmö, and had lived for two years in Rhodes where she was employed by a travel agency to greet tourists. "Swedes are more materialistic than Greeks," she said. "In Sweden life is only hard work and all the money goes to the government. Here life is casual. The Greeks are friendlier; they make you feel human."

"Greek people speak from the heart," said a thin blond man, a Stockholm television producer named Åke Starck. "In Sweden we are always so cold and serious. Look at us now, look what the Greeks do to us."

On the deck a ship's mechanic named Michalis was playing a guitar and three blond men were dancing in the Greek fashion. From below deck came the sounds of singing and hand clapping. Karin Persson dove into the turquoise waters and swam off like a fish. A dozen men leaped after her and soon splashing pink bodies filled the sea. We dropped anchor near some cliffs where the climax of *The Guns of Navarone* had been filmed. Bottles of *ouzo* appeared and trays of *mezédes*. Xenagos remembered past birthdays. "On my eighteenth birthday I met an English woman forty years old, owns many factories in Birmingham. She gave me much to drink and magazines with naked girls to make me hot. For two months every day she was putting in my pocket four and five quid. I was collecting a lot of money. Now I am thirty I have to pay, I have to buy the drinks. To fish you have to throw bait into the sea."

Our next port of call was in a beachcomber's cove named Kolimbia where we lunched on freshly grilled fish, and a great deal of wine. After the meal, a fisherman's wife, a small dark woman, played *bouzouki* records on a phonograph and led a serpentine line of Scandinavians wearing bathing suits in a leaping Rhodian dance called the *sousta*. On deck the *Trident*'s Greek crew, smoking cigarettes, watched the northern antics. A young Danish woman confessed that her charter flight was returning to Copenhagen that night. "There is so much snow I will not be able to find my car at the airport," she said. As gifts to friends she was taking four boxes of Rhodian strawberries.

On another day Xenagos took me to some inland villages. Of Rhodes' sixty-four thousand people, twenty-seven thousand are in the town and the rest are scattered in fifty villages. The roads, engineered by Italians, were the best of their kind in Greece. In Tholós, the first village, a produce peddler was selling oranges on the square while making a public speech against the fruit cartel that required him to go to Rhodes to buy oranges grown in Tholós to sell in Tholós. "Everything is a sickness," said Xenagos. "The three hundred men in the concilium [parliament] say they work for a better life for us. The only better life is to go to Germany or Australia." We visited a house abandoned three months before by a family emigrating to Canada. The windowless single room had an earthen floor and shelf beds. It was shown to us by the family's eldest daughter, a winsome brunette twenty years old named Tsambika, who lived nearby with her husband. Her mother, said Xenagos, had precipitated her conception with a pilgrimage to the mountain peak for which she was named.

We met hunters with guns stalking hares, partridges and woodcocks. "Rhodian hunters are bad sportsmen," said Xenagos. "They put glue on trees so birds cannot fly away." We passed through a pine forest and Xenagos, raising his nose, said, "Very dry, very nice. Smell! You must learn to understand nature with your nose."

Our next stop was in Embona, a windy village on a ledge of Rhodes' highest mountain, Attaviros. On the square men were slaughtering lambs for the feast of St. George next day. We called on an elfin old widow named Stamata Kounaki who was wearing her anti-snake goatskin leggings. Her house, one of the best in town, had a ceiling of cypress bark and olive branches. One whitewashed wall was covered with old plates. "Wedding plates," said the widow. "My marriage lasted four days and we needed many plates." Other walls were covered with family photographs and religious icons, among which were scattered photographs of Elvis Presley, a deity favored by three adolescent granddaughters. The room was furnished with hand-carved chests, a loom and a shelf bed under which there was a bin for wine, oil and vegetables. Doughnut-shaped pastries called *koulouria* were festooned on ropes from the ceiling and the widow filled our pockets with them.

The stinging high wind had driven everyone indoors and the streets were deserted. Men huddled in cafés. Scattered among the rows of white houses were dwellings brightly painted in blue, green, pink, and yellow, and combinations of these colors. "A colored house," said Xenagos, "means a daughter is looking for a husband. When the girl is engaged the house will be painted white again." We heard shouting male voices coming from a tailor shop, which we entered. The tailor, a thin nervous man of forty-five years named Chrisostomos Daskalakis, was arguing with his friend, a slight twenty-two-year-old farmer named Ioannis Papamichalis. Embona has no electricity and not a garment or a piece of cloth was visible in the dark little room. On the sewing machine lay a book, *The Virgin of Paris* by Victor Hugo. The tailor turned on me, the American, saying, "The newspapers tell us our government received twenty billion drachmae from your country. I need money to buy cloth. I cannot get a single drachma. Where is the money? Who gets it?" Xenagos had an answer. "It goes to the rich Greek capitalists," he said. "They send it straight to the banks of Switzerland. American aid is not for the poor, it's for the rich."

"It goes to the King and his mother," said the farmer. "Our royalty plays poker with your money."

"Does the money open a factory or a hospital?" the tailor went on. "No. It goes to the friends of the ministers. It would be better for us if all the concilium were dropped like cats in a net into the sea."

"American money goes to the police," said the farmer. "We are full up with gendarmes and police, one gendarme to a person."

"I wish with all my heart the Americans would send no more money," said Xenagos. "Is better for us to stop. Why steal money from the poor people of the U.S. to give to the rich men of Greece?"

They went on, indulging their Greek paranoia by translating national issues into personal terms. "Do you know the salary and expenses of the King and his family?" the farmer asked. I was looking at faded newspaper photos of King Paul and Queen Frederika pasted to a wall. "Same as England," the farmer shouted. "A poor country cannot afford it. You know how many roses at the wedding of Princess Sofia? A million! We break our backs carrying stones to pay for a million roses."

"You in America are a democracy," said the tailor. "You have no royal family. They tell us we have a democracy. How can that be? Must be a kingdom *or* a democracy."

"*Demokratia* was born in Greece," said Xenagos. "We gave the light to the world but we are dark."

"*Demokratia!*" The farmer, who had visited Czechoslovakia, spat on the floor. "Communism is the only democracy. In Czechoslovakia no one is so poor and no one is so rich as in Greece."

The tailor disagreed. "I cannot forget the old customs and traditions," he said calmly. "Rather than be a Communist I would end my life."

We left to seek some food. A man was running across the square at a diagonal, dragging by tethered front feet, a white kid which ran swiftly on hind feet, and was followed by some children and a dog. With horror I sensed what was going to happen. The man stopped in the center of the square, waiting for the children to catch up. He took a sharp blade from his belt and with one swoop sliced the kid's throat. Blood spurted over the stones. The goat kicked and gurgled, trying pitifully to rise. With another thrust the man severed the neck. The white legs on the headless body continued to lash the air and the flexed white tail twitched. The children, closing a circle, watched the dog's tongue lick the blood from the stones. No longer thinking of food, we got into the car and drove away.

At Chorion, a dusty cluster of hovels clinging to a mountainside, a small boy walking ahead announced us like a town crier, shouting, "*Amerikani! Amerikani!*" and three idiots followed, grunting, gesticulating, sputtering saliva. Half of the villagers were in Germany and Australia, Xenagos said, and only the indigent poor remained.

In the next town, Sianni, a new orange-colored American tractor stood outside the church. A thin old man scurried across the square, saying "Hello, hello. I am happy to welcome an American." His name was Anastasi Hagi; in 1907 when he was twelve years old he had gone with his father to Alaska to mine gold. The father died and the boy lived on a farm in California until 1919 when he returned to Rhodes to marry. In a small café which he owned he served us beer, cheese, salami and more *koulouria*. "Sianni is a town of old people," he said. "The young are in Australia and America." On the table were some back

issues of the New York *Times* and the Hartford *Courant,* sent him by
relatives. Two hundred Siannese were living in Hartford and in Tacoma,
Washington, he said. Dancing about, bringing more beer and an Edam
cheese from a back room, he recited the capitals of the United States,
including Alaska's and Hawaii's. "Ah, America! A good happy land,"
he said. "Greece is poor and unhappy." When we left he begged me to
send him Americans to Sianni to provide him with English conversation.

We drove on. A yellow and black snake curled in our path was one
of Rhodes' poisonous vipers. The mountains were covered with wild roses,
which some scholars believe are the traditional symbol of Rhodes. Others
say Rhodes' symbolic "roses" are really the hibiscus, still others the
pomegranate blossom. We descended into a long green valley toward
the western sea, and stopped at a tiny green-shaded village called Vathi.
At some café tables under bamboo thatching, men were playing cards.
Others read newspapers or silently fingered worry beads. Two women,
their mouths covered with scarves, were carrying hay on their backs.
"Is a tradition not to show teeth," said Xenagos. "You communicate with
girls only with eyes. You do not see mouth until you marry. Then you
can kiss her, and if she has no teeth it is too late."

We took a table and ordered some *ouzos.* When the café owner
discovered I was an American he sent his young son to spread the news.
Soon local *Amerikani* began to appear. The first was Steff Athanassiou,
a retired seventy-year-old Baltimore millworker who had just returned
to his home town after fifty years to spend the summer. After two weeks,
he was homesick for Baltimore. "It's too quiet here," he complained.
"No people, no movies, no TV. Houses are empty—the people have
gone to Germany, Australia, the U.S. No one works the land. All my
life I've looked forward to this and now I'm lonely."

A gray-bearded priest bustled up, fingering his beads like a rosary.
"How do you do," he said, "I am John Pappas. Was section foreman
fifteen years on Chicago Burlington Railways. I had one hundred men
under my jurisdiction. Came back to find better and found worse. Americans nice people, polite. Better than Greeks." He had a daughter in
Waterville, Connecticut, and five sons, all schoolteachers in Rhodes. One
was there in the café, reading a newspaper. A third man, thin and bald,
arrived and began, "Hi, fella. I was cameraman in Hollywood. Mary
Pickford, Tom Mix, Charlie Chaplin were my friends. I suppose is all
dead now." Only Tom Mix, I said. "Say hello to Mary Pickford for me,"
he said. "Tell her Mike the Greek wishes he'd never left."

We hurried back to Rhodes to keep an appointment with the mufti,
spiritual leader of Rhodes' twenty-five hundred Turks. The Moslem enclave of mosques, tombs and the mufti's residence was in an old Turkish

cemetery directly across the street from my hotel. The mufti padded up behind us in felt slippers, meeting us under an ancient sycamore tree. He was a frail, very old gray-bearded little man who leaned on the shoulder of a slant-eyed boy. He was wearing a black turban and a black sweater over a gray flannel shirt. "Welcome," he greeted us softly in Greek. "Do you know my friend Durrell?" he asked. I did not, but I had read of the mufti in Durrell's book on Rhodes. A gentle merriment shone from the old eyes. Padding softly in his slippers, using the boy as a cane, he led us through a garden to the funeral mosque of Mourat Reis, a Turkish admiral who died in a battle with pirates at the age of ninety. "He won the battle, even though he died," said the mufti. Inside the octagonal mosque an elevated sarcophagus was covered with a Turkish flag. Around the mosque were the tombs of four of the admiral's officers, and in the cemetery 150 Moslem graves were marked by stone columns carved with a variety of funeral hats to indicate social status, military rank and professions during the life of the buried corpses. High-crowned hats marked generals, turbans indicated sultans, prime ministers and a shah of Iran as well as poets. Thistle-blossom-shaped fezzes stood over the graves of ordinary men. Corpses were buried upright, facing east toward Mecca. As we walked through the cemetery, the mufti stopped several times and bent down, as if performing a religious rite. "Sometimes you find fresh eggs," he said, laughing. "The chickens come to lay." The cemetery was also a retreat for lovers, which made it necessary to lock the gates at night.

He asked us to remove our shoes and we followed him into a richly carpeted softly-lit mosque where the old man read from the Koran a hymn of praise to the olive tree, provider of man's food, oil for light, fuel for warmth, and shade from the sun's hot rays. Though the language was strange, the old man's voice swelled like bird song.

We dined that night in a Turkish restaurant outside Rhodes called Regep Spartali. Xenagos ordered a variety of roasted meats and salads, including *dzadziki,* cucumbers in yoghurt with garlic and dill. There was also a repertoire of Rhodian wines including an excellent rosé called "Chevalier de Rhodes." From another room we heard the merriment of a wedding party. "Is everyone hurrying to marry in April," said Xenagos. "Last Sunday was ten weddings in St. John's Church. Reason is we do not marry in May. May is month when donkeys make love so is considered bad luck for people." At the next table a Swedish couple in a frolicsome mood were dining with a young Rhodian. "Tonight the wife will make to bed with the Greek," said Xenagos. "Perhaps the husband also. Very agreeable in these matters, Swedish husbands." He showed me a note which had arrived that day in his office. "Please have a little

time for me tonight," I read. "I am so sorry with yesterday. Exquise!
Exquise! Inge."

"She wants an octopus," said Xenagos. "A lover with many hands."
He sighed. "I am a tired old man. I think tonight I will close this book."
Driving back to town, he continued about his experiences. "Swedish
women is not for trusting," he said. "I have a girl for fifteen days and
when she go back to Lund she write, 'You are my dream, my lover,
my chevalier.' One day comes my friend, a Turk named Tunz with a
letter from Sweden and he asks, 'Can you read?' I have great surprise.
Is from my girl friend. I am reading, 'You are my dream, my chevalier.'
He have her all day when I work and I have her after nine P.M. And
always she was saying I was her fucktotem."

At the edge of town we stopped at a cottage, the home of Xenagos'
friend and nighttime companion, a longshoreman named George. A tall
large-framed woman with deep breasts and flashing green eyes came to
the door. "He is gone," she said. "Off like a ram with the sheep." The
sight of Xenagos seemed to upset her. "This morning he came home at six
o'clock. Working in the harbor, he says. I know the work he does in the
harbor. All day he slept and tonight he could hardly wait to eat, so
busy is he in the harbor." Turning to me, she said, "In the summer
the women of Rhodes have no love. Always we are praying that no
Swedish woman will take our husband."

I asked Xenagos what would happen if a cuckolded Rhodian wife
went with a tourist male. Almost swerving the car from the road, he
said, "It would be an earthquake."

The next day, my last on Rhodes, was my birthday. To celebrate,
Xenagos took me to the nightclub outside of town, Rhodes by Night.
It was an eerily cheerless complex of grottoes with artificial green and
black stalactites lit with colored lights intended to represent a cave-age
cavern. Ironically it might also have been a bizarre air-raid shelter. The
underground revelries were appropriately primitive. A deafening din of
rock 'n' roll filled the caves. Gold- and silver-haired girls wearing blue
jeans, stretch pants or miniskirts, swayed and quivered in the arms of
sweating dark satyrs in blue jeans and open shirts, who were usually
shorter than their partners and frequently younger. Youths without girls
watched from tables, feasting their eyes on the fair ones. At the next
table three young Swedes also watched and one of them said, "For us
Rhodes is not very amusing. Our girls will not dance with us, only with
Greeks."

My own eyes were across the room on a solitary beauty alone at a
table. She was tall and high-breasted with neat slender legs, and she
wore an aqua dress which covered her knees in soft folds. Her hair was

a cloud of gold, her eyes were blue, and her skin had the pink freshness of film stars I had loved in my childhood. With dismay I noted she was chewing gum. Even so in the grotto of troglodytes and spastic nymphs she was an enchanted princess.

I wanted to ask her to dance but shyness held me back and she was swept away in the arms of a dark-jowled satyr. It was just as well. The dance was a wild *bostella*. Girls shimmied abandonedly, their limbs, hair and breasts dispersing like exploding rockets, and the youths, trying to match the silver sprites, jerked like puppets. My tall beauty was arching her back, trying to escape the pressure of a gigantic ring which her partner pressed into the small of her back. Unsuccessful, she remained pinioned.

The next dance was a tango. "I was not thinking Americans were so meek," said Xenagos. Spurred by his taunts and by drink, I leaped up and won the race to the coveted one.

"May I have the pleasure . . ." The words sounded absurd. I wondered what the young Greeks said.

She lifted her eyes and appraised me. "I'm sorry!" The voice was flat. "My feet are tired."

Drunk, desperately self-pitying, I pulled the stops. "It's my birthday," I said.

She looked at me coldly through narrowed eyes. "Well, happy birthday," she said, chewing her gum, glancing past me at an approaching young man. Before I could return to my table she was on the floor with the interloper.

Xenagos commiserated. "To dance with a Swedish girl you must be dark, have the intestines of a bull and no politeness," he said. "And you must be young. Not old like you and me."

Outside the night glittered with stars. A plane hummed overhead, beginning its spiraled descent. Xenagos sighed. "More snow princesses coming for melting by the Minotaur," he said. "No wonder we are in trouble."

XXXI

A Royal Journey

My host at the Plaka luncheon was a secretary from the Foreign Ministry, a tense nervous young man named Elias who spoke bad English with a stammer. When he guided the conversation to the subject of the King, I had the uneasy suspicion that the purpose of our meeting was an exploration of my political attitudes. Cautiously I described my pleasant impressions of the King at the Easter egg-cracking. I spoke of the King's youth, adding that he would have many years in which to mature and grow.

Apparently I passed muster. At the end of the lunch Elias said the King was preparing to make a week-long journey through towns and villages in Macedonia, and he invited me to join the tour's press corps. He would himself go along as interpreter. "You will be able to see how the King is loved, how he is adored," said Elias.

I received a detailed English-language itinerary. Except for names of the towns there was little variation in the daily schedule. A typical day read:

9:00   Depart Thessaloniki for Edessa.
11:30   Arrive Edessa. Go to church. Presentation to authorities.
          Her Majesty, the Queen, visits children's station.
1:30   Lunch with Mayor.
3:00   Depart for Veria.
4:30   Arrive Veria. Go to church. Presentation to authorities.
          Her Majesty visits Christ's Mother's children's station.
6:00   Reception with Mayor.
6:30   Depart for Thessaloniki.

Departure date was Monday, May 9. The evening before, Elias phoned to make sure I would be at the Foreign Office at 6 A.M. When I arrived a few minutes before six the offices were deserted except for two char-women, their feet bound in wet rags. They were scrubbing the floor by hopping over it in curious rabbit steps.

In five minutes Elias appeared. Thirty-five journalists, most of them photographers, were loading into a bus which filled narrow Zalokosta Street. Scattered among them were a few seasoned old-timers but most were young and a few appeared to be boys. Wearing unmatched jackets and trousers and dark sports shirts without ties, they looked like sports reporters on their way to a soccer match. I was the only foreigner.

Elias sat beside me. He explained that the bus was taking us to the Eleusis military air base where a plane was waiting to fly us to Thes-saloniki. The King and Queen would follow in a royal plane. From Thessaloniki the King would drive his own car and we would follow him in a chartered bus. "We try to keep up with the King," he said. "But is difficult. He drives very fast."

The plane was an unpressurized old Dakota C-47. Before we entered it I saw Elias cross himself three times and move his lips in a silent prayer. Revving up on the ground, the plane trembled like a vibrating machine. The pilot made a speech which Elias translated. "We will fly six thousand feet," he said. "It will be a little . . ." At a loss for words Elias made a wobbling motion with his hand. He looked pale.

At seven thirty we took off under gray-bellied clouds, barely clearing a circle of mountain peaks. My ears snapped. Beside me Elias was holding his nose, puffing out his cheeks. We flew out over the Aegean, followed the jagged coastline around snow-covered Olympus which shone coral in the morning sun, and passed over the green plains of Macedonia. On the airfield flags were flying. An army guard and band stood at attention and a flock of sheep grazed along the landing strip. A bus with twenty photographers and reporters from Thessaloniki was waiting for us. Elias herded us aboard, saying, "We must leave before arrives the King because in his car he runs a lot, about 140 kilometers, so we must go ahead to catch him."

We drove into Thessaloniki over Queen Sophia Avenue, which I remembered in September, filled with people to greet George Papandreou. Now it was empty. At a military base along the route some soldiers were standing at attention. At a corner I saw a cluster of persons who, it turned out, were waiting for a bus. Passing through the city, we continued north toward Kilkis, the first town on our itinerary, passing on the way a new jungle of refineries and reservoirs which the King was scheduled to dedicate the next day. It belonged to Esso Pappas, a Standard Oil of

New Jersey subsidiary. We followed a river through green meadows and blazing red fields of poppies. At a village crossroads a small cluster of twenty people and a group of smocked school children, shepherded by teachers, waited to see the King and Queen. Policemen guarded the road. "In any place where there are even a few people naturally he will stop to say hello," said Elias.

I began to read from a sheaf of English-language "Reference Papers" mimeographed by the Foreign Press Office, which Elias had given me.

"My strength lies in my people's love," I read. "As this motto indicates, the Greek Monarchy has an eminently democratic character. Indeed it has always been on the love of the people that the reigning dynasty has based the authority and prestige of the institution of the monarchy. . . ."

I turned a page, and I read, "The King reigns but does not govern. It may be said that the King of the Hellenes is also the Guardian of the Democracy in a country where democracy itself was born and flourished." There followed a biography of the King. "He was sent to Anavryta, a new public school operating on a system that was designed to develop character according to the Platonic principles of education. He read a great deal, developed a fondness for music and learned fluent English and German. He was a member of various teams and clubs and did well in track athletics, gymnastics, sailing and swimming. . . ."

In a village named Petrotón fifty people were waiting under a banner hoisted across the road which said *"Kalos Orissate!"* ("Welcome"). In another called Mendra a cluster of black-robed women were spinning wool beside the road. In Baltoi a banner said *"Zito o Vasilefs"* ("Long live the King"), but no one stood under it. In a field nearby twenty women in bright shirts and white kerchiefs were planting cabbages, paying no attention. As we passed through more and more villages I sensed a depression settling over Elias. "I think everyone has gone to Kilkis to greet the King," he said.

I returned to my papers. "The King is essentially a modern man," I read. "He combines unflagging energy with youthful drive. . . . He keeps himself constantly and thoroughly informed on national and international affairs. . . . He is one of the most accessible of monarchs, always willing to give of his time to others. Whenever possible, he relaxes reading a good book. . . ."

Ahead, at the foot of a wooded hill, lay Kilkis, an agricultural town of twelve thousand persons. Beyond were the dark mountains of Bulgaria. "Here you will see history," said Elias. "In 1912 the King's grandfather, Constantine I, personally led an army which liberated the people from Bulgaria."

We left the bus and began to walk up the main street. It was lined with soldiers, short men with sullen faces, standing five feet apart, armed with sabered guns. A reporter from a left-wing newspaper gleefully pointed out that few people were standing behind the fence of soldiers. A parade of several hundred schoolboys, carrying banners, marched from the south toward the center of the town where an arch of pine boughs with the banner *"Zitosan I Vasilis"* ("Hail to the King and Queen"), was set up. From the north came a similar parade of schoolgirls. Elias seemed cheered by the processions. I asked a general weighted with military decorations how many soldiers were in the lines. "I do not know," he said coldly in English. Smiling sardonically, he added, "I do not know anything that relates to the defense of Greece."

In a roar of motorcycles, the King and Queen arrived, riding alone in a green Mercedes convertible. They stepped from the car and, bowing and smiling to scattered groups, started walking briskly toward the cathedral. Outside a small curious crowd was waiting. Children waved paper flags. I entered the church ahead of the King and found a place behind the altar facing two thrones. The King and Queen entered and were greeted by the metropolitan, a white-bearded old man in gold robes who escorted them to the royal chairs. Assisted by several priests in blue and white vestments, the metropolitan sang a doxology. The Queen, young and lovely in a soft wool suit of canary yellow, listened attentively like a poised American college girl. The King's attention wandered. His cool gaze caught mine and I sensed a recognition, as if he knew who I was. His strong jutting jaw and the hard determination of his mouth and eyes reminded me of a young Richard Nixon.

A driver had brought the King's car to the church. When the service was over the Queen departed with some dignitaries for the orphanage and the King drove to a meeting with the provincial governor and other officials. "They will tell the King what problems they have here," said Elias. The meeting was held in a movie theater currently showing a film of rural lust called *Phovos,* meaning "Fear." Two thrones were set on a platform, under large blowup photographs of the King and Queen. The King sat on the left chair. Alone on the platform he appeared bored and restless. The governor, a large man with a small womanish voice, began a speech, saying "You take the place of your heroic grandfather . . ." In tediously monotonous tones he reviewed the history of the province, reciting its statistics—twenty-two thousand families of 110,000 people, five high schools, twenty-five boy scout troops, on and on. After him came the agricultural director, who said there were thirty-three *stremata* of land cultivated in fruit, cotton and tobacco. His droning voice put me to sleep and when I awoke an engineer was speaking of dams and power plants.

I heard a buzzing and the Queen entered. With quick long strides she paced down the aisle and took her place. With her arrival the King relaxed and seemed at ease. A health officer was speaking of the need for a mental hospital. Throughout the endless speeches the King said not a word and when they were finished he stood up, bowed curtly and with the Queen strode out of the theater. "In this case he did not say anything," said Elias. "But in some cases he asks for information more."

Outside an apathetically silent group of people were gathered about the royal auto caravan. The King and Queen entered the green convertible and roared away between the lines of soldiers. I joined some reporters at lunch in a small tavern. One of them, a middle-aged writer from the magazine *Ikones,* raised a bottle of beer and made an ironic toast. "God save the King!" he said.

On the ride back to Thessaloniki the bus driver turned a radio to a news broadcast of the royal visit, which described enthusiastic crowds and a warm reception. A dark-haired lean young reporter sitting beside me said, "As you can see, truth and myth have little to do with one another. The reception was rather cold. Of course, there *were* the school children, brought by their teachers." The reporter's name was Panagiotis Loudaris and he was from an Athens newspaper which supported the Papandreou Center Union party. "The coldness of the people toward the King is the result of last July," he went on. "The people did not like having their leader thrown out of office." A boy, the youngest member of our group, joined us and said in faultless English, "Greeks are not happy to see all this display of arms. We have suffered too much, we have had too many wars." The reporter's name was Spiros Voulos; he was nineteen years old. His sturdy boyish body and blond hair and fair skin made him seem even younger. He worked for a left-wing newspaper frequently called Communist by the right-wing press. "We see all these parades, all this marching and don't like it," he continued. "We say that the United States is responsible. *They* pay for our army, they need it. We don't."

"The people are against the King for what he did," said Loudaris. "They want elections."

"But Papandreou does not really want elections now," said Voulos. "He knows he is too old and he uses his present situation as a rallying point. His purpose is to groom and prepare his son. Unfortunately, this causes dissension in his own party."

Our next stop was at a new fertilizer plant which the King was to dedicate. Constructed as a joint enterprise by the National Bank of Greece and the French Pechiney–Saint Gobain Company, it stood next to the new Esso Pappas refineries, in the largest industrial development in Greece. A strong wind billowed clouds of fertilizer dust over the area, causing my sinuses to choke and my eyes to burn. Chairs were set up outside the factory for several hundred guests. Among them I recognized German bankers, foreign diplomats and many ministers and deputies from the government. A band was playing. A long red carpet led to two gold thrones and beside it, at an improvised altar, three priests waited, their robes and beards blowing in the wind. One of them was an archbishop from New York.

The King and Queen swerved into the field. More than ever they seemed like a pair of collegiates careening over the countryside in a new sports car. The King, who wore dark glasses, had changed from air force khaki to a blue admiral's uniform. The Queen, in a blue dress and white coat, seemed younger than ever. He kissed the presiding bishop's ring and both were sprayed with holy water from a sprig of basil. The priests intoned, "Long live the King," and the crowd repeated the words. The reception from financiers, industrialists and government officials was warmer than it had been from the people of Kilkis. But even here it seemed more ritualistic than spontaneous. The priests' resonant voices filled the afternoon like a pipe organ, singing, said Voulos, "a doxology for the factory."

During the long speeches my mind and eyes wandered across the fields, to the Greek and American flags flying over the oil refineries and a newly-built plant called "Hellenic Steel Company." Prime Minister Stefanos Stefanopoulos congratulated the French and Greek engineers for their "colossal project," and spoke of the importance of the new factory to the agriculture of Greece. To the southwest the sun was setting behind Olympus in a burst of orange. Around the complex with its acres of reservoirs and stacks like some bizarre city on the moon, sheep grazed in meadows. I watched the sickening gray clouds of dust rising from the place and rolling over the countryside, contaminating the bright Greek light and the sharp Greek air. I could hardly breathe.

Then it was over and everyone rushed pell-mell after the King, racing like demented lemmings through dust so thick it was impossible to see anything, on a hurried inspection tour, after which we gathered under an awning to drink Scotch and stuff ourselves with hors d'oeuvres. Later, entering Thessaloniki, Elias pointed out a statue of Constantine I, mounted on a horse. "See how exactly like the grandfather the King is," he said.

The hotel reserved for the press was a seaside inn in a village twenty miles from Thessaloniki, called Haghia Triada. A cow grazed outside my window and I fell asleep to the wash of the sea. In the morning, just before nine o'clock, Elias called through the door, saying, "We leave in ten minutes, please don't be late." On the bus I rode with the two young reporters, Loudaris and Voulos. My friendship with them, based on language, for they were the only two English-speaking members of our group, was misunderstood by Elias. Assuming I was aligning myself with the anti-royalist left-wing, he turned hostile and petulant. My companions were an amiable pair. The boyish Voulos was especially disarming. "I am happy to have the opportunity to know an American," he said. "In Greece we know your military, your sailors and your marines, and we don't know American civilians. Of course, there are a lot of tourists but their personalities are lost to us. They all seem the same, they are always in a hurry and they do bad deeds. They drink and have crude manners and they make very much noise. They don't care about people. So we don't like Americans, we don't like American thinking and the American way of life. Naturally we are proud and so we have some complex of inferiority because we are so poor."

The driver stopped at a newsstand where we bought the morning papers. In the English-language *Athens News,* I read, "King Konstantine and Queen Anna Marie were given a warm welcome in Kilkis. . . . By the time the Royal Couple reached the city thousands of people had lined the flag-bedecked streets. . . ." From his own newspaper Loudaris translated for me the story he had filed the night before. It began, "The King will not have reason to be especially satisfied with the first day of his campaign in North Greece. Sporadic applause here and there was all that the people offered him. . . ."

We were on our way to still another dedication, that of the new $200,000,000 Esso Pappas industrial complex. For weeks I had heard of preparations for the American-style party arranged by Tom Pappas, a Greek-born Horatio Alger from Boston. His name was well known in Greece. Above the familiar blue and white "Esso" gas station signs across the land, "Pappas" stood out in large letters.

The party was to be the largest public relations affair in Greek history. Four thousand guests, many of them Americans, were invited. Four hundred had sailed to Thessaloniki from Piraeus the night before on a chartered ship. A circus-like fete of bright awnings was set up on a hill facing the jungle of reservoirs, funnels and pipes. Bands played and American flags flapped against blue heavens. A canopy covered two gold thrones, and blue tents shaded tables set with four thousand places. Crowds of kibitzers crowded against a fence. In a press office at the gate hostesses handed out heavy folios of photographs and mimeographed speeches in several languages. Voulos and I found places at a table and I read a biography of Tom Pappas. It began, "He was a few years old when in 1906 the Papadopoulos family emigrated to the United States. In 1924 young Anthony became a United States citizen and changed his name to Thomas A. Pappas. Today he is considered one of the most able and successful businessmen in the United States." A list of eight American corporations of which Tom Pappas was a director followed. I read, "Today's realization of the Esso Pappas industrial complex is the realization of his ardent desire to help the land of his birth."

A peal of brass announced the arrival of the King's convertible. The Queen, in pink, was radiant as a rose. The crowd stood to applaud as they walked to the thrones. Beside me Voulos remained seated. "Considering that these are all rather rich people, the reception is really quite cold," he said. A priest, introduced as "His Eminence, Archbishop Iakovos of North and South America," read from the Gospels, the words, "Ye are the light of the world."

"He is speaking of Pappas," said Voulos.

The archbishop continued, "Let your light so shine before men that they may see your good works and glorify your father who is in heaven."

Tom Pappas mounted a platform facing the King and Queen and, addressing them in Greek, said, "I am an American citizen and proud of it. However, I do not forget that I was born a Greek. I did not come here as an industrialist seeking profit. It was my duty as a Greek to offer something to my country, something that would bear fruit and would constitute a symbol of the possibilities of our nation and would set an example to the younger generation. . . ."

He was a sturdy great-chested man with wide dark brows and a fringe of white hair circling a bald dome. Voulos whispered, "I can assure you his Greek is not very good, that he is making many mistakes."

Pappas continued in a hoarse voice, saying, "The flow of emigration must stop. Greek youth must remain in Greece. Young people of this land, you are destined for great and noble deeds. You have before you a fine example—a young king who at the age of twenty was acclaimed Olympic champion, following the tradition of his ancestors. With your king as an inspiration, you young people should work for the progress of your land. The future of Greece is in your hands."

The Queen stirred restlessly, crossing and uncrossing her white-gloved hands, running a hand over her hair. Across the valley the newly dedicated chemical plant belched rust-colored clouds into the air. Voulos said, "They will destroy the universe." Nine speakers followed Pappas on the platform, government ministers, American industrialists, the United States ambassador ("We Americans are proud!"), and the prime minister who, reading in a nasal voice from a manuscript held close to his short-sighted eyes, said, "Greece will soon enter into the family of economically advanced countries." During the marathon of oratory, Voulos began speaking to me softly of life and love in Greece. "We know love very young," he said. "Sex is the center of a man's life from age twelve. But then love goes. Greek young men are poor. To succeed in their lives they cannot marry their loves. They must find for marrying, rich women. In marriage men are the prostitutes, not the women. They marry for money instead of love.

"So it is necessary to make relationships without marriage. I am very lucky. I have at my age a mature love life. My mistress who is six years older than I gives me love and she finds the man in me."

Finally the speeches were finished. The King pressed a signal on a portable radio transmitter which set off factory sirens and freed a flock of white pigeons which fluttered nervously over the crowds and then, soaring, disappeared into clouds of chemical dust. The band played a march. The King and Queen walked briskly to their car and roared away.

Wine appeared on the tables and thousands of lunches, including both chicken and ham. "Would you like my hen?" asked Voulos. "I never eat birds. You see I like to make love in nature and if I ate birds I could not make love in nature any more. It's very simple."

The King's next appearance was at a field day at Anatolia College, an American-endowed school on the eastern edge of Thessaloniki. Our bus followed a sprinkling truck sent ahead to settle the dust for the royal caravan. The crowd in the athletic stadium included most of the Americans in Thessaloniki. It remained standing while the King and Queen climbed into a reviewing stand. Again Voulos slumped in his seat. Students in gym suits paraded across the field, boys behind a Greek flag, girls behind an American flag. "You'll notice the large bottoms on the girls," said Voulos. "Too much American butter. Greek women are beautiful only from the waist up." I watched the King's ungloved hand keeping time to the music. After some student gymnastics and field races, a group of girls danced a Virginia reel. "Not very lively, your American dances," said Voulos. "Perhaps they should have given the poor things some American whisky." The Greek and the American anthems were sung and then the King and Queen stepped down from their pavilion and drove away. The crowds, following instructions on programs, remained seated for ten minutes after the royal departure. "Why are you Americans so fluttery about kings?" asked Voulos. "You should have one."

The next morning it stormed. Rain was beating against the bus windows and *bouzouki* music blared from the radio as we drove before the King across eastern plains to Edessa. My friend Voulos was dressed like a college freshman in denim shirt, beige Levis, dark wool sweater and pigskin shoes. His attire irritated Elias who considered it inappropriate. "Let him go to hell," said Voulos. "The pants and shirt are American, the sweater English and the shoes Italian. Only my underwear is Greek."

We passed the ancient city of Pella, birthplace and capital of Alexander the Great. Processions of blue-smocked children waited in villages and clusters of old women huddled in the rain with priests. The rain had washed the landscape, the poppies in the green fields were like the blood of history soaked in the earth. The area was one of the most fertile in Greece. Sheep grazed in the tall grass between rows of fruit trees.

The plain ended abruptly at the foot of a thousand-foot cliff. Above on a plateau lay Edessa. As the bus snaked up the alpine landscape the rains stopped and sun flecked the snowy mountain peaks. The town was at the head of a waterfall. A crowd was waiting. "These peasants of the plains are calm and docile, they like the King," said Voulos. "But on the sea and in the mountains where men are sons of pirates and bandits, the King has no friends." Again rows of armed soldiers lined streets. Men in dark suits and women in bright prints stood apart from one another. Children were bright and scrubbed. At the town gate costumed girls waited with bowls of rose petals. Their rich brocaded dresses had a Byzantine grandeur. Bright ribbons fluttered from their filigreed metal caps.

Drums rolled and church bells rang, announcing the King and Queen. The Queen was wearing a chartreuse suit. As the King helped her from the car, the flower girls showered them with petals. We followed them up the winding shaded street toward the cathedral and petals fluttered also on us. The town of sixteen thousand persons was beautifully kept with fine old houses and new four- and five-story apartments. The prosperous, energetic and healthful atmosphere seemed northern.

After the service I followed the Queen on her visit to the *paidikós stathmos,* or "children's station." The orphanage was for boys up to eighteen years of age—two long lines of them dressed in blue blazers and gray knee pants and socks formed a cordon to the entrance. The yard was strung with hundreds of paper flags. Nearby the tall needle of a Moslem minaret pierced the skies. At the gate two tall youths wearing evzone costumes were waiting. One was a flag-bearer. He had a mustache and deep-set blue satyr's eyes. The other, tall and blond, held a bouquet of roses, which he presented to the Queen with a rhetorical speech. In his white-pleated skirt, embroidered jacket and red-tasseled fez, he looked like a young Rosenkavalier.

With long steps the Queen made a hurried tour of the orphanage. Elias and I trounced after her, up and down creaking stairs, past rows of double-decker beds. The scrubbed rooms smelled of disinfectant, the walls were hung with lithographs of heroes of the War of Independence. The inspection took under ten minutes. When it was finished the Queen, coolly gracious, her eyes shining, spoke a few words and Elias, wild with excitement, burbled, "She spiks Grik! She spiks Grik!"

The King's conference with officials was in a movie theater advertising a Jerry Lewis film called *The Family Jewels*. When the meeting was over we went with the King and Queen to the police headquarters for lunch. The fare was chicken which Voulos, reminded once more of love in nature, disdained. After the meal he and I went in search of a lavatory. We were pursued by Elias shouting, "Hurry, hurry. The King is ahead. We shall not be able to greet him in Veria."

Our bus caught up along the way. The King, his car gray with dust, had stopped to greet some farmers waiting for him at a crossroad on tractor-drawn farm wagons turned into bowers of flowers. We crossed fifteen miles of wheat plains and arrived in Veria in a shower of rain. A large crowd was waiting under umbrellas. The applause seemed real and spontaneous. Veria, suspended on a ledge facing Mt. Vermion, is the commercial center of the surrounding plains and the winter sports center of Greece. The shower ceased and the sun burst forth, bathing the town in blinding wet light. Voulos and I decided we'd had our fill of children's stations and governors' meetings, so we wandered to the square from which we had a silver-misted view of the sweeping Aliakmon Valley. Some young people, five boys in evzone costumes and five winsome girls in blue and white dresses, were waiting to dance for the King and Queen. We made some photographs. The boys, preening like cocks, kept standing in front of the girls so we made some pictures of the girls alone. "Country girls are very enticing," said Voulos. "Compared to them all city girls are like withered leaves." He interviewed the girls on what they thought of the King, and he reported, "They say he is a good-looking boy, like a cinema star, but that he does not look like a King." The King and Queen arrived on the square and the young people began to dance. The boys' roguish gestures, licentious winks and piercing whistles delighted the King who hugged himself laughing. When it was over the King and Queen drove away, waving to the dancers.

On the ride back to Thessaloniki, Voulos gave me his reason for the King's good show in Edessa and Veria. "The Right parties have very good organization in the provinces," he said. "You will see how the

villages are empty. The people are all taken into town to make a crowd."
It was, I remembered, the same explanation which the right-wing press
gave for the large crowds at the public appearances of Papandreou.

In the evening the King interrupted his tour to fly back to Athens for
the swearing-in of five ministers to replace some who had recently
resigned. For me the unvarying daily routine had begun to pall. I told
Elias I would leave the tour after one more day and he was distraught.
"You have not had your visit with the King," he wailed. "When he is
relaxed, when he is not having to think of official affairs, then he is very
friendly, very democratic." After three days I no longer believed in the
Prince Hal wassailings by the fireside and I had made other plans. Thanos
Simos had arrived in Thessaloniki and we were leaving in two days for
Mt. Athos.

On my last day with the tour I took Thanos on the press bus to Katerini
where the King was expected to arrive from Athens at noon. Thanos
was in a high mood—his family was politically royalist and in his childhood, during the civil war, he had lived with relatives in Katerini. We
drove south toward snow-covered Olympus, passing flat fields of sugar
beets, cotton and wheat. Except for the noble mountain rising above,
Katerini is a squalid, dusty town of decaying buildings, dirty streets and
poor shops. Banners across the main street said "Welcome" and "Long
live the King," but the crowd was pitifully small. There seemed to be
more musketed soldiers than usual. According to Voulos they were there
because the people of Katerini, followers of Papandreou, were expected
to be hostile.

The King and Queen arrived. She was wearing a turquoise suit. The
King, in his admiral's uniform, seemed tense and worn. They shook
hands with local dignitaries, were pelted with rose petals by costumed
girls and began their march to the church. Thanos and I were close behind. In front a band was playing a lively march. Suddenly the King's
buoyancy seemed to return. Walking briskly, smiling, he nodded from
one side to the other and waved to people on rooftops. "He is feeling
good," said Thanos. "The troubles in Athens are finished." A drunk
broke through the military lines and lurched into the road ahead and
the King, grinning, shook his hand. On the sidewalk a woman shrieked.
It was Thanos' aunt who had just sighted the tall form of her nephew
marching in the party of the King.

In the church the long-winded metropolitan droned on about the
King's father and grandfather. With the back of his hand the King wiped
sweat from his brow; the Queen kept braiding her fingers restlessly. Somewhere outside a band was playing the national anthem and its lilting

plaintiveness joined with the musical doxology inside in a strangely melancholy fugue.

On the way to a theater for the meeting with officials a curious thing happened. The King saw a one-legged man in a wheelchair and, stopping the procession, went up to the man, took his hand and spoke to him for several minutes. When the King resumed his march the gray-haired cripple could be heard crying loudly. The reporters dropped out of the procession and crowded around his wheelchair. Puffing on a cigarette which flapped between his lips, weeping uncontrollably, wiping his bright blue eyes with a dirty handkerchief, the man sobbed his story.

"His name is John Drianis and he is fifty-three years old," Thanos interpreted. "He was wounded in the Albanian war and ever since he has been a cripple. Now he has gangrene in his leg. His wife works as a washerwoman and as a porter, carrying luggage for tourists. The King asked him what he needed, what he could do for him and he told the King he has had four operations and now needs another operation to take away the leg but he has no money. The King said he would arrange for John to go to the hospital tomorrow. . . ."

The crippled veteran was sobbing too anguishedly to continue his story and some relatives wheeled him away. My own eyes were full and turning I saw tears in other reporters' eyes, even in the eyes of Voulos and those hostile to the King. It had been the first deeply human episode of the week.

After the meeting, and a visit to a children's station, the press was invited for drinks and food at a bar set up in a public garden. Suddenly, while we were drinking *ouzo* and Scotch, a gate opened and the King and Queen appeared and approached our noisy group. The men fell silent as the handsome young couple moved closer and then, standing alone, waited. No one spoke. In the silence which was anguishing I wanted to speak but I feared that my English words in a group that did not understand English would be a presumption. Finally, someone addressed a question to the King, asking if he felt the tour was a success, and he answered eagerly, rapidly, saying that he and the Queen had been moved and reassured by the devotion and loyalty of the people. Again, there was silence. The King took a glass, offered it to the Queen, who, smiling prettily, sipped from its edge, and he took another for himself. For several minutes they stood, smiling, nodding, and then they put their glasses down and walked out of the garden. The loneliness they left behind was felt by every man under the trees.

On the drive back a radio news broadcaster reported, "An enthusiastic welcome was extended to the royal couple by the people of Katerini."

Voulos smiled and he said, "I would not say the visit was a success. Of course, some people come to look from curiosity. As for those persons on balconies and roofs, naturally if you have a house with a window you will look. But you get more people at a Sunday football game."

XXXII

The Holy Mountain

Our sailing for the Holy Mountain might have been an embarkation for the Last Judgment. A cock crowed as our motorized caïque put-putted out of the tiny Aegean port; a lonely dog barked. When we steered east, the rising sun broke through the mists and turned the sea to a blinding gold.

We were a curious cargo of souls. Five monks sat on the port side of the hatch, a row of beards pointing toward shore. A garrulous Swiss, mixing English with German, was declaiming to a fat German who wore a blue nylon jacket and sniffed delicately at a great red rose. I had two tall and merry young companions, one Greek and one American. The Greek was Thanos Simos. The American was Jon Emerson, an architect from California with a black beard as full and shiny as any on board; the monks could not take their eyes from it.

The eldest monk, the pink skin of his face glowing through a nimbus of white hair like Father Time's, spread a blanket and invited us to sit. He was wearing two watches on separate chains. One, which he checked against Thanos', said 7:10. "Gregorian," he announced, holding it— shining new, with a luminous dial—above his head. The other, checked against the watch of the monk beside him, said 12:35. "Julian," he said, swinging it. Most of the monasteries on Mount Athos are on Julian, or Byzantine, time, in which each twenty-four-hour period begins at sunset, when clocks must be reset daily.

"What is the date?" asked Father Time, and Thanos replied, "May eleventh." The old monk shook his head. "April twenty-ninth," he shouted gleefully. His calendar was Julian too. Any sense of reality that I had brought with me was quickly slipping away.

On Mount Athos, contempt for the world's clocks and calendars is part of a monkish aloofness to history. For more than a thousand years it has been a semiautonomous state occupied exclusively by monasteries and their dependent estates and hermitages. Its residents like to boast that they have the oldest democracy in the world, and in the sense that the twenty monasteries are represented in a legislative body, this is true. But in the sense that the legislators are really administering God's law on earth, the government is theocratic. The thousand-year-old law barring all female creatures is credited to a pronouncement by the Holy Virgin, who, according to legend, saw Mount Athos and declared it to be her personal province, forbidden to all other women. The ban was extended to female animals on the premise that the spectacle of mating would offend souls intent on self-purification. Sex and women were simply declared out of existence. My curiosity about the monks had been goaded during the winter in Athens, where I had read about their being arrested for stealing icons, and had followed with interest the trial and imprisonment of a monk for growing and selling hashish.

The Holy Mountain is not easily accessible for men either. Regulations permit only males belonging to one of these categories: professors or students of theology, art or history; artists; writers and journalists; government officials from foreign countries; scientists, industrialists and businessmen. Jon Emerson and I had spent most of a day in Thessaloniki gathering the necessary permits and passes from the American Consulate, the minister of interior of Northern Greece and the Thessaloniki police department. The monks have lately turned wary of visitors because of the beatniks who took to invading the monasteries in alarming numbers. Monks are required by tradition to provide food and lodging for visitors, and the bands of wandering youths, mostly from Germany, were exploiting the monasteries for free holidays.

A young monk stood up near the crowded hatch and strode to the bow, where he stood, head back, like a dark sculptured figure. His black robe was new, his skin fair and scrubbed, his beard carefully trimmed. He shook out the shoulder-length black waves of his hair and let the wind ripple through them.

"Ah, Gerasimos," said Father Time. "He is only eighteen; he has a boy's vanity. He is a novice arriving for the first time."

The Swiss, finding the novice's aloofness a challenge, followed him to the bow and flexed his muscles. "I am a fighter," he said. "I am strong."

Gerasimos looked at him with contempt. "It is more important to be strong in the spirit," he said coolly in English.

"I could knock you into the sea," boasted the Swiss.

"And I would walk on it," said Gerasimos.

One of the monks, watching through field glasses, pointed toward shore. The glasses were passed along, coming finally to me, and I saw the foundations of an old castle, and beyond it a crumbling stone wall. We were passing the geographic frontier of Mount Athos, the boundary beyond which "no female animal or beardless person" might venture.

"You have come in the most beautiful month," said Father Time. "In May Athos is fresh and green. Flowers bloom, birds sing, the sea is peaceful." Because we were arriving by boat, I could not get rid of the feeling we were going to an island. Actually, Athos is a spiny-backed, six-mile-wide Macedonian peninsula extending southeast thirty miles into the Aegean. At its southern tip it rises to the 6700-foot Holy Mountain for which it is named. Now it was covered with clouds. What we saw was a forested wilderness dotted here and there with the deserted stone ruins of fortresses and castles. Several of the green mountains covered with yellow gorse, seemed to be wearing golden haloes. The coast was a rock cliff broken here and there with patches of beach. We could see down through green water, clear as a chlorinated pool, to the rocks far below.

The first stop was at a square stone tower, the boat dock for two monasteries named Zographou and Kastamonitou, hidden in the hills. A half dozen monks stood on the embankment, their black robes and beards flying in the wind. Three of them helped one another on board and took places on the starboard side. One, smaller and more animated than the others, listened to us speak and asked, "You are Englishmen?"

"Americans and Greek," I said.

"Tourists?"

"I am a writer," I said, remembering the regulations. "My friends are students."

"You will write about our death," he said. "You will tell how Athos is dying." Settling beside me, he drew a filthy handkerchief from a pocket and wiped his face. "Once we were ten thousand strong young men," he said. "Now we are fifteen hundred dying old men." His round, beaming face seemed more suited for joviality than despair. He wore a cylindrical cap under which billowed an untidy thicket of gray hair streaked with brown; the spirals around his ears were like a Talmudic scholar's. I asked where he had learned English.

"From books," he said. "I study beginning two years ago." His excellent pronunciation astonished me. "Here on Athos is no one for speaking," he went on. "Is my good fortune to meet you." We were embarking again, at the foot of a vast enclave of red roofs and green onion towers, a small city which might have been a summer palace on the Black Sea. "Is the great Russian monastery of St. Panteleimon," said the monk. "Before War 1914 was wealthiest and largest on Athos. Seven thousand monks lived here. Now there are twenty-seven and one-half. One is half-dead." Along the sea was a vast shell of a building, like a gutted hotel. On one of its terraces huddled a solitary figure, an old monk watching the passing boats. "Fire," said the monk beside me. "An old man with a samovar is a dangerous thing. There are many old men with samovars on Athos, many fires." He started to moan softly. "Athos is finished," he keened. "Finished, finished. . . ."

A half hour later we arrived at Daphne, the port of Athos. "Is very bad to go alone on Athos," our monk said. "You like me to go with you, to make explications?" The old man picked up his carpetbag and followed us. He took our documents and passports to the harbor police, then led us across a piazza to a small restaurant, where he ordered coffee and *ouzo*. I tried to pay, and he said, "Is impossible. Now you are in my country. When I come to yours, you will buy the coffee." We introduced ourselves. He wrote on my pad: "Monahos Nifon Dontakis, Kapsokalyvia, Mount Athos." Kapsokalyvia, he explained, was not a monastery but a skete, a village of independent monk artists who kept their own houses and gardens and made their living by painting icons.

The piazza bustled with the noisy masculinity of a frontier trading post. Black-robed, bearded monks were embracing, shouting, laughing, like a children's ballet of black bears. There were also beardless laymen in working clothes. These were "civils," said Father Nifon, employees in the monastery farms and lumber camps.

Father Nifon leaped up. The bus, Athos' only overland public transportation, was leaving for Karyai, the capital. He pushed us toward the faded, square-topped vehicle and climbed on with us, merry at the prospect of our company.

Gears ground, the motor churned like a tractor and we started slowly upward. The bus had a gamy odor, as though it had been transporting goats, and several seats ahead I saw the fat German still sniffing his rose. Monks and laymen were all babbling loudly. Thanos lit a cigarette and was ordered to extinguish it; cigarettes were not allowed on Athos. In addition to Greek we heard a variety of languages, for the monasteries of Athos represent many Orthodox countries—Bulgaria, Russia, Roumania and southern Yugoslavia.

We churned up through an idyll of green orchards and yellow gorse, through meadows of primulas, daisies and poppies. It took twenty-five minutes to climb the five miles to Karyai, a pretty village built around a church square, bright with geraniums, oleanders and bougainvillaea.

Father Nifon directed us into a side street and up several flights of stairs to the police station. The officer, a civilian youth hardly out of his teens, recorded the names of our fathers and our mothers' maiden names and told Thanos he hoped we would find Athos amusing. How, Thanos asked, did one amuse oneself?

"You can find almost anything you want," he said, rolling his eyes roguishly. "A kilo of hashish, an amiable companion."

"But there are no women," said Thanos.

"Ah, no women," the policeman said.

Pondering that, we all went across the square to the neoclassic government building, where we were received by a little man in baggy, Chaplinesque pants and a flat black cap embroidered with the two-headed Byzantine eagle. He disappeared with our documents. Through the open door I saw a wooden throne on a raised box covered with carpet. "For the governor," said Nifon. "He is our first monk, elected like your President." The man returned and demanded 200 drachmae from each of us. We paid him, and he gave us each an elegantly embossed document that said we might stay on Athos for seven days.

"Now we are free men," said Nifon.

Our first act was to visit the Church of the Protaton, after we found a monk to unlock the doors. Inside, every inch of space was richly frescoed by an artist who must have studied in Italy, for the Byzantine style was enlivened and softened by a humanism that suggested Masaccio and Giotto. The monk directed us to silver-covered icons, which Nifon and Thanos bowed to kiss, and to a Virgin and Child with faces too dark to see, which he said was painted by Saint Luke.

Karyai has one real street, which leads off into a network of cobbled lanes. There were several souvenir shops and grocery stores, barber and tailor shops, and a hotel. In a bookstore Father Nifon showed us some of his own art, small gypsum icons that were for sale. He suggested lunch at the hotel. The dining room was large and dirty, with sticky oilcloth tablecloths covered with flies. In the back was an all-black kitchen and a toilet of the Turkish variety, any description of which is best avoided. Nifon ordered bean soup, which was made with oil and was strong and thick. We followed it with a stew of veal and potatoes. Most of the other guests were civil workers. The waiter, a thin, hairy young monk, had jacked up his robes in order to move more quickly.

Father Nifon was enjoying the role of guide. Of Mount Athos' twenty monasteries, he told us, eleven are of the cenobitic rule, which insists on absolute spiritual obedience to an abbot elected for life. The monks function as a group. Meals, usually meatless, are taken in common. Nine monasteries are of the idiorrhythmic rule, governed by an assembly. In these the monks live in considerable freedom, retaining private property and preparing their meals, which may include meat, in the apartments. Visitors, not surprisingly, prefer the idiorrhythmic monasteries, which the cenobitic groups consider lax and undisciplined.

Some monasteries are extremely rich, collecting revenues from timber and real-estate holdings outside Athos. Others that once were supported by the churches and governments of Russia, Bulgaria and Roumania have fallen into moribund poverty. Monks also live in sketes, which may be subsidiary monasteries, or else villages built around communal churches. After the sketes there are kellions, which house small groups of monks living together, usually on farms. Still other monks are hermits who live alone in caves and shelters, and at the bottom of the scale are the "wanderers," who "live like snails," Nifon said. "They wander around very dirty, with a look of madness. No one can understand what is in their hearts, who is under those rags."

Our first night, Father Nifon decided, would be spent in the monastery of Iviron, a one-and-a-half-hour mule ride from Karyai. But the muleteer was taking a siesta and would not be ready for at least an hour, so we went to see the Russian skete of Saint Andrew's, only a ten-minute walk from the town.

On the way we passed a pink building that Nifon said was the "cemetery," a charnel house in which the remains of thousands of monks were crumbling to dust, and "always on top the pile is growing." On the edge of Karyai were several large villas with flower gardens and parks. These were the homes of governors. Every monastery that has a representative in the council of governors provides him with a house in town.

I seemed to be hearing high-pitched womanly laughter. Coming around a bend in the path, I saw what appeared to be a young girl approaching between two youths, all in black robes. Nifon said all three were boys from the school opened in Saint Andrew's for poor Greek youths, in the hope that some of them might be influenced "to make theologic" and remain as monks. Unfortunately, few did. "Young men no longer love God," he said. "All young men love is to make money, have women, go to the moon. These are the dreams of our times. God is no longer present in them." The boys went on, the one in the middle coquettishly tossing his long auburn hair and running a hand through it to bring out its fullness.

We arrived at a cluster of green onion domes and entered through an unhinged gate into a decaying compound of courtyards, chapels and arches. Windows were broken, doors sagged; fountains were dry, choked by tall grass and briars. One large building was a burned-out shell. "Old men with samovars, old men with candles," Nifon said. Except for a crow cawing in flight, the air was utterly silent. "Look," Nifon cried. "Built for the glory of God. Seven hundred monks!" The style was nineteenth-century Russian baroque. Saint Andrew's was the last of the religious communities to be built. Because it was patronized by the Czars, Greek politics prevented its formal recognition as a monastery. After World War I the Greek government, fearing Communist espionage, refused to admit Russian monks, and Saint Andrew's deteriorated more completely than any other Athonite community. "No souls," wailed Nifon. "It is a desert." Two mean-looking cats slunk through the weeds. A bell clanged. A solitary figure shuffled toward us, an ancient, bent, filthy old hunchback whose hair and beard were wispy, his face crinkled. He was one of five monks, all past seventy, who still lived in Saint Andrew's. In a tremolo voice he invited us to see the church; shaking with ague, his loose shoes flapping, he led the way.

The door creaked open, and we entered the largest church on Athos. Decorated in blue and white, it had a lovely delft quality. The iconostasi was an overwrought carnival in gold. The Virgin and Child encased in gold, said the old monk, was painted by Saint Luke. "Riches! Gold!" Father Nifon shouted, his voice echoing in the cupola. "All things crumble to dust!" As we walked back to town through a lane of cypress, he keened like a sorrowing woman. "All is empty, all is death."

The mules were waiting with two muleteers, a ruddy-faced, white-bearded priest and a swarthy fisherman who hired out mules when the sea was too high for fishing. Father Nifon, riding sidesaddle, and Thanos reined their own mounts. The priest led Jon Emerson's, and the fisherman, a sullen fellow, took charge of mine—a black perfidious beast called Judas. His method of getting rid of flies was to brush against briars, which covered me with stigmata like a quattrocento Sebastian; sometimes he went under branches, almost hanging me up like Absalom. He had a perverse piety, falling occasionally to his knees, nearly heaving me off. I closed my eyes and hung on, making myself think of the sure-footed beasts I'd heard carried tourists in and out of the Grand Canyon.

At the head of the caravan Father Nifon, whose mood shifts were Dostoievskian, was maniacally merry. "How many mules in New York?" he shouted back to me. "How long since you go to church on a mule?" Judas was lagging behind, munching tree branches and my driver bellowed, "Hooch!" and twisted his tail, causing him to spurt forward, almost dismounting me. When I caught up, Nifon was singing, "Gif my regardez zu Broadway . . ."

We looked down on a bright, wind-swept city of temples by the sea. At the gate of Iviron we dismounted and paid for the ride. Inside the gate two clocks faced each other, one showing Gregorian 4:30 P.M. and the other Julian 11:10 P.M. Nifon hurried us in to meet the *archon-*

daris, or guestmaster, a friendly little "civil" who served us coffee and *raki.* We were asked to sign the registry. Checking through a fortnight's thirty-two visitors, I found that twenty-two were from Germany and Austria and most of the others from Greece. After a second glass of *raki* we were free to look around.

All Athonite monasteries follow a single design, varying only in size and lavishness. Iviron, which owns forests and is rich, is one of the most spacious. Its three churches, all painted red, stand in a rectangular court of three- and four-story buildings, from the upper balconies of which open monks' cells and apartments. High towers served as a refuge in the days of pirate raids. As in most monasteries, the outside cortile of the main chapel is frescoed with scenes from the Apocalypse and the Last Judgment, to warn those who remain outside.

Inside the church it was almost dark. Then, as our eyes adjusted to the dim light, it turned into an Arabian Nights spectacle in burgundy and gold. A treasury of chandeliers and icons hung from the walls and ceiling. A heroic Christ stared down from the drum of the dome. Frescoes showed scenes from the lives of the Virgin and the Prophets.

A half dozen monks were murmuring a benediction in an unmusical monotone. Four were old. Two young ones, short and fat, with bushy black beards, appeared to be brothers. One, waving a censer, enveloped us in a cloud of smoke. I began to sneeze, and he burst into spasms of giggles. When the service was finished, the young monk took us to the chapel of the miraculous icon, a painting of the Virgin—by Saint Luke, of course—which, according to legend, floated to Iviron from the sea. The monk's reason for wanting us to see it was that it had been loaned to the Greek Orthdox Cathedral in New York, where, he said, it had been so homesick for Athos that its eyes had wept real tears.

"Same thing happens to me in New York," I whispered to Thanos. "It's the air pollution." Thanos broke into snickers and the monk, observing what must have seemed to him irreverence, clapped his hands angrily. "That's enough!" he cried and he herded us out.

We visited the refectory, a dining room meant for two hundred monks and now used as a gallery for an astonishing collection of five hundred icons, most of them painted on wood. Then we visited the library, where we were shown illuminated manuscripts dating from the tenth century.

The librarian, Father Athanasios, a white-haired, heavy man past eighty, could not stop looking at Jon Emerson's black beard. "Do men wear beards in America?" he asked.

"A few," said Jon. "Not many."

"God provided beards for men to wear," said the old man. "Saint

Paul, Michelangelo, Venizelos, all great men have worn beards. Beards got out of fashion when men were made to shave in Hollywood to play women's parts." He dwelt on this curious theory. "I'm glad to see you do not go with the sheep," he said to Jon, and turning to Thanos and me, he said, "You who shave your beards, you make yourselves women."

At seven thirty we were called for a supper of bean soup, olives, bread and wine. All monasteries lock their gates at sunset, when clocks are set. The monks, who are obliged to rise for prayers at midnight, are usually in bed by eight. The long, empty evening can be unnerving for visitors. After supper Thanos, Jon and I went to our room. There was no light to read by, the panes in the window were broken, the smell of the privy a few doors away was inescapable. We lay down on our hard, sheetless cots.

Suddenly we were aroused from our torpor by a frightful screeching below our window. At this moment Father Nifon appeared in the door to tell us we would not be expected to get up when the gongs called the monks to midnight prayer. The nerve-shattering hullabaloo outside continued.

"So there are no females on Athos," I said. "So mating is offensive."

"Ah," Nifon sighed, his expression resigned. "God sends us female rats. So are necessary female cats."

The morning was bright, with a strong wind. The sea was too high for a boat to sail around the southeast cape to Kapsokalyvia, so Father Nifon decided to return to Daphne and take a boat on the west side. After our thimble of coffee we said good-bye to him and promised to visit him in his village later in the week. Then the three of us went down to the jetty to wait for a boat that would take us on our way to Vatopedi monastery.

While we were waiting, Thanos decided to go for a swim. He undressed behind the sea wall and threw himself into the surf. An old monk, his thin white beard curved by the wind, appeared on the quay and beckoned him in. As Thanos came dripping from the sea, the old man cried, "Naked flesh! An insult to God!" Thanos dressed, and the old man released his apoplectic rage into the whistling wind, threatening to "report this scandal to the office of the governor." He started up the beach, then turned and watched us from the quay until the boat arrived. "He was waiting," said Thanos. "He was wishing for someone to undress. He had such a slyness around his eyes."

The sea was flecked with foam. At the second port, by the monastery of the Pantocrator, our skipper was unable to maneuver into the small harbor, and a barque came out to exchange passengers. After an hour we turned into a cove, and there ahead lay Vatopedi, a storybook village of red cupolas, blue balconies and pink columns. The harbor was a crescent of brightly painted houses, homes for civil workers, and behind them a sloping olive grove led up to the monastery, the center section of which was a hollowed ruin. A fire on a February night had destroyed its valuable library and icons; a monk had been tried and found guilty of negligence in causing it.

On our way up we heard nightingales singing in the olive trees, and peacocks screeching in a grove of medlars. We met a caravan of donkeys and mules carrying logs to the sea. Vatopedi is the second richest monastery; the monks were known to have shower baths, but these had been destroyed by the fire. In the sterner monasteries, where the Vatopedians are looked upon as self-indulgent sybarites, the fire was interpreted as divine retribution.

The burly monk at the gate was fascinated by Jon Emerson's beard. He called the guestmaster, who was likewise intrigued. We were taken to an upstairs drawing room, into an atmosphere of Victorian elegance, of damask curtains and baronial furniture. A Tiffany chandelier hung from the ceiling, but there was no electric power to light it. From a balcony we looked down on orange-lichened roofs, and groves of cypresses shading vine-covered gazebos and pavilions. After the ritualistic coffee and *raki* we were shown to our room, bright and clean, with soft beds and sheets and royal portraits on the walls. Almost immediately we were summoned to the dining room and served an excellent dinner of roast veal, salad, potatoes and all the wine we could drink. The guestmaster was eager to talk. He told us Vatopedi employed 150 woodsmen and owned sixty donkeys and mules; it collected revenues from real estate in Macedonia and various islands. The forty monks lived independently in their own apartments with kitchens, gathering only for social and religious events. At their merry New Year's Eve party it was the tradition to bake an English gold sovereign in a cake, a prize belonging to the lucky monk in whose piece it appeared. The peacocks were bred and raised for gifts to important visitors such as the King, who was expected to visit Athos with Ethiopian Emperor Haile Selassie within the month.

In the afternoon we undressed behind some piles of lumber by a water-driven mill wheel and went for a swim, and no one objected. At four thirty we heard bells and returned for vespers in the church. The service was short, with only three monks attending. At its close one monk stayed to show us icons and art treasures—a sculptured bronze door, the cortile Apocalypse, which was even more fantastic than Iviron's, and the large, richly frescoed refectory.

Our guide asked what churches we attended. Thanos passed muster, being Greek, and so did I, an Episcopalian. The Episcopal Church, said the monk, was very friendly with Orthodoxy. What he really wanted to know was the confession of Jon Emerson, and when Jon answered, "Christian Science," the monk's friendliness cooled, and he excused himself. We met no other monks. I caught a glimpse of one hanging laundry on a balcony railing and another watching us through an open window.

Outside the walls it was a magic evening. The nightingales were singing, and the swallows purred in their mud nests under the eaves. Bullfrogs croaked in the moats, and fat cats stalked them on the stones. Snapdragons, foxglove and roses covered the walls, and fig trees grew everywhere. The sea was molten orange. We turned boyishly larkish, picking cherries and shaking medlars from trees. Down by the sea we joined some boys gathering mussels from an old pylon; we cracked them with our teeth and ate them like nuts. A transistor radio in a boat was blaring *bouzouki* music, and Thanos linked arms with two woodsmen and began to dance the *hasapiko* on the quay. We helped some youths shoe a donkey, and then followed the beast to a corral.

Thanos explained that May is the month for donkey love, and the forty males in the compound were, in the manner of their species, almost exhibitionistically tumescent.

A handsome young monk was watching, listening to the ribaldries of the workmen. He told us his name was Father Elias, that he was from a village in Epirus and had been a monk only three years. "Yes, here life is free," he said. "We can do anything we wish. But I didn't know it would be so lonely. We are only four young ones." The gates would close in minutes, he told us; it was time to return to our rooms. We invited him to continue our conversation inside. He did not come, but later, after supper, we saw him hovering in the dark halls, from behind the damask curtains. A soft sadness filled the night.

In the morning our paradisiacal idyll turned into an inferno of frustration. We sensed hostility when the guestmaster brought us coffee. The sea was high, he said; there would be no boat to take us to Lavra monastery. The journey would take a good seven hours by foot.

The hike over unknown terrain was not one I intended to make. We discussed our dilemma with the gatekeeper, asking if we might stay another night. A messenger was sent to the prior. The answer was no. I asked to rent some mules and hire a guide, and again we were refused. For whatever reason—Jon Emerson's Christian Science affiliation, our innocent merriment in the garden, Thanos' dancing on the quay or even our fleeting friendship with Father Elias—the gates of Vatopedi had closed to us. We took our gear and started for the port. Looking back, I saw Father Elias watching from a window.

"They are sorry to be here," said Thanos. "They would like to leave and cannot. So they hate everyone who is free to leave."

At the port a policeman told us that boats were sailing on the west side. One would stop at the port of Zographou monastery at one o'clock. The trip across the peninsula would take two hours by mule. The officer called in a woodsman, who agreed to furnish us three mules, and his son as guide, for two hundred drachmae; it would take ten minutes for the mules to be unloaded of their burden of logs.

We waited an hour. The time was now eleven o'clock, and I remembered that the boat must be met at one. The sea was roaring. Horsetails spread across the sky—the weather was going to turn bad. The mulekeeper appeared to tell us he needed the mules to carry logs; in order to release them he must have three hundred drachmae. It took another ten minutes for the mules to be saddled. "You are learning to know the Greek character," said Thanos.

For an hour we climbed through yellow gorse. The boy, who said he was sixteen but looked twelve, walked beside Thanos, telling shocking stories about monks. I suspected his adolescent imagination was taking flight, but in my rage I was ready to believe him. He was from a village in Macedonia and longed to return to the world of women, to his mother and sister. "Where there are no women, men live like beasts," he said. "I don't know what to do."

At the summit four bulls were grazing in a clearing. They fled at the sight of us. We descended into woods, passing the Bulgarian monastery of Zographou, a gray Walter Scott fortress in the forest, and we entered a cool humid canyon filled with singing nightingales, thrushes and wrens. My watch, I noted, said seven minutes to one. The boy slapped the mules and I dismounted and walked to speed us along.

When we arrived at the harbor, the boat was disappearing around a distant cove. It wasn't the boy's fault, Thanos pointed out, but his father's. I paid the boy, and he disappeared quickly with the mules, leaving us stranded on the cement quay. A man was sleeping in a small fishing boat. I awakened him and asked if he would take us to Daphne. He could not, he said, without permission from the harbor police. I was sure permission would be forthcoming for a price, and I offered two hundred drachmae. Thanos said, "One thing you must remember. We are Greeks and it is not possible for us to do things as you Americans, with a system."

At three thirty we were back in Daphne. All the restaurant offered was boiled beans, which we ate with good Greek beer. A policeman, taking an interest in our dilemma, arranged for us to ride to Dionysiou monastery on a freight boat, and in a half hour we were at sea again, chugging toward the gray granite pyramid of Mount Athos, which was covered with clouds and streaked with snow. We passed Simopetra monastery, spectacularly set on a mountain cliff, and Gregoriou; then we arrived at Dionysiou, perched on a rock high above the sea. Two old monks, wearing gray tunics and boots like Tolstoian peasants, directed us on the long climb to the gate.

Until now we had visited idiorrhythmic monasteries. Dionysiou, of the cenobitic rule, was known as one of the strictest on Athos. The guest-master, a wispy-bearded old monk named Father Benedictos, introduced us to four other guests who had just arrived on foot from Lavra. They were an Austrian distiller of brandy and his twenty-year-old son, a German student from Cologne and an Australian engineer. Father Bene-dictos served the welcoming libations and took us out on a balcony, an aerie so lofty that the circling swallows would not fly up to it. Convulsed with giggles over our vertigo discomfort, the old monk playfully pretended to push Jon Emerson from the balcony.

A hearty supper of bean soup, spaghetti, olives and bread was served on the kitchen table. Father Benedictos and Father Efistratos, a cheerful, fat, younger monk, ate with us. Outside it was raining. The wind whistled around corners, flapping shutters. Indoors the fire crackled in the hearth, a pressure lamp hissed above us, and boxes of American detergents stood on the shelves.

We were given cloth napkins. Wine kept appearing in jugs, and when-ever a plate was empty, Father Benedictos filled it with food, exclaiming that we were seven growing boys. In outrageous English the young Austrian was explaining how the monks' pronunciation of Greek was in-correct. He said, "They are spikking old Grik like is now and not two thousand years ago. From ancient Grik is come Latin and so they have sometimes Latin pronunciation so is not old. In the Vienna Uni-versity our Grik pronunciation is the correct." Father Benedictos poured more wine and, smiling gently, said, "Drink! In the language of friendship pronunciation has no importance." Father Efistratos brought out a guest book. In 1965, he pointed out proudly, Dionysiou had entertained 6202 visitors from fifteen countries, beginning in this order: Germany, Austria, Holland, France and England.

It was after ten when we went to bed. We were awakened by a young "civil" who opened our door and said, "Watch service!" We stumbled into a cold morning. The monastery was so tightly squeezed on its rocky perch that it was difficult to find the church door. The interior was a warren of small rooms, almost dark. The two Austrians were in the first room with Father Benedictos, who waited to direct us into stalls. In the shadows inside, dark figures were moving; their murmurings were like the voices of ghosts. A candle flickered over the head of an old monk who was reading. Another burned beside the face of a youth giving the responses, lighting his smooth face like a painting by La Tour.

The church door opened, and a very fat monk with a great round head waddled in and took the stall beside me. He groaned softly with each breath. Suddenly he scowled at me, indicating that I was sitting when I should be standing. I stood, and he let forth a belch that rumbled through the labyrinths of the church. He frowned again, wagging his finger at me. Thanos explained that I had crossed my legs, which was disrespectful. I uncrossed them. The fat monk belched mightily. Inside, the young reader was bowing to the floor before an icon, and his hair fell in disarray over his shoulders. Once more the monk nudged me, wagging his head disapprovingly. I had no idea what it would be this time, and my confusion bordered on panic. The clouds of incense had affected my sinuses, and tears flowed from my eyes. The monk explained to Thanos that my hands were behind me when they should be folded in front. I drew them forward, and the monk nodded approvingly. Then he cleared his throat with great resonance and spat on the floor. With a resigned groan he waddled ponderously into an inner chamber and began kissing icons.

At eight fifteen the service was over. Father Benedictos showed us the illuminated manuscripts and the refectory, a great T-shaped hall covered with the most magnificent paintings of saints on Athos. Neither the light nor the time allotted was sufficient for us to see them. Monks take their riches of paintings for granted and cannot understand a visitor's preoccupation with them. Hanging from the refectory pulpit was a knotted rope, a "penance" rope, Father Benedictos explained; errant monks were required to clasp the knots while praying for forgiveness. I asked what were the sins for which a monk might be punished. "Quarreling with brothers, resentment in fulfilling obligations," was the reply.

After a breakfast of coffee and sweets we set out on foot for the next monastery, Saint Paul's. The path, following the sea, was fairly rugged, and we arrived in an hour at a gray, crenelated fortress in an alpine setting of waterfalls and snow patches. Outside the gate a thrush was singing in a bower of roses. In the courtyard inside, forty-five wine tuns were stacked against the church. A hunchbacked troglodyte, his head bent to the earth like a grazing beast's, was stroking a cat. He seemed also to be a mute, for he beckoned us with monosyllabic grunts to follow him up some stairs to a door marked RECEPTION. We knocked, and a jet-bearded, slight young monk soon appeared.

He had pale skin and wore horn-rimmed spectacles. He introduced himself as Father Theokletos, secretary of the monastery. He served the welcoming libations and told us at once that Saint Paul's was the most serious monastery on Athos, with the strictest discipline. Many of the forty-eight monks were young, he said, because pious youths were attracted by Saint Paul's earnestness of purpose. His words, coming in quick staccato breaths, sounded like a warning. While he spoke, several black-whiskered young monks with tense faces, all looking strangely alike, darted by the door. Scandal-prone Thanos, who was wearing a short-sleeved sports shirt, was reprimanded by one of them for exposing his naked forearms.

About noon we were brought some bread in our room. It was raining, so we passed the long afternoon reading and exploring the monastery, wandering through long corridors, reading signs that said, "Use of radios is forbidden," and "Visitors using the toilet are expected to be fully dressed to avoid a scandal." The toilet, a hole in the floor of a balcony jutting out of the wall at a height of seventy feet, was a scandal itself. In a tower four flights up we discovered a small, frescoed chapel of Saint George, the only thing of beauty we saw. In the courtyard below, a dozen monks were scrubbing the wine barrels, and the hunchback, his head near the ground, was sharing his supper from a tin pail with his familiar, the cat.

At six thirty we were beckoned to a small dining room for our own supper, an unappetizing combination of rice and spinach cooked together, bread, cheese and good dark wine. It was still raining when we finished, so there was nothing to do but go to our room. The strain was beginning to tell. Thanos was in a surly mood. Jon was silent, and I was depressed.

In a few minutes the door opened, and there was Father Theokletos, asking whether there was anything he might do for us.

The question seemed an excuse. Standing in the middle of the floor, gesticulating nervously, his beard jutting into the air, he told us his life's story, beginning with his boyhood in Athens and continuing with his education in Germany and his contented life in Saint Paul's. "There are ten thousand books in our library, and I've read them all," he said. Because of its piety, Saint Paul's was the happiest monastery on Athos, the best administered. If a monk misbehaved he was not flogged on the face as in centuries past, but assigned to fasting and prayer.

He finally left. In a few minutes there was another sharp tap on the door, and he appeared again to apologize for our solitariness, explaining that monastic rules did not permit monks to associate with visitors. Monks had work duties, he said, and religious obligations. They were not sophisticated men, and were unaccustomed to meeting foreigners. Each monastery based its life on the character of its founder. Saint Paul's patron was Saint Savas, a spiritual, reflective man.

Within the next hour Father Theokletos returned three times, always with a new discourse, the last of which was on ecumenicalism. Shaking

with passion, he said, "If God wanted all churches to be one, He would
have made them one. It is not true that Saint Peter founded the true
church of Christ. Saint Peter did not go to Italy, he was not martyred.
That is a Roman hoax. It was Saint Paul who established the church.
Peter fought to retain Judaism, but Paul founded the church in spite of
him." The only monastery that favored ecumenicalism was Vatopedi,
where *they also eat meat.* At Saint Paul's, he said, "We will fight with
our blood for the supremacy of Orthodoxy and Greek nationalism."

The monk's explosive visits had the curious effect of cheering us up.
We were free to leave in the morning; he and the other nervous little men
were destined for a lifetime in those dour corridors, protesting how
happy they were. If Vatopedi was the most permissive of monasteries and
Dionysiou the happiest, Saint Paul's was certainly the most neurotic.

In the morning we were aroused by bells and told to go to the dining
room. For the monks it was midday—they were gathering for their major
meal. On a platform a monk was reading from the life of Saint Xenia.
Three monks served everyone present with a tin bowl of salt cod cooked
in oil with spinach, a large head of romaine without dressing, and an
individual pitcher of wine. We munched like goats on the lettuce and
drank some of the wine; at that hour it was all we could manage. Our
disdain of the food angered our waiter, who reprimanded poor Thanos for
whispering during the meal.

The sea had subsided sufficiently for sailing, and we set out for the port,
walking the half mile through rain. Our seven days were running out, and
we still had to get to Lavra. We negotiated with the skipper, a barefoot
brown little man, and finally agreed on a price of three hundred drachmae.
The wild tip of Athos is an area of sketes, and we stopped at the ports of
several, taking on and letting off monks. The last one got off at Kapsokalyvia, where Father Nifon lived, a pretty village spread across the
steep mountainside. Our skipper pointed out the skete of Kerasia, from
which a monk had recently been imprisoned for growing hashish in his
barley.

We were in rough open sea and black waves pitched us like driftwood.
I imagined us lashed against the rocky cliffs, clinging to them as in rock-of-
ages Sunday school lithographs. Thanos disappeared. I found him in the
hatch, stiff and pale on a bunk, literally paralyzed by fright. Some icons
hanging on the walls of the boat were swaying like pendulums. We
passed the Cove of the Wicked Dead and in the mists ahead saw the port
of Lavra.

A policeman appeared on the deck to examine our documents. Our
skipper accompanied us up to the monastery. He took us to an upstairs
balcony, where the guestmaster served us coffee and *raki.* We looked out

on a disorderly medieval courtyard of turrets, parapets and outside stairways. Cats wandered across tile roofs, pigeons and swallows swooped in and out of eaves, mules grazed in the gardens, and bees buzzed over the roses. Lavra, which still has seventy monks, is the largest and oldest Athonite monastery. It was founded in 963 by a Byzantine monk, Saint Athanasios, as an autonomy responsible only to the emperor. The idea caught on. Four other monasteries were founded in the tenth century, and the others followed.

A young monk from America, Father Seraphim of Scranton, Pennsylvania, offered to guide us about. In the library we saw a fourth-century copy of the Epistle to the Galatians, and in the refectory a wall painting of the ladder of Saint John, up which a throng of frenzied souls were scrambling. On the left a swarm of devils were pulling the souls from the ladder and hurling them into the inferno below, while on the right, angels cheered the virtuous upward. I asked the American monk if he believed the childlike fantasies on the walls and he said, "Monks have a pious view." Mistakenly inferring that my attitude was hostile, he said, "I suppose you think of monks as dirty old men." I had indeed been giving the matter some thought. I said that cultures such as ancient Greece's and Rome's, which had a pragmatic view of man, seemed to value personal hygiene, and that in religious cultures, which emphasize spirituality, sanitation has been more or less disregarded. Father Seraphim said in reply to this, "Monks spend their time in prayer and meditation. If they spent time cleaning and washing, they would have less time for prayer. To them cleanliness has a spiritual rather than a corporal meaning."

I suspected that the social position of monks might have some bearing on the matter. Many Athonite monks come from the lower classes. They are there to escape poverty or some personal maladjustment not comprehended, or because of the influence of a relative in their childhood. They may bring with them a peasant's suspicion, superstition, sloth, vindictiveness and illiteracy. In the early centuries, when monks were often kings and scholars, monasteries had intellectual and political status. Now, because of a change in attitude toward religion in Orthodox countries, they are looked upon with contempt. Today's monks accept this attitude as a cross they must bear. What they know best is the peasant's sense of proprietorship. An intuitive understanding of land hunger makes them keepers of property and tradition, the indomitable landlords of the great medieval palaces, fortresses and villages built in the great monastic age, in which faith and mysticism flourished.

Our skipper shepherded us back to the boat. The sea was quieter. We decided to spend the night in Kapsokalyvia and asked our skipper to fetch us late the next day. He said he would signal us with a blast on his conch shell, which he demonstrated, filling coves and bays with echoing thunder.

It was a long climb to the village, where Father Nifon, who had watched boats for two days, was waiting. He took us to the Artists' House, a home for icon painters endowed by a rich monk. It had facilities for ten artists, but here too the population was declining, and only two were in residence. One, Father Ioannis, was old; the other, Father Antonios, was a smiling, dark little man of thirty-five who spoke halting English.

News of our arrival spread through the village, and a jolly dozen of Nifon's artist friends appeared to greet us. Kapsokalyvia has thirty-one houses perched on terraces facing the sea. Its population of forty-seven painters, sculptors, ceramists and lithographers all live from the income of their art. They do much mail-order business with Orthodox churches and Greek organizations in the United States and Canada. Thirty-two of the artists lived in pairs and fifteen lived alone. The monks maintain their own houses, each with a chapel and garden. "We are not like monastery monks," said Nifon. "Monasteries are rich, and no one works. Here we are poor, and work hard. In the communal life of a monastery, practical problems are easily solved. Each of us must face alone all the difficulties. In winter for three months doesn't come the boat and all is by feet in the snow. But we have our freedom. We are happy."

"There are old men on Athos who have never seen an automobile," said Father Ioannis. He had been on Athos forty-six years; an uncle monk at Lavra had brought him when he was fourteen. Father Antonios had not been off Athos for fifteen years, nor away from Kapsokalyvia for ten.

The two monks prepared a festive meal for us, and Nifon was invited. At a long table beside the kitchen fire we ate herring, a marvelous salad, cheese, hard-boiled eggs and oranges, and drank dark red wine. Father Nifon told how Kapsokalyvia, which means "burned huts," got its name. A fourteenth-century hermit named Maximos, who lived alone in the wild ravines, would frequently burn his hut as an offering to God and build a new one. Maximos had the gift of levitation, and soared through the air in company with the Virgin. He was fed with heavenly bread and lived to be ninety-five.

"Is there peace and love in America?" Father Antonios suddenly inquired of me.

"America is like every other country," I said. "There is love and there is also hate."

Antonios sighed. "Also on Mount Athos we have not peace and love in many houses," he said. "The Devil is here, keeping hate alive, keeping the troubles going." I looked at the young monk, his pale face glowing in the firelight, his eyes bright. "You would not know it, but here we fight a never-ending, invisible war. The Devil goes everywhere, even into the church. He knows that we are Christ's soldiers on earth, and he is furious and makes many evils." Father Antonios was terribly earnest. The child-like conviction, as true as the fantastic frescoes that had intrigued me everywhere on Athos, was very much like the innocent fears of my own childhood. My heart went out to him in a kind of love as he continued.

"The Devil *has* to tempt monks, for he knows we are Christ's soldiers, the keepers of His love. So there is much sin on Mount Athos. All the time, everywhere, we make this terrible fight. He tempts us through our imaginations. We pray. We make the sign of the cross. We beg Jesus' help to avoid the Devil's temptations."

While he spoke a black cat leaped softly on the open sill, causing me to jump. "We have many cats," said Father Nifon. "They protect us from rats and snakes."

It was after eleven when we finally went to our separate rooms. Mine had an iron stove with the legend ONWARD—FULLER, WARREN & CO., TROY, N.Y. 1865, and over it was a calendar from DOVER DRUGS, NEW HAMPSHIRE'S LARGEST DRUGSTORE. The bed had a soft mattress and a lace pillowcase, and over it hung a painting of Jesus in a small boat, quelling a storm. On the table was an old Italian edition of Dante, similar to one in my grandmother's house, which had been my favorite book when I was a boy. For an hour I lay with the light of a kerosene lamp, looking at Doré's drawings of the Devil tormenting souls.

Breakfast was *raki* and jam. Then we were shown our two hosts' paintings, which were gentle and sweet. Father Nifon arrived to lead us on the visit to his friends. Our first call was on another Father Antonios, a ceramist who baked small statues of clay. He served us *raki* and accompanied us to the house of Father Ananias, a twenty-eight-year-old wood carver from Crete. We drank more *raki* and saw the house and chapel, beautifully appointed and immaculate. Father Ananias' finely carved miniatures of saints were as painstakingly delicate as Oriental ivories.

We continued to a half dozen more houses, drinking *raki* and picking up a new companion in each, until we were a roaring caravan, bringing hilarious life to a Fra Angelico painting of paradise, stumbling up and down lanes that were swooningly scented with blossoming lemon and orange, roses, wisteria and Easter lilies.

Our last stop was at the home of Father Nifon, the largest and most disorganized house in town. One room was set up for painting, another for ceramics, and a third was a photography dark room. The monks settled on a balcony, toasting us, their visitors.

"When will you return?" asked Father Antonios. "Next year?"

"No, not next year."

"In two years?"

I could not say.

"Many of us are old," said Father Nifon, reverting to his melancholy mood. "In two years we will be only thirty in Kapsokalyvia. The others will have died."

Down at Artists' House, Father Antonios prepared another meal, which included a delicious lemon soup and, for us eaters of meat, canned corned beef. Father Nifon asked what I thought would happen to Mount Athos when the monks were gone. I suggested the possibility that the Greek government might nationalize the peninsula and develop it as a tourist attraction, the most astonishing museum of Byzantine art in the world. The seaside monasteries could be turned into hotels.

Father Nifon interrupted. "With women?"

"Of course."

"Never! No woman will set foot on Mount Athos. Even if the Queen would come with the King, she would not be permitted."

At that moment the conch bellowed up the mountainside. We gathered our things, and Father Antonios loaded us with bags of oranges and almonds and bouquets of roses. Grasping my hand, he whispered, "Our fight is bigger than anyone's in the world. Every day brings more temptations. We need so much strength."

He was assuming I understood, and he was right.

The sea was calm. As we slid out of the cove, I saw for the first time the cloud-free cone of Mount Athos silhouetted in an unnatural rosy dusk. The sun was disappearing behind the moon in an eclipse, and excited monks were passing smoked panes of glass back and forth. Standing at the prow in a high mood, Thanos shouted, "The sun is setting! Will all you Byzantine gentlemen set your watches, please." A wave of laughter filled the boat. I thought that if the King anchored the royal yacht close enough to shore, Her Majesty could at least hear the nightingales sing.

XXXIII

Message from Konstantine

From the Byzantine piety of Mount Athos we returned to Greece's strangest fusion of pagan and Christian worship, the fire-dancing of the religious cultists known as "Anastenarides."

Anastenarides are Thracians who were driven from their ancestral lands in the early decades of this century and settled in Macedonian villages. From Asia Minor they brought a uniquely ecstatic religion, a relic of ancient Dionysian worship combined with the worship of two Christian patrons, St. Konstantine and his mother St. Helen. The Anastenarides rarely attend church. They worship in an open-air sacred grove called "hagiasmata" or "sanctified place," and in a "konakia," the house of their supreme commander, where the sacred icons of Konstantine and Helen, brought from Thrace, are kept. Once a year for three days beginning with the feast of St. Konstantine on May 21, they perform bacchic rituals which include animal sacrifice and the exorcism of evil spirits by fire-dancing.

Of the four villages in which the Anastenarides settled, the most famous is Langadia, thirteen miles from Thessaloniki. At noon on May 21, I drove there with Jon Emerson, Thanos Simos, a nineteen-year-old voluntary staff worker at the American Farm School whose name was Betsy Hoffman, and Dimitrios "Jimmy" Halatis, a Farm School graduate who was a native of Langadia. The Anastenarides are a pastoral agricultural people—we passed fields of wheat, tomatoes and orchards of fruit. A hush lay over the town. Thousands of tourists, many from foreign lands, were ominously quiet. Somewhere drums were beating

like tom-toms in a jungle. The drums, said Jimmy, were in the house of
the chief of the Anastenarides, and he led us there. Outside the small
house, surrounded by a circle of tourists, a half dozen "bacchants," barefoot men and women carrying icons draped with jangling bells, embracing them as if they were infants, were jigging trancelike in the dust.
Others waved red kerchiefs.

A monotonously scraping melody accompanying the drums inside
sounded as if it were being played on a badly tuned violin. Policemen
at the door held off the crowds. I showed my press letter and we were
allowed inside. The small low-ceilinged room was steam-hot and pungent
with human smells. Icons hung from the walls. On one corner a cross
was planted in a flowerpot, and in other pots, candles were burning. In
the far corner a man was beating a drum and another was playing a lyre,
sawing a tortured tune, four five-beat bars, over and over. Three men
and eight women, their unseeing eyes like dead men's, stomped about the
room, bending their bodies, raising and lowering the icons in their arms.
The Anastenarides believe it is the icons that gives them the power to walk
on fire and it is only when the relics are in their hands that they can
endure the torments of their worship. The dancers were being trailed
around the room by relatives bearing towels who wiped their dripping
faces.

They had danced through the night and begun again at noon and
would not cease until 7 P.M., said Jimmy. In the morning a bull calf with
gilded horns and garlanded with flowers, had been sacrificed and its
bloody flesh hacked apart and distributed to the bacchants. The chief, a
short dark man of forty-five named George Emanuel, was dancing with
his wife and two daughters, aged twenty and sixteen. A heavy young
woman in a gray dress, her head thrown back, shook epileptically and
let out shrill cries which sounded like "Oink, oink, oink!" A tall man
with closed eyes, embracing his icon as if it were a woman, responded
with doglike barks, "Ach, ech! Ach ech!"

A small blond youth relieved the tall man, taking his icon, leaping
into the air with it, causing its silver bells to ring. The Anastenarides
believe the jangling of the icon bells drives away evil spirits; the sacred
kerchiefs tied to the icons were knotted "to tie up the Devil." The
women in gray began a chant, crying out, "St. Konstantine is riding
away on a horse."

A man answered, crying in anguished tones, "Tell us, why do you
leave, why do you leave us here?"

Other voices picked it up, saying:

"You are the strongest of men. Why have you left us?"

"I leave and I send you God."

"Almighty St. Konstantine, have pity on us."

"Holy Mother Savior, show mercy to your slaves."

"When we were slaves of the Turks and the Bulgarians the saints were free. Now that we are free, our saints are slaves in the churches on the soil of Greece."

The blond youth jangled his icon and cried, "These are our ancestral possessions brought out of slavery."

"Oink, oink, oink!" shrilled the woman in gray and men barked, "Ach ech!" The heat, the smells were making me ill, the hypnotic drums and the anguished cries filled me with a kind of terror. I fled from the room.

We walked toward the sacred grove. Cows wandered in the crooked earth streets, chickens scratched in the dust. The tree-shaded oval was surrounded by an arena of seats. Though it was only four o'clock and the dancing was not scheduled to take place for another three hours, the area was filled. Frantic police tried to control the stampeding crowds outside. I showed my credentials to an army general at the gate and he shook his head, saying, "Everyone has a letter from someone." Some Germans with cameras were allowed to pass. Remembering the camera-prone narcissism of all Greeks, we waved our cameras and were allowed to pass into a press section where we found chairs.

It was a turbulent scene. Men scrambled onto roofs. Boys hung from the trees like colonies of baboons. A jukebox was bellowing "Never on Sunday." Beyond the field a carnival merry-go-round blared. Touts peddled soft drinks, nuts and nougats. Balloons floated into the heavens and a pair of storks circled overhead.

A chicken was scratching on the dancing area, a circle of dark wet sand about eight feet square. At four thirty some men rolled out wheelbarrows of logs and children followed carrying bundles of kindling. "They're going to roast the hen," said Thanos. Greek and German film crews crowded into the field, blocking our view.

When the logs were piled high, a procession of Anastenarides elders arrived with candles and a cup of burning oil for the ceremonial lighting. The oil-soaked logs burst into flame and we could feel their heat fifty feet away. Two firewatchers stood at the edges of the fire, stirring it with long poles. A noisy group of relatives of the dancers arrived and took chairs reserved for them near the fire. There were about seventy-five, mostly women with children and babies. The men stirring the fire withdrew from the heat and were replaced by others.

By 6:45 the fire had burned down to a glowing mound of sizzling coals. The watchers raked it smooth and the hot air flickered. The amplified music stopped. The crowd hushed, listening to the drums approaching, louder and louder. Two rows of police formed an avenue through the crowd. Twenty-five barefoot bacchants ran into the field, men and women from sixteen to seventy years of age, prancing after the drummer and lyre player, their arms extended like blind persons', bearing icons and scarves. They closed on the circle of coals and then withdrew, as if driven off by the heat. The drums and lyres continued—the drum beats seemed to be synchronized with the beatings of my heart. The dancers whirled around the coals in short jigging steps, approaching and withdrawing, their in-and-out movements subtly sexual. The hands of those not bearing icons drew crosses in the air. Crying "Oink, oink, oink!" the woman in gray made the first leap into the coals. She ran across them several times until her feet were blackened with ash. With wild shrieks others plunged after her, scurrying over the sizzling circle, prancing in a frenzy of ecstasy in the outer oval of sand. Each dancer followed a single pattern, approaching the fire several times and backing away, and then plunging with a shrill cry onto the coals. Within moments all were streaking across the field. The younger daughter of the chief ran with her hands extended as if she were running in the dark. Several pairs of dancers embraced one another and leaped on the coals together. Most of the women danced a kind of fast two-step; men simply leaped. One elderly couple, a small thin man and his heavy thick-goitered wife, was unable to stop and, clutching an icon between them, they seemed to levitate over the coals. Their names were Satiros and Despina Lioros. The blond youth whom we had seen in the house of the chief embracing the large icon, was their son, Stamatis, aged twenty-four. Another son, Kostas, twenty, was among the dancers.

A lean youth in a green net shirt and dark trousers rolled to his knees, threw out his arms, taking the shape of a cross. Moaning deliriously, he pranced a half minute on the red bed. Two other youths, embracing, bending and unbending their bodies in unison, shaking the sweat from their bodies, joined him in a contest of endurance and the green-shirted one, baying, leaped through the air like a wounded dog. An old lady in black jumped up and down on one spot as if she would beat out the fire with her feet. A young husband and wife ran over the coals like lovers through a brook. Spreading his arms like wings, the chief leaped on the coals, spurring the others into a new frenzy of shrieking and leaping. Embracing himself, his eyes closed, the green-shirted one seemed about to collapse. Supported by another, he revived and stretching his arms toward the skies, raised himself upward like a burning martyr. Stamatis Lioros was spitting great globs of saliva. Three women interlocked arms and rocked together on the ashes. A man bent to stir up the dying coals with his hands and a young girl making strangely hissing noises danced on the ashes, her long braids whirling behind her.

Suddenly with no warning the relatives and friends of the dancers rose from their chairs and forming a circle around the field, brought it to an end. Following the chief, the dancers ran from the field. The green-shirted youth danced until he was out of sight. The fat woman's barking faded away and only the drums could be heard. The performance had lasted less than half an hour.

The circle of ash was gray and dead. Feeling it with my hands I found it only mildly warm. We followed the dancers to a concrete water tank where they were washing their feet. Cows lowed. Crowds gathered around to examine the dancers' feet. The chief offered his sole for me to touch. "Your feet are not the same as mine," he said defensively. The woman in gray was still bobbing and whirling, and Stamatis Lioros, clinging to his icon, continued to dance in the dust. I asked him why he did it, what drove him into the fire. "You get a message," he replied. "Konstantine tells you to do it." How did Konstantine speak to him? Smiling mysteriously, he said, "I don't know. I understand and that's all. I have danced for six years and my feet have never burned." He was delicately built, and his smile was like a saint's, beatific and gentle. I asked the same question of the green-shirted one who was drawing deeply from a cigarette and he replied with the same words, "Konstantine tells me." I spoke to the lady in gray and her answer was the same. Her name was Giorgia Hadzibuzina and she was thirty-seven years old. I asked if she would dance the next day and she said, "I don't know, I must wait for the message." How would the message be received, I asked. "I can't explain," she said. "It just happens."

Inside the hot little house the drums beat, the lyres played. I entered for a moment. The room was hot as a Turkish bath and cloudy with candle smoke. Some women were dancing. A black, shrouded grand-mother bobbed, jangling the bells on a red handkerchief. Another was weaving her arms in a swimming motion. A man barked, a child was shrieking. The dancing, said Jimmy, would continue through the night. A bacchant, ordered by Konstantine in a dream, would get up, build a fire, and arouse his fellow bacchants to dance.

Driving back to Thessaloniki, we discussed the phenomena we had witnessed, the emotional hysteria, the unparched feet. "They are peas-ants who work in the fields without shoes," said Thanos. "They have very tough feet." Jon Emerson confessed he had fought a desire to take off his shoes and run on the coals. Betsy Hoffman admitted suppressing the same impulse. Jimmy Halatis told the story of a German reporter and a drunken Greek sailor who one year had leaped onto the coals and had been hospitalized with their burns.

The next day, Sunday, we returned to Langadia, arriving at three o'clock. The photographers were gone and there were fewer foreigners. The crowd, as large as the day before, was almost entirely Greek. The streets smelled deliciously of *souvlaki* cooking over charcoal grills. We saw the green-shirted dancer, whose name was Panagiotis Gaitagis, tending bar in an outdoor tavern. He did not know, he said, whether he would dance again—Konstantine had not spoken yet. In the house of the chief the drums beat, the lyres played. The dancing had continued in relays through the night. Stamatis Lioros was kissing the icon in his arms. A fat woman, dripping sweat, was supporting, holding upright, a young woman who seemed to be in a faint. Giorgia Hadzibuzina, wearing a blue dress, was rocking convulsively. A young man, hands clasped above his head, bent to the ground and threw his body back like a sprung bow. An old woman with a towel passed among the dancers like a fight trainer, wiping their brows.

We went to the sacred field. The logs stacked in tepee fashion, were ignited and when they had burned the coals were raked. At seven o'clock the drum beats moved closer, bringing the dancers. There were only twelve. Panagiotis Gaitagis pranced to and from the fire like a runner waiting for the starting signal. Crying "Oink, oink!" Giorgia Hadzibuzina was first to plunge over the coals. Two thick-legged women followed her, rocking together in mutual embrace. The performance seemed less spontaneous than the day before, the excitement diminished for both performers and audience. I saw Betsy Hoffman get up and speak to a policeman. I could not tell whether the officer, a tall man, understood her and thought she was joking or whether he only pretended to understand. Looking down into her pretty young face, into her large dark eyes, he laughed and nodded his head. Had he lowered his eyes still further he would have seen her bare feet.

Jon Emerson, also barefoot, his black beard gleaming, got up and clasped Betsy's hand and together they ran toward the bed of coals. *"Ochi!"* the officer shouted, running after them. "No, no!"

He was too late. At the edge of the circle several of the bacchants tried to restrain the two intruders. One of the men wrestled with Jon. A burst of applause in the audience changed the bacchants' mood and they started to pull Jon and Betsy toward them, drawing them into the circle, to the hot center. Jon and Betsy leaped like fauns across the ash, turned around, ran back, and repeated the circle two more times.

The audience laughed and applauded. Men and women crowded into the field, forming a circle around Jon and Betsy, demanding to see their feet. How did it feel, they asked, and Jon said, "It felt kind of nice and warm." "It tingled," Betsy said. They sat on the ground and elevated their feet for people to see. A policeman brought a doctor who confirmed medically that the feet were not burned. Ignored by the crowd the dancers in the circle called a halt and ran out of the arena. Cheering the two Americans as if they were matadors, the crowd hoisted them into the air and carried them from the arena. Everyone demanded to see their feet. The idea spread that the bearded stranger was some kind of holy person. A strangely silent little girl in a pinafore clung to Betsy, following her everywhere.

We tried to escape and, running, made it to the car. But the cheering crowd followed us, encircling the car so we could not drive away. Faces filled the windows. The silent little girl gave Jon and Betsy two pieces of charred wood as if they were sacred relics. Speaking suddenly, her lip trembling, the child said, "Did Konstantine tell you to do it, did he send you a message?" Policemen cleared the street and we moved slowly away.

We stopped at Jimmy's house. His mother had heard that two Americans plunged into the fire and burned their feet. Neighbors arrived to see for themselves that the feet were not burned. In the country we passed two couples riding on a farm tractor. Recognizing us they shouted, "Didn't you burn?" When we arrived in Thessaloniki the news had already reached the city that two Americans, summoned by Konstantine, had walked on the fire and by the grace of the saint had miraculously not been burned.

XXXIV

Ghosts

I had waited until June, saving almost to the end, the island of Corfu. Looking down from my plane on the Ionian Sea, I remembered that it was on Corfu that Ulysses, his baggage lost at sea, emerged dripping naked before the astonished Princess Nausicaa, that Lawrence Durrell had identified Corfu as Shakespeare's setting for *The Tempest,* and that Austria's Empress Elizabeth, who built a palace on the island, called it "the most beautiful spot on earth."

An hour from Athens the plane descended toward mist-veiled green forests, golden wheat fields and turquoise lagoons. The air terminal smelled sweetly of *fraoules,* tiny strawberries, packed in green ferns, waiting to be flown back to Athens. The island capital, Kerkira, had Venetian ramparts and towers and islanders were speaking Greek in soft *Italiante* accents.

I met my guide, a pert self-possessed young woman named Elena Marondis, and Spyros, my driver, a muscular dark man, named, like half the men of Corfu, after the island patron, St. Spyridon. His large black 1961 Pontiac sedan shone like onyx and was a gift, said Elena, from a rich lady whom he had served as chauffeur.

We followed the sea out of town, driving through silver-misted valleys, through orchards of figs, peaches, almonds, and olive trees large as oaks. Cypresses and cedars added dark tones to a lush green Eden. "Our climate is so good we don't need to make things grow," said Elena. "The humidity keeps Corfu moist all the year so things grow by themselves. The fruits make themselves ready and we need only to pick. Olives fall

385

to the ground and we have nothing to do but gather them. So it is said we are rather lazy. Other Greeks are jealous of us and say we are mad."

She was thin as a gamin and had lovely changing dark eyes. She had learned English in Corfu's British Institute and she was president of the Guides' Association. "In Greece everyone wants to be a president," she said. "I never wanted to be so I am." There were, she said, forty-six guides of which thirty-two were girls. Did they, I asked, sometimes have romantic involvements with their clients? "We are daytime guides," she said, very business-like. "We do not have time for night attentions." How about Corfu by night? "For that there are special male guides," she said. "The clients are often elderly Swedish and German ladies who sometimes make arrangements." I asked how old she was and she replied sharply, "Never ask a woman that." To make everything very clear she told me she was married to a bank teller and had a son, aged two.

We turned inland. Ahead Mt. Pantocrator was covered with mists. We crossed the island to Paleocastritsa, a magically beautiful bay in a mountain inlet which, Durrell said, "lies in a trance, drugged with its own extraordinary perfection." The cove may have been the site of the palace to which King Alcinous' daughter Nausicaa, "tall, pale and beautiful as a goddess," brought the naked Ulysses. The surprised father took a dim view of the red-bearded interloper and packed him off "across the wind-dark sea."

On a precipice above the bay was a Byzantine monastery. Spyros snailed his car up part of the way and then, not wanting it scratched by trees and shrubs, parked, and Elena and I walked to the top. On the way she pointed out a "tree couple," a vertically thin male cypress and a rounded horizontally-limbed female standing side by side, a Mr. and Mrs. Jack Spratt posing for a marriage photo. "She is the only female allowed up here by the monks," said Elena. The monastery was rich, owning vast lands, but the monks numbered only three. One, young, short and hairy, was scurrying after some wayward sheep. Another watched us surreptitiously from behind a window blind and a third sat idly under a cypress smoking a cigarette. Straight down, perhaps five hundred feet, was the sea and the rocks in its bed shone like turquoise. "A girl was swallowed by a shark down there," said Elena. "So we have a little fear."

We looked at icons in the chapel and then Elena opened the door to a monk's cell and invited me inside. It was neat and spare. The bed was burlap-covered boards. A towel was draped over a washbasin, a robe hung from a peg in the wall. On our way out we passed a wooden vat. "In August," said Elena, her contempt apparent, "the monks will tromp the grapes with their feet. They hold up their skirts like dancing women."

We started down the path and on the way Elena bent over and

sniffed the ground. "See how the ground smells under the cypress," she said. "It is the resin. On Corfu there are always beautiful smells. When it rains in Albania we smell the thyme from the Albanian mountains. Now all of Corfu smells like linden. We dry the blossoms and make a tea which is good for the belly."

On Paleocastritsa Beach there was a restaurant and here in the sun we ordered lunch. Dark green lobsters, curling and uncurling their claws like condemned prisoners, were brought for our inspection and we selected two. While they were being prepared I went for a swim. The water was cold and so clear I could see the green floor three fathoms down. I splashed across the cove toward red and green cliffs, and I explored azure caves like a Homeric sailor in search of a naiad. When I returned, refreshed, to the table, Elena was reading a newspaper. In Athens there had been a new government crisis, a minister-without-portfolio had resigned. "He thought he should have a briefcase," said Elena. "But he didn't get one so it was no use being a minister without a briefcase." Spyros was in his automobile eating sandwiches. "He is very fond of that car," said Elena. "I don't know what he did to earn it, but he seems to have worked very hard." The lobsters came and with them a native white wine, shimmering gold with an herblike aroma. Elena confided that she enjoyed most guiding Americans. "I like Germans least," she said. "They never ask anything. You think you are leading mutes and when they move it is always together, like chickens or sheep." From a jukebox came the soft strains of a *canzonetti*. "Corfuans like music and singing," said Elena. "But we can't stand *bouzouki*. We're very calm people, not so hot-blooded like other Greeks. We never quarrel and this is astonishing to everyone." Our dessert was a large bowl of *fraoules* marinated in an orange liqueur. "Corfu is the only place in the world where wild strawberries are cultivated," said Elena. "Airplane passengers complained that the smell of the strawberries on the plane gave them headaches so now the strawberries have their own plane to fly to Athens."

Returning across the island we met women wearing the Corfuan costume of full gray skirts, white blouses and voluminous white headdresses in which they carried cargoes of laundry, cabbages, lemons large as grapefruit, slaughtered lambs and, at a building site, stones. Walking with stiff queenly majesty, they reminded me of the stone caryatids supporting the porch of the Erechtheion in Athens. On the east coast we drove north to the Castello Hotel, a former medieval castle in a forested park. Across the Bay of Gouviá were the mountains of Albania. The hotel, said Elena, "is rather popular with rich old people from England, Germany and Sweden." Nightingales and thrushes sang in the forest. "At night," said Elena, "there are also owls. Sometimes people move out of the hotel because of the birds." The palace was in baronial style with dark wood, rich red carpets and a wide staircase. The hunting trophies of a former owner hung from the walls. "As you can see, it's like a cinema," said Elena. It was tea time and a terrace, facing the sea, filled with elderly Swedish guests who were shepherded by a handsome Swedish girl wearing a purple silk scarf in her golden hair. "She's too pink," said Elena. "She reminds me of an advertisement of milk for babies." Foreign groups sometimes traveled with their own guides, explained Elena, "because if something happens like a death she is responsible." Disasters were not uncommon. "One Frenchman drank himself to death," said Elena. "And another, an underwater fisherman, swam out to sea and never came back. He even lost his body and left a wife with three children." Elena's strangest tale concerned an English wife whose husband died in Italy on the way to Greece. "She had the excursion for two," said Elena. "So she put her husband in a refrigerator in Italy and came here with an Italian boy friend to have her holiday. When it was over she went to Italy to take her husband out of the refrigerator and she took him home." A soft blue haze covered the sea which separated Corfu from Albania. "It is only two and a half kilometers," said Elena. "Corfuans swam there in the war to escape the occupation. Some didn't make it. In the morning we hear the Albanian cocks crowing." A waitress brought tea and cakes and the Swedes clucked over them. "Tourists are very strange," said Elena. "They get so enthusiastic over trifles which are really nothing. How marvelous the shish kebab! Nothing but a stick pushed through tough meat."

We returned to town and Elena left for the evening. Spyros suggested a night drive to the palace of the Empress Elizabeth and I arranged to meet him at nine o'clock. I took a table at an outdoor café under a long arcade, a copy of Paris' Rue de Rivoli built during the Napoleonic occupation. The remnants of history were around me. Beyond a row of tall Venetian houses was an English cricket field and nearby an ornate bandstand which might have been in Kensington Gardens. At a table local youths were drinking "tsin-tsi-berra," ginger beer, the popular soft drink of the island. Corfuan history is a series of occupations, by Corinthians, Romans, Byzantines, Sicilians and Turks. A kind of order was established in the fourteenth century when Venetians took the island and held it until the destruction of the Venetian Empire by Napoleon in 1797. In 1814, Corfu was occupied by the British who designed a water system still in use, built the cricket field and many public buildings, including a high commissioner's residence, now a palace of the Greek royal family, and a summer palace outside the town, called "Mon Repos," where the Duke of Edinburgh was born in 1921. In 1864, England ceded Corfu to Greece.

Three years before, the Empress Elizabeth, a beautiful and neurotic young woman in flight from an unhappy marriage and the stifling life of the Austrian court, had come for a visit and fallen in love with Corfu. Driving over the island she discovered a decaying Venetian villa in a wilderness of olive and myrtle, which faced the sea and across it the Albanian mountains. She bought it and in the 1890s she came back to build a secluded palace which she hoped would bring peace to her tormented life. Sparing no expense, the Empress commissioned a German scholar to build "a Phaecian palace with pillared colonnades and hanging gardens, safe from prying eyes."

Like her Wittelsbach cousin, the mad Ludwig II of Bavaria (whose brother Otto was the first king of Greece), Elizabeth was an artist without genius. When her designer died she summoned architects from Vienna and sculptors from Italy. During the building, Elizabeth's only son, Rudolf, committed suicide at Mayerling. She likened his death to the death of Achilles and named the palace "The Achilleon" as a memorial. She ordered every single article in the palace to be decorated with a dolphin's head, the dolphin being sacred to Achilles' mother, Thetis. The result was a hodgepodge of taste and styles—a swooningly romantic setting from Böcklin for a heroine out of D'Annunzio. To the natives of the nearby village of Gasturi, to whom the building brought a windfall of prosperity, the Achilleon, lighted by the torches of bronze goddesses, was indeed a fairy palace. Its black-veiled mistress darted over the countryside so swiftly the awed people named her "the locomotive."

The dream was not to be. The palace was hardly finished before the restless Empress contemplated selling it, a move from which she was dissuaded by her forbearing husband. One day in 1896, a new statue of Achilles, a monument to the dead crown prince, was unveiled in the garden. Rigid as a statue herself, the Empress sat through the ceremonies and on the same day left Corfu never to return. Two years later she was assassinated by an Italian anarchist on the quay of Geneva.

In 1907, the Emperor sold the palace to Kaiser Wilhelm II of Germany who used it as a holiday retreat until the outbreak of the World War in 1914. During the World War the Achilleon was used by the French as a hospital. In the Second World War it was successively a Greek, an Italian and a German hospital. In 1952, the palace came under the control of the Greek National Tourist Office, which operated it as a museum, and in 1960 it was leased to German businessmen who operate it as a gambling casino.

The mists which filled the twilight over the cricket field might have risen from Caliban's cavern. A young man drinking ginger beer with some German girls at the next table turned and asked, "Are you English?" I replied I was American and he introduced himself. His name, of course, was Spyros. He was, he said, a guide. He was small and dark with a sharp intelligence in his black eyes. I told him I had a very good guide and named her. "Ah, yes," said Spyros II. "She is very good. But some things is easier with a man guide. If you need I will help." I could not think of a thing I needed which Elena could not provide. "Perhaps tomorrow," he said, resuming an animated German conversation with the girls.

Spyros arrived in his black Pontiac. Nine kilometers south of the town we drove through Gasturi where Spyros, a bachelor, pointed out his house. Of the five hundred people in the village, he said, half were related to him. The Achilleon and its adjoining hotel and restaurant employed villagers as waiters, chars, kitchen helpers, parking attendants, gardeners, foresters and croupiers in the casino. "An old man named Efstathios Casfikis who worked for the Empress as gardener still lives," said Spyros. "Sometimes he remembers, sometimes not. When he has a spell of memory he tells of walking up the mountain with the Empress to a chapel. She climbed the mountain each day, either with him or with her Greek teacher whose name was Kristomanos."

Spyros was more interested in the Kaiser whom his father and mother had served as waiter and waitress. "During the period of the Kaiser everyone in the village worked in the palace. No one cooked. Such an abundance of food was cooked everyone was able to carry some home." The Kaiser, said Spyros, liked Greek women. "During the olive harvest he would stay in the olive groves, pinching and fondling the woman harvesters. One day he was lost. They found him in an olive grove eating bread with peasants. He gave the women earrings and perfume and cakes of palace soap. He went through villages astonishing everyone by throwing coins and soap cakes at women. Naturally the Kaiserin did not come to Corfu." It all came to an end in 1914 and Gasturi became a poor village. After 1962, when the Germans opened the casino, some of the old prosperity returned.

A great blue neon sign across the top of the palace was visible for miles. In its lurid light the white statues in the garden glimmered strangely. Corfuans are not permitted in the casino and Spyros waited while I entered the palace. Inside I was met by Corfu's tourist director, John Damaschinos ("man from Damascus"), a dapper friendly man who was the son of an English mother and had spent part of his life in England. To the right of the entrance was Elizabeth's chapel, unaltered since her time. The casino, as my man from Damascus pointed out, is the only one in the world with a chapel in which gamblers can pray for good luck on their way to the tables.

The palace rooms were a jumble of Victorian rococo, neoclassic and Bavarian baroque. Clusters of cherubs appeared to be leaping about the walls. The plangent theatricality of the palace seemed entirely suited to the astonishing woman who built it and the time in which she lived. We took an elevator to the third-floor restaurant where a gypsy orchestra was playing. The playing rooms were in Elizabeth's private suite. At the moment one table of baccara and four of roulette were in progress. The casino, said Damaschinos, was not the success which had been hoped. "Tourists are not gamblers," he said. "Except for Saturday nights when rich Athenians come to play, it is poorly patronized." Double sets of keys to the casino were held by the German lessors and the tourist office, and both were required to open the doors. "So it is necessary for me or someone from my office to be here every evening," said Damaschinos. "For me it is a peculiar thrill to come here. For us who were children on Corfu this palace was always something extraordinary. There is a bad-luck myth about the palace, we believe it is full of ghosts. Elizabeth was murdered, Wilhelm lost his throne. The French administrator of the hospital during the First World War shot himself. So did the interior decorator who supervised the restoration." In the summer, gaming tables are set up on the verandah, turning the Achilleon into "the only open-air casino in the world." "I hate the vulgarity of the blue neon lights," said Damaschinos. "But the Germans insist. In financial dealings they are scrupulously honest but there are diplomatic problems. Greeks are dedicated water drinkers and when a rich Athenian gambler was refused a glass of water he left in anger and never returned."

The palace was built into a hill and the third floor opened on a formal garden filled with statues. There was a row of nine simpering muses, one of which was sucking her index finger, and busts of Greek writers—Sophocles, Plato, Homer, Euripides—and one of Shakespeare whom Elizabeth considered worthy of the company.

A forest sloping toward the sea was filled with flickering fireflies, turning the universe topsy-turvy with star-filled heavens below. The sea glimmered through the trees. Cypresses and palms cast dark shadows on the statue of the dying Achilles. Vapory will-o'-the-wisps spiraled up through the forest. Except for the palms the romantically northern setting might have been the Starnberger See where Elizabeth's beloved cousin, Ludwig, was drowned, possibly a suicide. Only a German could have conceived a scene so yearningly evoking death. The orchestra playing waltzes and the gamblers around the tables accentuated the apocalyptic mood. The palace and its garden were a monument to death, the deaths of empires and king, and the necrological date was 1914.

Spyros was waiting to take me back to town. Driving through moonlit olive groves, he asked how old I thought he was. He flicked on a light and turned his profile. His brown face was smooth, his black hair was limned with gray. "Make a guess," he insisted. I ventured forty-five years. "I will be fifty-nine years old in December," he said proudly, turning off the light. Like his car he was well preserved. "But I don't feel old at all," he went on. "I have the body and strength of a boy of twenty." We were in the town. At the arcade he stopped the car. "It is early, not yet twelve o'clock," he said. "You like to see other things?" I was tired. "I'll see you in the morning," I said. "Good night."

I heard singing, a gently lulling male voice which I followed to a tavern. The singer was a fat dark man with hairy hands which he stroked softly across the strings of a guitar. Softly he lowed sweet-sad love songs like lullabies. It reminded me of the singing of Keti Apostolatou in Athens, and I remembered that she also was from the Ionian Islands.

In the morning I met Elena and she took me on a walk of the town, beginning on Moustoxilou Street, a narrow lane over which laundry flapped from facing terraces. "The balconies," said Elena, "were for the ladies to watch their knights fighting in the streets." The Venetian palaces were in run-down condition. "As there are four owners, one for each floor, they can never agree on restorations," said Elena, "so it looks very bad." We moved through a crowded market which smelled of strawberries, cherries and fresh fish. Soft voices babbled and canaries trilled in cages. We passed the courthouse, the steps of which were filled with men. "Ninety-five per cent of them are lawyers," said Elena scornfully. "We have so many lawyers in Greece because everyone needs a mediary for everything."

We entered the cathedral, a lavishly decorated basilica in neo-Byzantine style. An old priest bobbing up and down like a Moslem, was praying over a woman on her knees. When the prayer was finished she rose to her feet, opened her purse, gave the priest some money and left. Dropping the woman's money into his purse, the priest turned and invited us to see the body of St. Theodora, wife of the ninth-century Byzantine Emperor Theophilus. "The Emperor was against icons and ordered them destroyed," said Elena. "His wife was for the icons and saved them. Imagine what trouble that caused!"

The priest led us into a small chapel where, mumbling a prayer, he began opening a casket. The layers of silver and glass unpeeled like an onion. Deep in shadow I saw a headless black mummy and, reaching toward me, a black withered hand. The priest and Elena stooped to kiss the coiled fingers. Elena whispered, "It is tradition in Byzantine churches that the faces of dead monks and nuns be covered. When people see the head covered they say there is no head, but it is there." The priest was waiting for me to bend. When it was apparent to him that I was not going to bow to the frightful thing, he closed up the casket with a loud click and thud and pushed us from the chapel. Another woman arrived and began financial negotiations with the priest to reopen the casket. While the priest bickered over the sum, he peered into the woman's open purse. Terms were agreed upon and be began once more to open the casket.

We walked on to Corfu's most famous church, St. Spyridon. The fourth-century bishop of Cypress never visited Corfu. He became the island's patron when his body was brought there from Constantinople in the fifteenth century. His posthumous miracles are impressive. He is credited with saving the island from famine in the sixteenth century, ending the great plague which swept Europe in the seventeenth, and bringing about the military defeat of the Turks in the eighteenth. Four times each year his body is carried out in a colorful procession. His church, in Venetian style, is the richest on Corfu. "Everything," said Elena, "all the icons and chandeliers and lamps, are gifts from people who have been helped by Spyridon." We joined a long line waiting outside the crypt. A man was talking silently to himself, gesticulating in an animated argument with a nonexistent companion. "This is a type of Corfu madness that is very common," said Elena. The door of the chapel opened and a family came out. We moved slowly into a tiny dark room. Two priests were chanting, one at the head and the other at the foot of a catafalque lit by more than thirty filigreed oil lamps hanging from chains. A humming ventilator was unable to remove the stale smells of bodies and oil. We moved toward the casket. "You must kiss only the feet," Elena whispered. It was enough. The black head of the withered mummy beneath the glass leered toothily at me. I bent, not quite touching my lips to the glass, and I moved on.

Spyros was waiting on the esplanade. He drove us out of town in a southward direction along the east shore of the island. At an isolated beach he stopped and asked if I would like to swim. Elena waited in the car while Spyros and I climbed down an embankment and splashed for an hour in absolutely clear water. He swam vigorously; his body, was, as he reported, a young man's body, dark brown in color. "I wish to be dark as a Negro," he said. "The tourist girls have special desires for black men." We let the sun dry us and we dressed and drove three kilometers to the fishing village of Benitses where we found a garden restaurant dappled with sunlight. A stream flowed beside our table. Carnations and nasturtiums cascaded down its banks and mulberry trees dropped their black fruit into the water. We gathered a bowl of them for dessert. "We have white mulberries and black ones and red ones," said Elena. "The red ones are best."

In the afternoon we stopped at the famous belvedere of Kanoni. Spyros waited in his car while Elena and I climbed down to the sea and walked over the jetty to the tiny wind-swept convent called St. Vlacherna, standing in solitude on a reef. Two nuns were in charge. One, Sister Agapia, sat on the stones, legs spread like a Shakespearean bawd, joking with two fishermen. The other, Sister Kassiani, named for the abbess poet of Holy Tuesday, was whitewashing a wall with a broom. Her torn habit was streaked with lime. The place glistened. Steps to a bell tower were covered with pots of red geraniums. I asked the nuns how they lived and Kassiani, laughing like a happy Martha, said, "God and Christians provide." She said the sea was often so high in winter that they were sometimes marooned for weeks.

In the sea beyond was Mouse Island where it is believed Ulysses was shipwrecked in a storm. One of the fishermen offered to take us there in his motorboat. During the voyage, which took three minutes, Elena told me that the island was the inspiration for Böcklin's painting of Charon portaging souls to Hades, called "The Isle of the Dead." We climbed a rocky path toward a church on the summit, passing an English sign which said, "Well come foreigner to our little island. Don't go away without taking a souvenir." Outside the church a caretaker was waiting at a stand of postcards and cheap bric-a-brac. We bought some orangeade which he drew by a long rope dripping from a well. Suddenly the man began to shout, saying, "People come here and are discontent. What do they want? A ballet? An opera, a cinema? This is an island, God's handiwork. . . ."

"One of the crazy ones," said Elena. I understood the man's rage. Perhaps we were his only visitors that day. On the wall of a tiny church were two plaques commemorating visits by Elizabeth. The melancholy solitude which seemed to be unhinging the caretaker had drawn the Empress to this alien place.

Our helmsman returned us to the convent where Sister Kassiani gave us pink carnations. We climbed to Kanoni where Spyros was sleeping in his car. I asked him to take me to the Achilleon, so I might see it by daylight. On the way we passed the gates of the King's summer palace, "Mon Repos." Elena said, "When I was a little girl I picked cyclamens and anemones in the palace woods. I pretended I was Little Red Riding Hood." A woman carrying cabbages on her head waved merrily. "We are so calm and peaceful that a woman can walk any place alone at any hour," said Elena. "In Athens I could not do such a thing."

Spyros waited in his car at the palace gates and Elena and I walked inside, passing a statue of a satyr with cymbals and others of Hermes, Venus, Diana and Apollo. "Elizabeth was greatly impressed with Greek mythology," said Elena. We met a German croupier who nodded but Elena did not speak. "He was a storm trooper in Greece during the war and speaks Greek very well. I hate him," she said. In the palace we looked at portraits of the Empress, oil paintings, lithographs, photographs, catching her at every period of her life—as a lovely bride of sixteen, as a spirited matron with flowers woven into her long black hair, as a middle-aged woman in a cloud of chiffon, hiding her face behind a fan. Cases were filled with jeweled fans, many of them black for mourning. "She was always hiding her face because she did not wish that people recognize her," said Elena. The Empress had a strong mouth, flashing dark eyes, a high brow, firm nose and chin and, to the very end of her life, a wasp-slender waist. "She had her Swedish masseur pack her in warm seaweed to keep it thin," said Elena. In a final photograph made the year before she died when she was sixty, she appears entirely in black, regally poised in the high-busted fashion of the time, like a woman of thirty in a sorrowing trance. Nearby was a soulful portrait of Heine, the poet she loved above all others, a spiritual exile like herself who continued to yearn for the land from which he had been driven by anti-Semitism. An adjoining heavy-spirited room was filled with memorabilia of the Kaiser, with holiday photos, ship models and a heavy desk with a mounted saddle standing before it. "The Kaiser was a strange man," said Elena. "He did not like chairs and always sat in a saddle when he worked."

The Kaiser removed a statue of Heine from the garden because he considered the poet a "subversive Jew." It was taken by admirers to Toulon, in France. On its pedestal the Kaiser placed a statue of Elizabeth, slender-waisted in a Victorian gown, gazing across the sea toward the Albanian mountains, searching for the inaccessible dream. Nearby the statues of muses and poets gleamed in the sunlight. At the bottom of the garden, like a Wagnerian superhuman, stood the Kaiser's statue of a battling Achilles. "It has no artistic merit at all," said Elena contemptuously. "Fortunately an electric lamp on the end of the spear has been removed." So was a plaque which said, "From the greatest of the Germans to the greatest of the Greeks." Turtledoves cooed in the cypresses. Roses, bougainvillaea and hibiscus drenched the terraces with

color. Roses, delphiniums and petunias burgeoned like weeds. Albania
was lost in the mists, the town below was a silvery ghost. The drugged
island spread about us, a dream on a hot afternoon. "The Gods are
dead," wrote Oscar Wilde on Corfu.

> And yet, perchance in this sea-tranced isle,
> Chewing the bitter fruit of memory,
> Some God lies hidden in the asphodel.

XXXV

Museum on Corfu

DESPERATE FOR TOURISTS: The Greek government is so desperate for tourists that it not only has ordered all luxury and first-class hotels in Greece to reduce their rates by 20%, but it also is propagandizing the image of the Greek lover. The idea is to attract to Greece single women, American and Scandinavian schoolteachers, for example, who might be in the market for a bit of romance.

"Greece is one of the most love-conscious countries in the world," declares *Parikiaki*, a Greek publication. "The young Greeks are notorious lovers, and it is only a public secret that some beauties from the north come down to Venus land just to make sure about it. Another public secret is that the Greeks do have a special inclination towards foreign women."

A pocketbook recently published in Athens for the use of Greek guides contains translations of various amorous approaches, teaches the reader how to say in five different languages: "I love you . . . turn off the light, please, and come here . . ."

Parade Magazine, June 16, 1968

Twenty-four hours after they arrived on an Italian cruise boat, the three ladies from Newcastle had the hotel in an uproar. Because everyone involved in their story felt compelled to tell about it, it was as difficult as in *Rashomon* to learn precisely what happened. The night clerk whose name was Dimitrios told how Mrs. Garton called him twice to the room she shared with her daughter and her sister on the pretense that she could not get the Venetian blinds up or down. Antonio, a handsome bellhop, reported being snared into the elevator by the sister, Mrs. Allen, on the ruse that she was unable to operate it. The elderly night bartender said one of the ladies offered him money to come to their room. The desk clerk said, "They're all crazy, hysterical. They are sick." The telephone

397

operator said, "Never, *never* have we had anything like this in the hotel."
To which the concierge replied, "Once there was the American girl who
tried to get all the bellhops into her bed but after all she was only one
and these are three."

I met them in the lobby the day of their arrival. They had just had
lunch, Mrs. Garton said, and the wine, tasting of eucalyptus, had made
them sick. She was a good-looking blonde matron in her fifties. She introduced her sister, Mrs. Allen, brown-haired and heavier, and her niece,
Mrs. Beersmith, a fat sullen young woman.

They had rented a room on my floor into which the concierge had
moved an extra cot. "We get lonely in a room alone," Mrs. Allen said.
"None of us can stand it." They were returning from a cruise to New
Zealand. The trip, their first away from England, had taken two months
and for reasons not at once clear they had decided to leave the boat on
Corfu. "It's been one bloody trip, I tell you," said Mrs. Garton. "I'm
homesick. I miss my son Bertie who's twenty-two. I'll be glad to get
back." Mrs. Allen said, "My husband has heart attacks. As far as I know
he may be dead. I may not have a husband at all." Mrs. Allen's husband
was a "barrister," Mrs. Garton was the wife of a dentist, and Mrs.
Beersmith's husband owned a garage.

That evening I saw Mrs. Allen on the esplanade in colloquy with
Spyros II, the young guide I'd met the day before with two German girls.
A small dark fellow, he looked even smaller beside the buxom Mrs. Allen. Later I met Mrs. Garton and her niece in the hotel bar and they
invited me for a drink. Both appeared to be drunk. They were discussing
the absent Mrs. Allen.

"I think it's disgusting," said Mrs. Beersmith, "when old people don't
behave like old people and still want to be young." She was sitting with
her skirt pulled over the tops of black lace stockings on her fat crossed
legs. Mrs. Garton said, "Imagine! A mother of seven carrying on. In Italy
she fell in love with a soldier twenty-three years old named Renzo. She
told him she'd arrange to bring him to England and the boy's mother
became hysterical. Even though Renzo still had six months' national
service, the mother didn't stop weeping. I tell you, I've aged fifteen
years."

The revelations, which seemed to be motivated by a kind of revenge,
embarrassed me and I excused myself and went to bed. The next forenoon
I was sitting at a table outside the Corfu Bar. Suddenly Spyros II appeared and sat beside me. "Good morning," he said, yawning. "I am very
tired. I was very late with my grandmother."

"I saw you with her under the trees," I said. He grinned slyly. "She
was the oldest woman I ever had," he said.

"Your grandmother?" He laughed. His beaked nose and a slight curve of his thin back reminded me of a Neapolitan Pulcinella, or the bronze statuettes of masked satyrs with large noses and grotesquely upright phalli, which I had seen hawked to tourists in the Athens flea market. "She has very passion, very good," he said. "Body much young. Has many aesthetic operations not only on face but all over body. When lights is out is much the same, it does not make big difference how old. Trouble is she is not wanting to pay enough. For old woman is necessary to pay much."

"Pay who?" I asked.

He seemed surprised by my question. "Me, naturally," he said. "Is my business."

"What is your business?"

"To be lover. Excuse," he said, getting up and disappearing in the crowd. I saw Mrs. Allen, red-faced, her hair disheveled, weave toward the table. "What's the bloody little bastard been telling you?" she demanded angrily. Without waiting for an answer she sat down. "You could write a bloody book about what he's doing to me." She ordered a whisky and went on, saying, "I wanted to go to a hotel and he said he couldn't because people would recognize him." I remembered the argument under the trees. "He took me to his grandmother's house. Imagine! His grandmother! Someone opened a door and blankets and a mattress came flying out. He put them on the floor and that's where the bloody bastard . . . It was disgusting!" She shuddered primly. I called for the check, paid it and got up. "Where you going?" she called after me. "Got a bloody book to tell you . . ."

I walked to the cricket field where Spyros caught up with me. "What she say, what she tell you?" he asked.

"She said you took her to your house and your grandmother threw out some blankets."

"Not my grandmother, my brother," said Spyros, walking fast beside me. "My brother was ready to go to bed and my grandmother waked up. Please be quiet, I tell her, someone is drunk. My brother ask who I bring and I say a foreign lady and please be quiet, we will see what it will be. My brother went to his room to bring the blankets into the salon because he thought I wanted to sleep with her. But I don't want to sleep with her because I had been working twelve hours all day with Germans and therefore I was so terribly tired and didn't want to make any more love this night. You must, she said, you promised me. I told her we can do tomorrow. Tomorrow I will for a long time, I said. But she wanted me anyway at this time. We was together maybe an hour speaking of many things, solving the problems of the world, of Vietnam, of Cyprus, of the

Americans. Then she told me we will stay here until morning. I say no you can't. I told her do you drink something? She said yes. I brought her a bottle of *ouzo* and she drank enough and after I say to my brother, let's take her outside and put her in a taxi. So we took her and find a taxi and tell the driver to please if he will take her to the hotel. You see how I am a very tricky boy. I have been professional lover for ten years since I am fourteen."

"I think you are a liar," I said.

"Of course," he replied, disarmingly. "All Greek lovers are liars. We are liars because we must say nice things. When we go with someone, we must say, you are nice, I like you too much, perhaps I fall in love with you. I take for example myself. I say to everyone that I like you, you are so nice like the moon and I began to fall in love, I am afraid if you stay with me longer I will be really in love, and such things. Because if you do not say such things, even if you are nice, you cannot be professional lover. They must believe you. Of course, if foreign ladies know we are such big liars, they would not go with us. All my life I am terribly liar with girls. I am very surprised that anyone believes me."

I laughed. "Is very sad," he said. "I wish to speak truly which is not easy for me and you do not believe me." A kind of wistfulness had come into his voice. His concept of truth intrigued me. I was on my guard.

"Why do you tell me all this?" I asked.

"Because you are fine man who makes books. I will give you the story of my life which is very unique." Was it exhibitionism, or a need for confessional purification, that was urging him on? The loneliness of the alienated? "I will even show you my museum," he said.

"Museum?"

"My museum of love. Is in villa which is for my brother and me when our parents die, is where we make our business. Is on romantic little island where we take foreign ladies." Why, I wondered, hadn't he taken Mrs. Allen there. Seeming to read my thoughts, he said, "To go is necessary a little boat ride. Is much too drunk, Mrs. Allen, and I fear she fall into the sea. My brother is also lover but not so much as me. He is young and making studies at university so he can't have all the time women. We name our house the Villa Orgy. You like to see?"

"Yes," I said, not believing any of it.

"Good," he said, his face lighting with pleasure. "We will take picnic and have a sweet funny time. You will be interesting."

In the market he bought a small salami, a square of cheese, some bread and olives, a bag of cherries and a bottle of wine. We walked to the quay and got into a small rowboat which he untied. He rowed strongly and his small body bent over the oars seemed more clownlike than ever. Over his shoulder I saw a cluster of small rocky islands. The one on which he anchored was a reef of wind-swept pines almost hiding a small white stucco house. He unlocked a wooden door and invited me inside. The two white rooms were furnished with a table, some chairs and several beds. In the corner of one was a small kitchen. The walls were hung with photographs of women and girls of all types, large, small, fat, thin, dressed in slacks, dresses, bikinis. Most were blonde and many were wearing dark glasses.

"My museum," said Spyros, proudly. "My father make it with my mother so when they die and my brother and I are kings in our palace we begin to make business." There were pictures also of Spyros and of his brother, dark like Spyros but taller. Scattered among the photographs were assorted brassieres and women's undergarments. There was a shelf of books, mostly French, German and English paperbacks, and several calendars upon which dates were marked. A guitar hung on a wall. Tables held a radio, a phonograph and records and an assortment of costume jewelry, dark glasses, handkerchiefs and perfume vials. Everything was neatly labeled. There were also some cardboard files. Spyros said, "We bring here girls we meet from afternoon at the beach and invite to come for dancing in our house. When girls have eat and drink something and they are dancing they always begin to feel a little naughty. So you begin by kissing a little with nice music and you say, look, how quiet, how nice the sea so golden from the moon, how big and how near, look how near the stars looking so lovely so let's be happy. Look how close together are the stars like lovers between them and I am feeling like a star and therefore let's be lovers too. When you are romantic like that it is impossible to say no. Naturally we have big success. We are very different from one another, my brother and me, and when we bring girls together and girls like, we change. Many girls like different."

I was looking at a picture of a sad-faced middle-aged woman dressed in black. "Is my mother," said Spyros. "Is very sad for my mother to die. If she not die I would not be bad like I am. I would be good boy and make myself a student. But she die and now I am so bad." He drew open a file drawer jammed with cards covered with memorandums, addresses and monetary notations. "I am very careful for bookkeeping. Is necessary for successful business. Before Friedlind I have two hundred and fifty-seven girls and since another sixty-three . . ."

"Who is Friedlind?" I asked.

Spyros pointed to a row of pictures of one girl, a buxomly pretty blonde dressed in bikinis, in slacks and in skirts. "She is my fiancée for a year. I think I love her. Sometimes I am longing too much for her when I am alone or with others. I would like to get married with Friedlind because our love is not only sex love, is also platonic love. But is always problems. I think if I would get married I would have other girl friends. She told me I can have girl friends when we are fiancé, but when we will be married, never, she would kill me. And I think she do this. Her father do not trust me and will not give dowry to marry me. And I will never get married if my wife has not any dowry. Is a law of Greece. But still, Friedlind I love best. You can't think how many love letters she writes. She wants me, she will come this summer for three months just to be fiancée again. She says no one can love like me. She has much money, she has car. So is very stupid no dowry and we end." As he spoke Spyros kept moving restlessly around the room.

"For me is more naturally to have many girls. To make love is my summer law. In Corfu the climate is perfect for love, it is always wanting you to make love. From June to first days of October come thousands of ladies to Corfu every year for love. At home they are working so hard for ten or eleven months, it is so cold and they are always dreaming to go to a south country to find someone for love. And if someone is for one month alone in foreign country she need much love. They have in their minds before they come that it's better to go alone because they will be more free, nobody knows in their country or in their town. And they think, we would like to have a lot of different lovers. Why not, they like the change? Maybe not one hundred per cent but I think is about ninety per cent do this."

"Are there always lovers to accommodate them?" I asked.

"In Greece is perhaps five thousand professional lovers of which maybe one thousand is very good. Best are on Corfu and Rhodes and Corfu are the most famous I think. We have perhaps forty to fifty strong ones who can have different girl friends every day and night, who make the business. Then there are also many amateurs. Of course, some have other business, they sell rings or make guides in the day and are lovers at night. But maybe twenty-five of strong ones do nothing else, only to sell love with the foreigns day and night. You has to be an island man for doing this. The sea makes us more naughty than other people."

"How does the sea do that?" I asked.

"I don't know exactly. But men who live in big towns far from sea are different. When they come to Corfu from Thessaloniki, from Larissa, they are like a tourist, they are more careful in everything. We have the same houses, the same schools, the same cinema, the same everything. But the difference is that we have the sea. To have a reputation as a very great lover is necessary to live by the sea. Also my brother and I, I think we have the blood from my father. All his life he likes love, he has many girl friends. So you see with us it is the blood. The women of Europe and

England know about us and it brings an awful lot to Corfu. Past girl friends of mine send to me the girl friends of them."

"They refer new clients to you?"

"Yes, they say I am good boy, very sympathetic, so kind, a very good lover. And when new girls come to Greece they find me. Is very interesting to have a business constantly changing. It is necessary of course to speak many languages. I speak German and Italian and very good French and English."

"It must be a very tiring profession," I said, feeling fatigue merely from hearing of it.

"Is necessary to be young and very strong. After six or seven months of love we are in winter sometimes very tired. I take for example myself. I need always to rest for one or two months. Then sometimes I go to Athens, or to Europe for the rainy times to visit girl friends. I have been everywhere except Spanish, all Europe and to England visiting fiancées."

"All fiancées?"

"Many fiancées and sometimes just girl friends. If I am in a town about five weeks I like to go to the museums and theaters, of course, and see the nice things every town has. But mostly I am visiting girls. Last winter I am fiancé with Friedlind in Munich for three months. But being fiancé was not keeping me all the time busy. Is necessary to do something. In the same town I had other friends that I met in Corfu that wanted to see me with pleasure. What could I do?"

"But if you loved Friedlind so much how could you go out with other women?"

"Yes, I loved Friedlind terribly much but I like to go with others. That's all. Perhaps I loved her too much, I don't know. I was thinking all the time too much about her. I am longing too much, but I like to go with others too. This is the natural way for me. Then we have this trouble about the dowry. You think that is silly but for Greek it is the law.

"So when is finished with Friedlind I go to Hamburg and am fiancé for two months of a famous lady journalist, known by everyone in Germany. But I have another girl in Frankfurt, very pretty air hostess, and when my Hamburg fiancée finds out, she does not like. I try to explain I am very romantic and sweet so I will sometimes have other girls in my life. But she will not understand and she is very difficult. She finish our fiancée. I tell her, I love only you, I love you so much I can love no other. But she is smart, she is after all journalist. She doesn't believe me, she knows I am a liar. So then is soon time to come back for Corfu season."

I was looking at a colored photograph of a tall leggy girl wearing a tartan skirt which was blowing in the wind. "That is Edna, she is English," said Spyros. "A very nice girl, a very good one. But I have not been good to her so she is leaving tomorrow from Corfu. I like her, she is so nice, so smart, so sweet. But I could not very well give all my summer to her." We moved on to a round-faced pale-skinned blonde. "Is Monika from Holland. She is a teacher, very serious, very difficult. I mean she did not wish to come to my bed, but I think she was in love with me because when I met her for first time on beach and I ask do you want to come with me for dancing, she said, yes, I like. So we danced and after we make a walk alone and it was so nice a night, the sea was so quiet. So we take the boat. That first night was difficult, she didn't want. So I brought her back to her hotel and I said, good-bye. I didn't want to see her any more because I could not use my summertime with so difficult girls. Next day she speak to me on beach, she is sorry but she did not wish to be naughty with me because she is very Catholic, that she would sleep with a man only when she is married. After two or three days she said please talk to me, I want to see you at night. I said okay I would see her and the same night I met her and she said I think I love you. So this time was not difficult but easy. When she go back to Holland she make much correspond and she is longing to come again this summer here."

The next photograph was of a very young, dark-haired girl. "This is Renata, she is Italian, the youngest girl I ever had, thirteen years and a few months. She was very rich, her father had a factory." He pointed to another. "This is Lucy, the only America girl I ever had. Generally I do not waste time with Americans because ninety-nine per cent are difficult, they go out for dancing and kissing but not to sleep. Lucy was with my brother and I was with a Swedish girl who was my lover for a week. My brother said to me, please, will you make change because I can't do anything with her. I said, okay if you like. He is my brother, of course. So my Swedish lover goes with him and I with Lucy and we came here. I was very surprised. Lucy was so young and so sweet and so easy. Not like other American girls. The English and Scandinavians are terribly easy and the Germans are easy enough."

We were looking at a photograph of Spyros himself between two girls taller than he, his arms reaching around their shoulders. "These are two Swiss girls from Berne. I met them on the beach and before we speak we talk a lot with the eyes. They were not looking like Switzerland women at all. I call my brother and we bring them here. We are on the beach making swim without clothes. You feel very nice, you feel more free and fresh without clothes swimming. Then we started to kissing. I make love with the brunette and he with the blonde and then we change and start again. But I must tell you they are very naughty because when they make love it is not natural love. Yes, I like too, if someone is nice, and they have enough money, so we stay with them three days and three nights. I remember, I met another Swiss girl and she told me she was alone and she wants to stay with me. After two days and nights she met another boy friend she had before me. So I do not like Switzerland girls. They are too naughty." We moved on. "Here, are two Swedish girls from whom I took a lot of money because Swedish girls are very rich. I think they loved me and I perhaps them a little."

Spyros' easy equation of love with money struck me as awesomely pragmatic and his exuberant telling curiously innocent.

"No romance without finance," I said. "Is that how it is?"

"Of course in love money is important," he said. "When is business there's got to be money. Sometimes I meet girls that have not enough money or they don't want to spend for me and with them I will not sit for five minutes." The refrain of a Bessie Smith song was going through my mind, the words, "If I can't sell it I'll sit on it, I ain't gonna give it away."

"Because if there is no money," said Spyros, "how can you have all the time under the olive trees or on the seaside? You can't do that for many days. You can't sleep all the night on the seaside without to eat, nothing to drink. The money is the most important."

"And you never pay a girl?"

"Of course not. Perhaps when I get old I will have to pay for my girl friends. Now I am young, they have to pay. For me this is the natural way—when you are young to catch money from the girls and when you are old to pay for the girls."

Spyros' Leporello recital was growing monotonous. The photograph facing us was of a well-rounded matron in stretch pants. "That is Hedwig," he went on. "She was forty-two—no, fifty-two—the oldest lover I think ever for me. She had a nice sports car and lived in the Castello Hotel. I remember her on the beach. At that time I was nineteen years old. She had a bikini and was looking so nice I think everyone wanted to go with her. She has operations like this . . ." Spyros pinched his thin thigh and then his lean jowl. "She took the skin like that and put to other place so she had a nice hard body, like a girl in the legs. I was with her from the morning until the night, all the time in her hotel or on the beach. Her husband had been a pilot who put bombs on England so they shot him down. So she lose him and she was without love so many years, just a few times, because she had to work hard to give food to her children. Therefore when she comes to Corfu she was perhaps too hungry for love. I never remember so sex nights. She was so terrible I nearly died. But she love me and appreciate with money how I make for her.

"Women who are forty years past are sexiest. I remember a woman from Alaska, Blanche is her name. She has red hair and forty-five years. She had a body like a girl eighteen, and she was very easy. But since she is the only one in my life from Alaska I can't therefore say that the women from Alaska are all easy."

"How about Greek women?" I asked.

"Greek women don't pay," he said. "Therefore I am not able to go with Greek women. Only two times in my life have I been."

Spyros opened a file box filled with letters bearing a multitude of foreign stamps. "Is here all the letters from my fiancées and lovers," he said, drawing out a handful. "Here, read. I will make the picnic."

He began to slice the salami and the cheese. I unfolded a letter from Sweden and read, "I'm longing, dreaming and I'm often crying, thinking it will not be summer again. But suddenly a month is gone and we are nearer to the summer and I'm feeling closer to you. I wish to be close to you forever, I love you so much . . ."

A long letter from Denmark closed with: "I am watching the television, the opera *Cosi Fan Tutte*. It is about women who are not faithful to their boys. Soon I will sleep and dream about you. I love you always."

A girl in England wrote, "I am not prepared to leave England and my friends for the man I love. England is from a woman's point of view infinitely fairer. From what you told me I can only assume you have spent the last eight years of your life as a playboy. I am afraid you might find it difficult to alter those habits. Yes, Spyros, I love you— dearly. But I know I could never subject myself to an existence where a woman is obliged to take a place firmly in the background while my husband dominated me in total commandment."

A letter from France said, "I love you because you like the life, you like the sun, you like the love. Everyone here is very happy to think we will be married next year. I work in my factory, earning money for our honeymoon on Corfu. . . ."

A packet of letters were from Munich. "My dear Spyros," I read. "Please don't be sorry if I will come in two or three weeks. I have to see you. I don't want to make you sorry but I have to tell you that I am not all right in my body. What must I do? My love and kisses, your Friedlind." A letter dated a week later said, "I am terribly sorry I am not better in my body. *You understand why?* Please look for work in Athens so we can live there, away from Corfu. When you write me back, write on the letter the name of your brother in different letters than your handwriting. I told my parents I saw not you, only your brother. Kisses from your Friedlind."

"What does Friedlind mean when she says she's not well in her body?" I asked.

"She has a baby," Spyros said, continuing to slice bread. "I mean she start one. When I write I cannot make marry without dowry, she say she will kill the baby. She has a terribly difficult time to find a doctor. So I write to a nice girl friend, about twenty-eight, who lives also in Munich and I ask her to please find a doctor to kill a baby for Friedlind. If you will find the doctor, I say to the girl friend, I will be yours, I will come away from Corfu. She help and the doctor want a very much money. And when baby is killed I write the girl friend, I cannot leave Greece, I will stay here."

"Do you have this problem frequently of girls becoming pregnant?"

"Yes, I think so. The most time I make love without any preservative. I go with so many girls that some I'm sure start babies."

We sat on the tiny beach eating our lunch, passing the bottle of wine between us. Spyros sighed and said, "Those three English ladies in your hotel has very bad problems. They are many days on ship, a nice Italian ship with Italian sailors on it. Mrs. Allen met a sailor, a very young one, and the sister found another and the daughter another. But there was a big problem because they stay in one cabin for three persons and they make a war every night who stays in cabin. So the daughter goes into lifeboat with sailor to make love and . . ." Spyros lowered his voice to a whisper as if to keep the gulls flying overhead from hearing what he had to say. "The daughter gets a baby. And they want to find a doctor to make an operation. They tried in Germany, in France, in Italy but they couldn't find. I say they should go to Switzerland but it is about four months now so the baby is too big. The mother— you know she is fifty-five exactly and has seven children—is very cross and she told me everything, how the daughter has a husband in England and, of course, he will know it is not his baby. So they are in troubles and are so sorry and don't know what to do."

The water lapped at our feet. Mist covered Corfu like a gauze. "Is sad to have a life so bad with troubles and a world so beautiful," said Spyros, now in philosophical mood. "I am very romantic and this is a place especially for romantic people. Sometimes at night when we have full moon, I take boat and come here alone and I am dreaming that all my fiancées and girl friends, all that I have brought to this place, are here in the spirit and I speak to them and I tell them I love them all, not one but all, and this is because I am so romantic. But girls are not so romantic as me, they do not understand this." He threw a crust of bread on the waters and a gull swooped for it. "To sell love all the time makes me feel lazy. Sometimes I think I will change my business. When I am young and strong it is easy to be a lover. But is not so easy no more as was ten years ago and soon will be less easy. It makes me

tired to think of forever. So I think maybe I will make myself a ladies'
hairdresser or be the director of a hotel. I think you can have more
money by the hotel than by hairdresser. And in hotel if you see girl
you like is easy to arrange things. I don't know. I want to change but I
don't know." He scooped up some pebbles and splashed them into the
sea and the gulls, thinking them bread, swooped after them. "Maybe
one day I'll get married. I have been with so many and I think that
Friedlind is the girl especially for me. If only she could take the money
from her father, the money that belongs to her, then I would marry
with her. Two friends of me, two lovers of Corfu, get married with
foreign girls with much money who give their husbands a very good
life, the same I want with Friedlind." He exhaled a long breath. "Always
I am thinking I am in love with her. I am so very romantic."

We returned to the house and Spyros brought out a small metal box.
"I will show you now the most secret part of the museum, the naughty
pictures." He opened the box with a key. "I keep locked because once
before she die my mother open and find. She was terribly sorry because
she thought I was a good boy. Of course, I am good, but a little crazy,
that's all. She could not understand that." He handed me a handful of
photos. "Are of me and my girl friends without clothes, kissing, making
love. I have a nice automatic camera from Germany which can make
pictures alone. Are very naughty, no?"

They were indeed and also curiously pathetic. The thin dark little
body never quite covered the rounded forms over which it arched so
urgently, like a mantis over prey. The girls' faces, grinning sillily, con-
torted with lust and pleasure, had a terrifying similarity. There were
photographs of Spyros alone, looking, with his curved back, thin limbs
and shoulders, his beaked nose and upright phallus more than ever
like the little bronze satyrs. Only the horns and tail were missing. "Is
a picture my lovers take home for dreaming of me through the difficult
cold months," he said proudly.

Rowing back, he told me he had an appointment with Mrs. Allen.
"Why not?" he said. "If she pays enough she gets what she buys."
Watching his thin frame pulling on the oars, I wondered if he weighed
more than a hundred pounds. Late that evening I met him outside the
Corfu Bar. "Is too many difficulties with English ladies so I make
finish," he said. "Is very drunken, Mrs. Allen. I ask how much money
she has and she gives me purse and I count and is not enough. She says
she will cash check tomorrow but I don't trust. Now I am going to my
grandmother's to take some sleep. I am a little tired."

The hotel was in pandemonium. The night clerk told me the three
women had created such a disturbance in the bar that it had to be

closed. Mrs. Garton and Mrs. Beersmith had gone upstairs with two guests, Mrs. Garton with a Greek businessman and Mrs. Beersmith with an Australian sheep rancher who had arrived that afternoon. I found Mrs. Allen in siege at the elevator. Her hair was in disorder, her dress was slipping from her shoulders. She was holding a half-filled bottle in one hand and in the other a glass, from which whisky slopped on the floor.

"Coming to your room," she burbled. "Got a bloody book to tell you. All day I said to my sister, I got to see that bloody American bastard. She said you won't see *him* again. Like hell, I won't, I said. Got to talk to him, tell him a book like none he ever wrote. C'mon, let's go to your room . . ."

"I'm sorry, I can't," I said.

"Why not?"

"I'm working," I said. "I have notes and papers every place."

"I know," she said loudly. "You got a bloody woman in your room." The excuse was a better one than I had come up with and I nodded. "What the hell," she shouted. "Can't you bloody men go one night without a screw? O.K. we'll go to my room. I'm not proud."

I said it was impossible. Her loud voice drew a crowd and the night clerk begged me to get her on the elevator and take her to her door. It seemed a reasonable request. I could leave her there. Clutching bottle and glass she staggered with me into the elevator. Inside she fell on me, turning me into a human buttress. I piloted her to her room. She fumbled some keys and I took them and opened the door. The mess inside was beyond imagination. The baggage of three women was strewn about the floor. Corsets, underwear and an assortment of cheap and tasteless souvenirs littered the furniture.

It turned quickly into a nightmare. Clutching at me, pulling me inside, Mrs. Allen sobbed out a story of Spyros' betrayal, how he'd abandoned her when she'd not been able to produce more traveler's checks. I pulled myself away and she fell to the floor, taking a praying attitude, crying, "Oh dear God, help me. I love the little bastard. I looooooooove him . . ." Her cries turned into wails. I seemed to be caught in a Hieronymus Bosch dream; cold sweat covered my body. Clutching my knees, she sobbed, "I hate my husband. I've always hated him. He told me to go away and think it over and I've thought and I've thought and thought and I hate him more than ever. What do you do when you hate your husband, how do you explain it, what do you tell your children? I can't stand the bastard in my bed. I want everyone in bed but him. All these boys! Oh, my God, what will I do? How will it all come out?"

Grappling with me for support, she raised herself to her feet and she cried, "Someone *must* love me! I can't go back . . . can't . . . I'm a bloody lousy cheap bitch . . . I *need* someone. . . . What will I do? . . ."

She slid to the floor trying to pull me down with her. "Hold me . . . I know you got a bloody bitch waiting . . . I've been waiting for you . . . all day . . . I got to tell that bloody American my story I said to my sister . . . got to tell him . . . what will I do? . . . you don't know how it's been . . ." Raising her folded hands like a supplicating Gioconda, she prayed, "Oh, dear God! Help me, help me, *help* me . . ."

I slipped from the room and behind me I heard her crying, "Help me, help, help, help . . ." I went downstairs and told the night clerk to call a doctor.

In the morning I booked a flight for Athens. The word at the desk was that the three women were leaving. In the square I met Spyros having coffee with two Austrian women. He took me aside. "My brother is very busy with his studies," he said. "You are my good friend. If you stay in Corfu I make you a partner, introduce you to girls. Some like to go with men who are a little older, thirty-five, forty. You can make money very good . . ."

I said I didn't think I had the talent for his business, that I was sure I was too old. "Is a pity." Spyros sighed. "I think you are like me very romantic. I would like a romantic friend on Corfu. We would have sweet funny times."

I thanked him for showing me his museum. My gratitude was sincere —he had offered me some clues to the enigma of at least one Greek's character and I felt a kind of sympathy for him. We said good-bye.

In the hotel the concierge told me the ladies from Newcastle had decided not to leave after all. "Now the daughter is in the room with the Australian," he said. "He is a bachelor and I think the ladies have decided if she is with him one, two months, she can say, 'Oh, my, see, now I have a baby for you.' Many women have this idea of saying a baby belongs to another man. . . ."

XXXVI

The Kennedy Family of Crete

I flew to Crete to say good-bye to my friend Sokrates Kefalogiannis. Making the drive with me from Iraklion to Anoghia were Kostas and Marita Grammatikakis and Kostas' good friend, Kostas Kefalogiannis, a native of Anoghia and Sokrates' cousin.

Kostas Kefalogiannis was a burly, dynamic man in his forties. He was extraordinary-looking with a handsome round face, dark brown skin, black curly hair and mustache peppered with gray, and gold teeth which flashed when he talked. He was an exuberant conversationalist, speaking Greek in volcanic torrents which Kostas Grammatikakis and Marita were able to translate only in fragments. He wore a blue pin-striped suit and black shell-rimmed glasses and his nervous hands tugged on a silver chain of red worry beads which he flung from time to time into the air, gesticulating some conversational point. He was, said his friend, Kostas Grammatikakis, "so good, so honest, so brave!"

He had a kind of fame. In his youth he had served a prison sentence for kidnaping his sweetheart and hiding her in a mountain cave. The method of procuring a bride was common in Crete. Newspapers carry frequent stories of elopement-kidnapings, and Kostas K.'s "Romeo and Juliet" abduction had made the international press. The girl, from the town of Mirres, was returning from a movie accompanied by a brother-in-law when Kostas and three friends beat up the brother-in-law and escaped with the girl to a mountain cave. All served prison sentences. After Kostas' release the girl married him. Their short and stormy life

411

together ended in divorce and Kostas had married another woman by which he had four children.

Kostas K.'s father had been killed by Germans. In all, he said, thirteen Kefalogiannises were executed, including an uncle who was vice president of the National Bank of Greece in Athens and had returned to Anoghia to join the occupation. Kostas' mother was a Sbokos, a member of the family with which the Kefalogiannis maintained its Guelph-Ghibelline feud in Anoghia. Not surprising, the family of ten children was a turbulent brood. One brother was a deputy in parliament. Another who lost a leg in the war raced a motorcycle with one leg until he was killed in an accident. The youngest brother had driven his car off a cliff into the sea near Sounion. There were, he told me, three hundred Kefalogiannises in Anoghia, fifty in Iraklion where he lived, and more in Athens and western Crete. "We are the Kennedy family of Crete," he said.

He had phoned word of our arrival to Anoghia and a feast was being prepared. "God help us," said Kostas G. On the way we passed a herd of goats with tinkling bells, moving from seaside winter pastures into the summer highlands. Kostas K. was telling the story of a cousin named George who hid in the mountains for twenty years following the shooting of a doctor. The cousin returned to Anoghia when the police granted him amnesty. Why, I asked, had the cousin shot the doctor. Kostas K. replied, "My cousin and his two brothers were driving sheep through a village. The doctor complained the sheep were doing harm. There was an argument and the doctor killed one of the brothers. Naturally the doctor had to be shot."

We were entering Anoghia. Kostas K. put his head through an open window of the car and let out a yell. At once men ran from every direction. We stopped the car for a frenzy of embracing, hugging and kissing. As we drove slowly into the town Kostas K., his voice raspingly hoarse, conversed with the friends running beside the car. His eyes bulged with excitement. He pointed out the scorched ruins of a house and said the whole town had been like that when the Germans left it. Seven Kefalogiannis houses were destroyed and many were burned in the ruins. In the wreckage of another house stood a marble bust of its owner, a massacred resistance leader named Ioannis Dramoudanis, father of Kostas K.'s wife. We made our slow way to the house of Kostas K.'s sister, Irini, wife of a doctor. A strong good-looking woman, she looked enough like Kostas to be his twin. In temperament they differed for she was calm, quiet and reserved. She invited us to sit around the dining-room table, where we were served *raki* and coffee. While we drank Kostas and his sister recalled family legends, especially one of a cousin, Michael Kefalogiannis, a blond man who during the German occupation had come down from a mountain hideout for food and escaped detection by dressing as a woman. The Germans had whistled after him and made lewd suggestions.

We walked into the town, passing some children who waved from the yard of a new school, the gift of Anoghians in the United States. Whenever we came to a café we were forced to stop and have a drink. A messenger had been sent for Sokrates and when we were in the third café he arrived. He appeared gaunter, thinner than I remembered him, as if he had been ill. We embraced and managed, Sokrates speaking Greek and I English, to understand one another. His humbleness in the presence of other Kefalogiannises seemed to indicate a lower social position. Clearly the family of Kostas K. was of higher rank than Sokrates' more modest branch. Now, drinking *raki* he sat proudly beside me, smiling quietly, as if he wanted me to know that my coming to Anoghia to see him was giving him pleasure. We were, in our almost wordless bond, content and at ease with one another.

After an hour Sokrates excused himself. We had interrupted him at butchering lambs and he was going to finish. With a noisy band of Kefalogiannis relatives we continued our walk through the town, beginning at the town hall and the memorial plaque to the resistance dead. A cousin spoke of a newspaper story about an American consignment of military planes and heavy arms to Turkey. "Why don't you Americans understand the Turks?" he asked. "Why do you trust them? Don't you know if they find it advantageous to go with Russia they will?" A grizzled old uncle made a speech, saying, "Even if Americans give the Turks a thousand jets and tanks, we are not afraid. We will fight and we will win." Men repeated old stories of wars with Turks, how Turks had taken Anoghian women for the bordellos of Istanbul, how they tortured prisoners. I was shown some cherished guns, one used by a local hero to shoot a Turkish governor and another with which a resistance leader had shot a German captain.

The doors of houses were open and inside them women were busy at looms. We entered a dark earthen-floored basement where a Kefalogiannis cousin named Katerini Vrentzou moved her fingers across her loom swiftly as a harp player's fingers on strings. Whenever we paused a woman appeared with a tray of small glasses filled with *raki* and tiny cups of coffee. The impact of the liquor was causing us to reel. Kostas K. and I were photographed together in the remains of his boyhood home, a heap of rubble and crumbling walls. An aged blind priest, tapping his way with a cane, led by a covey of women, arrived and embraced Kostas. "Your beatings didn't make me a good man," said Kostas, his arm around the old priest. "A better man than I dared hope," said the priest, whose name was George Andraidakis and who was eighty-four years old. He rattled on, reminiscing about the Turkish occupation in his boyhood.

We arrived finally at Sokrates' small shop. I photographed him with a dozen lamb carcasses hanging upside down, blood dripping from snouts. An old lady who was Sokrates' aunt appeared with a tray of *raki* and then reappeared in a few minutes bearing coffee. Sokrates' small store was filled with meat, vegetables, hardware, pots and pans, soap and everything was crowded into a minimal space. Sokrates took a few minutes to wash and put on a suit and then I went with him and Kostas K. to the church where Kostas knelt to kiss icons and light candles while Sokrates stood stiffly by. Returning to the doctor's house we were followed by a band of children. Three girls addressed me proudly in a few words of school-learned English and Kostas invited them into a café and ordered ice cream for everyone.

In the doctor's house a feast was prepared. Except for Marita Grammatikakis, only men were seated around the dining table. Kostas' sister hovered over the table, watching for empty plates, directing the old women who served. There was roast lamb, salad, potatoes, a variety of condiments and pastries and a great deal of wine. In the rush of family conversation I was lost. Sokrates sat beside me smiling. I was toasted with wine and welcomed into the family and Sokrates said he hoped I would return for a longer stay, to live in Anoghia. But, he added, I might not find much diversion in the town, where pleasures were eating and drinking, singing, dancing and playing cards, sometimes until two o'clock in the morning. He told me he would be forty years old in September. I asked him why he was not married and he asked the same question of me. Our bachelorhoods provided a great merriment among Kefalogiannis relatives. When we married, said Sokrates, we would be each other's *koumbaros,* best man and brother-for-life. He spoke of it wistfully as a bond between us, seeming not to consider the brides we would in the circumstances be taking.

The night was clear and cold. A full white moon hung over the town. Music blared from a brightly lit café where some youths were frugging. Sokrates' mustache brushed my cheek, he embraced me and he said, "Come back."

I replied, "I will," and he helped me into the car. As we drove away I saw him standing alone outside the group of relatives, and I saw his hand snap in a salute. On the drive back Kostas K., his voice a whispering saw, continued with still more stories of the Kefalogiannis clan, stories of resistance and murder, of heroism and violence. "We are the Kennedy family of Crete," I heard him say and then I slept.

Before I left Crete I made a symbolic pilgrimage to a cave on Mt. Dicte where Cretans believe Zeus was born. Disliking caves, I had avoided the grottoes of Greece. A curious compulsion was urging me to this one.

The mountain in east central Crete stands at the edge of the plain of Lassithi, a high plateau totally enclosed by mountain peaks. To get there I followed the sea for fifteen miles and turned inland toward Potamies where I stopped and climbed to the mountainside Church of the Panaghia to see some twelfth- and fourteenth-century frescoes. The church walls were faded and blackened from candle smoke, but the pictures which covered them were wondrously human and alive. The earth-red color of the mortar shone through, so that the paintings seemed to glow with a soft rose light. The Christ Pantocrator in the dome had apple cheeks, a small mouth and a virile living warmth.

The terrifying mountain road followed unguarded precipices dropping off two thousand feet. Emerging from a pass, I saw below me, like a great flower bed of white daisies, the fans of more than a thousand windmills pumping water to irrigate a wide green plain. It was Lassithi, an arid agricultural plain kept green and fertile by its irrigating windmills. The valley has a river, the Megalos Potamos, which disappears mysteriously into a pit at its eastern end. The road circling the valley passed through a dozen villages built on hillsides so that every flat meter of land might be free to grow potatoes and cereals. Driving slowly to avoid hitting women and babies taking the sun in the narrow road, I arrived in Psychero, the village at the foot of Mt. Dicte.

A young man, lean and reddish-blond, waved as I passed and I waved back. He began to run and when I parked the car he had caught up. "*Yassu!*" he greeted, breathlessly. He introduced himself—his name was Nikolaos Dolapsakis and he was a guide who would take me into the cave. "The most sacred place in Greece," he said, speaking softly, almost whispering, as if he were pacifying a child. He was slight in build with soft blue eyes and great calloused hands which seemed out of proportion to the rest of him. "You will schauen the Zeus baby in stone and many Zimmer," he said. His gently confidential way of speaking made me uneasy; he seemed too intently persuasive. "I spik a little English and a little Deutsch," he said. "Is teach me tourists."

I said I was hungry and he took me into a dark wine shop. The shabby old man who ran it said he could serve me an omelet. My companion said he would not eat, that he had lunched at home. We ordered *ouzos* and while we drank he continued to speak, so softly I could scarcely hear him. Paging through my Greek-English word book for words, he told me he was a farmer, that he had six *stremata* of valley land upon which he grew potatoes. Contrary to its reputation, he said, the valley soil was tired and thin and not as fertile as it once had been. He had a wife and two little girls, he said, and he earned what he could from guiding tourists.

The old man returned with my omelet, some fried potatoes and a cabbage salad. He hovered over me while I ate, reassuring himself that I savored it. Holding my dictionary close to his nearsighted eyes, Nikolaos Dolapsakis told me that Swedes, Swiss and English and especially Germans visited the cave. "The Deutsch like good the Untergrund," he said. I remembered the troglodytes and the cavern settings for Wagner's operas and I was not surprised.

Slowly we started up the steep mountain, speaking little, saving our breaths. In his hand Nikolaos carried two slender brown candles. For one-half hour we climbed the path of stone and red earth and then we arrived at a moss-carpeted slit in the earth. I looked down into the bottomless darkness and felt an uneasy kind of panic. "Is easy, very easy," purred Nikolaos, going ahead, drawing me with his hand into the crevice.

The descent over smooth wet stone was almost vertical. My rubber soles slid over the moss-covered stalagmites as if they were ice. I remembered childhood nightmares in which I catapulted into black pits, or was flung alive into a grave. Finding each solid foothold, Nikolaos supported me, purring reassuring Greek words I did not understand, a gentle Pluto guiding me on an Orphic journey through the underworld. I wondered in the dark immersion about tour buses and their cargoes of aging ladies, how they managed the terrifying descent and if there were ever any casualties. Nikolaos' manner, so urgently comforting, so gently seductive, would be effective with ladies. No doubt they would follow, as I was following him now, anywhere he led. There was something unreal about the strength of him, such physical power in one so slightly formed. I looked behind me. The entrance was a thin slit of light, like the faraway opening of a well. We stopped and Nikolaos lit the candles, and gave one to me. The tiny flickering lights were like two fireflies. I wondered why my guide was not supplied with flashlights, whether it was because he was too poor.

I remembered how at the beginning of all things, Uranus, the first son of Mother Earth, cast his rebellious sons, the Cyclopes, into a gloomy underworld so far from the surface of the earth that it took a falling anvil nine days to reach its bottom. Several times I wanted to cry out that I could go no further, but I no longer had courage even for that. Without will, led on by my softly reassuring Charon, supported by his powerful embrace, I slid slowly down slimy walls, deeper, deeper into the terrifying darkness. We arrived at the bottom. Holding tightly to one another, we passed through dark room after dark room, bending under canopies of stalactites, slithering like moles through forests of stalagmites, and through the dark journey I was reassured by my guide's sibilant explications, the soft voice saying, "Cronus, the Meister von die Welt is marry with sister Rhea. He don't like for son to become Meister so he eat all children. Rhea very traurig. She come here for having baby Zeus. So Cronus father not know baby is safe."* Nikolaos raised his candle, bringing its feeble light to flicker on a stalagmite. "Baby, Zeus baby . . ." he murmured. The top of the wet rock seemed carved into the wizened face and form of a baby bound in papoose fashion. "Baby, baby, baby," Nikolaos said and his lulling repetition of the word was like the voice of a cello.

It was the moment for which I had come, for which I had made my underworld descent. Clasping my hand, Nikolaos continued to whisper, "Baby, baby, baby . . . ," and his voice was hushed as the voice of a man present at a holy birth. I wondered whether his piety was real or whether it was a studied performance for strangers like myself. The deep dark room around us seemed without walls. Turning my eyes upward to the ceilingless heights, I felt the fear and astonishment of the ancients and I understood why it had been so inviolably necessary that I come there into the Stygian depths of the earth. "Here is beginning," Nikolaos murmured. "Here is Zeus der Vater von die Welt."

Guided by the slit of light from above, our ascent from the pit seemed easy. With Nikolaos drawing me upward, it was no time at all that we were out in the sunlight. I lay on the ground, breathing deeply, absorbing the sun and air, the scent of thyme, the twitterings of birds, thankful as resurrected Lazarus, for my life.

Nikolaos stood beside me, admiring my corduroy jacket. "American?" he asked.

"English," I said.

"Is good, very good," he said and he indicated his own thin suit, patched at the knees and elbows. "Grik suit bad, kaputt," he said. We walked down to the village where he took me to his house to meet his family, a dark-eyed, dark-haired wife, roundly pregnant, and two little girls, Natalia, aged four, and Anastasia, aged two, both beautiful golden images of himself. He was teaching the children English, Nikolaos said

---

* Nikolaos' account of the Birth is a Cretan version. In *The Greek Myths*, Robert Graves places the birth on Mt. Lycaeus in Arcadia. In this version Mother Earth had nymphs transport the infant to the cave of Dicte on the Aegean Hill, where it was nursed by nymphs and fed on the milk of the goat-nymph, Amalthea. Perhaps there is more than one Zeus in the same way that there are many variations of the Madonna and saints in Christian mythology.

proudly, and he coaxed the elder to say "Gut mornin'." I thought how he must be praying for a boy this time, how girls would be a catastrophe to a poor man with land. He took the children on his lap, loving and fondling them, and the sweet beauty of the family brought tears to my eyes. We drank *ouzo* and made photographs and when I left it was with an exultation, as if I had experienced a miracle, as if the terrifying sojourn had been, like Orpheus' and like Persephone's, the beginning of a rebirth, a renewed sense of being alive.

XXXVII

The Tired American

A coolness had sprung up between Katsimbalis and me. It began at a dinner in the Plaka for a half dozen guests. As always with a group, Katsimbalis held the center of the stage and did not stop talking. I'd eaten a lot of roast pig and drunk much wine and the stories he was telling I'd heard a dozen times. Time passed and I nodded into sleep. In the next weeks I kept hearing that my old friend was referring to me as "the tired American."

But I could not think of leaving Greece without saying good-bye, and I called him. He invited me to lunch. We met at the Apotsos for a drink and went around the corner to the rooftop restaurant of the Hotel Astor, which has the most beautiful view in Athens. Behind us was the great rock of Lycabettus tufted with pine, and facing us was the Acropolis, the full sweep of it from the Parthenon to the Erechtheion, rising in the shining blue sky like a golden city in the Apocalypse. The bright city surrounded us. A hidden phonograph was playing Wagner's *Ride of the Valkyries*. It was perfect music, absolutely appropriate to the grandeur.

"Look at the sun over Salamis," said Katsimbalis. "Remember this when you go back to your puritan land: Helios is the patron of Greece. No vindictive Jew but young Apollo, the light-giver. Take him with you, keep him in your heart. You'll find he'll serve you well."

He spoke of the nudity of the landscape, of the harmony of stone and sky and, true to himself, he launched into a Rabelaisian account of some erotic adventures on the Acropolis hill. He told about his grandfather, a real-estate speculator who became rich in Athens' nineteenth-

419

century expansion. "Fortunately for him I was never a pauper," he said.
"Thanks to him I've had the resources for a reasonably rewarding life."

For me he had final thoughts. "You will have discovered we're an
utterly hopeless country. In a world becoming more and more organized
we're incapable of organization. We're much too individualistic. We have
cunning and shrewdness but your American kind of organizational logic
we don't have at all. We want to live in your modern world but we're
quite incapable of bringing it about. We've been a hopeless country
forever and Herodotus tells us why. 'Poverty has always been the companion of the Greeks,' he said, and you'll find it in the Penguin edition
of his works."

Undoubtedly, Katsimbalis was right, I was tired. I was also frightened.
The paranoia which seemed to be everywhere around me, even in the
air that I breathed, was settling over me. Ever since my visit with Andreas
Papandreou I had a sense of being watched, of conversations being
monitored. The traveler's easy and casual anonymity was lost to me.
I was seldom at ease. Perhaps I was imagining it all. But there was no
way to know. At the same time that I was feeling a deep sadness at leaving a beautiful land and good friends, I was anticipating with relief my
flight from the exhausting passions and anxieties, the labyrinthian con-
fusions and fears which were part of the daily lives of my friends and
which had become part of my own.

So I said good-bye. I lunched with George Theotokas, the wise friend
who more than anyone else had shown me, calmly and logically, the way
things were. "Americans are generous and humane beyond anything
known in history," he said. "But unfortunately for us, your country sees
only the obvious, you do not understand what is going on inside our
country. Why should the most powerful democratic country in the world,
in order to feel secure, need to support an undemocratic rightist government? Our reactionary regime is able to procrastinate elections because
of your support. If there is one message for you to take back to your
people it should be this: Greece has a potential revolution which can be
avoided in one way only, by social and economic reforms. We must
have democratic elections as soon as possible. The only possible outcome
of this continued postponement of elections is dictatorship and if that
comes to Greece, America, in its innocence, must share in the responsibility."

My last dinner was with Angelos and Leto Katacousinos. Of all my
friends, it was they I loved best, their beautiful apartment the place I
would most miss. "This is your home in Greece," said Leto. "You are our

family." On the terrace where I had spent many lighthearted hours we watched the moon rise over the temple of Zeus. In the bright night the temple's great columns cast dark shadows over the quiet, utterly serene city and I wondered with a premonition of despair when, if ever, I would stand in this place again.

The next morning just as I was leaving for my plane the phone rang and from out of it, as it had on a morning eight months ago, boomed the great voice of Katsimbalis.

"I'm in an agony of embarrassment," I heard. "I quoted Herodotus to you on the poverty of the Greeks. I've been up all night and I can't find the quote. It's not Herodotus at all. It must be Thucydides and I didn't have time to find it but I bloody will, and write you when I do.

"By the way," he went on, "my English governess had me memorizing Shelley when I was nine years old and there are some lines in *Peter Bell the Third* which I've never forgotten. They describe us Greeks very well. Let me give them to you:

> And this is Hell—and in this smother
> All are damnable and damned;
> Each one damning, damns the other;
> They are damned by one another,
> By none other are they damned."

XXXVIII

The Zorba of Monticello High School

It is a warm June night in a high school gymnasium in Wisconsin. While they wait for the graduation ceremonies to begin, ladies fan themselves with their programs; men are pulling at their ties and collars.

To be here I have flown from San Francisco. My seat is on the aisle. The organ peals out *Pomp and Circumstances* and the gowned graduates pass me on their way to the platform. Midway in the line a dark curly-haired youth hesitates by my chair, his eyes flash into mine, and he moves on. He is Alex Marlis, the "Zorba of Monticello High School."

During the student valedictories, through trumpet solos and vocal duets, my mind wanders, remembering how this unusual event had come to pass.

"It's quite impossible," a United States Embassy secretary had said in November 1965, when I inquired how I might help Alex Marlis come to America. Her certainty was a challenge.

The only possibility, I found, was a student visa for Alex to study in the United States. For this he would need an acceptance with a scholarship from an American school, plus the assurance of a home for two years. Both offered problems. Alex was a graduate of the American Farm School, equivalent to an American high school. But his English was too rudimentary for him to be accepted in a college. The home I could provide. But Alex was a farm boy and it did not seem fair to subject him at once to my bachelor quarters and busy academic life in San Francisco. A happy family atmosphere in a rural setting would be better.

I decided that Alex might perfect his English and familiarize himself with American life if he repeated two years in an American high school. I wrote to my friends Ken and Pauline Boss, in my home town of New Glarus, in Wisconsin. An offer for a home for Alex came from the next village, Monticello, from Gordon and Carol Schultz, a young farm couple with four children. Pauline Boss, herself a high school teacher, arranged for a scholarship for Alex in Monticello High School.

I had innocently believed that having Alex accepted in the United States would solve my problem. Now I found I had still to get him out of Greece. In this seemingly hopeless pursuit my greatest help came from Alex himself. With a patience, determination and an attention span unique to a Greek, he doggedly fought for permission to leave his country.

I kept a journal:

Feb. 21 (1966): An anxious phone call from Alex. He has sent his papers and wants to know if I have received them. Later in the day they arrived: his study record and recommendations from the Farm School faculty. The Embassy informs me no small high school in Wisconsin will be acceptable to the Immigration Service, that he would have to apply to the U. S. Attorney General. It appears hopeless but having gone so far, I feel a responsibility.

Feb. 25: Phone call from Al Croone, assistant director of the Farm School. There is considerable anxiety over the Marlis affair. If he is not cleared by April 15, he will be taken into the Greek Army.

Mar. 11: Phone call from Croone. The documents accepting Alex into Monticello High School have arrived. Since this was the crucial item, it appears now as if Alex may be on his way to Wisconsin.

April 1: Phone rang at 7 A.M. It was Alex, just arrived by bus from Thessaloniki, here to file for exemption from the army. If he gets this he will be on his way.

April 3: The army requires Alex to pass an English exam before they will defer him. He is insecure in the language and is frightened. Still he has an amazing will. He has to take the exam in Thessaloniki, and he has returned by bus. I called Bruce Lansdale at the Farm School and he said he would see that Alex has help in preparing for the exam.

April 9: Alex is back in Athens. He has passed the exam and was told he must now get his exit papers from the military. He knows a "general" from near his village who is now in Athens and he phoned this man and went for an interview. The general said he would ask for the papers and see if he could get them approved. Alex's determination is monumental. I invited him to spend the day but he said he had to begin at once the seven-hour bus ride back. If he is not back in the evening for milking his boss "will be angry."

April 12: Alex called in an anxious state. No word from the general. In the meantime his army induction is being delayed until the case is settled. Endless detail! I called the general and tried to shame him into some action.

April 18: Alex back. He and I sat all morning in government offices. Nothing accomplished. A new hurdle: since Alex is already a high school graduate, he cannot go to the U.S. as a high school student. Only a college will do. I have a final desperate idea and call Al Croone at the Farm School. If Alex were to take agricultural courses at Monticello, would the Farm School consider this as postgraduate work? Croone agreed and now we must write to Monticello for proper certification. Alex pushes on with fantastic persistence, saying little. This should never have been begun and I am filled with guilt for undertaking it.

May 20: At American Farm School to say good-bye to Alex. We are sad that I shall be leaving Greece without him. We walked over the fields —he showed me a crop of new American-strain alfalfa. He is full of enthusiasm, still believing that he will follow me to America. I am shamed by his faith for I no longer believe it.

June 3 (back in Athens): I tracked down Alex's papers, found them languishing on a desk in the Foreign Ministry. A clerk said the American letters and documents would have to be translated into Greek and no translator had had time. I asked if I might find a translator and he said it would have to be done by an "approved" translator. I spent my spleen on the clerk. He took me to a secretary who promised the translations would be made.

On June 10 I left Greece and four weeks later I was on my Wisconsin farm. On my first Sunday in Wisconsin I went to a community picnic in the village of Monticello. It was a beautiful summer's day. A band was playing in a lakeside bandstand. Church ladies barbecued chickens and cut pies. It was the best of American life and I was full of the euphoria of being home. I met the high school principal and he said, "Where's the young Greek?" I saw the Schultzes and their children, and Mike, aged four, asked, "Where's Alex?" Having three sisters he had looked forward all summer to the arrival of a "big brother." I looked across a wide green valley, over cornfields shimmering with summer's haze, at broad red barns and white farm houses. I was thinking of Alex, comparing his poor and hopeless life in Greece with the opportunities waiting for him in Wisconsin. That evening I wrote a letter to a friend in the Greek government. I described Monticello and the lakeside picnic, and I told how the people of the town were asking for Alex as they might for an absent friend, as if he were already a member of their community. I did not receive a reply and as the weeks passed I lost what small hope I'd spurred within myself by writing the letter. Then on August 30 —on a Tuesday—I received a wire from the American Farm School offices in New York and it said, "Alex Marlis arrives Madison Northwest Airlines Thursday nine-thirty P.M."

Ken and Pauline Boss, Gordon and Carol Schultz and I went to the airport. Alex stepped off the plane and blinked into the night. He was wearing a short-sleeved summer shirt. He carried a small bag and he seemed thinner than I remembered him. He appeared dazed, as if he were trying to make himself realize where he was. He was quiet— his English seemed even sparser than I recalled. Politely he pretended to understand when he did not and this made communication difficult. On the farm I had prepared a room for him, hung with Greek icons and some paintings from Crete. It was, he said, the first time he'd slept in a room alone.

In the morning we walked over Wilhelm Tell Farm. Its size—modest for Wisconsin—seemed incredible to him and most of his questions concerned sizes and prices of things. In the afternoon I took him to Monticello High School and introduced him to the principal and the teachers, and then we went to a clothing store and outfitted him with an American high school wardrobe. On Saturday five thousand people came to an amphitheater on the farm for the annual community production of Schiller's drama *Wilhelm Tell,* and in his confusion Alex seemed to have the idea that the multitude was there to greet him. It almost turned out that way for he charmed everyone he met with his gracious manners, his softly accented speech and his lean dark good looks. Worried, Pauline Boss said, "I hope he's not spoiled by all the attention, that he doesn't get the idea that life in Wisconsin is a never-ending party."

There was no need to worry. The day after Labor Day I delivered him to the Schultzes and he began school. After the first difficult weeks during which he struggled with the language barrier, he slowly began to comprehend and became an eager student. He played basketball and he made speeches about Greece before the young people's church groups and in other high schools. In the spring he was a member of the court in the junior prom. He fit easily into the home life of the Schultzes, becoming at once a member of the family. During Alex's first summer in Wisconsin he and I took a vacation together, fishing for bass and muskies in northern lakes and visiting Indian villages. One day we stopped for beer in a forest tavern. Rangers and fishermen were at the bar, the dark walls were decorated with deer heads and mounted muskies, and in a cage in the corner, cocking its red-fringed beak, was a black myna bird. The bartender told Alex to speak to the bird and Alex addressed it in Greek, saying, *"Kalimera, ti kanete?"* (Hello, how are you?). The bird turned its head quizzically and in a shrill voice it cried, "Hello, what do you know? Hello, what do you know?" His astonishment showing on his face, Alex said, "He understands Greek. But he doesn't speak it."

After the commencement there is a party for Alex's multitude of friends to celebrate his graduation. There is Greek music, ouzo to drink, and to eat there are platters of dolmades, pastitsio, and mousaka, all made by the Swiss-American ladies of Wisconsin from recipes in a Greek cook-book, and honey-soaked baklava and nut cakes sent by some Greek ladies in Madison. One of the guests is the president of the Monticello board of education, whose name is David Seeholzer, and he is speaking, saying, "Alex is going to be missed. In our tradition-bound small town school he broadened the horizons and opened doors to the outside world. There is now among students a great topical interest in Greece because they know Alex. Our school has been able to offer a richer educative experience because of him. He has brought something into the life of every student and I only wish we might find another like him."

As Mr. Seeholzer speaks Alex is outdoors leading some class mates in a *syrtaki,* dancing it by moonlight, like Zorba, whose name Alex's friends have given to him.

Alex's student visa expired upon his graduation from high school and he received official orders to leave the country. For two anxious months his friends worked at devising some strategy to keep him here. In August, at the very moment when his situation seemed most desperate, word came from Washington that Wisconsin's senior senator, William Proxmire, had introduced a bill in the Senate of the United States. It began:

FOR THE RELIEF OF ALEXANDROS MARLIS.

Be it enacted by the Senate and House of Representatives of the United States of America in Congress assembled, That, for the purposes of the Immigration and Nationality Act, Alexandros Marlis shall be held and considered to have been lawfully admitted to the United States for permanent residence as of the date of the enactment of this Act . . .

INDEX

427

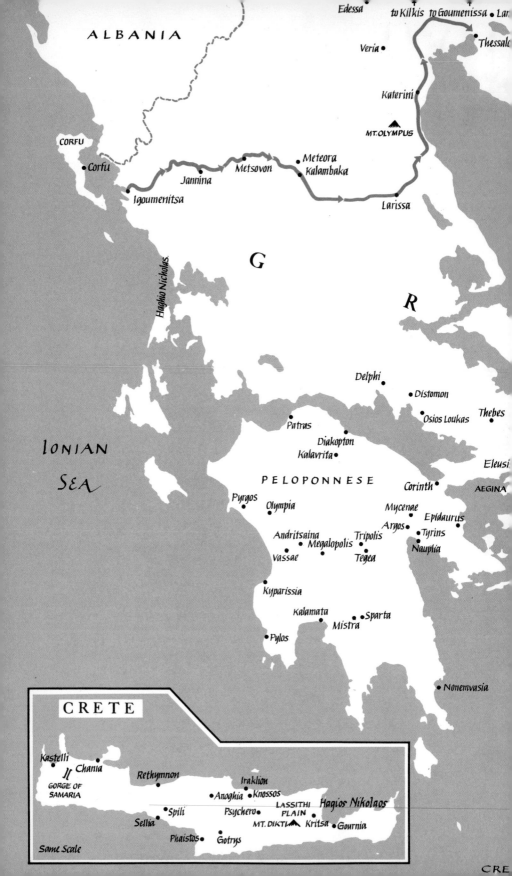